METHODS

AND

TECHNIQUES

OF

HAND

KNITTING

DRAWINGS BY KELLY J. HALL
AND JOANNA LYNCH

CHARTS BY BEVERLY J. BECKMAN

PHOTOGRAPHS BY JUNE HEMMONS HIATT
WITH THE HELP OF CHARLES FRIZZELL

THE PRINCIPLES OF
KNITTING

June Hemmons Hiatt

SIMON AND SCHUSTER   New York London Toronto Sydney Tokyo

Published by Simon and Schuster
A Division of Simon & Schuster Inc.
Simon & Schuster Building
Rockefeller Center
1230 Avenue of the Americas
New York, New York 10020
SIMON AND SCHUSTER is a registered trademark of
Simon & Schuster Inc.

DESIGNED BY BARBARA MARKS
Manufactured in the United States of America

10 9 8 7 6 5 4 3 2
Library of Congress Cataloging-in-Publication Data
Hiatt, June.
    The principles of knitting / June Hiatt.
        p. cm.
    Includes index.
    1. Knitting.   I. Title.
TT820.H65   1988
746.9′2—dc19   87-37665
                                              CIP

ISBN 0-671-55233-3

To Rob
and Jesse
For more than
can be said . . .

Acknowledgments

Writing is a solitary enterprise and an author is ultimately responsible for every word and thought set down, yet no book, particularly one such as this, takes form without considerable help from others. There were a great many people who provided me with stimulating ideas, valuable information, salutary advice, and much needed encouragement and support along the way. These people not only deserve credit, but it is my very great pleasure to mention them here.

I want first and foremost to thank my mother, Harriett Hemmons Nelson, who among many other things, taught me to knit when I was very young, so young that I remember my skinny legs and scuffed play shoes sticking straight out before me as we sat together. In doing so, she introduced me to the satisfying pleasures of working with my hands and the gratifications that come from making something both useful and beautiful. Well, I thought my childish efforts were beautiful, and because my mother never so much as hinted otherwise, with time they came to be just that. More important, however, the experience provided the strong, appealing taste of being both competent and creative, and that is an incomparably good thing to give a child.

Next I want to mention my deep indebtedness to the anonymous knitters all over the world and across many centuries who, through their creativity and skill, have incrementally added to the body of knowledge now available to us, their heirs. Furthermore, this book would not have been possible without the help of the many other authors who have toiled in these fields before me, particularly those who have gone out to visit and given voice to those unsung knitters, thus sharing with all of us the regional variations and innovations that might otherwise have been known only to an individual or community.

Closer to home, I would like to thank the members of the Bay Area Crochet and Knit Guild for their friendship and encouragement; they helped sustain me through years of very hard work. And while I am on the subject, I would also like to say how very much I value the guild concept. In bringing together people who share an interest in knitting, a guild fosters friendship and social ties as well as a greater knowledge of the craft. I wholeheartedly encourage you to seek out your local guild or, if one does not exist near you, to start one.

There were members of my guild who provided more than encouragement. Diane Baker, Wendy Bertrand, Carole Finnegan, Yvette Lehman, Emily Marks, Merrily Parker, and Nancy Wrisley, the members of my first class, shared their knowledge of knitting and graciously allowed me to test my ideas. I couldn't have had more intelligent students or a more satisfying introduction to teaching. Many of them also read and commented on parts of the manuscript, as did Melva Ruhaak, who knitted most of the lace samples photographed in the book. Christa Schreiber, Carole Finnegan, and Emily Marks also helped with samples when deadline pressures were upon me at the end. Candi Jensen assembled yarn, tools, and garments to photograph. Cigdem Brown, Susan Hodges, Stacey Keith, Karen Kempf, Pat Wheeler, and Maryann Zannini were the sources of information, questions, critique, and help that stimulated or filled in pieces of the puzzle.

There are two knitters whose contribution was especially gratifying and valuable. Barbara Walker's three fine books on stitch patterns inspired me to think that something comparable should be done in the area of techniques. I will leave it to others to decide if I have done that idea justice, but I am glad I made the attempt —I certainly know a great deal more about knitting now than when I began! More important, however, Ms. Walker graciously consented to do the technical editing, thus appeasing my fears of error and omission. She was the first to read a book I had been alone with for too long, and her flattering endorsement of my efforts meant more than I can say.

Toshiko Sugiyama is a knitter's knitter, a woman who has spent more than twenty years actively learning and testing every shred of obscure information she could find on techniques and who, by now, knows more about the craft than anyone I can think of. I was blessed to find her both neighbor and friend. She should have written this book, but as she told me, laughing, she was too wise to do so because she understood what a project on this scale can ask of one's life. Instead, she read the entire manuscript, in an astonishing four days, and then with great generosity, filled in all the missing pieces. I know Toshiko wanted to share her knowledge and I am enormously grateful that she chose me as her vehicle; it is a service I perform with pride. Toshiko also knits faster than most people think and without her calm and efficient help making samples as the deadline loomed, there would be fewer photographs to adorn my words: I couldn't have done it without her.

There are various other people in my local knitting world whom I want to mention. Kaethe Kliot of Lacis showed me the heights that knitted lace can achieve and loaned items from her collection for me to photograph. Linda Boroff of The Knitting Basket, Susan Druding of Straw Into Gold and Dierdre Sanchez of Wild Wools, are owners of the richly supplied stores I patronize with such pleasure. It was always good to leave the isolation of my desk and have them reassure me once again that the book was worth doing and that knitters were eager for it. I always returned home not just resupplied with yarn but reinvigorated.

I want also to mention the many people across the country who gave so generously of their time and knowledge when I was doing the research on fibers and yarns: Dr. Parvez Mehta of The Wool Bureau, Mr. Jim Coleman Jr. of Forte Mills on cashmere and qiviut. Sigrun Robinson of the Musk Ox Producers Cooperative on qiviut, Dolly Connelly for the beautiful photo of Oomingmak, which, while it could not appear in the book, now graces the wall over my desk. Richard Powers of Plymouth Yarns on alpaca, Lenore Schwartz of Conshohocken Yarns on cotton. Russell B. Pierce of Bartlettyarns on wool and spinning, Kristen Nichols of Classic Elite on mohair, The Mohair Council of America, Bonnie Allman on angora, Linda Anzelmo of the USDA on specialty fibers, Susan Druding and Susan Hodges on spinning, and my good friend Dr. Mary Alice Murphy for putting to rest the myths about allergies and wool.

In a book of this sort, words are not enough—I know most of you would struggle without good drawings and pictures to bring clarity to what I am trying to say. However, while I feel quite comfortable stringing words together, I have no gift whatsoever for drawing, nor did I, when I began, have the faintest idea of what was required to produce illustrations for a book. The artists, Kelly J. Hall, Joanna Lynch, and Beverly J. Beckman, began by teaching me how to tell them what I wanted, and then over many months of very hard work, they patiently interpreted my poor sketches, which I confess never improved much. I am enormously indebted to them for all they taught me, for their professionalism, their generosity, their friendship and encouragement, and most particularly for drawings that were so very beautiful.

When it came time to do the photographs, I was again ill prepared, being no more than the most casual and amateur chronicler of family events. Charley Frizzell gave me a shopping list of the equipment I needed and, more important, taught me to see through the lens. He critiqued my efforts whenever doubts arose and took those pictures I was not set up to handle. My dear friend and cousin, Eric Black, also advised me. I want also to thank the fine professionals at Custom Process in Berkeley, California, who handled all the developing and printing. I also appreciate the work of Jill Martin and her staff at Jam Graphics.

I must mention my dear old IBM PC, by now virtually an extension of my fingers and my mind, and the good people at FinalWord, particularly Rob Crutchfield in support, who created the program that saved me untold labor and made it so easy for me to polish my prose. I do not even like to speculate on how long it might have taken me to write this book without these technological marvels.

There comes a time when a book must leave its author's hands. I took my first step in that direction with the help of Barbara Tropp, who was extraordinarily kind to a stranger. My agent, Susan Lescher, placed the book and saw it through many vicissitudes into print; her counsel and advice in the early years were invaluable. The editor at Simon & Schuster, Carole Lalli, guided the team of people who worked to turn manuscript into book; she above all is responsible for the finished product. Marjorie Tippie had the daunting task of copyediting a large and complex text. Barbara Marks and Eve Metz should be credited with the design of the book and treatment of the illustrations. Kerri Conan, assistant to the editor, efficiently maintained the flow of communications and paper, and Jay Schweitzer and Rick Willett helped coordinate and organize all the various elements to make a finished book. Thanks also go to Simon & Schuster for providing the services of photo researcher Natalie Goldstein, who did so much on short notice. And finally, I must also thank Jerry Hiatt, who helped me greatly in the last few months.

And last, but by no means least, my family gave so generously of their encouragement, patience, and support over the long years that there is no way to adequately thank them. My husband, my rock, never lost faith, although I occasionally did. He helped in whatever way he could and in ways he never thought he might, taking over running the household when the hours at my desk filled the days and a good part of the nights for months on end—he learned empathy for those single working parents who bear all the burdens alone and became such a fine cook that I am reluctant to return to the kitchen. My son, Jesse, shared his mother with this book for a goodly portion of his childhood and did so with grace and good humor; a dose of benign neglect has apparently been good for him as he is growing into a fine and charming young man. Rob and Jesse must have wondered if life would ever return to normal, but they never complained. My only regret is that I have yet to persuade either of them to knit.

Contents

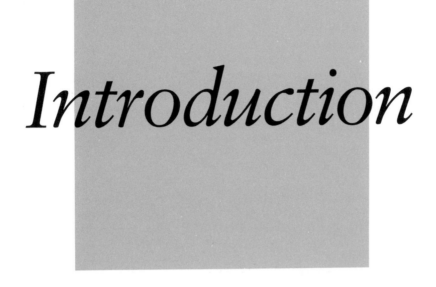

Introduction

Even the simplest hand-knit garment in this day and age is a luxury. In an era when ordinary men and women measure their lives and activities by tenths of seconds on digital watches, taking the time to knit a sweater, hat, or scarf must be justified by more than utility. If we simply wanted to keep warm, machine-knit garments would do the job. Why, then, do hand knits remain popular?

From the beginning of the machine age, people have expressed concern for the loss of individuality that mass-produced objects imply. The inherent uniqueness of anything handmade is a reassuring reflection of the individuality of each human being; it is a gesture of defiance against anonymity and monotony. Against a background of mass-produced objects, things handcrafted have taken on the luster of art. What had once been simply a fisherman's sweater or a peasant's warm mittens have come to be seen as desirable luxuries far from the small world in which they originated. As a result, the craft of knitting has been taken up by people who have no need to make their own clothing.

I don't think we can deny that the same motives are at work in knitting that operate when we acquire any other luxury object. In addition to aesthetic appreciation, there is both the awareness of the work and skill that went into its creation and the aura of status we assume in owning or wearing it. However, these are probably insufficient in themselves to impel most people to spend the long, long hours necessary to knit a garment. Fortunately, there is something about knitting that makes it an intrinsically pleasant activity.

Central to the appeal of knitting is that it works like meditation. Everything becomes quiet, still, and peaceful, and all the turmoil of life seems to succumb to the silent rhythm of the needles and the orderly progression of the stitches. There is a simple, sensual pleasure in the colors and textures of the yarns, and for me, inveterate adherent of the work ethic that I am, it provides an excuse to sit still, for after all I am accomplishing something worthwhile. I also find I do my best thinking when I knit, and I often keep a pad of paper nearby to jot things down as they come to mind.

In addition, knitting offers a creative outlet that accommodates itself nicely to busy lives. The tools and materials represent a modest investment, and the basic techniques are easily learned. The work is eminently portable, accompanying the knitter on vacations or to committee meetings, or helping to fill the empty hours on an airplane. Best of all, the result of the knitter's efforts is something attractive, practical, and unique. A hand-knit garment is also a special way of giving to the ones you love. When I see my husband or child wearing a sweater I have knit, I often think how every inch of the yarn has passed through my hands—it is almost as if I have my arms around them. The sweater is like a cozy talisman I have given them to wear out into the world.

However much we enjoy knitting, and hand-knit garments, there is no knitter who is not aware of the amount of time it takes to knit something. For some time now, in response to knitters wanting "quick knits," bulky yarns and large needles have become a major part of a yarn store's stock in trade, with patterns showing simplified styling and gauges of three or four stitches to an inch. Creativity has been expressed with color and texture rather than with detail or styling, and yarn manufacturers have responded with blended, fluffy yarns.

There is no doubt that this cheerful experimentation enlarged the domain of knitting to its benefit, but it did so to some extent at the expense of quality. Garments knit up with the idea of doing something quick and fun seem to have a short lifespan; they look dated, like last year's fad, all too soon. Certainly there is a place in our lives for things that are fun and ephemeral, but they should not be the sum of our efforts. There is a reawakened interest in classic style and the durable object, and I think the time is right for knitting to rediscover its more serious side as well. Instead of two quick knits you could as easily create one really choice sweater that will be treasured for a lifetime.

If you are going to knit something with more complex styling, a more difficult stitch, and finer yarn and needles, you will also want a mastery of technique that does justice to the effort. This book is intended to help you achieve just that. Of course, it will also help you make that next quick knit a better garment and one that is more satisfying to wear. Technique is the dry side of any art or craft, but it allows you to realize your ideas. How many of us have invested long hours in a knitting project only to have the result a disappointment because our skills were not adequate to the task?

Do not think, however, that you must master every esoteric element of knitting before you can turn out a quality garment. Far from it! Truly special knits that you would be proud to wear or give as a gift are possible using only a handful of the most elementary skills. And for all its emphasis on technique, this book was not meant to encourage technicians.

Those who knit up someone else's designs, however perfectly they do it, are good technicians and not masters of the craft. This is not to say that patterns and kits don't have a place in knitting—they most certainly do. You may not always have time to design your own garment—it can be twice as time consuming as simply knitting one—and there will always be occasions when even the most expert knitter will find that a kit or a commercial pattern is exactly what is needed. I think, however, that if you limit yourself to these you are missing half the fun and all the rewards of knowing that the finished product is uniquely yours.

Besides, what knitter has not been in the situation of discovering, in the back of the closet during spring cleaning, some yarn purchased three years ago? Perhaps you still like the yarn but wouldn't dream of making it up in the pattern you originally bought it for. Then, there is always that time when what you want to do more than anything else is to knit, but you've run into problems and the yarn store is closed—or you're on vacation and a store is miles away. Or perhaps you saw a gorgeous sweater in a store and you can't find a knitting pattern like it, or the pattern is close but the neckline or the sleeve is wrong.

My hope is that the information in this book will give you the confidence in your skills that will liberate you from dependence on instructors and patterns so you can create a garment that is exactly what you wish it to be. Knowing how a knitting pattern is put together, and how the stitches and techniques work, will help you to recognize errors when they occur in a commercial pattern (and they do), or to make any changes required to make a garment fit properly. You will be able to add elements to a pattern that the designer did not suggest, and as your confidence grows, you will want to begin to design your own patterns.

I do not believe in rote learning, nor in faithful adherence to recipes, so you will find few formulas here. I did not want to simply tell you how to do something; rather my goal was to explain the techniques so that instead of just going through the motions you would truly understand what you were doing. With this in mind, I have tried to be sensitive to the problems of description. Too often knitting books contain instructions that are incomplete, convoluted, or impossible to follow. Instead, the instructions here are given in a detailed, often lengthy, step-by-step manner. Please do not confuse length with difficulty. I think you will find these full descriptions easier to follow than the often brief and cryptic ones found in other books. I have also been most detailed in those descriptions likely to be of importance to a beginning knitter. As the techniques become more esoteric I become more brief, assuming that the knitter who would be interested in these needs less in the way of description.

In doing the research, I found that identical techniques were often referred to by different names or symbols in different books. In trying to decide which name was most appropriate, I found there was often no way to choose among the alternatives. In some cases I have simply abandoned all of them and settled on a term that conveys a sense of the operation performed or the resulting appearance. I hope I have not added to the confusion.

There is also a difficulty with certain relative terms commonly used in knitting, particularly "right side" and "wrong side," or "front" and "back." Both "right side" and "front" are generally used to refer to that side of the fabric which will show when the garment is worn. But "front," for example, could also mean the part of the garment worn on the front of the body, or it could be used to refer to the side of the work that happens to be facing the knitter. For the sake of consistency and clarity, I will use "inside" and "outside" to refer only to the faces of the fabric as it is intended to be worn or used. "Front" and "back" will be used only to refer to particular pieces of the garment, as in the front part of a sweater. "Right" will be used only with "left," as in the right or left side of a stitch or the right or left side of the fabric as you are looking at it. When we are discussing the position of the work in relation to the knitter, the position of the knitter's hands, or the placement of yarn or needles, I will use the terms "nearside" and "farside," meaning that side closest to the knitter or farthest away at that particular moment.

If you have read this far, you will have become aware that this is an affectionate but critical look at this fine old craft. Few knitters stop to really think about the techniques they use, but work the way they do because that's the way they were taught, and the well-worn path is the most comfortable one. Therefore, even the most advanced knitter will have a legacy of methods that may not really be the best in a given situation. I have gone back to the beginning and have questioned, examined, and tested even the most fundamental aspects of knitting, trying to look at each with new eyes. I wanted to know why a technique behaved the way it did, under what circumstances it worked best, and whether or not it could be improved or if there was an alternate method that worked better. In some cases, I found that what many believe to be separate techniques are simply different ways of doing exactly the same thing. I have tried to be exhaustively thorough, even including techniques that you should know about just so you can avoid them. In addition, there are countless regional variations and little oddments of knowledge that are not generally known. I have sought out and tested any obscure technique that I could find, rejecting some and delighting in others that I hope will find wider use.

This is meant to be a reference book, dipped into from time to time as the need arises, and is intended for every knitter, beginning, intermediate, or advanced. The beginning knitter should concentrate on the most basic techniques until they are mastered, and only then go on to something more complicated. If you are an intermediate knitter, it would be a good idea to review familiar techniques before delving into new material to make sure you are using the best methods of working, and then use the book as a reference when you want to try something new. As you keep knitting and solving problems associated with realizing your ideas, you will soon join the ranks of the expert knitters.

When I began this book, I already considered myself something of an expert knitter. Well, pride goes before the fall, and needless to say I completely underestimated the amount of time such an inquiry would take and how much there was to learn. Speaking from experience, I can unhesitatingly recommend to the most self-confident knitter that even the first chapters on fundamentals be read carefully. Just as I did, I think you may find some of your most cherished and dependable techniques called into question. On the whole, I hope the book will deepen your understanding, hone your skills, and provide you with new ideas and challenges.

THE PRINCIPLES OF
KNITTING

PART ONE

Working
the
Stitches

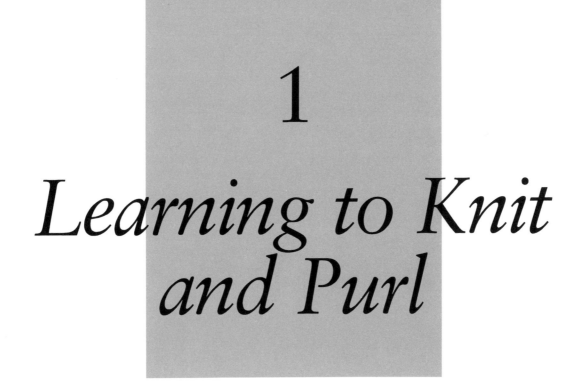

1
Learning to Knit and Purl

The most important thing to understand at the outset is that there is no one way to knit. In every region of the world where knitting is found, the craft has been enriched by unique ways of doing things, by new techniques, and by new stitch and garment patterns. I'm sure some of these innovations were developed because someone saw something he or she liked but had to figure out how to do it. Some were no doubt worked out in a conscious effort to improve speed. Others may be no more than mistakes that have been turned to advantage. While any method of doing something in knitting may be someone's favorite way of working, a comparison of all similar methods reveals that some work better than others, and a few may be highly suitable for some very specialized purposes but are less satisfactory when used for anything else. What I would like to encourage you to do, in this section as throughout the book, is to discard phrases like "But that's the way I've always done it," or "That's the way it should be done."

I will tell you a story. A man was in the kitchen watching his wife prepare dinner.

He realized that whenever she cooked this particular type of steak she would cut off a corner first and cook the remainder. He suggested that this was wasteful and asked her why she did it. She replied that that was the correct way to cook a steak of that kind. He asked her why it was necessary. She said, "Well, I don't know. My mother always did it that way, and that's the way I've always done it."

Next time his mother-in-law was at the house, the man asked her why she cut the corners off the steak. She replied, "Because the pan I had was too small."

I have a dear friend who has coined a word to describe that sort of thing; she calls them "falshoulds," and cooking and knitting are by no means the only areas in life where they are found.

In the following material I will give you a detailed analysis of different methods of holding the yarn and needles, compare them to one another, and discuss their pros and cons. There is a section on learning to Knit and Purl that is designed to teach the beginning knitter how to form these basic stitches, and that includes suggestions for improving speed and reducing fatigue.

While ostensibly for the beginner, these sections are actually recommended reading for every knitter. Even the advanced knitter will want to skim through in order to glean out those bits which are new and interesting. Once the foundation has been laid, we will move on to the material on the more complex stitches.

Holding the Yarn and Needles

I am sure you are all aware that not every knitter holds the yarn and needles in an identical manner. Most knitters knit one way or another because the person who taught them knit that way and they've gotten used to it. There are countless examples of exquisite knitting accomplished with every method.

I feel obliged, however, to recommend one of these methods over the others both to beginners and to those who are not that satisfied with their work. The method I recommend, which I call Right-Hand Knitting, is presented in detail on pages 8–12. This preliminary discussion is for those of you who already knit and are curious about the other methods, or for those who wonder if the way they knit is really the best. If you are comfortable with the way you knit, and pleased with the results, then there is no reason whatsoever to change. However, you should be able to make an informed choice about whether to continue with your present method, modify it in some way, or make a change.

There are five basic ways to knit, with quite a few variations on each theme. In four of the methods the yarn is held in the right hand; in the fifth it is held in the left. They all produce an identical fabric, but each one has certain advantages and disadvantages in terms of speed, fatigue, ease in working different techniques, and control of tension. In all but one minor method, the knitting needles are held with the hands on top, palms down.

Right-Hand Knitting

This form of knitting is described in such detail in the next section that I will give only a brief outline here. The hands are held fairly low, close to the lap. The yarn is held by the right thumb and forefinger, which control the tension. The right needle is released and rests on the lap as the hand moves left to pass the yarn around the needle tip. (This description doesn't do the method justice, as there are subtle movements involved that increase speed and reduce fatigue, but it is enough for you to recognize what method we are discussing.)

Right-Finger Knitting

This is the method that evolved out of that used by production knitters in Great Britain in the late nineteenth and early twentieth centuries.

The yarn is wrapped around the right forefinger, which acts as a shuttle, and around some combination of fingers on the right hand, which act as a tensioning device. The method of wrapping the yarn around the fingers seems to be rather individualistic—it's more a matter of what feels comfortable. A common method is: from the ball, starting from the palm side, completely around the small finger at the base, under the two middle fingers, then over the top of the forefinger to the needle.

Some people work quite close to the tip of the right needle, and the yarn is thrown with a flick of the forefinger. Others work farther back, either rotating the wrist up to bring the forefinger into position to pass the yarn around the needle tip or dropping the needle and moving their whole hand. The first method is much faster.

The original way of working Right-Finger Knitting included the use of either a knitting belt or stick. A knitting belt is worn around the hips; attached to it is a padded and stiffened oval leather pouch with holes in it. A double-point needle is inserted into one of the holes on the belt, which then supports it without assistance from the knitter. Since there are holes punched all over the pouch, the needle can be inserted into whichever hole will place the needle in a position that is most comfortable for the knitter. With the needle supported in this fashion, the right hand is free to work more swiftly as a shuttle.

A variation on the belt is the knitting stick—a carved stick with a hole in one end that could be tucked into the knitter's belt, or was tied into place with a ribbon. The knitting needle was inserted into the hole in the top of the stick, holding it in the same position a belt would.

As the right needle is fixed, the left needle must do somewhat more of the job. Instead of the right needle tip being inserted into the stitch to be knit, the stitch to be knit is put on the right needle tip. Instead of the right needle pulling the yarn through the old stitch, the left needle must pull the old stitch over the strand on the right needle tip and then pull back to release the discard stitch. The yarn is held in the same way as for Right-Finger Knitting, but the relation of right hand to needle varies from knitter to knitter. For me, the fastest way to work is to perch the thumb and other fingers on top of the needle. Wrapping the yarn then requires only a swift swiveling motion of the wrist and finger. Some people rest the hand on the needle much as they would if they were holding it, which reduces the speed of working a bit. Others work as for "pencil knitting" (see below), which is the slowest version.

The system works so smoothly that an expert knitter using a belt or a stick can achieve phenomenal speed. I should think the only reason this style of knitting has become so obscure is that it requires the use of double-point needles, which most people find awkward to handle and which have largely been replaced by circular needles. Also, the belts are not generally sold in the United States and accommodate only the smallest-gauge needles.

There are places, such as the Shetland Islands in Great Britain, where knitters combine this technique with the Left-Hand method of knitting (see below), holding one yarn on the left forefinger and another on the right forefinger. This enables the knitter to work with two colors at a time, one in each hand, shifting from one to the other without pause as the pattern requires. Should you ever want to do color pattern knitting, it would be well worth your while to learn this skill.

While few people in the United States are familiar with knitting belts, many people, without knowing why they do so, hold the right needle braced under their arm, giving much the same freedom to the right hand that the belt would. Undoubtedly they learned from someone who remembered the belt, but no longer had one and had improvised. Those of us who are farsighted find this impractical. I have tried bracing my right needle in the pocket of my jeans and it works quite well—rig up some improvisation of your own and try it.

Another descendent of the knitting belt is what I call "pencil knitting." The left needle is held from above and the yarn is wrapped as in Right-Finger Knitting; the right needle, however, is held from underneath almost as one would a pencil. For a knitter using a belt, it may be that it helped to tuck the thumb under the work to support the tip of the needle so it wouldn't sag with the growing weight of the fabric. Without the knitting belt, as it is done today, the entire weight of needle and fabric are supported in this way.

Left-Finger Knitting

This way of knitting is often called "Continental Knitting," as it is so common all over Europe. The needles are held from above, as in Right-Hand or Right-Finger Knitting. The yarn is wrapped once or twice around the left forefinger, which is held upright on the farside of the left needle tip. The right needle is inserted in the stitch, and the yarn for the new stitch is caught by the right needle tip and fished through the old stitch.

There is some evidence that this system may be descended from a very old method of knitting that relied upon needles that were hooked at one end. Without the hooks, there are some problems in bringing the yarn through the stitch, which makes this a problematic method of knitting, although widely used. While I don't recommend it for general purposes, the reasons for which I give below, it is excellent for use in a certain kind of color knitting, and for that reason I give detailed instructions for how to knit this way on pages 13–15.

The Pros and Cons

The problem with any method in which the yarn is wrapped around a finger lies with the precise control of the tension. When you pass the yarn around the needle, the yarn must slide through or across your fingers sufficiently to provide the yarn for a new stitch. When you pull the new stitch through the old one, a slight tension on the yarn is required so the stitch doesn't become too loose. It is this alternation in the tension requirements that presents the problem in a finger-wrap technique, as the only control is the amount of drag put on the yarn as it slides across the hand and fingers.

This is exacerbated in Left-Finger Knitting because of the difficulties with the way the Purl stitch is made. As a result, many knitters who use this method find the tension is different on the Knit and Purl rows. To compensate for this, some knitters give an extra tug on the yarn after each Purl stitch, others resort to working with two different-size needles, one for the Knit row and one for the Purl row. Regardless of compensatory techniques, it takes a very practiced hand indeed to get a smooth and consistent fabric. Because of this, it is difficult for a beginner, or even for the occasional knitter, to achieve a piece of work they can take real pride in.

The difficulty with forming the Purl stitches comes about because holding the yarn up and to the left works against bringing a new stitch through to the right. This isn't an issue so much with the Knit stitch because the strand gets caught against the top of the needle and thus is pulled through just fine. With the Purl stitch, however, the yarn is caught only against the side of the needle and must be dragged to the right by pushing the right needle against the left, and all the while the yarn is being pulled in the opposite direction. This is acknowledged to be awkward even by expert Left-Finger knitters. Some avoid the problem of the Purl stitch entirely by knitting in the round as much as possible, where they may use the Knit stitch row after row. Others wrap the yarn around the needle in the opposite direction, which makes it easier to pull through the stitch but causes the stitch to sit on the needle in the wrong position, and this creates more problems than it solves.

In addition, many specialty stitches are a problem with Left-Finger Knitting because the needle must move to pick up the yarn, rather than the yarn being brought to the needle. Having to fish for the yarn from within a stitch makes some techniques difficult to accomplish,

and stitches can be stretched out of shape by the motion of the needle.

Lest I sound altogether negative, there are merits to Left-Finger Knitting, as any of its adepts will tell you. It is a great advantage to at least know how to do it well enough to use it for the color knitting I mentioned above, as it makes the creation of some types of color patterns considerably faster and easier. For the beginning knitter who already crochets, Left-Finger Knitting would seem familiar and very easy to learn. The method is often suggested as a solution to the problems of a left-handed knitter (although I disagree, for reasons I give below). The main arguments in its favor are that because of its economy of motion it is not a fatiguing way to knit, and it is fast. In the hands of an experienced knitter, it really is *very* fast.

Right-Finger Knitting, because it is a finger-wrap method, has the same problem with precise control of tension as Left-Finger Knitting, but there are no real problems with doing any stitch or technique. Many Right-Finger Knitters achieve considerable speed. I suspect this is true because the nineteenth-century English and Scottish knitters refined the technique to a razor's edge, and those refinements have generally been passed down. One can read about these knitters racing along at two hundred stitches a minute, and turning out a sweater a week, but no occasional knitter should hold that up as a standard. It must be kept in mind that these knitters made virtually the same kind of sweater every time, with the same yarn, the same needles, and the same type of stitch pattern, and that they knit on a daily basis. It's a program designed to build speed, but not one modern knitters would wish to emulate. (I'm sure they were timed on plain Knit, aren't you?)

Some of the same "avoidance of Purl syndrome" is found with Right-Finger knitters. Unlike Left-Finger Knitting, there is no real difficulty with forming the Purl stitch, but because the right forefinger is held up on the farside of the needle, the route taken to throw the yarn around the needle tip is considerably longer for Purl than for Knit, and the motion is more awkward. This increases fatigue and cuts down on speed. Many knitters using these methods choose instead to work in the round at all times, even devising special methods of knitting across openings like armholes and necklines that allow them to be cut open and sewn, rather than shaped in the knitting—all done to avoid Purl!

While I can understand how it must have evolved, I have yet to discover any modern justification for the version I call Pencil Knitting, in which the right needle is held from underneath in the crook between thumb and forefinger. This is most certainly a system that requires it to be learned in trusting and uncritical childhood, because without the aid of a knitting belt or stick it is quite clumsy—I don't think many adults would put up with learning it. The thumb is trapped underneath the needle, where it restricts the movement of the hand and the forefinger. This is particularly noticeable with the Purl stitch. As the fabric begins to hang down from the needle, a chunk of it must be included between thumb and needle. This is not only a fairly awkward way to support any weight with the hand, so that most people will find it tiring, but the bulk of the fabric further restricts any motion. If someone you know knits this way, however successfully, and offers to teach you how, decline as politely as possible, but do decline. If this is the way you knit and you like the results, by all means continue to do so; the world needs its eccentrics to make it a more interesting place!

Right-Hand Knitting, the method I recommend, is not generally associated with the kind of speed that can be achieved by an expert with either of the other two methods, but with the refinements that I mention in the following detailed instructions, speeds are comparable to what most knitters manage using those techniques. With Right-Hand Knitting, because the yarn is held by the thumb and forefinger on top of the needle for Knit, and on the nearside of the needle for Purl, there is little difference in speed or agility when forming a Knit or Purl stitch—it is pretty much the same distance to cover whether you are wrapping the yarn around the needle tip on the nearside or the farside. In addition, because of the way the needles and yarn are held and manipulated, there is no limitation on hand movement. This allows easy formation of even the most complicated or awkward specialty stitches or techniques. No door in knitting is closed to the Right-Hand knitter.

As a matter of fact, one of the real advantages of the technique is its great simplicity. It is the most natural thing in the world to pick up the yarn with thumb and forefinger in order to wrap it around the needle; most beginners would do it that way if they were simply told to wrap the yarn around the needle with no instruction as to how to hold it. This makes it an easy method to teach, to learn, and to remember. But simplicity must not be confused with lack of refinement, and refinement is the great virtue of this method of knitting. The thumb and forefinger are the most sensitive of our fingers, and provide very precise control of the tension and the movement of the yarn. This allows even the occasional knitter to produce a superior fabric with smooth and even stitches, a fabric comparable to what could be achieved only by an expert with either of the other methods. In short, I think Right-Hand Knitting is by far the better method.

You now have all my arguments. If you are going to change, I know from trying it myself that it is especially difficult to learn a new method when you already know how to knit another way. If you can be patient with the inevitable feelings of clumsiness in the beginning, however, I think it will be worth your while. For those of you who already knit this way, and are feeling smug

and reassured as to the wisdom of your ways, please read the instructions for those refinements of technique I mentioned, which may help to increase your speed and reduce fatigue. If you prefer to continue in other, comfortable and well-worn paths, I hope that if you are ever in the position of teaching someone to knit, that with the help of this book you will teach Right-Hand Knitting. I think in the long run it will serve that person best.

Before we go on, however, let's digress a moment to discuss the implications of that statement for those of us who are not right-handed. Anyone faced with the problem of teaching a left-handed person to knit will also find this of interest.

Knitting for the Left-Handed

There is a bias in all knitting books, as in all society, toward the right-handed. But, fortunately, there is no real necessity for a left-handed person to learn a special way to knit—after all, one knits with two hands, and I know of left-handed knitters who knit the same way right-handed people do. However, if you are left-handed and have tried the usual way of knitting and it persists in feeling clumsy and slow, by all means knit Right-Hand Knitting "left-handed" instead. There are fewer problems than you imagine.

True left-handed knitting is "mirror reversed"; instead of knitting from right to left, one knits from left to right. Indeed, a mirror is the solution for the problems encountered by a right-handed instructor and a left-handed knitting student. A mirror should be positioned behind the instructor, and the student should mimic the movements seen in the mirror. The same technique could be used to follow the graphic diagrams in a book. No problem should be encountered in following directions for a stitch or garment pattern; whether you work from right to left, or left to right, will make no difference in the outcome so long as you are consistent. Any description of a technique that includes the words "right" and "left" need only have the directions reversed. Once the technique is mastered, there should be no further problems; you will simply work away from left to right, while the rest of us go from right to left. For those of you who are ambidextrous and looking for a challenge, you can Knit from right to left on one row, and from left to right on the next, and never have to turn the work around, or Purl!

I have given my reasons for not recommending Left-Finger Knitting (except in color knitting) above, at length, but because that method is so tempting to left-handed knitters, I would like to point out that, in that method, the right hand does all the work of stitch formation, the left hand being in charge only of tension control. Right-Hand Knitting done left-handed calls for the critical, dextrous work to be done with the left hand.

Learning to Knit and Purl

Whether you are a true beginner, or someone who is switching over from another way to knit, it will help a great deal to accept the idea that you will make mistakes and feel a bit clumsy to begin with. Children take that for granted when they try something new, and don't let it bother them, so they learn quickly and easily. Adults, however, are terribly uncomfortable when they feel ignorant or awkward—after all, we are supposed to be grown up and know how to do things—with the result that many get discouraged and give up. Don't let that happen to you. When you begin to feel frustrated, just say "That's okay, that's how I'm supposed to feel, but it won't last long and then I'll know how to knit." Keep in mind that it is much like learning to ride a bicycle—very awkward at first—but once you learn how you won't have to think about doing it. And I can promise you, there will be no skinned knees.

Before I go on to describe the techniques, it is important to clear up some terminology that confuses many knitters. The Knit stitch is by far the most common stitch, so fundamental that it has given its name to the craft. Therein we have a problem in determining whether we are talking about the craft or the stitch. In an attempt to ease this confusion, I will refer generically to knitting, with a small "k," and to the stitch in particular with a capital letter, as I do with the names of all the other stitches.

As if that confusion were not enough, the Knit stitch has a different appearance on each side, like a coin with two different faces. These two aspects of the Knit stitch have been given separate names, Knit for the way it looks on one side, Purl for the way it looks on the other side. When you form a Knit stitch, the Knit aspect of the stitch will be on the side of the fabric facing you, the Purl on the reverse. When you form a Purl stitch, the Purl aspect of the stitch will be on the side of the fabric facing you, the Knit on the reverse. You must, therefore, keep in mind that any mention of Knit or Purl simply refers to two sides of the same stitch, and that any instruction to Knit or Purl refers to the two different techniques used to control the direction in which the stitch will face.

While the stitch is the same no matter what method of knitting is being used, the instructions are presented in a manner that is appropriate for knitting a flat fabric rather than a circular one. (Information on knitting in the round can be found on page 110.)

Now let us begin.

Right-Hand Knitting

With this knitting method, both hands are actively used, although the right hand has more work to do in wrapping the yarn to form the stitches and manipulating the needle. The yarn is held between the right thumb and forefinger. As I mentioned in the previous section, it is not the fastest way to knit, but it is easy to learn and to do, it offers precise control with any technique, and produces very satisfying results even for beginning knitters.

For learning purposes, I recommend you use a soft knitting worsted such as Brunswick Germantown in a light neutral color with a pair of ten-inch needles in size 7 or 8. I will assume that you have used Half-Hitch Cast-on to place twenty or thirty stitches on the needle. A discussion of methods of Casting-on including Half-Hitch starts on page 123.

Holding the Yarn and Needles

1. Place the ball of yarn on your right side. Take up the needle holding the cast-on stitches in your left hand, the empty needle in your right hand. Sit in a comfortable position, with your elbows at your sides, and your hands holding the needles about four or five inches above your lap. The most important thing is for you to relax; tension causes fatigue and stitches that are too tight.

2. Hold both needles *lightly* with your hands on top, palms down, fingers about one or two inches back from the tips, with the shafts of the needles braced against the fleshy pads on the sides of your hands.

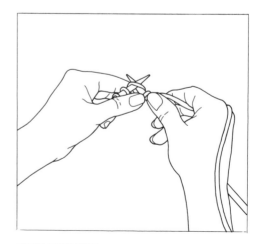

RIGHT-HAND KNIT

The weight of the needles should rest primarily on the last two fingers of the left hand, the last three of the right hand, leaving the other fingers relatively free to manipulate the yarn and stitches as required.

3. As you start, the yarn should come off the farside of the first stitch on the left needle and then up between the forefinger and middle finger of your right hand. It should lie all the way down in the gap between these two fingers and then just trail loosely over the back of your hand.

4. Grasp the yarn *lightly* with the thumb and forefinger of the right hand about one inch from where it comes off the first stitch on the left needle. Rest the side of your thumb on top of the needle until it is time to wrap the yarn.

Forming the Knit Stitch

This is the most basic stitch in all of knitting, the one all the other stitches are built upon, and the fastest to do.

1. Insert the tip of the right needle from left to right into the nearside of the first stitch on the left needle. As the needle enters the stitch, it should pass under the tip of the left needle.

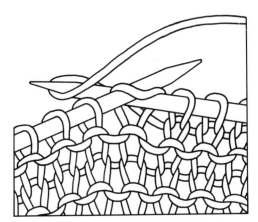

WRAPPING THE YARN TO KNIT

2. With the thumb and middle finger of the left hand, support the two needles just below where they cross and release the right needle. (It is supported by your left fingers, and the head of the needle will drop only an inch or so to your lap.)

3. Move your two hands together slightly. As the right hand moves left, carrying the yarn, the left hand should move right, carrying the work to meet the yarn.

4. Wrap the yarn under the right needle tip, up the nearside, over the top, and down the farside. Maintain a gentle tension on the yarn at all times.

5. Move your hands back to their original position, and pick up the right needle again.

6. Now pull the yarn wrapped around the right needle, through the stitch on the left needle as follows:
   • Push the tip of the right needle with your left forefinger, and at the same time pull the right needle back slightly with the last three fingers of your right hand. The right needle tip should slide under the left needle and back out of the stitch to the nearside.
   • Slide the tip of the right needle against the left needle as you pull it through the stitch so you do not lose the strand of yarn.
   • As the right needle clears the stitch, you will have the old stitch on the left needle, the new stitch on the right needle.

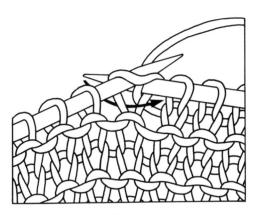

FORMING THE NEW STITCH

7. Now drop the stitch off the left needle by simultaneously pulling the needle back with the last two fingers of your left hand, and sliding the stitch off with the tip of your right needle. Notice that the yarn now comes off the farside of the new stitch on the right needle.

8. Repeat these movements with each stitch on the left needle. When all the original stitches have been Knit and dropped off the left needle, and the same num-

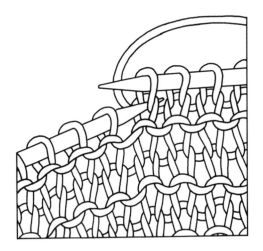

DISCARDING THE KNIT STITCH

ber of new ones are on the right needle, you have completed one row of knitting.

9. Transfer the needle with the stitches from your right hand to your left, and the empty needle from left hand to right, and repeat the process.

When you have completed several rows of knitting, examine your work. The fabric will have a corrugated appearance made up of horizontal rows of little nubs separated by rows of little Vs. Knit another row and watch the process carefully as you do so. As you release the old stitch from the left needle, it will fall below the new stitch on the right needle with the top of the stitch going toward the farside of the work. The bottom part of the stitch, on the nearside of the work, has the appearance of a little V. This is the Knit side of the stitch. If you look on the other side of the work, the head of each stitch will be lined up in a little row of horizontal nubs right beneath the new stitches on the needle. This is the Purl side of the stitch.

Complete this row, turn the work, and begin the next row. You will notice that the Purl side of the last row is now facing you. If you Knit back across all these stitches, exactly as you did for the last row, you will put a new row of Vs above the row of nubs. On the farside a row of nubs would appear above the row of Vs. Knitting every row like this is called Garter Stitch. A fabric made in Garter Stitch is nice and flat, with considerable vertical elasticity, and it has the same appearance on both sides.

The Subtleties

There are certain of the more subtle aspects of this process that I would like to call your attention to, as they are important factors in reducing fatigue and improving speed. These are the little things you would mimic while sitting with a teacher, and you might not even be aware you were learning them.

- Keeping your hands down low over your lap is an important factor in reducing fatigue. Holding the weight of arms, needles, and knitted fabric up at chest level, as many people do, is very tiring. However, holding the work low serves an additional purpose because this method requires that you release the right needle in order to wrap the yarn. If the work is held low, the head of the released needle will move down only an inch or two and come to rest on your lap. If you are holding it up too high when you release the needle, it could slip out of the first few stitches as you start the row. And finally, once you have some fabric hanging off the needles, it will rest in your lap, and you will find that it supports the needles, making it more effortless to work. This is even more true if you are working on circular needles (see the discussion on their merits on page 115).

- The reason you should have the yarn come up be-

tween your fingers and trail over the back of your hand is that then it is impossible for the yarn to get tangled up in the knitting, or caught between hand and needle. Fussing with the yarn slows you down. Holding the yarn in this way is aided by keeping the ball of yarn on your right side. If the strand of yarn were to head off to the left from your hand, it would tend to come out of your grasp. In addition, with the ball of yarn on your right side, you can easily pull more yarn free by simply raising your right arm, which allows quick return to the knitting.

- The left thumb and middle finger should always rest lightly on the near- and farside of the fabric between the needle tips, just below the first stitches. They shouldn't need to be moved into position in order to pinch and support the needle tips when you drop the right needle; they should be there all the time.

- Moving the right and left hand toward one another while wrapping the yarn is an important factor in increasing speed because it creates a real economy of motion, reducing the distance the hand has to travel in order to wrap the yarn around the needle tip. It is a gesture somewhat like playing a tiny accordion, and its success depends on keeping your elbows at your sides. Do *not* throw the yarn with your whole arm; that is wasted effort—after all, this is knitting, not tennis. Instead, with this method both arms move, but it is more like a slight drop of the hand from wrist or elbow. Because the needles are held by the left thumb and forefinger, as you move your left hand right and down, both needles will move to the right, bringing the needle tip under the right fingers so the yarn can be wrapped around it.

- Holding the needles lightly with the last three fingers of your right hand and the last two fingers of your left hand also has an important function. Because the right thumb and forefinger are always holding the yarn, they are otherwise occupied. The left thumb and middle finger are busy supporting the crossed needles while the yarn is wrapped, while the left forefinger is kept busy helping to push the needle back out of the stitch as the new stitch is pulled through. (The left thumb does this job when you Purl.) In addition to supporting the work, however, the other three fingers of the right hand work to move the needle in and out of the stitches. It is they that move the needle forward slightly to insert it into the stitch, and after the yarn is wrapped, they bring it back and then forward again to pull the new stitch through. The correct motion is only possible if you are holding the needle lightly; then a slight squeeze of the fingers toward the palm will bring the needle back. Try it and see. Once the new stitch is safely through the old one, the last two fingers of the left hand pull that needle back slightly in the same way to help the discard stitch drop from the left needle.

- The needle should be inserted well into the stitch, allowing you to wrap the yarn around the *shaft* of the needle instead of the tip. This determines the amount of yarn allotted to each stitch, and if the yarn is regularly wrapped around the tip of the needle, the stitches will be too tight.

Common Errors

It is difficult to absorb so many little details all at once. Go slowly and concentrate on one aspect at a time until you get it. Don't worry about how things look for now —I told you mistakes were inevitable—just go on as best you can and concentrate on developing facility with the stitch. If your work gets too messed up, discard that swatch and start again. As things begin to make sense, you will make fewer and fewer mistakes. The ones that are most common to beginners are fairly easy to watch for:

Position of the Yarn: Make sure the yarn is always on the farside of the work when you Knit. If you accidentally get it on the nearside and try to Knit the next stitch, the yarn will go over the needle, putting on an extra strand that shouldn't be there and will confuse you. If that has happened, either drop the strand off and ignore it, or Knit it together with the next stitch. It won't look right, but that isn't important now. The only correct way to fix it is to rip the work out to that point, and by the time you know how to do that, you won't make this mistake any more.

Dropped Stitches: If you drop a stitch, just pick it up as best you can and go on. In the material on the structure of the Knit stitch (see pages 12–13) there is a full discussion of the proper position of the stitch on the needle and how to pick it up correctly. When you are ready to refine your skill, I recommend you read that. For practice purposes, however, it really doesn't matter. If it dropped off and you didn't notice it until too late, you will have one fewer stitch on the needle, and the dropped stitch will probably run down a few rows. Don't think about it; pay attention instead to keeping your stitches back from the tips of the needles so they won't drop off. The first stitch on both needles should sit on the main shaft of the needle, right at the edge where the point begins the slope down to the tip.

Split Stitches: Another common problem is splitting stitches—inserting the needle through the yarn of a stitch, instead of through the center of the stitch. If this happens, you will notice a portion of the strand lying free on the near- or farside of the fabric. Here again, just ignore the mistakes already made and pay closer attention to correct insertion of the needle into the stitch, and gradually you won't do it anymore. Of course, there is a way to correct it, but it isn't necessary for you to worry about that now.

Forming the Purl Stitch

The second step in becoming a knitter is to learn how to Purl, of course. When you Knit, you drop the head of the old stitch off toward the farside of the work. When you Purl, it is simply the reverse; you drop the head of the old stitch off on the nearside of the work. In order to accomplish this, you must form the stitch in a slightly different way.

1. Pick up the needles as before, with the needle carrying the stitches in your left hand, and the empty needle in your right hand.
2. This time the yarn must come up the nearside of the needles to your right hand, where it is held as before. However, instead of resting on top of the needle, the thumb and forefinger should be on the nearside, with the nail of the forefinger resting against the shaft of the needle.
3. Insert the tip of the right needle from right to left into the nearside of the first stitch on the left needle. The tips of the needles will cross, the right needle on the nearside pointing left, the left needle on the farside pointing right.
4. Support the cross of the needles with your left thumb and middle finger to hold them secure and release the right needle.
5. Move your hands toward one another as you carry the yarn up the nearside, over the top, down the farside and under the right needle tip.
6. Continue to hold onto the yarn, move your hands back into position, and pick up the right needle.

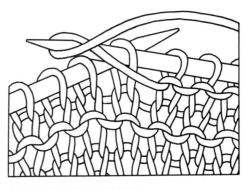

RIGHT-HAND PURL

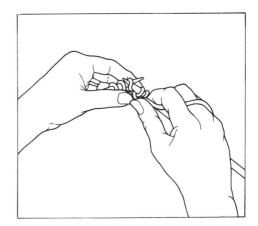

WRAPPING THE YARN TO PURL

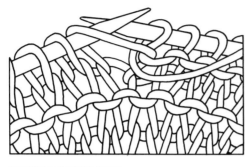

FORMING THE NEW STITCH

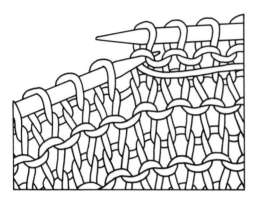

DISCARDING THE PURL STITCH

7. Maintain a gentle tension on the yarn as you bring the new stitch through the old one as follows:
   • Simultaneously push the tip of the right needle out of the stitch with your left thumb, and pull the right needle back slightly with the last three fingers of your right hand.
   • The right needle should pass under the left and out the farside.
   • Slide the tip of the right needle against the shaft of the left needle as you withdraw it from the old stitch so you don't lose the new one.
8. With the new stitch safely on the right needle, drop the old stitch off the left needle by pulling the needle back slightly with the last two fingers of your left hand, at the same time encouraging the stitch to drop off with the tip of the right needle.

Repeat these steps all the way across the row. Be sure to keep the yarn on the nearside of the work at all times. As you Purl, notice that you are dropping the head of the discard stitch off the left needle to the nearside of the work, and the little nubs are now appearing below your needle on the side facing you instead of on the reverse. If you look on the other side of the fabric, you will see that the little Vs are now back there.

Practice Purling, just as you did Knitting, until it feels almost automatic. Do not be surprised if, upon Purling every row, you discover that you are still making Garter Stitch. Of course you are! If you Purl every stitch and every row, you will be stacking nubs on top of Vs with results no different from when you Knit every row, stacking Vs on top of nubs.

Right-Finger Knitting

While I recommend the above method for most purposes, as we discussed in the previous section, Right-Finger Knitting has some advantages and it is worthwhile knowing how to do it as well. The method is excellent for certain kinds of color work, I prefer it for working small items in the round on double-point needles (see page 111), and it can be a less fatiguing method to use if you knit long hours at a stretch. However, I don't particularly care for it when I am working complex stitch patterns. It does require patient practice to develop an even tension. While the formation of the stitches is the same as that described above, the motion of the fingers and hands is somewhat different.

Holding Yarn and Needles
1. With the yarn at your right side, wrap the yarn around the right fingers as shown; the length of yarn between the last stitch worked and the wrapped forefinger should be no more than two inches.
2. Hold the needles lightly with the palms down and the needle bearing the stitches in the left hand. The palm of the left hand may rest on the needle, but generally most knitters lift the right hand off the needle slightly, holding it with the thumb and two or three fingers.
3. The forefinger should be held up, poised above and slightly to the farside of the needle tip.

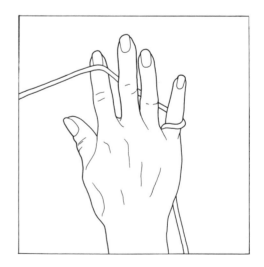

WRAPPING THE YARN FOR RIGHT-FINGER KNITTING

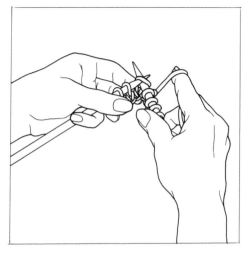

RIGHT-FINGER KNITTING

Forming the Knit Stitch

1. Insert the right needle tip from left to right into the nearside of the first stitch on the left needle. (If the needle is secured on a knitting belt or stick, rather than inserting the right needle into the stitch, move the left needle and put the stitch on the right needle in the same position.)
2. With a flick of the right forefinger, bring the yarn forward past the right needle tip and up the nearside between the crossed needles. (Depending upon how you are holding the needle, you may need to raise the right wrist slightly in order for the yarn to clear the tip of the needle.)
3. Maintain some tension on the yarn as you either pull the new stitch through the old one with the right needle, or use the left needle to lift the old stitch over the yarn and off the right needle, or a little of both; discard the original stitch.

Forming the Purl Stitch

1. Insert the right needle from right to left into the nearside of the first stitch on the left needle (or use the left needle to place the stitch on the right needle in the same way).
2. Rotate the right hand slightly toward you to bring the yarn into position, then move the right finger to pass the yarn down between the crossed needle tips, then under and up the nearside of the right needle tip.
3. Shift the right forefinger to the farside and maintain some tension on the yarn as you either pull the yarn through the original stitch or use the left needle to lift the original stitch over the yarn and off.

With either form of the stitch, try to make the movement of the right finger as economical as possible. Some people move the whole hand in order to pass the yarn around the needle, much as described above for Right-Hand Knitting, but this defeats the purpose of this method, cutting down on speed and increasing fatigue. While a very slight shifting of the hand may be necessary, the essential movement is a relatively small flick of the right forefinger. You will find the Knit stitch rather easy to accomplish, but the Purl stitch requires somewhat more maneuvering and practice. If you have trouble maintaining an even tension on the yarn, experiment with different methods of wrapping the yarn around your fingers until you find a pattern that works for you. Some people wrap the yarn over and under every finger, some give it a double wrap around the forefinger. In order to put more tension on the yarn with the wrap method shown, curl the little finger down on the yarn or press it against the ring finger.

Left-Finger Knitting

As you know, I do not recommend this way of knitting for general purposes, but it is extremely useful to know how to do it well enough to use it in one method of color knitting, so I am going to describe it in some detail for those of you who might wish to learn how.

Holding the Yarn

- With the ball on the left side, and the needles held in the usual way, wrap the yarn once or twice around the left forefinger, which is held up, poised above and slightly to the farside of the needle. (The yarn should come off the nearside of the finger to the stitch.)

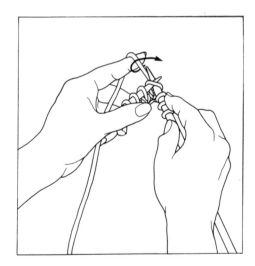

LEFT-FINGER KNITTING

Forming a Knit Stitch

1. Insert the tip of the right needle into the stitch in the customary way, then around the farside of the strand of yarn from right to left.
2. Draw the yarn through to the nearside and drop the discard stitch from the left needle. (Some people use the middle finger of the left hand against the farside

of the strand to hold it in position for the right needle; others move the forefinger to pass the yarn around the needle tip. I have also seen some knitters hook the right forefinger around the yarn between left forefinger and needle to help pull the new stitch through.)

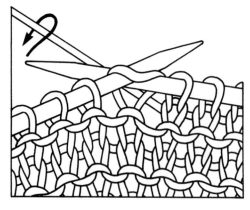

CATCHING THE YARN FOR LEFT-FINGER KNIT

Forming a Purl Stitch

1. Move the shuttle forefinger to the nearside of the needle.
2. Insert the right needle into the stitch in the customary way to Purl, then move the needle up the nearside of the strand of yarn, over the top, and down the farside.
3. Here it is necessary to make a quick downward motion of the needle tip, which helps the yarn slide to the right of the point where the two needles cross. With the tip held down, the right needle must then slide against the shaft of the left needle, drawing the yarn under the needle tip and out the farside. If the

contact between the two needles isn't maintained, the yarn will escape and slip off the needle. (Some people reach the forefinger over the needle and hook the yarn around the needle tip.)

Reverse Left-Finger Knitting

There is a variation on Left-Finger Knitting used by some knitters who have found it difficult to form the Purl stitch in the manner described above. While the alternate method of Purling is much easier to do than the other, it results in the stitch being reversed, or turned on the needle. As a result, on the following row each stitch must be worked through the farside to prevent it from crossing on itself on discard. (For more information, see the discussion on the correct position of the stitch on the needle on page 18 and the section on "Crossed Stitch" on pages 32–36.)

Reverse Left-Finger Knitting presents no real problem as long as all the knitter wishes to do is Knit and Purl, but difficulties can arise in following the instructions for many of the decorative stitches and special techniques that are written for normal stitches. Therefore, it is really not wise to get into the habit of knitting in this manner because of the limitations it imposes.

The yarn and needles are held in the same way as with Left-Finger Knitting.

Turning the Stitches

- Insert the right needle into the stitch on the left needle in the usual way, but move the needle tip up on the farside of the strand, over the top, and down the nearside. The tip of the needle is held down slightly as the new stitch is pulled through the old one.

Notice that the left side of the new stitch is on the nearside of the needle.

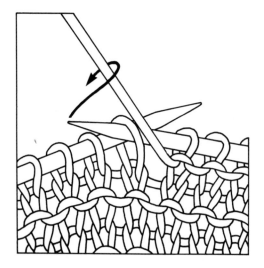

CATCHING THE YARN FOR LEFT-FINGER PURL

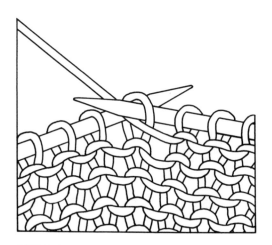

CATCHING THE YARN TO TURN STITCH

Knitting the Turned Stitches

- Insert the right needle into the farside of the stitch on the left needle and catch up the yarn in the normal way. The discarded stitch will be a normal, uncrossed stitch in the fabric.

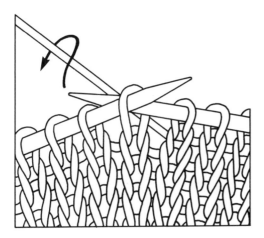

KNIT FARSIDE ON TURNED STITCH

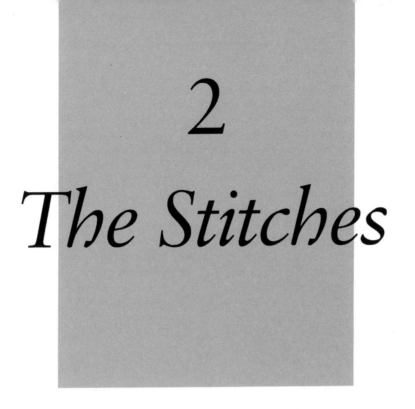

2
The Stitches

All the wonderful variety of knitting is based on a single principle, that of pulling one loop of yarn through another. The basic techniques of Knit and Purl were introduced on pages 8–15. These and some twenty other fundamental techniques have been elaborated into a seemingly infinite vocabulary of stitch patterns as all the possible variations, permutations, and combinations are exploited by knitters. As the alphabet stands to language, the fundamental stitches are to knitting. Even the most complex stitch pattern is no more than a combination of basic stitches, each one simple in itself. Once you have mastered these basic techniques, the whole world of knitting is laid open to your imagination.

This chapter, then, will focus on the building blocks of the various patterns, not on the stitch patterns themselves. There are many fine books on the market that contain nothing but stitch patterns, foremost among them Barbara Walker's exhaustive three volumes, which I recommend highly.[1] I am sure the Walker books could keep the most compulsive knitter happy for a lifetime, and all knitters owe her a debt of gratitude. Instead, the material here is designed to help you understand those stitch patterns, and perhaps design some of your own. I am going to explain the elements of which the patterns are made up—how to do each technique, what its structure is, and what uses it is put to. With this material available to you, you should find any pattern much easier to learn, and you will be able to analyze a pattern should you wish to

1. *A Treasury of Knitting Patterns*, 1968; *A Second Treasury of Knitting Patterns*, 1970; *Charted Knitting Designs*, 1972; Charles Scribner's Sons, New York.

vary it, improve on it, or combine it with some other. The information will be valuable in helping you decide whether or not a particular pattern is appropriate for the kind of garment you plan to make. Eventually, you will be able to look at a knitted fabric and figure out how a stitch is done. Information on how to read either written or charted stitch pattern instructions can be found on pages 459–485.

In discussing this material, there are some simple terms you should be familiar with. As you work, the stitch being formed on the right needle is called the new stitch. The stitch that is worked into and then dropped from the left needle is the discard stitch. It is the discard stitch that takes the form in the fabric that the technique gives to it. The new stitch is neutral, and has no form until it is manipulated and discarded in turn on the next row. Let's first look at how the normal stitch sits on the needle. Notice that the yarn comes from the stitch to the right, up the nearside of the needle, over the top and down the farside, and then travels to the stitch to the left. The correct position of the stitch, therefore, is with the right side of the stitch on the nearside of the needle. This is true whether you are looking at the stitch from the Knit side or the Purl side. A stitch not in this position is said to be "turned," and if a turned stitch is worked in the usual manner, it will cross on itself and be visibly different from the other stitches.

When you look at the completed stitch in the fabric rather than on the needle, the normal path of the yarn is from the stitch to the right, up the right side of the V of the Knit stitch, then to the farside to form the Purl nub, back to the nearside, down the left side of the V, and then to the stitch on the left.

The strand of yarn that passes from one stitch to the other is called the running thread, and it lies on the Purl side of the fabric next to the head of the discard stitch that forms the Purl nub.

There are two sets of nubs for every row: One set, curving down, is made up of the heads of the stitches from the row below; the other set, curving up, is made up of the running threads that lie between the bases of each stitch in the row above. You will also see the running thread where it stretches across the gap between the two needles, passing from the base of the stitch on the left to the base of the stitch below the new one on the right needle.

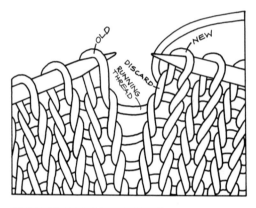

TERMS FOR ASPECTS OF THE STITCH

The Knit and Purl Stitches

The basic methods of forming the Knit and Purl stitches have already been discussed in full on pages 8–15. This material further elucidates the characteristics and behavior of the stitch and some of the ways in which it can be used.

All of the other stitches start here, each of them no more than an elaboration of this Janus-like stitch. With just the two aspects of this single stitch, you have the capability of creating a wealth of textured patterns on your fabric; indeed, the possibilities are limited only by your imagination. While I am sure you will want to explore all of the specialty stitches, you really need go no further. There are examples of exquisite knitting in the textile collections of museums that do no more. In addition, when you really understand the structure of Knit and Purl, you will have a great deal of confidence as you work, other stitch techniques will be more readily understood, errors will be easy to recognize and correct, and there will be far fewer of them.

Stockinette Stitch

If you Knit on top of Knit stitches, and Purl on top of Purl stitches every row, you will create a fabric with all

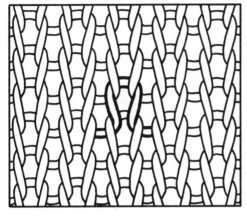

STOCKINETTE/KNIT STITCH

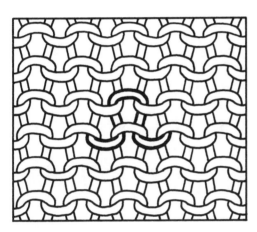

REVERSE STOCKINETTE/PURL STITCH

Knit stitches on one side and all Purl stitches on the other side. The Knit side is most often called Stockinette or Stocking Stitch, the Purl side, Reverse Stockinette, and this is the most commonly used stitch pattern in knitting. The Stockinette Stitch is the pattern we think of as "knitting" and is appreciated for its smooth face. Attractive enough in itself, it also acts as the perfect background for a wide variety of other stitches and techniques.

Proportion and Resilience

A Knit stitch is wider than it is tall, so Stockinette will produce a gauge that has roughly 70 to 75 percent as many stitches as rows. A fabric done in this stitch pattern is far more expansive in the horizontal dimension than in the vertical. Because the yarn travels from stitch to stitch horizontally, if you stretch the fabric that way it is quite easy for the stitches to flatten out and provide more yarn to the running threads. When you release the fabric, the stitches take the yarn back up again and re-

turn to normal size. However, while each stitch is linked to the one above and below, they are not connected by a continuous strand of yarn, so when you stretch the fabric vertically you will find it far less expansive. The stitches in the columns can only borrow a bit of yarn from their own running threads and one or two stitches on either side; most of the stretch provided is that of the yarn itself. You should keep this in mind if you are considering knitting a sweater horizontally rather than vertically.

Curl

Left to its own devices, the top and bottom edges of Stockinette will curl up toward the Knit side. If the fabric is quite narrow, the side edges will roll toward the Purl side. If you look at Stockinette Stitch in cross section, it becomes apparent why it has this tendency to curl. The stitch is narrow at the bottom where it is pulled through the stitch below toward the Knit side; at the top it is arched back and widened out where the stitch above is pulled through. Think of it as a little soldier at attention, heels together, shoulders thrust back, back arched, and the chest puffed way out. In a very narrow fabric the effect is so pronounced that the fabric itself mimics the stance of the stitch and the side edges will curl toward the Purl face. As the fabric widens this tendency is gradually overcome, with the vertical curl only slightly evident at the very edge, and when the fabric is wide enough, the natural resilience of the yarn begins to work against the tension in each stitch and then the bottom and top edges curl up instead.

While this curling is a nuisance in many cases, and can only be overcome by placing a border of some noncurling stitch pattern along the edges, it can be used to advantage as well. Allowing the fabric to roll up at the lower edge of a sleeve or along a neck edge can add a charming design element to a garment. This design element is called Rouleau, the French word for "roll."

HORIZONTAL AND VERTICAL CURL

IRREGULAR ROW TENSION

Tension

Stockinette is so commonplace, and seemingly so easy to do, that knitters typically underestimate its challenge. In fact it is one of the most difficult stitch patterns to handle successfully, and it takes a very practiced hand to do it justice. The smooth surface of a Stockinette fabric betrays any error in technique or irregularity in tension with a vengeance. This makes it particularly problematic for beginners, and for those of you who knit using one of the finger-wrap methods. Fortunately, there are ways to compensate, and with time and experience the problems can be overcome.

- You must, of course, be careful to correct any errors. There cannot be any stitches that are split, accidentally crossed, or slipped.
- Be very careful to knit each and every stitch with a precise, even tension.
- Many people find it requires a firmer tension on a Purl row than on a Knit row in order to make the stitches of both rows exactly the same size. If you are having trouble with this row-by-row tension, you will see the evidence on the Purl side of the fabric, which will have what looks like two-row horizontal stripes defined by a wider "gutter" between one row of Purl nubs and the next, as you can see in the photograph above.
- Some knitters compensate for this problem by using two different-size needles. This, of course, only works if the difference between one row and the next exactly matches the difference in needle size, but it may not. Also, using that as a permanent solution will restrict you to straight needles. It is far better to practice on a swatch, adjusting the tension, perhaps a little looser on Knit or a little tighter on Purl, constantly checking the Purl side, until all the rows balance out. With time, your hands will become used to working the correct way, and you won't have to think about it.

While you are learning, it is an excellent idea to use yarns that are fuzzy, loosely spun, or highly textured with slubs or a crimp, or one that is a variegated or tweedy color, because any of these qualities will camouflage a multitude of errors.

Garter Stitch and Horizontal Welts

In the material on forming the Knit and Purl stitch, we already discussed the method of working that produces Garter Stitch. Let's go back to it a moment and discuss its behavior. This stitch pattern, and others related to it, encourage the curl that is inherent in a Knit stitch. If you were to look at a fabric of Garter Stitch in cross section, you would see that it is made up of tiny scallops with one row curling to one side, the next to the other side. This gives the fabric great vertical elasticity and resilience. Also, because each row curls in the opposite direction, one cancels the other out and the fabric itself lies perfectly flat.

I don't find it a very attractive stitch pattern, but the fact that it is easy to work and well behaved ensures its utility and popularity. It is especially good for beginners because the rough surface distracts the eye, hiding any

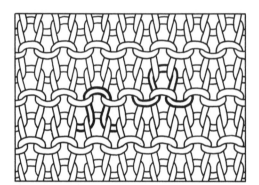

GARTER STITCH

GARTER STITCH AND HORIZONTAL WELTS

small errors, and since it is all in Knit, the tension is easier to control. Typically the gauge of Garter Stitch will show that it has twice as many rows as stitches, which is unusual among patterns. This means that any fabric done in this manner will require a great many more rows for the same length than many other patterns and will thus take considerably more yarn and more time to produce. It will, however, provide excellent thermal benefits because the curl enhances the stitches' ability to trap warm air.

If you alternate a few rows of Stockinette with a few rows of Reverse Stockinette, you will create horizontal stripes, first smooth, then nubby. Since Stockinette curls toward the Knit side horizontally, the Knit portion will be slightly recessed and the Purl portion will protrude, and for this reason is often called Horizontal Welting. The fabric will have some of the same elasticity as Garter Stitch, but the more rows there are in each stripe, the less elastic the fabric will become (see pages 211–216 for more information on this and other welts).

Ribbing or Vertical Welts

Another variation possible with Knit and Purl is to alternate the two stitches on the same row. If you work one or two Purl stitches and then one or two Knit stitches, and always stack the Knits on top of Knits and the Purls on top of Purls row by row, you will create alternating columns of Stockinette and Reverse Stockinette.

Moving the Yarn

If you are going to work this way, there is one important detail that you must keep in mind. I mentioned in the instructions on how to form the stitches that you must *always* have the yarn on the farside for a Knit stitch, and on the nearside for a Purl stitch. If you have just completed one and want to do the other, the yarn must be carried to the opposite side of the work through the gap between the needle tips, never over the needle. Passing the yarn over the needle is a specialty stitch called a

Yarnover, and it creates a new stitch with a hole under it. It is a mistake when you don't intend to do it, and a beautiful stitch when you do. (For a full discussion of the Yarnover, see pages 73–76.)

In all knitting instructions, it is assumed that the knitter knows to switch the yarn properly when changing from Knit to Purl; the instructions will simply say, for instance, K1 P1 (Knit one stitch, Purl one stitch). However, you will occasionally encounter instructions to move the yarn from one side of the needle to the other as if you were switching from Knit to Purl, but for some other purpose. In this book an instruction to do this is referred to as "yarn nearside" or "yarn farside" and is abbreviated *yns* or *yfs*. Most other knitting books refer to "front and back," or "forward and back," rather than "nearside" and "farside," but for reasons I spelled out in the Introduction, I find those terms too ambiguous.

Proportion and Behavior

The behavior of these patterns is opposite to that of Garter Stitch and Horizontal Welting. The narrow columns will show evidence of vertical curl with the columns of Knit stitches protruding, the columns of Purl stitches receding to produce a fabric of great horizontal elasticity with absolutely no horizontal curl. These patterns are used for the edges of most sweaters and are called ribbing in the U. S., and welts in Great Britain.

The most common plain rib patterns are Single Rib and Double Rib, but there are many others that introduce more decorative elements. Single Rib is made up of one Knit stitch, one Purl stitch (K1 P1), alternated across the row. It is trim, tailored, and elastic, being about 30 percent narrower than Stockinette stitch. It tends to lie very flat, as the curling tendency of each stitch offsets that of its neighbors. Double Rib has two Knit stitches, two Purl stitches (K2 P2), alternated across the row. It is a chunkier, more pronounced rib that is even more elastic, about 40 percent narrower than Stockinette, and 20 percent narrower than Single Rib. Double Rib is the peak; beyond two stitches per column the ribbing again begins to lose elasticity.

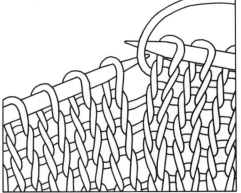

BRINGING YARN BETWEEN NEEDLE TIPS

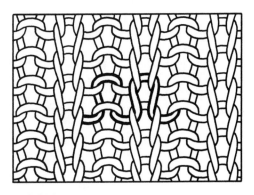

SINGLE RIB

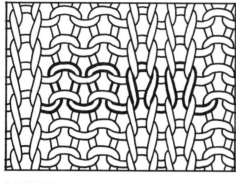

DOUBLE RIB

SEEDED CHEVRON

While many people do not bother to do so, at their cost, it is just as important to do a stitch gauge for a rib pattern as for any other stitch pattern. It does require special care in measurement because of its elasticity (more information can be found on page 424). Most patterns and instruction books recommend that the ribbing be done on a needle one or two sizes smaller than that used for the stitch pattern on the remainder of the garment to encourage elasticity. Actually, you can hardly use a needle too small; the finer it is, the less likely the ribbing is to stretch out and lose its elasticity with wear.

Tension

Rib is another stitch pattern that often shows evidence of tension problems. In Double Rib you may notice that the left stitch column in each Knit rib will be enlarged; in Single Rib it may be that every other Knit stitch in each column will be larger. Generally, these irregularities can be corrected if you are careful to tension the yarn firmly on the Purl stitches, particularly when you switch from Knit to Purl. You will quickly accustom yourself to the rhythmic change in tension that is required, and you will find your ribbings much improved in appearance.

Brocade Patterns

The nub created by Purl is used to create a wealth of patterns on the smooth face of a Knit stitch ground. You can put them wherever you want in order to create boxes, diamonds, diagonal lines, zigzags, butterflies, flowers, or windmills—any shape that can be reduced to the simple geometry of stitches. They are referred to as brocade patterns because many of them were originally inspired by weaving patterns created with texture rather than color.

Because Knit and Purl are just two aspects of the same stitch, and what is Knit on one side is Purl on the other, and vice versa, many of these patterns are reversible. If you create a shape in Purl stitches on a Knit ground, when you turn the fabric over you will have the

BISCUIT BROCADE

DUTCH WOOL PETTICOAT IN FIGURATIVE BROCADE PATTERN, PROB. LATE 17TH CENTURY

same shape created out of Knit stitches on a Purl ground. The more balanced the number of Knit and Purl stitches on each face of the fabric, the less tendency the fabric has to curl, but the more it widens. Seed Stitch, for instance, is a common texture pattern, imparting a nice nubby quality to the fabric. It is basically a broken Single Rib—one Knit stitch, one Purl stitch alternated across the row—but instead of forming columns, each subsequent row breaks the pattern with a Knit stitch placed above a Purl, a Purl stitch placed above a Knit. (Yes, there is a Double Seed version, which is a broken Double Rib.) Seed Stitch is 30 percent shorter than Stockinette, and 18 percent wider. Watch your gauges carefully on these stitches because of this widening.

Turned Knit and Purl

There are several occasions when it is necessary and appropriate to turn the stitches so the left side of the stitch is on the nearside of the needle. This is frequently done as a part of certain stitch techniques, either to create a particular effect or to facilitate working. A turned stitch that is Knit or Purled in the normal way, by inserting the right needle into that half of the stitch on the nearside of the needle, will cross on itself. This can be used decoratively, and the technique is discussed on page 32. On the other hand, a turned stitch that is Knit or Purled by inserting the right needle into that half of the stitch on the farside of the needle instead will not cross on itself; it will become a normal stitch in the fabric.

Most often, a stitch is turned immediately before it is worked, but a whole row of stitches can be turned by wrapping the yarn in the opposite direction, as follows:

KNIT OVER

- Insert the right needle into the first stitch on the left needle in the normal way to Knit, wrap the yarn from the farside *over* and down the nearside of the right needle tip. Pull the new stitch through and discard.

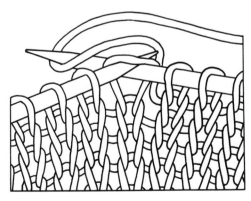

WRAP FOR KNIT OVER

PURL UNDER

- After you insert the right needle into the first stitch on the left needle in the normal way to Purl, wrap the yarn from the nearside *under* the right needle tip and up the farside. Pull the new stitch through and discard.

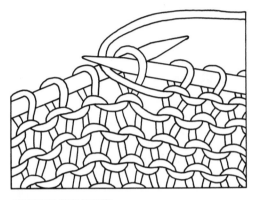

WRAP FOR PURL UNDER

When you examine the results, you will see that the new stitches on the right needle are turned, with the left sides of the stitches on the nearside of the needle. However, you do not want these turned stitches to cross in the fabric, so the turn must be "undone" as you work the stitches on the next row, as follows:

KNIT FARSIDE

- Insert the right needle into the farside of the turned stitch on the left needle, wrap the yarn under the needle in the normal way for Knit, and draw through the new stitch.

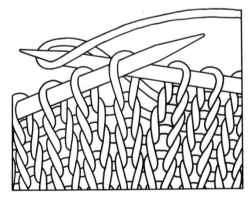

KNIT FARSIDE ON TURNED STITCH

PURL FARSIDE

- Reach around and insert the right needle into the farside of the turned stitch from left to right, wrap the yarn over the needle in the normal way for Purl, and draw through the new stitch.

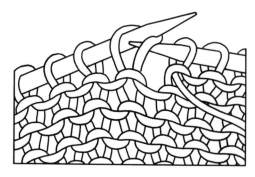

PURL FARSIDE ON TURNED STITCH

The new stitch will sit on the right needle in the normal position, and the discard stitch will lie uncrossed within the fabric, as it should. If you are knitting a flat fabric, it is easiest to use Purl Unders on one row and Knit Farside on the next. If you are knitting a circular fabric, you will have to work one row with Knit Overs and the next with Knit Farside.

Turned Knit and Purl can sometimes be of use when working with yarns that are rather tightly spun or inelastic. These yarns may cause the fabric to go on the bias, an effect that is permanent and cannot be steamed out. The problem occurs because the process of wrapping the yarn around the needle for each new stitch adds additional twist to the yarn, and as the twist gets tighter, the whole fabric may start to skew. Most knitting yarns are relatively loosely spun, so any additional spin put on by the knitting itself will not produce a noticeable effect in the fabric. Nevertheless, it is something to guard against, and you most certainly will have to take it into consideration when working with any yarn that is overspun. There are several solutions. A very simple one is to clip or pin the yarn to the ball every few rows, then let the ball of yarn hang from the work and so untwist itself. Another is to use Turned Knit or Purl on every other row so that whatever twist is imparted on one row will be undone on the next.

Many Left-Finger knitters regularly use a Purl Under, described for that knitting method on page 14, because it is much easier for them to work than the normal Purl. Working Turned Purl on one row and Knit Farside on the next is fine for a plain Stockinette fabric, but because the instructions for all other stitch techniques are written for stitches that are not turned, you will encounter difficulties with any other sort of pattern. Of course, if you really understand how a given technique works, you can deal with a stitch in either position, but it adds a layer of complexity that is really quite unnecessary.

Slip Stitch

When instructions call for a Slip Stitch, all that is required is to move a stitch from the left needle to the right needle without working it. The yarn is simply passed loosely either on the nearside or the farside of the stitch to be slipped, and the next stitch is worked as required. There is probably no simpler technique in all of knitting, but this simplicity is quite deceptive, for a Slip Stitch plays many and various roles, some structural, others decorative, some obvious, and others very subtle.

Basic Slip Stitch

There are two ways to make a Slip Stitch, knitwise and purlwise. We will do the latter first as it is more commonly seen.

SLIP STITCH PURLWISE

• Insert the right needle into the first stitch on the left needle just as you would to Purl, and allow the stitch to transfer to the right needle without working it.

This transfers the stitch directly, maintaining its correct position on the needle, with the right side of the stitch on the nearside of the needle.

Structurally, when a new stitch is not formed on a subsequent row, the old stitch will be forced to occupy the space that would normally be filled by two stitches, one on top of the other. This elongates the Slip Stitch, and it does so by drawing on yarn from the stitches on either side of it, which tends to tighten them up and draw the fabric in slightly. The elongation will be somewhat incomplete so there will also be a certain amount

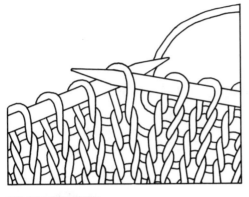

SLIP STITCH PURLWISE

of compression that occurs, drawing the row above and the row below together. When a stitch is slipped over more than one row, this compression is exaggerated. It is possible to achieve the same effect while minimizing distortion of the surrounding fabric by using one of the elongation techniques described elsewhere in this chapter. These techniques elongate the stitch so that it can be stretched over several rows without drawing on yarn from adjacent stitches.

SLIP STITCH KNITWISE

• Insert the right needle into the first stitch on the left needle just as you would to Knit, and allow the stitch to transfer to the right needle without working it.

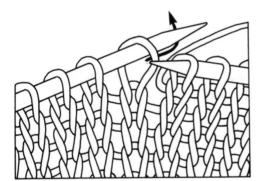

SLIP STITCH KNITWISE

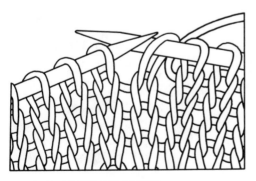

SLIP STITCH TRANSFERRED KNITWISE

This turns the stitch as it is transferred, and it will sit on the right needle with the left side of the stitch on the nearside of the needle. Most often this is done as one step in some other technique where it is necessary for the stitch to be turned, and it will not be carried over more than one row, as it is in the method above.

Stranding the Yarn

Now that you know how to transfer the stitch from one needle to the other, let us turn our attention to the problem of what happens to the yarn before, during, and after this otherwise simple process. Because one stitch has been skipped, the running thread passing from the last stitch worked to the next stitch worked is elongated and lies at the base of the slipped stitch. This elongated running thread can be hidden on the inside of the fabric, or can be used to decorative advantage on the outside. Here is how to place it where you want it.

SLIP STITCH YARN NEARSIDE

If you have Knit the stitch preceding the Slip Stitch, the yarn will be on the farside of the work.

1. Pass the yarn between the needle tips to the nearside and then slip the stitch either knitwise or purlwise.
2. If the following stitch is to be Purled, leave the yarn on the nearside and Purl.
3. If the following stitch is to be Knit, move the yarn between the needle tips to the farside and Knit.

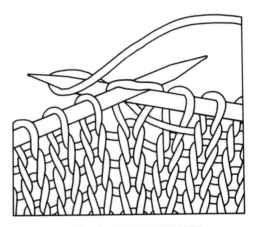

SLIP STITCH WITH YARN STRANDED NEARSIDE

If you have Purled the stitch preceding the Slip Stitch, the yarn will already be on the nearside of the work.

1. Slip the stitch knitwise or purlwise without changing the position of the yarn.

2. If the following stitch is to be Purled, leave the yarn on the nearside and Purl.
3. If the following stitch is to be Knit, move the yarn between the needle tips to the farside and Knit.

SLIP STITCH YARN FARSIDE

If you have Knit the stitch preceding the Slip Stitch, the yarn will be on the farside of the work.

1. Slip the stitch knitwise or purlwise without changing the position of the yarn.
2. If the following stitch is to be Knit, leave the yarn on the farside and Knit.
3. If the following stitch is to be Purled, move the yarn between the needle tips to the nearside and Purl.

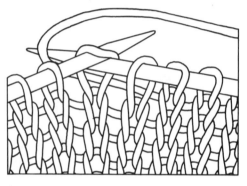

SLIP STITCH WITH YARN STRANDED FARSIDE

If you have Purled the stitch preceding the Slip Stitch, the yarn will be on the nearside of the work.

1. Pass the yarn between the needle tips to the farside and slip the stitch either knitwise or purlwise.
2. If the stitch following the Slip Stitch is to be Knit, leave the yarn on the farside and Knit.
3. If the following stitch is to be Purled, move the yarn between the needle tips to the nearside again and Purl.

Whether you pass the yarn on the nearside or farside of the Slip Stitch, you must be careful not to tension it

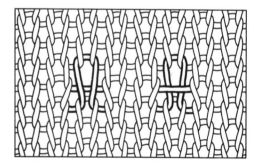

SLIP STITCHES

too tightly or the adjacent stitches will pull together and bunch up the fabric. With practice you will accustom yourself to allowing sufficient yarn to the running thread when you form the next stitch.

Multiple Slip Stitches

As mentioned before, it is also possible to slip several stitches, one after the other, which elongates the bar of the running thread into a strand. The only limit on the length of the strand is the problem of snagging it when the garment is worn; ¾ inch is a reasonable limit. The number of stitches required to create a strand of that length will, of course, depend upon your stitch gauge—you must be careful in this regard with stitch patterns that call for this if you are working in bulky yarn on large needles, for the strand could turn out to be longer than is practical.

If you are required to slip several stitches in a row, maintaining the correct tension on the strand becomes a more critical issue. A good trick to ensure adequate length to the strand is to stretch the slipped stitches out

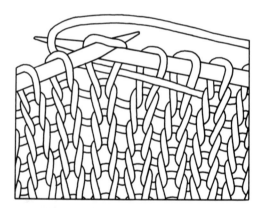

STRANDING YARN PAST TWO STITCHES

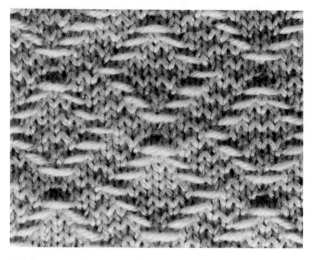

WOVEN DIAMOND, DONE WITH MULTIPLE STRANDING

on the right needle as far as they will go before working the next stitch. This way they are at their limit of expansion, and you can be sure that the running thread will not inhibit the natural resilience of the knitted fabric in any way. There are a few situations in which the running thread is deliberately kept taut when stitches are slipped. This is used to create vertical Welts (page 214) and Cording (page 155).

The strand created by Multiple Slip Stitches can also be caught up by a stitch on a later row to create quilted or lattice effects. Say you have stranded the yarn across five Slip Stitches. Three or four rows later, work to the stitch that lies above the center of the strand. Now we face deciding among the alternate methods knitters have devised to catch that strand.

LATTICE TECHNIQUE #1

1. With the tip of the right needle, reach down on the nearside of the strand and pick it up with the left side of the strand on the nearside of the needle.
2. While holding the strand on the right needle, Knit the first stitch on the left needle, drawing the new stitch through the discard stitch and under the strand from farside to nearside.
3. The strand will drop from the right needle as you pull the new stitch through; drop the discard stitch from the left needle in the normal way.

When you are done, examine your work and you will see that the strand is caught behind the base of the new stitch, with the discard stitch lying behind it.

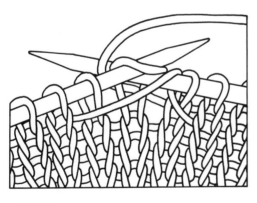

LATTICE #1

LATTICE TECHNIQUE #2

1. Lift the strand onto the left needle with the left side of the strand on the nearside of the needle.
   • Lift it up with the right needle and put it on the left needle, or
   • Pick it up directly on the left needle by moving the

left needle tip down between the fabric and the strand.
2. Insert the right needle through the strand and into the first stitch on the left needle and Knit in the normal way.
3. Drop both the discard stitch and the strand from the needle at the same time.

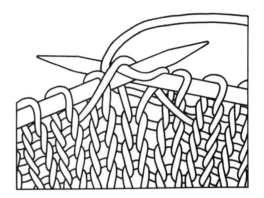

LATTICE #2

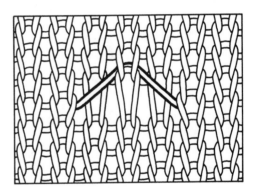

TWO-ROW LATTICE

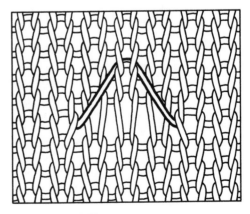

THREE-ROW LATTICE

QUILTED LATTICE

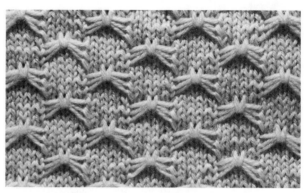

LITTLE BOWS, A MULTIPLE LATTICE PATTERN

When you examine your work you will see that it produces exactly the same result as Lattice technique #1. It is only a matter of preference which one you choose to use. I use Lattice technique #1, as I find it slightly easier and faster to work.

LATTICE TECHNIQUE #3

This last method for catching up strands produces a different result, which is less successful and more trouble to do. I have seen it in several patterns, however, and wanted you to be able to recognize it if only to avoid it.

1. Reach the tip of the right needle down on the near-side of the strand and catch it up.
2. Wrap the yarn around the needle as to Knit and draw a loop under the strand.
3. Knit the first stitch on the left needle and then pull the loop holding the strand over this new stitch and off the needle.

In this case, the loop holding the strand will cross on itself and will encircle the base of the new stitch and lie below it. It is therefore pulled up one row less than in the methods given above. Also, because of the route the yarn takes in this method, the loop holding the strand is pulled to the right, which distorts the pattern.

MULTIPLE LATTICE

The Lattice technique can also be used on multiple strands, i.e., two to five strands worked one above the other and then gathered up with one stitch. It creates a little bowknot effect that is quite charming.

Slipping so many stitches in one small area, as is required for patterns like this, can distort the fabric. It is important to watch the tension carefully, and in most cases it will steam out. If you are not happy with the result on a swatch, however, look in the section on elongation later in this chapter, where you will find some tricks for subtly elongating the slipped stitches.

Applications

The Slip Stitch can be combined with a Drop Stitch technique (page 44) to pull the stitch on a diagonal, creating hatch marks. These are often seen as a decorative surface on a column of Knit stitches; the patterns resemble cable stitches, only they lie flat. It can also be used as an allover textural device, and you will occasionally see it used to create the stem and leaves of tiny flower motifs.

The use of the Slip Stitch technique to create texture is found mainly in a family of stitch patterns commonly called Brioche, or Honeycomb (see page 85) where a Slip Stitch is combined with a Yarnover, creating a cell-like structure. These patterns produce very fluffy, soft fabrics with excellent thermal properties.

The tendency of the Slip Stitch to pull the rows above and below it together is used to create a variety of highly textured "blister" or "puff" patterns. When Slip Stitches bracket a section of the fabric containing a normal complement of stitches, the Slip Stitches pull the rows above and below together, forcing the fabric in between to bunch up. Depending on how the technique is used, the blisters or puffs will either protrude or recede, and can be made large or small to create many charming effects.

The running thread formed when a stitch is slipped can also be quite decorative when placed on the outside of the fabric. The small horizontal bars can be used to form vertical or diagonal lines, and patterns that make use of this aspect of the Slip Stitch produce very handsome, tailored fabrics. The more Slip Stitches used, the more dense the fabric will be. In some cases, this firmness is desirable, as for outerwear; in other cases, it might be less so, and can be overcome to some extent by using needles a size or so larger than normal for the yarn.

The Slip Stitch technique is exploited in many ways in color knitting, both as a means of facilitating the handling of yarn and stitches, and for its characteristics as a stitch (see the material on page 256 for more information). And finally, as I mentioned above, it is often an integral part of other stitch techniques.

Knit Below

Simply put, this technique involves knitting into a stitch one or more rows below the first stitch on the left needle. There are several different ways to accomplish this and they produce very different effects. One of the most common and important ways the technique is used is in a family of stitches called Brioche, or Honeycomb, which produce textured fabrics with a cellular structure and excellent thermal properties (see page 85).

Basic Knit Below

This is a deceptively simple technique, as its structure is rather interesting and complex.

KNIT VERSION

1. With the yarn on the farside, insert the tip of the right needle from nearside to farside into the center of the stitch that lies directly below the first stitch on the left needle.
2. Wrap the yarn as for a normal Knit stitch and pull the new stitch through.
3. Drop the stitch above from the left needle.

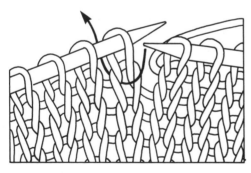

KNIT BELOW

PURL VERSION

1. With the yarn on the nearside, insert the tip of the right needle from farside to nearside into the stitch below the first stitch on the left needle.
2. Wrap the yarn in the usual way to Purl and draw the new stitch through; drop the stitch above from the left needle.

I want you to observe what happens to the discard stitch as the new stitch is completed. Either as soon as it is discarded, or when you begin to work the next stitch on the left needle, you will see that the discard stitch will unravel from the stitch below, which you have just Knit. Don't worry, it won't go anywhere; it has become a strand instead of a stitch and is caught up by the new stitch you have made. Because of the unraveling, however, a Knit Below can be worked no more frequently than every other stitch in every other row; the adjacent stitches are necessary to anchor the strand.

You might well say that the stitch worked into now resembles a Slip Stitch, and you would be right; it is now a single stitch that spans two rows. The complicating factor here is that instead of lying at the base of the Slip Stitch like a proper running thread, the strand is caught up with it by the new stitch above, and it is longer than it would be in that situation. Of course it is longer because it was once wrapped around the needle to form a stitch.

The really interesting thing about this stitch, however, is that the identical effect can be achieved by using a Slip Stitch combined with a Yarnover. (For a description of how to do that, see the material on Honeycomb on page 85.) Whether worked as a Knit Below, or as a Slip Stitch/Yarnover, the fabric will be the same, although many books present these patterns as if they were totally different techniques. Now that you know they are two different ways to accomplish the same

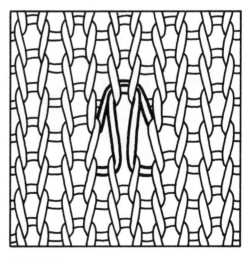

KNIT BELOW

thing, you can decide for yourself which way of working is better for you. In some cases, the Slip Stitch/Yarnover produces a better result, sometimes the Knit Below is simpler to do, and in a few of the more complex patterns, one or the other technique may be necessary. The Slip Stitch/Yarnover requires two rows, one for the Slip Stitch/Yarnover and one for the decrease that joins them and restores the stitch count. The Knit Below is a one-step process, being worked at the desired point with no preparation necessary. The difficulty with the latter, however, is that it is easy to split the stitch below as you insert the needle, and in some nubby or fluffy yarns, it can be hard to see where you are going. I use them both, sometimes one, sometimes the other, depending on the stitch pattern and the yarn I am working with.

GARTER STITCH KNIT BELOW

Knit Below is often used in rib or Garter Stitch format. The latter is interesting. Due to the structure of the stitch, what you work as Garter Stitch turns into Seed Stitch. It seems the Knit Below technique is full of metamorphoses. Here's how it works.

In a Garter Stitch, one Knits every row, which creates alternating rows of Knit and Purl stitches on both sides of the fabric. Purl stitches will always lie directly below the stitches on the left needle as you are working the next row. Now, if you work a Knit Below on every other stitch, look what happens. When you work a regular Knit stitch, the Purl nub will lie below the discard stitch on the right needle. When you work the next stitch as a Knit Below, you will be working into the Purl stitch, and when the stitch above unravels, the Purl nub will be eliminated. What started out as a row of Purl now alternates Purl and Slip Stitch, creating a rib effect that can be arranged in columns, or broken by alternating the pattern every other row as you would for Seed Stitch.

Now let's expand the possibilities somewhat.

method of working is identical. As with Basic Knit Below, the stitches above the one you work into will unravel once the discard stitch is released from the left needle, and will become Yarnover strands caught up by a Slip Stitch. If the strands don't unravel easily when you have completed the row, stretch the fabric horizontally to its maximum, then tug on it vertically. This evens out the stitches and will undo the bunching up that can occur.

In this case, a Multiple Knit Below is easier than trying to create the same effect with multiple Yarnovers —the Yarnovers stack up on the needle and become clumsy to carry row by row. You will, however, occasionally come across a pattern that calls for that, and if you find it awkward, just rewrite the pattern for Knit Below instead.

There are two other methods of working a Multiple Knit Below.

UNRAVELED KNIT BELOW

Sometimes you will see patterns that ask you to unravel the stitches before working the stitch in the row below. The effect will be the same, and it is more trouble to unravel on purpose when the stitches will unravel themselves, so why bother? Well, some yarns don't unravel readily, even when stretched out, so it's worth knowing how to do should you need to. Also, if the yarn is fuzzy or nubby and you are having trouble counting down the correct number of rows, by all means unravel first so you are sure you are working into the correct stitch.

1. Drop the first stitch off the left needle.
2. Insert the tip of either needle under the running thread alongside the dropped stitch and pull up gently until the stitch unravels. Repeat this process the desired number of rows.
3. Insert the left needle from nearside to farside into the

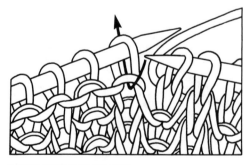

GARTER STITCH KNIT BELOW

Multiple Knit Below

It is just as easy to Knit two, three, or four rows below as it is to Knit one row below; the basic principle and

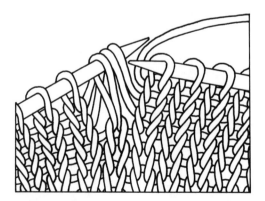

PICKING UP STITCH AND STRANDS FOR UNRAVELED KNIT BELOW

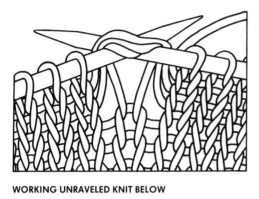

WORKING UNRAVELED KNIT BELOW

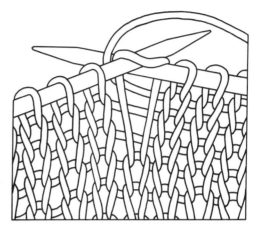

KNIT BELOW LADDER

center of the stitch remaining and under all the strands above it, making sure you pick the stitch up in the correct position, with the right side of the stitch on the nearside of the needle, and Knit in the normal way.

4. Drop the discard stitch and the strands from the left needle together.

Alternately, you can proceed as follows:

1. Pick up the stitch and the strands on the right needle, again going in from nearside to farside.
2. Wrap the yarn as to Knit and pull the new stitch through. The discard stitch and the strands will drop from the needle as the new stitch is formed.

With the latter method, you have only one needle tip forming the new stitch. Some people find that awkward, although I think it can be a little faster way to work.

If you are uncomfortable about dropping stitches but want to deliberately unravel, you can insert the right needle into the desired stitch in the row below and then drop the stitch from the left needle. Using the tip of the left needle, unravel the strands down to the stitch you are holding on the right needle. This way there is no danger of going too far.

Knit Below Ladder

The Multiple Knit Below can also be worked without including the strands.

• Unravel the strands down to the desired stitch, pick up only the stitch on the left needle and Knit.

This way of working turns that stitch into a long Slip Stitch with a backdrop of strands that are not gathered up by the new stitch. Because the background strands were once stitches, and have the extra yarn that provides, they will spread horizontally behind the Slip Stitch, creating a small, round barred opening in the fabric that is quite charming.

Applications

The Multiple Knit Below and the Knit Below Ladder are used primarily for spot patterns. Multiple Knit Below and Knit Below Welting (see page 212) create puffy textures and decorative distortions of the fabric. The Basic Knit Below technique is found primarily in the Honeycomb stitches (page 85). There are Stockinette, Garter,

HONEYCOMB

KNIT BELOW PUFF

and Rib varieties, open and closed versions, and those that run on the diagonal. If you want a soft, warm, and cozy fabric, these are the patterns to turn to. They are marvelous when done in more than one color, creating rich tweedy fabrics. Once you make yourself familiar with these stitches, I think you will find you turn to them again and again—and there is a rich variety of patterns to choose from. And now that you understand the structure of these stitches, you can make up your own!

Crossed Stitch

You will find that Crossed Stitch is rather ubiquitous, used on its own merits as a decorative stitch either alone or in combination with other techniques, and frequently as a behind-the-scenes player, where its role is more structural and it is used to enhance another stitch. Because it is so basic, it is important to understand just how it works.

As you know from the discussion of the structure of the Knit/Purl stitch, as you look at it from the Knit side the stitch lies flat and open, with the yarn coming from the right forming the right side of the stitch, and the yarn coming from the left forming the left side of the stitch. The two sides of a Crossed Stitch are switched, with either the right side of the stitch crossing over to the left on the Knit face of the fabric, or vice versa.

Left Crossed Stitch

The Left Crossed versions are easier to do, so let's look at them first.

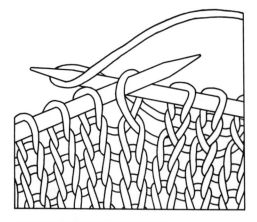

LEFT CROSSED STITCH/KNIT FARSIDE

KNIT LEFT CROSSED STITCH

1. Insert the right needle tip into the farside of the first stitch on the left needle from right to left.
2. Wrap the yarn in the normal way to Knit, pull through the new stitch, and drop the discard stitch from the left needle.

If you watch, you will see the discard stitch cross on itself as it drops from the left needle, with the right side of the stitch crossing over to the left at the outside, the left side crossing behind it to the right.

PURL LEFT CROSSED STITCH

1. Insert the right needle tip into the farside of the first stitch on the left needle from left to right.
2. Wrap the yarn in the normal way to Purl, pull through the new stitch, and drop the discard stitch from the left needle.

This produces the identical stitch as the Knit version; when looked at on the Knit face of the fabric, the

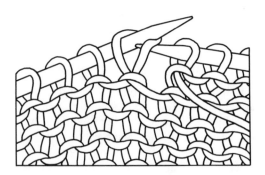

LEFT CROSSED STITCH/PURL FARSIDE

stitch will cross to the left. It is quite a bit easier to do the Knit version than the Purl.

In most knitting instructions, a Left Crossed Stitch is not often referred to by name; usually the knitter is simply told to Knit or Purl "through the back of the stitch." You may recall Knit and Purl farside from the discussion on Turned Knit and Purl on page 23. The technique is precisely the same, but the type of stitch it is used on makes all the difference.

Right Crossed Stitch

If you Knit or Purl a normal stitch through the farside, it will cross to the left, as discussed here. If you Knit or Purl a turned stitch through the farside, it will not cross, but if you Knit or Purl a turned stitch through the nearside in the normal way, it will, and it will cross to the right, which is just what we want next.

KNIT RIGHT CROSSED STITCH

In order to cross an isolated stitch to the right, just slip the stitch knitwise in order to turn it, return it to the left needle and either Knit or Purl normally. However, if you must work an entire row of Right Crossed Stitches, it is far more efficient to turn the new stitches on one row and cross them on discard on the next.

1. On an inside row, work every stitch as for Turned Purl (page 23), wrapping the yarn under the needle tip. (The discard stitch in this case has been handled in the normal way, and will not cross, but the new stitch will be turned on the needle.)
2. On the return row, Knit into the nearside of the turned stitch as you would normally. (The turned stitch will cross over on itself to the right as it is discarded.)

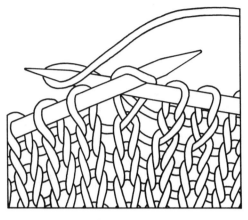

KNITTING THE TURNED STITCHES

PURL RIGHT CROSSED STITCH

1. On an outside row, work every stitch as for Turned Knit (page 23), wrapping the yarn over the needle tip. (The discard stitch has been handled in the normal way, and will not cross, but the new stitch will be turned on the needle.)

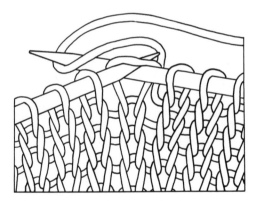

TURNING THE STITCHES FOR PURL RIGHT CROSSED

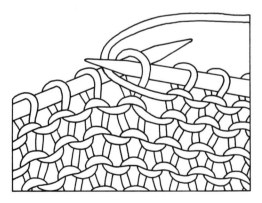

TURNING THE STITCHES FOR KNIT RIGHT CROSSED

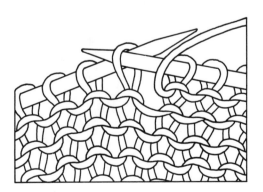

PURLING THE TURNED STITCHES

2. On the return row, Purl into the nearside of the turned stitch in the normal way. (The turned stitch will cross over on itself to the right as it is discarded.)

When a stitch has been turned, half of the stitch on the nearside of the needle will be pulled to the left, the half on the farside will be pulled to the right, opposite to the way a normal stitch presents itself. This makes the stitch more difficult to work into in general,

but it is more so with Knit than with Purl. Therefore, if you want every stitch on every other row to be crossed, it is best to use Knit Over on the stitches of one row with plain Purl on the return. If you want every stitch of every row to cross to the right, you would do a Knit Over on one row, and a Purl Under on the next.

When a stitch is crossed on itself, whether to the right or the left, it will be considerably tighter than a plain Knit stitch. If the stitch is placed in a column on a Purl ground, the Crossed Stitch will have an embossed appearance, being both narrower and more raised than a plain Knit stitch would be if used in the same way. When used on every stitch, the resulting fabric will be tailored and quite firm. In addition, if every stitch on every row is crossed to the left, the fabric will take on a left bias, while if every stitch is crossed to the right, it will take on a right bias. When the stitches of every other row are crossed, the bias will be less pronounced, but still there. The bias is permanent and can not be removed. The only way to avoid incurring this bias effect is to cross every other row in the opposite direction, but that is somewhat more complicated.

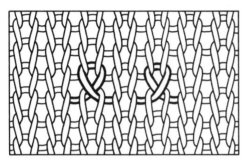

RIGHT AND LEFT CROSSED STITCHES

CROSSED STITCH BIAS

Crossed Stitch Combinations

The bias tendency of the Basic Crossed stitch can be overcome by combining the right and left versions in certain ways or by mixing Crossed and plain stitches.

BALANCED CROSSED STITCH

Working one row of Left Crossed, one row of Right Crossed stitch cancels the bias and produces a handsome, allover texture pattern. Unfortunately, it is slow going unless worked at a fairly loose tension, and the concept is, therefore, most useful when applied in small sections rather then for an entire fabric. There are stitch patterns, for instance, that call for blocks or sections of Left Crossed Stitch that would probably be more successful if done in Balanced Crossed Stitch because of the lack of bias. If you are considering using a pattern like that, you might want to try it both ways and see which you prefer.

1. On the first row, insert the needle into the farside of the stitch and wrap the yarn over the needle. (In other words, use both Knit Farside and Knit Over on every stitch. This crosses the discard stitch to the left and turns the new stitch at the same time.)
2. On the return row, Purl into the nearside of the turned stitch in the normal way. (This crosses the

discard stitch to the right and places the new stitches on the needle in the normal position.)

Of course, it is possible to Purl into the farside of every stitch, wrapping the yarn under the needle and using plain Knit on the return row. That produces the identical result, but the return row is more difficult to work.

used more for its appearance than for its ability to draw in, it can be very successful as a pattern. Crossing every stitch by working Knit one farside, Purl one farside, will produce an even less elastic fabric that tends to widen out. Another version places Balanced Crossed Stitch on just the knit columns on the outside of the fabric by alternating Knit one farside, Purl one on the outside, and Knit one, Purl one farside on the inside.

BALANCED CROSSED STITCH

CROSSED STITCH RIBBING

There are some books that recommend ribbing in Crossed Stitch, claiming that it is tighter and more elastic than conventional ribs. This is not true, as you would discover if you were to make a comparison. On a twenty-stitch sample, Single Rib produced 7.0 stitches per inch, Crossed Rib produced 5.7. In an actual garment, this means that the number of stitches that would produce a twenty-inch width in Single Rib, would turn out to be twenty-four inches in Crossed Rib. Because the stitch is crossed on itself, it actually has reduced resilience; it is harder for it to stretch out and recover. Crossed Rib is usually done as a Single Rib with every Knit stitch worked farside, so that every other stitch in each column will be crossed (the Purl stitches are worked normally). The rib does lie nice and flat and has a rather attractive appearance, with each column being more textured and irregular than a plain ribbing. When

TWO RIBBINGS IN CROSSED STITCH

Applications

Aside from being used for an entire fabric, or to create geometric patterns within a fabric, Crossed Stitch has many other applications. It is sometimes used on Cable Stitches to give them a more embossed appearance and is commonly used to form stems and the spines of leaves, or to add definition to the very tip of a leaf. There are many Twist Stitch patterns that create zigzag

FACETED DIAMOND

BEADED CHAIN

lines, and a Crossed Stitch is often used at the point where the line changes direction or where two lines intersect. It is frequently used in lace patterns, to tighten up a stitch that lies between two Yarnovers, and in one

type of Beading to prevent the beads from slipping through to the inside of the fabric. In short, because you will encounter the stitch in so many situations, it is well to understand exactly how it works.

Elongation

This is a group of very simple techniques that allow you to make some of the stitches larger than they normally would be on the size needle you are using. There are a variety of ways to do this, depending on the effect you wish to achieve.

Stitch Elongation

The Stitch Elongation methods are used to add a measured amount of additional yarn to otherwise normal stitches so they are enlarged in comparison with the other stitches of the fabric. The choice of technique depends on whether the effect is wanted on an entire row, or only on certain groups of stitches. These techniques are used both for their own decorative merits, and as part of other stitch techniques.

NEEDLE ELONGATION

If you want one entire row of stitches elongated, simply use a larger needle in the right hand. When the stitches have been worked off the larger needle on the return row, don't forget to return to the needle you were originally working with. You will have to go up approximately four needle sizes in order to make the stitches half again as large as the rest of the stitches in the fabric; however, any change in the size of the needle will be visible. (See the chapter "Materials" for information on the irregular size increments in American needles.)

If you wish to elongate more than a row or two, you will begin to enter the territory of a technique called regauging, which is a method of altering the stitch gauge, and therefore the size of the fabric, by means of changing needle sizes. The technique has some very interesting applications, which are discussed on page 423.

OPEN STRIPES DONE WITH NEEDLE ELONGATION

MULTIPLE WRAP ELONGATION

This method is used to elongate individual stitches or small groups of stitches, or to enlarge an entire row more than you could with the needle method, above.

1. Work stitches in the normal way, either Knit or Purl, but wrap the yarn two, three, or four times around the needle.
2. Pull all these wraps through the discard stitch and leave them on the right needle.
3. On the return row, Knit or Purl only one of the

wraps of each stitch, dropping the remainder from the left needle.

When you have completed the return row, it is a good idea to tug down on the fabric to even out the elongated stitches. Each wrap will add roughly half again as much to the length of yarn provided to the stitch. For instance, if each normal stitch requires one inch of yarn, a double wrap will take about one and a half inches and a triple wrap about two inches.

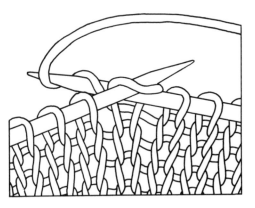

DOUBLE WRAP FOR ELONGATED STITCH

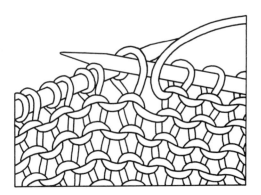

PURLING AN ELONGATED STITCH

SEAFOAM, A YARNOVER ELONGATION PATTERN

YARNOVER ELONGATION

The Multiple Wrap method can often be awkward, what with pulling all those wraps through the discard stitch, especially if you are working with a bulky yarn. Here is another approach that avoids that problem. It also provides about one quarter as much more yarn on each wrap instead of one half, and this smaller increment may create just the effect you wish.

1. Knit or Purl the stitch you wish to elongate, and then work a Yarnover (page 73).
2. On the return row, drop the Yarnover from the needle, insert the right needle into the next stitch (the one that will be elongated), and give it a tug to help it take up the extra yarn provided by the Yarnover. Then Knit or Purl the elongated stitch in the normal way.

For a more elongated stitch, of course, you simply work several Yarnovers, one after the other, dropping them all from the left needle on the return row, or work one Yarnover on either side of the stitch in question.

CROSSED ELONGATED STITCH

Any elongated stitch can be crossed once on discard using the techniques described for Crossed Stitch above. With Needle Elongation and Yarnover Elongation, it is quite straightforward. With a Multiple Wrap Elongation, one must simply be careful to work into the farside of the strand on the left needle just where it emerges from the stitch below—if you work into the extra wraps it won't cross. If you want the stitch to cross in the other direction, remember the principles for Crossed Stitch, and wrap the yarn in the opposite direction from normal as you work each elongated stitch; when you work these on the return row, they will cross.

Here is a clever way to create a Twice Crossed Elongated Stitch. The technique seems a bit complicated at first, but once you get the hang of it, it works up very quickly, and it's quite a lovely, old-fashioned stitch.

Veil Stitch
1. Insert the right needle into the first stitch on the left needle as to Knit.
2. Pass the yarn under the right needle tip as to Knit, but·do not draw through a new stitch. Now wrap the yarn around the left needle—under and up on the nearside, and over to the farside, then once again around the right needle tip as to Knit.

Now to pull the new stitch through the discard stitch, you must be careful about the route of the right needle tip. If you look at the left needle, you will see that the stitch and the wrapped yarn are crossed, form-

ing an X. The one on top, stretched between the two needles, is the stitch; the one under it is the wrap.

3. On the farside of the left needle, move the right needle tip between the stitch and the wrap at the top of the X. As the right needle comes under the left needle toward the nearside, bring it out between the stitch and the wrap at the bottom of the X. Discard stitch and wrap together.

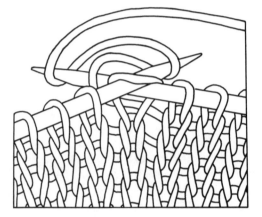

VEIL STITCH, THE WRAP

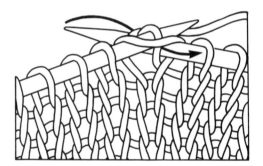

VEIL STITCH, DRAWING THE NEW STITCH THROUGH

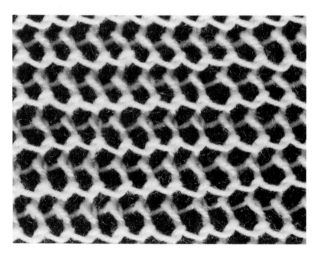

VEIL STITCH

Once you've done it a few times, you won't need to peer around on the farside to see where you're going, and it will all seem quite natural.

Elongated stitches are used as horizontal stripes of contrasting texture, and if width is planned carefully, can be threaded with ribbon. With Needle Elongation it is possible to graduate the size of the stitches in each subsequent row by using several different size needles, one after the other, row by row.

Multiple Wrap or Yarnover Elongation is most frequently used to create spot patterns, giving a deliberate distortion to the regularity of the fabric. There are also some Slip Stitch and Drop Stitch patterns in which the stitch is pulled over so many rows that it provides a neater result if the stitch is first elongated to some degree. And last but not least, the techniques are an important part of many Threaded Stitch patterns (see that section later in this chapter).

Loop Stitch

This technique allows you to make loops that hang off the face of the knitting.

The loops can be used all over a fabric, in horizontal stripes, in small tufty sections, or as borders. This is one to be playful with. Keep in mind that the loops will add considerably to the warmth of the garment, especially when they are used on the inside, where they can trap body warmth. Mittens and hats knitted in wool with loops on the inside are the warmest of all.

There are two methods of making the loops, one in which they are secured as they are being worked, and the other in which they are knotted in place later.

KNOTTED LOOP STITCH

With the traditional methods of working, the loops formed were not very secure in the fabric, either in the making or in the wearing. Here is a new approach that keeps them in place quite dependably.

1. Insert the right needle into the first stitch on the left needle and Knit, but do not drop the stitch from the left needle.
2. Pass the yarn to the nearside between the crossed needle tips, around the left thumb, and back through the needle tips to the farside.
3. Knit the same stitch on the left needle again, and then drop it from the needle and extract your left thumb from the loop.
4. Next pinch the loop against the fabric with the right thumb while inserting the tip of the left needle into the nearside of the two new stitches thus created on the right needle, then hold the loop with the left thumb and wrap the yarn around the right needle tip as to Knit. Pull both stitches over the yarn and off the needle.

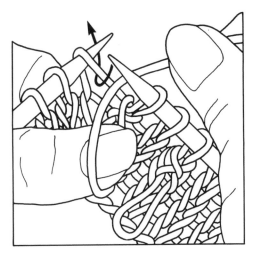

WRAPPING THE YARN FOR A KNOTTED LOOP

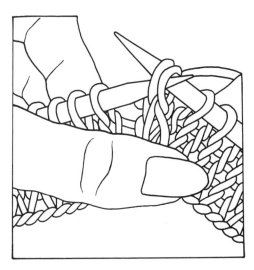

SECURING THE LOOP

The last step is a Crossed Left Decrease, which restores the stitch count. Once these loops are tightened up, they will hold quite nicely because the decrease crosses the stitches. One way to tighten them up after a row is completed is to insert the free needle into all the loops across the row and then tug up on the needle holding the stitches, down on the one holding the loops. More simply, grab a bunch of them at a time and tug down, repeating across the row.

KNOTTED LOOP STITCH

Loop knitting can be worked in Stockinette, or in Garter Stitch, which would prevent curling, or introduced in rows, columns, or spots with any number of other stitch patterns. Should you wish denser fluff, knit with two or three strands of fine yarn held as one—which provides you as well with the opportunity to blend colors and textures. Wrapping the thumb and knitting the stitch twice in succession creates a double loop. This puts three stitches on the needle to work together with the decrease. With a fine yarn, you could make a triple loop, working four stitches into the decrease. And if you *really* want loops, work in Garter Stitch, making loops on every row so they are on both the inside and the outside of the fabric. To reduce the number of loops, work them every other stitch, staggered every other row. Needless to say, the technique absorbs a great deal of yarn; plan carefully (see the information on calculating yarn yardage on page 428).

One or the other of the two variations that follow are found in most books that discuss the technique. Unfortunately, the loops made with either method are not held securely in the fabric. I want to give you the instructions for them only so you will know to avoid them, and not mistake them for something new or different if you encounter them elsewhere.

TRIPLE LOOP STITCH

1. Insert the right needle into the first stitch on the left needle as to Knit.
2. Hold the left forefinger extended along the farside of the crossed needle tips and wrap the yarn three times around both the forefinger and the right needle tip in the following way:
   • Pass the yarn up the farside of the forefinger, under the right needle tip, over the top of the needle, and back under the forefinger.
3. Pull all three wraps through the discard stitch just enough so that they sit like stitches on the right needle and then release the discard stitch from the left needle. The loops will hang on the farside of the work.

Some instructions leave it at that, and some ask that you return the three loops to the left needle and then Knit all three together through the farside, or insert the left needle tip into the nearside of the three loops on the right needle and Knit them together that way—which amounts to the same thing. Others just suggest that you work Crossed Stitch on the return row. Regardless of which way you do it, these loops tend to unravel all too easily, which is the very large demerit I must give to this method; I really don't see how it would survive wearing, when it barely manages to stay together during knitting.

KNIT-TOGETHER LOOP STITCH

This next method is slightly more difficult to do but gives a somewhat better result. It restricts itself to a single loop, but that provides plenty of fluff.

1. Insert the right needle into the first stitch on the left needle as to Knit.
2. Wrap the yarn once around both forefinger and right needle tip in the following way:
   • Pass the yarn up the farside of the forefinger, over the top, and down the nearside between the crossed needle tips.
3. Draw through the new stitch, but do not drop the loop off your forefinger, nor the discard stitch off the left needle.
4. Knit together through the farside both the new stitch and the discard stitch in the following way:
   • Insert the left needle tip into the nearside of the new stitch on the right needle, but do not release it from the right needle; then insert the right needle tip into the farside of the discard stitch on the left needle. Once you have both needles through both stitches, Knit the stitches together. Then, and only then, extract your finger from the loop.
5. Use Knit Left Crossed Stitch on the return row.

These loops are also formed on the farside of the work. The Crossed Knit on each intervening row helps to secure the loops, and while better than the first version, it still has a tendency to pull out if one is not careful. In addition, it's very awkward to do all that manipulation with one finger tied down.

BOW KNOTS

Here is another form of loop, developed by California knitter Barbara Aytes.[1] In this case, however, the elongated strand is pulled out on the face of the fabric and secured with a knot to form a little bow.

1. Depending upon the size loop desired, make a double, triple, or quadruple Yarnover. Knit or Purl the next stitch, then make another multiple Yarnover of the same size.
2. On the return row, drop the Yarnovers from the needle, pulling the long loops to the outside of the fabric. At your convenience, stop, pull the loops out firmly to tighten up the stitches on either side to the correct size, and knot the two loops together with a square knot.

Several pairs of Bow Knots can be clustered together. For instance, you could put a pair on one row, a pair on the next row and knot them corner to corner, one pair on top of the other, or stack the pairs one above the other in columns. Do three in a row on two rows, or two in a row on three rows and knot six together. This works very well on Garter Stitch done every other row. You can also place a multiple Yarnover on either side of several Knit or Purl stitches and knot them over the intervening stitches to cluster them together. Do the same with intervening rows. Use your imagination and place them where you will; they are especially charming on a garment for a little girl, but I can also see them in a metallic yarn on an evening sweater, and no doubt there are many other possibilities between those two extremes.

BOW KNOTS

Cable Stitches

The extravagance and seeming complexity of a garment covered with the sinuous lines of Cable stitches looks daunting to the knitter who has never tried to make one; however, these fabrics are more works of care and patience than of esoteric skills. It is the elaboration of patterns that sets the challenge—the knitter must pay careful attention to each step—but the technique itself is quite simple, albeit slow and somewhat tedious to do.

I am going to describe here only the basic techniques involved. (For a discussion of how to plan and carry out a Cable knit project, see page 425.) Also, these patterns are infinitely more easy to follow on charts than in written instructions. Please see the section on Stitch Charting (page 449) for an explanation of its benefits; it will simplify your task enormously.

The fundamental principle of Cable knitting is that certain groups of stitches exchange places in a precise way in order to create a pattern. In order to do this, a group of stitches is removed from the left needle onto a holder of some sort (see below). These stitches are then held either on the nearside or farside of the fabric while a number of other stitches are worked. The stitches on hold are then either returned to the left needle to be

1. Barbara Aytes, *Adventures in Knitting* (New York: Doubleday & Co., 1968).

worked in turn, or worked directly off the holder. There are endless variations on this theme, but nothing more complicated than that.

Two different cable holders are found in knitting stores, as pictured in the chapter "Tools and Materials." The choice between the two is really up to you; both will do the job, as will a plain knitting needle. (Toothpicks and common nails can also be used, but they have a tendency to fray or split yarn and are really useful only when the knitting compulsion is at full strength and the proper tool is not available.) If you are going to do any serious Cable knitting, you will want to make this very minor investment. I find the straight one easier to handle and prefer it, but many knitters feel that the stitches on hold are a little more secure on the curved one. Try them both and choose the one that suits you.

Before we go on to the details of the techniques, I want to define some terms. Cable patterns are basically one-sided—that is, they are only decorative on one face of the fabric. The stitches that cross in front of the others on the outside of the fabric will be called facing stitches, the ones behind them will be called backing stitches. When the instructions mention "cable to the right or left," therefore, they refer to the direction the facing stitches take on the outside of the fabric. The entire group of stitches comprising the Cable pattern will be referred to as the Cable unit. In the abbreviation used in written instructions, the stitches to be cabled within each unit will be designated by numbers separated by a slash mark, which means "over." Therefore, if the instructions say "2/2," the Cable unit has four stitches, and two will be crossed over the other two.

With all that in mind, let us go on to look at the basic principles of how these stitches are done, beginning with the most elementary and common Cable.

Basic Cables

Cables are generally worked on the outside of the fabric because it is easier to see what you are doing and to make sure the stitches cross over one another in the right way. While Purl stitches can certainly be used within a Cable, Knit is traditional.

KNIT RIGHT CABLE

The Cable unit is made up of four stitches, and the two on the left will be the facing stitches, pulled to the right on the nearside of the other two. Working on the outside:

1. Slip the first two stitches on the left needle to a cable holder. Move the holder to the farside of the work and either let it hang or pinch it against the fabric with the fingers of your left hand.
2. Knit the next two stitches on the left needle.

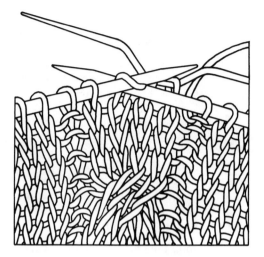

HOLDING THE STITCHES FARSIDE FOR KNIT RIGHT CABLE

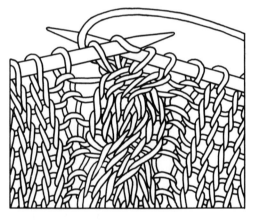

COMPLETING A KNIT RIGHT CABLE

3. Return the two stitches from the cable holder to the left needle and Knit them.

If you are using the straight cable holder, you will take the stitches onto the holder on the left point, and either return them from the same point, or Knit them off the right point. If you are using a curved holder, take the stitches onto the needle with the long point if you are going to return them before you Knit them. If you are going to Knit them from the holder, take the stitches on with the short end and knit them off the long end.

When knitting the Cable Stitches directly off the holder, you must be careful that the stitches on the left needle don't drop off; have those stitches pushed back from the tip a bit more than usual, and pinch the holder against the fabric under the needle with the tip protruding into the gap between the two needles. Working this way eliminates a step, and anything that makes a Cable Stitch faster to do is worth the effort of learning.

Because of the distance over which the four stitches must stretch, there will be something of a gap between them and the adjacent stitches. This can be minimized, although not entirely overcome, by tightening up on the running thread before working the first stitch of the Cable and the first stitch after the Cable.

Please note that when the stitches are transferred between the left needle and the cable holder, they must be slipped purlwise in order to maintain their correct position on the needle. While it is certainly possible to work Cables using Crossed Stitches, that should be done by choice and not by error.

KNIT LEFT CABLE

The Cable unit is made up of four stitches, and the right two will be the facing stitches.

1. Slip the first two stitches on the left needle to a cable holder. Move the holder to the nearside of the work and either let it hang or pinch it against the fabric with the thumb of your left hand.
2. Knit the next two stitches on the left needle.
3. Return the two stitches from the cable holder to the left needle and Knit them.

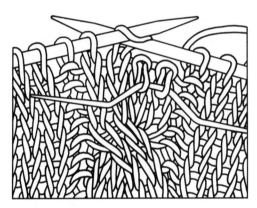

HOLDING THE STITCHES NEARSIDE FOR KNIT LEFT CABLE

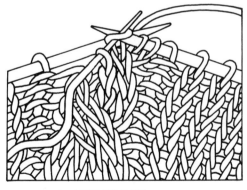

COMPLETING A KNIT LEFT CABLE

Should you want to create some special effect that requires a Cable that has Knit stitches on the outside, but must be worked on the inside, here is how to do it.

PURL RIGHT CABLE

The Cable will cross to the right on the outside of the fabric.

• Slip two stitches to the cable holder, hold them on the farside, and work the Cable in Purl, two stitches from the left needle and then two stitches from the cable holder.

PURL LEFT CABLE

The Cable will cross to the left when viewed from the outside.

• Slip two stitches to the cable holder, hold them on the nearside, and work the Cable in Purl, two stitches from the left needle and then two stitches from the cable holder.

FOUR RIB BRAID

Cable Variations

In most Cables, both the facing and the backing stitches are worked in Knit, with the Cable itself set off on a background of Purl stitches. Cables can be done, however, with only the facing stitches in Knit, blending the other stitches of the Cable unit into the Purl background. They can also be done entirely in Seed Stitch or half Seed, half Stockinette.

Using the same basic Cable technique, it is possible to cross two stitches over one (2/1), three over three (3/3), two over three (2/3), four over two (4/2), or any combination you care to come up with between 2/1 and 4/4, but that is generally the outside practical limit beyond which the stitches don't want to stretch (if necessary, it is possible to elongate the Cable stitches to allow them to stretch further; see page 36).

You will notice that I have not mentioned 1/1 Cables, although that would logically be the most fundamental unit. That is because there are alternate ways of working them without the use of a cable holder that makes them much faster to do, but there is no law that says you can't use a cable holder for them if you want to. One of those alternatives, Drop Stitch, is described next; the other will be found in the section on Twist Stitch later in this chapter.

SEED STITCH CABLE

Drop Stitch

A Drop Stitch is just what it says it is—a stitch that is dropped off the needle and picked up again when it's time to work it. There are a variety of uses for it, one of which is a 1/1 Cable without the use of a cable holder. Most knitters get nervous just at the thought of a dropped stitch, and the idea of doing it purposely is not a comfortable one. In fact, there are times when this technique should not be used and others when it is perfectly satisfactory.

Any Drop Stitch can be accomplished with a cable holder in the same way a true Cable Stitch is done, and that is the method of choice when the yarn is at all slippery and has a tendency to run easily. There are many yarns, however, that do not run all that easily, particularly wool but also any yarn that is fluffy or nubby, and this technique is then preferable because it is so much faster than using a cable holder.

LEFT CROSS DROP STITCH

1. Drop the first stitch off the left needle on the nearside of the work.
2. Knit or Purl the next stitch on the left needle.
3. Insert the left needle into the dropped stitch from nearside to farside, and Knit or Purl.

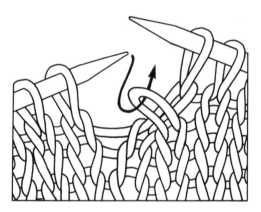

DROP STITCH/LEFT CROSS

RIGHT CROSS DROP STITCH

1. Drop the first stitch off the left needle on the farside of the work.
2. Knit or Purl the next stitch on the left needle.
3. Insert the left needle into the dropped stitch from nearside to farside, and Knit or Purl.

There are two things you must be careful of: One is not to split the yarn of the stitch when you pick it up, and the other is to make sure that the stitch is picked up in the proper position, with the right side of the stitch on the nearside of the needle. Frequently it helps to secure the dropped stitch against running by pinching it against the fabric with either your left thumb or right forefinger.

The result is a true 1/1 Cable Stitch, and unlike a Twist Stitch, as we will see in the next section, the stitches are not stacked or bunched together; they are unrestrained and lie side by side. Also, like a true Cable, either stitch can be worked in a Knit or a Purl. A single Drop Stitch can be pulled over three or four stitches, but there are not too many patterns that call for anything beyond that. It is also possible to use the technique on a stitch that was previously slipped, which pulls the stitch not only to the right or left, but up at an angle over a row or two. A stitch stretched over some distance like this can often benefit from elongation so the surrounding fabric lies flat and without distortion. In that case, the only limit, really, is the problem of snagging those long floating stitches when the garment is worn.

There's certainly no law against using the Drop Stitch technique for any Cable Stitch, but most people feel more comfortable with the cable holder when more than one stitch is going to be moved.

CHAIN LINK, A SIX-STITCH AXIS CABLE

Axis Cables

These Cables are made with three or more stitches, with the center remaining in position while the flanking stitches cross.

FACING AXIS CABLE

Here is a five-stitch Cable in which pairs of flanking stitches cross behind a single center axis stitch.

1. Slip three stitches to the cable holder and hold on the nearside.
2. Knit two stitches from the left needle.
3. Return the center stitch to the left needle, move the cable holder to the farside, and then Knit the center stitch.
4. Knit the two remaining stitches from the cable holder.

BACKING AXIS CABLE

To demonstrate an Axis Cable with the flanking stitches crossing in front, we'll use a six-stitch unit, with two stitches forming the axis.

1. Slip four stitches to the cable holder and hold on the farside of the work.
2. Knit two stitches from the left needle.
3. Return the center two stitches to the left needle and move the cable holder to the nearside.
4. Knit the two center stitches and then the two stitches remaining on the cable holder.

It is possible to have up to four stitches on either side of the axis, but the axis itself should probably not be larger than two stitches. The direction of the cross can, of course, be right or left, depending on whether you have the cable holder on the nearside or farside. One could also make the axis stitches in Purl and the flanking stitches in Knit.

Interspersed Cables

Here is another interesting Cable variation, in which a number of stitches are transferred to the holder and then interspersed with the stitches on the left needle one by one.

LEFT INTERSPERSED CABLE

1. Transfer up to four stitches to the cable holder and hold them on the nearside of the work.
2. * Knit one stitch from the left needle, Knit one stitch from the right side of the cable holder *. Repeat between * and * until all four stitches are worked off the cable holder.

RIGHT INTERSPERSED CABLE

Follow the steps as for Left Interspersed Cable, but keep the cable holder on the farside of the work. The effect will be heightened if each facing stitch is worked in Knit and the backing stitches are worked in Purl.

Rotated Cables

Here is a last simple and interesting but rarely seen way to make a Cable Stitch.

ROTATED CABLES

LEFT ROTATED CABLE

1. Transfer all four stitches of the Cable unit to the holder.
2. Give the cable holder a half turn, toward you to the left, so that the stitches that were on one side are now on the other.
3. Knit all the stitches off the cable holder. (They will be tight—it's too much of a struggle to return them to the left needle.)

This produces a Cable with a narrower waist than the others because the outside stitches trade places.

RIGHT ROTATED CABLE

• For the right version, rotate the cable holder away from you to the right.

You will find that there are seemingly endless variations on these themes. Once you are familiar with the principles, and the way these stitches are charted, you will find that you can easily modify a pattern to suit you, or to invent one of your own. No one has elaborated on Cables more than Barbara Walker, and anyone interested in Cable knitting, particularly those of you who would like to try your hand at designing a pattern, will find guidance and inspiration in her book *Charted Knitting Designs*.[1]

Twist Stitch

A Twist Stitch is first cousin to a two-unit Cable Stitch, but because of the way it is normally made, its appearance and structure are slightly different. Like a Cable, the pattern is decorative only on the Knit side, although it can be worked in either Knit or Purl.

There are three families of Twist Stitches, and within each family we must become acquainted with both Knit and Purl Right Twist, and Knit and Purl Left Twist. I am going to introduce you to the version I prefer first, although it is not the one most commonly encountered in stitch patterns. However, this method produces a superior result and is far easier to work than the other; I recommend that you use it in most patterns where a Twist Stitch is called for. Do look over the material on the other versions, however; because they are so frequently encountered in patterns, and used by so many knitters, I want to discuss their limitations and

possibilities even though I don't recommend them for most purposes. Once you are familiar with them, you will be able to select the one that will create the effect you wish to achieve.

Knit-Together Twist Stitches

This family of Twist Stitches relies on a Knit or Purl Two Together decrease technique that stacks the two discard stitches up, giving the stitch a very neat, trim, and consistent appearance, with the Right and Left Twists perfect mirror images of one another. In addition, the size of the Twist Stitches is the same as the stitches in the intervening rows. Although the technique can be used in any circumstance, it is particularly suc-

1. New York: Charles Scribner's Sons, 1972.

cessful when the intent of the pattern is to create a diagonal line of stitches.

KNIT RIGHT TWIST

1. Knit the first two stitches on the left needle together.
2. Knit the first stitch again.
3. Drop both discard stitches from the left needle.

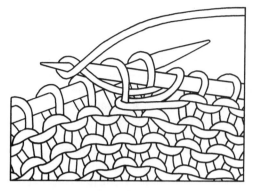

PURL RIGHT TWIST/THE SECOND STITCH

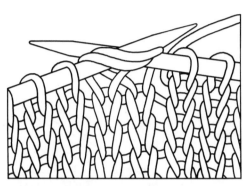

KNIT RIGHT TWIST/THE FIRST STITCH

KNIT TOGETHER RIGHT AND LEFT TWIST

KNIT LEFT TWIST

1. Slip two stitches knitwise. Return them to the left needle in their turned position.
2. Knit the second stitch farside.
3. Knit the first and second stitch together farside.
4. Drop the two stitches from the left needle together.

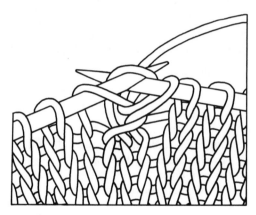

KNIT RIGHT TWIST/THE SECOND STITCH

PURL RIGHT TWIST

1. Purl the second stitch on the left needle.
2. Purl the first two stitches on the left needle together.
3. Drop both discard stitches from the left needle.

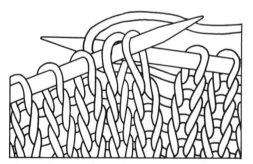

KNIT LEFT TWIST/THE FIRST STITCH

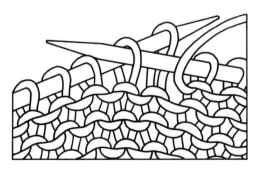

PURL RIGHT TWIST/THE FIRST STITCH

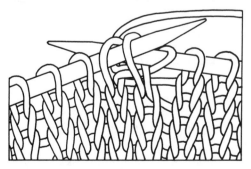

KNIT LEFT TWIST/THE SECOND STITCH

Left Twist is a little more complicated because the stitches must be turned on the needle prior to working the stitch, in order to prevent them from crossing. As a result, this is a rather slow way of working, and the slip/return step can, if not done with care, enlarge the discard stitches and change their appearance slightly. A faster method, which avoids that problem, is to turn the stitches to be twisted on the preceding row with either a Purl Under, or a Knit Over. It can be difficult to anticipate just which stitches you need to turn in a complex pattern, however, so this alternate method is best used only when the Twist Stitches are in predictable locations —in the same place row by row, in sections, or occupying an entire row.

PURL LEFT TWIST

1. Slip two stitches knitwise. Return the stitches to the left needle in their turned position.
2. Purl the two stitches together through the farside.
3. Purl the first stitch through the farside.
4. Drop both discard stitches from the left needle.

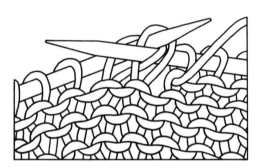

PURL LEFT TWIST/THE FIRST STITCH

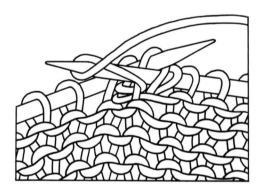

PURL LEFT TWIST/THE SECOND STITCH

Cable Twist Stitch

This group produces the identical result that would be obtained with the use of a cable holder.

KNIT RIGHT CABLE TWIST

1. Insert the right needle from left to right into the nearside of the second stitch on the left needle. Do not allow the right needle tip to pass under the left needle; instead, move the tip of the needle around the nearside of the first stitch.
2. Wrap the yarn as to Knit and pull the new stitch through.
3. Knit the first stitch in the normal way and drop both discard stitches from the left needle together.

That first step enlarges the discard stitch and is a bit awkward to do, although with familiarity it goes reasonably well.

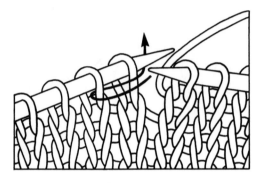

KNIT RIGHT CABLE TWIST

PURL RIGHT CABLE TWIST

1. Insert the right needle into the nearside of the second stitch on the left needle and Purl.
2. Purl the first stitch.
3. Drop both stitches from the left needle simultaneously.

Blessedly simple—if you want a Cable Twist, consider working it on the Purl side. This version is structurally identical to the Knit Right version, a true two-stitch Cable; however, because it is simple to do, no distortion occurs, so it doesn't really match the Knit version. If you were going to need a Twist Stitch done on every row, therefore, it wouldn't work out very well.

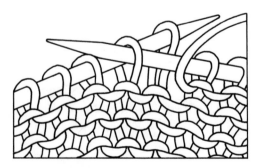

PURL RIGHT CABLE TWIST

KNIT LEFT CABLE TWIST

1. Slip the first stitch purlwise and the second stitch knitwise. Return the two stitches to the left needle, maintaining the turned position of the second stitch.
2. Knit the second stitch farside, then Knit the first stitch normally and discard both.

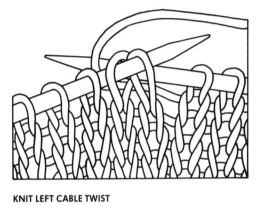

KNIT LEFT CABLE TWIST

Many people use this version of a Twist Stitch, but don't bother with turning the second stitch. The problem with that is that the second stitch will cross on discard. It is possible to dismiss this as utterly inconsequential, and indeed at times it is. But it does make a subtle difference in the appearance of the stitch, and if the point of the pattern is to use mirror image pairs of Twist Stitches, this won't work. As you know, a Crossed Stitch is considerably tighter than a plain Knit stitch, and when it is, in addition, pulled around another stitch, it will be even more so. The combination of the two things will cause a slight but obvious hole to appear to the left of the Twist Stitch. In a smooth yarn at normal tension, the hole will be visible; in a fluffy or highly textured yarn, particularly at a loose tension, it won't matter a whit, and knitting the second stitch on the farside is much faster and easier. In any case, you will encounter suggestions in stitch patterns to work the Knit Left Twist in this manner; now that you know the consequences, you may substitute another method of working if you choose.

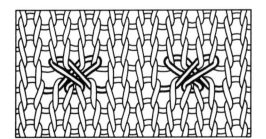

CABLE TWIST STITCHES

PURL LEFT CABLE TWIST

1. Slip the stitches as described above for the Knit version.
2. Purl the second stitch farside, then Purl the first stitch normally and discard both.

Purling the second stitch farside is not easy to do, but it is possible, and the result is identical to the Knit version. There are easier ways to do Twist Stitches, however, so I'm not sure there is much to recommend this method.

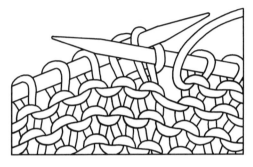

PURL LEFT CABLE TWIST

Wrapped Twist

There are only two versions of this, the others being impossible. But the two we have are simple to do, and their appearance is bold and distinctive, and very decorative when used in columns. Actually, this is more like a Wrap or Couching Stitch (see below) than a Twist Stitch, but so many people use it as if it were one, I find I must talk about it here.

WRAPPED KNIT RIGHT TWIST

1. Insert the right needle into the second stitch on the left needle in the normal way—the needle should enter the stitch on the nearside from left to right and pass under the left needle.

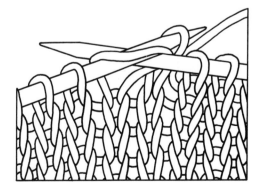

WRAPPED KNIT RIGHT TWIST

2. Wrap the yarn around the right needle and pull through the new stitch.
3. Knit the first stitch.
4. Drop both discard stitches from the left needle at the same time.

When you work a Knit Right Twist in this manner, the yarn passes behind the first stitch (just as it would for a Slip Stitch), the second stitch is worked, and the new stitch is pulled across the first stitch. What this does is to wrap the first stitch front and back so it is locked into position. As a result, the finished stitch will be quite bunched together. Also, whereas in all other Twist Stitches it is the discard stitch that crosses on the face of the fabric, with this version it is the new stitch, which tends to be quite enlarged.

Wrapped Purl Left Twist

1. Insert the right needle tip from farside to nearside into the second stitch and under the left needle.
2. Wrap the yarn as to Purl and pull through the new stitch.
3. Bring the right needle back around to the nearside again and Purl the first stitch.
4. Drop both discard stitches from the left needle together.

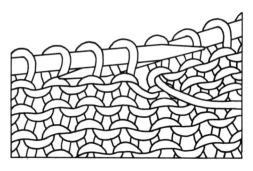

WRAPPED PURL LEFT TWIST

Rotated Cable Twist

There is one other way to make a true two-stitch Cable without the use of a cable holder. I have never seen this technique anywhere, but it works and is relatively easy to do—it's related to a Rotated Cable. Some of you might prefer this way of working to the others. It shouldn't be used on the diagonal, but it is nice for a column, and if worked with care, the right and left versions match pretty well.

Rotated Knit Right Twist

1. Insert the right needle on the nearside, into the first two stitches on the left needle from left to right as to Knit, and allow them to transfer together to the right needle.
2. Return both stitches one at a time to the left needle.
3. Knit the two stitches one at a time through the farside.

The two stitches switch places during the rotation. They also get turned, with the left side of the stitch on the nearside of the needle. They must either be returned to their correct position on the needle while being transferred back, or worked through the farside to prevent them from crossing.

Rotated Knit Left Twist

1. Insert the right needle into the first two stitches on the left needle on the farside from left to right.
2. Transfer the stitches together to the right needle.
3. Return both stitches to the left needle, one at a time, by inserting the left needle tip into the stitch on the farside from right to left.
4. Knit the two stitches.

Rotated Purl Right Twist

1. Slip two stitches together knitwise.
2. Return the stitches, one at a time, by inserting the left needle tip into the stitch on the nearside from right to left.
3. Purl the two stitches.

Rotated Purl Left Twist

1. Slip two together farside.
2. Return them, one at a time, by inserting the left needle into the stitch on the farside from right to left.
3. Purl the two stitches.

Multi-Stitch Twists

The final variations possible with Twist Stitch are to enlarge the number of stitches involved. One could, for instance, Knit the fourth stitch, then the first, second, and third; or Knit the fourth, then the third, second, and first. Here again, the stitches will bunch up considerably—they will never flatten out like a true Cable and are not a substitute for one—but in many ways the appearance is attractive, giving a knotlike effect.

Applications

Well, after all this, what do we do with them?

Twist Stitches are used to create allover texture, diagonal lines, zigzags, crossing points, and columns. The allover texture is achieved by using a Twist Stitch scattered evenly across a row and staggered row by row. Different effects can be achieved by how closely together or far apart the Twist Stitches are placed; they can be as close as every pair of stitches in every row, every other pair of stitches in every other row, or with four, five, or more stitches and rows in between.

The more Twist Stitches there are in a fabric, the tighter and denser it will be. Worked on every stitch of every row, one row with a Right Twist, the next with a Left Twist, a dense basketweave is created. Worked in cotton, it will produce a fine potholder; done in wool,

it would make an extremely durable and windproof jacket fabric. A larger-size needle in these cases will help to keep the fabric supple.

Twist Stitches are freqeuntly combined with other stitches to produce diagonal lines. Sometimes it lends no more than a slight ridge or small sideways curl to a pattern. More often it is used to create zigzag and serpentine lines of Knit stitches on a Purl ground by working the Twist Stitch one stitch to the right or left on each subsequent row. There are many strikingly beautiful patterns done this way. The slope of the diagonal can be adjusted by working the Twist Stitches on every row, every other row, or every third or fourth row.

When the Twist stitches are stacked on top of one another, a column is created. The columns are usually set off by flanking stitches of Purl. If the Twists are worked on every row or every other row, they will be tight and quite embossed. If worked on every third or fourth row, they will take on the appearance of a narrow and delicate Cable. These little Twist Cables are often found interspersed with other larger Cables, or used to bracket a column of lacy openwork.

RIBBED LEAF

WICKERWORK

RIGHT: CABLE TWIST, LEFT: WRAPPED TWIST

Threaded Stitch

This technique is somewhat related to Twist Stitch, but the resulting appearance is quite different. Instead of stitches pulled past one another, here they are pulled through one another.

Basic Threaded Stitch

The right and left versions of Threaded Stitch are well-balanced mirror images of one another that can be set in vertical columns or in alternating horizontal rows. You will find few stitch patterns for this technique, but it is very attractive and deserves wider use.

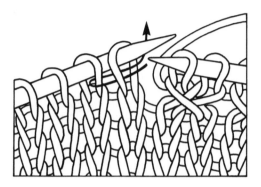

LEFT THREADED/THE FIRST STITCH

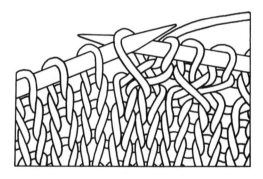

LEFT THREADED/THE SECOND STITCH

AN ALL-OVER PATTERN IN THREADED STITCH

LEFT THREADED STITCH

1. Slip the first stitch on the left needle knitwise, then replace it in its turned position.
2. Insert the needle tip into the first stitch as to Purl, then into the second stitch as to Knit. Pull the second stitch through the first one and Knit it; drop only that stitch from the left needle.
3. Now Knit the next stitch (it used to be the first one) through the farside and drop it from the needle.

The first stitch will encircle the second, and that half of the stitch which shows on the outside of the fabric will slant upward to the left across the other stitch. There are books that suggest that the second stitch be Knit through the farside before the first stitch has been discarded from the left needle. Although it produces an identical result, it is difficult to insert the needle into the proper strand on the farside of the needle without looking to see where you are going, and that slows you down.

Turning the first stitch before working the technique prevents the first stitch from crossing when it leans to the left. This guarantees that the left version matches the right version (below), but it is not essential and, in fact, it is much faster to work if you don't bother to do so. With the unturned version there is more of a gap between each pair of stitches, and the facing strand is slightly longer. Whether the stitch is turned or not, it must still be worked farside, and all other steps in the process are the same.

RIGHT THREADED STITCH

1. Insert the right needle tip into the second stitch on the left needle as to Knit (do not allow the right needle tip to pass under the left needle—it must remain on the nearside), wrap the yarn, and pull

through the new stitch. Lift the discard stitch over the first stitch and off the needle.

2. Knit the first stitch and discard it also.

In this case, the encircling stitch slants upward toward the right. It is admittedly difficult to insert the needle into the second stitch without catching the first. You may wish to try the method below, which produces the same result.

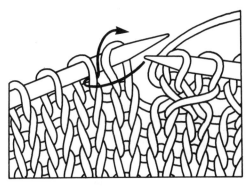

RIGHT THREADED/THE FIRST STITCH

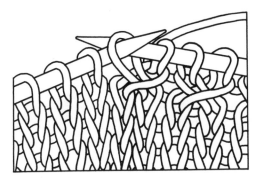

RIGHT THREADED/THE SECOND STITCH

RIGHT AND LEFT THREADED STITCH

ALTERNATE RIGHT THREADED STITCH

Here is an alternate way of working, which, as it adds a step, is not necessarily any faster and has its own little difficulties, but it's nice to have a choice. Perhaps this will suit you better than the other.

1. Insert the right needle tip into the second stitch as to

Purl, and lift it over the first stitch to the tip of the needle.

2. Hold the first stitch back with the thumb of your left hand while you change the position of the right needle in the lifted stitch from Purl to Knit. Now Knit that stitch and discard it.

3. Knit the first stitch.

Because of the awkwardness of working either method of Right Threaded Stitch, it is not much used, but should you have a pattern where a left slant on one row and a right slant on the next is what is needed, it has its place.

BOLD THREADED STITCH

Basic Threaded Stitch will work up rather dense; here is a way to make it softer and more open, and in this version, the Right Threaded Stitch is much easier to work.

1. Work with one needle about three sizes larger than the other. Purl the row prior to the pattern stitch row with the larger-size needle in the right hand.

2. Use the smaller-size needle in the right hand on the pattern row in exactly the same manner as for Basic Threaded Stitch, above.

The Needle Elongation provides slightly more yarn to the stitches to be threaded, making them easier to work and allowing them to stretch into position without constricting the fabric as much as in the basic version. Otherwise, the pattern is structurally the same.

A STRIPE USING BOLD THREADED STITCH

MULTIPLE THREADED STITCH

And last but not least, a true openwork version. In this case, several stitches are threaded through one another. For the sake of example, let us work with a unit of six stitches, three to be threaded through the other three.

1. On the row prior to the pattern row, Purl every stitch with two to four extra wraps of yarn.
2. On the pattern row, slip the six stitches of the unit to the right needle one at a time, dropping the extra wraps as you do so.
3. Now reach over with the left needle tip and pick up as one the three stitches on the right, pull them over the other three and hold them on the left needle. Then transfer the remaining three stitches as well.
4. Knit the six stitches, one at a time, in the order in which they present themselves on the left needle, Knitting the first three normally and the last three farside.

The instructions above will result in the outside stitches slanting upward to the left. If you wish the stitches to slant to the right, work in exactly the same way, but make the pattern row a Purl row instead.

The number of stitches involved is really up to the knitter—you can work with two through two, three through three, or four through four—but I have never seen more than that used. With each increase in the number of stitches involved, it may be necessary to increase the number of wraps. While a stitch pattern will call for a certain number of wraps, those things aren't sacred. If you work up your sample and think the result is too tight or too loose, add or subtract a wrap until you get the look you want to achieve.

OPENWORK CROSS

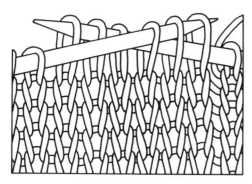

MULTIPLE THREADED/PICKING UP THE STITCHES

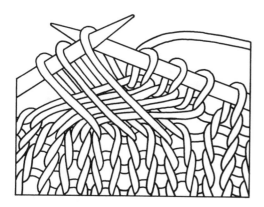

MULTIPLE THREADED/WORKING THE STITCHES

Applications

Threaded Stitches can be worked as a narrow horizontal insertion to form stripes, as a spot pattern on a ground of some other stitch, or as an allover pattern. In the latter case, the pairs of Threaded Stitches can be stacked, one on top of the other, or staggered by working one plain Knit stitch at the beginning and end of the next pattern row to throw the pairs one step to the left. The more Threaded Stitches used in a fabric, the more density must be taken into consideration.

Wrap Stitch

Here is a very simple technique that offers some nice textural possibilities. It's a way of wrapping a number of stitches with yarn to cluster them together.

The simplest Wrap Stitch uses one strand, but the position of the strand can be changed somewhat by a slight variation in the method of working. When more than one strand is used, the effect is quite bold and begins to resemble a Knot.

SINGLE WRAP (VERSION 1)

1. Working on the outside and with the yarn on the farside, slip two stitches to the right needle, bring the yarn between the needles to the nearside, then return the two slipped stitches to the left needle.
2. Move the yarn back to the farside. Knit the two stitches, and continue with the row.

As you can see, the yarn is now wrapped around the base of the two discard stitches, tying them together. If you wrap the strand loosely, it will somewhat resemble what you would get if you slipped stitches with the yarn stranded on the outside of the fabric. If you wrap the strand tightly, the two stitches will bunch together, providing more of a textured effect. You can, of course, work the technique on a Purl row in much the same way.

There is a reason for wrapping the yarn counterclockwise. Should you wrap it clockwise, you will find that the first wrap is pulled out of line to the right and the symmetry of the stitch is lost. Both the number of wraps and the number of stitches you try to wrap should be held to a reasonable limit, which depends entirely upon your gauge. I should think a one-inch wrap would be a very generous outside limit, but since on a heavy yarn that might be three stitches, while in a fine yarn it might be ten stitches, don't pay as much attention to the number of stitches called for in a pattern of this sort as to what is appropriate to your stitch gauge and the effect you wish to achieve.

This Wrap Stitch is very closely related to the Pull-over technique (see page 82), which is somewhat more versatile, and in fact this version differs from a Yarnover Pullover only in the direction of the wrap.

SINGLE WRAP (VERSION 2)

If you intend to pull the stitches tightly together, you may find it difficult to Knit the two stitches after they are wrapped; here is a method for Knitting them first

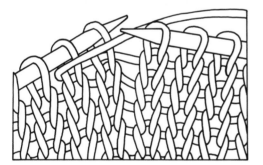

WRAP STITCH/VERSION ONE

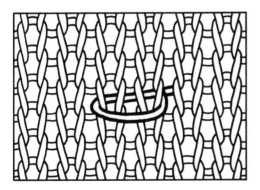

WRAP STITCH

SMOCKING PATTERN USING THE WRAP TECHNIQUE

and wrapping them second. The wrap will lie at the base of the new stitches instead of at the base of the discard stitches.

1. Knit two stitches and then bring the yarn between the needle tips to the nearside.
2. Transfer the two new stitches back to the left needle, being careful to maintain their correct position on the needle. Bring the yarn between the needle tips again to the farside, and return the two stitches to the right needle. Continue with the row.

   With this version, the stitches can be worked in Purl to add a nubby bit of texture.

MULTIPLE WRAP

Here we extend the technique to more than two stitches and to more than one wrap.

1. Knit the number of stitches you want to wrap.
2. Transfer the new stitches from the right needle onto a cable holder.
3. Wrap the yarn around the stitches that are on the cable holder in a counterclockwise direction as many times as is desired or practical.
4. Return the stitches to the right needle and continue with the work.

   It is possible to slip the stitches onto the cable holder from the left needle, wrap them, and then Knit them off the holder, but once they are wrapped they become more difficult to work. I recommend the above method as the easiest way.

As with the Single Wrap, the stitch may be done very tightly, or loosely, as you please. The combination of several stitches and several wraps bunched together provides a rather pronounced texture, almost like a small Bobble (see page 90). If done loosely, the wraps will appear as multiple horizontal strands, most often seen in a spot pattern of some kind. The stitch is very effective when used in a little bouquet motif to wrap the stems together, or to tie together the ribs of a Twist or Cable Stitch, where they intersect, giving something of the appearance of smocking. There is also the possibility of using a contrasting color to cluster the stitches (see the material on Stranded Knitting on pages 255–258).

BELLS CREATED WITH BOBBLES AND MULTIPLE WRAPS

3
Decreases and Increases

Increases add stitches, decreases take them away. Their primary purpose is to serve as the fundamental units of shaping. With more stitches on the needle the fabric will widen, with fewer stitches it will narrow. Shaping with stitch techniques can be accomplished in three different ways: The shaping units can be distributed evenly across the fabric, they can be paired in the center, or they can be placed at the edges, depending upon what it is you want to achieve. In each case, you may wish to make the increases or decreases as invisible as possible, or take advantage of their structure as a design element. A familiarity with the basic methods and the ways in which they can be varied puts a valuable tool at your command. Many knitters simply use their one favorite method regardless of the situation or what is called for in the pattern. If that is what you have always done, I think you will have real fun discovering what variety there is available to you, and seeing how much improvement there is in your work when you use the right technique for the purpose you have in mind.

In addition to shaping, however, increases and decreases are also an integral part of many decorative stitch patterns, where they are used for their appearance rather than to change the number of stitches on the needle. In these situations, the selection of one technique rather than another will alter a stitch pattern in a subtle but appreciable way. Familiarity with the different methods at your disposal will help you to analyze and understand a stitch pattern quickly and perhaps improve it.

The nomenclature and customary abbreviations for increases and decreases tend to be rather unspecific in many pattern instructions, and the knitter is left to decide which method to use. In the following material I have provided names for each technique; however, other than the exceptional case, a knitter would rarely need to be told whether to use the Knit or Purl, or right or left version of a particular increase. Common sense will serve, and the context makes things clear.

However, for those exceptions most patterns spell out the details of how to work the increase, sometimes within the instructions, sometimes as a preliminary note with the instructions then simply referring to *inc* for "increase," or *M1* for "make one." If a pattern isn't clear, you might wish to add an abbreviation or a note of your own. Also, patterns will occasionally suggest the use of a technique that is not really the best in a given situation. With the information provided in this chapter, you may choose to ignore an instruction and use a method you think would be more appropriate, in which case you will want to alter and rewrite the pattern. Personally, I prefer to work from a chart and recommend that you learn both how to read them and how to write them so that you can translate any written stitch pattern to its charted form (see the section on reading and writing charted patterns on page 459).

There is another way to shape a knitted fabric called regauging, which depends upon a change in needle size rather than a change in stitch techniques. It's an important concept to know about, and once you are familiar with it you will find frequent occasions to make use of it. It does not properly belong in this section on stitch techniques, but a thorough discussion can be found on page 423.

Decreases

There is really only one basic principle by which the number of stitches on the needle is decreased, and that is to work two stitches together so that one new stitch is formed in the position where two had been. Depending upon how the decrease is worked, one of the stitches will slant across the other on the outside either to the right or the left. I will frequently refer to the stitch on the outside as the "facing" stitch of the pair, and the covered one as the "backing" stitch. While there are Knit and Purl methods of working both variations, the slant is really visible only on the Knit side of the stitch. Properly determining the direction of the slant is important when the decrease is used in a way that exploits its decorative possibilities.

The right decrease, in either its Knit or Purl version, is very straightforward and is all that the novice knitter need be concerned with. It is generally the one used unless the pattern requires the other for some special reason. While it is possible for anyone to follow the directions given here for the left decreases and double decreases, and they can be done in a rote fashion with perfect success, these procedures will be difficult to really understand without prior knowledge of the material on the Slip Stitch techniques (page 24), and that on Crossed Stitch techniques (page 32). I recommend you familiarize yourself with that material first.

There are quite a few occasions in knitting where it is necessary to have mirror-image pairs of right and left decreases. They may be set at either side of a fabric, at either side of a stitch repeat, or flanking a center stitch. Unfortunately, although the two forms of the decrease are identical in structure except for the direction of the slant, it is not easy to get them to match in appearance. The reason for this is that the process of working the decrease enlarges the first stitch of the pair, whether this be the facing or the backing stitch. As we discuss each technique, I will point out which opposite version you can pair it with.

Right Decreases

The standard Knit and Purl versions of the right decrease are by far the most common techniques used, and with good reason, as they are neat, unobtrusive, and very easy to do. On the Knit side, the left stitch of the decreased pair is the facing stitch and will slant to the right.

KNIT TWO TOGETHER

1. Insert the right needle into the first two stitches on the left needle, on the nearside from left to right, just as you would to Knit a single stitch.
2. Pass the yarn around the needle in the normal way and pull the new stitch through both stitches.
3. Discard the two stitches from the left needle simultaneously.

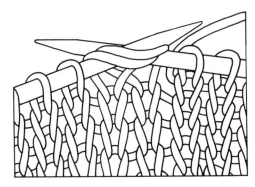

KNIT TWO TOGETHER

When you examine the result, you will see that both discard stitches encircle the new stitch at its base. The new stitch will be directly above the backing stitch, with the facing stitch slanting toward them, and the column of stitches will continue above the facing stitch. This behavior is true of decreases in general.

The facing stitch on this decrease is small and neat. Its only true pair is the Slip Slip Purl Decrease, below. Unfortunately they must be placed on separate rows, one on a Knit row, one on a Purl. In those situations where the decreases are sufficiently separated that the eye will not notice they are on different rows, or when the pattern calls for them to be on different rows, this works out very nicely.

PURL TWO TOGETHER

Exactly the same as the Knit version in structure, but in this case it is the facing stitch that will be enlarged. The closest left pair is the Slip Slip Knit Decrease, below.

1. Insert the tip of the right needle into the first two stitches on the left needle, on the nearside from right to left, just as you would to Purl a single stitch.

2. Pass the yarn around the needle in the normal way and pull the new stitch through both stitches.
3. Drop the two stitches from the left needle simultaneously.

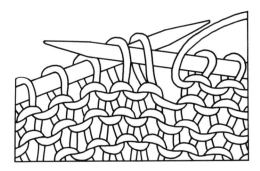

PURL TWO TOGETHER

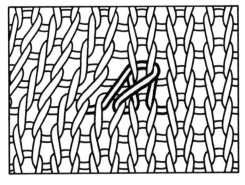

RIGHT DECREASE

KNIT RIGHT PULLOVER

Here is a considerably slower method of making a right decrease, but because it enlarges the facing stitch, it will look more like the left decrease for those occasions when it is important that the two match precisely and both be on the same row.

1. Knit the first stitch of the decrease pair. Slip the new stitch to the left needle.
2. Insert the right needle into the nearside of the second stitch on the left needle as to Purl. Pull this stitch over the first and off the needle, dropping it beneath the needle tip.
3. Return the new stitch to the right needle.

PURL RIGHT PULLOVER

The same decrease, done in Purl.

1. Slip the first stitch of the decrease pair, Purl the second stitch.
2. Reach around on the farside with the left needle tip

and pick up the slipped stitch. Pull it over the new stitch and off the needle.

Left Decreases

None of the left decreases are as quick to do as the Knit or Purl Two Together right decreases. However, as I mentioned above, except for the direction in which the facing stitch slants, the structure is identical. Because they are slow, these methods are used only when a decrease with a left slant is a necessary asset in a stitch pattern, or on the fabric.

SLIP SLIP KNIT

In terms of the ease of working, this is the best left decrease. In an ideal world it would be the natural mate to Knit Two Together; unfortunately, here it is the facing stitch of the decrease that is enlarged, so they do not match. Under most circumstances, the difference between the two is slight, and this would still be the decrease of choice when their respective appearance is not easily compared or is obscured by other techniques. However, if the paired decreases must be precisely the same, it is best to use this as the left decrease and the Pullover version of the right decrease, in which case both facing stitches will be slightly enlarged.

1. Slip two stitches knitwise, one at a time.
2. Insert the left needle from left to right into the nearside of the two turned stitches on the right needle.
3. Wrap the yarn as to Knit, and with the left needle pull both stitches together over the strand and off the needle.

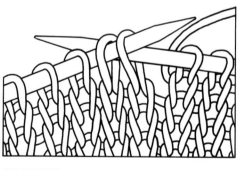

SLIP SLIP KNIT

Knitting the two stitches together through the farside is what causes them to slant to the left; slipping the two stitches knitwise is necessary to prevent the stitches from crossing on themselves when that is done. While a Crossed Decrease has decorative possibilities, you should not do it unwittingly; see below for Crossed Decreases.

SLIP SLIP PURL

This is the Purl version of Slip Slip Knit, identical in structure but slightly improved in appearance. While Slip Slip Knit doesn't match a Knit Two Together, Slip Slip Purl is much closer, but of course they will, of necessity, be on different rows.

1. Slip two stitches knitwise, one at a time.
2. Insert the left needle into the nearside of both slipped stitches and transfer them back to the left needle in their turned position.
3. Reach the right needle tip around to the farside and insert it into these two stitches from left to right. The needle tip should come through the stitches and pass under the left needle tip to the nearside.
4. Wrap the yarn in the normal way to Purl and draw through the new stitch.
5. Drop both discard stitches from the needle simultaneously.

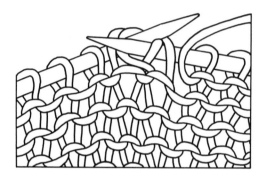

SLIP SLIP PURL

SLIP PULLOVER

This left decrease will seem quite different when you do it, but the path the yarn takes is identical to the Slip Slip Knit Decrease. Many patterns give the knitter the impression that it is a separate technique entirely, but it's just an alternate way of working. I find it stretches the facing stitch of the decrease out even more than the Slip Slip Knit method, so I don't generally use it. There are occasions, however, when a left decrease is part of a series of steps within another technique, and this one turns out to be the easiest way to work. Knowing that you can switch from one to the other with impunity is therefore helpful.

1. Slip one stitch knitwise, then Knit the next stitch.
2. Insert the tip of the left needle into the slipped stitch (now the second stitch on the right needle) on the nearside from left to right and pull this stitch over the new stitch and off the needle.

You will encounter stitch patterns that do not specify that the Slip Stitch should be transferred knitwise, in

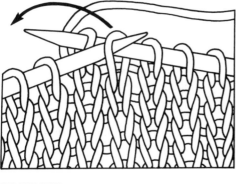

SLIP PULLOVER

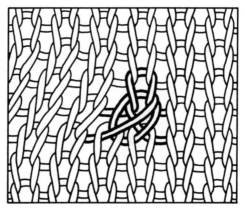

CROSSED RIGHT DECREASE

which case it will cross when it is pulled over the other stitch. You will want to substitute the method given here unless you want the decrease to be more obvious (see Crossed Decreases, below).

Although it is possible to do a Purl version of this decrease (much like the Knit Right Pullover), it is complicated, and there is really no need for it.

CROSSED LEFT DECREASE

• Knit or Purl two stitches together through the farside.

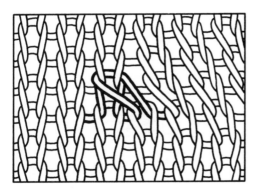

LEFT DECREASE

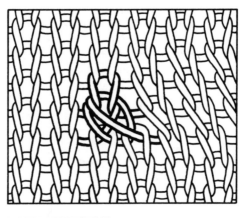

CROSSED LEFT DECREASE

Crossed Decreases

The uncrossed decreases we have been discussing are suitable for every purpose; however, it is possible to work any decrease so the discard stitches are deliberately crossed in order to enhance their decorative nature. It's a subtle but noticeable difference, especially when done repetitively, and as with any Crossed Stitch, it tightens the stitches. (Again, look at the detailed material on Crossed Stitches on pages 32–36 if you are not familiar with how this works.)

CROSSED RIGHT DECREASE

1. Slip two stitches knitwise, one at a time.
2. Transfer them back to the left needle in their turned position.
3. Knit or Purl two together.

Double Decreases

A double decrease is one in which two stitches must be removed at once. While it is possible to simply work a pair of single decreases side by side, generally what is meant by a double decrease is that one new stitch is formed on three discard stitches, reducing the number of stitches by two. Depending upon how the decrease is worked, one of the three discard stitches will dominate on the Knit face of the fabric; the others will slant behind it. The configuration of each stitch is discussed as if you were looking at it on the Knit side. You may choose any one of them, depending only on whether or not it enhances your stitch pattern in some way; they all have the same effect structurally.

There are quite a few traditional patterns, particularly in lace, that use double decreases, and I have found they frequently gain in clarity and symmetry when some other method than the one given is used. I have included the Purl versions for you to look up as needed.

KNIT CENTER DOUBLE DECREASE

The center stitch will be on the nearside, the right stitch in the middle, the left stitch on the farside.

1. Insert the right needle into the first two stitches on the left needle as for a Knit Two Together and slip them to the right needle.
2. Knit the next stitch.
3. Pull the two slipped stitches, one at a time or together, over the new stitch and off the needle.

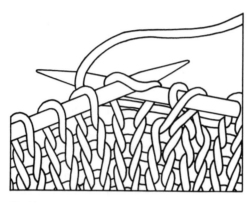

CENTER DOUBLE DECREASE/THE THIRD STITCH

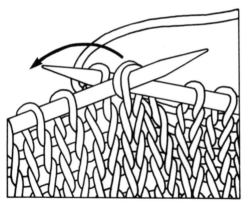

CENTER DOUBLE DECREASE/THE PULLOVER

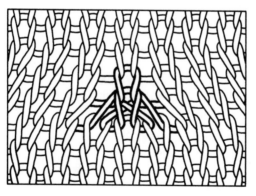

CENTER DOUBLE DECREASE

PURL CENTER DOUBLE DECREASE

The same result as the Knit version but done on the Purl side.

1. Slip the first two stitches knitwise, one at a time.
2. Insert the left needle into the two slipped stitches on the nearside from right to left and allow them to return to the left needle. (The stitches will exchange position in this return; the one that had been first on the left needle will now be second.)
3. Insert the right needle into all three stitches on the nearside from right to left. Wrap the yarn in the normal way to Purl and pull through the new stitch. Discard the three stitches together.

KNIT RIGHT DOUBLE DECREASE

The left stitch is on the nearside slanting to the right, the center stitch is in the middle, the right stitch is on the farside.

1. Insert the right needle into the first three stitches on the left needle on the nearside from left to right.
2. Wrap the yarn in the normal way to Knit and draw through the new stitch.
3. Discard the three stitches together.

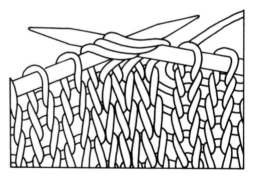

KNITTING THREE TOGETHER

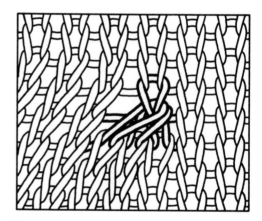

RIGHT DOUBLE DECREASE

PURL RIGHT DOUBLE DECREASE

Same as above, done on the Purl side.

1. Insert the right needle into the first three stitches on the left needle, on the nearside from right to left.
2. Wrap the yarn in the normal way to Purl and draw through the new stitch.
3. Discard the three stitches together.

The facing stitch of the right decrease tends to be somewhat more enlarged than its counterpart the left decrease. Work it carefully to minimize the distortion as much as possible. These decreases are rarely used in balanced sets, so usually it doesn't matter whether they are exact mirror images of one another.

KNIT LEFT DOUBLE DECREASE

The right stitch will be on the nearside, the center stitch in the middle, and the left stitch on the farside. There are two alternate methods of working, one identical, one virtually so; choose whichever method of working seems comfortable to you.

1. Slip two stitches knitwise, one at a time.
2. Knit the next stitch.
3. Pass the two slipped stitches over the new stitch and off the needle either together or one at a time.

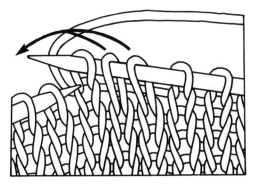

LEFT DOUBLE DECREASE/THE PULLOVER

ALTERNATE KNIT LEFT DOUBLE DECREASE #1

Same as above, done a different way.

1. Slip three stitches, knitwise, one at a time.
2. Wrap the yarn around the needle as to Knit and pull the three slipped stitches over one at a time. (They can be pulled over all at once, or one and then two, etc., if you find it easy to do that.)

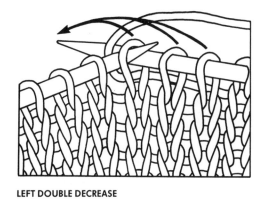

LEFT DOUBLE DECREASE

ALTERNATE KNIT LEFT DOUBLE DECREASE #2

This puts the right stitch on the nearside, but the center stitch on the farside and the left stitch in the middle.

1. Slip the first stitch knitwise.
2. Knit the next two stitches together.
3. Pass the slipped stitch over the new stitch and off the needle.

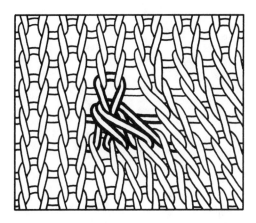

ALTERNATE LEFT DOUBLE DECREASE/THE PULLOVER

PURL LEFT DOUBLE DECREASE

Same as the Knit versions above. It can be a bit awkward to do, but if you really need it, it works. On the outside, the left stitch will be on the nearside, center stitch in the middle, right stitch on the farside.

1. Slip three stitches, knitwise, one at a time.
2. Return the three stitches to the left needle in their turned position.
3. Reach around on the farside, insert the needle into all three stitches from left to right and Purl.

ALTERNATE PURL LEFT DOUBLE DECREASE

The last step of the above decrease can be difficult if you are working at a firm tension. There is an alternative, but it requires more steps. On the outside, the left stitch will be on the nearside, the center stitch on the farside, the right stitch in the middle.

1. Purl two stitches together. Slip the next stitch on the left needle knitwise and return it (in other words, turn it on the needle).
2. Return the new stitch (the one on the Purl Two Together) to the left needle.
3. Pull the turned stitch on the left needle over the new stitch, then return the new stitch to the right needle.

You can simplify this slightly by not turning the third stitch, but it will then cross on discard. Because that stitch is the facing stitch of the decrease, the result won't match the Knit version; you will have to decide for yourself whether or not that matters to you.

THE DOUBLE DECREASES

Multiple Decreases

There are some stitch patterns that call for more than two stitches to be decreased in one position. Of course, it is possible to simply work several single decreases in close proximity, and this is occasionally done, but usually the point is to bunch the stitches together closely.

MULTIPLE SLIP DECREASE

This is a pullover decrease, very similar to the double decreases above, and it reduces five stitches to one.

1. Slip two stitches knitwise, one at a time.
2. Knit three stitches together.
3. Pull the two slipped stitches over the new stitch and off the needle.

Alternatively, you could slip three knitwise, Knit two together, and pull the three slipped stitches over the

new stitch and off. Reducing four stitches to one can be done by slipping two knitwise, Knitting two together, and pulling the two slipped stitches over the new stitch and off.

WRAP AND PULLOVER DECREASE

The discard stitches are crossed in this procedure, which tightens them up and gives a neat, compact look to the decrease.

1. Knit three to five stitches.
2. Wrap the yarn around the right needle as to Knit.
3. Starting with the first, pull each new stitch, one by one, over the strand and off the needle.

TIGHT PULLOVER DECREASE

This is worked in basically the same way as the decrease above, but the order in which the stitches are pulled over the strand and off the needle is reversed, with the one farthest away pulled off first and the closest one last. It is very knotty, and so tight that it generally requires five to seven stitches to create the same effect as the one above with only four or five. It is also very difficult to pull the last stitch over. I mention the technique only because it is found in some books, but I do not recommend it.

Joinery Decreases

I have had some difficulty deciding whether this is truly a decrease or actually a casting-off technique, which suggests that it is probably both. It is highly specialized, but when it is appropriate it works very well indeed. You will have occasion to use it in Joinery Cast-off (page 153), in Double Knitting (page 239), for securing the tops of pleats (page 215), or on any small section of fabric that must be overlapped.

Rather than joining two stitches that are side by side, these decreases join the stitches of two different fabrics, or two different sections of fabric. There are two ways to work.

TWO-NEEDLE JOINERY DECREASE

Have the two sets of stitches on two separate needles held side by side with the tips aligned at the point where the yarn comes off one of the stitches. You may have to slip one set of stitches onto a double-point needle, or work an extra row on one set so that the stitches can be positioned properly. You may work all in Knit, all in

Purl, or in any combination of the two as required to maintain the stitch pattern on the outside of the fabric.

1. Work either a Knit or Purl Together Decrease on one stitch from the near needle and one stitch from the far needle. A stitch from the near needle must be the left stitch of each decrease pair.
2. Continue in this manner until all of the stitches have been joined.

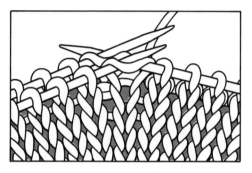

TWO NEEDLE VERSION/KNITTING TWO TOGETHER

SINGLE-NEEDLE JOINERY DECREASE

This method produces the same result as the one above. If you find you are frequently dropping stitches when working with the two-needle method, try this approach instead.

1. Line the stitches up on two needles as above, then take up another circular or double-point needle and

SINGLE NEEDLE VERSION/INTERSPERSING THE STITCHES

SINGLE NEEDLE VERSION/KNITTING TWO TOGETHER

slip first one stitch from the far needle, then one stitch from the near needle. Continue in this way until all of the stitches are interspersed on one needle.
2. Slide the stitches to the right needle tip where the yarn comes off the first stitch and begin the decreases.

Starting with a stitch from the far needle is not optional, as it places the stitches in the correct relationship to one another. It is essential that a stitch from the near needle be the left stitch of each decrease pair. If this is not done, the decrease will cause the two stitches to twist around one another in an unsightly way, and the continuity of the columns of stitches will be lost.

In Double Knit, the stitches will already be interspersed on a single needle. If for some reason the first stitch is one from the near fabric, work that stitch alone to establish the correct sequence, then begin the decreases on the next two stitches; the last stitch will also be worked alone. There may be other occasions when you have an uneven number of stitches interspersed on the needle, in which case you may have to work either the first or the last stitch by itself, but not both. This is inconsequential and will not affect the result.

GLOSSARY OF DECREASE TECHNIQUES

Crossed
Similar to right and left decreases. More obvious.

Double
Removes two stitches. Right, left, and center versions.

Joinery
Related to right decrease. Highly specialized. Joins two fabrics or two sections.

Left
All-purpose decrease. Slants to the left. Unobtrusive.

Multiple
Removes three or more stitches.

Right
Most common all-purpose decrease. Slants to the right. Unobtrusive.

Slip Pullover
Alternate method of working left decrease.

Increases

An increase allows you to put two or more stitches into a position where formerly there was just one. There are five basic techniques, each having qualities that are desirable in some situations and not in others. Some are very quiet and unobtrusive, some are quite decorative. In addition to the simple function of adding stitches, increase techniques are also an important part of many stitch patterns. Knowing the structure and behavior of these techniques will allow you to select the one most appropriate for what you are trying to accomplish, or to recognize when a stitch pattern might be enhanced by substituting another decrease for the one given in the instructions.

Keep in mind that when you are doing an increase, one new stitch replaces the discard stitch and is therefore not an increase; only the extra stitch or stitches are increases. Thus, if you have worked three stitches into one, you have increased the total number of stitches on the needle by two, not by three.

Bar Increases

This type of increase is quite noticeable on the Knit face of a Stockinette fabric, and therefore can be rather decorative when placed in pairs, or when used in columns a few stitches in from a side edge. It is also ideal as a hidden increase in ribbing, or other Knit and Purl stitch patterns.

KNIT BAR INCREASE

This is probably the most common increase, as it is very easy to do.

1. Knit into the first stitch on the left needle, but do not discard the old stitch.
2. Knit into the farside of the same stitch, then discard it.

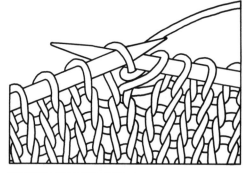

WORKING A BAR INCREASE

If you look at the two stitches you have just made, you will notice that the first looks like a normal Knit stitch, but the one on the left looks like a Purl stitch. This is the "bar" in the name of the stitch. The bar is actually the head of the discard stitch where it is wrapped tightly around the base of the second new stitch.

When making use of this stitch, you must keep in mind where the bar will fall—it is always on the left side of the increase. For instance, say you want decorative, paired edge increases, both done on the Knit face of the fabric, two stitches in from either edge. You would increase in the second stitch on the right side so the bar will fall between the second and third stitches. On the left side, however, you would have to increase in the third stitch from the left in order to have the bar fall between the second and third stitches. If you want the bars to flank a center stitch, you must increase in the stitch before the center one and in the center one itself.

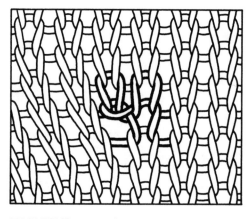

BAR INCREASE

PURL BAR INCREASE

Here is how to do the same increase in Purl.

1. Slip the stitch knitwise and return the turned stitch to the left needle.
2. Bring the right needle tip around and insert it from left to right into the farside of the turned stitch, wrap the yarn as to Purl, and draw through the first new stitch.
3. Now Purl into the nearside of the same stitch and discard.

While this increase is structurally the same as a Knit

Bar Increase, on the Knit face of the fabric the bar will fall to the right of the increase stitch, instead of to the left.

TURNED BAR INCREASE

Here is a subtle improvement on the basic Bar Increase. Done the usual way, there can be a tiny hole below the bar; this closes it.

1. Slip the first stitch on the left needle knitwise.
2. Insert the left needle into the nearside of the stitch, now on the right needle, and Knit one farside; do not discard.
3. Knit into the nearside of the same stitch.

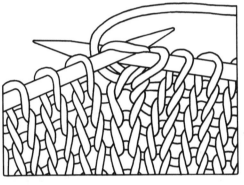

WORKING A TURNED BAR INCREASE

For the Purl version, work as follows:

1. Purl, but do not drop the stitch from the left needle.
2. Now bring the right needle tip around and insert it from left to right into the farside of the same stitch, and Purl again.

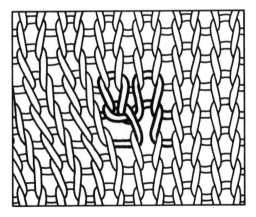

TURNED BAR INCREASE

MULTIPLE BAR INCREASE

While it is possible to work more than two new stitches into the discard stitch using the Bar Increase technique,

it has limitations. Since the discard stitch is crossed each time an additional stitch is made, the more stitches you add, the more difficult it becomes to work, especially in Purl. The resulting increase is clustered tightly at the base, and in those patterns where clustering is the point, this works out quite nicely. In many other situations, however, it would not be at all appropriate, although it is commonly recommended in many stitch patterns. Whenever you encounter a Multiple Bar Increase, therefore, I suggest you analyze the pattern carefully to see what purpose the increase serves, and decide for yourself whether it is suitable or not.

Rib Increases

A Rib Increase is made in nearly the same way as the one above, but the result is quite different. The technique is the preferred one for placing a single increase on a Yarnover strand, but it is not terribly successful when done on a regular stitch.

KNIT/PURL RIB INCREASE

1. With the yarn on the farside, Knit into the next stitch, but do not drop it from the needle.
2. Move the yarn to the nearside and Purl into the same stitch and then discard.

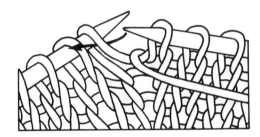

RIB INCREASE/THE KNIT-PURL VERSION

Needless to say, the stitch could certainly be worked with a Purl stitch first, and a Knit stitch second. Some books specify that this will change the appearance when the increase is used on a Yarnover strand, but if it does, it is very subtle, and analysis does not reveal any reason for a difference. The two methods of working produce an identical structure, but one is the mirror image of the other.

In the Knit/Purl version, the first stitch is brought up on the nearside of the discard stitch and the second stitch is brought up on the farside of it; in the Purl/Knit version, the first stitch is brought up on the farside and the second stitch on the nearside. The relationship between the two stitches is the same on both sides of the fabric; if you work the increase on the outside using a Knit stitch first, a Knit stitch will be the first of the pair on the inside as well. Either way, there will be a small

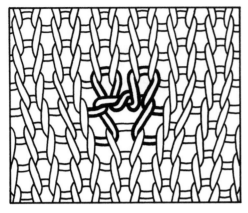

KNIT/PURL RIB INCREASE

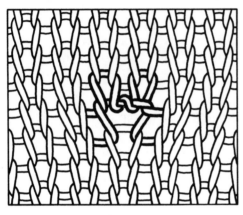

PURL/KNIT RIB INCREASE

nub between the two new stitches that is formed when the yarn switches from one side to the other for the second stitch. The nub will be more obvious when the increase is worked at a loose tension. Work whichever way seems easiest for you; if you find the nub is too obvious, or not obvious enough, try the other method and see if there is any change.

MULTIPLE RIB INCREASE

The Multiple Rib Increase is worked in the same manner as above; simply shift the yarn to the appropriate side to form the next stitch until the required number have been placed on the needle. When handled in this manner, the discard stitch becomes enlarged and the base of the new stitches is ridged. I don't really care for its appearance, although it is commonly used as a multiple increase in Eyelet and lace patterns. Whenever you come across it, I recommend you substitute the Multiple Yarnover Increase, which is described on page 76.

Raised Increases

A Raised Increase is the best all-purpose increase, and the most unobtrusive. It should be used when it is im-

portant to have the increases hidden. It is ideal when you must increase many times across the width of the fabric, but it serves well in almost any situation. It cannot be used, however, when it is necessary to make an increase in the same position every row; there must be at least one row intervening, and it is only hidden when the Knit aspect of the stitch is on the outside of the fabric.

KNIT RIGHT RAISED INCREASE

1. Working on the outside, reach the tip of the right needle around on the farside and insert it up under the Purl nub below the first stitch on the left needle.
2. Lift this stitch onto the left needle tip with the right side of the stitch on the nearside of the needle.
3. Knit the stitch in the normal way and discard it.
4. Knit the stitch above it in the normal way and discard it.

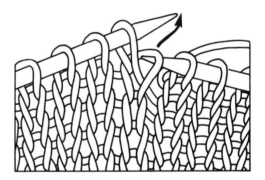

LIFTING THE STITCH FOR RIGHT RAISED INCREASE

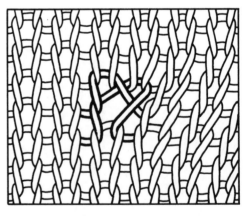

RIGHT RAISED INCREASE

It is possible to simply insert the right needle tip down into the Purl nub and Knit without lifting the stitch onto the needle. It is more difficult to insert the needle properly, making it easy to split the stitch, but it does stretch the stitch out less. I think, on the whole, the method I have given you is best, but do be careful not to stretch the lower stitch up any further than necessary, and work on the tips of the needles. It also helps to keep your left forefinger on the stitch above to keep it from slipping through the stitch below once it is on the needle.

Either the raised stitch or the one on the needle can be worked as Knit or Purl if that would help to blend the increase into a stitch pattern. Notice that on the Knit side the increased stitch lies to the right of the other. The left version follows.

KNIT LEFT RAISED INCREASE

In order to balance pairs of these increases, you will want to be able to put the increased stitch to the left of the stitch, rather than to the right.

1. Knit the stitch above the one into which you will work the increase.
2. Insert the left needle tip under the *second* Purl nub below the new stitch, and lift this stitch up into position to work it.
3. Insert the right needle into the *farside* of the raised stitch and Knit or Purl. (Do not work into the nearside of the stitch, as it is turned on the needle wrong and would cross on itself.)

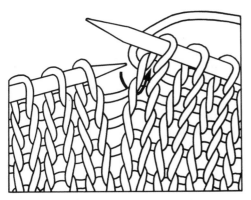

LIFTING THE STITCH FOR LEFT RAISED INCREASE

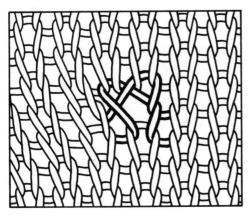

LEFT RAISED INCREASE

The reason you must reach down two rows instead of into the row below is easy to understand once you think about it. The stitch you want to place the increase on is the one below the stitch on the left needle. If you want the increase to lie to the left of that stitch, you must first work the stitch on the needle. You will then have a new stitch on the right needle, the stitch that was on the left needle will be just below it, and the one you want to increase into will now be two rows down.

PURL RIGHT RAISED INCREASE

Please note that a Raised Increase placed on one side of a Purl stitch will be on the opposite side of the Knit face of that stitch.

1. Working on the inside, insert the tip of the right needle under the Purl nub that lies on the nearside, below the first stitch on the left needle.
2. Lift this stitch up on to the left needle tip. The right side of the stitch will by necessity be on the farside of the needle.
3. Purl into the farside of the raised stitch and discard it.
4. Purl into the stitch above in the normal way and discard it.

PURL LEFT RAISED INCREASE

1. Purl the first stitch on the left needle.
2. With the left needle, reach on the nearside and pick up the second Purl nub below the new stitch.
3. Purl into the raised stitch in the normal way.

If the Purl nub lies on the outside of the fabric, this increase does not work very well. The nub will be stretched out of shape, and the increase will be quite obvious. You can still use the increase on Brocade patterns, but place them on the Knit stitches rather than the Purl.

SLIP RAISED INCREASE

This variation, I find, produces a slightly more subtle result.

1. For the right version, Knit or Purl the raised stitch, then slip the stitch above. For the left version, slip the stitch, then Knit or Purl into the stitch one row below.
2. Work the slipped stitch and the increased stitch normally on the return row.

In the normal way of working, both the increased stitch and the new stitch occupy the position that would normally have a single stitch in it. With this variation,

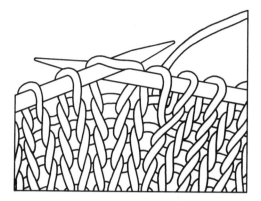

KNITTING A STITCH AFTER A SLIP RAISED INCREASE

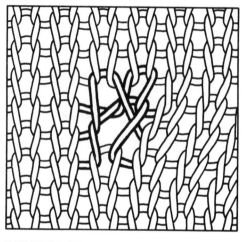

SLIP RAISED INCREASE

the Slip Stitch is pulled up slightly toward the row above, leaving the increased stitch in the row below. Rather than sitting side by side, they are staggered slightly, which causes less distortion of the columns of stitches on either side. There will be a Slip Stitch running thread on the Purl side of the fabric, so the technique is only appropriate if the Knit side will be the outside of the garment.

DOUBLE RAISED INCREASES

There are a variety of ways to use this increase to place three stitches where one had been. Each has a distinctive appearance, which is emphasized when placed in a column, one every other row.

Version 1:
1. Work a Right Raised increase.
2. Knit the stitch itself.
3. Work a Left Raised increase on the other side of the stitch.

This makes quite a decorative increase; the raised stitch is pulled open into a tiny Eyelet.

Version 2: Work as above, but Knit the center stitch farside.

A very slight change in method makes a rather large difference in the outcome. Developed by Barbara Walker, this is plain and unobtrusive with no holes whatsoever—as close to an invisible double increase as one can have.

Use a fairly easy tension on the new stitches or you may find it difficult to work the next one. You will have to take some time to learn to recognize the left half of the stitch into which you must work the third increase, because it is fairly tight at this point and obscured by the stitch above.

DOUBLE RAISED INCREASES/RIGHT: VERSION ONE, LEFT: VERSION TWO

The next two variations are not technically double increases because they require more than one stitch, but they serve the same purpose. The first should be used on an uneven number of stitches, the second on an even number.

Version 3: On three stitches, work a Left Raised Increase on the first stitch, Knit the center stitch, then work a Right Raised Increase on the third stitch.

The result is a center column of tight Knit stitches, framed by vertical strands. It is attractive, tailored, and has no holes.

DOUBLE RAISED INCREASES/RIGHT: ON THREE STITCHES, LEFT: ON TWO STITCHES

Version 4: On two stitches, first work a Left Raised Increase, then a Right Raised Stitch Increase.

The result is a center column of strands that resemble a raised, upside-down Knit stitch. It is quietly decorative.

MULTIPLE RAISED INCREASE

Although it is not commonly done, it is possible to use this technique for a multiple increase simply by working one increase into the stitch below from the right side, a multiple increase into the stitch on the left needle, and then another increase into the stitch below on the left side.

UNDERSTITCH INCREASE

This is worked in a manner very similar to the Raised Increase, but the effect is much more obvious. The increase can be highly decorative, especially as a double.

1. Insert the right needle tip from nearside to farside into the center of the stitch directly below the first stitch on the left needle. Wrap the yarn as for a normal Knit stitch and pull the new increase stitch through.
2. Knit the stitch above in the normal fashion.

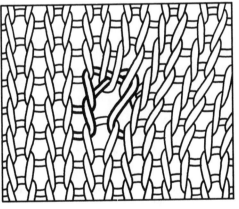

UNDERSTITCH INCREASE

For the Purl version, simply insert the needle from farside to nearside. The Double or Multiple Understitch Increase is worked on the same principle as the Double or Multiple Raised Increase, but through the center of the stitch. Should it prove useful, the stitch on the left needle could be worked as either Knit or Purl, regardless of how you worked the increase.

The reason the two look so different is that in the Raised Increase, the increase stitch is pulled through just the stitch below; in the Understitch Increase, it is pulled through both the stitch below and the stitch on the needle.

Running Thread Increases

This type of increase is not made on another stitch, but between two stitches. In appearance, it is not quite as obvious as a Bar Increase, and not quite as unobtrusive as a Raised Increase. Generally speaking, it is rarely used as a structural increase, being more commonly found as a part of other stitch techniques. However, should you need a quiet increase that can be done every row in the same position, you might use this because the Raised Increase wouldn't work. As you will see when we get to that section, a Running Thread Increase is little sister to a Yarnover, and the basic version, given first, will produce a tiny Eyelet below the increase stitch.

OPEN RUNNING THREAD INCREASE

1. Insert the left needle tip from nearside to farside under the running thread that lies between the two needles.
2. Knit or Purl into this strand as if it were a normal stitch.

The strand must be picked up so the right side of the strand is on the nearside of the needle. It is possible to

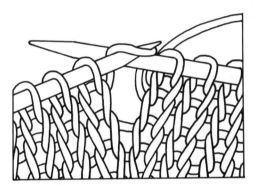

KNITTING THE RUNNING THREAD

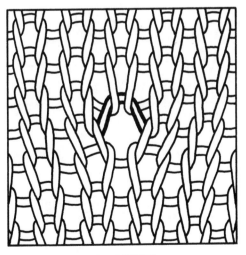

OPEN RUNNING THREAD INCREASE

simply insert the right needle under the strand from farside to nearside, wrap the yarn, and pull through the new stitch. It is sometimes hard to get the new stitch through safely, so I generally work in the way I've given above, but try both and use whichever you prefer.

LEFT CROSSED RUNNING THREAD INCREASE

In this version, the running thread will cross on itself to the left.

1. Insert the left needle tip under the running thread as above.
2. Knit or Purl into the farside of this strand.

It is somewhat difficult to insert the right needle tip directly into the farside of the strand, so don't place any tension on the strand as you work.

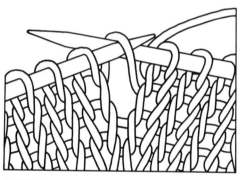

KNITTING THE RUNNING THREAD FARSIDE

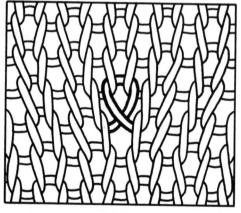

LEFT CROSSED RUNNING THREAD INCREASE

RIGHT CROSSED RUNNING THREAD INCREASE

This will cross the running thread to the right.

1. Insert the left needle under the running thread from farside to nearside. The left side of the strand should be on the nearside of the needle, as for a turned stitch.
2. Knit or Purl the strand as if it were a normal stitch.

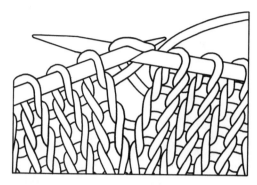

KNITTING A TURNED RUNNING THREAD

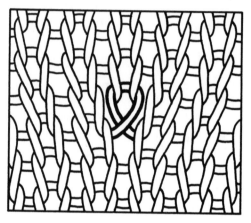

RIGHT CROSSED RUNNING THREAD INCREASE

Either Crossed version provides a quiet, attractive little increase, but however subtle, they will definitely show up if used repetitively, or close to one another. I think the nicest version for edge increases is to have the stitch cross toward the edge rather than away.

DOUBLE RUNNING THREAD INCREASES

Here again, there are several ways to work a double increase on a running thread, and all of them have personalities of their own.

Version 1: This produces two small columns of Eyelets flanking the center stitch.

- Work an Open Running Thread Increase on either side of a center Knit stitch.

Version 2: Very slightly different from the one above, but the center stitch column looks tighter and neater.

- Work as above; Knit the center stitch farside.

Version 3: This one is very attractive and quite decorative, with a slightly embossed and elongated center column of stitches; the Eyelets have virtually disappeared. I find this particularly handsome in Chevron

DOUBLE RUNNING THREAD INCREASES/FROM RIGHT TO LEFT: VERSIONS ONE, TWO, THREE

DOUBLE RUNNING THREAD INCREASES/RIGHT: VERSION FOUR, LEFT: VERSION FIVE

stitch patterns, and it makes a beautiful foldline for a bias strip (see page 173).

• Work as above; slip the center stitch.

Version 4: Here the center column of stitches has a somewhat beaded look, as one stitch is prominent and rounded, while the one above it is very tiny.

• Work a Right Crossed Running Thread Increase; Knit one; work a Left Crossed Running Thread Increase.

Version 5: The Rib Increase can also be used to place two new stitches on a running thread. In effect, this works like a double decrease, but is particularly appropriate if you have an even number of stitches on the needle. The result is slightly less open than the same technique used on a Yarnover.

A Yarnover is no more than a very simple increase, but so important a one that it merits a section of its own.

Yarnovers

A Yarnover is a very common and very simple technique. It may be common partly because it is simple, but more likely because of the many lovely effects it creates. It is at one and the same time the most elementary increase, and the basis for all of lace knitting, as well as appearing in many other guises that lie between those two extremes. What is this chameleon? Only the act of passing the yarn over the needle prior to knitting the next stitch. You know from the discussion on Knit and Purl (page 21) that it is important to pass the yarn between the needle tips, not over the needle, when switching from one to the other. While passing the yarn over the needle is a mistake in most cases, it is a lovely stitch when appropriate. Here is where it is appropriate, and how to do it correctly. Although simple, it cannot be done just any old way.

The correct formation of a Yarnover causes it to sit on the needle in exactly the same way a stitch does, with the right side of the strand on the nearside of the needle. The reason for this is that while a Yarnover is no more

than an elongated running thread, once it is made it will be treated in exactly the same manner as any other stitch. The strand will be Knit or Purled in some way, then discarded in the row above where it was made, causing a hole to appear in the fabric below it. This is more politely, and more deservedly, known as an Eyelet and is much more decorative. The Yarnover can be used alone as a decorative increase, but more often than not it is used in conjunction with other stitch techniques, many times in such a way that no hole is formed.

In any case, the essential nature of the technique must be kept in mind; each one used will add a stitch and therefore widen the fabric. For this reason you will rarely see a Yarnover without a companion decrease that restores the stitch count. The decrease is most often placed right before or after the Yarnover, but can also occupy any position in the same row or the next one. Its placement depends as much on the appearance of the decrease and the effect it has on the pattern as on the need to cancel the increase aspect of the Yarnover.

Single Yarnovers

The way the Yarnover is formed depends upon whether the stitches before or after it are Knit or Purl. Most patterns will simply call for a *YO* (or an *O*), and it will be up to you to choose the correct manner of working it within the pattern. I am going to spell out the "formulas," but the concept is really very simple. If you're working away and can't remember the formula, just use common sense; formulas always make things seem much more mysterious than they are. Keep in mind that the yarn must begin on the nearside of the right needle, must pass over the needle, and then must be placed in the correct position, near or far, to form the next stitch. If you're not sure you did it correctly, look at the Yarnover; does it sit on the needle the way a stitch should? Here is how it is done:

KNIT-TO-PURL YARNOVER

YARNOVER/KNIT TO KNIT

- Knit one, then bring the yarn between the needle tips to the nearside. Knit the next stitch.

    If you have the yarn on the nearside of the needle and you Knit the next stitch, the yarn will automatically go over the needle as you wrap the yarn around the needle tip to form the new stitch.

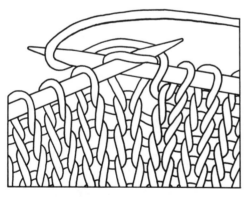

KNIT-TO-KNIT YARNOVER

YARNOVER/KNIT TO PURL

- Knit one, then bring the yarn between the needle tips to the nearside, over the needle, and forward again between the needles. Purl the next stitch.

    The yarn always slightly resists being brought from farside to nearside—it likes to be on the farside best—so give it a good tug or the running thread will be longer than you might want it to be.

YARNOVER/PURL TO PURL

- Purl one, then pass the yarn over the needle to the farside, then between the needle tips to the nearside again. Purl the next stitch.

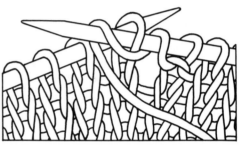

PURL-TO-PURL YARNOVER

YARNOVER/PURL TO KNIT

- Purl one, do not move the yarn. Knit the next stitch.

    Because the yarn is already on the nearside, when you Knit the next stitch, it will automatically go over the top of the needle to form the Yarnover.

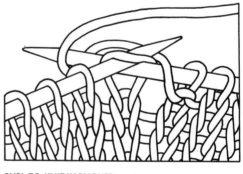

PURL-TO-KNIT YARNOVER

Double Yarnovers

If you wish to enlarge the Yarnover, all that is required is to wrap the yarn twice around the needle. On the

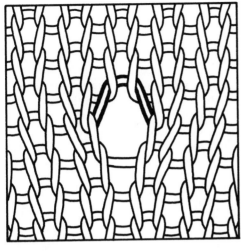

YARNOVER

return row the extra wrap is dropped from the needle, leaving a single Yarnover twice as large as it would normally be. I will give you the instructions for double Yarnovers; triple Yarnovers simply follow the same principles.

DOUBLE OVER/KNIT TO KNIT

• Knit one, then bring the yarn between the needle tips to the nearside, over the needle to the farside, and between the needle tips to the nearside again. Knit the next stitch.

For the first wrap, you must pass the yarn completely around the needle; the second wrap will happen automatically as you Knit the next stitch.

DOUBLE OVER/KNIT TO PURL

• Knit one, bring the yarn between the needle tips to the nearside, over the needle to the farside and between the needle tips to the nearside twice. Purl the next stitch.

DOUBLE OVER/PURL TO PURL

• Purl one, then pass the yarn over the needle to the farside and between the needle tips to the nearside twice. Purl the next stitch.

DOUBLE OVER/PURL TO KNIT

• Purl one, then pass the yarn over the needle to the farside and between the needle tips to the nearside. Knit the next stitch.

Just as with the Knit to Knit version, the first wrap must pass completely around the needle; the second wrap will happen automatically as the Knit stitch is formed.

Crossed Yarnover Increases

While the Yarnover is most often used to form the openings in knitted lace, in which case it is always accompanied by a decrease to maintain the stitch count, it can also be used as a structural increase to widen the fabric. Worked as described above, of course, this would be very decorative, but a quieter more unobtrusive increase may also be had by working the strand so that it crosses. There are, then, two versions based on the Crossed Stitch techniques already discussed:

LEFT CROSSED YARNOVER INCREASE

• On one row, work a normal Yarnover in the position where you want the increase. On the next row, Knit or Purl the strand farside.

RIGHT CROSSED YARNOVER INCREASE

• On one row, work a turned Yarnover (place it on the needle so the left side of the strand is on the nearside of the needle). On the return row, Knit or Purl the turned strand on the nearside.

This decrease is structurally identical to a Crossed Running Thread Increase, but the appearance in the fabric is slightly different. Because the Crossed Running Thread Increase is so tight, the stitch above is pulled down and the crossed strand is pulled up slightly, leaving a tiny hole beneath. These distortions draw attention to the decrease, which it is not really attractive enough to merit. The same technique done with a Yarnover is more successful because there is more yarn in the strand. As a result, the crossed strand is more relaxed and occupies the full position a normal stitch would, leaving the stitch above in the row where it belongs. A Crossed Yarnover Increase, therefore, draws much less attention to itself; it is quite unobtrusive and quietly attractive.

When using this increase in series adjacent to the selvedge, the best result is obtained if you use the Right Crossed version at the right side, the Left Crossed version at the left side. When used a few stitches in from the edge, cross the strand in the same direction the bias stitches will travel. This is also quite a good technique to use when you want to hide an increase in a color pattern, both because it is relatively unobtrusive and because it allows precise control of stitch color.

Multiple Yarnover Increases

A Multiple Yarnover Increase can be used to form three or more stitches on a stitch, a running thread, or on another Yarnover strand. It is most often found as a part of other stitch techniques, most particularly the Bobble, but as a double increase stacked in a Chevron-type pattern (see page 171) it is very open and decorative. There are two versions, the first and most common for an uneven number of stitches, the second a modification allowing an even number.

MULTIPLE YARNOVER: UNEVEN NUMBER

1. Insert the right needle as to Knit, wrap the yarn, and draw through a loop, but do not drop the discard stitch from the left needle.
2. Yarnover.
3. Knit the same stitch again and then drop the discard stitch.
4. For five stitches, add another Yarnover, Knit one before discarding.

The instructions are the same for doing the increase in Purl; simply substitute Purl for Knit.

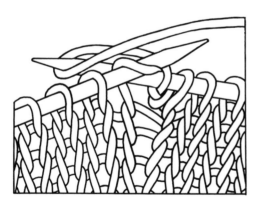

THREE STITCH MULTIPLE YARNOVER INCREASE

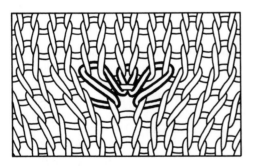

MULTIPLE YARNOVER INCREASE

MULTIPLE YARNOVER: EVEN NUMBER

With the following modification in the last step, it is possible to produce an even number of stitches, but only when done on a Yarnover strand.

- After completing the last Yarnover in the increase, if the next stitch is to be Knit, insert the right needle tip into the stitch and under the Yarnover strand, wrap the yarn, and draw through the new stitch.
- If the next stitch is to be Purl, insert the needle tip under the Yarnover strand and then into the stitch, wrap the yarn, and draw through the new stitch.

By working the adjacent stitch through the strand, the final Yarnover within the increase is secured. If this is not done, it will behave like a true Yarnover and have a hole under it, which in this case would not be desirable.

GLOSSARY OF INCREASE TECHNIQUES

Bar
Hidden in Knit/Purl patterns. Decorative in sequence, or flanking center stitch. Multiple version tightly clustered.

Raised
All-purpose. Right and left versions. Nearly invisible. Cannot be done every row. Double and Multiple very decorative.

Rib
Best for single increase on Yarnover. Multiple version. Fairly unobtrusive.

Running Thread
Quietly decorative. Can be done every row. Open, Crossed, and Double versions.

Slip Raised
More subtle version of Raised.

Understitch
Similar to Raised. Decorative.

Yarnover
Not generally used as a structural increase. Double and Multiple versions. Decorative.

4

Decorative Increases and Decreases

his chapter introduces new applications of the increase and decrease techniques just detailed. There, the function of the techniques was structural; they were used to widen or narrow the fabric by adding or subtracting stitches. Here the focus is on their decorative qualities. In order to be used in this way, however, it is necessary to counteract the effect they have on the number of stitches on the needle. What was wanted of these techniques before we will now work to prevent, in order to reveal their other aspects. This is done by always pairing a decrease with an increase—what one removes, the other will restore, thereby keeping the number of stitches on the needle constant. With this seemingly contradictory procedure, extraordinarily varied effects are possible, with every minor change in the components or their position revealing another aspect.

Texture Stitches

In the following material, I am not really going to introduce any new techniques, so much as show how ones already introduced can be combined to produce different stitch patterns. Most often these patterns are used to add textural qualities to a knitted fabric, and all of them, as I have said, rely upon the increase and decrease principles already discussed.

There is such an enormous variety of these stitches, however, with each slight change in technique producing quite a different pattern, that I am only going to give a few examples in order to show the general principles involved. Fortunately, they all fall into just a few family groups, and once you become familiar with how each group works, you will be able to identify any similar stitch pattern you encounter. In some cases, these instructions will be more formulaic than is normally the case, but they seem to require that treatment for reasons of space and efficiency. (If any of the abbreviations used are not familiar to you, see "Reading Written Garment and Stitch Patterns" on page 407.)

Multiplying Stitches

This is a rather miscellaneous category of techniques that share a single common trait, that of working every stitch on the needle more than once. Three of the techniques are used all over or in large sections, creating fabrics that are dense, gathered, or highly textured. The last, although very closely related to the others, does nothing of the kind; it results in a flat, refined horizontal stripe, another illustration of how a very small change can make a very large difference.

RUCHING

This technique creates horizontal gathered insertion bands.

1. Increase into every stitch across the row, doubling the number of stitches on the needle.
2. Work to the depth required for the effect you wish to achieve, the number of rows depending upon your stitch gauge.
3. Decrease every stitch across the row, restoring the original number of stitches to the needle.

The recommended increase is the Raised Stitch Increase, and the decrease a simple Knit or Purl Two Together. Either Running Thread Increase could be used, as could a Bar or Rib Increase, but they will be more obvious and less of a match to the decrease row. Some patterns call for a needle a size or two smaller to be used on the

RUCHING

increased number of stitches, an option that is particularly important on medium- to heavy-weight yarn. In any case, your stitch gauge sample will tell you if you are achieving the effect you wish.

In most garments making use of Ruching, the bands are worked repeatedly over the entire length of the fabric. The gathered portion may equal the normal portion in width or be considerably wider or narrower, depending upon the effect desired. Either the gathers or the bands dividing them could also be worked in another color, and/or a differently textured yarn. For another method of creating the same effect that does not require increases or decreases, see Regauging (page 423) or Twice Knit, below.

As a note of interest, the word "ruching" is a dressmaking term referring to horizontal bands of frilling, made of heavily gathered ribbon or other fabric inserted on a skirt or sleeve. It is also the French word for "beehive," and it is not too hard to make the shift from the image of an old woven-straw beehive, with its stacked, rounded curves, to the gentle puffy bands of ruching.

CLUSTER STITCHES

This effect is created by increasing and decreasing several stitches in close proximity in order to cluster them together.

The simplest way to form a Cluster Stitch pattern is to Knit Two Together on every pair of stitches across the row. On the return row, either a Bar Increase is worked on every stitch, or a Running Thread Increase between every stitch in order to restore the correct number of stitches to the needle (just like Ruching with no intervening rows). A somewhat bolder version calls for a

Knit Three Together across the row, and on the return a Multiple Yarnover Increase on every stitch. Of course, the increase can be worked first and then the decrease.

Another variation is to work a decrease, then a comparable increase, alternating one then the other across the row. On the return row, the alternation is switched so the increase is worked above a decrease, and the decrease above an increase.

There are a few situations where the increase and decrease are both done in one spot. An example of this would be to Purl three together, Knit three together, Purl three together all on the same three stitches, or Purl three together, Yarnover, Purl three together on the same three stitches. A slightly different approach is to Knit three together, Knit the first stitch again, and then Knit the other two stitches together again. Another calls for a Raised Stitch Increase, return the new stitch to the left needle, and Knit two together.

As you can see, these are all very closely related, easy to do, and fun to play with. The textures they produce are as nice used for an entire fabric as they are to form horizontal bands or vertical columns between other stitch patterns, and they are frequently found combined with other stitch techniques.

They could also be used in the same way Purl stitches are used on a Knit ground to create geometric patterns. When used all over a fabric and done on relatively small needles, the fabric will be thick and warm; when done on larger needles, the stitch can sometimes be quite open, as the decreases pull the stitches together and leave gaps between one cluster and the next.

CORAL KNOT, A CLUSTER PATTERN

TWICE KNIT

Here we have a family of stitches that uses just a simple decrease, but with much more complex results. They produce fabrics that are extremely dense, and it is advis-

able to work them on needles three or four sizes larger than you would normally use for the yarn.

- *K2tog, dis1*k1fs.

After you have Knit the two stitches together and are ready to discard, put your left forefinger on the top of the second stitch, slide the needle tip back slightly, and allow just the first stitch to drop off. The second stitch remains on the needle to be Knit together with the next stitch in the same way. Knitting the last stitch farside prevents a loop forming at the side edge. Follow the same basic method for working in Purl. A fabric can be worked in a Stockinette version, Knitting one row, Purling the next, or in Garter, by Knitting or Purling every row.

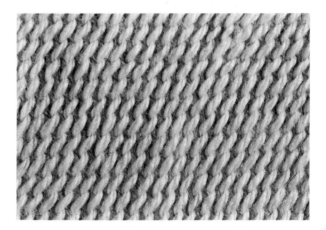

BASIC TWICE KNIT

For Crossed Twice Knit, work as follows:

- *K2togfs, dis1*k1fs.

If you stretch the fabric and examine the structure, you will see that it looks almost like embroidered cross stitch, with each stitch overlapping the stitches to the right and left of it. Relaxed, however, only half of each stitch is visible, slanting up toward the right. On the Purl side, the slope of the stitches is more oblique, giving each row a corded appearance. The appearance of the stitches made with Crossed Twice Knit is very similar to that of Basic Twice Knit, except that the slope is up toward the left instead of to the right.

A variety of stitch patterns can be created by combining the Knit, Purl, and Crossed versions in different arrangements. For instance, a row of Crossed Twice Knit and a row of Purl Twice Knit will produce a horizontal herringbone pattern. On the other side, the corded effect also alternates to right and left with each row and, interestingly, looks almost like columns of Knit stitches resting on their sides. Using these techniques with other types of stitches should be done with care, however, because few other stitch techniques are quite this dense.

GARTER STITCH TWICE KNIT

HERRINGBONE TWICE KNIT

Because of the density of fabrics made with Twice Knit patterns, I have seen it suggested that a Twice Knit Cast-on be used (just like Knit Cast-on, but worked with Knit Two Together for each new stitch instead). It is an extremely difficult cast-on technique and not really worth it; a firm Half-Hitch Cast-on or Cable Cast-on works just fine. At the other end, a regular Pullover Cast-off can be used if done rather tightly, or use the same technique but pull one stitch over two, instead of over one. Increase and decrease techniques require special mention as well. Probably the easiest and quietest increase is accomplished if you work the pair of stitches together as usual, then slip the first stitch purlwise to the right needle instead of discarding it. Alternatively, you can Knit or Purl the pair together, then work the first stitch again; discard just the first stitch and proceed as usual. For a decrease, if you simply work the pair of stitches together and then drop both of them from the needle together, it will be quite obvious unless done at the very edge. The best decrease within the fabric looks complicated, but is not. Knit three together, discard one; Knit three together, discard two; continue in pattern. Work in the same way for Purl, if necessary.

I don't know if anyone still knits potholders, belts, or slippers, but those are the purposes for which Twice Knit is generally recommended. However, while these are all very well and good, it's an interesting technique and I find it hard to believe that something more can't be done with it. For instance, since we were just discussing Ruching, the horizontal compression of Twice Knit would automatically gather or ruffle any regular stitches worked above or below it, without any need to increase or decrease stitches. It would also do nicely for tailored vests, jackets, and hats if knit up softly.

HORIZONTAL STITCH

Here is a fascinating stitch technique from Mary Walker Phillips' book *Creative Knitting*,[1] which forms a horizontal chain of stitches on the outside of the fabric. It's a combination of Twist Stitch and Twice Knit, but it certainly doesn't look like either one.

Row 1: On the inside, work all stitches of the row with a Purl Under so they are turned on the needle.
Row 2: On the outside, work a Turned Bar Increase in the first stitch, then proceed as follows:

- Step 1: Insert the left needle directly into the first stitch on the right needle and slip it left.
- Step 2: Knit the second stitch on the left needle farside, then Knit the first stitch on the left needle farside; discard the two stitches.

Repeat these two steps across the row.

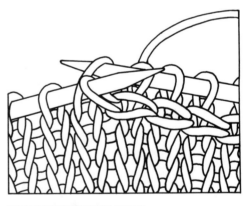

WORKING HORIZONTAL STITCH

It is very easy for the new stitches to become enlarged. This can be used to decorative advantage—if you use two rows of Horizontal Stitches, the stitches in the middle will look almost like a band of open insertion. If you do not want the open look, carefully tighten each stitch as you work or hold a smaller needle in the right hand.

1. William and Shirley Sayles (eds.) (New York: Van Nostrand Reinhold Co., 1971), p. 74.

HORIZONTAL STITCH

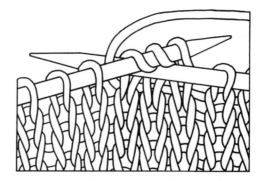

WORKING A COUCHING STITCH

If you are going to work more than one row of this stitch technique, you can eliminate the Knit Two Together at the end of row 2 and the increase at the beginning of every row after the first; one compensates for the other.

If you want to get fancy, the technique can be done in two colors. On each Twist Stitch pair, Knit the second stitch farside with one color, and the first stitch with the second color; the chain will be in the second color.

Couching

Couching is an embroidery term for a thread that is tacked down to the fabric at intervals by other stitches. There are a variety of ways to create somewhat the same effect in knitting through the use of Slip Stitch (page 24) or Pullover techniques (see below). But the technique that is actually called Couching involves forming an extra loop of yarn that is then attached to one of the stitches in the fabric. There are two ways to work:

HORIZONTAL COUCHING

1. On the outside of the fabric, insert the right needle tip from nearside to farside between two stitches on the left needle, wrap the yarn as to Knit, and pull through a stitch.
2. Retain the loop on the right needle and continue with the work.
3. On the return now, Purl the loop together with the following stitch.

Which two stitches to insert the needle between is a matter of your stitch gauge and the length of the Couching strand desired. Care must be taken to provide sufficient yarn to the loop on both the near and the farside of the fabric so no gathering occurs.

HORIZONTAL COUCHING PATTERN

ALTERNATIVE HORIZONTAL COUCHING

1. Insert the right needle tip from nearside to farside between two stitches on the left needle, wrap the yarn as to Knit, and pull through a stitch.
2. Slip the next stitch knitwise.
3. Insert the left needle from left to right into the nearside of the two stitches on the right needle, wrap the yarn as to Knit and pull the stitches over and off the needle.

The step that joins the Couching stitch and the first stitch on the left needle is just like a Slip Slip Knit decrease. (The Couching stitch is technically an increase; the Slip Slip Knit restores the stitch count.) Don't try to return the loop to the left needle and work this as a Knit Two Together; the loop will wind up behind the discard stitch and it won't look right at all. (You can, of course, use the Alternate Left Decrease, sl1kw, k1, psso, replacing the Slip One Knitwise by the Couching loop, then Knitting the stitch on the left needle and pulling the loop over the new stitch and off.)

The difference between the two methods is subtle. In the first, the loop is joined to the stitch on the right, in the second it is joined to the stitch on the left. With either method it is difficult to control the tension on the loop and the surrounding stitches; too much yarn in the loop will cause the stitches to enlarge, too little will gather the fabric. The first method above seems to perform quite a bit better in this regard than the second and can be used to create very satisfactory texture patterns.

Actually, Couching can be used to deliberately gather the fabric. Done tightly, the technique will create much the same effect as Cluster stitches, Welting, or to what can be achieved with either the Wrap or Pullover techniques.

VERTICAL OR DIAGONAL COUCHING

Here is another variation, combining Couching with the Knit Below technique, allowing you to create a Couching strand that is either vertical or on a diagonal.

1. Insert the tip of the right needle either into a stitch in a row below, or between any two stitches. Wrap the yarn around the needle and draw through a loop.
2. Attach the loop to the fabric using one of the two methods above.

If you are using the first method, wrap the yarn forming the loop in the normal way to Knit; if you are using the second method, use a Knit Over to prevent the loop from crossing as it is worked into the decrease joining it to the fabric. Vertical or Diagonal Couching can be worked on any stitch within half an inch or so of where you are working.

In some patterns, this form of Couching can be used to create much the same effect as an elongated Slip Stitch, either one that is vertical or drawn at an angle across the fabric through the use of the cable technique. However, Couching will create a double strand on both sides of the fabric, using considerably more yarn and adding additional bulk to the fabric. In addition, as mentioned above, it is difficult to control the tension on the loop and the stitches immediately preceding and following it, a problem not encountered with the Slip Stitch, and one that frequently leaves rather obvious deficiencies in a fabric done with Couching. When you encounter one of these patterns, consider whether a Slip Stitch could be used to create the effect desired; if not it might be better to use embroidery.

Tight Vertical Couching spaced across a fabric will force the intervening stitches to puff out forming what are known as "blister" patterns, although the true Knit Below technique is more commonly and successfully used for this effect.

Pullover

There are a wide variety of Pullover techniques, all of which involve passing a stitch on the right needle over one or several stitches to the left of it. When a stitch is discarded in this way, it encircles the base of the stitches it was pulled over, bunching them together. This is basically a decrease technique, so in order to maintain the number of stitches on the needle, a compensating increase must be worked nearby. This increase may or may not be the same stitch as the Pullover. When it is, it is called an Increase Pullover; when it is not, it is called a Stitch Pullover.

STITCH PULLOVER

1. Knit three stitches.
2. Pull the third stitch on the right needle over the first two stitches and drop it off beneath the needle tip.

The number of stitches involved in the Pullover depends upon the particular stitch pattern (two was used in this example, but it might have been one or three, etc.). The compensating increase may be worked before or after the Pullover, directly above it on the next row, or be included within it. For instance, the pattern might call for Knit one, Yarnover, Knit one, then pull the third stitch over the other two, so that the Yarnover increase compensates for the stitch that was pulled over. Many patterns will use a Slip Stitch Pullover. Note that if the Pullover stitch is slipped knitwise, it will not cross, so it will be slightly looser than if the stitch is slipped purlwise.

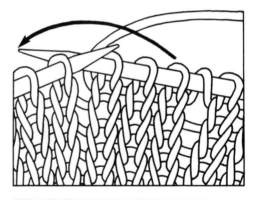

YARNOVER FOLLOWED BY A STITCH PULLOVER

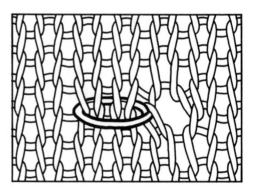

STITCH PULLOVER REPLACED BY A YARNOVER

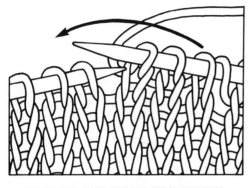

YARNOVER FOLLOWED BY A SLIP STITCH PULLOVER

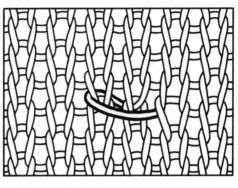

YARNOVER PULLOVER

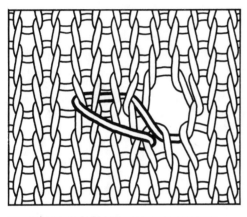

SLIP STITCH PULLOVER REPLACED BY A YARNOVER

INCREASE PULLOVER

• Yarnover, then Knit two stitches. Pull the Yarnover over the two stitches and off the needle.

In this case, the Yarnover is both the increase and the Pullover decrease, so it compensates for itself. Other versions of this type of Pullover use a running thread or Running Thread Increase. The Yarnover version is virtually identical to a Basic Wrap Stitch (page 55), and can be made exactly the same by using a Reverse Yarnover (wrapping it so the left side of the strand is on the nearside of the needle).

Pullovers made on the outside of the fabric will slant toward the left; those made in Purl on the inside of the fabric, following the same general principles, will slant toward the right on the outside.

Tunisian Knitting

A step up in complexity combines a Yarnover Pullover with a Slip Stitch in another way. These stitches are based on Arabic knitting techniques and in British and American books are referred to as "Tunisian stitches." I suspect they are little known and oft neglected because the common way of working them is rather difficult. I am going to give you a better way to work these stitches, and I think you will find that once the easier method is adopted, the possibilities of this technique become more attractive.

SINGLE TUNISIAN

The pattern begins on the inside.

Row 1: Yns, *sl1, yo*, repeat from * to * across the row.
Row 2: *Sl1 (the Yarnover), k1, psso*, repeat from * to * across the row.

In the first row, the Yarnover is done like a Purl to Purl; starting on the nearside, the yarn must pass over the needle to the farside, between the needle tips to the

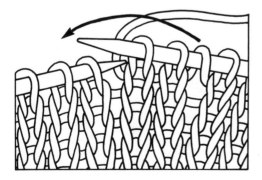

WORKING A YARNOVER PULLOVER

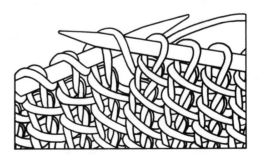

SINGLE TUNISIAN/SLIPPING THE YARNOVER

SINGLE TUNISIAN/KNITTING THE STITCH

nearside. The Yarnovers will not lie between the stitches but on top of them, and no stitches are knit on this row. As the needle is turned to begin the next row, the last Yarnover must be held on the needle, as it is not secured.

On the return row, the first Yarnover will seem strange when you slip it; the yarn must pass from the farside of the first stitch on the left needle, over and then under the right needle. Once the first stitch has been Knit and the Yarnover pulled over it and off the needle, it will be secure, and subsequent Yarnovers will be easier to handle.

What happens is that the Yarnover process in the first row simply winds the yarn around the needle, one wrap for each stitch. If you take the needle out to unravel that row, you would see that the yarn is not attached to any of the stitches and will fall free the minute the needle is withdrawn. On the return row, when the wrapped yarn is pulled over the stitch, it encircles it, much in the same manner as the Slip Knot in the baseline of Half-Hitch Cast-on. Instead of lying at the base of the stitch, however, it slopes up toward the left because it is caught up by the running thread between each stitch on the row above. The fabric produced in this manner is very attractive, quite tailored and geometric in appearance, and nicely resilient.

SINGLE TUNISIAN

Here are the instructions as normally given, so you will know what has been changed, and why, and so you will recognize it and not mistake it for something new.

TRADITIONAL TUNISIAN

The pattern begins on the inside.

Row 1: Yns *sl1kw, yo*, repeat from * to *.
Row 2: K2togfs on every pair of stitches.

The only difference on the first row is that the stitches are slipped knitwise, but in all other respects it is the same. On the return row the Knit Two Together farside includes the stitch and the Yarnover strand. It is really a struggle to insert the right needle, and I am sure this has persuaded many people that the technique is not worth the trouble.

The slip one knitwise from the first row is a bit confusing; once it is turned, if Knit normally on the return row it would cross, but as it is Knit through the farside it is restored to being a normal Knit stitch. The reason that step is necessary is because the Yarnover strand must be Knit through the farside in order to cross on itself, and since they will be worked together, the Knit stitch must be turned in order not to cross. Are you still with me? The gist of the story is that the method is unnecessarily complicated and hard to do.

DOUBLE TUNISIAN

Let's turn our attention to the first variation on the Tunisian theme. With a slight modification, the Yarnover strand will encircle two stitches instead of just one. The pattern begins on the inside.

Row 1: Yns, sl1, *sl1, yo*, repeat from * to *.
Row 2: K1, *sl1yo, k1, psso*, repeat from * to *.

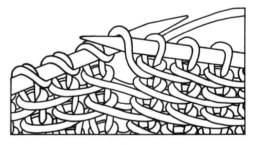

DOUBLE TUNISIAN/SLIPPING THE FIRST YARNOVER

DOUBLE TUNISIAN/KNITTING THE STITCH

The first row is pretty straightforward—it is worked exactly like Traditional Tunisian except than an extra stitch is slipped at the beginning of the row. The next row can be a little confusing at first; however once you've done it a few times, you will find it's quite simple. With the left forefinger, pull the first Yarnover strand back to the left, out of the way so you can Knit the first stitch. Now you will be faced with a Double Yarnover Wrap, the one you pushed to the left and the next one. Slip the first wrap to the right needle, push the second one to the left as above, and Knit the second stitch. Pull the wrap on the right needle over the stitch and off. Repeat across the row, slipping the first wrap, holding the second back as you Knit the stitch, and pulling the wrap over and off.

If you find Knitting the stitch under the Yarnover awkward, there is an alternative method, borrowed from Traditional Tunisian. Work the Slip Stitches in the first row knitwise, which turns them, and on the return row Knit them farside (which returns them to plain Knit so they will not cross after all). The reason for this is that the farside of the stitch is less obstructed by the Yarnover, and you may find it somewhat easier to do this way. In all other respects, work the pattern the same way. Either method produces an identical result; it is simply up to you to decide which way you like to work.

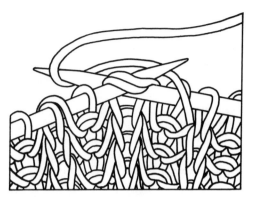

HONEYCOMB RIB/THE DECREASE

SYNCOPATED BRIOCHE, A HONEYCOMB PATTERN

Honeycomb (Brioche) Stitches

Here is a group of stitches that is very closely related to Tunisian, in that it uses a Slip Stitch and a Yarnover, but instead of the Pullover Decrease, it uses a Knit Two Together. However, there couldn't be a better example of how a few small changes in knitting technique can produce a vastly different fabric, for Honeycomb patterns look nothing whatsoever like Tunisian ones. Look for these stitch patterns, as they provide beautiful texture as well as a cellular structure that enhances the thermal properties of a knitted fabric. The version given here produces a deeply textured, well behaved ribbing used more for its appearance than for its elasticity, although it is gently resilient.

HONEYCOMB RIB

Cast on an even number of stitches.

1. Preparation Row: *Yns, sl1, k1*, repeat from * to *. (Because the yarn is on the nearside when you Knit, it will pass over the needle and across the slipped stitch, forming a Yarnover.)
2. All subsequent rows: *Yns, sl1, k2tog*, repeat from * to *. (The Knit Two Together will join the slipped stitch and the Yarnover.)
3. Final row: *K1, k2tog*, repeat from * to *.

What is happening here is that instead of stranding

the running thread directly past the slipped stitch, it is elongated by wrapping it over the needle with the Yarnover technique as the stitch is slipped. On the next row, the Knit Two Together joins the strand and the slipped stitch, and when the two are discarded, the elongated running thread is pulled up over the slipped stitch like a little tent. Because the strand originates at the bases of the stitches adjacent to the slipped stitch, the technique can be done no more frequently than every other stitch.

There are many wonderful patterns that use the Honeycomb technique. The Yarnover and Slip Stitch can be flanked by Knit stitches instead of Purls as they are here, or the pattern can be staggered to form a broken rib or set on a diagonal with intervening stitches. There are a variety of these patterns, in some of which the Yarnover strand is carried up an extra row before working it. However it is done, any stitch pattern that is predominantly Honeycomb will tend to compress and widen, and the patterns also change markedly in appearance, depending on whether they are done on larger or smaller needles.

As an aside, I became curious about how Brioche, a word we commonly associate with a sweet and buttery French bun, came to be used for a knitting stitch, that doesn't really resemble a bun at all. The word has its origins in an old Norman word for grindstone. Now, presumably Norman grindstones were round, explaining how the word came to be applied to a plump round bun. Somewhere along the line, however, the word started being used as a slang term for a mistake, or a blunder. I have yet to find a French etymologist who can explain how it got from "bun" to "blunder," but it is easy to see how the knitting stitch might come to be discovered by working into the row below by mistake. What we seem to have is a fancy-sounding French word for "mistake stitch." I do think it creates such lovely patterns, however, that they deserve better than to be called that, so I prefer the nice English word "honeycomb," which is so descriptive of these stitches' cellular appearance.

There is an alternate way of working Honeycomb Stitches, discussed in the section on Knit Below (page 29), and I recommend you go over that material thoroughly if you are interested in these stitches. Once you are familiar with the two different methods of working, you can decide for yourself which method is the easiest for you, given the stitch, yarn, and needle combination you have at hand.

Embossing

Embossing is another technique that makes use of increases and decreases to create motifs of various shapes that stand out from the surface of the fabric. There are two different types. In the first, stitches are added in the position where the motif is wanted. These extra stitches are worked along with those of the background fabric until the motif is the desired size and then the stitch count is returned to normal, either gradually or all at once. These are often found in fanciful shapes such as bells or flowers and can be very charming. With the other type, the extra stitches are added on and worked in whatever manner is appropriate, and then the stitch count is restored to normal, all before the background fabric is continued. Nubs, Knots, Bobbles, "peppercorns," or "popcorns," whatever they are called, they are charming additions to any garment, and it's easy to toss them into a pattern that doesn't have them to liven it up. However they are made, these stitch techniques can give a fabric a lavish, almost encrusted look that is quite delightful.

Embossed Motifs

With this method of embossing the fabric, the motif is worked along with the background stitches. They maintain a much lower profile than the Knots and Bobbles discussed in the next section. But while they are more subtle, they are also more versatile. There are basically three types, defined by the placement and handling of the extra stitches.

Semidetached Motif

This technique produces some of the more charming and decorative of the embossed patterns. The additional stitches for the motif are formed with casting on rather than with increases, creating an opening at the base of the motif.

THE INCREASES

1. Knit to the point where you wish the motif to appear, turn the work, and use Cable Cast-on (page 143), Woven Knit Cast-on (page 143), or Chained Cast-on (page 144) to add the number of stitches required for the base of the motif, plus one.
2. Turn the work back to the Knit side, transfer the extra cast-on stitch to the left needle, and Knit it together with the next stitch in a right decrease (Knit Two Together) and continue with the row. (This step eliminates a gap that tends to appear between the lower left corner of the motif and the main body of the fabric.)
3. The additional stitches provided for the motif are then worked along with the rest of the fabric until you wish to decrease them.

It is important that this cast-on edge be smooth and neat. Most patterns will call for Simple Cast-on or Knit Cast-on, but a much better result is obtained with one of the methods I have recommended.

THE DECREASES

The decreases may begin on the very next row, or after a few intervening rows, and should be placed within the motif.

- If a left decrease is placed on the right side, and a right decrease on the left, the motif will be outlined by the slanting stitches of the decreases. If the reverse pattern is used, no outline will be created and the motif will be smooth.
- If all of the decreases are placed along one side of the motif, the stitches within the motif will slant on the bias (for more information on bias, see page 172).

The most popular motif making use of this technique is that of a bell. The bells are seen both internal to a fabric or used as an edging, and the shape is created by delaying the decreases for a few rows. If the decreases are begun immediately, the shape would be more of an inverted V. Generally these motifs are embedded in stitches of contrasting texture, most commonly Purl (Reverse Stockinette), but any stitch that helps to set them off may be used.

CARILLON, A SEMI-DETACHED MOTIF

Attached Motif

In this case, the increases are added gradually over a number of rows, just like the decreases. As a result, there is no gap at the base. The increases and decreases are internal to the motif, but can be either all on one side or the other, or balanced on both sides. Again, a contrasting ground is used.

Various increases can be used depending upon what enhances the pattern. The Running Thread Increase would be the most hidden, the Yarnover Increase the most decorative. If an Eyelet is desirable but a Yarnover makes too large an opening for the scale of the motif, use an Open Running Thread Increase instead. When the increases are on the left side of the motif and the motif is placed on a background of Purl, the Bar Increase could be used, as it throws a Purl nub to the left of the increase stitch.

Gauge must be checked carefully on a swatch large enough to show the effect of the embossing on the width of the fabric. While the motifs will protrude from the face of the fabric, the extra stitches will also add a bit of width overall, which too small a gauge will not dis-

cover. The most common motif shapes are diamonds, ovals, petals or leaves.

FUCHSIA, AN ATTACHED MOTIF

Exchange Motif

With these patterns, the number of stitches on the needle remains constant at all times. As the size of the motif is increased, a comparable number of stitches are decreased from the background; as the motif is decreased, the background is increased. In some patterns, the motifs are staggered side by side so that as one motif decreases the adjacent motif increases. The motifs are divided by a few stitches of Purl, which helps them to puff out and sets them off visually.

CANDLE FLAME, AN EXCHANGE MOTIF

Nubs

These are the smallest members of the family and are very easy to do. Because they are so tiny, they are most often found distributed all over a fabric in fairly close array. Some patterns refer to them as "peppercorns," which is really quite apt.

CHAIN NUB

This creates a subtle texture by working one stitch several times—not horizontally as one would with an increase, but vertically.

1. Knit or Purl the first stitch and allow the discard stitch to drop from the left needle.
2. Pass the yarn around the right needle tip as if to either Knit or Purl and then pull the new stitch over the yarn and off the needle. Repeat two more times.
3. When you have chained four stitches, simply continue with the row.

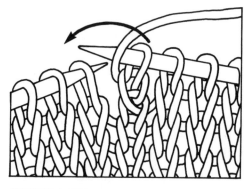

WORKING A CHAIN NUB

Needless to say, the number of stitches is arbitrary, but one stitch more or less will change the appearance. More than four stitches tends to get rather droopy, two creates such a small effect it's hardly worth it, three might be better than four in a bulky yarn. On the other hand, you could chain five or ten stitches and let them form a loop that hangs from the face of the fabric. In the small versions, I find the outcome a little nubbier and more effective if the stitch is done in Purl. Whether Knit or Purl, the technique leaves gaps on either side of the chain that may or may not be important to you.

RUNNING THREAD NUB

Here's another way to do much the same thing, and it eliminates the gap should you wish to do so.

1. Work a Running Thread Increase and chain the stitch three more times, as above.
2. When you have completed the last stitch of the chain, continue with the row. On the return row, Purl the chain stitch and the preceding stitch together.

DOUBLE RUNNING THREAD NUB

This is another, slightly larger version.

1. Work a Rib Increase on the running thread.
2. Work just these two stitches for four rows in Stockinette, Reverse Stockinette, or Garter Stitch. Continue with the row.
3. On the return row, work two decreases, one stitch of the chain with the stitch to the right, and one with the stitch to the left.

Whether you are working in Knit or Purl, work the decreases so that the stitches of the chain are the backing stitches of the decrease—first a Knit Left, then a Knit Right Decrease; or on the Purl side, first do a Purl Right, then a Purl Left Decrease.

THREE-STITCH NUB

This is a nice, very small, compact little nubbin, and it is quick and easy to do.

1. Work a three-stitch Multiple Bar Increase.
2. On those three stitches, work a Wrap and Pullover Decrease.
3. As you prepare to work the next stitch, push the Nub toward the nearside with your left forefinger.

FIVE-STITCH NUB

Slightly larger, just as easy to do.

1. Work a five-stitch Multiple Bar Increase.
2. On those five stitches, work a Wrap and Pullover Decrease.

PEPPERCORN PATTERN

3. As you prepare to work the next stitch, push the Nub toward the nearside with your left forefinger.

A word of caution appropriate to all Nubs, Knots, and Bobbles: After you have completed the Nub, firmly tighten the stitch holding the Nub, and keep the running thread taut as you work the next stitch. On the return row, do the same with the stitch following the one holding the Nub. This helps to bind the Nub to the fabric and prevents holes from appearing on either side.

Knots

Now we move up to the Knot family. The thing that distinguishes them from the Nubs is that we add a row of knitting between the increases and the decreases.

SLIP STITCH KNOT

Row 1: Work a five-stitch Multiple Yarnover Increase, turn.
Row 2: Purl the five stitches, turn.
Row 3: Slip all five stitches to the right needle, one at a time, and then work a Wrap and Pullover Decrease.

After the increase and the first turn, it is a good idea to tighten up the first stitch and work it with a firm tension so the edge stitches don't enlarge. This Knot is quite nubby, but compact and fairly symmetrical. It's not my favorite, but it is intermediate in size between the Five-Stitch Nub and the next Knot, and so may be of use to you sometime. Notice that this, and all subsequent techniques, use the Multiple Yarnover Increase instead of the Multiple Bar Increase; the former tends to be more centered and, therefore, works better for the larger Knots and Bobbles.

DOUBLE DECREASE KNOT

This is somewhat larger, compact, and nicely centered —altogether, an excellent Knot.

Row 1: Work a five-stitch Multiple Yarnover Increase, turn.
Row 2: Purl the five stitches, turn.
Row 3: Knit three together, turn, Slip Slip Knit. Pull the second stitch on the right needle over the first and off the needle.

Tighten the first stitch after each turn and work it with a firm tension so the edge stitches don't enlarge. The center stitches of the Knot will be the facing stitches of the decrease, which helps them to protrude. Remember to bind the completed Knot tightly to the adjacent stitches as explained above.

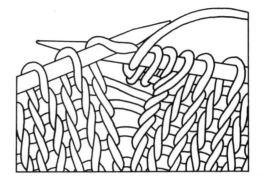

MULTIPLE INCREASES FOR A KNOT

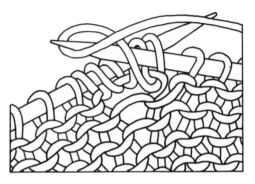

PURLING THE SECOND ROW OF A KNOT

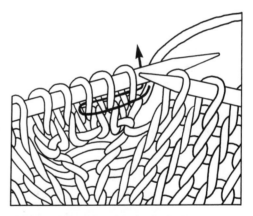

WORKING THE FIRST DECREASE OF A KNOT

CENTER PANEL IN BOUQUET, A KNOT PATTERN

Bobbles

Now let's turn to the Bobbles. Again, these are just bigger Knots. The bigger they get, of course, the more work they are, and no Bobble is quick to do (I suppose it's a bit like puppies or children: It's only because they are so charming that we put up with them at all).

There are almost as many ways to create a Bobble as there are patterns containing them, and I've knit my way through every one I have encountered. You will undoubtedly come across other methods that achieve much the same thing, but many of them are not as successful as one would like. I will not go into the details of the rejects here, since I have already outlined the pros and cons of the different multiple increases and decreases upon which they depend. I promise you, I have tried them all, and after a good deal of experimenting, I've come up with a Bobble I really think is better—I hope you like it as well as I do.

THE BETTER BOBBLE

Row 1: YOinc3, turn.
Row 2: P1, YOinc3, p1, turn.
Row 3: K5, turn.
Row 4: SSP, p1, p2tog, turn.
Row 5: Sl2togkw, k1, p2sso.

There are several new things to notice here. First, the increases and decreases require two rows. This adds to the symmetry of the Bobble. Second, the final decreases are planned so that the outside stitches converge behind the center stitches, allowing the latter to protrude as much as possible.

If you want to make the first decrease in Row 4 slightly easier to do, use Knit Under on the last two stitches of the K5 on the previous row so the stitches are already turned for the left decrease. The Bobble is even nubbier if it is done in Purl; just reverse the instructions, working Purl where it says Knit, and Knit where it says Purl.

You will encounter many patterns that call for the first stitch of each row of the Bobble to be slipped, but this enlarges the edge stitches, making them more prominent, and tightens the adjacent stitch within the Bobble, making it less so. I find the result quite unnattractive and recommend against this practice.

Last but not least, as I mentioned with the Knots, make sure to tighten up the last Bobble stitch and maintain a firm tension as you Knit the next stitch of the row to bind the Bobble to the fabric. On the return row, do the same with the stitch following the one holding the Bobble. You may find the fabric surrounds the Bobble more firmly if you slip the Bobble stitch on the return row, stranding the yarn past it firmly.

Keep in mind that any Knot or Bobble can be worked as easily on a running thread as it is on a stitch.

This is useful to know if you ever want to introduce one or the other into a stitch pattern that is based on an even number of stitches where there is no "center" stitch. After the Bobble is complete, restore the stitch count on the next row by working a Purl Two Together on the remaining Bobble stitch and the preceding stitch.

ATTACHED BOBBLE

There is one remaining problem with the Bobble just described, and that is the gaps on either side. Now people have worked Bobbles with gaps on either side for hundreds of years and gotten along just fine, so perhaps it isn't a problem at all, but I began to wonder if they couldn't be eliminated. The solution rests on a technique borrowed from another area of knitting entirely.

Bobbles are already somewhat tedious to do, and this adds a few more steps, but I think the outcome is worth it. Here is a Bobble that is plump, symmetrical, and firmly attached to the fabric with no gaps. The Bobble is the same—the only difference is that during its construction the two stitches on either side of the Bobble are wrapped with the yarn. Once the Bobble is complete, these two stitches require special handling as the knitting progresses.

The Bobble
Row 1: YOinc3, turn.
Row 2: P1, YOinc3, p1, sl1 yfs ret1 yns, turn.
Row 3: K5, sl1 yns ret1 yfs, turn.
Row 4: SSP, p1, p2tog, turn.
Row 5: Sl2togkw, k1, p2sso.

Because of the wrap, the first stitches on either side of the Bobble require special treatment. The wrap lies at the base of each stitch and must be worked just as for Wrapped Short Rows (page 176), where the technique is illustrated. The wrap to the left of the Bobble is dealt with immediately, the wrap to the right will be taken care of on the next row. Because one is on an outside row, one on an inside row, the techniques differ slightly.

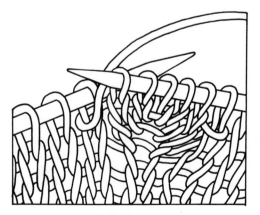

WORKING THE SECOND WRAP FOR AN ATTACHED BOBBLE

First Wrap

1. Transfer the stitch to the left of the Bobble to the right needle.
2. With the left needle tip, lift the wrap up onto the needle to the right of the stitch.
3. Transfer both stitch and wrap back to the left needle and Knit or Purl two together, depending upon your stitch pattern.

The wrap will become the backing stitch of the decrease, hidden on the inside of the fabric.

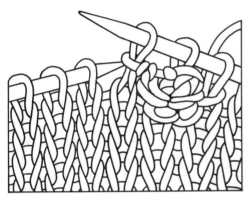

LIFTING THE WRAP TO ATTACH THE BOBBLE

Second Wrap

1. Work the stitch holding the Bobble.
2. Slip the next stitch to the right needle knitwise, lift the wrap up and to the right of this stitch, and work a Knit or Purl Two Together farside.

THE BIGGER, BETTER BOBBLE

Here is a larger Bobble, constructed on the same principles. It can be done without the wrapping steps, of course, but because of the extra row, the gaps are even larger, and I think the outcome is much nicer if they are used.

Row 1: YOinc3, turn.
Row 2: P1, YOinc3, p1, turn.
Row 3: K5, sl1 yns ret1 yfs, turn.
Row 4: P5, sl1 yfs ret1 yns, turn.
Row 5: K3tog, SSK, wrap the yarn as for Knit, and pull the two stitches over and off the needle.

Continue with the knitting, working the wraps as described above. With a Bobble of this magnitude, it becomes especially important to work all the edge stitches with a firm tension.

You may encounter advice to "lock" the last stitch of the bobble by working it one more time and tightening the discard stitch firmly. While this neatens up the last stitch and prevents it from being enlarged, it also adds length and causes the Bobble to droop. I think it is

HOLLOW OAK, WITH BOBBLES, CABLES AND SEED STITCH

better to just put good tension on that stitch as you go to work the next one.

AFTERTHOUGHT BOBBLE

If you have grown weary of a sweater that is just too plain, or you'd like to dress up an older brother's hand-me-down but still perfectly good sweater for a younger sister, or you have just finished something and wish you'd thought of Bobbles in the first place, here is how to add them on to anything, anywhere, at any time.

1. Leave a ten- to twelve-inch end of yarn and place a tight Slip Knot on a relatively small needle.

2. On that single stitch, work a Bigger, Better Bobble, firmly, as described above.
3. Allow ten to twelve inches and break the yarn. Pull the end through the last stitch and tighten it down.
4. Use a crochet hook to bring the two ends through the fabric from outside to inside, one above and one below either a running thread or a stitch head. Tie the ends together in a firm knot and weave them into the adjacent stitches as described on page 380.

If you want to cluster several Bobbles closely together, don't weave in the ends; it will thicken the fabric too much. Just tie the knots, cut the ends off, and leave them there to tickle the wearer, or stuff them inside the Bobble to fatten it up.

The result is a perfectly respectable Bobble with no gaps on either side, but it is definitely more trouble to do than the knitted-in sort, and you are left with all those knots and ends. Nevertheless, when it works, it works very well indeed.

SLIP BOBBLE

One of the wearying aspects of working a Bobble is turning the fabric back and forth, particularly when it has grown heavy. Here is a way to eliminate the turns and produce a very smooth, very handsome Bobble.

1. Use a Multiple Bar Increase to place five stitches on the needle.
2. Slip the five stitches to the left needle, draw the yarn firmly across the farside, and Knit the five stitches.
3. Repeat the last step, working one or two more rows, depending on the size Bobble required.
4. K2tog, K1, SSK, slip the remaining three stitches to the left needle and then Sl2togkw k1 p2sso to complete the Bobble.

On the center row(s) of the Bobble, draw the yarn slightly less firmly across the farside then on the first and last rows to allow the Bobble to take on a round shape. It is also possible to work the Bobble on a pair of short, double point needles. This allows you to slide the stitches from the left point to the right point at the end of every row, eliminating the need to slip the stitches from one needle to the other. It also permits using a smaller size needle for the Bobble than for the main fabric, giving the Bobble a neat, compact appearance. Work with the fabric supported in your lap and push the other stitches back from the needle points somewhat so they don't slip off during Bobble making.

Stitch Bias and Lace

In the preceding sections we have looked at how increase and decrease techniques can be used to give texture to the surface of the fabric. Here is another application of the very same fundamental techniques. In this case, however, a slight change in the placement of the shaping units produces a smooth fabric with stitches that travel at various angles instead of staying in nice neat columns and rows. The choice of one particular technique rather than another can make an enormous difference in the outcome, as we shall see. When shaping units with a subtle appearance are chosen, the effect relies entirely upon the changing paths of the stitch columns. The most dramatic effect is achieved by using the Yarnover Increase; the result, of course, is knitted Lace.

Bias Stitch Patterns

In order to create bias, increases and decreases must be strictly paired, but separated horizontally by several plain stitches. When this is done repeatedly, the new columns of stitches generated by the increases will travel at an angle until they are swallowed up by decreases several rows later. The shaping units may be stacked up vertically, the decreases may be stacked while the increases step toward them (or vice versa), or groups of shaping units may be clustered or staggered in the pattern. In most cases, the bias set up will affect the top and bottom edges, causing it to scallop. (For more information on bias, see "Bias Fabrics," page 172).

The resulting patterns are many and varied indeed, ranging from the tailored and formal geometry of Chevron patterns to those containing soft, undulating curves.

Chevron Patterns

There are many handsome stitch patterns that form alternating columns of bias across the entire width of the fabric; no more than strips of Double Bias set side by side. The baseline angles will alternate beneath each strip, forming a scalloped or serrated edge that does very well as the bottom edge of a garment without the need for a ribbing or other edge; however, it requires special consideration in casting on (see page 132). A ribbed edge can certainly be used, even though the lower points of the Chevrons may bulge out somewhat (although this is not so noticeable when the columns of bias are narrow or the fabric is well gathered by the ribbing). Care must also be taken at shoulder seams where it is sometimes necessary to seam straight across, turning the contour into the selvedge in order to create a smooth line.

The bias will also affect any plain rows of stitches inserted between pattern areas. For instance, a few rows of Reverse Stockinette or Garter stitch inserted between bias rows and themselves worked without any increases or decreases will still undulate, following the contours

of the Chevrons. And finally, these patterns are particularly beautiful when done in variegated yarns or in color stripes.

Stepped Patterns

Another variation on the theme is to hold one set of shaping units in a vertical column while the other set shifts position row by row, each time on a new column of stitches. Remember, the columns of stitches between the shaping units will always move away from the increases and toward the decreases. Any stitches outside of the paired shaping units will remain vertical.

If, for instance, you step increases toward a column of double decreases, you will create a diamond shape. If both the increases and the decreases are vertical for a while and then the increases begin to slope toward the decreases, the bias stitches will move in a soft curve.

Similarly, the increases and decreases can be stepped in parallel fashion, always the same number of stitches apart, causing columns of bias stitches to travel across columns of vertical stitches.

DRAGON SKIN, WITH STEPPED SHAPING

Cluster Patterns

Although these stitch patterns definitely contain bias, it is created not so much on the chevron or stepped shaping principles we have been discussing, but rather in a manner similar to that described for gathering. Instead of organizing the paired increases and decreases in vertical lines and slopes, they are grouped horizontally across the width of the fabric with several increases clustered together and an equal number of decreases clustered to one side. Several rows later a cluster of decreases is placed above one of increases; a cluster of increases above one of decreases setting up a soft wave motion in the columns of stitches. These patterns are closely related to the Embossing patterns described on page 86 and, like them, the side edges of the fabric also undulate.

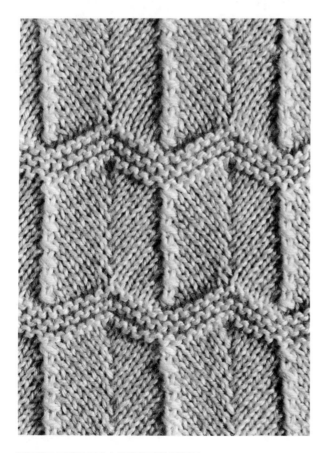

WELTING FANTASTIC, A CHEVRON PATTERN

Shaping Techniques for Slope and Bias

In the above material, I have not specified which increase or decrease to use because basically you can use any technique that you think will enhance the pattern. Nevertheless, there are some general guidelines you will want to keep in mind.

Since the sloped columns of stitches converge on the decreases, give some thought to whether you want the bias columns to form the facing or the backing stitches of the decreases. For instance, if right decreases are used at the right side edge, the bias columns will extend as far as possible. If you wanted the bias columns of stitches to cover a column of vertical stitches to the right, you would use right decreases, whereas if you wanted the bias to disappear behind the vertical portion, a left decrease would be in order. The opposite would be true if the vertical column of stitches lay to the left of the bias.

When a double decrease is used, you will recall there are three to select from, with either the left, right, or center stitch being the facing stitch. Many stitch patterns are not particular about this, and you will want to choose one that enhances the pattern, or perhaps substitute a different one than that called for. The Center Double decrease makes a lot of sense, of course, but it is quite dominant, and you may prefer to use one of the others to gain a more subtle effect.

As with the decreases, analyze each stitch pattern and decide for yourself whether or not the increase suggested is the best one in that situation. In this case the most important consideration is whether the increase is closed or open, and to what degree, and whether you want a quiet or a highly decorative effect. The most decorative increase, of course, is the Yarnover, which, when combined with the concepts of bias, opens the door to all the beauty and variety of Lace, as we shall see next.

Lace

For such an important and seemingly complex aspect of knitting, you will find this section oddly small. That is because we have already discussed two of the most important elements of Lace knitting in the sections on Yarnover and Bias, and Lace makes supreme use of the principles of both. The third element, Eyelets, follows this section directly. Here I want only to show you that you already have the knowledge to make sense of even complex patterns that make use of those principles. To prove that to you, let's take the basic bias shapes we were just looking at and substitute a Yarnover Increase for the closed increases we used there. The result will be some very common and popular Lace patterns, which you will no doubt recognize.

Let's look first at what a Chevron looks like when a Yarnover increase is used.

PURL BARRED SCALLOP

Here's an example using Yarnover Increases stepped toward a column of decreases forming soft curves.

HORSESHOE LACE

The next has the decreases angling toward a column of Yarnover Increases, creating a formal diamond shape.

LEAF PATTERNED LACE

There is a variation on the Chevron principle that uses clustered groups of increases next to similar groups of decreases. Here is a very famous old pattern that illustrates the technique very nicely.

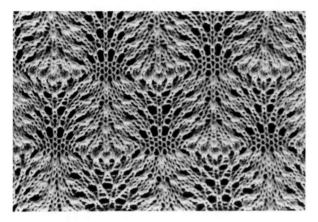

OSTRICH PLUMES

And finally, an example of parallel increases and decreases used to push the columns of stitches into lovely petal shapes.

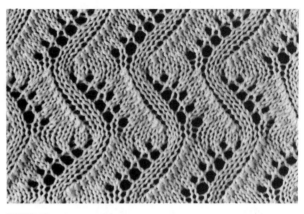

MEANDER

These few samples show you the general manner in which a Lace pattern is constructed. Once you know how the techniques work, and what the effect on the fabric is, you should have no trouble analyzing and understanding any Lace stitch that makes use of them, or even in creating one of your own. Lace includes far more than this, however, and it is time to turn our attention to the Eyelet family, where the Yarnover and the decrease are never separated as they are here.

Eyelets

Usually we think of an Eyelet as a small hole, or group of holes, in an otherwise smooth fabric. Making an Eyelet is easy—no more than a paired decrease and Yarnover. Two things—the relationship between the decrease and the Yarnover, and how the Eyelets are placed on the fabric—create astonishingly varied effects ranging from true Eyelets through Lace to Mesh. It is sometimes difficult to decide whether a stitch is an Eyelet pattern or a Lace pattern, but there are two primary elements that distinguish them.

First, an Eyelet pattern generally has less openwork and more background stitches than a Lace pattern. Second, in an Eyelet pattern the increase and the decrease are always side by side, whereas this is not necessarily the case with Lace. Mesh bridges the two; it is technically an Eyelet because the increases and decreases are next to one another, but there are virtually no background stitches, making it the most open of any knitted fabric. There are hundreds of patterns that call for some

form of Eyelet. Once you understand how the different versions are constructed, and what their limitations and possibilities are, you will find any pattern easy to decipher. You will also then have the confidence to experiment in order to improve or modify a pattern, or even to create your own.

The instructions given here are for just the Eyelets, with nothing said about background stitches or the arrangement of the Eyelets on the fabric. I have deliberately isolated them in this way so as to make the method of forming them and their structure perfectly clear. I am going to give all the instructions in the manner in which an Eyelet is most commonly done in flat knitting with the Eyelet formed in Knit on one row and plain Purl worked on the next row, and I will assume that you are trying them out on a swatch of Stockinette. The instructions notwithstanding, the Eyelet can most certainly be worked in Purl with Knit on the next row, or in Garter Stitch. Simply keep in mind what the principles are and the conversion to another way of working will be no problem.

Generally, it is the Knit face of an Eyelet that is the most attractive; when viewed on the Purl side, the nubs tend to overshadow the opening. This is especially true when the fabric is worked in Garter Stitch, where the size of the opening is also reduced because of the vertical compression inherent to that pattern. Some of that can be overcome by stretching the fabric open in finishing, and many lovely patterns are worked this way.

In order to understand this material, you should already be familiar with the decrease stitches (pages 58–65) and the Yarnover technique (page 73). If you are unfamiliar with any of the abbreviations used in the instructions, please refer to page 407.

Single Eyelets

These are the basic Eyelets on which all the variations are built. There are subtle changes in appearance, depending upon the relationship between the decrease and the Yarnover and the type of decrease used. Remember that on the Purl row the Yarnover is worked as if it were a normal stitch, and therefore it should be formed so it sits on the needle in the correct position, with the right side of the strand on the nearside of the needle.

LEFT SMOOTH EYELET

This way of working leaves unbroken columns of stitches on either side of the Eyelet. The removed stitch is hidden behind the left stitch, and the Eyelet is nice and round.

Row 1: YO, k2tog.
Row 2: Purl.

As you can see, the number of stitches remains the same; the stitch removed by the decrease is restored by the Yarnover.

RIGHT SMOOTH EYELET

This has the same general appearance as the one above, but the removed stitch is hidden behind the right stitch.

Row 1: SSK, YO.
Row 2: Purl.

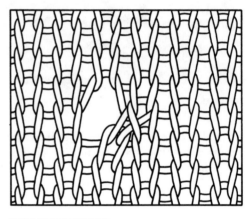

RIGHT SMOOTH EYELET

LEFT BROKEN EYELET

In this case, the removed stitch is the facing stitch of the decrease, covering the stitch to the left of the Eyelet. The appearance of the Eyelet is less round because of the angled stitch in the lower corner.

Row 1: YO, SSK.
Row 2: Purl.

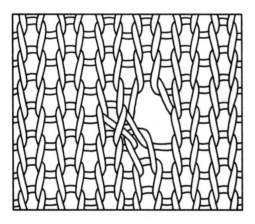

LEFT SMOOTH EYELET

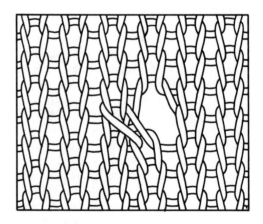

LEFT BROKEN EYELET

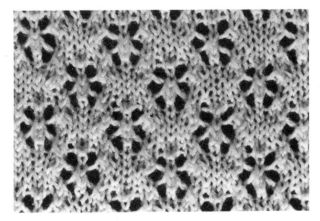

SNOWFLAKE PATTERN, WITH SMOOTH EYELETS

MIXED EYELET RIB

RIGHT BROKEN EYELET

The appearance of the Eyelet is the same as the one above, but the removed stitch covers the stitch to the right of the Eyelet.

Row 1: K2tog, YO.
Row 2: Purl.

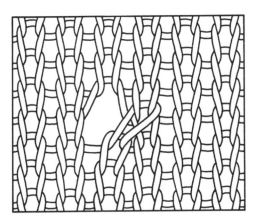

RIGHT BROKEN EYELET

General Comments

Whenever possible, the Left Smooth Eyelet and the Right Broken Eyelet are the ones to choose because they make use of a right decrease (K2tog), which is quicker and easier to do. Actually, the Purl Right Decrease (P2tog) is even faster, so if you are working a simple Eyelet pattern, you might want to consider working the Eyelet on the Purl side of the fabric, with a Knit row on the return. If the pattern is complex, it may not be worth the rewriting that would be necessary.

Also, when the above instructions call for a Yarnover followed by a left decrease, I have specified the Slip

Knit version rather than the alternate Slip Pullover way of working. With the latter, the Yarnover strand covers the Slip Stitch, which makes it difficult to pick up in order to pull it over the stitch and off the needle. Regardless of their respective difficulty, either decrease produces the same result.

Half Double Eyelets

We can increase the size of the Eyelets by removing two stitches, one on either side on the Yarnover. The Yarnover restores one of the stitches, and on the next row an increase worked on the Yarnover restores the other.

SMOOTH HALF DOUBLE EYELET

This Eyelet is round at the bottom; the removed stitches are hidden behind the stitches to either side of the Eyelet.

Row 1: SSK, YO, K2tog.
Row 2: Purl, working a Rib Increase on the Yarnover.

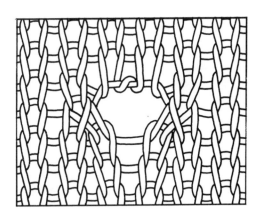

SMOOTH HALF DOUBLE EYELET

BROKEN HALF DOUBLE EYELET

Similar in principle and size to the one above, but the Eyelet is angled at the bottom due to the slanted, facing stitches of the decreases.

Row 1: K2tog, YO, SSK.
Row 2: Purl, working a Rib Increase on the Yarnover.

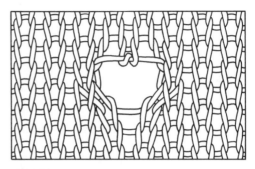

SMOOTH DOUBLE EYELET

BROKEN DOUBLE EYELET

Here the removed stitches slant out at the bottom, and the strands of the Yarnover slant in at the top, making the Eyelet angular at both the top and the bottom.

Row 1: K2tog, YO2, SSK.
Row 2: Purl, working a Rib Increase on the Yarnover.

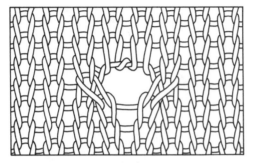

BROKEN HALF DOUBLE EYELET

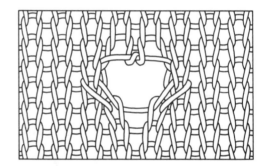

BROKEN DOUBLE EYELET

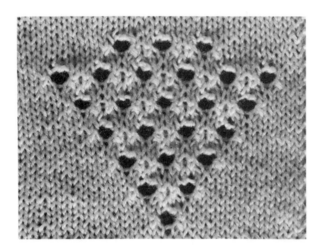

ARROWHEAD, WITH HALF DOUBLE EYELETS

Double Eyelets

These are identical to the ones above, except they make use of a Double Yarnover, increasing the size of the opening.

SMOOTH DOUBLE EYELET

This Eyelet is very open but less round at the top. The two removed stitches are hidden on either side at the bottom, but the top is somewhat more angular, due to the length of the Yarnover strand.

Row 1: SSK, YO2, K2tog.
Row 2: Purl, working a Rib Increase on the Yarnover.

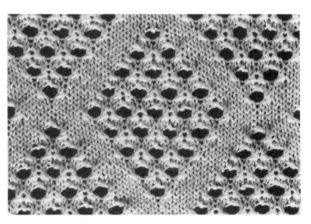

DIAMOND PATTERN WITH DOUBLE EYELETS

General Comments

Many people work into the first wrap of a Double Yarnover, discard it from the left needle, and then work into the second wrap. However, that approach sometimes causes the new stitches to wind up off to the right side of the Yarnover strand, leaving the left side to be taken up by the adjacent stitch, which enlarges it. It is generally better to drop one of the Yarnover wraps from the needle first and then work the two stitches. This helps to balance them on the center of the strand.

The instructions above call for a Rib Increase, without specifying whether it should be worked Purl/Knit or Knit/Purl. I have seen some books that claim that the two produce an Eyelet with a different appearance, the latter forming a small "picot" or knot at the top center. This is puzzling, because the basic structure of the increase is the same regardless of which way it is made as discussed on page 66.

I thought for a while that the nub might lean toward the Knit side if worked one way, and toward the Purl side if worked another, but countless trials have failed to prove this. The nub does become more obvious when the increase is worked loosely and is quite unobtrusive when worked with a firm tension. When the nub is prominent, it gives the Eyelet a charming, slightly heart-shaped appearance, and when it is not, the Eyelet is round. Since most Eyelets are worked in Knit with Purl on the return row, and the increase is worked on the Purl side, I like to use the Purl/Knit sequence. When I work the Eyelet on the Purl side and the increase on the Knit side, I use the Knit/Purl sequence. The important thing is to be consistent about which increase and what kind of tension you wish to use.

Extra-Large Eyelets

You will encounter other variations, and patterns that call for even larger Eyelets, all constructed on much the same principles as the ones discussed above. Whenever three or more stitches must be worked onto a Yarnover strand, I highly recommend the Multiple Yarnover Increase (page 76). There are some patterns where the Yarnover is made on one row and paired decreases are worked on the next row, on either side of the increase on the Yarnover strand. There are others that place a multiple decrease to one side of the Eyelet instead of using pairs on either side, and some that make use of multiple Yarnovers. There is even one that is triangular in shape, making use of casting off at the base with increases worked over several rows to gradually restore the stitch count. If you are familiar with the repertoire of increase and decrease stitches and the formation of a Yarnover, not even the more complex of them should remain mysterious to you for long.

Eyelet Insertion

What I call Eyelet Insertion patterns are those that create vertical, diagonal, or horizontal lines of Eyelets on a solid background. Though the traditional term for this work, derived from British usage, is "faggot stitch," or "faggoting," I shall refer to a single opening in the fabric as an Eyelet, and any series of Eyelets as Eyelet Insertion in order to use terminology that relates to the

structure of the stitching. (Insertion work is the more general term in embroidery for rows or columns of openwork.) Knitted Lace includes Eyelets and Eyelet Insertion arranged in various patterns, but it also makes use of Yarnovers separated from their decreases by a number of intervening stitches, or even rows, as we discussed in the previous section.

As you can well imagine, it is quite easy to arrange basic Eyelets in rows. The most open version would be created by working an Eyelet on every pair of stitches across the row; less open patterns would have a stitch or two between each Eyelet. These rows are a charming way to set off a border, they can act as a division between two other stitch patterns, or they can define a yoke or a collar edge. A row of Eyelet Insertion is frequently used in patterns to create the holes through which to thread a ribbon. When used as the turning row of a hem (see page 203), the result is a "toothed" edge, which is quite charming.

A column of openwork can also be created by stacking Eyelets one on top of another. When placed in columns in this way, each decrease includes the stitch made on the previous Yarnover. The strands that divide one Eyelet from another are made up of the yarn from the Yarnover and the running thread from the stitch made on the Yarnover. In the basic Eyelet, the appearance was changed by using one decrease rather than the other. When stacked in columns, those effects are magnified.

RIBBON EYELET, AN INSERTION PATTERN

SMOOTH LEFT EYELET COLUMN

The line of stitches to the left of the Eyelets will be unbroken, with the removed stitches hidden behind them. The strands dividing one Eyelet and the next slant upward to the left.

Row 1: YO, K2tog.
Row 2: Purl.

On subsequent rows, the decrease will include the stitch on the previous Yarnover and the one to the left.

CORDED LEFT EYELET COLUMN

Here the removed stitch is the facing stitch of the decrease, giving the column of stitches to the left of the Eyelets a corded appearance. The strands of yarn dividing the Eyelets slant upward to the left.

Row 1: YO, SSK.
Row 2: Purl.

    On subsequent rows, the decrease will include the stitch on the previous Yarnover and the one to the left.

SMOOTH RIGHT EYELET COLUMN

The line of stitches to the right of the Eyelets will be unbroken, with the removed stitches hidden behind them. The strands of yarn slant upward to the right.

Row 1: SSK, YO.
Row 2: Purl.

    On subsequent rows, the decrease will include the stitch on the Yarnover and the one to the right.

CORDED RIGHT EYELET COLUMN

The removed stitch is the facing stitch of the decrease, and the column of stitches to the right of the Eyelets will have a corded appearance. The strands of yarn slant upward to the right.

Row 1: K2tog, YO.
Row 2: Purl.

    On subsequent rows, the decrease will include the stitch on the Yarnover and the one to the right.

General Comments

As with individual Eyelets, it is faster and easier to use a right decrease than a left—either the Smooth Left Eyelet Column or the Corded Right Eyelet Column—and even faster if the Eyelet is done on the Purl side.

DOUBLE DECREASE EYELET COLUMN

The eyelet columns discussed above are frequently seen in pairs, a right and left flanking a plain stitch or two. A common variation on that theme is a column made up of pairs of Eyelets flanking a center double decrease. The appearance changes slightly depending upon which of the three double decreases is used, but the basic technique is the same.

Row 1: YO, DblDec, YO.
Row 2: Purl.

DOUBLE DECREASE EYELET COLUMN

Eyelet Mesh

Eyelet Insertion Columns placed side by side, with no intervening stitches, will create a mesh that can be used in sections or for an entire fabric. When this is done, the Eyelet columns will begin to move on the bias, drawing the fabric with them. The effect will exist to a minimal extent with even a single column of Eyelet Insertion, but will be pronounced when multiple columns are used side by side. The direction of the bias will always be toward the Yarnover. In other words, if the Yarnover lies to the right of the decrease, the fabric will have a bias to the right; if the Yarnover lies to the left of the decrease, the fabric will slant to the left.

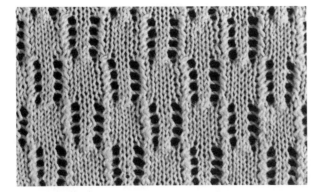

CHECKERED ACRE, EYELET COLUMNS

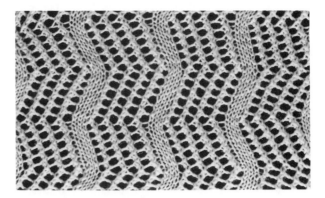

RIB FANTASTIC, EYELET MESH BIAS

BALANCED EYELET MESH

A mesh without bias can be formed by alternating the decreases. For a flat fabric entirely in mesh, you will need one edge stitch at each side to anchor the first Yarnover of one pattern row, the last Yarnover of the other pattern row.

1. On the first two rows, work Smooth or Corded Left Eyelet Columns.
2. On the next two rows, work Smooth or Corded Right Eyelet Columns.

There is an alternate method of working that produces a nearly identical mesh fabric; the difference between the two is quite subtle, but you may like one more than the other. Work on an uneven instead of an even number of stitches, and work a single Knit stitch at the beginning of one pattern row and a single Knit stitch at the end of the next pattern row to stagger the Eyelets.

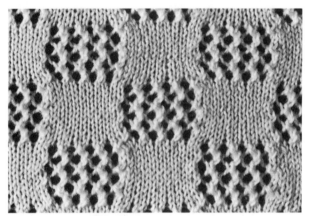

LACE CHECK, A BALANCED MESH

DOUBLE EYELET MESH

Here is another way to avoid bias, but whether used as a column or to create a mesh, the effect is much more open.

Row 1: SSK, YO2, K2tog.
Row 2: Purl, working a Rib Increase on the Yarnover.

DOUBLE EYELET MESH

With subsequent Eyelets, each decrease includes one of the stitches made on the Yarnover.

SQUARE EYELET MESH

One of these Eyelets alone is not terribly attractive, but when used to create a mesh, it is interesting because of its square shape. It is most commonly seen as the basis of an old netting technique called Filet Lacis (Lace Net), where the Eyelets are arranged in patterns on a background of Garter Stitch squares containing the same number of stitches as the Eyelets.

1. Yarnover; slip two stitches knitwise, one at a time, pass one slipped stitch over the other and off the needle; slip a third stitch knitwise and pull the second one over and off the needle. (This is Slip Pullover Cast-off; see page 150.)
2. Now insert the left needle into the nearside of the remaining slipped stitch and Knit it through the farside. (The reason for slipping the last stitch knitwise and then knitting it through the farside is only that that is the fastest way to work. If it were slipped directly, it would be necessary to return it to the left needle prior to knitting it in the regular way.)
3. On the return row, either Knit or Purl the stitch, then work a Rib Increase on the Yarnover strand.

SQUARE EYELET MESH

Because a casting-off technique is used rather than a decrease, the Eyelet is not pulled into a curve as in other techniques, but instead lies very flat. Traditionally, the instructions for this mesh call for a Double Yarnover, but I think the Single Yarnover gives a better result. A Double Yarnover stretches out much wider than the space occupied by the two stitches that are removed, and as a result the fabric tends to splay out. If you want a larger Eyelet, use a Double Yarnover, remove three stitches instead of two, and use a Multiple Yarnover Increase to restore the stitch count. Whether you use a Single or Double Yarnover, these fabrics widen considerably, and you will want to use one of the methods of casting on that will not restrain the edge. Also note that because the stitches cast off for each opening are not first knit, this fabric is difficult to unravel; it is necessary to undo each cast-off stitch individually.

Trellis Insertion Columns or Mesh

When Eyelets are used on every row instead of every other row, quite a bit changes. First, the shape of the Eyelets is more angular. Then, instead of there being one Eyelet on top of another, they are staggered within the column. As with Eyelets made on every other row; the type of decrease used affects the appearance. Here, however, mirror-image decreases are placed to the left of the Eyelet on one row, to the right on the next and as a result no bias is created in the fabric. You will frequently encounter Trellis columns, either individual ones or groups, used as part of stitch patterns to create openwork; the columns can, of course, be placed side by side all the way across to produce Mesh fabric.

Four-Stitch Trellis

In a four-stitch unit, the two plain stitches are always placed on the previous decrease and the Yarnover strand, and the new decrease includes the previous plain stitches. The difference between the two versions is seen not in the Eyelets, which have the same hexagonal shape, but in the appearance of the stitches between them, either relatively smooth or corded, with the latter being more popular. The patterns are given in Stockinette; either is also attractive in Garter Stitch.

SMOOTH TRELLIS

Row 1: SSK, YO, K2.
Row 2: P2tog, YO, P2.

CORDED TRELLIS

Row 1: K2, YO, SSK.
Row 2: P2, YO, P2tog.

FOUR STITCH TRELLIS, TWO VERSIONS

FROST FLOWERS, A TRELLIS PATTERN

Three-Stitch Trellis

The next two variations are worked on a three-stitch unit, making the Eyelet column narrower than the ones above. The plain stitch is worked on the previous decrease, and the new decrease includes the previous Yarnover strand and the adjacent plain stitch. Because the Yarnover strand is included in the decrease, the Eyelets take on a diamond shape. Here again, the decrease chosen affects the appearance of the columns of stitches to each side of the Eyelets. It is possible to work either of these in Garter Stitch, but it is not terribly successful, as the Purl nubs tend to overshadow the Eyelets.

SMOOTH DIAMOND TRELLIS

Row 1: SSK, YO, K1.
Row 2: P2tog, YO, P1.

THREE STITCH TRELLIS, TWO VERSIONS

CORDED DIAMOND TRELLIS

Row 1: K1, YO, SSK.
Row 2: P1, YO, P2tog.

Two-Stitch Trellis

And finally, three variations that are based on a two-stitch unit. Each decrease includes both the previous Yarnover strand and the decrease. The different methods of working change the appearance of the single stitch dividing the Eyelets, making each one quite distinctive. In addition to the pattern repeats, you will need one edge stitch at each side to anchor the Yarnovers at the beginning or end of a pattern row.

ZIGZAG DIAMOND TRELLIS

Row 1: YO, SSK.
Row 2: YO, P2tog.

TWO STITCH TRELLIS, TWO VERSIONS

KNOTTED DIAMOND TRELLIS

Row 1: SSK, YO.
Row 2: P2tog, YO.

GARTER STITCH TRELLIS MESH

You will recall I mentioned above that using a Purl Right Decrease (P2tog) is the fastest way to make an Eyelet. Well, the fastest, and one of the handsomest Eyelet Mesh fabrics is made in the same way in Garter Stitch. It is very open, and the division between the columns is narrow and knotted.

• Work either a Purl Two Together followed by a Yarnover, or a Yarnover followed by a Purl Two Together, it really doesn't matter which, on every stitch and every row.

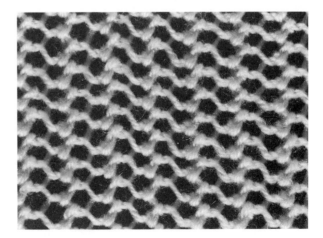

GARTER STITCH MESH

Diagonal Eyelet Insertion

Eyelets can be placed on the diagonal without creating bias in the fabric by stepping them one stitch to the right or left on each pattern row. There are two different ways of working, each resulting in a very different appearance. In the first group we will look at, the Eyelets are divided by a decrease that produces a heavy bridge, either smooth or corded, between one Eyelet and the next. In the other group, the Eyelets are more open, divided by just two interlaced strands, and there is the option of forming a chain of stitches at the base of the diagonal.

Bridged Diagonal Insertions

The appearance of the bridge between one Eyelet and the next changes from smooth to corded depending upon the type of decrease used and its position relative to the Yarnover. The slope of the insertion column, whether up to the right or to the left, is controlled by the position of each Eyelet unit relative to the one below.

If you want the diagonal to slant upward to the left, each decrease must include the stitch made on the previous Yarnover and the stitch to the *left*, with the new Yarnover following the decrease.

LEFT SMOOTH BRIDGE

Row 1: K2tog, YO.
Row 2: Purl.

LEFT CORDED BRIDGE

Row 1: SSK, YO.
Row 2: Purl.

If you want the diagonal to slant upward to the right, the new Yarnover will be followed by the decrease, which includes the stitch made on the previous Yarnover and the stitch to the *right* of it.

RIGHT SMOOTH BRIDGE

Row 1: YO, SSK.
Row 2: Purl.

RIGHT CORDED BRIDGE

Row 1: YO, K2tog.
Row 2: Purl.

BRIDGED DIAGONAL INSERTIONS/RIGHT: SMOOTH, LEFT: BROKEN

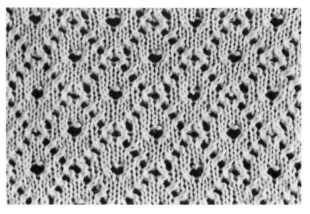

TIN LANTERN, WITH BRIDGED INSERTIONS

Open Diagonal Insertions

In these variations we can choose between creating a chain of stitches below the line of Eyelets or not, depending on which decrease is used and the position it is in. Here again the direction of the slope of the Insertion column is controlled by the relationship between each Eyelet unit and the one below.

For a left diagonal, work the stitch on the previous Yarnover, then the new Yarnover and the decrease.

LEFT CHAINED DIAGONAL

Row 1: YO, SSK.
Row 2: Purl.

LEFT PLAIN DIAGONAL

Row 1: YO, K2tog.
Row 2: Purl.

For a right diagonal, the decrease is on the two stitches to the right of the previous Yarnover, followed by the new Yarnover.

RIGHT CHAINED DIAGONAL

Row 1: K2tog, YO.
Row 2: Purl.

RIGHT PLAIN DIAGONAL

Row 1: SSK, YO.
Row 2: Purl.

OPEN DIAGONAL INSERTION/LEFT: CHAINED, RIGHT: PLAIN

Zigzag and Diamond Insertions

While Diagonal Eyelet Insertion often is used to create simple diagonal lines of openwork on the fabric, the Chained version is favored to form zigzag and diamond shapes, as the stitches at the base of the Eyelets emphasize the lines. However, the way this is done in most patterns results in there being a break in the chain where it changes direction. Should you wish to connect the chain, it is necessary to add two rows to the pattern at the point where it switches direction; it is best to work out the change on a stitch chart.

Shifting from left to right:

• When the last Left Diagonal Chained Eyelet has been completed, work a Left Diagonal Eyelet with a Smooth Bridge, then begin the Right Diagonal Chained Eyelets.

Shifting from right to left:

• When the last Right Diagonal Chained Eyelet has been completed, work a Right Diagonal Eyelet with a Smooth Bridge, then begin the Left Diagonal Chained Eyelets.

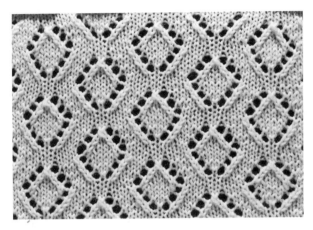

MRS. MONTAGUE'S PATTERN

EYELET CHAINS

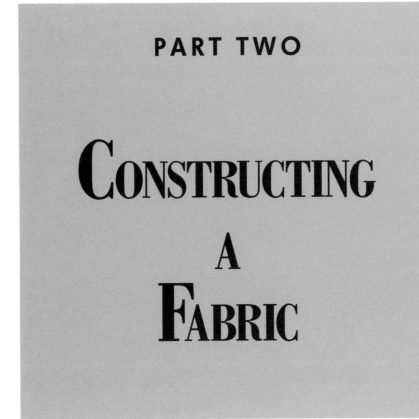

PART TWO

CONSTRUCTING A FABRIC

5
Circular and Flat Knitting

There are a variety of approaches one can take in constructing a knitted fabric. Conventionally, a fabric is worked from the bottom of the garment up to the top, but it is also possible to work from the top down, from side to side, or at an angle. Regardless of which direction you choose to work in, the various sections of the garment may be constructed separately as flat pieces and then sewn together. When working from the top down, virtually the entire garment can be worked in the round, forming an interconnected group of tubes that require no seaming of any kind. When working from the bottom up, sections such as the midriff and the sleeves can be worked in the round, while the sleeve caps and upper body sections are generally worked flat. Working flat can be done on any sort of needle, but working in the round requires a set of three to five double-point needles or a circular needle.

Whether to knit flat or in the round is one of the areas in knitting that seems to provoke rather intense convictions. I'm not sure why this is so, but people have their enthusiasms or get comfortable with a certain way of doing things and would like the world to follow in their footsteps. But fads and habits are poor recommendations for most things. As with every other aspect of knitting where there is some choice involved, the decision as to which way to work should first and foremost be made on the basis of an understanding of the advantages and disadvantages of the techniques themselves, and only then should personal preference come into play. If you really like to work one way rather than the other, at least you should know what you are gaining and what you are giving up when you do so.

Knitting in the Round

Knitting in the round is simplicity itself. The stitches are cast on in the normal way and then drawn into a circle, and the knitting proceeds around and around without interruption, with the outside of the fabric always facing the knitter.

The strongest adherents of knitting in the round are those who dislike Purling and those who enjoy working color patterns. With the outside of the fabric always facing you, it is easy to see a color pattern develop and avoid mistakes. Also, there is a special method of working certain types of color patterns where one yarn is carried in each hand (see page 257). The method is very fast in skilled hands, especially so when a knitting belt is used (see page 5).

Instructions for any stitch pattern must be written specifically for circular knitting; any pattern for flat knitting will include alternating outside and inside rows and would have to be rewritten. By far the easiest type of stitch pattern to follow is one in charted form, and all written instructions, whether intended for flat or circular knitting, can be converted to the same charted pattern. While the chart itself will be the same, the way it is read will be different depending upon which way you are working. (For detailed information on reading and writing pattern charts, see page 449.)

There are two kinds of needles used for knitting in the round, circular and straight double point; they both produce an identical fabric, the difference being that double points accommodate a fabric of any size while circular needles have limitations in that regard, as we shall see. For a long time double points were the only kinds of needles available and were used for both knitting flat and in the round. The advent of single-point needles eclipsed them for knitting flat because the head of the needle prevents the loss of any stitches, at least at one end. Double-point needles continued to be used for knitting in the round until circular needles, which are far more comfortable to hold and easier to work with, were introduced. For most knitters, double-point needles are now reserved for making sleeves in the round and for items like mittens, socks, and hats that won't fit on even the smallest circular needle. The exception is the knitters in those areas of the world who still use the knitting belt along with the long, fine-gauge double-point needles to produce some of the finest sweaters made. For more information on the different kinds of needles available, see page 333.

The general principles regarding how a fabric is constructed in the round are the simplest to understand when a circular needle is used, so let us start with that.

Working Rounds on a Circular Needle

A circular needle will have two pointed needle shafts just long enough for the hands to grasp. Many of them have a slight bend built in to the shaft to make them more comfortable to hold and to work with. These needles are connected to one another by a length of fine-diameter, flexible nylon cord. The needles come in all the standard sizes and the nylon cord comes in various lengths.

• The length of the circular needle *must* be smaller than the circumference of the fabric or you will not be able to join the stitches into a circle.

The needle measurement is tip to tip, and the smallest length is sixteen inches. The tips on a sixteen-inch needle are often quite short, and many people find them awkward because there is little room for their hands. For a fabric smaller than sixteen inches, you must resort to double points.

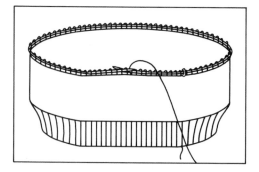

WORKING IN THE ROUND ON A CIRCULAR NEEDLE

Casting On and Joining the Round

1. Cast on the number of stitches required for the full circumference of the fabric and then bring the two needle tips together. Be careful to see that the cast-on edge lies flat under the needle and at no point passes over it.
2. The yarn should come off the first stitch on the right needle, which is the last stitch cast on. The first stitch on the left needle is the first one cast on, and as you knit it, the running thread will span the gap between the two stitches and join the cast-on edge into a circle. This happens again at the end of every row so the fabric becomes a seamless web.
3. Place a ring marker between the first and last stitch to mark the end of a row and carry it up as you work. (While in most cases you can clearly tell which stitch is the first of the row by examining the fabric, the ring marker makes things obvious and you don't have to stop and think about it.)

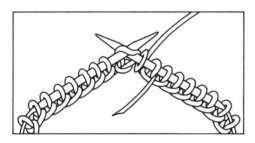

JOINING CAST-ON EDGE IN A ROUND

Casting on to a circular needle can often feel like working with a live snake; it does wiggle about without the weight of a fabric to stabilize it. I prefer to cast on to a single-point needle and then slip the stitches one at a time to the circular needle to begin working. It's an extra step, but I have found it improves casting-on speed and produces a more consistent and attractive edge.

If you discover as you knit the first row that the baseline has twisted over the needle, it must be corrected. Fortunately, that is very easy to do. Work to the end of the first round. Pass the left needle tip under the running thread that joins the last stitch cast on to the first stitch Knit, then rotate the entire edge over the left needle until the twist disappears. After the first row you won't be able to make this correction, so make sure to check the edge carefully.

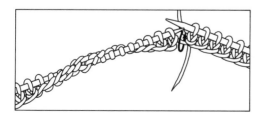

CORRECTING A TWISTED BASELINE

That's all there is to it; just keep going round and round for as many rows as you require. Information on openings can be found below; for attaching a new supply of yarn and hiding ends, see pages 376–379.

Working on Double-Point Needles

Double-point needles come in all sizes and in various lengths, usually in sets of four or five. One is reserved for use in the right hand; the remainder fill the same role as a circular needle, with all of the stitches evenly divided among them and drawn into a circle. There are two ways to begin, with the method I recommend given first.

Casting On Double Points

1. Using a single-point needle, cast on all of the stitches required for the width of the fabric.
2. Hold the needle with the cast-on stitches in your left hand and begin to slip the stitches, one at a time, to the first double-point needle.
3. When that needle contains one third of the stitches, pick up a second double-point needle and hold it on the nearside and parallel to the first, with the tip extending forward of the other.
4. Slip another third of the stitches to this second needle. Note that as the number of stitches on the second needle increases, it will become impossible to continue to hold the two needles side by side. First making sure that the stitches are well back from the tip, drop the first needle.
5. Pick up a third needle, hold it in the same fashion, and slip the remaining stitches.

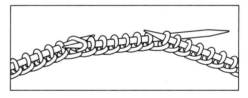

SLIPPING CAST-ON STITCHES TO DOUBLE-POINT NEEDLES

Alternatively, the stitches can be cast directly on to the double-point needles, holding them in the same manner as above when the stitches are being slipped. The problem with this approach is that it often causes an overlong baseline stitch at the point where you switch from one needle to the other. While the above method requires an extra step, I think it is an easier way to work and produces a smoother result.

Joining the Round on Double Points

1. Draw the stitches into a circle, just as you would with a circular needle, being careful that the cast-on edge lies below the needles all the way around. The

yarn must come off the first stitch on the right needle.

2. Pick up the yarn and the empty needle in your right hand and hold the needle bearing the first cast-on stitch in your left hand (where the end of the yarn is). As you work the first stitch, draw the running thread tightly between the first and last cast-on stitches to bind the circle.

3. When you come to the end of the stitches on the first needle, drop the needle bearing the new stitches, transfer the empty needle from left to right hand, and begin knitting the stitches on the next needle to the left.

4. As you begin each new set of stitches, move both tips of the needle bearing the stitches to be worked next so they rest on top of the adjacent needles. (This is important so you can grasp the needle effectively with the least interference from the points of the adjacent needles.)

5. Rest the empty needle on top of the needle to the right as you insert it into the next stitch to be worked. Always work this first stitch with a very firm tension.

6. Continue around the circle, handling the intersection between two needles in the same fashion each time.

7. Place a ring marker between the first and second stitch of the row and carry it along as you work.

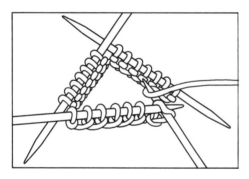

JOINING THE ROUND ON DOUBLE-POINT NEEDLES

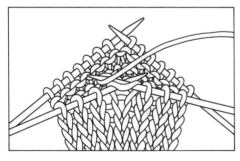

WORKING IN THE ROUND ON DOUBLE-POINT NEEDLES

Probably the most difficult aspect of working in the round on double-point needles, aside from learning where to put your hands and trying not to get stabbed on all those points, is controlling the tension on the stitches at the intersection of two needles. What happens all too often is that the running thread that passes between the last stitch on one needle and the first stitch on the next is elongated, and when this occurs row after row a distinctive vertical line will appear in the fabric. Positioning the needle as described above will help. In addition, you can hardly work the first stitch on each needle too tightly. Should you find consistent irregularities, it is best to rip down and try again. Should you find occasional ones, once the fabric is completed it is possible to work some of the extra yarn out of the running thread and into the stitches on either side with the tip of a knitting needle or a tapestry needle. It would be very tedious to have to do this on every row of an entire fabric; it's best to keep a constant watch on those areas of the fabric in order to avoid the problem.

Some books recommend that you shift the intersection from time to time, I suppose on the premise that if the problem is staggered it won't be quite so obvious. What this means is that you would work across a group of stitches on one needle, and maintaining the needle holding the new stitches in your right hand, knit one or two stitches off the next needle. This is done with each needle so the number of stitches on the needles remains constant, although the individual stitches gradually shift from one needle to the other. It seems to me that rather than solving the problem, this would produce a fabric full of irregular stitches. There are many beautiful examples of knitting done on double-point needles that bear no evidence of the intersection and therefore offer proof that the problem can be solved with a little time and practice.

Shetland Three-Needle Method

Shetland knitters often work with just three needles instead of four or five. It's an interesting method and in many ways easier. For items of any size, longer double-point needles are required than are generally available in stores in the United States, or you must revert to working with four needles.

1. Divide the stitches onto two needles, half to each, and knit with the third needle.

2. As you work the first few stitches on a particular needle, the two needles bearing the stitches are held parallel, side by side, with the yarn coming off the first stitch on the far needle. Have the stitches on the far needle well back from the tip so they won't drop off as you work. (If you are working the first few stitches in Knit, when you insert the working needle into the stitch, the tip will emerge up between the two needles.)

3. After you have knit a few stitches, insert your left forefinger down between the two needles to separate them slightly. By the time you have knit an inch or

two the three needles will begin to form a triangle and you can release the far needle and just hold the one with the stitches being worked.

4. When you get toward the last few inches of stitches on the needle, you will again experience interference from the other needle. I tuck the point of the far needle between the second and third fingers of my left hand to keep it out of my way.

5. At the end of a row of stitches on one needle, turn the work as you would with flat knitting and slide the stitches up to the other tips of the needle to begin the next row.

Working this way there is one less intersection and two less points to worry about.

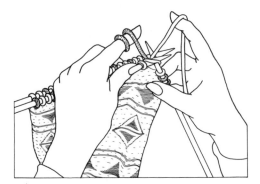

SHETLAND THREE-NEEDLE METHOD OF WORKING IN THE ROUND

Openings in a Circular Fabric

Working in the round poses problems with center front and armhole openings, as you can imagine, but knitters are creative people, and where there's a will there's a way. Certainly you can switch from working in the round to working flat any time an opening is required, but for knitters who do not like to Purl or have no skill with the stitch, that is no solution at all, particularly when, as often as not, their stitch gauge is likely to change if they do so.

There are three basic methods that allow you to construct the body of a sweater as a tube from waist to shoulders and later open it to allow for armholes, or divide the front for a cardigan.

The Steek

Some traditional sweater designs employ a temporary insert called a Steek, which makes it possible to continue to work in the round right across the armholes or center front opening without dividing the front and the back. In finishing, the Steek is cut open and the edges secured against unraveling. The technique is found in many areas and worked in locally idiosyncratic ways, but the general principle is roughly the same everywhere. Let's look at how it is used to make the armholes of a sweater.

1. When you reach the armholes, rather than dividing the fabric into front and back sections to be worked flat, cast off or place on holders one or two inches' worth of stitches for the base of the armhole.

2. On the next row, cast on a minimum of the same number of stitches and continue to work the garment up to the shoulders. These extra stitches are called the Steek.

3. Now release the stitches of the Steek and unravel them down to where they were cast on. Cut each strand in half and knot pairs of strands along the edges of the armhole to secure them against unraveling.

OPENING A STEEK

The number of stitches to cast on for the Steek is determined by how much yarn you want available in order to tie the knots, and that depends upon your stitch gauge. Instead of casting on and knitting the stitches of the Steek, Multiple Yarnovers (page 76) can be used; however, many are required to make the strands long enough to handle once they are cut. The Yarnovers from each row are dropped before the ones of the next row are made. This is not as successful a way to work because the loose strands allow the stitches on either side of the Steek to enlarge, and this must be corrected before the knots are tied. Alternatively, run a bit of contrast-color yarn through the stitches as for Stranded Cast-off, but keep the stitches on the needle and just continue to work, thus avoiding the need to cast on. When you unravel, this yarn stitch holder will be there waiting.

Usually this type of garment has little or no shaping; the shoulder line is straight and worked off with Joinery Cast-off (page 153) or grafted together (page 371). The neckline stitches can be placed on a holder and later knit up in some sort of a ribbed border. Once the shoulders are joined, use double-point needles to pick up sufficient stitches around the armhole for the circumference of the sleeve, working so that the knots turn to the inside as described on page 188, and knit the sleeve in the round from shoulder to wrist, shaping as required where a seam might have been.

Gussets

A straight sleeve without a cap can be rather tight under the arm. To correct for this, in some areas a Gusset is worked at the underarm, which acts to provide ease for arm movement. To form the gusset:

1. Start about two inches below the armhole and gradually increase one stitch on each side of the center of the armhole until a little triangle of fabric has been introduced.
2. Place the Gusset stitches on a holder, then cast on and work the Steek as described above.
3. Pick up the stitches for the sleeve around the armhole, including those of the Gussett, and work the sleeve in the round, decreasing the Gusset stitches within the sleeve in the same manner as they were increased within the body.

UNDERARM GUSSET

Knitting Flat on the Outside Only

Here is an alternative to working a Steek, which produces the identical result.

1. At the armholes, divide the work front and back, placing one group of stitches on a holder.
2. Continue to work on a circular or long double-point needle.
3. At the end of every row, break the yarn, slide the stitches to the tip of the needle on the right side, and reattach the yarn. Knit every row.
4. Whenever you have a pair of ends at each side, knot them together to secure the stitches along the edges.
5. Work in the same way on the other half of the garment.

Both the Steek and this technique are very clever, but you are left with all those knots and ends of yarn on the inside along the seam. If one of the merits of working in the round is to avoid the bulk of a seam, as many people argue, this could certainly cancel out that potential benefit. However, I have a beautiful traditional Shetland Fair Isle sweater that was made in this way. There was no attempt made to hide the ends of yarn; they were just cut off short near the knot and left like a little fringe around the armhole. There is no evidence of them on the outside, nor am I aware of them on the inside, but then these sweaters are made in a very fine yarn, and that is the critical difference.

Cut Openings

Here is another way of knitting in the round to the shoulders that offers an alternative to a Steek and the knots it leaves behind.

1. Ignore the armholes and the center front opening, if there is one, and knit a tube from waist to shoulders.
2. When the work is done, use a tapestry needle and a contrasting color yarn to mark a guideline on either side of where the opening should be.

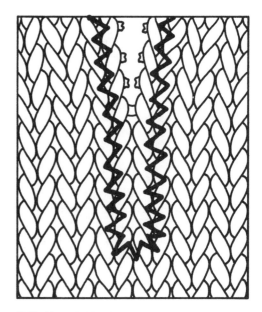

CUTTING AN OPENING

3. Run one or two lines of tight machine stitching along this line in what will be the selvedge (don't catch any of the contrasting yarn in the stitching) and then cut the knitted fabric open between the stitching lines and remove the marking yarn. The machine stitching will prevent any of the stitches from unraveling.

It requires some care to prevent a knitted fabric from stretching out as the sewing foot pushes it under the needle. Most of the stretch can be eliminated by easing the armhole to the sleeve to restore it to its proper dimensions, but there are also special sewing machine feet on the market that "walk" a fabric under the needle and help prevent the problem. Alternatively, work the contrast-color yarn that marks the sewing line in such a way that it helps to stabilize the fabric, or sew over tearaway interfacing that has been basted in place.

Once the armhole has been cut, work the sleeve as for a Steek, picking up the stitches around the opening so that the frayed edge and the line of sewn stitches is turned to the inside. Sometimes the sleeve is worked with a wide selvedge at the top that is sewn over the raw edge on the inside to hide it and make the armhole smooth. The raw selvedge down a center front opening can be encased in a double bias facing (see page 173), or you could work a hemmed border done on picked-up stitches (see page 188).

Knitting in the Round from the Top Down

When you work in the round from the top down, it is far easier to avoid any necessity to switch to working flat in order to make openings. There are some limitations on the type of garment designs that can be worked in this way, but many of the standard ones can be managed, and the approach has even suggested some new ones. It will change the appearance of color patterns and some other stitch patterns, although that is not necessarily bad, but Stockinette and Garter Stitch look the same no matter which way you work.

The most important consideration is that it can be daunting to construct a garment with this approach because all of the shaping required for shoulders, neckline,

armholes, and sleeve caps is going on all at the same time rather than piece by piece, as in flat knitting. If you have any difficulty in following a pattern, or cannot give undivided attention to your work, don't attempt this. However if you want to try something new and enjoy a challenge, look for Barbara Walker's *Knitting from the Top*.[1] Elizabeth Zimmerman also has some top-down designs in her books. One of the advantages claimed for working this way is that you can try it on in progress and find out before you have gone too far whether things are going along as they should. However, this should by no means be relied upon entirely because of problems with the gauge differences that can exist between a dressed and undressed fabric (see page 418).

Circular Knitting: The Pros and Cons

One of the things that makes knitting challenging and creative is that the knitter is designing and constructing both fabric and garment simultaneously. Circular knitting is the most direct method of doing this, as it allows the knitter to construct any tubular element of the garment without the necessity for seaming; the garment itself seems to grow off the needles. Certainly there are many advantages to working in the round, and in some situations it is the best way to work. Garments such as skirts, hats, gloves, mittens, and socks are so much nicer without a seam of any kind. In many other circumstances, however, it is arguable whether knitting in the round is the best way to construct a garment because the method has problems and limitations that must be taken into consideration.

To Seam or Not to Seam

Even knitters who don't mind Purling often prefer working in the round because they wish to avoid the possibility of a bulky or rigid seam. However, a Steek or a cut armhole, unless worked in fine yarn, will frequently be bulkier than a sewn seam or the join produced by picking up stitches around an armhole worked on a flat fabric where there are no knots or cut edges.

Nevertheless, irony abounds, and one of the criticisms leveled at circular knitting is that there are no side seams! The argument is that the side seams of a sweater add definition to the garment, and that without them it tends to look like you're wearing a barrel. Actually, I think there is some merit to this, but it depends on the style involved.

The barrel effect is particularly evident when a straight midriff is set over a ribbed edge, which is unfortunately the most common sweater style. If the garment is intended to be tailored, with nice straight lines along the body, a seam does help to maintain the shape. Also, there are some stitch patterns that are quite stretchy and may sag out in wear more than you expected, in which

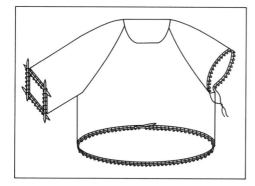

KNITTING IN THE ROUND FROM THE TOP DOWN

1. New York: Charles Scribner's Sons, 1972.

case side seams and sleeve seams will restrain the tendency and support the fabric. On the other hand, if the style is loose and fluid, the seam may be irrelevant or actually impair the intended effect. The question, as always, is whether or not a seam is appropriate given how it behaves in the fabric.

In the absence of a real seam, devotees of working in the round frequently create the illusion of one with a Seam Stitch, made by working a Slip Stitch every other row on the stitch that lies where the seam would have been if the fabric had been worked flat. This is done to correct the barrel look, and because it constricts the fabric, it will help support it in somewhat the same way a seam does. A seam stitch, either Slipped or Purled, appears in some old patterns in the role of a marker, establishing an easily visible line around which the increases or decreases are worked, but I should think a ring marker would serve much better and eliminate the unnecessary vertical line in the garment. If you need a seam, make a proper seam, and if you need a marker, use a temporary one.

Aside from the support it provides, however, a proper seam offers itself for other purposes. It is a very useful place to tie on new balls of yarn, to hide ends of yarn, and to carry other colors of yarn up until they will be worked again. There are ways to carefully tie on a new supply of yarn in the middle of the fabric (see page 352), and handled with care it can work out well in certain circumstances. However, with any openwork pattern, or a fabric worked at a loose tension, it is far more difficult to do this successfully. A seam selvedge functions like a little closet where you can tuck away things you don't want to show in the fabric; when you work in the round, you don't have that option.

Problems with Horizontal Stripes

There is a problem when working horizontal stripes in the round whether created by stitch pattern or by color pattern, although it will be more pronounced with the latter. At the end of a row of circular knitting, the running thread travels from the last stitch of one row to the first stitch of the next row above. Therefore, instead of the end of the row being level with the beginning of the row, as it would be if you seamed it, it is pulled up level with the next row. In effect, the knitting is not a series of rows stacked one on top of the other, like the rims of stacked plates, but a continuous, tightly coiled spiral.

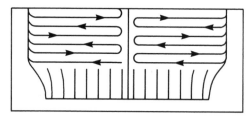

ALIGNMENT OF ROWS IN SEAMED FABRIC

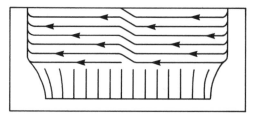

STRUCTURE OF ROUNDS IN CIRCULAR FABRIC

In a plain, single-color fabric, or one with a vertical pattern, this shift up is not that noticeable, but even so knitters are careful to place it at what would have been a side seam, so that it is somewhat hidden in wear by the arm. However, in any strongly horizontal pattern the distortion becomes quite obvious, particularly at the point of a color change, and placement at the side seam doesn't really hide it much at all. Even so, this can be reasonably unobtrusive when working in a fine yarn, especially if the pattern is complex enough to distract the eye; however, with a simple pattern and a bulky yarn, the distortion of the stripe will be quite visible. I think horizontal patterns are generally more successful when worked flat and seamed carefully to align the stripes correctly, but then I don't mind Purling a bit, and the distortion offends my sense of symmetry and design. You must establish your own standard on the matter.

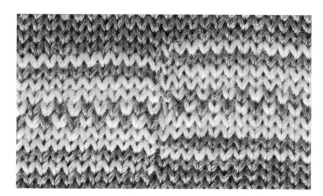

EFFECT OF CIRCULAR KNITTING ON HORIZONTAL STRIPE

Problems with Pattern Repeats

Regardless of whether you are working a horizontal or a vertical pattern, working in the round also presents some problems with the pattern repeat. More information on pattern repeat can be found on page 526, but, briefly, it is the number of stitches that are worked in a particular way to produce the stitch pattern, with identical groups worked repeatedly across the width of the fabric. Some designs make use of a variety of stitch pattern repeats set side by side in columns. The number of stitches used to make the fabric must be a multiple of the number of stitches in the repeats, unless shaping is taking place. Generally speaking, partial repeats make visual sense when they lie along a seam, but it is very difficult to successfully blend together two partial repeats at the point where they meet in a fabric worked in the round.

There are ways around the problem; occasionally it is possible to use slightly more or fewer stitches than required for the width of the garment in order to work with full repeats. If this can be done successfully, working in the round is ideal because no seam intrudes between the pattern repeats. Unfortunately, some pattern repeats can include ten or twenty stitches, which makes it impossible to add or subtract one repeat without an appreciable change in the size of the garment. If you are working in a fine yarn, you can get away with more, but even so you may be forced to select a pattern different from the one you wanted. If you do not wish to switch patterns, a Seam Stitch (page 116) helps or you can introduce a narrow section where a seam would have been that is worked plain rather than in pattern.

Other Problems

Finally, there are several other things about knitting in the round that don't affect the form or quality of the garment but rather the work itself. As the fabric grows, the full bulk and weight of the garment is in your lap and being supported by the needles. You may not have to turn the work around abruptly at the end of a row as in flat knitting, but you must turn it constantly in a circle as you go along, and as it gets heavier I find this becomes a tiresome chore. I think it is faster and far less cumbersome to work on relatively small sections at a time; the work remains conveniently portable, and stays cleaner.

Some designs require fairly complex shaping at armholes and neckline, and when you are working in the round this is happening all at once. It requires a great deal of concentration to get every shaping technique in just the right place. I find it much easier to work on one section of the garment at a time.

Perhaps the most important consideration to my mind, however, is the one of mistakes. All of us are faced with the necessity of ripping down to correct an error from time to time, and when you rip out a circular fabric it will cost you *twice* as much effort as when you rip out a flat one. Think about it—instead of ripping down two or three inches on the front, you must by necessity rip out as much on the back, which may have been knit perfectly! I would rather sew seams than take the chance of having to do all that knitting over again unnecessarily.

All in all, it seems to me that knitting in the round brings with it certain risks and quite a few compromises, and unless the garment is one that would be particularly enhanced by being seamless, it should be avoided.

Knitting Flat

Working this way is really quite straightforward, and there are very few things you can't make on a pair of straight needles. Each section of the garment is designed, cast on, and worked separately, and when all the sections are complete, they are sewn together using techniques appropriate to a knitted fabric, but otherwise in the same fashion a garment of woven fabric would be.

A flat fabric is generally worked on single-point needles—short ones for small articles, long ones for larger items—but it can also be done on a pair of double-point needles or a circular needle. Regardless of what kind of needle is used, the basic method is that described in "Learning to Knit." On one row, all of the stitches are worked in a way appropriate for the outside of the fabric, the fabric is then turned, and on the next row all of the stitches are working in a way appropriate for the inside of the fabric. Because of this alternation of inside and outside rows, the only written stitch patterns that can be used are those intended for flat knitting; however, any charted stitch pattern can be used for working either flat or in the round (see page 459).

Flat Fabrics on Circular Needles

With this method, the needle forms a circle while you are knitting, but the fabric never does. Because the fabric is not joined into a circle, the length of the circular needle is of no importance when working flat; you can work a two-inch width on a thirty-six-inch needle if that's all you have.

Casting On and Working Flat

1. Cast on to a single-point needle and transfer the stitches to a circular needle to begin.
2. Draw the needle into a circle to bring the points

together so they can be used just as one would a pair of single-point needles.

3. At the beginning of every new row, the yarn must come off the first stitch on the needle tip in your left hand.

4. At the end of a row, open the needle out, turn the work around and re-form the circle with the other side of the fabric facing out in order to work back across the row.

5. Continue in this way, always turning the fabric at the end of every row as you would on straight needles.

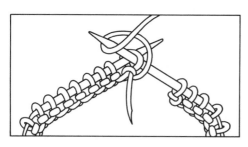

WORKING FIRST STITCH OF ROW/FLAT FABRIC ON A CIRCULAR NEEDLE

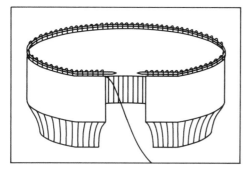

WORKING A FLAT FABRIC ON A CIRCULAR NEEDLE

There are several very nice things about working with a circular needle. It's impossible to lose the "other" needle as can happen with a pair of single points. It also is by far the most considerate way to knit when you are traveling because there are no ominous-looking needles waving at your neighbors or poking at them in a careless moment, and you and your circular needle will fit comfortably into even the narrowest airplane seat. When you must put your knitting away, the stitches can be pushed back from the tips to ride just on the nylon filament, causing the needle to act as a stitch holder.

Flat Fabrics on Straight Needles

Straight needles have a point at one end, with which to manipulate the stitches, and a head at the other, to prevent any of the stitches from falling off as you work. They come in ten- and fourteen-inch lengths and in all

sizes. Because a flat garment is constructed in pieces, one at a time, and because the fabric can be bunched up on the needle, the fourteen-inch size will accommodate even quite large garment sections, although anything larger than about twenty-four inches would be much easier to handle on a circular needle.

Knitting on straight needles is the same as described above for a circular needle except instead of re-forming the circle, when the right needle is filled with all of the newly worked stitches, it is transferred to the left hand and the empty needle to the right hand to begin the next row.

When working with a long straight needle, every small manipulation of the tip of the needle causes a much larger range of motion at the head of the needle, and as the fabric grows weightier, this becomes quite fatiguing and tends to stretch out the selvedge stitches. The problem doesn't exist with a circular needle, and since it is also lighter in weight, you will find you can knit for much longer periods of time without tiring. In addition, if you use the Right-Hand method, which requires that you remove your hand from the needle to wrap the yarn, the needle won't go anywhere when you do so, especially once there is some fabric resting on your lap to support it.

Generally speaking, I work small items on ten-inch single-point needles, and use a long single-point needle to cast on wider fabrics and then switch to a circular needle to work them.

Circular Fabrics on Straight Needles

Yes, it is possible, but it requires the use of a special technique called Double Knitting, which is discussed in full on pages 233–247.

Flat Knitting: The Pros and Cons

There are several disadvantages that should be mentioned regarding this way of working.

First, great care must be taken to work the same number of rows and the same shaping techniques front and back, or in each sleeve. Actually I think great care should be taken to work the correct number of rows regardless of how you are constructing the fabric, so I don't take this criticism very seriously. One way of assuring that things match up is to use two balls of yarn and cast on and work paired sections such as sleeves or the side fronts of a cardigan at the same time, but I'm not sure it's worth the trouble, and you still must match the front and the back. Rows can be counted if you have trouble keeping track of them as you knit.

Then, many people quite justifiably do not like rigid or bulky seams in their lovely soft sweaters. A well-done seam should be neither, although it can be difficult to avoid the latter problem when working with heavy yarns. The section on seams on pages 362–371 has a full discussion of when a seam is appropriate and how and when to avoid them.

In addition, many people like to knit, but many knitters do not like to sew. This is a prejudice that is much harder to dismiss or argue with. However, I suspect some of that prejudice has come about because people are unhappy with the seams they produce, or are unsure of the correct methods to use and how to do them. It is a shame to limit the kinds of things you can knit because of the lack of a skill that is relatively easy to acquire. Since it is the rare design that will allow you to avoid seams entirely, you might as well learn to do it well. Sewing may never be your favorite part of a knitting project, but it will take less time once the skills are mastered, and at least you can look on the results with pride and satisfaction.

Finally, all that is left is the problem of Purling, but as you know, I recommend learning Right-Hand Knitting because with that method the Purl stitch is virtually as easy to do as the Knit stitch, and once you've worked a few garments flat it won't seem the problem it once was. Even if it is still a bit slower for you, speed isn't everything; the quality of the finished garment and expanding your options to include all of what is possible in knitting count for a great deal more.

There really are no limitations in terms of what kind of design can be done when working flat and it is far easier to manage complex patterns and subtle shaping or to introduce special design elements to just one portion of a garment. All of the material in this book is discussed in terms of flat knitting. When a technique must be modified in some way in order to be used for knitting in the round, I will mention it unless it is only a matter of changing Purl stitches to Knit stitches.

Medallion Knitting

There is a type of knitting that is generally referred to as Medallion work because it creates flat fabrics that are roughly circular at the outer edge. The technique is most often used for shawls, doilies, table mats, hats, and baby bonnets.

Traditionally, Medallion Knitting begins at the center of the fabric and is worked in ever-widening concentric circles to the outer edge, but it can be done from the outer edge toward the center. The decorative increases or decreases necessary to accomplish this are placed so that they create straight lines like the spokes of a wheel, or ones that are sloped or curved. The fabric that lies between these lines can be worked plain, or in a lace or other decorative stitch pattern. While the technique is most often used to create rounds, it can also be used to make a square, or any number of polygonal shapes. More information on Medallion Knitting can be found on page 529.

Working from the Center

In order to start a fabric worked from the center out, most patterns call for somewhere between three and nine stitches to be cast on and distributed among three needles. However, it is very difficult to keep the needles from falling out of the stitches at this point, and I am sure many a knitter has given up and decided to make something else because of this. The frustration can be almost entirely alleviated by working on three needles, Shetland style (see page 112). Because the two needles bearing the stitches are held side by side in your left hand, it is impossible for the needles to fall out. As the diameter of the fabric increases, switch to four needles

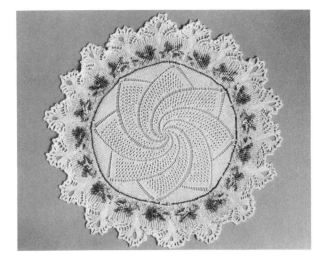

LACE MEDALLION WITH BEADED BORDER

WORKING A MEDALLION FROM THE CENTER

if you like, and if it gets large enough, to a circular one.

Regular methods of casting on can leave something of a hole at the center of the fabric. When working in a lace pattern this is of little consequence, but for the most part it is nice to close it as much as possible. Here's a method I like:

THREE-STITCH START

1. Using a double-point needle, cast on three stitches with Picot Cast-on (page 137), tightening the baseline firmly.
2. Slide the stitches to the other end of the needle and Knit the first stitch, work a Bar Increase (page 66) on the second, and Knit the third. There are now four stitches on the needle.
3. Take up a second double-point needle and divide the stitches, two to a needle. Fold the two needles side by side with Purl to the inside, slide the open end of the stitches to the needle tips and begin working in the round, beginning each round with the yarn coming off the first stitch on the far needle.

SLIP KNOT BASELINE

Here's another method to use when you would like to start with six or eight stitches instead of just three.

1. Wrap the yarn around the first two fingers of your left hand as described for starting a Slip Knot (page 89).
2. Pick up a needle and the yarn to the ball (the lower left arm of the X) and wrap the yarn around the needle as for a Purl-to-Purl Yarnover (page 74).
3. Insert the needle under the top right hand arm of the X, wrap the yarn as to Purl, tighten to draw the needle firmly against the circle of yarn on your fin-

gers, and then bring the new stitch under the strand.

4. Make another Yarnover and then continue alternating a Purl stitch and a Yarnover until you have the required number of stitches, ending with a Purl.
5. Distribute the stitches on two needles and begin to work in the round, using the Shetland Three-Needle method (page 112).
6. At your convenience, pull on the tail of yarn to tighten the baseline circle to nothing, then secure and hide the end of the yarn.

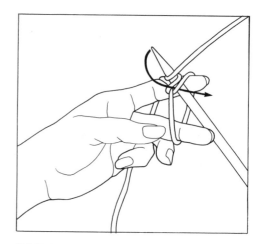

SLIP KNOT BASELINE FOR MEDALLION

CROCHET START

It is much easier to work a tiny circle of this sort in crochet than in knit.

1. Form a Slip Knot, leaving it about ½ inch in diameter. Hold the Slip Knot with the knot to the right, the loop to the left.
2. With a hook, work several stitches in Single Crochet,

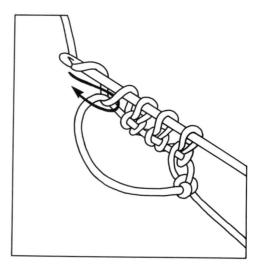

CROCHET START FOR MEDALLION

using the Slip Knot as a baseline and allowing the stitches to accumulate on the hook.

3. Transfer the resulting stitches to the double-point needles, join in a round, and begin working the Medallion. At your convenience, tighten the Slip Knot to close the circle at the center.

Alternatively (although it leaves a hole at the center of the Medallion), crochet a short chain, join it into a circle, place the single stitch on a double-point needle, and pick up the required number of stitches into those of the chain, distributing them on two needles.

DOUBLE KNIT START

This is my favorite. It results in a nearly invisible join at the center, but it requires some familiarity with the techniques of Double Knit (page 233).

1. Use a very fine double-point needle and cast on four stitches with Alternating Cast-on. Use a Twist Start as the first stitch, Half-Hitch Cast-on for the last. Turn.
2. Work one full round with Double Knit.
3. You may immediately separate the four stitches onto two double-point needles of the correct size for your gauge and begin working in the round with the Shetland Three-Needle method, or while the stitches are still interspersed, you can increase into every other stitch and then transfer six stitches, three to a needle.

Working from the Outer Edge

Tradition notwithstanding, there are two distinct advantages to starting at the outer edge. First, there are more options with casting on than with casting off, making it easier to match the edge to the stitch pattern. Second, as you approach the center and must work on only a few stitches, you can switch to three needles, Shetland style, and that plus the weight of the fabric hanging down makes it somewhat easier to manage than if you had started in the center. And finally, the last few stitches at the center can be grafted together (see page 371), or you can use Stranded Cast-off (page 156) and draw them tightly into a circle to finish things off.

MEDALLION WORKED FROM OUTER EDGE

6
Casting On

Casting on (or binding on, as it is sometimes called) is the means by which a baseline of stitches is placed upon the needle in order to begin knitting. This baseline forms the edge of your fabric and, therefore, its appearance and behavior can make quite a difference in whether or not you are satisfied with what you have made. There are many ways to cast on, and each method has unique characteristics. It isn't just a matter of whether or not this one or that one is quicker or easier to do, but whether or not its particular qualities complement those of the stitch pattern it will be used with.

There are questions of elasticity or stability that must be taken into consideration in light of how the fabric will be used. Good stretch and resilience are necessary at the edges of ribbed cuffs and waistbands. However, the same method of casting on, successful in that case, might turn loose and loopy when used with a pattern that is firm and inelastic. Some patterns have a great deal of lateral spread, and require a method of casting on that will not constrict the edge. Then there are many lovely stitch patterns that create a scalloped or indented edge, which, when measured along the contour, is much longer than the body of the fabric is wide. These require special handling so that the casting on will follow the contours of the pattern. And finally, you may want one method of casting on because of its rather decorative appearance, or another because it is so unobtrusive. It is therefore worth your while to gradually acquire a knowledge of all these techniques so you can readily apply the one that is most appropriate. We will discuss all the techniques, not just those that are best, because in some cases knowledge of a lesser method will enhance your understanding of a better one; in other cases, when a method I do not recommend is actually quite commonly used, I want knitters to know what my criticisms are so they may be persuaded to use something better.

If you are a beginning knitter, I recommend that you look at Simple Cast-on (page 126) and Half-Hitch Cast-on (page 127). The former will enhance your understanding of the latter, and the latter is the best all-purpose casting-on technique. It is easy to learn, fast to do, and could very well be used, with reasonable results, for anything you knit. The other techniques can be added to your repertoire when you are ready for something new, or when you find a situation where Half-Hitch Cast-on doesn't work as well as you would like it to. When you have finished learning to cast on, just skip over the rest and turn to the chapter "Learning to Knit and Purl" on (page 3).

Attaching the Yarn

Before we go on, let's pause a moment and discuss a few simple knotting techniques used to tie the yarn on to the needle in order to begin the casting-on process, or to tie one yarn to another.

SLIP KNOT

Many methods of casting on start with a simple knot placed on the needle and counted as the first stitch. Here is how to do it.

1. Pick up the yarn six or eight inches from the end, with the yarn from the ball in your left hand.

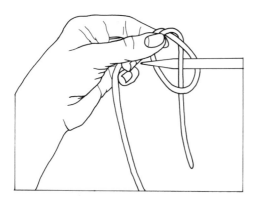

MAKING A SLIP KNOT

2. Make a circle of yarn about two inches in diameter, with the end of the yarn on top.
3. Drop the end of the yarn on the farside so it hangs down behind the circle, and hold the circle in your left hand.
4. Reach the tip of a knitting needle through the circle, catch up the strand of yarn, and pull it through to form a loop.
5. With your left hand, pull down on both strands of yarn to tighten the loop on the needle.

ALTERNATE SLIP KNOT

Here is another way of doing the same thing. Try them both and use the one you feel most comfortable with.

1. Pick up the end of the yarn with your right hand.
2. Extend the first two fingers of the left hand to the right. Starting on the nearside, wrap the yarn twice around your fingers—over the top, down the farside, and up the nearside, then over the top again, crossing the second wrap over and then to the left of the first.
3. Put the end of the yarn in the palm of your left hand, where it is held along with the yarn from the ball.
4. With the needle held in your right hand, reach the tip through the first circle of yarn and around the farside of the second strand to the left; catch this

strand up on the needle and bring it through the circle.

5. Drop the strands of yarn off your fingers and tighten the knot.

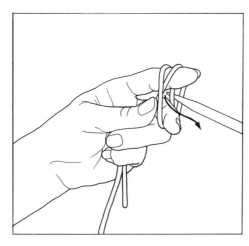

SLIP KNOT/ALTERNATE METHOD

TWIST START

This is a simple way of forming the first stitch by wrapping the yarn around the needle. I think the Slip Knot is a better way to start, as it gives a nice neat corner, but this isn't bad, and many books suggest it. It is used only with the Finger methods of casting on, not the Knit methods.

1. Extend the left thumb and forefinger.
2. Wrap the yarn up the nearside of the thumb, over the tops of both fingers, and down the farside of the forefinger. Hold the tail of yarn and the yarn from the ball in the palm of the hand with the other three fingers.

3. Insert the needle down into the circle formed by thumb, forefinger, and strand.
4. Bring the tip of the needle under the strand, point it toward you, and then raise it up in the normal position to knit.

The strand to the forefinger will pass down the nearside and under the needle to the right of the strand to the thumb; the strand to the thumb will pass down the farside and under to the left. This is the correct way to start for most purposes. Should you wish to twist the yarn in the other direction, and there are times when it works better to do it that way, point the needle away from you as you bring it out of the circle.

YARN BUTTERFLY

Should you wish to allow sufficient yarn for seaming at the end of a cast-on or cast-off edge, wind the yarn into a "butterfly" and let it dangle from the fabric until you need it.

1. Hold the end of the yarn against the palm of your hand with the last two fingers.
2. Extend the thumb and third finger and wrap the yarn around them in a figure eight as many times as needed.
3. Make an e-loop (See "Simple Cast-on," page 126) with the yarn around the thumb and first two fingers of your right hand and draw the butterfly off your thumb and through the loop of yarn. Tighten and repeat the knot one or two more times to keep the yarn from unraveling.

A Yarn Butterfly can also be used as a substitute for a bobbin when working a form of color knitting called Intarsia (page 270).

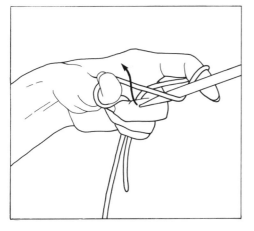

TWIST START

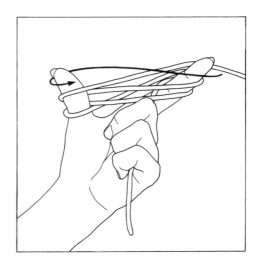

MAKING A YARN BUTTERFLY

TEMPORARY KNOT

There are times in knitting where it is necessary to tie together two ends of yarn that will later have to be untied. Here is a knot that makes the tying and the untying very easy.

1. Wrap two yarn ends around the fingers of your left

hand exactly as described above for the Alternate Slip Knot.
2. Instead of using a needle, reach your right fingers through and grab the far left strands, and pull them through the right strands to form a loop. Hold on to all four strands with the left hand as you pull up on the loop to tighten the knot.
3. When ready to untie, just pull on the end and the knot will come undone.

Finger Cast-on Techniques

As the title suggests, this family of techniques relies on the use of the fingers and a single needle to place the first stitches on the needle. There are such a wide variety of ways to accomplish this that it may seem confusing at first, but by the end of the section I think you will find that we have reduced their numbers to those few that are truly useful.

Elementary Finger Cast-ons

The basis of this first method is the half-hitch, sometimes called an e-loop from its appearance. In fact, the yarn is simply looped in a circle onto the needle. Almost any means of doing this that is easy for you is fine. The easiest way I know is as follows:

SIMPLE CAST-ON

1. Place a Slip Knot on a needle held in your right hand. Your hand should be on top of the needle, palm down. Hold the knot in position with your right forefinger, about one or two inches back from the tip.
2. Hold the yarn with the last three fingers of the left hand. The yarn should then pass from the palm of your hand, up the outside and around the back of your thumb, and then between the thumb and forefinger to the needle. Hold your left hand with palm facing the right needle and thumb up, and place a slight tension on the yarn.

3. Insert the tip of the right needle under the yarn against the outside of the thumb. As you pick up the yarn on the needle, release it from your thumb. Tighten the yarn gently around the needle with a downward movement of the left hand, keeping light tension on the yarn with the last three fingers.
4. Bring your hand back up into the starting position, and as you do so, pick up the yarn around the thumb again in the same manner as before by placing the back of the thumb against the farside of the strand.
5. Continue in this way until you have the number of stitches you require. It will be necessary to maintain

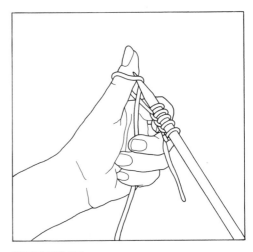

SIMPLE CAST-ON

some tension on the yarn while you form the stitches, as it is not really knotted around the needle and will unravel easily.

The virtues of this method are that it is very simple, and it gives a reasonably elastic base for most purposes. I find it rather unattractive, however, as it rides along the Knit side of the work rather than sitting down along the base of the stitches. In addition, it is very awkward to work the first row of stitches into the baseline. As you will see, there is another technique that renders this one more or less obsolete, but you should know about it because it is commonly recommended, it reappears as part of other methods, and knowing about it will aid your understanding of them.

TWISTED SIMPLE CAST-ON

This is a Simple Cast-on with an extra twist in the loop, giving it a tighter, neater appearance, but the edge is slightly less elastic. Like Simple Cast-on, it is difficult to knit the first row of stitches.

1. Make a Slip Knot and place it on the needle held in the right hand; wrap the yarn on the left thumb as described for Simple Cast-on.
2. Swivel the left hand slightly to the right so the strand coming off the back of the thumb crosses over the strand between thumb and needle.
3. Move the tip of the needle around the nearside of the strand passing from thumb to palm and reach under and pick up the strand passing to the needle. Drop the yarn off the thumb, picking it up again below the newly formed stitch.
4. Tighten the yarn gently on the needle and continue in this manner until you have the required number of stitches.

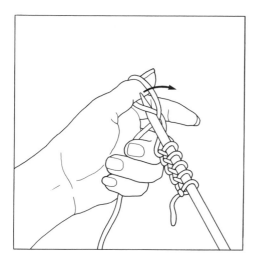

TWISTED SIMPLE CAST-ON

Half-Hitch Cast-ons

This next family of cast-ons is very fast, provides a neat and attractive edge that is easy to knit up from, and is reasonably elastic. It is the method preferred by most knitters and the one I recommend as the best, all-purpose cast-on.

Half-Hitch Cast-ons require that you calculate half the length of yarn you will require for your foundation stitches, since you begin the casting-on process at the midpoint of the yarn required. Generally speaking, you will need to measure off a tail of yarn, allowing one-half to one inch per stitch, depending on the size of needles and yarn; the larger the needles and yarn, the more you will need. I am sure you will not waste very much yarn using this rough guideline, but if you wish to be more precise see my note on page 140 for a more accurate way to measure.

KNIT HALF-HITCH CAST-ON

1. Calculate the length of yarn you will need based on the number of stitches required. Make a Slip Knot, place the knot on the needle, and tighten gently. (You do not absolutely need to use a Slip Knot here —many people just drape the yarn over the needle and begin—but it is more consistent with the rest of the cast-on row if you do so, and I think it gives a nicer corner.)
2. Hold the needle in your right hand as for Simple Cast-on, above, with the tail hanging down on the nearside and the yarn from the ball hanging down on the farside. With the right forefinger, hold the knot on the needle one or two inches back from the tip.
3. With the last three fingers of your left hand, hold both strands of yarn about five or six inches below the needle. Now insert your left thumb and forefinger between the two strands, spread them apart slightly, and raise your hand and the needle tip so they are directly opposite one another, catching the strands on the backs of those fingers as you do so. Place a slight tension on the yarn and begin as follows:
   • With the tip of the needle, slide under and pick up the yarn on the outside of your thumb. This will form a loop between thumb and needle; do not drop the yarn from your thumb.
   • Now move the needle to the yarn along the nearside of your forefinger, and pick it up by going over, down the farside, and up under the strand.
   • Move the tip of the needle toward you, carrying the strand from the forefinger through the loop held by the thumb. As you do so, bend your thumb down to allow the loop to fall off and transfer to the needle.

• Catch up the tail of yarn below the new stitch onto your thumb as before and tighten the new stitch gently on the needle by spreading thumb and forefinger apart and pulling on both strands.

4. Continue in this manner until you have as many stitches as required.

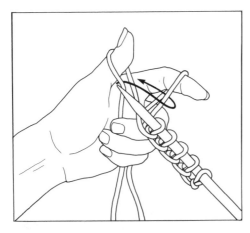

HALF-HITCH CAST-ON/PICKING UP YARN FOR STITCH

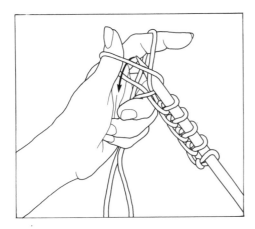

HALF-HITCH CAST-ON/DRAWING STITCH THROUGH LOOP

If this method is new to you, or you have used it for years but never analyzed it, let me explain that what you have done with this swift motion of the fingers is to form a series of Slip Knots on the needle. Another way to think of it is that you have formed half-hitches around the bases of your first row of stitches. Do it again and watch carefully. The strand from your thumb forms the half-hitch, the strand from your forefinger becomes the stitch. It is nearly identical to what you would achieve by using Simple Cast-on and then working the first row; the yarn takes a slightly different route in the baseline, which improves the appearance while retaining the elasticity.

You may sometimes encounter advice to cast on using a larger needle than you plan to use for the body of the knitting in order to give the edge more elasticity. Because of the structure of this edge, this is a futile effort. The size of the needle will only determine the size of the stitches in the first row, not the half-hitch, and it is the half-hitch that determines the elasticity of the edge. Remember, the strand to your thumb and the strand to your forefinger are not connected after the first stitch, so the stitch lends no yarn for stretch to the half-hitch; their relative elasticity is independent one from the other. (If you doubt me, I recommend you try Contrast-Color Half-Hitch Cast-on, below, which reveals the structure quite clearly.) All you can do to modify the degree of stretch this edge will have is to tighten the thumb strand very gently, just enough to make it neat and consistent with its fellows. It helps if you don't tighten the stitches so they are actually side by side on the needle—leave about a yarn's width between one stitch and the next. What this does is to elongate the half-hitch as it passes from one stitch to the next, and the greater length of yarn provided will allow it to stretch more in use. (There is another, more complex way of accomplishing the same thing discussed under Double-Needle Cast-on below.)

Because this cast-on incorporates the first row of knitting, it has a Knit side and a Purl side, which must be taken into consideration when you go to knit the first row. You must decide whether you wish to establish your pattern with the outside face of the fabric above the Purl side of the baseline or above the Knit side of the baseline. If you use the Purl side as the outside, there will be a tiny row of knots along the edge; if you use the Knit side as the outside, there will be smooth sloping

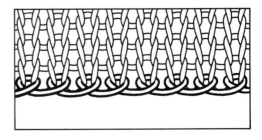

HALF-HITCH CAST-ON/KNIT SIDE OF EDGE

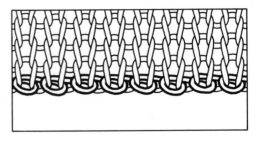

HALF-HITCH CAST-ON/PURL SIDE OF EDGE

strands along the edge. Both are attractive but quite different, and the former is more obvious than the latter.

The Knit side of the edge will be facing you as you cast on. To place it on the outside when working a circular fabric, join the edge in a round and begin with an outside row of the stitch pattern; if you are working flat, turn and begin with an inside row of the pattern. If the stitch pattern starts with an outside row when what you need is an inside row (commercial patterns are likely to refer to "right side" or "wrong side" instead), there are two solutions. One is to start with the last row of the pattern instead of the first. The other is to recall that this cast-on has already produced one row of stitches, so if the first row of the pattern is plain, you may be able to proceed directly to the second row. It is easier to judge what to do if the pattern is charted (see page 407).

CONTRAST-COLOR HALF-HITCH CAST-ON

Here is a way to do the same cast-on, using two different yarns. As you work, you will see that the first row of stitches is made with the main color and the half-hitch that forms the foundation is in the contrasting color. This is the best way I know of to display the actual structure of this technique.

1. Take one ball of yarn in the color you plan to use for your garment, and another ball of yarn in a contrasting color (and/or texture). Tie the two yarns together with the Temporary Knot described on page 126.
2. Put the knot on *top* of the needle, with the yarn in contrasting color on the nearside and the main color farside. (Do not count this as the first stitch.)
3. Pick up the yarns as for Half-Hitch Cast-on with the contrast-color yarn around your thumb and the main color on your forefinger. Use Half-Hitch Cast-on for the required number of stitches.
4. When you have finished casting on, and have Purled to the end of the first row, do not Purl the knot—simply allow it to drop off the needle where it can hang harmlessly at the bottom of your work until you finish.

You can use this as a decorative device, should you like the idea of a thin line of contrasting color forming the edge of your fabric, and for added interest at the edge, the yarn could be a double or triple strand, or a bulky, textured yarn. If you do not like measuring off a tail of yarn for casting on, you can tie together two balls of yarn in the same color, cast on as many stitches as you like, and be guaranteed that you will not run out of tail—a particularly useful trick when you are casting on a large number of stitches and the consequences of miscalculating the amount of tail required would be a great deal of wasted effort.

HALF-HITCH CAST-ON WITH CONTRAST COLOR EDGE

There are occasions in knitting when it is necessary to unravel the cast-on edge in order to knit in the opposite direction, or to graft two sections of fabric together. Half-Hitch Cast-on is not the easiest of the casting-on techniques to unravel, but the Contrast-Color variation simplifies things. When it comes time to pick up the edge stitches in order to knit in the opposite direction, they will be clearly outlined by the contrasting color of the baseline.

PURLED HALF-HITCH CAST-ON

Now that you know Knit Half-Hitch Cast-on, here is how to Purl. Knowing both, you can select which one works best for the pattern you plan to use, or even rib if you wish.

1. Hold the needle and yarn in exactly the same manner as detailed above in Knit Half-Hitch Cast-on.
2. With the tip of the needle, pick up the yarn on the farside of your forefinger (the one that goes from forefinger to palm). As you bring this strand forward, it will cross the yarn between forefinger and needle, forming the half-hitch.

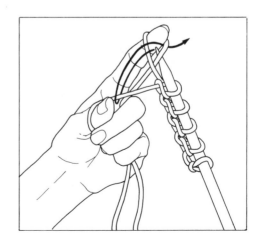

PURLED HALF-HITCH CAST-ON

3. Now bring the needle tip forward and pick up the strand between needle and thumb, going under and up on the nearside. (Do not go over the strand or the stitch will be on the needle the wrong way.) Take this strand back through the loop formed between forefinger and needle.

4. Drop the loop off the forefinger and pick the yarn up again in the same way below the newly formed stitch. Tighten the stitch gently on the needle.

It is sometimes difficult to maintain the tension on the forefinger in this variation. If you have that problem, give the strand to your forefinger a half-hitch around your little finger first.

If you are going to rib this cast-on, you might also try using the Contrast-Color method, above. An edge done in that way is an excellent choice for a fabric made in Double Knit (page 237).

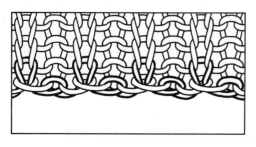

RIBBED HALF-HITCH CAST-ON EDGE

TWISTED HALF-HITCH CAST-ON

Here is another variation that puts an extra twist on the e-loop. It is a little tricky to do at first, and even when mastered is not as fast as the regular Half-Hitch Cast-ons. It does provide a neatly tailored, albeit less elastic edge.

1. Calculate the tail, make a Slip Knot, place it on the needle, and hold the yarn and needle in exactly the same way as for Knit Half-Hitch Cast-on.

2. Move the tip of the needle around the nearside of the strand that passes from thumb to palm, then go under and pick up the strand that passes from thumb to needle. As you bring the needle back up into the starting position, you must hook the thumb down to hold onto the loop.

3. Now pick up the strand between forefinger and needle, going over and down the farside, then move the needle forward and your thumb back to bring the strand through the loop.

4. Drop the loop off your thumb, reach down to pick up the tail of yarn as before, and tighten the stitch gently on the needle.

RIGHT-FINGER HALF-HITCH CAST-ON

There is an alternate way of doing Half-Hitch Cast-on and Twisted Half-Hitch Cast-on. The method can really be used effectively only by someone who knits Right-Finger style (see the discussion on different knitting methods in the chapter "Learning to Knit and Purl," but even then it is slower unless you are using a knitting belt (page 5). I can't imagine using it in preference to the faster, simpler version given above, especially when you consider that they produce identical edges. If you doubt me, do both, slowly, watching the formation of the stitch carefully as you do so. You will see that they

TWISTED HALF-HITCH CAST-ON/PICKING UP YARN FOR STITCH

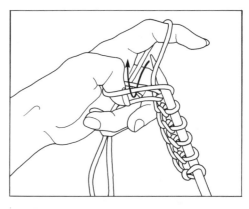

TWISTED HALF-HITCH CAST-ON/DRAWING STITCH THROUGH LOOP

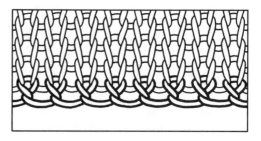

TWISTED HALF-HITCH CAST-ON EDGE

are precisely the same, albeit often presented as two different techniques in many knitting books.

1. Calculate the amount of tail you will need, make a Slip Knot, and place it on the needle. Wrap the tail of yarn around your thumb as for Simple Cast-on—from the palm, up the outside and around the back of the thumb, and then to the needle.
2. With the needle held in the right hand, take up the yarn from the ball just as you would in order to Knit. Pick up the yarn from the outside of the thumb as in Simple Cast-on. Do not drop the loop off your thumb.
3. Wrap the yarn in the right hand around the needle as you would to form a Knit stitch. With the tip of the needle, pull this yarn through the loop formed between thumb and needle. Then drop the loop off the thumb, pick up the yarn below the new stitch on the thumb as before, and tighten the stitch on the needle.

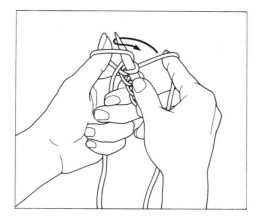

WRAPPING YARN FOR RIGHT-FINGER HALF-HITCH CAST-ON

TWISTED RIGHT-FINGER HALF-HITCH CAST-ON

For those knitters who use the Right-Finger method, there are two other ways of working the same edge achieved with Twisted Half-Hitch Cast-on. I find these are slow to do unless you are working with a knitting belt (page 5). In the first version:

1. Calculate the amount of tail required, make a Slip Knot at that point, and place it on the needle. Hold the yarn as described above for Right-Finger Half-Hitch Cast-on.
2. Pick up the strand from beneath the thumb as described in Twisted Simple Cast-on and hook the thumb down to keep hold of the loop. Wrap the yarn with the right finger as to Knit.
3. Bring the yarn wrapped around the needle through the loop, then drop the loop off the thumb. Pick the yarn up again below the newly formed stitch and tighten the yarn gently on the needle.

TWISTED RIGHT-FINGER HALF-HITCH/VERSION ONE

The second version is used in the Shetlands and was taught to me by Liz Allen at the Textile Workshop in Edinburgh.

1. Hold the tail of yarn in the palm of your hand and wrap it from farside to nearside over the top of the thumb, then all the way around again so the second wrap crosses the first to the left. The yarn should form an X on the top of the thumb, with the strand to the needle lying on top.
2. Reach the tip of the needle under the top right hand arm of the X, wrap the yarn with the right finger as to Knit and draw the new stitch under this strand, bringing the tip of the needle out between the upper and lower arms on the right side of the X.
3. Drop the yarn from the thumb and gently tighten down the knot that has been formed at the baseline.
4. Rewrap the yarn on the thumb as above and continue.

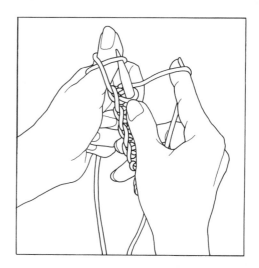

TWISTED RIGHT-FINGER HALF-HITCH/VERSION TWO

You will get pretty quick at wrapping the yarn around your thumb, but tightening the knot at the baseline is a slow operation, as the yarn will not pull through quickly and you must pay attention to making each baseline stitch the same size. The edge has a definite Knit and Purl side, which it is wise to take into consideration even when working a rib.

KNOTTED CAST-ON

This is a nice old variation on the Half-Hitch Cast-ons that produces a handsome, tailored edge that is very expandable. When done in a contrasting color, with a heavier yarn, or with one that is doubled, the effect is quite bold.

1. Using Half-Hitch Cast-on, place twice as many stitches as required on the needle. Turn.
2. *Pull the second stitch on the left needle over the first and discard it. Purl one stitch*. Repeat from * to * across the row.

KNOTTED CAST-ON EDGE IN CONTRAST COLOR

This edge is best used with stitch patterns that widen; if you want to use it with other patterns, work with a firm tension on the thumb strand so the edge won't splay out.

The instructions normally given for this method of casting on are cumbersome and tedious. They call for two stitches to be cast on and one pulled over, two more cast on, another pulled over, etc. The problem with this is that the yarn must be dropped from the left hand and a needle picked up in order to work the pullover step, then the needle set down and the yarn picked up again to work the next two new stitches. The instructions I have given you here accomplish an identical edge, but it is considerably easier to do.

DOUBLE-NEEDLE CAST-ON

I have saved the best of this family for last. Here is a variation that creates a very handsome, unobtrusive, fully expandable edge suitable for every stitch pattern I've tried it on. This one is the hands-down winner. For one thing, it works beautifully with Double Rib, for which none of the other methods is adequate. Perhaps more important, it handles an irregular edge with aplomb. Let us consider for a moment why this is a breakthrough.

Whenever one knits a pattern that creates a scalloped or angular edge—and there are many lovely patterns that do—the baseline tends to be too tight, causing the edge to curl. In most cases, this curling cannot be steamed out. Why does this happen? If you were to measure along every little curve or angle of an edge like that, and compare the measurement to that of the width of the fabric, you would find an enormous diference—the edge can sometimes be twice as long as the fabric is wide. There simply aren't enough stitches, and therefore yarn, along the cast-on edge to stretch that far. With Double-Needle Cast-on, additional yarn is provided to the edge, allowing it to accommodate itself to any contour the stitch pattern creates.

You will remember from the discussion of Knit Half-Hitch Cast-on that the elasticity of the edge is determined by the half-hitches that encircle the base of each stitch. The trick here is to form the stitch on one needle and the half-hitch on another, smaller needle, thus assuring adequate yarn to the baseline for expandability. The instructions will seem complicated at first, but keep in mind that you already know this cast-on—it is just modified. Don't learn it just by rote, but watch carefully as you go and make sense of the process so you really understand it. With practice the technique goes smoothly, although it is impossible to do it as fast as one can do Half-Hitch Cast-on.

Here are the instructions (remember, it's worth it):

1. Allow for a tail of yarn, make a Slip Knot and place it on the needle held in the right hand, with the tail of yarn hanging down on the nearside.
2. Take up a second, smaller needle and line it up under the first one, holding the two needles as one. The Slip Knot will be between the two needles, the yarn hanging down on either side of the small one.
3. Pick up the two strands of yarn in your left hand as for Knit Half-Hitch Cast-on.
4. Pick up the yarn on the outside of the thumb with the tips of both needles.
5. Pick up the strand from forefinger to needle *with just the top needle*, going over (the strand will pass between the two needles from farside to nearside), down the farside, and under the strand.
6. Bring this strand through the loop formed between thumb and needles, but before you drop the loop off

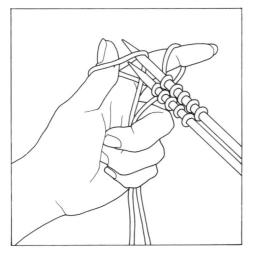

DOUBLE-NEEDLE CAST-ON/PICKING UP LOOP

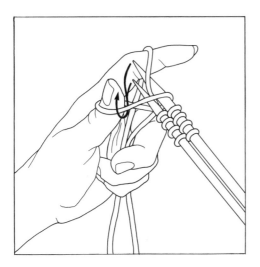

DOUBLE-NEEDLE CAST-ON/BRINGING STITCH THROUGH LOOP

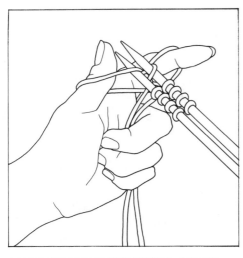

DOUBLE-NEEDLE CAST-ON/CATCHING LOOP ON LOWER NEEDLE

the thumb, bring the top strand of the loop between the two needles from farside to nearside so it is caught on the lower needle.

7. Now drop the loop from the thumb and pick the strand up again below the newly formed stitch. Apply tension to both strands to tighten the stitch on the top needle and the half-hitch on the bottom needle. The half-hitch should be tightened firmly.

8. Holding both strands steady with the left hand, rotate the two needles away from you with the right hand so the tips draw a complete circle around the taut strands of yarn, and at the same time, the two needles should rotate around each other, with the top one going down to the farside, under, and up into position again. This crosses the two strands under the bottom needle. (Don't eliminate this step; without it the edge tends to be somewhat undisciplined.)

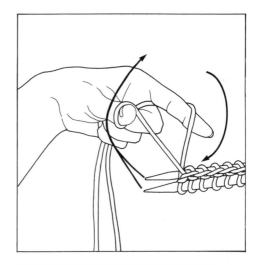

DOUBLE-NEEDLE CAST-ON/ROTATING NEEDLES

9. Continue in this manner—making a stitch, then rotating the needles—until you have the required number of stitches. When you do, pull the *bottom*, smaller needle out of the stitches, turn the work and begin your stitch pattern with an inside row.

As you can see, the top needle determines the size of the first row of stitches, while the size of the bottom needle determines the amount of yarn allowed to the half-hitch. The bottom needle should be a minimum of two sizes smaller than the top needle. When you rotate the needles, the yarn that forms the stitches will pass under the yarn of the baseline, which ties it against the fabric to keep it neat.

Just as with Half-Hitch Cast-on, there is a Knit and Purl side to this edge; if you are working flat, turn and start with an inside row. After you have worked a row or two of your pattern, stretch the material out to its maximum. This smooths out the funny little loops left when you pulled out the bottom needle, and at the same time you will see how beautifully expandable this edge is. I used this technique for the first time on a young boy's sweater—the ultimate test of the ability of an edge to stretch rather than break with hard use—and it has performed superbly.

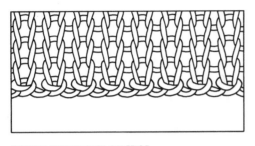

DOUBLE-NEEDLE CAST-ON EDGE

Braided Cast-ons

Here are three highly decorative casting-on techniques that can be done in either solid or contrasting colors. They are little known, and generally associated only with the Herringbone Braid and Braided Knitting knitting techniques (see pages 264 and 266), but they should be more widely used than they are. Although they are slow to work, they would provide nice edges for any number of stitch patterns and garment styles. The working methods are related to the Half-Hitch Cast-ons we have been discussing.

BRAID OR CORD CAST-ON

The first two edges are made in an almost identical way, but a slight change in technique produces a markedly different result. The instructions are given for working with two yarns in different colors.

1. Holding two yarns as one, tie a Slip Knot and place it on the needle. Count this double strand knot as the first stitch.
2. Hold the two yarns as for Knit Half-Hitch Cast-on, with the yarn that is the color of the Slip Knot stitch closest to the needle tip on your thumb. Make the second stitch in the normal way.
3. Before making the next stitch, switch the yarns, placing the yarn that was on the thumb on the forefinger, the one on the forefinger on your thumb. The direction in which you switch the yarns determines the outcome.
   • *Braid:* Switch the yarns clockwise: near yarn left to forefinger, far yarn right to thumb.

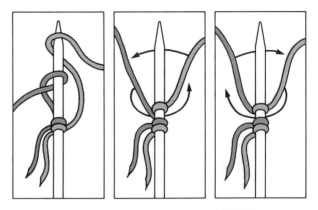

LEFT: BRAID OR CORD CAST-ON/CENTER: BRAID VERSION
RIGHT: CORD VERSION

   • *Cord:* Switch the yarns counterclockwise: near yarn right to forefinger, far yarn left to thumb.
4. Continue in this way, switching the yarns after every cast-on stitch, until you have the number of stitches you require. If you are going to continue with a Stockinette-based stitch pattern, Purl the first row if you are knitting flat, Knit if you are working in the round, or continue immediately with Horizontal Braid (page 264). Knit or Purl the two stitches of the Slip Knot together as if they were one stitch.

You will find that the yarns from the balls twist together as you work. This isn't too much of a problem for a relatively short distance, but can be a nuisance when casting on a longer edge, and you may have to stop and untwist them—a lazy susan tray would help here. Please note that working the row of Knit on the outside after casting on is essential in order to preserve the appearance of these edges with any pattern except the Horizontal Braid, which is done on the Purl side.

The structure of the Corded version is very similar to that of Double Needle Cast-on, above, but is slightly

CORD CAST-ON EDGE

less resilient, although both of these edges are nicely expandable. If you are using two different colors, remember that the first row of stitches will also alternate colors. This is quite obvious with the Cord, which lies directly beneath the fabric at the baseline, but the stitches are entirely covered by the Braid, which turns its face up to the world.

If you are going to do the edge in a single color, you do not need two supplies of yarn unless you are going to continue in a Herringbone Braid or Braided Knitting pattern, in which case begin as for any other Half-Hitch Cast-on. If you are going to work the edge in two colors and continue in a single color, simply abandon the contrast-color yarn after casting on, and work the end in at a later time.

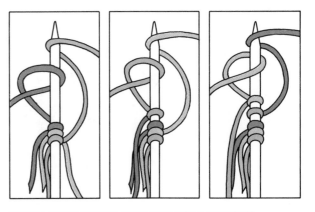

TRICOLOR CAST-ON/LEFT: YARN ONE/CENTER: YARN TWO RIGHT: YARN THREE

TRICOLOR CAST-ON

This version, as the name implies, is frequently done with three different color yarns, although it is very handsome in a solid color. The working method is related to the Right-Finger Half-Hitch Cast-on.

1. Tie the ends of all three yarns together in a single Slip Knot and place the knot on the right needle. Flatten the yarns under the knot as best you can so they are lined up, counting from the needle tip, first, second, and third.

2. Pick up the first yarn on your thumb as for Right-Finger Half-Hitch Cast-on, then pick up the third yarn with the right hand, or right finger. (This technique is much easier to manage if you use a knitting belt, page 5; in the absence of that handy piece of equipment, tuck the needle under your arm, or support it in some other way.)

3. Insert the tip of the needle under the thumb strand, bring the third yarn on the farside past the second yarn and wrap it as to Knit. Draw the yarn through the thumb loop, then drop the loop and tighten the baseline on the new stitch. Leave the thumb yarn hanging on the nearside.

4. Reach your left hand around and transfer the yarn from right hand to left hand, bringing it under the needle tip to the nearside and wrapping it on your thumb to serve as the baseline for the next stitch.

5. Pick up the yarn not used in the last stitch in your right hand, and use it to wrap and form the next new stitch.

6. Repeat these last three steps until you have the number of stitches required. If you are going to continue in a Stockinette-based stitch pattern, Purl the first row if working flat, Knit if working in the round, or continue with Herringbone Braid. Knit or Purl together all three strands in the Knot as if it were a single stitch.

This is slow, but a lot easier to do than you might think. Keep in mind some basic rules. The stitches on the needle will line up in groups of three, one in each color. The next stitch is always formed with the yarn that is the color of the first stitch on the needle carried on the thumb for the baseline, and the yarn that is the color of the third stitch on the needle wrapped for the new stitch. When the stitch is completed, always drop the thumb strand on the nearside, and transfer the yarn from right hand to left hand, then pick up the yarn that is the color of whatever stitch is then third on the needle.

Alternating Cast-on

Here is a wonderful method of casting on if you are planning to use Single Rib (page 21), or as an edge for a fabric made in Double Knit (page 234). It is fast, simple to do, fully expandable—in fact, there is no cast-on edge at all, simply the first row of stitches. Seems impossible? Try it and see! You'll find it very attractive, although it does not work for any other stitch pattern.

ALTERNATING CAST-ON FOR SINGLE RIB

1. Allow a tail of yarn, make a Slip Knot and place it on the needle, and hold the yarn as for Knit Half-Hitch Cast-on. (The edge is improved by the use of a slightly smaller needle than that used for the fabric itself.)

2. There are two alternating steps:
   • Step 1: Reach the tip of the needle over and down the farside of the strand that passes from needle to forefinger, then under and up the nearside of the strand from needle to thumb. Bring this strand back under and up the farside of the first strand and return to the starting position. This forms a "Purl" stitch.
   • Step 2: Reach the tip of the needle over, down the nearside, and then under the strand of yarn that

ALTERNATING CAST-ON/FORMING A PURL STITCH

ALTERNATING CAST-ON/FORMING A KNIT STITCH

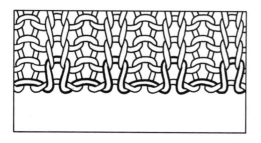

ALTERNATING CAST-ON EDGE

passes between needle and thumb. Then move the needle over and down the farside of the yarn that passes from needle to forefinger. Bring this yarn back under the first strand and return to the starting position. This forms a "Knit" stitch.

3. Make the last stitch with Half-Hitch Cast-on.

Work neatly and firmly, making sure that the yarns cross underneath the needle so each stitch is the same size. There is nothing to secure these stitches against

unraveling, so don't let go of the two strands until you have made the last stitch with Half-Hitch Cast-on. If you want to stop and count stitches, pinch the two strands with your left fingers to hold the last stitch in position. If you must set the work down, work a single Half-Hitch Cast-on stitch; rip this stitch out before you continue.

If you are working flat, turn and begin the Single Rib or Double Knit pattern with a Knit stitch. If you wish to start with Purl, begin casting on with step 2 first, step 1 second, and finish with a Purled Half-Hitch Cast-on. If you are working in the round, you can use the Twist Start (page 125), then end with step 1. Hold onto the baseline as you join the edge into a round and begin the ribbing with a Knit stitch.

If you have been watching carefully as you cast on, you will see that each stitch is made with alternating strands of yarn, one stitch off the thumb, the next off the forefinger. Each stitch encircles the running thread of the two adjacent stitches, one pulled under the running thread to the nearside, the next pulled under the other running thread to the farside, giving the two steps a Knit/Purl appearance.

Most instructions call for this cast-on to be followed by two rows of Double Knit prior to beginning Single Rib. That is really quite unnecessary, and it reduces the elasticity of the ribbing, but it does give the edge a slightly more rounded appearance that you may find attractive. That same rounded appearance can be achieved by other means that do not compromise the performance of the ribbing. However, while you need not use Double Knit with Alternating Cast-on for Single Rib, Alternating Cast-on is the ideal edge for any Double Knit fabric (see page 233).

ALTERNATING CAST-ON FOR DOUBLE KNIT

The structure of Alternating Cast-on is so similar to that of a Double Knit that it forms an ideal edge for those fabrics. Do be careful to coordinate the edge with the Double Knit pattern you plan to use so that you work those cast-on stitches that come up the nearside of the strand as Knit and slip those that come up the farside. If you are planning a color pattern in Double Knit, you will want to think about applying the Contrast-Color yarn principle as well; see the Half-Hitch version above, which can be adapted to Alternating Cast-on without modification.

There is also a clever way of using Alternating Cast-on to avoid a seam, particularly in situations where you are working a garment from the top down. See Double Knit as a substitute for grafting (page 245). And finally, it can be used to advantage as a way of starting Medallion knitting (page 119).

ALTERNATING CAST-ON FOR DOUBLE RIB

Here is a way to adapt Alternating Cast-on for use with Double Rib. I'm not sure it's worth it, as it distorts the edge somewhat, but this is less obvious when the garment is being worn, and if you are intent on a rounded, expandable edge and Double Rib, you might find it satisfactory. Personally, I recommend Double-Needle Cast-on for a superior result, but since this technique appears in so many other books, I feel I must discuss its merits.

1. Work Alternating Cast-on for Single Rib, casting on a multiple of four stitches.
2. Work two rows of Double Knit as follows:
   • Rows 1 and 2: *Knit one, bring the yarn to the nearside, slip one, return the yard to the farside*, repeat between * and * across the row, ending with a Slip Stitch.
3. After the two rows of Double Knit, work as follows:
   • Step 1: Knit the first stitch.
   • Step 2: Bypass the second stitch, Knit the third stitch by inserting the right needle into the nearside of the stitch from left to right. Do not allow the right needle to pass under the left needle; it must move around the nearside of the second stitch. Wrap the yarn and pull through the new stitch. Do not discard.
   • Step 3: Bring the yarn between the needle tips to the nearside and Purl the second stitch. Discard the second and third stitches from the needle together.
   • Step 4: Purl the fourth stitch.
4. Repeat steps 1 through 4 across the row.

If you find step 2 awkward, you may use a cable holder (page 338), holding the second stitch on the farside while you work the third, or use a Drop Stitch technique (see page 44).

What the process does, of course, is to alter the sequence of the stitches, so that instead of K1 P1, you have K2 P2. The cast-on edge and the rows done with Double Knit will remain in the original sequence, however, and where they are pulled into the new pattern, a certain distortion occurs. It is possible to eliminate the two rows of Double Knit, but the distortion is then somewhat worse. Look at it expanded, as it would be while worn, before you decide whether or not to use it.

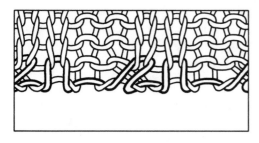

ALTERNATING CAST-ON EDGE WITH DOUBLE RIB

Other Finger Cast-ons

There are three other cast-on techniques closely related to those we have been discussing, but producing very different results. One is decorative, one purely functional, and the other is common, but flawed, and so must be mentioned only to be dismissed.

PICOT CAST-ON

Here is a technique combining Half-Hitch and Alternating Cast-on, which Barbara Walker calls Picot Ribbing in her *Second Treasury of Knitting Patterns*[1]; it is quite charming with Single Rib.

1. Use the Twist Start (page 125), then proceed as follows:
   • Step 1: Make a stitch using Knit Half-Hitch Cast-on.
   • Step 2: Make a "Knit" Alternating Cast-on stitch, bringing the forefinger strand under the thumb strand.
2. Repeat these two steps across the row, ending with a step 1.
3. Begin Single Rib on row 1 with K1 P1. If you require an uneven number of stitches, eliminate the Twist Start.

The baseline of this cast-on forms a half-hitch below every other stitch and a running thread below the intervening ones. One side of the edge is attractive, while the other is not. If you are working flat, when you turn to work the first row, use this as the outside edge. The "Purl" side of the half-hitch will form the little Picot below the Knit columns. If you are working in the round, start with a Slip Knot, then use the "Purl" ver-

PICOT CAST-ON

1. New York: Charles Scribners Sons, 1970.

sion of Alternating Cast-on in step 1 and the Purl version of Half-Hitch Cast-on in step 2; end with a step 1 and immediately join the work into a round and begin the ribbing with K1 P1.

If a slightly tighter edge is desired, it is possible to put the yarn on the other way around in step 2, above, by reaching under the strand to the forefinger instead of over it. On the first row of knitting, you will notice that these stitches are on the needle the wrong way, with the left side of the stitch on the nearside of the needle. When you work them in the normal way, they will cross.

I have seen instructions for a similar cast-on that, instead of using Alternating Cast-on in the second step, calls for a simple Yarnover done with the yarn from the forefinger. When this is done, however, the baseline strand is attached only to those stitches made with Half-Hitch Cast-on, and it strands loosely past all the stitches made with the Yarnover. I see no reason to use the technique.

STRANDED CAST-ON

Here is another edge, quite similar to Alternating Cast-on. It is altogether too homely to serve as a visible edge; it is, however, a wonderful backstage player. It is the ideal cast-on to use when the edge must be removed to free the stitches so they can be picked up and worked in some other way. For reasons why you might be tempted to do that, see page 190. Because it provides a completely unrestrained edge, it is sometimes appropriate for stitch patterns that widen considerably, and can also be used to gather the fabric.

1. Allow a tail of yarn slightly longer than the fabric will be wide. Make a Slip Knot and place it on the needle. Hold the two strands as for Knit Half-Hitch Cast-on.
2. Now there are two steps, repeated alternately until you have the desired number of stitches:
   • Step 1: Reach over and down the farside of the strand to the forefinger, pick it up on the needle, and return to the starting position.
   • Step 2: Reach the needle tip over, down the nearside and under the strand to the thumb, then over and down the farside of the strand to the forefinger; bring this strand under the strand to the thumb and return to the starting position.
3. The second-to-last stitch should be a step 1, then make the last stitch with Half-Hitch Cast-on.

Work with a firm tension and make sure the yarns cross evenly under the needle so the first row of stitches will be a consistent size. Hold onto the two strands at all times or the edge will begin to unravel; if you must stop to count stitches, pinch the two strands beneath the needle tip. The last half-hitch will hold the edge securely; should you need to set the work down tempo-

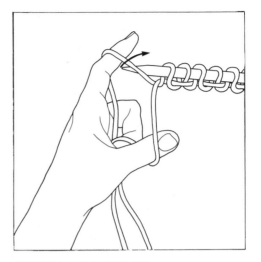

STRANDED CAST-ON/STEP ONE

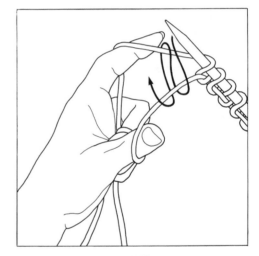

STRANDED CAST-ON/STEP TWO

rarily before you have cast on sufficient stitches, work a stitch with Half-Hitch Cast-on and rip it out before you continue. The sequence given is for an even number of stitches, starting and ending with step 1 followed by a half-hitch. For an odd number of stitches, start with step 2 and end with step 1 and the half-hitch.

If you have been watching carefully as you do this, you will see that the first stitch is like a Yarnover; the second is pulled under the baseline strand, just as in Alternating Cast-on. The stitches are all made from the strand on the forefinger and are therefore connected side by side. The baseline strand comes off the thumb and simply runs through the running threads of every other stitch. After you have worked a few rows, examine the edge. You will notice that the baseline strand acts as no more than a stitch holder. In order to adjust the width of the edge, either to gather it or stretch it out, pull out the yarn end where it doubles back through the last stitch. If you are planning to start knitting immediately after casting on, by not using the half-hitch at the end you can eliminate the nuisance of having to unravel the strand in order to adjust the baseline. Work so that you end with step 2, then hold the baseline strand firmly against the needle until you work the first stitch; once that is done the edge is secured and will not unravel.

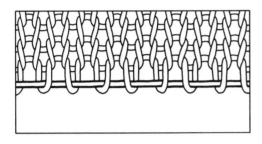

STRANDED CAST-ON EDGE

Should you want to use this cast-on for later removal, it helps to work with a contrast-color yarn for the baseline. Tie the two yarns together and let the knot sit on top of the needle as you start to cast on. Hold the contrast-color yarn on your thumb and the main-color yarn on your forefinger; after casting on and working the first row, drop the knot off the needle. The contrasting color makes the baseline clearly visible when it comes time to remove the stitches.

There are several situations when working a garment from the top down in which this technique provides a clever way to avoid a seam. The shoulder seam can be eliminated if you cast on at the top of the back and work down that side. Then pick up the stitches for the shoulders where they are held by the Stranded Cast-on and work down the front. The stitches across the back of the neck can later be picked up and worked into a collar.

You might also find the principle useful when working a garment from side to side. Use Stranded Cast-on on one side and Stranded Cast-off (page 156) on the other. When you are ready to join the front and back, pick up the stitches of the front left side on one needle and those of the back left side on another, and work Joinery Cast-off (page 153). Repeat with the stitches of the right side. If you want a drop shoulder, you can knit front and back side to side in one piece. You can then pick up the armhole stitches and work the sleeve down from shoulder to wrist. Join the sides as described above; the only seam is that of the sleeve.

I also recommend Stranded Cast-on for use with gauge samples, particularly with stitch patterns that tend to widen, because it allows an unrestrained edge, thus permitting more accurate measurement (for information on gauge, see page 415).

You may come across another method of working Stranded Cast-on. It is frequently referred to as Looped Cast-on, or something similar. The left hand is swiveled,

so that for one stitch the thumb is on the nearside and for the next the forefinger is, with all the stitches taken off the thumb strand and the strand on the forefinger forming the baseline. It accomplishes the same thing, but is awkward and slower to do. I mention it only so that you will recognize it and not think it an entirely different technique.

INVISIBLE CAST-ON FOR SINGLE RIB

In many knitting instruction books you will encounter a cast-on called by this or some similar name, and it is often highly recommended because it produces a rounded edge. Unfortunately, the instructions are usually lengthy and complex, the procedure itself is somewhat challenging, and the outcome is of dubious value. Alternating Cast-on is much faster and easier to do and produces a far better result with Single Rib. Nevertheless, this method merits discussion if only so you will recognize it and know not to bother with it.

The instructions normally call for half the required number of stitches, plus one, to be cast on using Simple Cast-on. On the next row these are Knit, with a Yarn-over placed between each stitch. This results in an even number of stitches, with every other stitch secured by a half-hitch. This is traditionally followed by four rows of Double Knit (see page 234). The half-hitches in the baseline strand must then be unraveled from every other stitch.

This is not only a good deal of trouble to do, but the structure of Double Knitting, which is necessary here to secure the stiches, both cuts down on the expandability and causes the edge to splay a bit under Single Rib. Using only two rows of Double Knit instead of the usual four helps a bit, but the edge is still not nearly as resilient or as attractive as the one produced by Alternating Cast-on, which is, in any case, far better should you actually want to work in Double Knit.

Another option offered by some instructors is to work the Single Rib twice the required length, fold it in half and hem it into place. This forms a rounded, fully elastic edge, although the fabric is twice as thick and may, therefore, be bulky. It also creates a tube through which you can insert elastic should the resilience of the ribbing give out. Please see Joinery Hem (page 203).

Other Uses for Finger Cast-ons

There are times in knitting when it is necessary to widen the fabric in such a manner that increases will not suffice; instead, the additional stitches must be cast on at one or both sides. It is also necessary to cast on within a fabric for such things as pocket openings or buttonholes. Typically this is done using Simple Cast-on or one of the Knit Cast-on methods, (pages 141–148), but it is also possible to use any one of the Finger Cast-on methods, and I think they produce a much nicer edge for the new stitches. The compromise involved is that it requires the use of an extra strand of yarn for the baseline, and when that is done, two additional tails of yarn will have to be hidden on the inside during finishing.

FINGER CAST-ON AT SIDE EDGE

1. At the edge where you wish to cast on, take up a second, separate strand of yarn of adequate length for the baseline. Hold the tail of this yarn below the right needle against the nearside of the fabric.
2. Wrap this extra strand around the thumb, and the yarn you have been working with around the forefinger in the usual way for any Half-Hitch Cast-on, and add the required number of stitches.
3. When you are done, abandon the strand and continue working according to your pattern.

HALF-HITCH CAST-ON AT A SIDE EDGE

The technique can also be used to increase on every other row in a series of steps.

1. Allowing sufficient length in the strand for the entire cast-on edge, cast on the first group of stitches as above.
2. Drop the strand, turn and slip the first cast-on stitch, then work across the row in pattern.
3. Turn and work back. At the edge, pick up the strand and cast on the next group of stitches.
4. Continue in this way until you have cast on as many additional stitches as are required.

There will be two rows of stitches between one step and the next. Carrying the baseline strand from step to step and slipping the first stitch of the row helps to slope

the turning point between one step and the next to provide a smooth line.

Alternatively, cast on the full number of stitches required and use Short Rows (page 179) to slope the edge.

FINGER CAST-ON WITHIN THE FABRIC

The same method of adding stitches at the side edge using one of the Finger Cast-on techniques can also be used when it is necessary to cast on stitches within the body of a fabric. This might happen, for instance, if you are working up the front and down the back of a sweater, casting off and then casting on again for the neck opening. There are several casting-on and casting-off techniques that create identical structures along an edge, and it is nice to match them up when they will be in close proximity like this. Keep in mind that Stranded Cast-on (like Stranded Cast-off) is equivalent to placing stitches on holders so they can be picked up and worked in another way, at another time. Half-Hitch Cast-ons can be used to make a rather nice buttonhole (see page 221).

Calculation of a Tail of Yarn for Casting On

There is a precise way to calculate the length of yarn required for any technique that requires a measured tail of yarn. It is very frustrating to estimate and come up short, and have to rip out the cast-on edge and start over again. Here is how to be sure you will not run out:

1. With the needle and yarn you plan to use, cast on ten stitches.
2. With your left thumb and forefinger, pinch the tail of yarn where it emerges from the last stitch cast on. Slide all the stitches except the Slip Knot off the needle and unravel the stitches by pulling apart the tail of yarn and the needle holding the one stitch.
3. The length of yarn between your fingers and the needle is the amount of tail required to cast on ten stitches. Measure it, and multiply that measurement by one-tenth the number of stitches you plan to cast on.

If the corner where you begin casting on will later become the start of a seam, allow an extra length of yarn for sewing up. Form this into a Yarn Butterfly (page 125) and allow it to dangle at the bottom of your work until you need to sew the seam. This avoids having to hide two ends of yarn at finishing, one from casting on and one from seaming—instead there will be none at that corner, which is far neater, much less work, and eliminates bulk in the seam.

Knit Cast-on Techniques

ere is a family of techniques that calls for the use of two needles and the basic Knit stitch itself to cast on the first stitches.

Knitted Cast-ons

This method of casting on is extremely common, probably because it is so much like knitting, and therefore easy to remember how to do. For many knitters, the basic method is the only one used. In fact, it is rather slow to work, produces an edge that is only moderately attractive, and while it is fairly elastic, has a tendency to pull out of shape. There are ways of varying the basic technique, however, that make it very nice for certain specialized uses, so it must not be dismissed, simply placed in proper perspective.

KNIT CAST-ON

1. Form a Slip Knot ten to twelve inches from the end of the yarn. Place the knot on the needle and tighten it. This will be your first stitch. (A tail that long will be easy to thread through a tapestry needle and weave in on the inside when you are finished; see page 380.)
2. Hold the needle with the stitch on it in your left hand, and the other needle in the right hand. The short tail of yarn should hang off the nearside of the needle and the yarn from ball to needle should hang down the farside. Place your left forefinger on the top of the stitch to hold it in position about one inch back from the tip of the needle.
3. Knit one stitch and transfer the new stitch to the left needle by putting the tip of the left needle into the new stitch on the nearside from left to right. The farside of the stitch on the right needle should go to the farside of the left needle.
4. Withdraw the right needle, reinsert it into the new stitch as before, and then tighten the stitch around the needle gently before wrapping the yarn to make the next stitch. (Most people tighten the stitch first and insert the needle second, but it is much harder to do that way, and produces a tighter, less elastic edge.)
5. Repeat this process, each time forming a new stitch by pulling a loop of yarn through the last stitch formed and placing the new stitch on the left needle with its fellows.

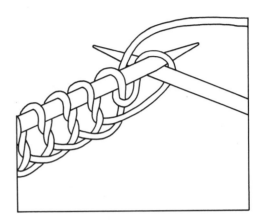

WRAPPING THE YARN FOR KNIT CAST-ON

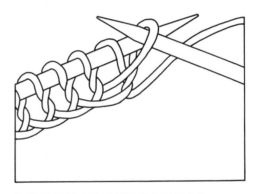

TRANSFERRING A STITCH FOR KNIT CAST-ON

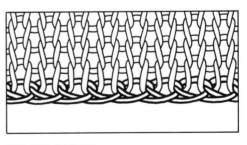

KNIT CAST-ON EDGE

When you are finished, the stitches will all be on the left needle and ready to knit. The two sides of the edge are identical, and it does not matter whether you begin your pattern with an inside or an outside row—the result will be the same. If you examine the edge, you will see that it is made of a series of strands that pass from the left side of one stitch to the right side of the stitch to the right. Since this strand passes across the width of two stitches, it gives the edge a tendency to snag and get pulled out of shape. Many people use a larger needle for casting on as a way of adding elasticity to the edge, but the larger the needle, the longer this strand will be, which exacerbates the problem. Therefore, it is probably best to cast on using a needle one or two sizes smaller than you plan to use for the stitch pattern.

By the way, for those of you who are familiar with crochet, this edge is identical to that which would be obtained by crocheting a simple chain and then knitting into one side of each stitch of the chain. (See also Chained Cast-on in this section for another method of knitting a "crocheted" edge that is far more versatile than this one.)

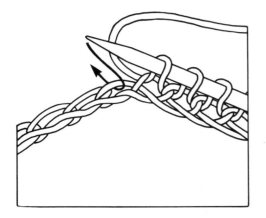

KNIT CAST-ON EDGE PICKED UP ON CROCHETED CHAIN

PURL CAST-ON

If you can Knit it on, you can certainly Purl it on, and knowing how makes the technique more versatile. Purl Cast-on forms exactly the same edge as Knit Cast-on, but it is considerably faster to do. Personally, I use it in

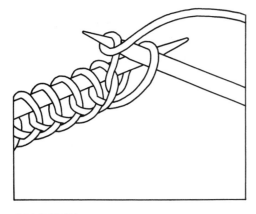

PURL CAST-ON

preference to the Knit version whenever I have occasion to use the technique. It is particularly useful if you must start your stitch pattern with an inside row.

1. Place a Slip Knot on the right needle.
2. Insert the left needle directly into the stitch on the right needle so it emerges on the farside. Wrap the yarn around the right needle as to Purl, and draw through the next new stitch. As you work this new stitch, the previous stitch will be transferred to the left needle, where it is retained. Repeat this step as many times as necessary.

KNIT-PURL CAST-ON

And if you can Knit it on, and Purl it on, it follows that you can rib it on, and it makes a rather nice edge, too. Simply make one stitch with the Knit method and the next with the Purl, taking the needle under the yarn each time and alternating the two until you have the required number of stitches. Obviously, you could also vary the Knits and Purls to accommodate any number of different rib patterns. The ribbed version is more elastic, and splays considerably less than plain Knit or Purl Cast-on.

There are several other variations on this technique that you may find useful or interesting. I have never seen them discussed in any of the numerous books on knitting that I have consulted, but they are so simple and logical that I can't believe I am the first to think of them. They also provide an excellent illustration of just how small a change is required to produce a very different effect in knitting, and a lesson on why it is wise to pay attention to the details.

OPEN KNIT CAST-ON

This version would look very nice under a Lace stitch as it produces tiny Eyelets along the edge. The Eyelets also provide very convenient openings for knotting on a fringe.

• Cast on in exactly the same way as detailed in Knit Cast-on above, but when transferring the new stitch to the left needle, insert the left needle tip on the nearside from right to left instead of from left to right.

You will find that this is actually a considerably faster way to work Knit Cast-on, as the right needle need not be withdrawn from the stitch and reinserted in order to work the next stitch. Just slip the tip of the right needle under the left one and continue.

When the required number of stitches have been cast on, Knit across the row and examine the result. (It does not matter whether you begin the first row with Knit or

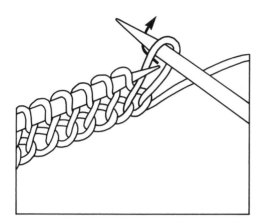

TRANSFERRING STITCH FOR OPEN KNIT CAST-ON

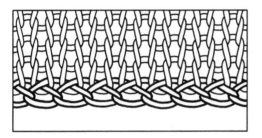

OPEN KNIT CAST-ON EDGE

with Purl.) In this case, the bottom strand passes from the right side of one stitch to the left side of the one to the right, and adjacent strands are twisted in between. The long strand is therefore gone, but the twist opens things up, producing the Eyelet.

WOVEN KNIT CAST-ON

The edge we get with this variation has a complex, woven appearance that is neither loopy nor open, and it has little tendency to curl. It would be excellent for use on a tailored garment without ribbing. Care must be taken to balance it with the stitch pattern, however, for it is quite dense and inelastic and will not do with a pattern that widens. You may find you get a better result if you cast on with a larger needle.

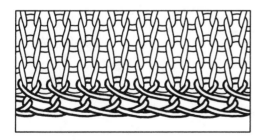

WOVEN KNIT CAST-ON EDGE

• Cast on and transfer the stitches as in Knit, Purl, or Open Cast-on, above, then Knit the first row of stitches through the farside so they cross.

The difference created by using one or the other method of casting on is so subtle as to be not worth worrying about; simply choose the one you feel most comfortable working with. The result with Knit or Purl Cast-on is slightly deeper and more complex.

Cable Cast-ons

These next variations of the Knit-on technique are frequently encountered with a claim that the edge produced is more elastic than the others. In fact, it is one of the least elastic edges that knitters have available to them. When not touted for elasticity, it is touted for its strength. The edge is firm and dense; however, as with a reed that bends in the wind, the real advantage of a knitted garment under stress is that it stretches, so I don't look upon an inelastic edge as particularly strong. The edge does have a rather neat and uniform appearance, almost like a cord, and there are good uses to which it can be put. Cable Cast-ons are particularly appropriate with stitch patterns that are rather dense and inelastic themselves, and are a good choice for adding stitches within the body of a fabric, as for a semi-detached motif (see page 86) or a buttonhole.

KNIT CABLE CAST-ON

1. Make the first two stitches in the same way as described in basic Knit Cast-on, above.
2. For all subsequent stitches, insert the right needle tip from nearside to farside *between* the first two stitches on the left needle. Pass the yarn around the needle as to Knit, draw the new stitch through, and place it on the left needle in the same manner as in Knit Cast-on.

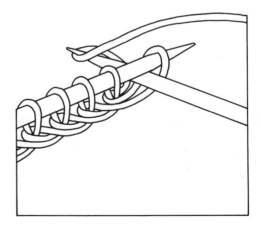

KNIT CABLE CAST-ON

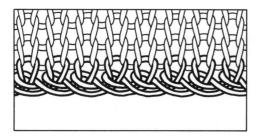

KNIT CABLE CAST-ON EDGE

3. Continue in this way, pulling the yarn for each new stitch between the last two stitches on the left needle until you have the required number of stitches.

PURL CABLE CAST-ON

There is a Knit side and a Purl side to this cast-on edge. If it is more convenient for you to start your stitch pattern on an inside row, there is a Purl version of Cable Cast-on.

• The instructions are the same as above, except the right needle tip is inserted between the first two stitches on the left needle from farside to nearside and the yarn is thrown as to Purl. The new stitch is transferred in the same way.

Chained Cast-on

A Chained Cast-on is a technique worth knowing about. It not only creates a decorative and elastic edge that can be used with any stitch pattern, but can be an excellent choice for casting on within the body of a fabric, such as for a semidetached motif (see page 86) or for a neckline or other opening. In addition, it exactly matches Pullover Cast-off (page 150), which makes it very nice to use when both the top and bottom edges of a fabric will be visible, such as on a blanket or a scarf. There are several different methods of creating this edge; choose the one you are most comfortable with.

CHAINED CAST-ON WITH TWO NEEDLES

1. Make a Slip Knot and place it on a needle held in the left hand.
2. Proceed as follows:
   • Step 1: Take up the other needle in the right hand, and wrap the yarn around it as for a Purl-to-Purl Yarnover: up the nearside, over the top, down the farside, and under the needle tip to the nearside again.
   • Step 2: Purl the stitch on the left needle and discard. (There are now two new stitches on the right needle, a Yarnover and a regular stitch.)

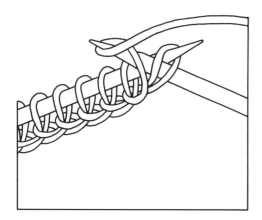

PURL CABLE CAST-ON

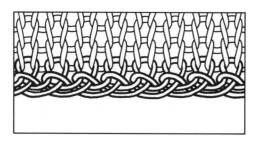

PURL CABLE CAST-ON EDGE

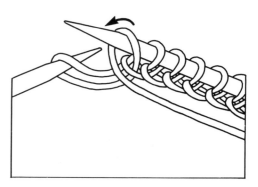

CHAINED CAST-ON/MAKING THE YARNOVER

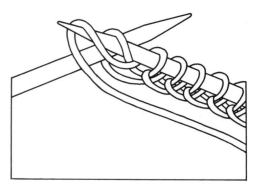

CHAINED CAST-ON/PURLING THE STITCH

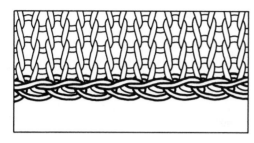

CHAINED CAST-ON EDGE

- Step 3: Transfer this last new stitch from right needle to left needle, leaving the Yarnover on the right needle.

Repeat these three steps until you have the required number of stitches, ending with step 2.

The Yarnovers will be the new stitches on the needle, and the stitch transferred back to the left needle is the one you will work into and discard next. The discarded stitches form a resilient chain at the base of the cast-on edge. No Eyelets will be produced; the Yarnovers will behave like normal stitches when they are worked. It is important to maintain a fairly firm tension as you work to ensure that each stitch of the chain is a nice consistent size. If the baseline stitch seems enlarged as it is discarded, first pull up gently on the first stitch on the right needle to tighten it, then firmly tighten the stitch on the left needle as you work the next Yarnover. You may wish to use a needle somewhat smaller or larger than the one you plan to use for the body of the fabric, depending upon the type of stitch pattern the edge must accommodate itself to. If the edge is highly contoured, try Chain Loop Cast-on, below.

CHAINED CAST-ON WITH HOOK AND NEEDLE

Here is the usual method of creating the same edge, using a crochet hook and a needle together. The needle determines the size of the first row of stitches, the hook the size of the stitches in the chain.

1. Make a Slip Knot a few inches from the end of the yarn and place it on the crochet hook, then hold the hook in your right hand.
2. Take up the needle in your left hand. Wrap the yarn around the left forefinger as to crochet. The yarn should pass from the hook, under the needle, to the finger.
3. Proceed as follows:
   - Step 1: Hold the hook against the nearside of the needle, and chain one stitch firmly against the needle. (As you do so, the yarn will pass over the needle, forming a new stitch; the crochet chain will form the baseline of the cast-on edge.)
   - Step 2: With either your right forefinger or the hook, return the yarn under the knitting needle.

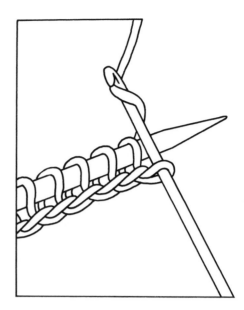

CHAINED CAST-ON WITH HOOK/FORMING A STITCH

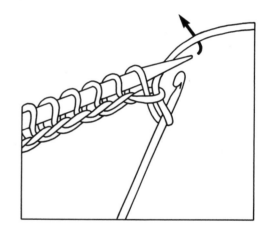

CHAINED CAST-ON WITH HOOK/RETURNING YARN TO FARSIDE

Repeat steps 1 and 2 until you have one less stitch than required. Transfer the last stitch on the crochet hook to the needle.

I think you will find Chained Cast-on with Two Needles simpler to do. The only advantage this version offers is that the needle and hook can be different sizes, offering more precise control over the size of the stitches in the baseline, but the same thing can be accomplished by picking up stitches along a chain.

CROCHET CHAIN CAST-ON

As with Knit Cast-on (page 141), it is possible to create the same edge using a crocheted chain. There are two different ways to pick up stitches on a chain, one way creating Knit Cast-on, the other this. If you examine a crochet chain, you will see what looks like a series of Knit stitches on one side and a series of nubs, like a little spine, on the other side. The nubs of this spine are created by that portion of the yarn which runs between one stitch and the next, what I call in knitting the running thread. If you pick up one side of each stitch of the chain on a knitting needle, you will create an edge exactly like that of Knit Cast-on. If you pick up the nubs instead, it will be identical to Chained Cast-on.

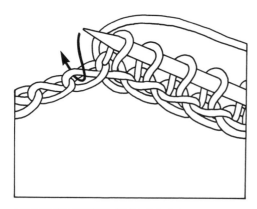

PICKING UP CROCHET CHAIN CAST-ON

CHAINED CAST-ON FOR REMOVAL

With a slight modification in technique, Chained Cast-on is an excellent method to use if you are planning to later remove the cast-on edge in order to work in the opposite direction. (For a discussion of what circumstances might prompt you to do that, and how to pick the stitches up properly, see Picking Up and Knitting in the Opposite Direction, page 190.)

1. Work the same as in Chained Cast-on with Two Needles, only use a contrast-color yarn for casting on.
2. Change to the main color and work the body of the fabric.

When you are ready to work in the opposite direction, follow the instructions under Removing Chained Cast-on (page 191).

CHAIN LOOP CAST-ON

Here is another variation on the technique that makes this cast-on more decorative and suitable for even the most acutely indented edge. Work tightly, or on quite a small needle, as this can turn sloppy if not done with care.

1. Make a Slip Knot, and place it on the needle held in your left hand.

2. Proceed as follows:
   • Step 1: Form a Purl-to-Purl Yarnover on the right needle.
   • Step 2: Purl the stitch on the left needle and discard.
   • Step 3: Insert the left needle into the farside of the new stitch on the right needle, wrap the yarn as to Purl, and pull the stitch over the yarn and off the needle.
   • Step 4: Transfer the last new stitch from right needle to left needle.
3. Repeat these four steps until you have the required number of stitches, ending with step 2.

What this does is place an extra chain in the base between each Yarnover. Of course, you could chain as many stitches between each Yarnover as you wish. Adding one, as given here, will produce an Eyelet effect when used with most stitch patterns; add a number of them and you will create a chained loop between one stitch and the next. The technique can be used as a decorative solution to the problem of a scalloped or indented edge, because the extra chains add length to the edge. (For a discussion of why contoured edges require special handling, see Double-Needle Cast-on, page 132.) The loops also provide a convenient hanger for fringe.

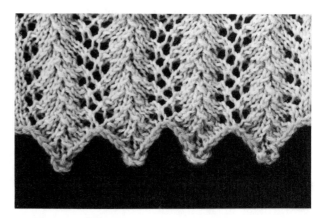

A DEEPLY INDENTED EDGE WITH CHAIN LOOP CAST-ON

The same edge can be created using crochet, picking up every second, third, or fourth nub, etc., instead of every one. Needless to say, if you do know how to crochet, you can work any sort of a decorative edge you wish, then pick up the stitches and begin to knit. Once the concept is grasped, the possibilities are too numerous to mention.

Border Cast-ons

There are many beautiful stitch patterns that are knit narrow and long to form borders that can be sewn on to the edge of a knitted fabric. It is also possible to pick up stitches along the selvedge of one of these borders so it will form the lower edge of the fabric, with no sewing required. Here is just one to give you the idea of how it works. Many of the patterns used for this purpose are lacy; this one is particularly open.

EYELET CAST-ON

This cast-on is quaint, highly decorative, and very easy to do.

To make the chain, proceed as follows:

1. Make a Slip Knot and place it on a fairly small needle. Make one additional stitch with Half-Hitch Cast-on. Turn and pick up a second needle in the right hand, working as follows:
   • Step 1. With the yarn farside, bring the needle tips together. Wrap the yarn over the top of the right needle to the nearside, then under the needle tip to the farside, to make a turned Yarnover.
   • Step 2. Insert the right needle into the farside of

the two stitches on the left needle and knit them together, wrapping the yarn over the needle.

2. Turn and repeat these two steps until you have a chain as long as you require for the cast-on edge. When the chain is complete, Knit the last two stitches together farside without forming a new Yarnover, leaving one stitch on the needle.

3. To pick up stitches along the chain, insert the needle into the first Yarnover loop on the side of the chain, wrap the yarn as to Knit, and pull through a new stitch. Continue in this way across one side of the chain, working one new stitch into each Eyelet loop.

The turned Yarnover produced in making the chain replaces the stitch removed by the decrease in the next step, which maintains a constant number of stitches on the needle. Wrapping the yarn over the needle in the decrease turns the new stitch. When the turned Yarnover and the turned stitch are Knit together farside on the next row, they will form an uncrossed Left Decrease. Turning these stitches with the wrapping method is easier than having to turn them with the needle tip prior to the decrease.

The size of the needle you use will determine the size of the loops you make, so do a few versions on different sizes to see which one will give you the appearance you like; as with any lace pattern, a small needle produces the most attractive fabric. Also, the Eyelets you knit into may be worked in either open or crossed versions—for the open version, Knit into the nearside of each loop; for the crossed version, Knit into the farside.

This cast-on works with any stitch pattern, but you will want to coordinate the length of the border to the width of the pattern carefully. You can use a larger or smaller needle, or work twice into each Eyelet using a Knit/Purl Rib Increase (see page 67). The border can be frilled or ruffled by using it with a pattern that compresses, such as a rib. It has a good deal of lateral spread, so it works well with stitch patterns that widen.

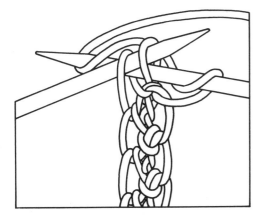

WORKING THE DECREASE FOR EYELET CAST-ON

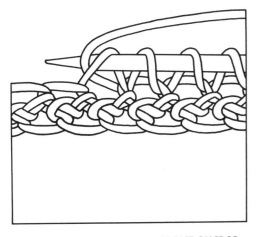

PICKING UP STITCHES ALONG EYELET CAST-ON EDGE

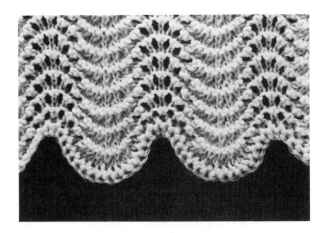

OLD SHALE PATTERN WITH EYELET CAST-ON EDGE

Other Uses for Knit Cast-ons

The knitted-on techniques are traditionally used to place additional stitches at a side edge in order to widen the fabric abruptly, or to cast on stitches within a fabric such as for buttonholes and neck openings. As you know, I'm not terribly fond of plain Knit or Purl Cast-on for any purpose, including this one. A Cable Cast-on generally works better, although care must be taken that the edge is not too constricted. (Also, see page 139 for information on using one of the Finger methods for this purpose, which I think often gives a far better result.)

GLOSSARY OF CASTING-ON TECHNIQUES

Alternating
Used primarily for Single Rib or Double Knit. Invisible, highly resilient. Identical to Invisible Cast-off. Very fast.

Braid or Cord
Slight variation in technique produces two different edges, one decorative, one tailored. Can be done with contrast or solid color. Resilient. Slow to work.

Cable
Good for motifs, buttonholes, and compact stitch patterns. Tailored, firm, and inelastic. Knit, Purl or Rib versions. Slow to work.

Chained
All-purpose; good for contoured edge, patterns that widen, and later removal. Decorative. Matches Pullover Cast-off. Very elastic. Slow to work.

Chain Loop
Suitable for contoured edge or patterns that widen. Decorative. Similar to Chained; highly expansive. Slow to work.

Double-Needle
All-purpose; good for ribs or contoured edge. Neat and unobtrusive. Identical to Half-Hitch but highly elastic. Slower to work.

Eyelet
Decorative. Slow to work.

Half-Hitch
Best all-purpose. Neat and unobtrusive. Good elasticity. Identical to Half-Hitch Cast-off. Purl, Alternating (Rib), and Twisted versions. Very fast.

Knit
All-purpose. Moderately attractive; tends to be loose. Average elasticity. Slow to work; Purl version faster.

Knotted
All purpose. Tailored, decorative. Quite elastic, good expansion. Very slow to do.

Open Knit
All-purpose; suitable for lace or fringed edge. Decorative version of Knit Cast-on. Faster to work.

Picot
Used with Single Rib. Decorative. Fast.

Right-Finger Half-Hitch
Optional version for Right-Finger knitter. Outcome same as Half-hitch. Twisted version. Slower to work.

Simple
All purpose. Produces loose, unattractive edge. Twisted version tighter and neater. Fast and very easy to do, but stitches difficult to work into.

Stranded
Primarily for later removal. Unrestrained edge. Matches Stranded Cast-off; equivalent to placing stitches on holder. Very fast.

Tricolor
Three-color, highly decorative. Tailored when done in solid color. Very slow to do.

Woven Knit
Decorative version of Knit Cast-on. Tailored. Inelastic.

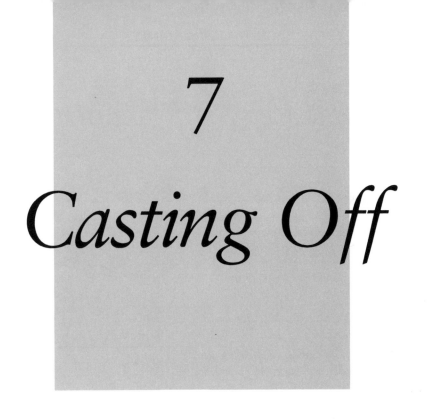

7
Casting Off

Casting off is the process by which the finished fabric is taken off the needle in a manner that secures the last row of stitches and prevents them from unraveling. Here, as with other basic techniques, there are quite a variety of ways to accomplish the task.

Some methods of casting off are versatile, working well in almost every situation, while others are more specialized. Just as with casting on, the elasticity or stability of the cast-off edge must be taken into consideration in light of how the fabric will be used. Often, a cast-off edge will become part of a seam and its appearance is not critical. At other times, the edge will remain a highly visible part of a garment—as at the end of a scarf, for instance—and its finish will be important. There are also some situations where the finished appearance is enhanced by matching the cast-off and cast-on edges, and fortunately there are several techniques that allow this to be done.

Knitted Cast-off Techniques

Because they rely upon the basic stitch techniques, the following methods of casting off are very easy to do. The first group is made up of no more than simple variations upon a very common theme. The last two groups have very specialized applications, one utilitarian, the other decorative, and both are very useful to know about.

Chained Cast-off

While you will find quite a few methods of working here, there is, in fact, but one Chained Cast-off. All of the variations are no more than different ways to accomplish exactly the same edge. The only criteria for choosing among them is to find which one is comfortable for you to do and gives you the best result—an edge that is neither too loose nor too tight and in which all of the stitches are an even, consistent size.

Pullover Cast-off

The following method is the most common. It is certainly easy to do, but it requires that you really pay attention as you go along in order to make the edge smooth. An excellent all-purpose technique, it is the only one a beginning knitter needs to be concerned with. There are many people who have used the method exclusively throughout a lifetime of knitting. It is identical to that created by Chained Cast-on, should you wish to match the two edges.

1. Work two stitches.
2. Insert the tip of the left needle from left to right into the nearside of the second stitch on the right needle, and lift this stitch over the first one and off the needle.
3. Work another stitch.
4. Repeat steps 2 and 3 until there is only one stitch left on the right needle.

As you work the last row and cast off, keep in mind that the discard stitches will form the last row of your fabric, while the new stitches will form the cast-off edge. Therefore, you must maintain your stitch pattern, knitting the Knit stitches and purling the Purl stitches. Occasionally it is difficult to do this with a complex pattern, in which case just Knit or Purl, whichever you think will work best.

The important thing is to maintain a smooth, even tension, and to avoid making the edge too tight. One

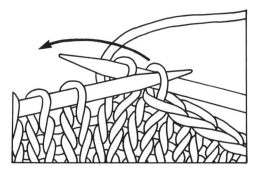

PULLOVER CAST-OFF

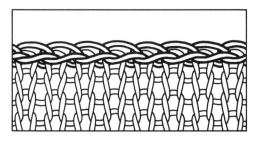

PULLOVER CAST-OFF EDGE

sure way to avoid that is to hold a needle two or three sizes larger than the one you worked your fabric on in the right hand as you cast off. Unlike Half-Hitch Cast-on, in this case a larger needle will affect the length of the cast-off edge because the size of each new stitch forming the edge is determined by the size of the needle, and larger stitches provide more yarn for stretch.

There are two ways to finish off the last stitch, depending upon whether you are working flat or in the round.

When working flat:
1. Break the yarn, leaving ten to twelve inches, which can later be threaded through a tapestry needle to hide the end on the inside.
2. Elongate the last stitch until the end of the yarn pulls through the stitch below, or wrap the end around the needle tip as to Knit and pull the last stitch over and off, then draw the end through and tighten it down firmly. This last version is more secure.

When working in the round:
1. Break the yarn and pull it through the stitch as above. Thread it through a tapestry needle.
2. Pass the needle from farside to nearside under both sides of the first cast-off stitch.

3. Insert the needle down into the center of the last cast-off stitch, coming out on the nearside.
4. Insert the needle from nearside to farside through the center of the stitch below the last cast-off stitch.
5. Hide the end on the inside of the fabric in the usual way (see page 379).

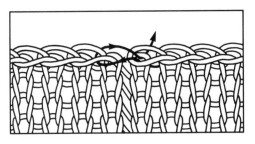

FINISHING A CIRCULAR PULLOVER CAST-OFF EDGE

DECREASE CAST-OFF

This way of working is very easy to do and produces a nice, even edge; in fact, it is no more than Slip Slip Knit decreases worked all the way across. I rather prefer this to the traditional Pullover method.

1. Knit the first stitch.
2. Slip the next stitch knitwise.
3. Insert the left needle tip from left to right into the nearside of the two stitches on the right needle, wrap the yarn as to Knit, and lift the two stitches over the yarn and off the needle.
4. Repeat steps 2 and 3 across the row until there is one stitch remaining on the right needle.
5. Break the yarn and finish the last stitch as in Pullover Cast-off, above.

As with Pullover Cast-off, work on a larger-size needle for added stretch, but use a fairly firm tension to aid in obtaining a consistent edge.

I have seen this method written with instructions to Knit two together farside, return the new stitch to the left needle, and repeat. The effect along the edge will be the same, but the discard stitches forming the last row of your fabric will be crossed. If you are working in Crossed Stitch, you might wish to use that modification, but otherwise the one above is correct.

It is possible to Knit two together, return the new stitch to the left needle, and repeat, but it has an odd outcome. The new stitches forming the cast-off edge are pulled through the discard stitches and lie horizontally within them. The discard stitches are lined up sideways, with the right side of the stitch on the nearside of the fabric, instead of lying flat. The edge formed tends to be rather rigid, but the spaces between the stitches afford an opening convenient for tying on a fringe. If that's just what you need, give this variation a try.

SUSPENDED CAST-OFF

Another variation, which also provides the identical edge as those above. It works well to prevent inconsistencies but is more trouble to do.

1. Work two stitches.
2. With the tip of the left needle, lift the second stitch on the right needle over the first one and off the needle, but do not discard it.
3. With the right needle, reach around the suspended stitch and Knit the next stitch on the left needle.
4. Discard the suspended stitch and the last stitch worked at the same time.
5. Repeat this process across the row until a single stitch remains.
6. Break the yarn and finish the last stitch as described in Pullover Cast-off, above.

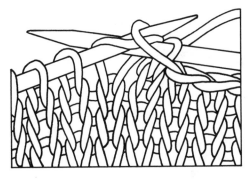

SUSPENDED CAST-OFF

When you hold the pulled-over stitch on the left needle in this manner, it accomplishes two things. First, it enlarges that stitch slightly, thereby providing adequate yarn to the edge for expansion; and second, it prevents the stitches from being enlarged in an inconsistent way as one is pulled over the next.

I find Suspended Cast-Off awkward, and don't really like to use it regardless of its merits, but for some knitters who have trouble obtaining a nice even edge, this is a good solution.

SINGLE CROCHET CAST-OFF

If you like working with a crochet hook, and you have trouble obtaining a smooth edge with Pullover Cast-off, you might like to try this alternative. The route of the yarn, and the finished appearance, will be absolutely the same. If necessary, use a larger-size hook than the equivalent knitting needle in order to add length to the edge.

1. Hold the needle bearing the stitches in the left hand, and wrap the yarn around the left forefinger in the normal way to crochet.

2. Insert the crochet hook from left to right into the nearside of the first stitch on the left needle and slip the stitch to the hook. Hook the yarn and draw through a loop.
3. Slip the next stitch to the hook in the same way, hook the yarn, and draw the loop through both stitches on the hook. Repeat this step across the row.
4. Finish the last stitch as in Pullover Cast-off, above.

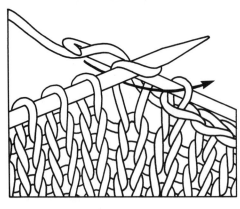

SINGLE CROCHET CAST-OFF

It is possible to hook the loop through while the stitch is still on the knitting needle. The reason I recommend against this is because more precise control of tension, and the resulting size of the cast-off stitches, is obtained by working off the hook. Needless to say, you can reproduce Picot Chain Cast-off by simply working extra Single Crochet chains between each stitch.

Picot Chain Cast-off

Here is a variation of Chained Cast-off that inserts an extra stitch between each pullover step. It can be used to add a decorative note, or to add length to an edge that finishes off a scalloped or indented pattern. Work on a small needle as follows:

1. Knit two stitches and pull the right one over the left as for Pullover Cast-off, above.
2. Insert the left needle directly into the nearside of the stitch on the right needle, wrap the yarn as to Knit, and pull the stitch over the yarn and off the needle.
3. Knit the first stitch on the left needle and repeat the pullover step.
4. Continue in this manner, knitting the new stitch that remains on the right needle a second time before working each pullover step.
5. Finish the last stitch as in Pullover Cast-off.

If you add two or three extra stitches instead of just one, you will form a small Picot Loop.

Slip Stitch Cast-off

Here is another version of a Pullover Cast-off that provides an edge with the same structure as those above, but it is very even, firm, and inelastic. It is a good method for use on stitch patterns that are themselves dense and inelastic, and can be used when you are required to cast off within the body of the fabric, such as for buttonholes. That application is discussed on page 221. Here I will simply give you the instructions appropriate for when it is used to cast off stitches across the entire row.

1. Work the last row onto a double-point needle, circular or straight, or slip the stitches one at a time from one needle to the other.
2. Starting at the end opposite where the yarn comes off the last stitch, hold the needle with the stitches in the left hand as usual and slip two stitches to the right needle.
3. Pass the right stitch over the left as for Pullover Cast-off, above.
4. Slip another stitch to the right needle and repeat the pullover.
5. Continue in this way until one stitch remains.
6. Finish the last stitch as in Pullover Cast-off.

The reason this version is tighter is that the amount of yarn allowed to the edge is fixed when the last row of stitches is worked, and therefore no additional yarn is imparted as each stitch is pulled over and off as is the case with the others. Should you need to make the edge looser, you must use a larger-size needle in the right hand to work the last row before casting off. Note that if you need to unravel this edge, you cannot just pull on the yarn and have it zip off as with the others; it is necessary to pick each stitch free one by one.

Stepped Cast-off

There are occasions when it is necessary to create a slope and cast off at the same time. Most gradual slopes can be handled with decreases, but when the slope is more acute than can be created by decreasing one stitch on every row, it becomes necessary to resort to casting off in order to remove several stitches at a time. This may occur, for instance, with the shaping of a shallow sleeve cap, the top edge of a dolman sleeve, or more commonly, with a shoulder line. There are other ways to work a Stepped Cast-off, which we will discuss below, but this version is the most successful.

Each group of stitches that are cast off together will be referred to as a step, and the intersections between steps are called "turning points." Details on how to do the calculations for a slope of this kind can be found on page 439. All casting off should be done while maintaining the stitch pattern. The instructions are for Pullover Cast-off, but any other method of working a chained edge can be used as well.

1. At the beginning of a row, use Pullover Cast-off on the stitches of the first step, then work the remaining stitches of the row normally. Turn and work as follows:
   • Step 1: Work back across the next row to the last cast-off step and when two stitches remain on the left needle, if you are on the outside work a Knit right decrease, if on the inside a Purl left decrease. Turn.
   • Step 2: Slip the first stitch, Knit or Purl the next, pull the slipped stitch over to remove the first stitch of the next step (a Slip Pullover Left Decrease), then continue with Pullover Cast-off on the remaining ones; work to the end of the row.

2. Continue in this way, always working a decrease at the beginning of each step and another between two steps until all of the required stitches have been removed.

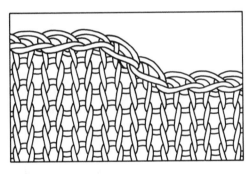

STEPPED CAST-OFF EDGE

It is important to use the correct decrease so the removed stitch slants in the same direction as the slope. Many people use either the decrease or the Slip Stitch rather than both, but the slope will not be as smooth that way.

If you examine the structure of a Stepped Cast-off, you will see that there are two full rows of stitches between each step. The method given above eliminates one stitch at the edge of each of those rows, creating a slope between two steps. If you were to eliminate one or both of these decreases, the edge would resemble stair steps, with each step two rows higher than the last. The bulkier the yarn the more pronounced this sharp change of level will be. Think about it in relation to the gauge. If you have a gauge of eight rows to the inch, the two rows between each step of the slope represents ¼ inch; if you have six rows to the inch, it will be a jump of ⅓ inch, and in a bulky yarn at four rows to the inch, it will be a whopping ½ inch. In order to sew the seam in a straight line, the extra stitches would have to be

turned into the shoulder seam, making it bulky. Also, when just one decrease is used, there is frequently a small gap at the turning point. With this method, the gap virtually disappears, but it is still wise to work the stitches involved fairly firmly.

There is another way of creating a sloped line that makes use of an interesting and versatile technique called Short Rows (page 175). Instead of casting off the steps, each group of stitches is left unworked row by row, so that at the end of the process a slope has been created but all of the stitches involved are still on the needle. A final row is then worked across all of these stitches. At this point, several things can happen. The stitches can be cast off on that final row and seamed in the normal way, or the stitches can be cast off and seamed at the same time, using Joinery Cast-off (see below), or they can be grafted (page 376) to another set of stitches for a seamless join.

Joinery Cast-off

This technique allows you to cast off and join the stitches of two separate garment sections all in one process. It produces an excellent seam, and I'm sure you'll make regular use of it once you see how well it works. Joinery Cast-off is ideal for shoulder seams, especially when used in conjunction with Short Rows (page 178) to slope the shoulder line, but there are many other applications.

GARMENT SECTIONS SEAMED WITH JOINERY CAST-OFF

BASIC JOINERY CAST-OFF

With this method, the stitch columns of the two fabrics are lined up perfectly, head to head. On the inside there will be a single slim line of Chain Cast-off stitches, producing a smooth join with no bulk whatsoever.

1. The fabrics should be positioned with their outside faces together, the needles parallel, with the tips lined up side by side. (You may have to work an extra row on one or the other in order to accomplish this.)
2. Insert the right needle into the first stitch on the near needle and the first stitch on the far needle and Knit two together.
3. Repeat with the next two stitches, then pull the second stitch on the right needle over the first to cast off.
4. Repeat across the edge.

When working the cast-off, it does not matter whether you use a Knit or Purl decrease, because they will be hidden on the inside and the result on the outside will be the same. Personally, I think the Purl Two Together decrease is easier to do, but try them both and choose the method that is comfortable for you. What is important is that the stitch on the near needle be the left stitch in the decrease pair. If this is not done, the two stitches will twist around one another, distorting the smooth line of the seam.

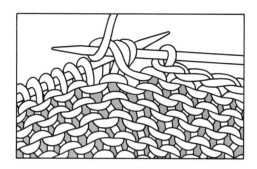

JOINERY CAST-OFF IN PURL

If you find that you are having trouble working this way, you can first transfer all the stitches from both needles to a circular or double-point needle, taking first a stitch from the far needle, next a stitch from the near needle, alternating in this fashion until all the stitches are interspersed. Since the stitches will tighten up when you do this, it's a good idea to place them on a slightly smaller needle, but use your regular-size needle or a larger one in your right hand as you cast off. Then work the Joinery Cast-off just as described above, using either a Knit or Purl Two Together on every pair of stitches across the row. The pullover step remains the same—when there are two new stitches on the right needle, pull the right one over the left and off the needle.

REVERSE JOINERY CAST-OFF

It is possible to work Joinery Cast-off so the horizontal line of cast-off stitches will be visible when the garment is worn. If done carefully, so that each of the cast-off stitches is smooth and the same size as all the others, the effect is quite decorative. In order to work it this way, simply place the inside faces of the fabric together and then work the technique in the same manner as detailed above.

GARMENT SECTIONS SEAMED WITH REVERSE JOINERY CAST-OFF

JOINERY CAST-OFF ON RIB

If you are joining two sections of ribbing, you must plan carefully before you knit so the columns of Knit and Purl stitches will line up properly. It is all too easy to get this wrong, so let's look at how it works.

If on both garment sections you establish a Knit/Purl sequence on an even number of stitches, the first stitch of every row will be a Knit and the last stitch of every row will be a Purl. Therefore, when you turn one fabric around so that the outside faces of the fabrics are together for joining, the last Purl stitch of one section will then be facing the first Knit stitch of the other section. Of course, the same phenomenon holds true for Double Rib. The easiest way around the difficulty is to work on an uneven number of stitches so you begin and end the rib with the same type of stitch. If you are working Double Rib, you would have to have a multiple of four plus two. Alternatively, just establish the ribbing sequence so the same type of stitch is at each armhole, front and back. If you start one side Knit/Purl, you may have to start the other Purl/Knit.

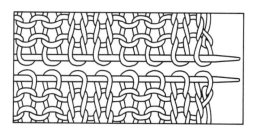

LINING UP RIBBING FOR JOINERY CAST-OFF

Although it is important to line up the columns of Knit and Purl stitches, it is not necessary to maintain the Rib pattern while casting off; simply work either all Knit Two Together or all Purl Two Together; it will make no difference to the outcome.

Border Cast-offs

This is very clever, and being clever, quite a bit of fun. It's a technique that allows you to cast off an edge and add a border at the same time. Since the same principles apply here as for attaching a border to picked up stitches along a selvedge, which is discussed in detail on page 194, I will not repeat myself. These instructions refer only to those aspects which are different when the border is worked on existing stitches rather than on ones that are picked up.

GARTER STITCH BORDER CAST-OFF

Whereas a border worked on picked-up stitches is knit up in the same direction as the main section of fabric, in this case it will be worked perpendicular to it, but the technique is otherwise the same. The decrease joins one stitch from the border and one stitch from the main fabric every other row. The stitch that is removed by the decrease is from the main fabric, effectively casting it off, while a constant number of stitches is maintained in the border.

GARTER STITCH BORDER CAST-OFF

As with borders attached to picked-up stitches, Garter Stitch is the most common stitch pattern used because of its resilience; with other patterns, matching the gauge of the border to that of the fabric becomes critical. If this is not done, the border will either splay out or constrict the edge, and the result will not be satisfying at all. If there is not too great a discrepancy in the two gauges, the fabrics will ease together when they are dressed; if the difference is large, regauging may be the solution. Should you require more or fewer stitches than the existing fabric provides, work evenly spaced increases or decreases on the last row so you have half as many stitches as there will be rows in the pattern, or use one of the joining methods described on page 193.

CORDED CAST-OFF

This is a close relative of Border Cast-off, combining it with the technique for making a cord.

1. After you have completed the last row of the fabric, use Cable Cast-on to add three stitches at the top right corner. On these stitches, work as follows:
   • Step 1: K2, then work an SSK or Slip Pullover decrease on the next two stitches.
   • Step 2: Slip the three border stitches back to the left needle one at a time, maintaining their proper position on the needle.
2. Repeat these two steps, drawing the yarn very tightly across the farside of the stitches as you Knit the first stitch in step 1.

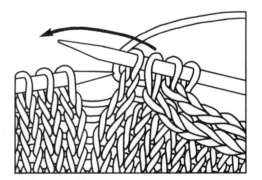

WORKING SLIP PULLOVER DECREASE FOR CORDED CAST-OFF

CORDED CAST-OFF EDGE

The decrease in step 1 works just as it does in Border Cast-off, eliminating one stitch along the top edge of the fabric while maintaining a constant number in the border. Drawing the yarn tightly across the farside of the border in step 2 pulls the first and last stitch together, forming a rounded cord.

Because the basis of this technique is Stockinette, gauge becomes an issue since it takes more rows than stitches to make an inch. Since these stitches are slipped in order to form the cord, there is only one row of cording for each column of stitches in the main body of the fabric. For a short distance this will not be critical, but at some point it will begin to constrict the edge. To compensate for this, you can hold a larger needle in the right hand. It is best to do a stitch gauge on a sample cord, and if regauging is an insufficient adjustment, you may have to increase on the last row of the fabric in order to have more rows in the border.

Corded Cast-off can also be worked in the same way on stitches released from a cast-on edge (see page 190), or on those picked up along a selvedge (see page 194).

Sewn Cast-off Techniques

Here we have a group of casting-off techniques that are done with a tapestry needle. The advantages of these methods of finishing the edge are that they tend to be more expandable and more subtle in appearance than those that are knit off the needle. The disadvantages are that they are quite a bit slower to do and they require skill to make the stitches a consistent size.

Because the entire length of yarn must be pulled through each stitch, the wider the edge, the more the yarn will fray. This fraying is exacerbated in any yarn that is nubby or fluffy, and some yarns may be impossible to use at all. Therefore, unless the ends can be easily hidden so that several shorter lengths of yarn can be used rather than one long one, or the yarn is particularly smooth and strong, these techniques must be restricted to relatively short distances. For those situations where they are appropriate, the outcome is worth the extra effort.

out concern for fraying. It is not at all attractive, but still has its merits. It matches Stranded Cast-on and like it, is ideal when a completely unrestrained edge is needed for a stitch pattern with a great deal of lateral spread. It can also be used as a gathering strand, for instance at the top of a stocking cap. Last, but not least, it can be used as a temporary stitch holder when the stitches must later be picked up and worked in some other way.

1. From the last stitch measure a length of yarn equal to the width of the fabric plus an extra twelve inches or so.
2. Thread the end through a tapestry needle.
3. Slip the stitches off the knitting needle onto the tapestry needle one at a time. Wait to draw the yarn through several stitches rather than pulling it all the way through each one.

Elementary Sewn Cast-off Methods

This first group of techniques are all very simple to do. The first two are really quite utilitarian and would not be used on an edge that would show. The next matches a common cast-on edge and earns its keep for that reason alone. The last is simply a pleasant edge, useful when you want something quieter than the ubiquitous Chained Cast-off.

STRANDED CAST-OFF

This is the simplest possible method of securing the stitches and can be used on any number of stitches with-

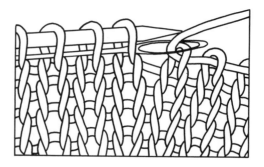

WORKING STRANDED CAST-OFF

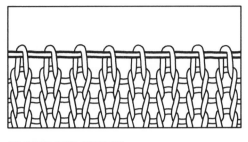

STRANDED CAST-OFF EDGE

DOUBLE STRANDED CAST-OFF

Here is a tighter version of Stranded Cast-off. The strand wraps twice around each stitch, reducing them considerably in size. For that reason, this works a bit better for gathering, as it looks neater and holds better.

1. Thread a sewing needle with the measured length of yarn, hold the needle bearing the stitches in your left hand, the sewing needle in your right.
2. Insert the sewing needle into the first two stitches on the nearside from right to left.
3. Draw the yarn through and drop the first stitch from the needle.
4. Repeat across the row, inserting the needle in the same way through the single last stitch.

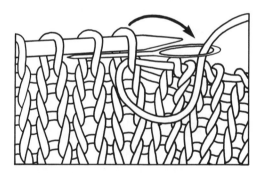

WORKING DOUBLE STRANDED CAST-OFF

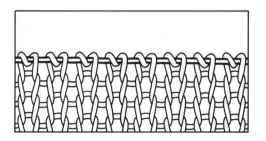

DOUBLE STRANDED CAST-OFF EDGE

HALF-HITCH CAST-OFF

This casting-off technique provides a perfect match for Half-Hitch Cast-on in appearance and structure, and is just as versatile.

In order to calculate the amount of yarn required, cast on ten stitches using Half-Hitch Cast-on, unravel it, and measure the length taken up by the baseline (the strand off your thumb). This measurement will be equal to what you need for casting off ten stitches. (If you are really organized and have inordinate amounts of foresight, you will write that figure down when you are casting on for your fabric, knowing that you will need it later for casting off.)

Thread the sewing needle and hold the needle bearing the stitches in the same way as for Double Stranded Cast-off, above.

If you are working on the outside:

1. Insert the sewing needle into the second stitch on the left needle as to Knit, allow it to pass under the knitting needle and out of the stitch on the right farside.
2. Draw the yarn through the stitch and tighten gently until the first two stitches are pulled together side by side.
3. Insert the sewing needle into the first stitch on the nearside from right to left, as to Purl.
4. Draw the yarn through the stitch and tighten gently. Drop the first stitch from the knitting needle.

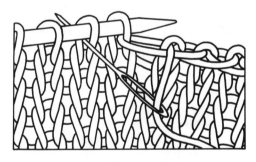

WORKING THE FIRST STITCH OF HALF-HITCH CAST-OFF

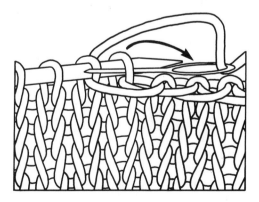

WORKING THE SECOND STITCH OF HALF-HITCH CAST-OFF

5. Repeat these four steps across the row.

6. When a single stitch remains on the knitting needle, pass the sewing needle through this stitch from nearside to farside, and then under the casting-off strand that runs between this stitch and the preceding one. Tighten to form a Slip Knot.

If you are working on the inside:

1. Insert the sewing needle into the second stitch on the left needle from the farside, allow it to pass under the knitting needle and out of the stitch on the nearside.

2. In the second step, insert the sewing needle into the first stitch on the nearside from left to right, as to Knit.

3. Draw the yarn through the stitch and tighten gently. Drop the first stitch from the knitting needle.

Worked in this manner, the outside edge will be identical to Half-Hitch Cast-on with Purl as the first row. If you prefer it to match Half-Hitch with Knit as the first row, work the inside version on the outside or vice versa.

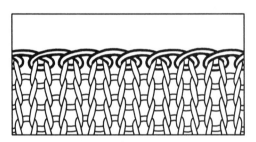

HALF-STITCH CAST-OFF EDGE

Try to maintain a gentle, even tension as you pull the yarn through the stitches. As you work, stretch the edge out from time to time to make sure you aren't making it too tight or too loose. It will be difficult to correct any inconsistencies if they are too far back, but if you catch them quickly, you can use the tip of your needle to even things out, working a little yarn back to a tight spot or out of a loose one. Be very careful to work through the center of each stitch; don't let the sewing needle split the yarn, as a split stitch will be unsightly and impossible to adjust. It helps if you wiggle the sewing needle while it is inside the stitch to make sure it has cleared. After using the technique a few times, you will develop a practiced hand and get good results.

I have seen an alternate method of working this from left to right. The needle bearing the stitches is placed in the lap or on a table with the tip to the left. It seems to me that you work against yourself that way; I find it much easier to do as I've suggested above.

BACK STITCH CAST-OFF

This method doesn't resemble any of the casting-on techniques, but it is easy to do and it's rather attractive. Because of the path of the yarn, the discard stitches forming the last row of the fabric are pulled slightly sideways and there is a little nub at the top of each column of stitches.

1. Thread the sewing needle and hold the needle bearing the stitches exactly as for Half-Hitch Cast-off, above.

2. Insert the sewing needle from right to left through the nearside of the first two stitches and draw the yarn through.

3. Insert the sewing needle from left to right through the nearside of the first stitch again.

4. Drop the first stitch from the needle.

5. Repeat the last three steps across the row.

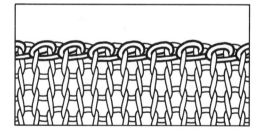

BACK STITCH CAST-OFF

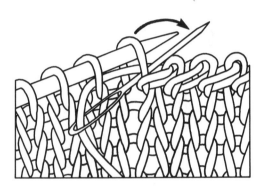

BACK STITCH CAST-OFF EDGE

Invisible Cast-off

Here is a marvelous technique that is actually related to grafting (page 371), but here used to cast off. Unfortunately, it is suitable only for Single Rib and Double Knit, but for those it is ideal both in terms of appearance and of elasticity. The edge produced is identical to that achieved with Alternating Cast-on and is essentially invisible.

Because of the problem of fraying, the technique is not generally used on wide edges, but I will provide instructions for how to use several short strands to get around this problem. That makes this technique available where it is most needed, casting off the edge of a Single Rib neckline. For that purpose alone, I urge you to make the effort to add this to your repertoire.

I suspect too few knitters use the technique because the instructions make it seem difficult. Well, the instructions may look lengthy, but the process itself is easy to do. Practice on a few sample swatches, going through things slowly, step by step, and you will have it in no time. It will be well worth the small investment in time.

There are two ways to work this cast-off, on the needle or off. I will show you the off-needle method first because it is most obvious with that version what it is you are doing and what path the yarn takes. The most accurate way to calculate the amount of yarn required is to cast on ten stitches using Alternating Cast-on, unravel the stitches, and measure the total amount of yarn used. This length will be equivalent to what is needed to cast off ten stitches. Allow a little extra, break the yarn at that point, and thread the sewing needle.

INVISIBLE CAST-OFF: OFF NEEDLE

After completing the last row of the fabric, remove the needle from the stitches. Place the fabric, with the yarn coming off the last stitch on the right side, on a table or some other firm surface and gently pat it flat. You will see that the Purl stitches line up in a row slightly behind the Knit stitches, with a trough between the two. The instructions are written for a Single Rib that starts with a Knit stitch.

1. Insert the sewing needle into the first Knit stitch from farside to nearside, then through the first Purl stitch from nearside to farside. Draw the yarn through and proceed as follows:
   • Step 1: Pass the needle again through the first Knit stitch, but from nearside to farside, then through the second Knit stitch from farside to nearside. Draw the yarn through.
   • Step 2: Pass the needle again through the first Purl stitch, but from farside to nearside, then through the second Purl stitch from farside to nearside. Draw the yarn through.
2. Repeat the last two steps, working a pair of Knit stitches, then a pair of Purls across the row.

Study the illustration carefully so you will understand the path the yarn is taking. Notice that the first stitch of each pair is the last stitch of the previous pair, and therefore the sewing needle will pass through each stitch twice, once in each direction. For each pair of stitches, Knit or Purl, the needle enters the first stitch

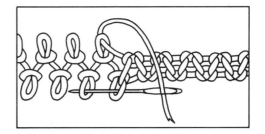

INVISIBLE CAST-OFF: OFF NEEDLE/WORKING TWO KNIT STITCHES

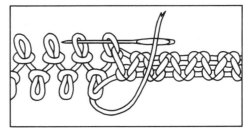

INVISIBLE CAST-OFF: OFF NEEDLE/WORKING TWO PURL STITCHES

from outside to center, then moves to the left in the little trough between the two ranks of stitches, and comes back out the second stitch of the pair. I find I say a little litany to keep myself on course—"to center and out, to center and out . . ."—as I work each pair. If you are having trouble keeping adjacent stitches from unraveling, pinch them with your left thumb and forefinger as you draw the yarn through the others. It is more difficult to avoid splitting a stitch with this method of working; make sure your sewing needle is blunt and watch carefully to see that you are truly going through the center of each stitch.

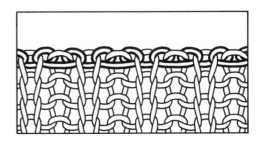

INVISIBLE CAST-OFF EDGE ON SINGLE RIB

INVISIBLE CAST-OFF: ON NEEDLE

This version is a little more confusing to learn, but once you grasp the idea I think you will find it easier to do than the off-needle version. There is less chance of splitting a stitch, and because there is no danger of having an unbound stitch ravel down, it is easier to draw the yarn through and tighten up the edge evenly.

Keep in mind that this is Single Rib—each pair of Purl stitches that must be linked together is separated on the needle by a Knit stitch, each pair of Knit stitches is separated by a Purl. Keep the illustration at hand the first few times you try this and be encouraged—it only looks difficult.

Calculate a length of yarn in the same way as given in the off-the-needle version, above. Hold the needle bearing the stitches in your left hand. I am going to assume that the first stitch is a Knit stitch.

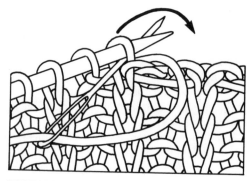

INVISIBLE CAST-OFF: ON NEEDLE/WORKING THE FIRST KNIT STITCH

1. Insert the sewing needle into the first stitch as to Purl. Draw the yarn through and proceed as follows:
   • Step 1: Insert the sewing needle from farside to nearside between the first and second stitches, pass it around the nearside of the Purl stitch from right to left and back through the center of the stitch to the farside. Draw the yarn through the center of the stitch to the nearside.
   • Step 2: Insert the sewing needle into the first Knit stitch on the nearside from left to right as to Knit, drop it from the knitting needle, and draw the yarn through toward the nearside.
   • Step 3: Insert the sewing needle into the nearside of the second Knit stitch from right to left as to Purl. Draw the yarn through the stitch.
   • Step 4: Insert the sewing needle into the first Purl stitch from right to left as to Purl, drop it from the knitting needle, and draw the yarn through.
2. Repeat these four steps across the row, each time working a pair of Knits or a pair or Purls.

Once you become somewhat familiar with the motions, you will recognize that you are working into the first two stitches as to Knit and into the second two as to Purl.

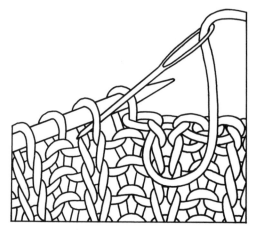

INVISIBLE CAST-OFF: ON NEEDLE/WORKING THE SECOND KNIT STITCH

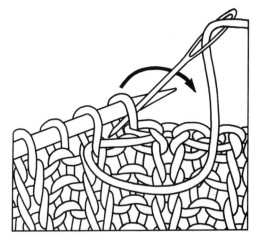

INVISIBLE CAST-OFF: ON NEEDLE/WORKING THE SECOND PURL STITCH

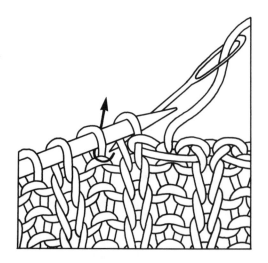

INVISIBLE CAST-OFF: ON NEEDLE/WORKING THE FIRST PURL STITCH

INVISIBLE CAST-OFF FOR A WIDE EDGE

It is only possible to use Invisible Cast-off on a wide edge with the use of more than one strand for sewing in order to limit fraying. The two ends of yarn that result every time a new strand is introduced must be carefully secured and hidden so that no evidence of them can be seen. Try this on a sample before you attempt it on your actual garment, and if it doesn't work well, select another method of casting off.

As you pass the needle between two Knit stitches or between two Purl stitches, you will be forming a Purl-like nub that lies in the trough between the two tiers of stitches. It is here that you can join another strand of yarn.

1. After working step 4, above, leave an end of yarn about eight to ten inches long and abandon the original strand.

2. Pick up another strand, leave a similar length end, then work step 1 above and continue with the casting off.

3. To finish the edge, thread the end that emerges from the left-edge stitch into a tapestry needle. On the inside, wrap the two strands around one another to interlock them, then pass the needle under the side of the Knit stitch to the left. Work the end down the side of the column of Knit stitches to hide it, duplicating the path of the yarns in the right half of each stitch.

4. Adjust the interlock at the edge so it is unobtrusive and then work the other end down the column of stitches to the right in the same manner.

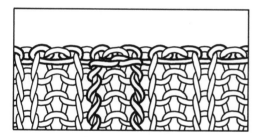

HIDING ENDS ON WIDE INVISIBLE CAST-OFF EDGE

Working between steps 4 and 1 places the ends on the farside and should be used if you are grafting with the outside facing you. If you are grafting with the inside of the fabric facing you, change strands between steps 2 and 3 instead. You will be able to find where this was done if you look for it on the inside, but it will be completely invisible on the outside and it will not restrain the edge in any way.

INVISIBLE CAST-OFF FOR DOUBLE RIB

While it is possible to use the same grafting technique to cast off Double Rib, it is more difficult than the Single Rib version. The result is somewhat less elastic than is desirable, but in practiced hands it is reasonably attractive, although it distorts the two/two pattern of the rib somewhat.

The instructions for doing the cast-off with the

stitches on the knitting needle are so complex I doubt I could persuade any of you to try it, so I'm not going to bother with that. With the stitches off the needle it is frequently difficult to keep them from unraveling, so the best thing is to take only as many stitches off the needle at a time as is absolutely necessary.

Keep in mind that the principle is basically the same as that for Single Rib, and the initial preparatory step is the same. You will be working pairs of stitches, first a pair of Knit stitches on the nearside, then a pair of Purls

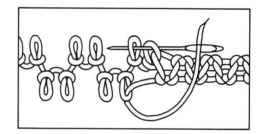

INVISIBLE CAST-OFF FOR DOUBLE RIB/WORKING AN ADJACENT PAIR OF PURL STITCHES

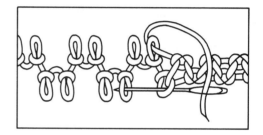

INVISIBLE CAST-OFF FOR DOUBLE RIB/WORKING A SEPARATED PAIR OF KNIT STITCHES

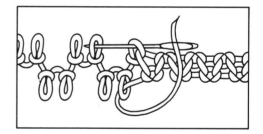

INVISIBLE CAST-OFF FOR DOUBLE RIB/WORKING A SEPARATED PAIR OF PURL STITCHES

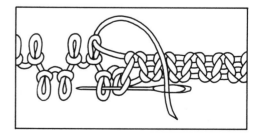

INVISIBLE CAST-OFF FOR DOUBLE RIB/WORKING AN ADJACENT PAIR OF KNIT STITCHES

on the farside. Each stitch must be worked twice, so the first stitch of each pair will be the last stitch of the preceding pair on the same side. Any pair of Knits will be worked from near to far on the first stitch, from far to near on the second; any pair of Purls will be worked from far to near on the first stitch, from near to far on the second, just as with Single Rib.

The only real difference lies in the fact that Double Rib has a two/two pattern, so if you have last worked a pair of Purl stitches that are side by side, the next pair will consist of Knit stitches that lie to the right and left of the two Purl stitches. Next you will work two Purl stitches that have a pair of Knits between them, then a pair of Knits that are side by side, and again a pair of Purls that are side by side, and so on. Refer to the diagrams as you go and it will soon make sense.

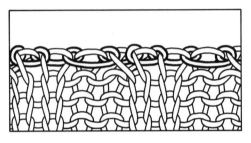

INVISIBLE CAST-OFF EDGE ON DOUBLE RIB

GLOSSARY OF CASTING-OFF TECHNIQUES

Back Stitch
Sewn technique. Decorative. Creates consistent edge. Easy to do.

Border
Used to work border and cast-off simultaneously.

Corded
Similar to Border. Produces corded edge.

Decrease
Identical to Pullover. Excellent method for creating consistent stitches. Easy to do.

Double Stranded
Sewn technique. Similar to Stranded but tighter, excellent for gathering. Easy to do.

Half-Hitch
Sewn technique. Identical to Half-Hitch Cast-on. Versatile. Easy to do.

Invisible
Sewn technique. Identical to Alternating Cast-on. Excellent for Single Rib and Double Knit. On and off needle versions.

Invisible for Double Rib
Sewn technique. Possible, but not particularly attractive.

Joinery
Used to join and cast off two fabrics simultaneously. Plain and decorative versions.

Picot Chain
Pullover with added length. Good for contoured edge.

Pullover
All-purpose. Identical to Chained Cast-on. Easy to do.

Single Crochet
Identical to Pullover. Made with crochet hook.

Slip Stitch
Identical to Pullover in structure. Creates firm, inelastic edge. Especially good for dense patterns, motifs, and buttonholes. Easy to do.

Stepped
Method of sloping a cast-off edge. Generally used for shoulder lines.

Stranded
Sewn technique. Matches Stranded Cast-on. Unrestrained edge; useful for gathering. Unattractive. Very easy to do.

Suspended
Identical to Pullover. Controls size of stitches. Awkward to do.

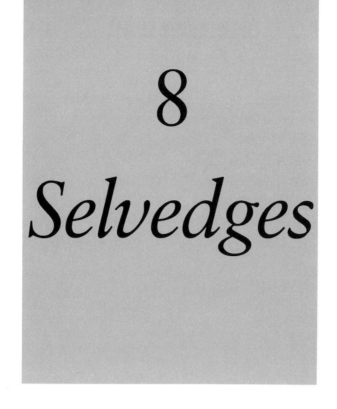

8
Selvedges

T he selvedge consists of one or two columns of stitches at each side edge of the fabric. These stitches are frequently worked in a different way from the stitches in the main body of the fabric in order to create some special effect. Most commonly, the aim is to create an edge that is easy to seam, easy to pick up stitches along, or that will lie flat and look attractive if left unfinished in any other way.

The appearance and function of the selvedge is an aspect of knitting too often ignored. The various techniques are all very simple to do, but it is important that the one chosen is appropriate for the purpose it must serve and that some thought be given to its relationship to the stitch pattern and any shaping units placed along the edge to create a slope or curve. Let's look first at the methods of making selvedges, and then we will turn our attention to how they are used.

Basic Selvedges

The two basic selvedges used by most knitters on virtually every fabric they knit are the Stockinette and the Chain. I'm not sure why they elicit so much controversy, but they do, with adherents of one or the other claiming it to be the only acceptable way to work. Actually, they both have something to offer, and much depends on the circumstances. A little knowledge about what is really going on here is obviously in order.

STOCKINETTE SELVEDGE

This is a good all-purpose selvedge, excellent for seams and a good choice if you plan to pick up the stitches along the edge to knit in the other direction (see page 190).

Outside row: Knit the first and last stitches.
Inside row: Purl the first and last stitches.

When you Knit or Purl the last stitch of the row and turn the work, you will immediately Knit or Purl that last stitch again. The yarn doubles back on itself as it goes from the stitch below to the one above, creating a bit of a nub on the Purl side of the selvedge column. The result is not particularly attractive—if you are working

an edge that will show, you may want to choose one of the more decorative selvedges described below.

CHAIN SELVEDGE

This version of Chain Selvedge seems to be the easiest to describe, and for a knitter to remember.

• Slip the first stitch of every row.

A Chain Selvedge produces an enlarged column of Stockinette along the edge, each stitch spanning two rows. Unlike regular Stockinette Selvedge, there is no nub, as the yarn does not double back on itself. It is attractive, although quite open, and the stitches are a consistent size, so it is suitable for use on edges that will show. It does nothing to prevent curl, but could certainly be used with any stitch pattern that lies nice and flat.

When I first began to look at the Chain Selvedge, it seemed odd that there were so many ways to do one when the edge itself was so simple. Upon close examination it became clear that the variations don't produce different results; they are just different methods of working, some of them more or less efficient than others, which simplifies matters quite nicely.

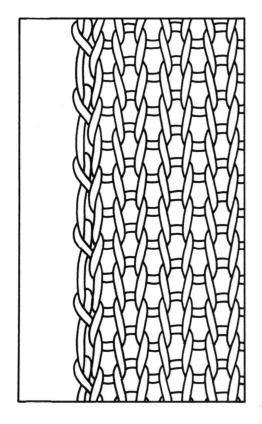

STOCKINETTE SELVEDGE

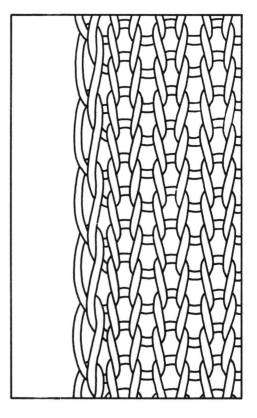

CHAIN SELVEDGE

The most common variation is to slip the first and last stitch of one row, and Purl these stitches normally on the return row. Now if you stop to think about it, this creates the identical chain as the selvedge above, with the edge stitches worked only every other row, the only difference being that the stitches are slipped on the same row insead of alternate rows. The problem here is with the left selvedge. When you turn the work after the Knit row, you will find the yarn coming off the second stitch on the left needle. You must then draw it from left to right across the slipped stitch and then work it. This is rather awkward. I have also seen a Chain Selvedge pattern calling for the knitter to slip the last stitch of every row. This simply creates the problem on both sides. I can't see any advantage whatsoever in either method, especially since the outcome is fundamentally the same.

Another variation is to slip the first stitch of every row knitwise. You can certainly do that if you wish, but if you were to forget for a few rows and start slipping the stitches purlwise, I'm sure you couldn't tell the difference. I have also seen instructions to slip the first stitch on the Knit row from the farside, and slip the first stitch of the Purl row knitwise. This turns the stitch in toward the fabric on the Knit side, but the turn is undone when you work the stitch on the next row, so there's no point in going to the trouble. It winds up looking and behaving just like the others.

CHAIN SELVEDGE FOR STOCKINETTE

There is one variation on Chain Selvedge that is technically superior because of its ease in working with any stitch pattern based on Stockinette. The advantage is lost, however, if you are not working Knit on one row, Purl on the next. When you are, this is the way to go.

Knit row: Slip the first stitch knitwise.
Purl row: Slip the first stitch purlwise.

Since the outcome is basically the same whether you slip the stitch knitwise or not, the two selvedges will have the same appearance. What's the point? As you know, the correct position of the stitch is with the right side of the stitch on the nearside of the needle. When you complete a row and turn the work, notice that the yarn comes down the nearside of the needle, passes through the stitch below and hangs down right under the needle tip. If you wish to Knit, slipping the first stitch knitwise turns the stitch on the needle, bringing the yarn to the farside, in the correct position to Knit the next stitch. If you wish to Purl, however, the yarn is already in the correct position on the nearside and there is no need to turn the stitch.

Stockinette vs. Chain

The Stockinette Selvedge works well for seaming or for picking up stitches on a fabric made in medium weight yarn. With one selvedge stitch per row it is easy to work into, and there will be no gaps at the join. However, when working with a heavy yarn, having so many stitches turned inside may cause the join to be unacceptably bulky. In that case, the Chain Selvedge may be preferable as it contains only half as many stitches; it does, however, require a special way of working a seam or picked-up stitches to prevent gaps appearing. At the other end of the spectrum, when the fabric is worked in a very fine yarn, the stitches in a Stockinette Selvedge can be so tiny that they are difficult to see, whereas those of a Chain Selvedge are a much more manageable size and yet small enough to make a smooth join.

There are two very important discussions that I recommend you read before deciding which one of these selvedges to use, one on how they behave when seamed (page 366) and the other for when stitches are picked up along the edge (page 184).

Decorative Selvedges

Here is a group of selvedges that are nice to use along an edge that will not be seamed or have stitches picked up along it, and they are all very easy to do.

GARTER STITCH SELVEDGE

This is a very neat, trim selvedge, quite decorative, and generally used for edges that will be visible. It is, of course, the ideal edge for any pattern that relies primarily on Garter Stitch, but it has attributes that make it more generally useful. Because of its great elasticity, it works well for patterns that are either compressed, or that spread vertically, or for those which have a contoured edge to which it will generally adapt nicely. It also lies quite flat and therefore works to prevent some of the vertical curl of Stockinette Stitch. Although it is easy to see what you are doing, it is not a particularly good edge to seam or pick up stitches on because it produces a very nubby selvedge, but it can be handled well enough should that be necessary.

• Knit the first and last stitch of every row.

One of the odd things about this very old, very common selvedge technique is that the right and left sides actually look slightly different from one another when used on a fabric other than Garter Stitch. Should you really want them to match exactly, work as follows:

Outside row: Purl the first stitch, Knit the last.
Inside row: Knit the first stitch, Purl the last.

GARTER STITCH SELVEDGE

DOUBLE GARTER STITCH SELVEDGE

This selvedge multiplies all of the good characteristics of Garter Stitch Selvedge; it will lie flatter and have more vertical elasticity.

- Knit the first two stitches and the last two stitches of every row.

PENULTIMATE SELVEDGE

Isn't that a wonderful word? It means second-to-last and sounds ever so much more lovely. There are two versions of this type of selvedge and they are both quite decorative.

Penultimate Garter Stitch Selvedge
This forms a Stockinette Selvedge adjacent to a column of Garter Stitch. It is used when you want to work a border on stitches picked up along the edge.

Outside row: Knit the two stitches of the selvedge.
Inside row: On the right side, P1 K1: on the left side K1 P1.

When the stitches for the border are picked up, the selvedge will be turned to the inside leaving a column of Garter Stitch between the border and the main fabric.

Penultimate Chain Selvedge
This forms a Chain Selvedge with a column of Purl stitches in the second position. It may be used alone as

DOUBLE GARTER STITCH SELVEDGE

PENULTIMATE CHAIN SELVEDGE

a decorative edge or with a border picked up so as to turn the selvedge to the outside. In either case, the Chain Selvedge will close over the column of Purl stitches on the outside, hiding it completely.

Outside row: On the right side, Sl1kw, yns, P1; on the left side: P1 K1.

Right Inside: On the right side, Sl1pw, yfs, K1; on the left side: K1, P1.

SEED STITCH SELVEDGE

An attractive two-stitch selvedge that will steam nice and flat, is easy to do, and also has good resilience. I think it is prettier than the Double Garter Stitch Selvedge.

• K1 P1 on the first two stitches, P1 K1 on the last two stitches of each row.

SLIP KNOT SELVEDGE

Here, each selvedge stitch is formed of a pair of vertical strands with a tiny knot at the base. It is very similar in appearance to Garter Stitch Selvedge, but this one is not as elastic. It is quite attractive.

Outside row: Bring the yarn around the edge of the fabric to the nearside, Slip the first stitch, then take the yarn between the needle tips to the farside.

Inside row: Bring the yarn around the edge of the fabric to the farside, slip the first stitch, then take the yarn between the needle tips to the nearside.

This wraps the yarn around the slipped stitch and tightens it up. The area behind the double strands is quite open unless you are careful to keep good tension on the slipped stitch as you work the second stitch on the needle.

GARTER CHAIN SELVEDGE

This is so close in appearance to the Slip Knot Selvedge given above that they are indistinguishable. It's really a matter of which way you like to work.

Outside row: Slip the first stitch knitwise, Purl the last stitch.

Inside row: Slip the first stitch purlwise, Knit the last stitch.

YARNOVER SELVEDGE

This puts a Yarnover at the beginning of each row, which makes the selvedge quite open and decorative.

Outside row: YO, k2tog on the first two stitches, use Knit Over on the last two stitches (wrapping the yarn over the needle instead of under; see "Turned Knit," page 23).

Inside row: YO, p2togfs.

SEED STITCH SELVEDGE

YARNOVER SELVEDGE

In order to make the Yarnover on the Knit row, simply hold the yarn on the nearside as you insert the needle into the first two stitches; it will automatically pass over the needle as the decrease is worked. The Knit Over at the end of the Knit row turns the two decrease stitches on the needle in preparation for working them together on the next row. It is easier to do it this way than to have to slip and return them at the beginning of the row. If you forget to wrap the yarn the proper way, however, just turn the stitches as you would for Slip Slip Purl. On the Purl row, first wrap the yarn around the right needle as for a Purl-to-Purl Yarnover (up to the nearside, over the top, and under the tip to the nearside again) and then insert the needle for the decrease. In order to make the two sides even, wrap the Yarnover on the Knit side fairly loosely, the one on the Purl side somewhat tightly as it has further to go.

Selvedges Along Slopes or Curves

It is important to consider the placement of shaping techniques in relation to the selvedge. There are several alternatives, depending upon whether you wish to hide the increases or decreases as much as possible, or take advantage of their appearance decoratively.

Increases or decreases can be made on the edge stitches if you are using Stockinette Selvedge, but it will compromise seaming or picking up stitches (see page 365). It is far better to place the shaping units adjacent to the selvedge. Placing them right next to the selvedge will make them quite unobtrusive; placed a few stitches in from the edge will produce decorative bias (see page 171).

Making the Selvedge Neat

Particular care must be taken in order to make the selvedge stitches neat when they will show on the finished garment. Always place a good firm tension on the yarn as you work the selvedge stitch after a turn, and as you work the next stitch.

If you find that your selvedge stitches are enlarged despite your efforts to control the tension, this is probably because you are working on long straight needles. While you knit, the tips of your needles will be making relatively small movements, but the range of motion at the head of the needle is much broader. With the weight of the fabric hanging off the needle, a great deal of stress is placed on the selvedge stitches. This constant movement tends to enlarge them by pulling yarn out of the adjacent stitches. Not only will the selvedge be enlarged, but the nearby stitches will be constricted.

The best solution is simply to switch to a circular needle. If you cannot do that, work with your knitting down in your lap so that the weight of the fabric is well supported and try to reduce the amount of "wagging" your needle does.

Selvedges and Stitch Patterns

When the side edges of a garment are to be seamed, stitches for the selvedge must be added to the number of stitches required for the width of the fabric. A moment's thought will convince you: if no additional stitches were allowed, and four stitches, two on each side front and back, are included in the seams, you will reduce the overall width of the garment by whatever measurement four stitches represents in your stitch gauge. What's more, these stitches will be removed from the stitch pattern, which may distort it on either side of the seam.

It is not always evident whether selvedge stitches have been included in a commercial pattern. Presumably the pattern will turn out the correct size whether they have been explicitly included or are there by default. Nevertheless, if you would like to check, divide the number of stitches used for the width of the fabric by the pattern repeat and/or the stitches per inch of the gauge. If there are two left over, they are likely to be selvedge stitches.

To find out if they are included in a stitch pattern, you will either have to knit a sample or chart the pattern. The latter is not only quicker, but you will then have the chart to knit from. For more information, see page 412.

9
Contouring the Fabric

Certainly there are charming garments that can be made up out of simple squares, rectangles, and tubes. Elementary knitting patterns rely almost exclusively on simple shapes of that sort, and there are many venerable traditional styles that do as well. For the most part, these garments rely on color and stitch pattern rather than fashionable shape for their charm, and the best of them are very beautiful. However, as we all know to our respective despair or delight, human beings are not quite so simple; we have any number of curves and angles in our shapes, and the most comfortable garment is one that reasonably follows our natural contours. In order to accomplish that, we must turn our attention to the techniques that will allow us to shape the edges of the fabric in slopes or curves or create three-dimensional shapes more complex than a tube.

There are two basic concepts used for these purposes. One of them, by far the most common and versatile, has to do with the adroit placement of increases or decreases either within the fabric or at the edge. As the stitch count changes, the contour of the fabric will change as well. The other is a technique called Short Rows, which allows you to work some columns of stitches more than others. The latter is considerably less well known and more limited in application, but what it does it does very well indeed, and you will find many interesting and useful things to do with it.

Slope and Bias

In the introduction to the section on how to work the various increases and decreases, I mentioned that they can be used either to shape the fabric or for decorative purposes. Let's look more closely at how they can be used to make fabrics with slopes and curves. When used for shaping, the techniques may be placed in such a way as to either gather the fabric, force the edges to slope at an angle or in a curve, or change a flat fabric into a three-dimensional one. Used in a different manner, the same techniques will cause all or some of the stitches to move on the bias. The methods used for making bias fabrics are discussed here; that on bias stitch patterns can be found on page 471.

Shaping the Fabric

As you know, each increase or decrease technique has a distinctive appearance, whether quiet or decorative. However, in terms of altering the dimensions and contour of the fabric, the particular technique chosen is less important than the number and distribution of the shaping units, as they all behave in much the same way in this regard.

Edge Slope
In order to make more than a simple square fabric, it is essential that you understand how to slope the side edges. The angle of any slope is determined by how many stitches are added and how frequently the shaping units are spaced along the edge of the fabric. If one increase or decrease is worked every row, for instance, the fabric will become wider or more narrow relatively rapidly, while if worked every other row, or with several rows in between, the change will be more gradual. The calculations for working out a pattern for a slope of any kind can be found on page 437. For slopes more abrupt than can be achieved by working one increase or decrease per row, it is necessary to use casting on or casting off, but the same concepts apply.

When increases are distributed row by row along one side of the fabric in this manner, that edge would begin to slope out while the bottom and the other side edge remained perpendicular to one another. The columns of stitches that continue up from the original portion of the fabric, and those generated by the new stitches, will be vertical and perpendicular to the baseline. When decreases are used in the same way, the side

SLOPED EDGES

edge along which they are placed will slope in toward the fabric and the stitch columns eliminated will simply end where the slope cuts across them at an angle.

We are all familiar with the simple slopes used to taper a bodice or a sleeve, but the truth of the matter is, you can create any sort of shape you have in mind. For instance, two slopes can be alternated along one side of the fabric forming an attractive serrated edge that can be a nice way to treat the sides of a scarf or blanket; it is best done in Garter Stitch to avoid the problem of curling.

Edge Curves
Probably of more interest, however, is the use of the technique to create curves such as for armholes, sleeve

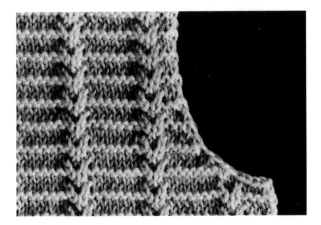

CURVED EDGE

caps, etc. In order to change a slope into a curve, use a series of short slopes, one after the other, all at a slightly different angle. Because a knitted fabric is so resilient, these small straight slopes will smooth out into a single long curve. If, for instance, you were to work a series of decreases, for a while working them one per row, then another group one every other row, then one every third row, the angle of the slope would be continually changing and thereby form the curve. More information on working out the pattern for a curve can be found on page 445 and page 522.

Gathering

Shaping units distributed in a horizontal pattern produce a very different effect than when they are placed vertically along a side edge. For instance, quite a lot of them spaced out evenly across a single row of the fabric will change the width abruptly. Using increases in this manner will cause the new portion of fabric to be gathered in soft folds; decreases will gather the original fabric in relation to the narrower new section. The columns of stitches and the side edges of both sections will remain vertical, except in the portion directly adjacent to the gathers, where the edge will be forced to curve just like the gathers do.

Everyone is familiar with the gathering that occurs where a ribbed wasitband meets the body of a sweater or where a ribbed cuff joins a sleeve. In that case, re-gauging (page 423) is used to change the width of the fabric. However, increasing and decreasing can be used in the same way to create ruffles, gathered peplums, shirred bodices, etc., without the need for a Rib pattern.

Changing Contour

When fewer shaping units are distributed across a row and several similar rows follow the first, the fabric will change size less abruptly. Instead of gathering, the columns of stithces will either converge or expand in a gentle slope or curve and the side edges will follow suit. Actually, the columns of stitches remain vertical, but what had been a flat two-dimensional fabric is forced to transform itself into a three-dimensional one; in effect, the entire center portion of the fabric puffs out like one large gather, producing a dome shape. The technique is commonly used to shape hats and mitten tips, and you may be familiar with certain of the Icelandic and Scandinavian sweater designs where the yoke and shoulder section is worked in the round and decreased in this manner.

A more specialized application of the principle of distributing shaping units within the fabric can be found in the techniques used to make Medallions (see page 119). These are flat fabrics worked with circular rows, either from the center out or from the edge to the center. The shaping units are positioned in such a manner as to push the outer circumference into curves or slopes.

Shaping with Bias

There are other methods of distributing increases and decreases within a fabric that, instead of forming gathers or domes, will not only shape the fabric but force certain of the columns of stitches to move on the bias.

If you stack a series of increases one on top of the other within the fabric, the columns of stitches to one side will remain vertical while those generated by the increases will slant away. When decreases are used instead of increases, the columns of stitches will march toward the line of decreases where they are absorbed.

The effect this has on the fabric is commonly seen on armholes for raglan sleeves in which, for decorative reasons, the decreases are placed three or four stitches in from the edge. The stitch columns between the edge and the decreases will run on the bias, parallel to the slope created and cutting across the vertical columns of stitches in the body of the sweater. A similar effect can be created by placing the increases used to shape a sleeve

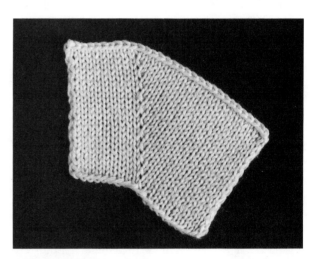

STACKED INCREASES

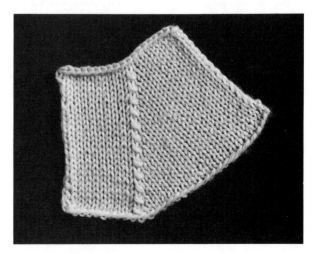

STACKED DECREASES

SLOPED EDGES WITH DECORATIVE BIAS

a few stitches in from the edge. Here again, the new stitches generated by the increases will move out from the fabric on the bias, parallel to the sloped edge.

As an aside, I understand this decorative element became popular with the introduction of inexpensive, factory-made knitwear cut and sewn from knitted cloth in much the same way any garment is made from woven cloth. In reaction, the bias was used by knitters as evidence that the fabric was made and shaped by hand rather than being cut and sewn. Its origins being long forgotten, it has remained a part of knitting far more because people are in the habit of working that way and now consider it fashionable than that they feel they have something to prove. Of course, once it was accepted as a mark of quality and fashion, the better machine-knit garments incorporated the bias as well. Do it if you like the way it looks, but by no means do it because you think that is the way an armhole or sleeve must be done.

Bias Fabrics

In the above examples, the shaping units not only created bias, but made the fabric wider or more narrow. When increases and decreases are strictly paired horizontally, and pairs are evenly spaced up a fabric, the bias is preserved but the number of stitches on the needle is held constant, and the fabric therefore remains the same width.

In Single Bias, the columns of stitches run at an angle from one side edge to the other. In Double Bias, the columns of stitches either converge from the edges to the center, or emerge out of the center and slope to each side. Anything from narrow strips of bias fabric, such as might be used as facings or to enclose the edges of a fabric (see page 210), to entire garments can be made in this fashion, although the latter can be quite complicated to plan and work. Regardless of the width, an understanding of how these bias fabrics are made is not only useful in and of itself, but will aid your understanding of the bias concept in general and will be particularly important when you come to the discussion on the use of bias in stitch patterns, below, which are far more

common than bias fabrics. Let's look, then, at how to make bias facings.

SINGLE BIAS FACINGS

When a series of increases is placed along one side edge and a matching series of decreases is placed at the other side edge, the stitch columns will move at an angle, emerging out of the increases and disappearing into the decreases, but the columns of stitches will remain perpendicular to the top and bottom edges. Therefore, the shape of the fabric will be that of a trapezoid. If you hold the side edges vertical, the bottom and top edges will be parallel but run at an angle with the lowest points at the decrease side, the highest points at the increase side. If, instead, you hold the top and bottom edges horizontal with the stitch columns vertical, the two side edges will slope.

There are a variety of techniques that can be used to create a narrow bias strip. I like the results of the method given here, which uses a rather specialized, but very simple and effective increase, and produces a bias running up from right to left. If you want the bias to run in the other direction, turn the strip upside down.

1. Cast on the number of stitches that, according to your gauge, will give you the width you require.
2. On the outside, make a Yarnover around the right needle at the beginning of the row, Knit to the last two stitches and work a Slip Slip Knit.
3. On the inside, Purl to the end of the row, Purl the Yarnover strand farside.
4. Repeat these two rows until the strip is the length you require, and cast off.

One important aspect that you must keep in mind when planning a bias strip, is that not only will it be narrower than the same number of stitches worked plain, but it will narrow further as it is pulled length-

SINGLE BIAS FACINGS, FLAT AND FOLDED

wise. To compensate, add a stitch or two more than your gauge would require for the width you want and then measure for accuracy before you continue; if necessary, rip out and adjust the number of stitches. A knitted bias strip does not have a great deal of stretch either horizontally or vertically; however, this is one of its advantages when used as a facing.

SINGLE BIAS WITH FOLDLINE

A Single Bias facing will fold along its length quite readily, although the result will be quite rounded. If you want a crisper foldline, you will have to create one at the center of the strip. I have seen books that recommend using a Twist Stitch to create a foldline, but I don't think it works very well. It is far better to use a Slip Stitch, exactly as for a Vertical Foldline on a normal fabric (see page 205), but it has some interesting characteristics when done on a bias fabric that have to be handled correctly.

- Work as for Single Bias, above, but on every inside row, Purl half the stitches, Slip one, Purl to the end of the row.

Both because the stitch to be slipped next does not lie directly above the last stitch slipped due to the bias, and because the stitch count changes on the Knit rows because of the increases and decreases, it is easier to make sure you are slipping the right stitch if you work it on the Purl rows.

Notice that the foldline falls along one side of the Slip Stitch instead of down its center and the slipped stitches are slightly enlarged and quite visible on one side of the folded strip, but not on the other; neither half is unattractive, but you may wish to take this into consideration when you apply it to your garment. If the center stitch of an odd number of stitches is slipped, the fabric will be wider on one side than the other, which may be an advantage in some circumstances.

DOUBLE BIAS FACINGS

In order to make a Double Bias strip, where the stitch columns move in two opposite slopes either toward or away from the center, it is necessary to use a second pair of shaping units. If, for instance, you were to increase at the right edge, work two decreases side by side at the center (or one double decrease) and another increase at the left edge, the baseline between the first paired increase and decrease will slope up to the right, the baseline between the second pair (a decrease, then an increase) will slope up to the left. The columns of stitches will be perpendicular to their respective baselines and will thus appear to run on the bias, converging where they are swallowed up by the decreases in the

DOUBLE BIAS FACING WITH CENTER INCREASES

center. The lowest point of the fabric will be in the center, below the decreases.

Should the decreases be placed at the outside edges, and the increases at the center, the shape will be reversed. The baseline between the first decrease and the increase will slope up to the left; the baseline between the increase and the second decrease will slope to the right. The columns of stitches will move out from the center toward the side edges where they are swallowed by the decreases. The lowest points of the fabric will be at the outside edges, again below the decreases.

While a Double Bias strip can be made using either method, generally the fabric folds more crisply when double increases are used in the center. In addition, there are more decorative increases to choose from, each of them producing a distinctively different foldline. If you are using a true double increase, cast on an uneven number of stitches for the fabric, using the center one for the foldline; if you are using paired single increases, cast on an even number of stitches.

CURVED DOUBLE BIAS

There is one double increase, which when used for a bias foldline, will pull the entire strip into a pronounced curve.

1. Cast on twice the number of stitches required for the width of the bias, plus one extra for the foldline.
2. On the outside, Knit two together, Knit to the center stitch. Make a Running Thread Increase, Slip the center stitch, make another Running Thread Increase. Knit to the end of the row and work a Slip Slip Knit.
3. On the inside, Purl across the row.
4. Repeat until the strip is the length desired.

Because the center stitch is slipped, the length of the strip along the foldline will be less than that along

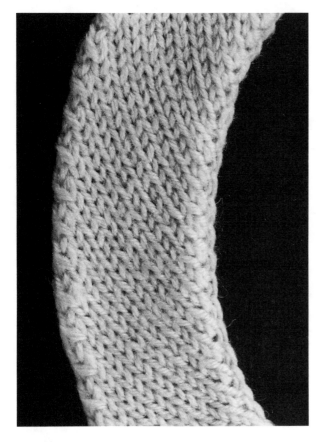

CURVED DOUBLE BIAS FACING

the selvedges, which when combined with the bias pulls the strip into a curve. It also tightens up the running threads on which the increases are made, minimizing the tiny Eyelet usually formed with that technique.

Barbara Walker provides an alternate version of this strip in her book *A Second Treasury of Knitting Patterns*,[1] which has two center stitches worked plain, flanked by Raised Stitch Increases. I find the increases less attractive and the foldline a little bulkier than the version I have given you here, but try them both and see which one you like.

Squaring the Corners

Whether you are making a narrow bias strip or an entire fabric, the bottom and top edges present problems because of their strong slope. While it is less important for a narrow strip, which can often be stretched or folded into place adequately, it is essential that the corners be squared on a bias fabric to be used for any garment other than a scarf. This can be accomplished by using Short Rows (see page 175) to fill in the missing areas of fabric.

First, of course, it is necessary to work out a pattern for the Short Rows, and in order to do so, you must

1. Barbara Walker, *A Second Treasury of Knitting Patterns*, New York: Charles Scribner's Sons, 1970.

determine what slope you need to achieve. On a narrow strip it is relatively easy to knit up a small sample and simply measure the width of the strip and the height of the missing portion (the length between the lowest point below the decreases and the highest point below the increases). Then use your stitch gauge to determine how many stitches and rows this involves and calculate the number of stitches per row to reactivate.

For Single Bias:
1. At a bottom edge, cast on the number of stitches required for the width.
2. Immediately inactivate all of the stitches and begin Increasing Short Rows at the side where the bias increases will be placed. It is not necessary to wrap the turning points.
3. Gradually reactivate all of the stitches row by row according to your pattern and then begin working the bias pattern.
4. At the top edge, work in the same but opposite way, this time gradually reactivating stitches from the side where the decreases are toward the side where the increases are.

For Double Bias with center increases, cast on the number of stitches for the full width, and start Increasing Short Rows at the center, working out to both sides. At the top, square first one side, then when that is done, work across the stitches of the other side and repeat the Show Row pattern on that half. If you have decreases at the center, work one side at a time at the bottom, then from the center out at the top.

Bias Garments

You will rarely see patterns for true bias garments, and with good reason. The effect that bias has on the top and bottom edges becomes more dramatic as the fabric becomes wider. Rather than work something like a sweater with true bias, generally the illusion of bias is created with stitch patterns of one sort or another that create a diagonal line, of which there are many.

It is certainly possible to design a garment that takes advantage of the edges created by bias. For instance, a garment front done in Double Bias with center decreases would have a deep V pointing down at the center. At the bottom, the edge would slope up toward each side; at the top the V could be used for the neckline. In one done with center increases, the V would point up. At the bottom the center would be at the waist and the edge would slope down toward each side. At the top, the point would have to stop at the neck and the edge would slope down toward the underarms, functioning somewhat like raglan armholes which would need to be filled in with sleeves of some sort.

Some patterns use ribbing to straighten the bottom edge, and in an oversized garment with little shaping this works reasonably well, but the lines of stitches will look distorted and there will be considerable blousing in certain areas and none in others.

The only way to work a true bias garment with a normal contour all the way around is to lay the entire garment pattern at a forty-five degree angle to the stitch columns and rows and use increases and decreases to accurately shape the slopes of every edge. A pattern of this sort can be done with a schematic drawing on graph paper and then the proportions carefully transferred to a garment chart from which you can work (see the section on Schematic Drawings and Garment Pattern Charts, page 511), but I'm not sure why anyone would go to the trouble.

Short Rows

Here is a fascinating technique that adds extra rows to a limited section within the body of a fabric. It can be used to form sloped or curved edges or the equivalent of darts. Most commonly it is used for shoulder lines and to turn sock heels, but it can also create a contoured edge, or add extra depth to cover a rounded back.

Short Rows work very much like either decreases or casting off, except that the stitches removed are only temporarily set aside, and are held inactive on the needle while the remaining ones are worked additional rows. The number of stitches being worked gradually increases or decreases row by row, progressing on a slope. Once the extra rows are completed, all of the stitches are brought into play again and the work continues in the normal way, or the sloped edge can be cast off. These slopes can be designed to move up from the outside edges of the fabric toward the center, or up from the center toward the outside edges. The exact nature of the slope should be worked out like any other, using the information in Calculating Steps and Points (page 437).

There is an elementary and an advanced way of working, both of which will be explained in detail. The former is more commonly known and used, but the latter produces by far the better result.

Decreasing Short Rows

This is the most direct and most common way of working Short Rows, and it is really quite easy to do. The structure of the fabric formed with Short Rows resembles a staircase. Generally the stitches are inactivated in groups called "steps" (although a step may consist of just one stitch), and the place between two steps will be referred to as a "turning point." The number of active stitches is decreased step by step, row by row until the slope is complete, at which point all the stitches may be

cast off, or reactivated. The elementary method of working Decreasing Short Rows forms a good introduction to the principles, so let us look at that first.

BASIC METHOD

In this example, Short Rows are used to create a slope starting from the left edge on the outside and moving up toward the right.

1. Starting on the outside, work across the row until only the number of stitches in the first step remain on the left needle. Turn.
2. Slip one stitch and work back across the row. Turn.
3. Work across the row until the stitches of two steps remain on the left needle.
4. Repeat the second row above and continue in this way, each outside row adding a step's worth of stitches to those which are inactive on the left needle, and slipping the first stitch of each inside row.
5. When there are no more stitches to be added to those which are inactive, work across the entire row, reactivating all of the stitches or casting them off.

In order to produce a slope from the right side up to the left, begin on an inside row, but otherwise work in the same way.

Each time a step is set aside, the adjacent stitches are worked two rows, one approaching the step, the other

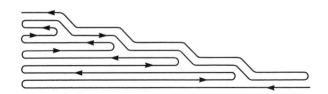

DECREASING SHORT ROWS

working away from it. Therefore, it is important to slip the stitch at the turning point to provide a smoother transition between one step and the next.

When you have reactivated all of the stitches, examine the work and you will see a small gap at each turning point. This can certainly be exploited as a decorative element, if you wish, and may very well be hidden by a highly textured yarn or stitch pattern, but most knitters prefer to find a way to avoid leaving this hole in the fabric.

WRAPPED METHOD

This method of working Short Rows produces a superb result with a nearly invisible transition from one step to the next. The technique is built on the basic method above, but includes some additional steps designed to close the gap. The result is so superior that I'm sure you will feel, as I do, that the extra effort is well worth it.

The trick in this case is to work a running thread from one side of the turning point, together with a stitch on the other side of the turning point, in order to pull the gap together. The precise method of working changes slightly depending upon whether the Knit or Purl face of the fabric will be the outside of the garment, and whether the slope is up to the left or up to the right. The important thing, here as always, is to grasp the underlying principle; once you understand how the technique works, you won't find it difficult to do. Let's look first at the same sort of slope discussed above.

Working the Short Rows

1. Knit the first turning point, slip one stitch, bring the yarn to the nearside, and return the slipped stitch to the left needle. (This wraps the running thread around the first stitch on the inactive side of the turning point.)
2. Pass the yarn to the farside, return the slipped stitch to the left needle, and turn the work.
3. Purl the next stitch with a very firm tension, drawing the two stitches on either side of the gap into a clus-

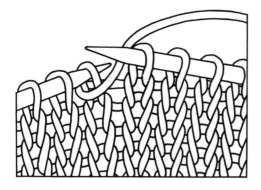

WRAPPING THE STITCH AT THE TURNING POINT

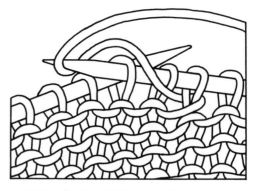

WORKING THE FIRST STITCH AFTER THE TURN

ter with the new stitch, then Purl across the remainder of the row normally.
4. Work the remaining turning points in the same way.

Reactivating the Stitches

1. Knit to the first turning point and slip the wrapped stitch to the right needle.
2. Insert the left needle tip up under the wrap at the base of the stitch and then into the stitch itself, transferring stitch and wrap to the left needle. Knit the stitch and the wrap together.

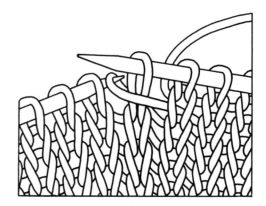

LIFTING THE WRAP AT THE TURNING POINT

Let's look at what has happened here. When the stitch is wrapped, the running thread passes from the last active stitch, across the gap at the turning point, around the inactive stitch on the other side, back past the stitch it emerged from, which is slipped, and into the next stitch. In other words, it detours to wrap around the stitch across the gap. The first stitch after the turn is slipped in order to make a smoother transition between steps. The reason for tensioning the yarn so tightly at the turning point is to prevent the running thread from being so long and loose that it will not close the gap effectively once it has been released from the stitch and worked into the decrease. When the stitches are reactivated, the clustered groups will relax into their normal positions within the fabric.

Wrapping from farside to nearside causes the strand

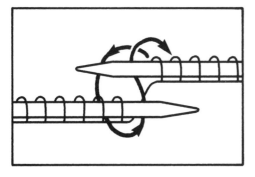

PATH OF YARN AT WRAPPED TURNING POINT

to cross over itself before it moves past the slipped stitch. Worked in this way, it will get caught up neatly against the inside of the fabric. If you do it the other way around, there will be a loose strand on the inside of the fabric and it will put less tension on the gap. And, of course, the decrease must be worked so the wrap is hidden on the inside.

Rules for Wrapped Turning Points

The above example is for just one slope, but Wrapped Turning Points can be used with any form of the Short Row technique. Here, in as concise a way as I can put it, are the basic rules for working Short Rows with Wrapped Turning Points in any situation.

- Always start the wrap with the yarn on the inside of the fabric.
- Always strand the yarn past the slipped stitch on the inside. (The wrap should cross over itself as you bring the yarn to the correct side of the fabric to strand past the slipped stitch.)
- Always cluster the stitches tightly at the gap.
- If you are reactivating the stitches on an outside row, join the stitch and the wrap with either a Knit or Purl Two Together in order to hide the wrap on the inside.
- If you are reactivating the stitches on an inside row, slip the wrapped stitch *knitwise*, reach down with the left needle and lift up the wrap, then transfer the turned stitch back to the left needle. Join the stitch and the wrap with either a Knit or Purl Two Together *farside* in order to hide the wrap on the inside.

Those of you who are already familiar with the technique will find these instructions slightly different from what you are accustomed to. In the way it is usually presented, the Short Rows are worked as in the basic method above, but without the Slip Stitch at the turning point. When the stitches are reactivated and a gap is reached, the tip of the left needle or a cable holder is used to retrieve a running thread from between the two stitches to the right of the gap. The running thread is then worked in a decrease with the stitch to the left. While the outcome is much the same, it is a real nuisance to dig up that running thread and get it onto the needle in the correct position, and the absence of the Slip Stitch makes the slope less refined. Finally, most instructions pay little attention to the direction of the wrap or the form of the decrease, which can lead to confusion and inconsistent results.

Shaping a Fabric with Decreasing Short Rows

If you cast off the stitches on the row after you reactivate them, the edge of the fabric will slope up because the columns of stitches along one side have progressively more rows in them than those on the other side. If, instead, you continue working, the sections of fabric above and below the slope will be set at an angle to each other, with the Short Rows forming a wedge lying between the two. The bottom line of the wedge will be perpendicular to the columns of stitches in the lower portion, and the top line of the wedge will be perpendicular to the columns of stitches in the upper portion. If you work a right slope, the section above will angle off to the left; if you work a left slope, it will angle off to the right.

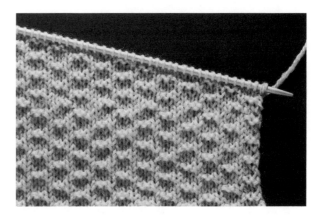

SHORT ROW SLOPE

When you work Short Rows at both sides simultaneously and then continue to work on all the reactivated stitches, the center of the fabric will have more rows in it than it has at each edge and will protrude in the center in exactly the same manner that a woven fabric does when you sew a dart at each side.

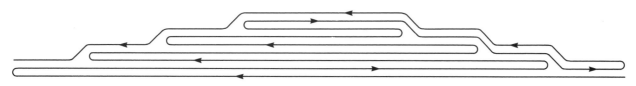

SHORT ROW SLOPES AT BOTH SIDES

It is, of course, important to balance the two sides so they have an equal number of steps and an equal number of rows. The extra rows inserted in the center will always be an uneven number. When the Short Rows are complete and it is time to reactivate the stitches, you will have to do so one side at a time. The first side to be reactivated should always be the one where the first step of the first Short Row lies. If you find yourself going down the other side, something is wrong.

Increasing Short Rows

In all the above situations, the Short Rows gradually retreat from the side edge, step by step. Much the same effect can be achieved by working in the opposite way, with Short Rows that gradually increase step by step. Decreasing Short Rows are far more common, but there will be times when working this way makes more sense or is essential. The sequence of things, although not the substance, is slightly different.

First, all of the stitches involved in the slope are immediately inactivated, and then reactivated step by step, so the number of stitches being worked continually increases. As before, it is easier to understand how this works when using the basic method.

BASIC METHOD

The illustration is for a single right slope.

1. On the outside, work one step, turn.
2. Slip one stitch and work back across the active stitches. At the edge, turn.
3. Work across two steps, turn.
4. Repeat the second row, and continue in this way, working one more step on each outside row and always slipping the stitch at the turning point.

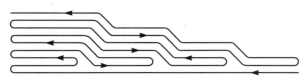

INCREASING SHORT ROWS

Notice that you must work across the turning point of the step in the previous row in order to reactivate the next group of stitches. If you wish to work a left slope, begin on an inside row instead.

When working from the center out, just as with Decreasing Short Rows, you must have an equal number of steps on each side with an uneven number of rows at the center. The first complete row before the Short Rows and the first complete row after will both be worked in the same direction on the same side of the fabric.

WRAPPED METHOD

The method of wrapping the turning points on Increasing Short Rows is basically the same, but because you must work across the previous turning point in order to activate the next step, you will be working first the decrease that closes the gap at the previous turning point, then a new step of stitches, then a new wrap, and so on. In short, instead of having the wrapping process and the decreases separated as they are when the Short Rows decrease, they are together here. The basic rules of how to wrap and slip the stitches and work the decreases remain the same as outlined above.

Decreasing vs. Increasing Short Rows

How do the two approaches differ in regard to the structure of the fabric? If the slopes contain the same number of stitches in each step for the same number of steps, the angle of the slopes will be identical. However, with Decreasing Short Rows, all the turning points will be at the top of the sloped section, directly under the row that reactivates all of the stitches. With Increasing Short Rows, all the turning points will be just above the last complete row at the bottom of the sloped section. Knowing this, you may decide for yourself where to place the turning points, depending upon where they will fall within the garment section and in relation to the stitch pattern you are using. This is, of course, more important to keep in mind if you are using basic Short Rows than ones with Wrapped Turning Points; but for all that the gaps disappear with the latter method, the way the rows lie will be subtly different. For some reason I can't explain, I find that Decreasing Short Rows produce a smoother fabric; that may be becuase I prefer working that way, but you could find that your hands produce just the opposite result.

Applications

Now that you understand the principles, let's take a look at the types of situations where Short Rows can make a difference in the quality and shape of a knitted fabric. Some of these applications are traditional, some are new, and once the technique is familiar to you, you will undoubtedly find innovative ways of your own to put it to use.

Short-Row Shoulder Lines

One of the simplest and most effective ways to use Short Rows is to slope a shoulder line. Once the slope is completed, the stitches of the back and front may be joined either by grafting (page 371) or by Joinery Cast-off (page 153). This produces a much smoother and more refined shoulder line than that achieved with Stepped Cast-off and a sewn seam.

SHORT ROW SHOULDER LINE SEAMED WITH JOINERY CAST-OFF

I am sure the technique hasn't been much used for this purpose because the basic method is the only one commonly known, and it leaves visible marks in the fabric. Since the shoulder line is at eye level, the marks are quite obvious. With the wrap technique, the result is so smooth you will find it difficult to locate the turning points even if you look for them. I now use this on virtually all of my shoulder lines, and I recommend you give it a try.

Short-Row Darts

Short Rows can also be used to add horizontal darts at each side of a garment front for a full bustline. The Short Rows will slope the darted portion, leaving fewer rows at the side edges than in the center. Choose whichever approach, Increasing or Decreasing, you feel will enhance or blend in with your garment design and stitch pattern. If you are working a fancy stitch pattern of some kind, continue the pattern as it is being worked on the active stitches without regard to which row of the pattern was last worked on the inactive stitches. There will be a break in the pattern along the line of the slope, more or less obvious depending on what sort of pattern it is, but this is no different than what would occur with a sewn dart, and the result is much smoother.

Shaping Length with Short Rows

Those of you with a rounded upper back will find that Short Rows provide a very nice solution to the problem of garments that don't hang correctly. In this situation, you will not want an obvious line such as a dart produces, so don't work all of the Short Rows consecutively. Using your stitch gauge and your pattern draft, determine how many extra rows are required at the center top back, and how wide they must be. Generally Short Rows that decrease in width from the shoulder blades toward the neck will work best. Distribute the extra rows evenly so you work one Short Row, then several rows on all of the stitches, then another Short Row, so as to blend them in as unobtrusively as possible.

Do keep in mind the effect on stitch pattern of having rows that are not worked all the way across. Distortion can be minimized in some patterns by placing the turning points adroitly so that the rows blend in as much as possible. On the other hand, if hiding them is impossible, consider turning the Short Rows themselves into a design element and make them very obvious instead.

Contouring a Cast-on Edge

There are several situations where Short Rows can be used to advantage along a cast-on edge in much the same way they are used to slope a cast-off one.

A useful example is that of a dolman sleeve, for which the stitches for the sleeves must be cast on at the side edges of the body. Generally these stitches are added gradually to produce a slope from side edge to wrist. Unfortunately, just as in Stepped Cast-off, Stepped Cast-on produces true steps, especially in a bulky yarn, and this can cause problems in seaming. The solution is to cast on all of the stitches required for the

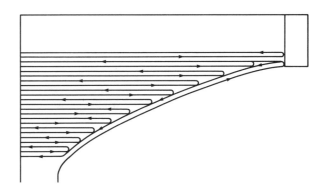

DOLMAN SLEEVE SHAPED WITH INCREASING SHORT ROWS

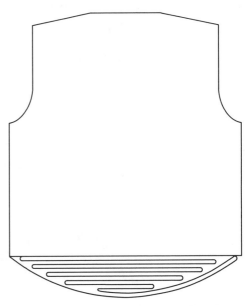

CURVED LOWER BACK SHAPED WITH SHORT ROWS

length of the sleeve at once, and then use Short Rows to gradually activate the stitches according to the same pattern you would have used for casting on. The edge will be perfectly smooth for seaming, and the Short Rows will take care of filling in the fabric above the slope.

Short Rows can be used in the same manner to curve any lower edge. The concept offers you a great deal of latitude in contouring the shape of an edge, either as a decorative element on its own, or in order to control the position and amount of blouson above a ribbing, for instance, where you might want more fullness at the center back than at the sides, or some at the sides and none at the center front. Detailed information on calculations for curves can be found on page 445.

Turning Sock Heels with Short Rows

The most common traditional use for Short Rows is turning sock heels. There are many different styles of socks and a variety of heel styles found in the pattern books, but for the latter they all employ somewhat the same principles. Due to space considerations, I cannot provide a full discussion on socks but can only touch on how this technique is applied.

Work the sock in the round from the ribbing down to the ankle, at which point temporarily inactivate half of the stitches at the instep. Work the remaining stitches flat into a square for the heel flap. This brings us to the heel cup, which is shaped with Short Rows combined with decreases. The Short Rows cup the fabric at the end of the heel flap by placing more rows in the center

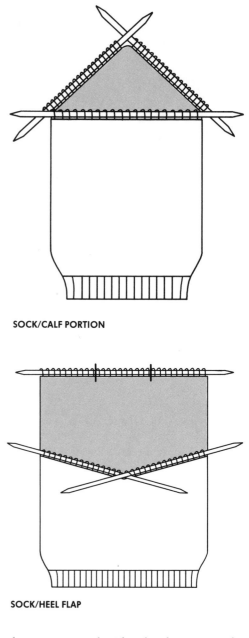

SOCK/CALF PORTION

SOCK/HEEL FLAP

than there are to each side; the decreases reduce the number of stitches, forcing the sides to curve in. Heel cups can be worked in slightly different contours depending on preference and the shape of the foot.

- For a wedge cup, work Short Rows that start on the center third of the heel flap stitches and lengthen one stitch per row to both sides, each one followed by a decrease prior to the turn. When there are no more stitches that can be decreased, the cup is done. This is a shorter cup, providing a good fit for a narrow heel.

- For a square cup, use Short Rows worked on a constant number of stitches at the center of the flap, with a decrease at the end of every row. The cup can be made narrow and long or wide and short, depending

CUFFED SOCKS FROM SWEDEN

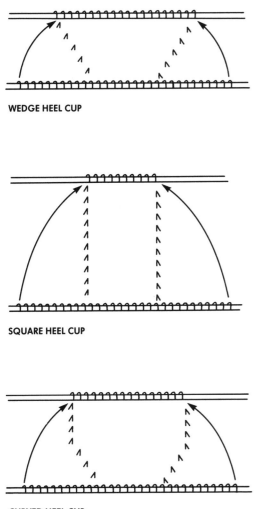

WEDGE HEEL CUP

SQUARE HEEL CUP

CURVED HEEL CUP

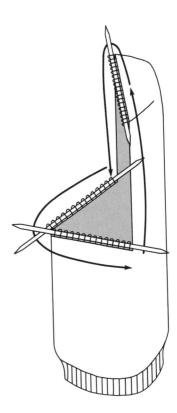

REACTIVATING THE STITCHES AFTER TURNING THE HEEL

upon the number of stitches used for the Short Rows.
• For a curved cup, combine the two, working first as for a wedge-shaped cup, then continuing as for a square cup. I think this produces the most natural shape.

Once the cup is turned, reactivate the instep stitches and pick up new stitches along the selvedge of the heel flap to rejoin the round. Gradually reduce the number of stitches with decreases to form Gussets at the juncture of heel flap and instep. When the number of stitches is correct for the circumference of the foot, continue the sock on a constant number of stitches to the toe. Shape the toe with decreases as necessary to create a comfortable fit, placing them to one side, to both sides, or all around, reducing the stitches to a few, which are then grafted together.

Working a sock is a good way to get a sense of how Short Rows can be used to form a cup shape. With that in mind, it is not too far to travel to discover the method of making a shaped hood or a cap such as a baby bonnet. See the chart for a sock on page 531.

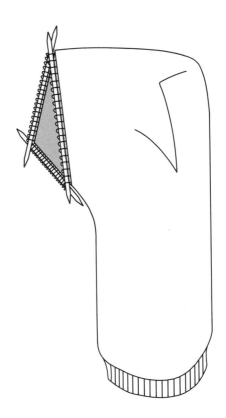

WORKING THE INSTEP

Short-Row Miter

There may be occasions when you will want to work a border pattern that must be knit narrow and long, either to be sewn on or attached simultaneously to picked-up stitches (see page 194). If the border is required to pass around a corner, such as it would on a square shawl, for instance, it will need a Miter. A Miter is a slope placed across the width of the fabric that causes the columns of stitches above the slope to run perpendicular to those below it. (The method of measuring for and calculating any Miter can be found on page 442.)

The most common method of working the slope of a Miter is with decreases. When all the stitches but one have been removed, the same number are picked up along the slope and gradually reactivated with Short Rows to complete the Miter.

Instead of using decreases and picked-up stitches, much the same effect can be had with Decreasing Short Rows. Gradually inactivate all but one of the stitches, then reactivate them again according to the same pattern with Increasing Short Rows. If Basic Short Rows are used, there will be rather large Eyelet-like holes along the line of the slope. You may consider these holes attractive or not, depending upon what it is you are trying to achieve and the sort of border pattern being used. The holes can be closed with Wrapped Turning Points, or the following method, which gives a slightly different look.

On an Outside Row

1. Work the active stitch(es), slip the first inactive stitch knitwise.
2. Insert the tip of the right needle as to Knit under a strand at the center of the gap between the slipped stitch and the next inactive stitch and pick up a new stitch. Pass the slipped stitch over the new stitch and off the needle.
3. Turn, slip one, and work to the end of the row.
4. Repeat as necessary until all the stitches are active again.

On an Inside Row

1. Work the active stitch(es), slip the first inactive stitch directly.
2. With the tip of the right needle, pick up the center strand in the gap, then insert the left needle into the farside of both strand and slipped stitch and Purl.
3. Turn, slip one, and work to the end of the row.

Short-Row Curve

A Miter is not the only way around a corner. Short Rows can also be used to push the side edge of a fabric into a curve. Generally speaking, this works best when the fabric is fairly wide and there are sufficient stitches for shaping so a curve results instead of an angle. In-

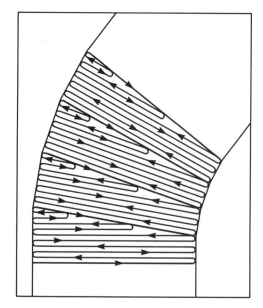

CURVING SIDE EDGES WITH SHORT ROWS

stead of the single sloped line of a Miter, in this case there are several slopes spaced out across the entire length of the curve. Working out a pattern for this sort of thing requires some care and attention, and it is necessary to make a full-scale draft so you can see clearly what is at work.

On your pattern draft, draw a pair of lines directly across the width of the fabric to identify where the curve begins and ends. Measure the length of the inner and outer curve between these two lines and multiply these measurements times your row gauge to determine how many rows are required for each one. The difference between the two is the number of extra Short Rows that are needed at the outer edge to create the extra length for the curve.

Divide the inner and outer curves into an equal number of segments, and draw lines directly across the width, dividing the curve into a series of equal wedges, like pie slices. Use Calculating Steps and Points (page 439) to work out the pattern for the slope of one wedge, or draw the wedge on graph paper in order to do so (see the information on garment charting, page 521). As you work, use the same Short Row pattern on each wedge to form the curve.

In this, its simplest form, all of the Short Rows lie at the top of each segment of the curve. In a complex stitch pattern, you may want to intersperse the Short Rows across the length of each segment in order to work them into the pattern in the most unobtrusive way. Barbara Abbey provides some exquisite examples of fine lace collars with this technique in her challenging and inspiring book, *Knitting Lace*.[1]

1. New York: Viking Press, 1974.

10
Picking Up Stitches

There are a variety of occasions when it is necessary to pick up stitches along an edge and knit them up in another manner, or in another direction. Actually, it is a method of joining two sections of fabric that should be used more often than it is, because then the line between them is far more resilient than if it had been sewn. On many traditional sweaters the stitches are picked up along a drop shoulder in order to work the sleeves from the top down, a convenient way of making sure the sleeve is the correct length, and when the cuff or elbow gets worn it can be ripped back and reknit. The technique can be used to add a collar to a neckline or a border to a cardigan, and to turn a sock heel. There are even occasions for picking up stitches within a fabric rather than at an edge, such as for applying pockets or ruffles.

Many knitters pick up stitches in a sort of hit-or-miss way, and patterns are frequently vague in their instructions on this point. The material here should help you feel confident about these situations, and once you get the idea you will never again stall about adding a neckline or border, or rush to the knitting shop hoping someone there will do it for you.

Picking Up Stitches Along an Edge

If you are planning to pick up stitches along an edge, you will need a selvedge stitch in addition to the stitches of the fabric because all or most of it will be absorbed into the join. As you know, there are a variety of these, but some of them work better than others for picking up. I think Stockinette Selvedge gives the best result in most circumstances, so I will use it to introduce the basic principles at work when you pick up along any edge. Other selvedges are then discussed with those concepts in mind so their limitations can be understood.

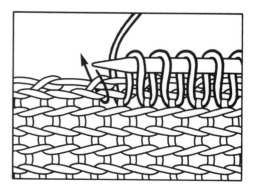

PICKING UP UNDER FULL SELVEDGE

Picking Up Along an Edge

Before you begin, examine the column of edge stitches so its structure and appearance are familiar to you. There are three possible ways to pick up these stitches. One can pick up the outer half of the selvedge stitch at the very edge, the inner side nearest the fabric, or both sides of the stitch. Each method of working will produce somewhat different results, which is worthwhile taking into consideration.

FULL SELVEDGE

This is the easiest method of picking up along an edge and forms an attractive but slightly bulky join between the two sections of material. When worked in this way the entire selvedge stitch is turned toward the inside of the fabric and will look like a chain. On the outside, there will simply be a row of Knit stitches perpendicular to the columns of stitches in the main fabric, and the two fabrics will be joined firmly and smoothly together.

1. With a single knitting needle in your right hand, hold the fabric in your left hand, with the outside facing you and the edge to be picked up on top.
2. Insert the tip of the needle from nearside to farside under both sides of the selvedge stitch. Wrap the yarn as to Knit and draw through a new stitch.
3. Continue in this way, bringing one new stitch under each selvedge stitch.

Another way to think of the process is that you are working into the spaces between the first two columns of stitches. The running threads of the new picked-up stitches will be wrapped around the running threads

BORDER WORKED ON FULL SELVEDGE

that lie between the selvedge and the adjacent column of stitches. Therefore, if you have trouble locating the next selvedge stitch to work under, the best way to find it is to stop looking for it. Stretch the fabric out slightly until you can see the space between the stitches and insert the needle into the next gap to the left.

You may encounter instructions in other books to use a crochet hook in picking up stitches. The outcome is the same, but the method given above is so easy to do, and so much less cumbersome than having to transfer stitches from hook to needle, that there is nothing to recommend that way of working unless you have inadvertently made the selvedge stitches so tight that you are having trouble bringing the yarn through with the knitting needle. In that case, the hook will undoubtedly help.

INNER SELVEDGE

With this version, only half of the column of selvedge stitches is turned to the inside, where it will look almost like a sewn whip-stitch hem. On the outside there will be a fairly complex, woven row between the original portion of the fabric and the new one done on the picked-up stitches. This is not particularly attractive, but it's acceptable, quite narrow, and is generally hidden behind the adjacent column of stitches from the main body of the fabric. This slight compromise in the appearance is compensated for by the reduced bulk of the join compared to the method given above.

• Work as above, but instead of inserting the needle under the entire selvedge stitch, insert it under only that side of the stitch which lies nearest to the fabric.

You will notice that one selvedge stitch is much like a normal Knit stitch and easy to pick up into, the next is knotted and more difficult. You may want to use a slender needle in the left hand for picking up, and the correct size in the right hand for forming the new stitches, working each stitch just as you would to Knit.

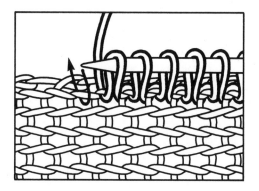

PICKING UP UNDER INNER SELVEDGE

If you have any problem locating the next selvedge stitch, let the adjacent column of stitches guide you, as they are more regular. You should keep your eye on those stitches in any case, to be sure you don't inadvertently work into the side of one of them. If you find you have, rip back and undo it, as it will destroy the smooth regularity of the juncture between the two fabrics.

This method of picking up does not work well if you have knit the original fabric at a loose tension. Because you are placing the new stitch on the side of a previous one, the latter is quite likely to stretch out, and gaps will appear at the join between the two fabrics.

OUTER SELVEDGE

If you pick up under the outer side of the selvedge stitches, the join will have no bulk whatsoever. Half the selvedge stitches will remain on the outside, and when the technique is used on a Stockinette fabric, they will blend in and be fairly inconspicuous. With any other stitch pattern, however, this half column of stitches would be quite obvious, in which case it may not be suitable to work this way. The first row of new stitches will be slightly irregular if you examine them closely, but generally look as they should. If your fabric was worked at a loose tension, you will have the same problem with gaps at the join as described above. In short, this isn't perfect, but the lack of bulk may be a priority for you in certain circumstances.

• Work as above, but instead of inserting the needle under the side of the selvedge stitch closest to the fabric, insert the needle above it, into the center of the selvedge stitch.

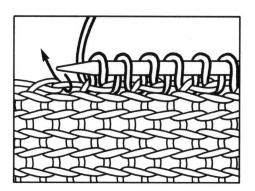

PICKING UP UNDER OUTER SELVEDGE

Here again, you may want to work with two needles instead of one, a small one in the left hand, the correct size in the right hand. When picking up into the "knotted" stitch, reach well around on the farside to pick up the strand at the outermost edge.

CROSSED SELVEDGE

If you have worked your selvedge stitches at a loose tension, and you want to pick up under one side of the selvedge stitch, the stitches will stretch out and gaps will appear, as I mentioned above. By far the best solution is to work under both sides of the selvedge stitch instead, but if you feel that reducing the bulk of the selvedge is critical, you may be able to correct the problem if you pick up in such a way that the selvedge stitch will cross on discard. This will also work if you are picking up along a Chain Selvedge (see below).

- Use two needles. Work as above, but insert the left needle into whichever side of the selvedge stitch you wish to pick up so the right side of the strand is on the nearside of the needle, then, with the right needle, Knit or Purl farside.

On a Stockinette Selvedge it is very difficult to cross the tighter selvedge stitches; cross only the open ones and either skip the tight ones or work them plain.

Picking Up as to Purl

It is easiest to work into the selvedge correctly if you do so with the outside of the fabric facing you, and in most cases that is the way you will be working. However, there are times when it is essential to work the other way in order to begin knitting at a particular point. In this case, you must work as to Purl so the selvedge is turned toward the inside of the garment.

- With the inside of the fabric facing you and working from right to left, insert the needle under the selvedge stitch from farside to nearside and wrap the yarn as to Purl.

You may pick up in any of the ways discussed above, although should you need to do so, crossing the selvedge stitches will be a bit more awkward. If necessary, in order to make sure you work under only the selvedge stitches, curl the edge toward you so you can also see the adjacent column of stitches, then insert the needle.

Alternate Method of Picking Up

Many books suggest a method of picking up where a relatively slender needle is slipped under all of the selvedge stitches along the edge. You can then begin knitting as if these were regular stitches on the needle. Unfortunately, working this way is somewhat awkward to do, it cannot be used to pick up under the entire selvedge stitch, and it tends to stretch the selvedge stitches out. Since it otherwise produces the same result, there is little to recommend it.

Picking Up Along Other Edges

There are a wide variety of edges along which you might want to pick up stitches, some of them with other selvedges than Stockinette, some with no selvedge at all. Let's look at how to deal with the other possibilities.

CHAIN SELVEDGE

In many books, Chain Selvedge is recommended as the best one to use for picking up stitches. It does have certain merits, and under some circumstances works well, but I do not think it is successful in most cases.

It is very easy to work into this selvedge because of the size of each stitch and the gap between it and the fabric, but on the other hand, the selvedge tends not to hold the new section of fabric firmly against the existing one. If you are picking up under both sides of the stitch, the join between the two fabrics is often reasonably good unless you have worked the fabric at a fairly loose tension, or the garment is planned to fit snugly and the join will be stretched out in wear. If you work under just one side of the selvedge stitches, the problem is exacerbated and the gaps in the seam can become quite obvious, although this can be largely corrected if you work as for Crossed Selvedge, above.

Because there are only half as many stitches in a Chain Selvedge as in a Stockinette Selvedge, there will be less bulk at the join. This can be a real advantage when working with heavy yarns, but you are likely to find yourself with considerably fewer stitches to work into than you require for the new section of fabric. You can work increases along the selvedge (see "Spacing Picked-up Stitches," pages 188–189), or pick up two stitches under each chain just as if it were Stockinette Selvedge. This is possible because while you have only half the number of stitches, you do have the full complement of running threads in a Chain Selvedge, one for each row.

As you know when you work under both sides of any selvedge stitch, you are really placing new stitches between the running threads. Technically, therefore, you can place one picked-up stitch on each row of a fabric with a Chain Selvedge without increasing. Unfortunately, while it is very easy to work into the gap that lies between each pair of running threads, the paired running threads themselves lie so close together it isn't easy to insert the needle tip between them. You may find it easier to skip a few stitches on a Stockinette Selvedge than to work this way along a Chain Selvedge.

Turning a Selvedge to the Outside

One of the very nicest ways to handle the edge along which you pick up stitches is to turn it to the outside rather than to the inside. This is particularly effective for use with a border on a center front opening, or

TURNING A SELVEDGE TO THE OUTSIDE

around an armhole for either a border or a sleeve knit from the top down.

1. Use a two-stitch selvedge, with the outer stitch done as either Stockinette or Chain Selvedge and the inner one in Reverse Stockinette.
2. On the inside, the inner stitch of the selvedge will form a column of Knit. Hold the fabric with the edge to the right and pick up into these stitches, inserting the needle from right to left under just that side of the stitch which lies closest to the edge and wrapping the yarn as to Purl.

The picked-up stitches tighten the inner column of stitches of the selvedge, and they virtually disappear, while the column of stitches at the very edge are turned to the outside and completely cover the join between the two fabrics. If you have used Stockinette Selvedge, it will look like a column of tiny braid; if Chain Selvedge, like a smooth, enlarged column of Knit stitches. Both

are very attractive, but the former is more subtle and hardly noticeable, the latter far more decorative.

Because of the way the pickup process tightens up the adjacent stitches, it is necessary to pick up into every stitch in the column to avoid irregularities. If your border pattern requires fewer stitches than that (see the discussion on spacing picked-up stitches along the edge, below), there are two solutions. First, you could pick up with very small needles, and then switch to the size needle you require and place a few carefully spaced decreases on the first row of the border. The small needle will make the picked-up stitches smaller and help to hide the decreases behind the selvedge. (They also make the pickup process easier to do, so you might want to use them in any case.) Second, you could regauge your border (see page 423) if this will not compromise its appearance or behavior; regauging is particularly effective with Rib patterns, which always look nice when they are done firmly.

If you are going to use this on an edge that will require shaping, such as an armhole, place any shaping techniques adjacent to the column of Reverse Stockinette, leaving it undisturbed. If you use a right decrease on a left edge, a left decrease on a right edge, the slope of the facing stitch of the decrease will follow the slope of the selvedge when it is turned out.

It is possible to achieve somewhat the same effect by picking up on the inside into the running threads adjacent to a selvedge. This tends to tighten up the adjacent stitches too much, it is more difficult to do (you need two needles and must use Purl farside), and it is not easy to find each running thread along a Chain Selvedge. Also, if you don't work into each one, the edge will be seriously constricted. It is far better to plan ahead with the two-stitch selvedge described above, or, if you have not done that, to turn the selvedge to the inside.

GARTER STITCH SELVEDGE

Because Garter Stitch compresses vertically, it generally has twice as many rows as stitches per inch in its gauge. This is very convenient if you are going to pick up stitches to add a second section also in Garter Stitch; just pick up along the edge, working under the full selvedge between the Purl rows.

If you are working with some other stitch pattern that requires more stitches than that method would provide, you can work two stitches between each Purl row. If you examine the structure of the fabric carefully, you will notice that there is a running thread that lies between the Purl rows; make one new stitch to the right of this thread and one to the left.

Both because it is so compressed, and because it switches from Knit to Purl, this makes a rather nubby selvedge, but it's very neat.

BORDER ATTACHED WITH SLIP STITCH JOIN

FABRIC WORKED ON STITCHES PICKED UP ALONG KNOTTED EDGE

Cut or Knotted Edges

If you prefer to knit in the round, you can knit a tube from waist to neck and cut the openings for armholes, neckline, and a center front opening. The cut edges can be secured with machine stitching, or by using a Steek and knotting them (see page 113). Regardless of how you secure the edges, the pickup process is basically the same as when you pick up along a selvedge.

• Insert the needle between the running threads of each row, adjacent to the stitching that secures the edge.

Horizontal Edges

When it is necessary to pick up stitches along a top or bottom edge, it is far better to remove the edge and free the stitches (discussed on page 190). However, there is one interesting and decorative way to make use of picked-up stitches along a Chained Cast-off edge that is similar to turning a selvedge to the outside.

• Work on the inside of the fabric, and insert the needle as to Knit under both sides of the cast-off stitch in order to pick up new stitches or insert the needle down into the head of the stitch discarded below the cast-off edge.

A CAST-OFF EDGE TURNED TO THE OUTSIDE

The former is the easiest way to work, but I think the latter gives a better result. In order to accomplish it, however, you must study the edge and learn to see the stitch you need to work into.

You will see that the entire chain of the cast-off edge is turned to the outside of the fabric, forming a decorative row of stitches running perpendicular to the columns of stitches. It's really quite attractive, and there's no reason to restrict its application to the juncture between fabric and border—it can also be used to create horizontal stripes within the body of the fabric itself, or along a slope created by Short Rows (page 175). Simply cast off using a Chained Cast-off on the Knit side, turn the work, pick all the stitches up again, and continue.

Spacing Picked-up Stitches

The number of stitches to be picked up is calculated in the normal way on the basis of the width required for the new section of fabric and the stitch gauge of the pattern you will be using on it. The rule for doing this correctly is to avoid working with a measurement taken from the edge along which you will pick up the stitches, because it is nearly impossible to do that accurately on a fabric as stretchable as a knit. What you want is the measurement the fabric *should* be once it is cleaned and dressed, and information on how to obtain that is to be found on page 351.

The number of selvedge stitches available along an edge is almost never the same as the number of stitches that it is necessary to pick up. You may wish to try regauging the border pattern (see page 423), using a larger or smaller needle as necessary; however this may be more work than spacing the stitches along the edge in such a way as to pick up the necessary number.

When you require more stitches than there are rows available, you must work into some selvedge stitches twice; if you require less, you must skip some selvedge stitches. Those stitches which are either skipped or worked twice must be spaced at regular intervals along the entire edge in order for the two sections of fabric to fit together smoothly. The method for working out this sort of pick up pattern can be found in "Calculating Steps and Points," page 444.

Spacing Along Stockinette Selvedge

On the existing fabric, each Stockinette selvedge stitch represents one row. This is true regardless of whether the edge is straight, sloped, or curved. If there are more selvedge stitches than you require, simply skip the appropriate stitches according to your pickup pattern; the skipped stitches will not be noticeable, particularly if you are working under the full selvedge. If there are less selvedge stitches than you require, it will be necessary to increase on some of them.

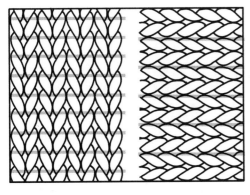

COORDINATING STITCH COLUMNS AND ROWS

Increasing on the Full Selvedge

- Pick up the first stitch under the inner side of the selvedge stitch, the second under both sides of the same stitch.

Increasing on the Inner Selvedge

- Pick up the first stitch under the inner side in the normal way. Then take up a second needle in the left hand and insert it from farside to nearside into the outer half of the same selvedge stitch and Knit farside.

Don't attempt increases when picking up on the farside of the selvedge stitches; the result is not attractive.

Spacing Along Chain Selvedge

Chain Selvedge contains half as many stitches as rows in the fabric, however, as we discussed above, you can pick up one stitch per row by working between each running thread. Therefore, when you need less picked up stitches than there are rows, work just as for Stockinette Selvedge and skip one running thread from time to time; it will not show at the join. However, when picking up one stitch per row will not produce enough stitches, it is impossible to use the increasing method described above for Stockinette Selvedge, as it will show. Instead, it is best to work increases spaced along the first row worked on the picked-up stitches. Unfortunately you cannot use the nice, quiet Raised Increase for this; however, there is a reasonable alternative.

- After picking up the stitches, turn and work an inside row, picking up an extra stitch as needed by reaching down into the side of a selvedge stitch where it lies at the base of the new fabric, much as you would to Purl a Running Thread Increase.

Spacing on an Irregular Selvedge

There may be times when the selvedge presents problems and it is difficult to see where each stitch lies. You

may have forgotten to add proper selvedge stitches, the stitch pattern may distort the edge, the yarn may be fine or fuzzy or a dark color, and you could find yourself frustrated with the precise approach I have described above. In these cases, you have to mark off intervals along the edge and work into it as neatly as you can. Again, it is best to work with a measurement from your pattern, not from the edge itself. Once you have the correct measurement, proceed as follows:

1. For a straight edge or a slope, draw a line the length the edge should be on a piece of paper. Mark one-inch intervals along the line. If you are dealing with a curve, do the same on a full-scale pattern draft.
2. Pin the knitted fabric to the paper, stretching the fabric out gently or easing in fullness as necessary.
3. Mark the fabric at one-inch intervals with safety pins and remove the pattern.
4. Use the information in Calculating Steps and Points (page 444) to work out a pattern for exactly how many stitches to pick up between each pin.

If you are improvising and do not have a pattern, lay the edge down flat on a wide ruler and use it as a guide for placing the pins.

There are occasions, usually around a neckline, in which some stitches are on holders, while the others must be picked up along a selvedge. With some commercial patterns, the instructions will indicate how many stitches to pick up just along the selvedge, while others will simply indicate the total number required for the neckline, including those on holders. In this latter case, subtract the number of stitches on the holders from the total required. Mark the inches off along the selvedges as above and divide the remaining stitches evenly among them.

Whenever you are picking up stitches along an edge that has had increases or decreases worked near it, or that lies adjacent to some cast-off stitches or stitches on holders as is often the case on a neckline, an occasional gap will appear between the picked-up stitches and the fabric. There is no simple formula for correcting these situations, but the gaps can generally be closed. Keep an eye on things as you work, and when you see a gap, stop and examine the structure of the fabric to determine what is causing the problem. Look for the side of a stitch or a running thread right below the gap that you might be able to work into instead of the selvedge stitch. Only then rip back to that point and try one thread or another until the gap closes; sometimes crossing whatever you pick up into will do the trick. Running threads often work the best, especially if crossed, because once you have worked into them, they will tighten up the stitches on either side, yet the first stitch of the fabric will remain undisturbed and look as it should. Alternatively, use the equivalent of a Raised Increase.

Picking Up and Knitting in the Opposite Direction

There are occasions in knitting when it becomes necessary to free the stitches at the lower edge, pick them up on a needle, and knit down in the opposite direction. In most cases this is done in order to make alterations or repairs. While the technique is not much used, when you need it you'll be glad to have it. Actually, I suspect it is less used than it might be because it seems daunting to the average knitter; however, it needn't be. Once the process is understood, you'll see that it is quite straightforward. The explanation will be considerably more clear if you really understand the structure of the knitted fabric, and I'm going to assume that you are completely familiar with the material on pages 3–15 on Knit and Purl. Nevertheless, let's take a look at the fabric again with this particular problem in mind.

If you turn a Stockinette fabric upside down, you discover that it looks exactly the same that way as it does right side up. The path of the yarn is identical, and all the stitches still look like Knit stitches. However, there has been a subtle metamorphosis that must be taken into consideration. Let's look at how it works. Hold up your hand with the fingers spread. Think of the tips of your fingers as the top of the stitches and the gully between each finger as a running thread. You have five stitches and four running threads, right? However, with the fabric upside down, the running threads become the heads of stitches, and the heads of stitches become running threads, which means there will be one less stitch than before. In addition, what had been the two sides of one knit stitch when right side up have now, when upside down, been transformed into halves of adjacent stitches. (The best way to witness this metamorphosis is to do it with a piece of knitting where two colors alternate stitch by stitch.) While the stitch count is one stitch short, the reality is that half a stitch is missing at each edge, but you can't pick up half a stitch either. I'm sure many a knitter has searched for that missing stitch and then given up in frustration. Rest assured, it isn't there.

In some cases, depending upon your gauge, the missing stitch is no problem at all, and it's probably best to just ignore it. However, if you are working with a bulky yarn, even one stitch can make quite a difference, and it may then be wise to add it back in. Since the fabric is

STRIPED STOCKINETTE UPSIDE DOWN

actually missing half of a stitch at the right side, and half at the left side, the best place to add the stitch back in is at the center. Use a Raised Stitch Increase (page 68) so it will be as invisible as possible.

If the original fabric is in Stockinette, and you use the same yarn and needles on the portion knit in the opposite direction, there will be no discernible difference between the two sections. If, however, the main fabric was worked in some other stitch pattern, or in a color pattern, any attempt to continue the pattern will not work, as the new portion will be offset a half stitch. There are several tricks for getting around the situation, but there is no way to match the patterns up, not even by adding in the missing stitch. You must instead turn the limitation to decorative advantage by introducing some new element. Even a row or two of a different pattern or color will provide a sufficient visual break between one portion and the other that the offset will not be visible.

Removing Cast-on Edges

Freeing the edge stitches is much easier to accomplish with some casting-on techniques than with others. If you have been very clever and planned all this out ahead of time, you will have used either Stranded or Chained Cast-on with a contrast-color yarn for good measure. When it comes time to remove the edge, it helps to work with the fabric on a table, or at least in your lap, so the needle bearing the stitches that have been picked up is supported and the stitches don't come off while you free the next one from the baseline.

Removing Stranded Cast-on
This is by far the easiest method of casting on to remove, and it is even easier if you have used a smooth contrast-color yarn for the baseline strand.

1. Turn the fabric so the cast-on edge is up and the end of yarn is at the upper right corner.
2. Remove the half-hitch from around the base of the first stitch and place the stitch on a needle.
3. Tug on the end of the yarn until you can clearly identify the baseline thread that passes through the first row of stitches.
4. Pull up on the end until you see where it passes through the next stitch, and then insert the needle into the stitch from right to left.
5. With your fingers or another needle, pull the baseline strand out of the stitch to the left.
6. Repeat across the row, picking up each stitch and removing the strand.

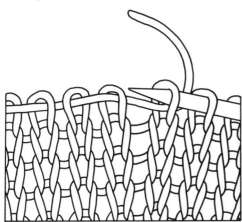

REMOVING STRANDED CAST-ON

Should you have any trouble picking up the stitches, insert the tip of the needle between the first and second stitch and pull up some of the baseline strand so you can tug up on the stitch from both sides. Be careful to pick the stitches up on the needle in the correct position, with the right side of the stitch on the nearside of the needle. In order to be sure, work the first row on these stitches carefully, checking the position of each one so you can correct any of those in the wrong position.

If you feel that your stitches and yarn will behave reasonably well, you can, of course, pull the baseline strand out of all the stitches at once. However, when working with a very smooth yarn, you take the risk that some of the stitches will run before you have a chance to pick them up, and with a nubby or fluffy yarn, the baseline may snag in the stitches as you draw it out and cause some of them to unravel. For these reasons, I

don't generally recommend this approach. As a compromise, it speeds things up somewhat to free the stitches in groups rather than one at a time; pinch the freed stitches between thumb and forefinger, to keep them from running as you draw out the baseline.

Removing Chained Cast-on
This is one of the easiest methods to use because the chain unravels so easily it doesn't generally pull at the stitches much. You can zip the whole chain off at once, take it off groups of stitches, or remove it gently, stitch by stitch, depending upon your sense of how well the stitches will hold. Chained Cast-on only unravels from its last stitch, not from its first stitch, so you must use a separate strand of yarn for the cast-on edge. As long as you must, you may as well also use a contrasting color that helps distinguish between stitch and edge.

Removing Half-Hitch Cast-on
Half-Hitch Cast-on is more tedious to remove than either of the two methods above, but it isn't difficult. As it is the most common method of casting on, and as removing an edge is not always something one has planned for, it is well to know how to handle the situation. You might want to practice on a swatch with a contrast-color baseline (see page 129). This reveals the structure of the edge so well you will be able to see quite clearly what you are doing and gain the necessary confidence before you tackle the actual garment.

1. Turn the fabric upside down. The end of the yarn should come out of the fabric at the upper right corner on the nearside.
2. Look on the farside of the fabric and tug on the end of yarn gently to identify the path it takes. Pull the first strand out on the Purl side from left to right.
3. You will now be able to see where the strand passes through the stitch. Insert the needle into the stitch from farside to nearside so the right side of the stitch

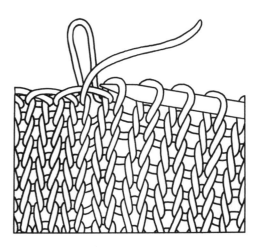

REMOVING HALF-HITCH CAST-ON

is on the nearside of the needle, then pull the strand out of the stitch on the nearside from right to left.
4. Repeat across the row.

As with the methods above, it is possible to free all of the stitches before picking any of them up on the needle. However, because the baseline forms a half-hitch around each stitch, there is quite a bit of drag as the strand is withdrawn, and it is all too easy to unravel a whole group of stitches as you try to free just one. You will probably save time in the long run by capturing each stitch on a needle as it is freed from the baseline. Cut the unraveled yarn off from time to time to keep it short.

Removing Knit Cast-On

This is very similar to the process of removing Half-Hitch Cast-on.

1. Turn the fabric upside down with the end of yarn in the upper right corner.
2. Tug on the end of yarn gently until you identify the path it takes on the farside of the fabric. It will pass through what looks like two stitches to the left of the one you wish to pick up. Pull the strand out of the two stitches to the farside.
3. The end of yarn will now be on the farside, and it will pass through the stitch you need to pick up next. Insert the needle into the stitch from farside to nearside, so the right side of the stitch is on the nearside of the needle. Pull the yarn out of the stitch to the nearside.
4. Continue in this way across the row.

REMOVING KNIT CAST-ON

Removing Alternating Cast-on

Because adjacent stitches along an edge made with Alternating Cast-on are from different strands of yarn, it is impossible to unravel it. Should you need to knit in the opposite direction, it is far better to separate the fabric a row or two above the cast-on edge (see below).

Dealing with Ribbings

While one can certainly remove a cast-on edge along a ribbing, pick up the stitches and work in the opposite direction in some other pattern, it is important to note that one cannot rip a ribbing from the bottom up. Because the path of the yarn alternates through the stitches, the running threads are effectively knotted into the fabric structure. Therefore, if it is necessary to redo a ribbing, or for that matter any pattern of mixed Knit and Purl stitches, the yarn must either be withdrawn stitch by stitch or the fabric divided on a plain row in order to remove the patterned portion entirely; obviously the latter approach is far more efficient.

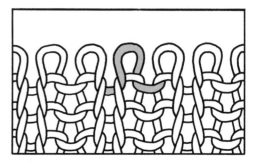

FREED STITCHES IN RIBBING

Separating a Fabric

Instead of releasing the edge and ripping back, there are occasions when it is faster to just separate two portions of the fabric in order to rework the garment in some way.

1. Determine where you wish to divide the fabric.
2. With a knitting needle, snag one of the stitches and pull it out firmly until you can slip a scissors into the loop and cut it.
3. Using the needle, gently unravel the cut ends from the rows of stitches on either side. Rather than drag the entire length of yarn through each stitch, periodically cut the end so it stays relatively short.
4. Once the fabric has been completely separated, pick up the stitches along one side onto the needle.

SEPARATING A FABRIC

If you find the stitches difficult to pick up in the correct position, there are two possible remedies. One is to rip down one additional row, either after the stitches have all been picked up, or as you are picking them up (see page 356). The other is to check each stitch as you knit the first row on the picked-up stitches, correcting its position if necessary and working up any that have run down.

The most common reason to release an edge is to lengthen a child's sweater. They do grow (not the sweaters, unfortunately, but children). If the sweater has been made with sufficient roominess in the body, all that may be necessary to give it another year of good wear is to remove the edge, rip back the ribbing from waist and sleeves, knit down a few inches in some decorative border pattern, and reknit the ribbing. (This is considerably easier to do if the garment was worked in the round; if not, it will first be necessary to release the seams.)

Either for design purposes or because the garment has worn spots, it may be better to separate the fabric at some point. In that case, it is possible either to knit the full length in new yarn, or to knit a new length of fabric on one section and then graft the two separated sections back together again. This is a good way to salvage a ribbing, for instance, which is time consuming to knit. There are some drawbacks to grafting a wide fabric, however, so before you tackle something like that, see the discussion on grafting (page 371).

Working in the opposite direction also offers the possibility of making stylistic changes in a garment. Perhaps you have knit up a sweater with a straight tailored edge, and you suspect that it would look much nicer if it had some ribbing at the bottom. Perhaps you have a short-waisted sweater finished with ribbing, and you decide that it would look stunning with the addition of a peplum in some lace stitch, or it would be enhanced by the addition of a tailored hip portion below the ribbing to make it longer. If you think the garment would be more attractive without the lower ribbing, separate the fabric above the ribbing, remove it, and knit down with a flat border or a hem instead. Of course, the technique also makes it possible to turn a short-sleeved sweater into one with long sleeves, or vice versa.

Whatever you have in mind, don't count on using yarn left over from when you made the sweater for this purpose. A number of things—washing, the sun, wear and tear—will have altered the appearance of the yarn in the sweater sufficiently that it will probably no longer match yarn still in the ball. If it is still in good condition, recycle the yarn ripped out of the garment. If it isn't reusable, it's best to be creative and find some yarn that adds a note of contrast and makes no attempt to match. If the yarn is of a different weight than the original, get a stitch gauge on it and either increase or decrease on the picked-up stitches so you don't alter the dimensions of the garment.

Last but not least, there is one situation in which releasing the edge is done as a deliberate part of the garment construction. There are many beautiful border patterns that are knit narrow and long. One can knit them up separately and sew them on; however, it is also possible to release the stitches at the lower edge of the garment, pick them up, and then use Border Cast-off (page 155) to knit the border and join it to the fabric all in one operation. The technique also provides a solution if you discover when you clean and dress the garment that your cast-on edge is too tight for the stitch pattern. Releasing the stitches and adding a two- or three-stitch width of Seed or Garter Stitch Border Cast-off will solve the problem nicely.

Picking Up and Joining

In the situations described above, all of the stitches are picked up along the edge and then the new section of fabric is worked on those stitches, perpendicular to the original. It is also handy to know how to work a section of fabric on a separate set of stitches and simultaneously attach it to another set of stitches that have been picked up along an edge.

The most interesting use for the technique is to attach borders or work a sleeve cap from the top down. While the method is rarely used, I suspect this is because it is little known, for it offers several very nice advantages, the first being that there is no seam to sew and the second that the join is more elastic than if it had been sewn.

Joining Borders

There are many beautiful border patterns, knit narrow and long, that are meant to be sewn on to the edge of a fabric. Any of them can be attached using this method instead. Let's look at the simplest first and then expand the possibilities.

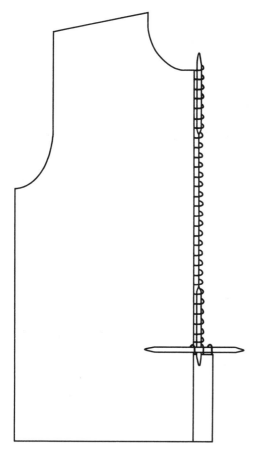

JOINING A BORDER TO PICKED-UP STITCHES

Garter Stitch Border

By far the most common use for this technique is a border worked in Garter Stitch. It lies flat and has great vertical elasticity, so it adapts itself readily to a fabric made in almost any other stitch pattern. It may need to be stretched or eased in slightly with blocking or a bit of judiciously applied steam, but it is very accommodating. This is really quite easy to do and introduces the principle nicely.

1. Use Chain Selvedge on the edge along which you will pick up the stitches to reduce the bulk of the join.
2. Starting at the top edge, pick up under every stitch of a Chain Selvedge or every other stitch of a Stockinette Selvedge. Work either as to Knit or Purl, depending upon whether it is the inside or the outside of the garment that is facing you.
3. When all the stitches are picked up, turn and use either Knit or Purl Cable Cast-on to place the re-

quired number of stitches for the width of the border on the same needle carrying the picked-up stitches.

4. The first row will be worked toward the join. If the outside is facing you, Knit across the row until only one border stitch remains on the left needle, then use a Slip Pullover Decrease to join the last border stitch to the adjacent picked-up stitch.
5. If you are working an inside row toward the join, work the Garter Stitch pattern entirely in Purl so you can use a Purl Two Together Decrease on the last border stitch and the picked-up stitch.
6. Turn and Knit or Purl back out to the edge of the border.
7. Continue in this way, using a decrease to join one border stitch to one picked-up stitch on every other row until only one picked-up stitch remains on the left needle.
8. On the last row, use Pullover Cast-off, working toward the join. When only one stitch remains on the right needle, break the yarn, allowing sufficient length to thread through a tapestry needle, and finish off the stitch (see page 150).

As you will see when you do it, the decreases consume the picked-up stitches one at a time, while the

GARTER STITCH BORDER ON PICKED-UP STITCHES

number of stitches in the border remains constant. Take care to work the decreases as given so the picked-up stitch is hidden on the inside of the garment. Because Garter Stitch looks the same right side up as it does upside down, you can pick up and work the border in whatever way makes it easiest for you, but if you are going to work a pair of borders on either side of a center front opening, for instance, you will want to be careful to match the cast-on edge of one border with the cast-off edge of the other.

This border is generally worked in the same type of yarn and on the same size needles used for the main section of fabric. If you have used a stitch pattern for the main section that tends to compress, you might try a smaller needle for the border; if the stitch pattern is expansive, try a larger one. For more information on refining the fit between the border and the other section of fabric, see the material below on working a border in another stitch pattern.

Other Borders

There are two approaches to using other stitch patterns for this technique, and with either of them you may use whatever size needle and yarn is appropriate to the border, regardless of how the main section of fabric was worked. Certain preliminary steps are the same for both:

1. Make a stitch gauge for the border pattern and calculate exactly how many rows will be required for the length of the edge.
2. Use Calculating Steps and Points (page 444) to plan the pickup. Remember that you will want to pick up half as many stitches as there are rows in the border pattern because you attach the two only every other row. It is best to use a Stockinette Selvedge on the main fabric section, as a Chain Selvedge may not provide enough stitches for picking up and will make spacing difficult.
3. Pick up and cast on just as for the Garter Stitch Border, above.

Garter Stitch Join

1. Cast on sufficient stitches for the border, which will be worked in whatever pattern you have chosen, plus two or three stitches between the border and the join to be worked in either Knit or Purl Garter Stitch.
2. Work the border in pattern and the intervening stitches in Garter Stitch, joining the last border stitch to the selvedge with a decrease just as described above.

Slip Stitch Join

This second approach requires some additional small changes in the method but avoids the necessity for any Garter Stitch between the border and the main section of fabric.

1. Calculate the number of rows for the border and plan the pickup as above. Cast on sufficient stitches for the border, plus one extra stitch.
2. Work the border stitches in pattern. Work the decreases on the extra border stitch and a picked-up stitch the same as for a border of a Garter Stitch, but after each decrease turn the work and slip the joining stitch instead of working it again on the next row.
3. Finish in the same manner, casting off toward the join.

BORDER WORKED ON SELVEDGE TURNED TO THE OUTSIDE

In this last version, the join is formed by a column of Slip Stitches, one enlarged stitch for every two rows. It is smooth and attractive, although quite obvious. If you work the join stitches after the turn instead of slipping them, the ones not involved in a decrease will be smaller and less bulky than the ones that are, and the column of stitches will have an irregular appearance that may be very obvious with smooth stitch patterns (it is completely hidden by Garter Stitch). It is also possible to pick up twice as many stitches and attach the border at every row, but the decreases can be awkward to do and the join tends to thicken; I don't think it is worth the trouble.

The selvedge may be turned to the outside, but re-member, with that method you must pick up into every stitch. If the number of stitches required for the border is less than that, knit one row on the border stitches, working decreases as required to adjust the number of stitches, and then begin to work and join the border. It is important to use a small needle for the pickup in this case so the adjustment will be hidden.

Joining to Other Edges

There is no rule that says that this method of attaching a border must be restricted to a vertical edge; it can just as easily be done on stitches released from a cast-on edge or on those which would otherwise have been cast off (see page 155). Should you wish to work around a corner, it will be necessary to work a Short Row Miter, (page 182).

One of the more popular ways of doing a border on a cardigan is to knit it at the same time as the garment. After the shoulder line is cast off, you must continue working the border stitches to form the portion that goes behind the neck. In finishing, the two ends are grafted together at the center back and the side edges are seamed to the back neck edge. Instead, work the two fronts and the back, place the back neck edge and the border stitches on holders and use Joinery Cast-off on the shoulders. Pick up the stitches on holders and knit the border and attach it at the same time, first up one side to the center back, then up the other. Graft the two sets of border stitches together, working from the border edge toward the garment.

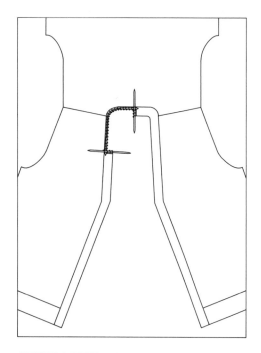

JOINING A CENTER FRONT AND NECK BAND

Alternate Method of Starting

If you do not like the look of Cable Cast-on for the edge of your border, here is a way to use a half-hitch method.

1. Use the stitches-per-inch calculation from your gauge and measure a length of yarn appropriate for both the total amount of border stitches and the picked-up stitches.
2. Tie a Slip Knot at this point and place it on a double-point or circular needle. Cast on the border stitches, then, using the tail of yarn, pick up the stitches along the selvedge. Make sure the running thread between the last cast-on stitch and the first picked-up stitch is drawn up firmly so there is no gap at the intersection.
3. When the pickup is complete, slide the stitches so the other point of the needle is at the border edge where you began, then slip the border stitches to a second needle. When you reach the yarn at the intersection between the border and the picked-up stitches, turn and begin to work the border pattern from join to edge and continue as described above.

Picking Up as You Work

This is a more informal way of working, if you will, and it is often useful when it seems otherwise difficult to get the yarn into the correct position to begin knitting. The method does, however, have some limitations, which must be kept in mind. First, it is best used only when the pickup pattern is simple and the selvedge easy to deal with; improvising a complex pickup along an edge never works well. Second, with this approach, the join will be thickened.

When you pick up all at once, the running threads of the new stitches will lie under the selvedge, but when you pick up stitches as you work, the running thread will pass around the entire selvedge stitch on its path from the last stitch of the fabric to form the next picked-up stitch, and this adds considerable bulk to the join.

On the whole, I think picking up all at once is easier to do and produces a superior result in almost every case, and I recommend that you work that way when-ever possible, but should you want to try this approach, here are the instructions for working a border.

1. Cast on the number of stitches required for the bor-der and work the first row toward the join.
2. On an outside row, slip the last stitch of the border knitwise, insert the tip of the right needle under the first selvedge stitch and Knit, then pass the slipped stitch over the new stitch and off the needle.
3. On an inside row, slip the last stitch of the border, pick up the selvedge stitch with the right needle as to Purl, insert the left needle into the farside of both the selvedge stitch and the border stitch, and Purl two together.

4. After the turn, work the joining stitch if you are using Garter Stitch, slip it if you are not.

Joining a Fabric at Both Sides

If you can join a fabric like this along one side, you can certainly join it on both sides. The technique is most commonly used for a saddle, or epaulette, shoulder line, where a one- to two-inch gap at the top of the shoulder is filled with fabric knitted perpendicular to the front and back sections. This strip can, of course, be sewn into place, but is much nicer when joined with decreases as described here.

Joining an Epaulette and Straight Sleeve

You can work an Epaulette shoulder on a sleeve done from the wrist to shoulder or from shoulder to wrist.

Working Wrist to Shoulder

1. Have the two sets of shoulder stitches on separate needles.
2. Cast off all the sleeve stitches but for a group at the center, where the sleeve meets the shoulder line, for the Epaulette.
3. As you work the Epaulette, join it to the front and back shoulder stitches at the end of every row. Use a Slip Pullover Decrease on an outside row, a Purl Two Together on an inside row.
4. The sleeve must then be sewn into the armhole.

Working Shoulder to Wrist

1. Have the two sets of shoulder stitches on separate needles.

2. Use Stranded Cast-on to place the stitches required for the width of the Epaulette on a needle (so they can be picked up later for the neckline border).
3. Work the Epaulette, joining on both sides as described above.
4. At the armhole, pick up the stitches all the way around for the sleeve and continue in the round to the wrist.

Joining a Sleeve Cap

Attaching a sleeve with a cap is somewhat more complicated, but the basic principle is the same. Plan the pickup pattern carefully (see "Calculating a Pick-up pattern," page 444) in order to set the sleeve in smoothly.

1. When working the body of the garment, leave the stitches at the base of the armhole on a holder instead of casting them off.
2. Along each armhole selvedge pick up one stitch for every other row of the cap, plus however many stitches are required for the small flat portion at the top of the cap where you will begin knitting. (If you worked an Epaulette, start with those stitches where they meet the armhole.)
3. Use three double-point needles for the picked-up stitches, one at the top and one at each side.
4. Begin working on the group of stitches at the top, joining a sleeve stitch to a picked-up stitch at the end of every row.
5. In order to shape the width of the cap, use increases where you would normally have used decreases in working the cap from the bottom up.
6. When you have absorbed all of the picked-up stitches at each side, incorporate the stitches on holders at the base of the armhole and continue working the sleeve in the round.

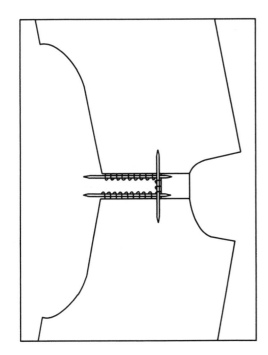

JOINING AT BOTH SIDES/EPAULETTE

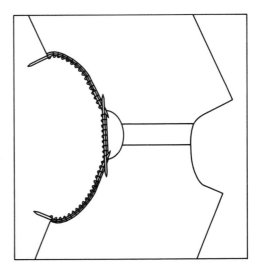

JOINING AT BOTH SIDES/SLEEVE CAP

Picking Up Within the Fabric

These techniques are not often used, but they are definitely worth knowing about. They make it possible to apply flat collars or ruffles to a finished fabric without sewing. The discussion necessitates the use of the words "right" and "left," and before we go any further I want to make sure we agree about how they will be used. I am going to presume that you are looking at the outside of the garment section, in other words, not right and left as it will be once the garment is being worn, but as it is while you are working on it.

When it comes to stitch gauge, picking up stitches internally is no different from picking up stitches along an edge. You must take into consideration the stitch gauge of the fabric that you will be working on the picked-up stitches and coordinate it with the gauge of the existing fabric. It may be necessary to skip a stitch now and then as you pick up, or to work into a stitch more than once in order to obtain the correct stitch count.

When picking up stitches within a fabric, it is not always easy to keep track of where you are going and just which stitch comes next, particularly if you are working on a slope, if the yarn obscures the stitches, or if the stitch pattern is complex. Because of the resilience of a knitted fabric, it is very difficult to "eyeball" something like this correctly. As you insert the needle, it will pull the fabric a little bit this way and a little bit that way, and instead of a nice straight line, you may wind up with a wavy one. I recommend against that sort of improvisation. The solution to this is a bit of advance planning; see page 349 for how to set markers within the fabric as you knit.

Perhaps the pickup process is an afterthought. In that case, it is best to mark the pickup line with a tapestry needle and a length of contrast-color yarn or embroidery thread (be careful not to split any stitches). The tapestry needle will not pull the fabric out of alignment as you work in the way a knitting needle does.

Once you are clear about where you are going, it is quite easy to pick up the stitches with a single needle in much the same way as working along an edge. However, when you pick up along an edge in the normal way as to Knit, the Purl row that is formed is turned toward the inside. When you are picking up on a surface instead of at an edge, this Purl row will be visible on the outside of the fabric. You must consider how the new fabric will lie on the existing one and plan the method of picking up so it covers the Purl row. If you Knit the pickup, the Purl row will appear above the needle; if you Purl the pickup, it will be below. There are a variety of ways of working into the stitches.

Picking Up into Stockinette

This is a nice smooth fabric to work into, making the process very easy. There are two methods, the choice between them depending upon the angle at which you must work.

CENTER PICKUP

This is a very straightforward way to work and is a particularly good method to use when you are picking up along a horizontal line or a moderate slope, as the new stitch emerges from the center of the stitch.

Always work from right to left as follows:

• To Knit, insert the needle into the center of a stitch and back out the center of the stitch above. Wrap the yarn as to Knit and pull through the new stitch.

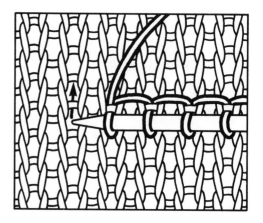

CENTER PICKUP/KNIT

- To Purl, insert the needle into the center of a stitch and back out the center of the stitch below. Wrap the yarn as to Purl and pull through the new stitch.

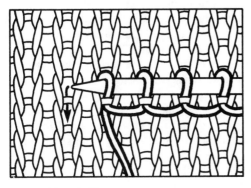

CENTER PICKUP/PURL

SIDE PICKUP

When you are picking up along a vertical line, or that of a steep slope, working into the side of the existing stitches gives a smoother effect. Turn the fabric sideways so the columns of stitches are horizontal, and work from right to left. You must decide whether to work into the right or left side of the stitch, and this is determined by how the new fabric will lie on the existing one. Whereas above the concern was only with where the Purl nubs would lie, here it must also be with the remaining half of the stitch into which you work.

- To Knit, insert the needle up under the side of a stitch, wrap the yarn as to Knit, and pull through a new stitch.
- To Purl, insert the needle down under the side of a stitch, wrap the yarn as to Purl, and pull through a new stitch.

If the new fabric will lie to the left, pick up as to Purl into the right half of the stitch so both the remaining half of the stitch and the Purl nubs will be covered. If the new fabric will lie to the right, pick up as to Knit into the left half of the stitch.

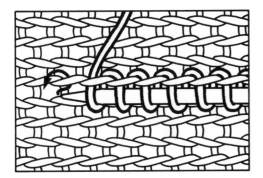

SIDE PICKUP/KNIT

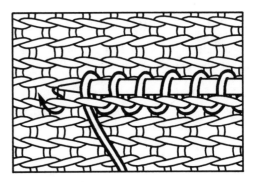

SIDE PICKUP/PURL

Picking Up Into Other Patterns

Fabrics made in stitch patterns other than Stockinette present more of a challenge, but they can be handled well if you take the time to understand the structure of the pattern.

REVERSE STOCKINETTE

When picking up on the Purl side of a fabric, always work into the heads of the stitches for a horizontal line or a low slope. The principle is the same as that outlined above for working into the center of a Stockinette stitch. Insert the needle up under the head of the stitch for Knit, down under the head of the stitch for Purl. If you are picking up on the vertical or a steep slope, you can also work into the heads of the stitches, but a better result is obtained by reaching into the fabric between the Purl nubs to pick up the side of a stitch. It's quite hidden; stretch the fabric out so you can clearly see where it lies. After a bit you won't need to do that—your needle will find it without much trouble.

Mixed Stitch Patterns

If you will be picking up on a fabric that combines Knit and Purl stitches, work into the centers or the sides of the Knit stitches and into the Purl nubs.

You may wish to pick up stitches within a fabric worked in a complex stitch pattern, one that does not provide simple Knit and Purl stitches nicely lined up in rows and columns. You can work into the stitches as best you can, but the result may be less than satisfactory. The best approach is to pick up on the running threads instead, as regardless of what is going on with the stitches, they will be perfectly normal, plain running threads, and all in their proper places. Work in the same manner as for picking up into the center of a stitch, going up under the running thread for Knit, down under it for Purl. This does not work well for picking up on a horizontal line because the columns of stitches of the new fabric will be slightly offset, but it works very well for any slope or a vertical.

Picking Up Through the Fabric

Here is an alternate method of dealing with a mixed fabric that also avoids having a row of Purl on the outside. Work on the outside of the fabric, but hold the yarn for the picked-up stitches underneath on the inside. The challenge here is that once the stitches have been picked up, the yarn you need in order to continue knitting must be on the outside. There are two solutions. You can either pick up with a separate strand of yarn, or calculate the length you will need for picking up and draw that end of the yarn through the fabric from outside to inside.

Pick Up with Separate Strand

1. Work with the outside of the fabric facing up; hold the yarn underneath on the inside and leave a ten-inch end of yarn as you start.
2. Reach the tip of the needle through to the inside, either into the center of a stitch or between two stitches, wrap the yarn, and draw a stitch through to the outside.
3. Pick up as many stitches as required, then break the yarn off leaving another ten-inch end.
4. Before you begin to knit on the picked-up stitches, turn to the inside and use a tapestry needle to secure and hide the ends of yarn so they will not pull free as you work (see page 379).
5. Attach a new supply of yarn on the outside where you wish to begin working.

Pick Up with Tail of Yarn

1. Work on the outside just as described above, but use a double-point needle to pick up stitches from the tail of yarn.
2. When all of the stitches have been picked up, return to the other end of the needle where the yarn supply is and begin to work.

If you have difficulty pulling the yarn through, you may find it helps to hook the yarn with a crochet hook and then transfer the stitch to the needle.

11

Hems, Facings, and Folds

A hem is created by folding a portion of a fabric back on itself and sewing it down in order to finish an edge. A facing performs the same function, but is a separate piece of fabric that is sewn on as a backing for an edge, a collar, or a lapel. Some books recommend against hems or facings entirely, arguing that they are appropriate to woven fabrics but unnecessary in knitting. There is something to be said for this, as hems are not without their problems and knitters have many other nice ways of finishing the free edges of a knitted fabric.

However, there are knitters who enjoy using a hem, if for no other reason than that it forms a convenient, secret place to knit in someone's name or initials and perhaps a date or some tender message to the wearer. Also, one can simply get tired of having a rib at the edge of every sweater one makes. But these aren't the best reasons for adding a hem. The decision should be made on the basis of whether or not a hem or facing will enhance the design and wearability of a garment, and that in turn comes from a thorough knowledge of the different ways to make a hem and what the advantages and disadvantages are. In some situations a hem is the perfect solution to a design problem, and at other times it wouldn't be in the least appropriate.

The main problem with a knitted hem or facing is that of bulk, and with the problem of bulk comes the additional one of impairment of the natural movement of the fabric. With a lightweight knit garment, for instance, particularly one that should move, such as a skirt, a hem might work against the desirable soft qualities of the fabric and should be avoided. There are other situations, however, where it might work to solve a design problem. If you don't wish to have a border or ribbing of any kind, a hem can help to hold the fabric flat and smooth. In other situations, such as that of a tailored cardigan or jacket, a hem is not only a smooth finish for the edge, but it helps support the geometrical shape of the design, particularly if there are buttons. The fact that it cuts down slightly on the resilience of the fabric is in this case a plus, for a garment of this sort without a hem can often pull out of shape at the edges. Finally, there are collars and lapels that might be limp and lack shape without the support of a hem or facing.

Folds may also be made within the fabric to form Welts, Pleats, and Tucks. Handled correctly, these design elements can add great charm to a garment, but again the bulk and resilience of the fabric must be taken into consideration. With Pleats and Tucks, for instance, the thickness of the fabric is tripled rather than just doubled as it is with a hem. For the most part, therefore, these techniques are reserved for use with relatively fine yarns.

Hems

Because there are legitimate occasions for a hem, we are fortunate that there are also some quite clever ways to reduce their bulk, and when handled correctly, they can become a nice addition to a garment. For the most part, Stockinette works best for a hem, as it is smooth and flat. In the instructions below, even if I don't mention it, I am assuming that that is what will be used. I have included a discussion on how to handle working a hem on a garment section done in some other stitch pattern.

Foldlines for Horizontal Hems

Any hem is hidden on the inside of the garment, so its structure and behavior are far more important than what it looks like. The foldline, on the other hand, will form the edge of the garment, and therefore its appearance is critical. There are four methods of making a foldline, and you will want to choose one or the other depending on its suitability to your garment.

ROUNDED FOLDLINE

This method produces a gently rounded edge and is by far the simplest approach.

1. Cast on the required number of stitches for the width of the garment section. Knit the depth of the hem in Stockinette according to your stitch gauge and then continue with the main garment section.
2. In finishing, the hem is sewn invisibly to the inside.

A Rounded Foldline of this sort absorbs a certain amount of the length that you knit, more so in a heavier yarn than in a finer one. If you use your gauge to calculate how many rows for the hem, it's a good idea to add one to three rows extra for the foldline, depending on the weight of the yarn. For a more accurate approach, fold your swatch in half to the depth of your hem, mark the row where the hem would be sewn down, and count the rows between the mark and the cast-on edge.

STOCKINETTE FOLDLINE

If you want a very unobtrusive edge to a hemmed garment, but prefer a less rounded effect, work as follows:

1. Cast on and work the depth of the hem.
2. Change to a needle two sizes larger and work one row. Return to the original size needle and continue with the main garment section.
3. Fold along the enlarged stitches and sew into place.

This makes the stitches of the foldline larger and softer than the rest of the fabric, and when turned under the hem will be flatter than the above version.

PURL FOLDLINE

This is the most common method of working, and is very easy to do. It produces a crisp, tailored edge suitable for most purposes.

1. Cast on the required number of stitches for the width of the garment section, and work the hem in Stockinette to the depth you require.
2. Then work a single row of Purl on the outside of the fabric, either by Purling across on the Knit row, or Knitting across on the Purl row, as the case may be.
3. Continue with the work in the normal way. When the garment is assembled, fold along the Purl row and sew the hem invisibly to the inside.

You will be working Knit stitches above and below the single row of Purl so the Knit side of the hem faces out as well. You will find that the fabric folds readily along the line of Purl nubs, making measuring the hem unnecessary.

PURL FOLDLINE

PICOT FOLDLINE

And finally, here is a lovely variation that produces a decorative foldline.

1. Work the hem to the required depth in the same manner as described above, and then proceed as follows:
   • On an outside row: K1, *K2tog, YO* K1 or,
   • On an inside row: P1, *P2tog, YO* P1.

PICOT FOLDLINE

2. On the next row, work into the Yarnovers as if they were normal stitches and continue with the main garment section.

When the hem is folded to the inside for sewing, the decreases will form little pointed teeth separated by gaps created by the Yarnovers. If you prefer to space the gaps out a bit, work it *K2tog, YO, K1* instead.

Horizontal Hems

Here are several ways to work basic hems that either make the result more successful or make the job easier to do, plus a method of adding a hem as an afterthought.

Casting On and Sewing Hems

The most successful method of sewing any hem into place is called grafting (page 377). The reason it works so well is that it preserves the full elasticity of the fabric, the grafted stitches being just as resilient as any others. In addition, there is little suggestion on the outside of the fabric as to where the hem is attached. Such is not the case with the usual methods of sewing. The technique is not difficult, and I strongly recommend that you learn how to do it; the discussion includes tips for working into the correct row and for working into stitch patterns other than Stockinette.

Grafting can be used to sew any cast-on edge to the fabric, but many of these edges are not themselves terribly elastic, which more or less cancels the benefit to be had. Stranded Cast-on offers an excellent solution. When the garment is assembled and you are ready to sew the hem into place, fold it up into place, and as you graft the stitches to the inside of the fabric, remove the baseline strand. You may find it easier to do this if you first pick up the stitches of the edge on a separate needle, removing the baseline strand as you do so, and then graft the stitches off the needle. If you have used some other cast-on edge, many of them can be removed to free the stitches (see page 190).

JOINERY HEM

Here is way to work a hem up from a cast-on edge that is easy to do and does not need to be sewn into place. It results in a nearly invisible join.

1. Use Stranded Cast-on with a contrasting-color yarn to place the required number of stitches on the needle.
2. Work the hem exactly as described above, using either a Purl or Picot Foldline. When you have worked the same number of rows above the foldline as there are below the foldline, proceed as follows:
3. On a double-point needle, pick up the stitches along

the cast-on edge, removing the baseline strand as you do so.

4. When all of the stitches have been picked up, fold the hem up with the needle holding the picked-up stitches on the farside. Holding the two needles side by side, work the entire row with Joinery Decreases (see page 64). Alternately, intersperse both sets of stitches on a single double-point needle, first one from the main fabric, then one from the hem, and then work the decreases.

5. Continue with the remainder of the garment section in the normal way.

Hems for Ribbing

Some people like to double a ribbing at waist or wrist, and a very neat effect may be obtained by making the fold permanent using the above techniques. In this case, a foldline would cut down on the resilience of the cuff, so it is eliminated and a Rounded Fold used instead. You may work the Joinery Decreases in rib or in Stockinette, depending upon what will blend best with the stitch pattern used on the sleeve proper. The result is a nice, plump cuff. A more tailored version with greater holding power can be achieved by regauging the hem portion of the cuff (see page 423).

I have seen it suggested that a small Stockinette hem be placed on a ribbed edge, but frankly I don't understand what purpose it could serve, as it would work against the resilience and elasticity of the ribbing. It may have originally been intended as a corrective for a poorly cast on edge, but I think it far better to correct the casting-on than to hamper the ribbing. Should you wish a rounded edge, but not a hemmed ribbing, try working just a few rows of a Double Knit Hem (see below) before going on with regular Single Rib (it does not blend well with Double Rib), although it, too, will restrict the edge.

HORIZONTAL HEM ON PICKED-UP STITCHES

In all the above methods, the hem is worked as an integral part of the garment section. However, if you did not work a hem, and later decide that the garment would be enhanced by one, it is possible to pick up stitches, use the cast-on edge as a foldline, and knit the hem in the other direction. The instructions are given for Half-Hitch Cast-on, which works the best, and the approach depends upon whether the Knit or Purl side of the edge is on the outside of the garment.

Knit Half-Hitch Edge: Pick up the first row of Purl nubs that lie directly above the horizontal strands of the the cast-on edge. Work the hem to the depth required and then graft into place.

The horizontal strands will form the foldline and create a fairly attractive edge.

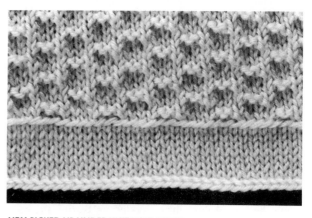

HEM PICKED UP UNDER KNIT HALF-HITCH

Purl Half-Hitch Edge: Pick up stitches under the horizontal strands along the cast-on edge. Work the hem to the depth required and graft into place.

This leaves a row of Purl nubs along the turned edge, almost identical to what it would look like had you worked the hem continuously with the garment and used a Purl Foldline.

If you have used some other casting-on technique, test what will happen by adding a hem to a swatch worked just like your garment. If the result is not attractive, the solution is to unravel the cast-on edge or separate the fabric in order to free the stitches (see page 190). Once the stitches are picked up, work a foldline, if you wish, and then the required number of rows for the depth of the hem.

Casings

The above hems are all worked at the bottom of a garment section. They can just as easily be worked at the top in order to form a waistband or a casing for elastic or a drawstring.

• Do not cast off. Instead, work the last row of the garment section as a foldline, work the depth of the hem, and then sew the stitches off the needle to the inside with the grafting stitch (page 377).

If you are using a casing for elastic or a drawstring, keep in mind the problem of bulk. Not only will there be two layers of knitted fabric and one of elastic, but the elastic will gather the knitted layers up, making them even thicker. Consider reducing the stitches to the minimum required for the width of the area so there is less gathering. Also see the material on refining the hem, below. Other solutions are to use a woven fabric facing (see below) or a Sewn or Crochet Elastic Casing (page 381).

Double Knit Hem

A simple hem offers a perfect opportunity to use the clever techniques of Double Knitting (page 233). The result will be identical to the Joinery Hem, but there is no need to pick up any stitches, which makes it far more efficient. It can also be used at the top of a garment for a waistband or casing. There are a variety of edges that can be used at the foldline, some of which can only be achieved with Double Knit.

Once you understand how Double Knitting works, you will quickly see how readily it can be applied to these purposes. The discussion of that technique is rather extensive, however, so I will not repeat it here. While Basic Double Knit is all that need be learned in order to use it for a hem, a mastery of the technique will allow you to work it in two different colors, in two different color patterns, or in two different yarns. The latter case affords the opportunity of using a split yarn to reduce bulk (see below), an important refinement in creating a successful hem.

Vertical Hems

The most successful approach to working a hem along a vertical edge is to knit it at the same time as the main garment section. Because a knitted fabric has less stretch in the vertical dimension than it does in the horizontal, a hem worked in this way gives good support to the edge. We don't have the foldline options with a vertical hem that we do with the horizontal one, but the one that is available is quite easy to do.

VERTICAL FOLDLINE

1. In addition to the stitches cast on for the main garment section, you must cast on one for the foldline, and then the required number of stitches for the width of the hem. Work the hem portion in Stockinette.
2. Every other row, slip the foldline stitch purlwise, with the yarn stranded on the inside, and then either Knit or Purl it on the return row in the normal way.

Slipping the stitch every other row reduces the bulk in that column of stitches, and this helps to create a smooth, flat edge when the facing is folded back. This is one of the few times when you should strand the yarn behind a Slip Stitch with a firm tension; it encourages the fold to turn and lie flat. When the garment is assembled, sew the hem invisibly to the inside (see page 377). When the hem is worked at one with the garment, as described here, it will be impossible to use the refining techniques described below. If you need to refine a vertical hem, you can knit it separately and simultaneously attach it to picked-up stitches (see page 194).

If the hem is for a vertical hemmed border, you must of course cast on enough stitches for the width of the border, a stitch for the foldline, and a number equal to those of the border for its hem.

VERTICAL FOLDLINE

VERTICAL HEM ON PICKED-UP STITCHES

If you did not work the hem at one with the garment section, and later decide that you need one, it can be knit on stitches picked up along the selvedge, in much the same way as the Horizontal Hem on Picked-up Stitches, above. Worked in this way, the stitches of the hem will be perpendicular to the stitches of the main section of fabric, and the hem will be worked over a certain number of rows, depending upon your gauge. As I mentioned above, a knitted fabric has more resilience in the horizontal dimension than it does in the vertical dimension, so a hem worked this way will not support the edge as successfully as one that is worked at the same time as the main garment section; you will, however, be able to use regauging techniques if you wish.

When working a hem on picked-up stitches, the selvedge stitches are turned to the inside, causing a certain amount of bulk because the fold falls right along the line where the two fabrics meet. To minimize that, pick up in Knit, then work a Purl or Picot Foldline, then the depth of the hem. This offsets the foldline one row away from the selvedge stitches. Alternatively, pick up so as to turn the selvedge to the outside (see page 186).

The edge can be cast off and then sewn down, but a better result is obtained if the stitches are sewn directly off the needle (see "Grafting to a Selvedge" on page 376).

For a hemmed border on a vertical edge, pick up the stitches and work the width of the border in rows, work the foldline in Purl on the outside, and then work the hem the same number of rows as were done before the foldline. Sew it down in the same way.

VERTICAL BIAS HEM

A Vertical Bias Hem is worked at one with the garment, and must therefore be made with the same yarn and needles.

1. Cast on the stitches for the width of the bias, in addition to those for the width of the garment, plus one extra for the foldline.

   • If the bias is on the right side of the garment: On the outside work a Knit two together at the edge, Knit to the foldline, work a Crossed Running Thread Increase, then slip the foldline stitch. Continue across the row on the garment stitches.

   • If the bias is on the left side of the garment: Slip the foldline stitch, work a Crossed Running Thread Increase, then Knit the stitches of the bias hem, working a Slip Slip Knit on the last two.

2. On the return row, Purl the foldline stitch and those of the bias hem.

   I happen to like the effect of a Running Thread Increase in this situation, but you could also use the Crossed Yarnover Increase.

Hems at Corners

In some situations, you may want both a vertical and a horizontal hem that meet in a corner, such as for a center front opening. In order to prevent bulk, the two hems must be mitered so they do not overlap. It is a simple matter to calculate the slopes required on each section of hem, and all the information for how to do so can be found on page 442.

These hems can be handled either by working them at one with the main garment section, or on stitches that are picked up along the edge in the same way as detailed above.

MITERED HEM FROM CAST-ON EDGE

With this version, increases are used to slope the side of the horizontal hem and the base of the vertical hem where they will meet at the corner.

1. Cast on the number of stitches required for the inner edge of the horizontal hem. Work the hem, increasing as required at the corner for the Miter. When the hem is the correct depth, work the horizontal foldline.

2. Begin working the main garment section, adding one stitch for the vertical foldline, then increase in the same way as for the horizontal part of the Miter until the vertical border is the correct width.

3. During finishing, seam the Miter and sew the hem into place on the inside.

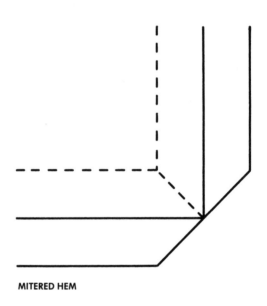

MITERED HEM

MITERED HEM ON PICKED-UP STITCHES

A mitered hem worked on picked-up stitches can be done in two ways. The simplest approach is to work the horizontal and vertical hems separately.

Separate Mitered Hem

1. Pick up the stitches along the cast-on edge and work the horizontal hem, decreasing according to the pattern you have developed to form the miter. Do not cast off; sew the stitches off the needle with the grafting stitch (page 377).

2. Pick up the stitches along the selvedge for the vertical hem and work the Miter in the same way you did on the horizontal hem section. Sew the stitches off the needle with the grafting stitch, and then overcast (page 366) or use Selvedge Seam (page 364) to join the two edges of the Miter together.

A nicer approach is to work the vertical and horizontal hems at the same time on a circular needle. Worked in this way, there is no need to sew the edges of the Miter together where they meet at the corner.

Continuous Mitered Hem

1. On a circular needle, pick up all of the stitches along the bottom cast-on edge, and the required number along the selvedge.

2. As you knit the hem, use double decreases, either decorative or plain, to shape the Miter according to your calculations. Sew the stitches off the needle with the grafting stitch.

Curved Hems

In order to work out the correct shaping for a hem that must follow the contours of a curve or a circle, you must first determine whether the hem lies within the circle represented by the outside edge or outside of it. An inner curve is one that lies within the circle; an outer curve, one that lies outside of it. You can see precisely what is required if you work with a full-scale pattern draft and draw a line representing the edge of the hem where it will be sewn to the inside of the garment. Depending upon whether you are working from the edge of the hem toward the garment edge, or the other way around, you must increase or decrease the number of stitches so the hem will lie flat and smooth on the inside of the garment.

HEM FOR AN OUTER CURVE

The hem done around a circular neckline provides a familiar example of an outer curve.

1. Using your pattern draft, measure both the outer edge of the garment and the inner edge of the hem by standing your tape measure on end and "walking" it around. The outer edge will have a smaller measurement than the inner edge.

2. You will be working on stitches picked up around the outer edge, and working toward the inner edge, so you must use increases to shape the hem. Subtract the two measurements to obtain the number of stitches that must be increased within the hem.

3. Using the number of rows required for the hem, dis-

tribute so many stitches per every other row (do not put increases in the row next to the outer edge of the garment, as they will distort it) and then use Calculating Steps and Points (page 437) to distribute the stitches to be increased in each row evenly around the circle.

HEM FOR AN INNER CURVE

A curved corner on a center front opening is a good example of an inner curve. The outer edge of the garment will have a larger measurement than the inner edge of the hem, where it will be sewn down to the inside. Because only some of the hem is curved, the measurements required for the calculations are slightly more complicated than those for a circle.

1. On the pattern draft, draw a line across the hem marking the point where the vertical edge begins to curve, then another where the horizontal edge begins to curve.

2. Measure the inner and outer edges of the hem between these two lines, and calculate the number of stitches they represent according to your gauge. Subtract the smaller number from the larger to obtain the number of stitches that must be increased or decreased in order to shape the curve.

3. Use Calculating Steps and Points (page 437) to work out how to space the increases or decreases evenly over several rows within the corner, so many in each row, in order to make the change in size smooth.

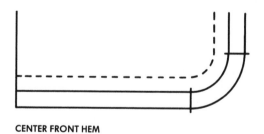

CENTER FRONT HEM

CURVED CORNER HEM ON PICKED-UP STITCHES

By far the easiest way to work a hem around a curved corner is to do it on picked-up stitches, working the vertical and horizontal sections and the curve simultaneously from the garment edge to the inner edge of the hem. While the instructions are for a bottom corner, the principle would be the same for a top corner, or for both.

1. On a circular needle, pick up the required number of stitches along the cast-on edge and along the selvedge, spacing them as required.

2. Work the hem in Stockinette, decreasing to shape the

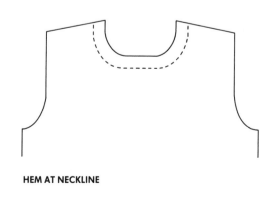

HEM AT NECKLINE

curve according to the pattern you worked out as described above.

3. Sew the stitches off the needle using the grafting stitch (page 377).

CURVED CORNER HEM WORKED FROM INNER EDGE

It is also possible to work a curved hem continuous with the main garment section, casting on at the inner edge of the hem and working toward the outer edge of the garment, but it is complex. Again, the example provided is for a bottom corner. The hem is worked in two sections, the vertical portion down to the point where the curve begins, and the horizontal portion, which includes the entire curve.

1. Cast on the number of stitches required for the inner edge of the horizontal hem, including the curve. Knit the required number of rows for the depth of the hem, working the spaced increases necessary for shaping in the corner. Work a Stockinette Foldline.

2. Now, begin working the main garment section. In order to shape the curved edge of the garment itself, use Short Rows (page 177), which gradually lengthen row by row at the corner. The first Short Row should stop at the point where the curve begins along the lower edge, the last where it ends along the vertical edge.

3. When the curve is complete, and all of the stitches have been reactivated, pick up the number of stitches required for the foldline and the width of the vertical hem along the selvedge of the horizontal hem. Continue the work normally.

The method of drafting and calculating a curve of this kind is found on page 445.

The Stockinette Foldline is the most similar in appearance to a Vertical Foldline. A Purl Foldline will not match, but if you want to use it, one way to blend the

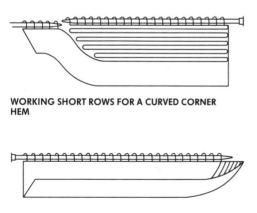

WORKING SHORT ROWS FOR A CURVED CORNER HEM

PICKING UP HEM SELVEDGE

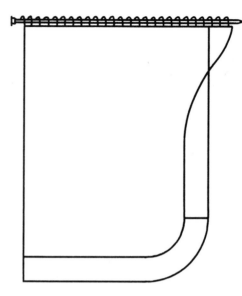

CURVED CORNER HEM ON INSIDE

two together is to eliminate the Purl Foldline at the outer edge of the curved portion. The Short Rows will work to provide a fairly crisp turn to that part of the hem and form a transition between the two dissimilar foldlines.

Refining the Hem Facing

The way most hems are done, the edge of the garment will have a round, rather fat look compared to the main portion of the fabric. This is because there is the same amount of fabric in both the hem and the main garment section, and the former pushes against the latter, causing it to protrude slightly. There are three ways to solve the problem, two of which reduce the width of the hem and one that also reduces its density. These techniques can be used on any horizontal hem and any vertical hem worked separately or on picked-up stitches.

If just the hem section is made very slightly narrower, it will have less tendency to push out against the main fabric. In addition, the hem must then be stretched in order to seam it into place and this tension helps to support the hemline. Generally speaking, a 5 to 10 percent reduction in the width of the hem will do the trick. What this means in practice is that if, for instance, you have a garment that is twenty inches in width, the hem facing will be about one inch narrower with a 5 percent reduction, or a half-inch difference on each side. With a 10 percent reduction, the hem will be about two inches narrower, or a difference of an inch at each side. It is no problem for the fabric to stretch this far as long as you avoid any restraining cast-on or cast-off edge on the hem. Therefore, use Stranded Cast-on for a hem worked in one piece with the garment section, or if you are doing an opposite-direction hem, don't cast off. In either case, you can then use the grafting stitch (page 377).

Decreasing the Hem

The simplest way to reduce the size of the hem is to reduce the number of stitches it contains.

1. Calculate the number of stitches required for the width of the garment section, reduce this figure by 5 or 10 percent, and use Stranded Cast-on to place the smaller number of stitches on the needle.
2. Work the hem to within two rows of the foldline and then increase to the full amount of stitches required, spacing the increases evenly across the row. Use Calculating Steps and Points (page 437) to work out the proper spacing.
3. Work one more row on the larger number of stitches, then the foldline. Continue with the main garment section.

It is important to work the increases or decreases one row away from the fold. If this is not done, the edge of the garment will have a slight distortion where each shaping technique was placed. Sew the edge into place with Grafted Hemstitch or use Joinery Decreases. Because there are a different number of stitches in the hem than in the fabric, use Calculating Steps and Points to determine which stitches in the main section to skip as you sew in order to adjust the width of the hem to the width of the fabric. If you are using Joinery Decreases, work with the stitches on two needles and from time to time knit a garment stitch alone.

If you are working a hem on picked-up stitches, simply work the decreases in the same position as the increases are worked above; otherwise, the approach is the same.

Regauging the Hem

Once you grasp the principle of this technique, you will find other applications for it. In brief, instead of reducing the number of stitches, the width of the fabric is decreased by using a smaller-size needle for the hem section than that used for the main garment section. Using a needle one size smaller on the hem will give you approximately a 5 percent reduction in the width of the fabric. Using a needle two sizes smaller will reduce the width of the hem by about 10 percent.

Regauging has an advantage over the above method, where width is reduced by decreasing, in that it is easier for the hem to be sewn down when the number of stitches in both sections is the same. As with those methods, however, it is important to make sure there is no restraining edge to the hem.

The difficulty with using regauging for a hem is that when you reduce the needle size, you increase the density of the fabric. This might be advantageous when the hem is being used on a jacket, or other sporty design, especially if it is intended to support buttons and but-

tonholes, but on a lightweight garment it may become too stiff. One solution that minimizes the density is to work those few rows closest to the foldline in the same size needle used for the main fabric, then use a needle one size smaller for the center rows of the hem and another two sizes smaller for those at the edge.

Hem with Split Yarn

One of the nicest ways to both reduce the width and the density of a hem is to work it on the same needle and number of stitches, but with a finer-weight yarn. Now few of us will have just the right sort of fine yarn about the house when we wish to do a hem, it's expensive to buy a whole ball for the small amount of yarn used in a hem, and one can't count on finding a compatible color. Whenever possible, therefore, the best thing to do is to split the yarn being used for the garment (see page 363).

If you use a split or finer-weight yarn, the hem will be quite open, light, and delicate, and it will stretch out readily to the width of the main fabric. (My experience is that it will nearly double its width, if pulled.) A hem of this sort is particularly appropriate for a neckline, or for any garment where maintaining the flexibility and movement of an edge is essential. In addition to these qualities, the technique has the advantage of maintaining the same number of stitches in the hem as there are in the main fabric, which makes joining the two easy.

As a rough guideline, if you have a four-ply yarn, using three of the plies on the same size needle for the hem will be roughly a 5 percent reduction in width, while using two of the plies for the hem will be about a 10 percent reduction. You may also reduce the size of the needle, but this might cause the hem to be too narrow for a garment worked with straight sides. If, however, the hem is to back up something like an A-line skirt, which gradually narrows, by all means both split the yarn and use regauging.

If you are in doubt as to how the hem will behave, it is best to work it up in a trial swatch; one five or six inches wide will give you a pretty good idea of what will happen. In order to save effort, work the hem in the opposite direction, then should your first attempt not be what you have in mind, you need only rip out the hem and try again, leaving the swatch itself intact.

Hems with Other Stitch Patterns

As I mentioned above, I have discussed all of these hems as if they were done in Stockinette for a garment done in Stockinette. Certainly there will be times when you wish to have a hem on a garment done in some other stitch pattern. While you could work the hem in the same pattern as the garment, if it is either bulky or lacy and open, that approach may not be the best one. On the whole, it is better to do the hem section in Stockinette regardless of the pattern used on the garment, but this presents problems in regard to stitch gauge, as the two patterns are unlikely to match. You will have to work a Stockinette stitch gauge for the hem in addition to one in the stitch pattern of your main fabric, and use the approaches outlined above in Refining the Hem to coordinate the two. I strongly recommend trying any

hem on a swatch first in order to make sure that it will behave the way you wish it to on your garment, but it is particularly important in this case. It seems like a lot of extra effort, but it may save many hours of work and spare you a great deal of frustration or disappointment in the long run.

Facings

In the above discussion we concentrated on finishing edges with hems worked continuously with the garment or on stitches picked up along an edge. For those occasions when any knitted hem, however refined, would be too bulky, or when what is wanted is to prevent the edge from stretching out, a facing is ideal. There are two kinds of facings used in knitting, knitted bias or woven. The former works much like a hem, but it has somewhat less stretch than a normal knitted fabric, so it both faces the edge and provides more rigid support. Woven facings are much finer than any knitted hem could be and can be used either straight grain or bias, depending on whether you want the edge to stretch or not.

Woven Facings

There are a variety of commercial hem tapes on the market that can easily be used to face a knitted fabric just as well as a woven one. Aside from these tapes, which are specifically intended for this purpose, keep in mind the possibilities of decorative ribbon, either satin or grosgrain, or of making your own facing from a piece of china silk, crepe, satin, batiste, faille, netting, organdy, or chiffon. It is important to select a fabric suitable to the work it must do. For instance, while a grosgrain ribbon is just right for a button stand on a cardigan, you might prefer to use a soft chiffon for the neckline facing on an angora bed jacket. Be sure to use fabrics or tapes cut on grain for straight edges, and cut on the bias for curved edges.

Applying the Facings

The edge along which you will apply a fabric facing should be finished with a flat or decorative selvedge, or with a few rows of crochet edging, and the facing should be set back from this edge on the inside. As an alternative to a decorative selvedge or crochet edging, you can

also make a "mini-hem" using one of the regular hem techniques given above. The mini-hem includes a foldline and just one or two rows of hem. The hem itself is not sewn down; instead, one side of the woven facing is sewn to the edge of the mini-hem, and the other side is sewn down to the inside of the garment.

The garment must be assembled and dressed first (see page 387), and the facing should be preshrunk. (Wetting the facing and ironing it dry is ordinarily sufficient to shrink it.) It is best to cut the facing according to the pattern, not to the garment. All too often the soft resilience of a knitted fabric will betray you in a measurement of this sort and shouldn't be relied upon. If you have modified the pattern and must take the measurement from the garment, do so with the fabric lying perfectly flat and patted gently into shape, or use the number of rows you have actually knitted and your stitch gauge to determine the length the fabric should be.

Once your facing is prepared, pin it carefully to the sides and in the center, and then add more pins between these, gently easing the knitted fabric to fit the facing. Baste into place, if necessary, and try the garment on or put it on a dressmaker's dummy to make sure that the facing neither puckers the garment nor allows it to sag or splay out. If the facing is the correct length, but the knitted fabric puckers slightly between the pins, a little judiciously applied steam should smooth things into place (see "Steaming," page 394.) If the puckers are not corrected by steam, this is evidence you have measured your facing incorrectly, and you will have to cut a new, longer one. If the garment sags or splays out, the facing is undoubtedly too long. Carefully measure how much it should be shortened, cut the facing, and repin. Don't sew until you get things right, and don't expect your facing to correct problems in sizing. Sew with regular sewing thread, using a nice, hidden hemstitch (see page 382).

There are several ways to handle the challenge of

backing a buttonhole band with a woven facing. The facing itself is applied along the edge like any other, but then must be cut open and attached to each buttonhole. The different methods of doing this are all described in the section on pages 218–227.

Regardless of which approach you choose, I cannot urge you strongly enough to try it out on a swatch before you ever attempt it on your actual garment; you will save yourself endless frustration.

Enclosing Cut Edges

There were many charming traditional sweaters, especially in the Scandinavian countries, which were worked in the round from waist to shoulder and then cut like fabric to make the openings for armholes, necklines and center fronts. These edges were then finished off with decorative woven bias tapes, which enclosed the cut edges, rather than with knitted borders. This isn't much done these days, but you might find it a quaint and old-fashioned touch for a sweater or vest.

Knitted Bias Hems and Facings

There are some situations in which a bias facing offers the right solution to the problem of finishing an edge. These facings are generally knitted separately, can be made whatever width is suitable, and can be worked in fine or split yarn or in an entirely different type of yarn or color, if you wish. On a Single Bias strip, the bias runs from edge to edge with or without a foldline; on a Double Bias strip, the bias runs from a center foldline out to the edge. Bias facings are ideal for curved edges, such as at a neckline or the bottom corners of a center front opening, and a lightweight facing of this sort does very well when applied over the selvedges of the seams in a knitted fabric that has been cut in order to finish

them neatly (see "Openings," page 114), or to hide a zipper tape on the inside.

For a more detailed discussion of how to knit a bias fabric, see Slope and Bias (page 170). You will find that once you are familiar with the general concept, it is easy to work out a simple pattern for whatever width or type of facing you wish to make.

Single Bias Strips

Single Bias is the easiest to make and the most versatile. It is generally sewn down flat to the inside of the garment just back from the edge to lend support, or to cover a cut edge or a zipper tape. You can also sew one side of the bias strip to the outside, the other to the inside, in order to completely encase the edge and produce a round, corded finish.

A bias strip will adapt itself to a simple curve, but not to an S-curve. For instance, if you have knit a strip with a left bias it will follow the contour of a curve in which the inner, smaller curve is on the right side and the outer, larger curve is on the left, but it will not go the other way. In order to accommodate a curve in the other direction, you must either knit a right bias strip, or turn the left bias strip upside down. That's easy enough, but don't expect it to go first one way, then the other, as in an S-curve.

Double Bias Strips

A Double Bias strip has bias running out from the center to both edges and has a pronounced foldline. It is sewn down so that it completely encases the edges of the garment. If the bias is sewn to the very edge, keep in mind that it will add width to the fabric, just as any other border would. In the section on Slope and Bias you will also find instructions for a Curved Double Bias facing that can be used for necklines.

Welts, Pleats, and Tucks

These design elements are made using many of the same principles found in Hems, above, the major difference being that they are internal to the fabric rather than at the edge. All of them add a certain amount of bulk or stiffness to the fabric because it is folded back on itself. Therefore, with the exception of the Welt, which has a robust charm that would en-

hance even a bulky knit, the others should be restricted to the fine yarns. Also, I would like to encourage you to be playful with these concepts. Welts and Tucks are not well enough known, and I'm sure clever knitters can find interesting ways to use them. Pleats seem confined to skirts in most people's minds, but they shouldn't be, as there are other design applications.

Welts

A welt is a narrow ridge, either horizontal or vertical, that protrudes from the surface of the fabric. It is made like a tiny hem in that the fabric is folded back on itself and secured in place, but there is no foldline, so the effect is rounded rather than flat.

STOCKINETTE WELT

The simplest way to create a horizontal Welt is by making use of the natural tendency of Stockinette to curl toward the Knit side. All that is necessary is to work a few rows of Reverse Stockinette on a background of Stockinette (see page 20).

The number of rows in the Welt can vary, depending upon the effect desired and your stitch gauge. One row of Purl stitches will simply form a nubby horizontal line against the smooth ground of the Knit stitches and is rather a minimal Welt. As you add rows, however, Stockinette curl will show its effects, and the Welt will begin to protrude from the face of the fabric in a softly rounded shape. Beyond about one-half inch the effect begins to diminish somewhat and will eventually flatten out. Of course, you must be careful not to subdue the Welt in the process of cleaning or steaming the garment.

A closely spaced series of these Welts will behave like horizontal ribbing, but will have less elasticity than vertical ribbing. If they are used within the fabric, rather than going from edge to edge, they will cause gathering on either side, just as any ribbing does to the fabric above and/or below. Very small sections of horizontal welting are often found in stitch patterns to produce a highly textured surface.

The vertical counterpart to the horizontal Stockinette Welt relies on the tendency of narrow columns of Knit stitches to protrude, just as they do in ribbing. Simply isolate a few columns of Knit stitches in a ground of Reverse Stockinette. As the Welt approaches about half an inch in width, the fabric will begin to flatten and lose the tendency to curl. Stretching the fabric out during washing or steaming will destroy the effect.

ROULEAU WELT

Here is a very charming variation on the Reverse Stockinette Welt that cannot be pulled open by the weight of the fabric.

1. At the point where you want the Welt, if you are not already doing so, begin Stockinette with Knit on the outside of the garment, and work between one-half and one inch of fabric. Cast off across the row.
2. On the inside, pick up the same number of stitches below the first row of the Welt, working as to Purl

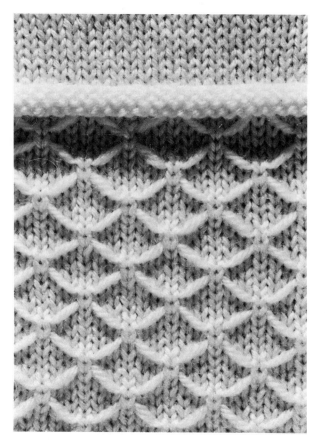

A ROULEAUX WELT DIVIDING TWO STITCH PATTERNS

into the heads of the stitches. Continue with the work as before.

The Welt will curl down over the outside of the fabric like a little rolled awning, attached only at its base. You can certainly create the same effect vertically, by working the Rouleau on picked-up stitches.

KNIT BELOW WELT

A horizontal Welt can be made permanent through the use of a Knit Below technique. When this is done, it cannot be pulled flat by the weight of the garment or diminished by cleaning or steaming. Because this Welt does not rely on Stockinette curl for its effect, it can be done in Knit, which gives it a nice smooth appearance.

Generally these Welts are a minimum of three rows, the maximum being determined by your gauge and the effect you are trying to achieve. A good way to determine how many rows to allow is to use a flexible tape to measure the circumference of something like a pen or pencil that is the size of the Welt you are trying to make. Use that measurement and your stitch gauge to make the calculation. Keep in mind that the extra number of rows inserted where the Welt is to be worked are *not* counted as rows that contribute to the length of the garment. This makes it very easy to add a Welt to an existing pattern, as the row count for the pattern remains unchanged.

If you are working on the inside:

1. Slip the first stitch on the left needle.
2. Reach the left needle tip down and insert it up under the Purl nub in the appropriate row, directly below the slipped stitch.
3. Raise this stitch up, and place it on the left needle in the correct position, with the right side of the stitch on the nearside of the needle.
4. Return the slipped stitch to the left needle and Purl two together (the returned stitch and the raised stitch).
5. Repeat these four steps across the row.

The reason that you must slip the stitch, and then return it after picking up the stitch below is that the latter must be the left stitch of the decrease pair. If this is not done, the raised stitch would be twisted around and show on the outside.

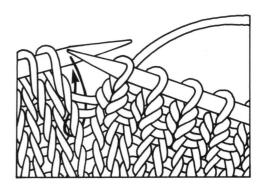

WORKING A KNIT BELOW WELT ON THE OUTSIDE

KNIT BELOW WELTS ON SEED STITCH

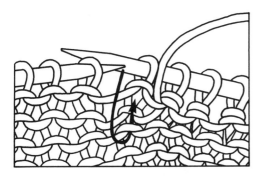

WORKING A KNIT BELOW WELT ON THE INSIDE

If you are working on the outside:

1. Reach the right needle tip down on the farside and insert it under the Purl nub in the first row of the Welt, directly below the first stitch on the left needle.
2. Raise this stitch up and place it on the left needle in the correct position, with the right side of the stitch on the nearside of the needle.
3. Knit two together (the raised stitch and the stitch to the left).
4. Repeat these three steps across the row.

In this case, the raised stitch must be the right stitch of the decrease pair in order to hide it on the inside.

It is a little more difficult to work this way as you must try to find the nub on the farside of the fabric. If you have trouble working into the correct row below, it may be worthwhile to take the time to mark it with a contrasting color yarn as a guide. An easy way to do this is with the weaving-in technique, (page 282), but if you are not familiar with the special knitting technique

required, you can also thread the yarn into a tapestry needle (page 350) and accomplish the same thing.

A Welt of this sort offers many opportunities for creativity. It can be made in a different color or color pattern. The last row before the Welt and the first row after the Welt can be worked in a different color, with the Welt worked in the same color as the main fabric. It can also be worked in a different yarn, or in Stockinette against a fabric worked in some other stitch pattern. In these two cases, however, you must be careful about your stitch gauge and if necessary increase or decrease on the first and last rows of the Welt in order to make the Welt the same width as the main fabric.

Most commonly a Welt is worked across the entire width of the fabric, but it is possible to make smaller Welts and scatter them across the fabric as a decorative motif. Simply decide according to your stitch gauge how many stitches and rows to include, and how to space the mini-Welts out on the fabric. If you use just a few stitches and rows, it will have a puff or blister shape. If you include enough stitches for the Welt to be an inch or two long, the effect will be of barlike ridges.

If you do not like the process of picking up the stitches in the row below, you might be interested in the Double Knit Welt (page 241).

SLIP STITCH WELT

Here is a vertical Welt made on the same principles used to create a knitted cord.

Row 1: Work the Welt, wrapping the yarn twice for each stitch.

Row 2: Slip the Welt stitches with the yarn stranded on the inside, dropping the extra wraps as you do so. Pull the yarn very tightly across the slipped stitches to bunch them together as you work the next stitch, then continue the row at normal tension.

Because the stitches of the Welt are worked on one row and slipped on the next, they will have half the number of rows as the surrounding fabric. The stitch elongation works to balance the two so the Welt does not tighten up in relation to the surrounding fabric and cause it to be distorted.

If the extra wrap on each stitch of the Welt lengthens them too much, there are two other ways to control the amount of additional yarn provided to the stitches of the Welt. Slightly less yarn is provided by inserting a Yarnover between each Welt stitch. These Yarnovers are dropped on the return row and the extra yarn is taken up by the adjacent stitches. The least amount of elongation is created by using an extra wrap on just the center stitch of a three-stitch Welt. (For more information on these techniques, see page 36.) The correct approach should be worked out on a swatch before you begin.

You may also work the Welt in Reverse Stockinette on a Stockinette ground. If you are working the Welt on a background done in any other stitch pattern you must be even more careful about matching the gauge of the Welt to the gauge of the fabric.

Wrapped Vertical Welts

There are several other stitch techniques that can be used to work Welts, some producing a more pronounced effect than others. A firmly worked Couching Stitch (page 81) or a tight Wrap Stitch (page 55) will all create welts if they are repeatedly worked on the same columns of stitches and spaced about one-quarter to one-half inch apart. In these cases, of course, the wrap that pulls the Welt together shows on the outside, making all of them quite decorative.

If you are modifying a pattern to include a Welt of this sort, keep in mind that the Welt will add a slight amount of width to the garment, as the stitches are not pulled together so tightly that the stitches on either side of the Welt are side by side.

Sewn Welts

Instead of working the Welt at the same time as you knit the fabric, the welts can be sewn into place later. Add the number of stitch columns you want to include

A SEWN VERTICAL WELT

in each Welt to the number of stitches needed for the width of the fabric. In order to guide you in sewing, run a length of contrast-color embroidery thread up the columns of stitches to each side of those to be included in the Welt. Working on the inside, use Seaming Reverse Stockinette (page 368), working into the running thread lying adjacent to the columns of stitches of the Welt and drawing it up tightly; be careful not to pucker the fabric.

This is a very nice way to add a series of tiny welts just at the yoke that, once drawn together, will gather the bodice below. Done the length of the fabric, a few adroitly placed Welts of this sort can also serve to reduce the width on a garment that is too large; you must, however, be careful of the effect it has at the top and bottom; tapering the Welts is one solution.

On the same principles, it is just as easy to work a Sewn Welt horizontally as vertically. Here again it is best to mark the rows above and below those of the Welt and sew into the running threads.

Pleats

There are a variety of Pleat styles, all of which can be created in a knitted fabric. Knife Pleats are all folded in one direction, a Box Pleat has two foldlines that meet at the center, with an Inverted Pleat the two foldlines face away from one another, and Accordion Pleats—well, they look like an accordion, one foldline protruding, one receding. The latter is generally done with stitch patterns rather than construction techniques and is not dealt with here. All of the former are made much like they would be in a woven fabric, being folded and pressed into place and secured at the top edge. However, unlike a woven fabric, a knit requires a foldline that is built in in order to hold the shape of the Pleat and give it a crisp edge.

Consider working Pleats on a peplum, either all the way around or just a few placed front and back. You can add interest to the wrist of a straight sleeve, or add moving ease with a Box Pleat down the center back, or knife pleats at each side of the front and back. As you can well imagine, Pleats are most successful when done in fine yarns.

Foldlines for Pleats

Regardless of which type of Pleat you plan to use, there must be two Vertical Foldlines (page 205), one for the inner foldline, one for the outer foldline, each requiring an extra stitch. In addition to the stitches required for the width of the fabric and those for the foldlines, you must also add extra stitches for the foldback and the underlay. Multiply twice the width of the Pleat times your stitch gauge, plus two additional stitches for the foldlines, to find the number required for each Pleat.

Determine which way the Pleat will be folded, to the right or left. As you work on the outside of the fabric, the inner foldline will be first, the outer foldline second for a Pleat folded to the right; the reverse is true for a Pleat folded to the left. The inner foldline stitch lies between those of the foldback and the underlay. You may find it helpful to identify them with two different-color ring markers, at least until the pattern is well established.

To work the Pleat:

• Every other row, slip the stitch of the inner foldline with the yarn stranded on the outside of the fabric, slip the stitch of the outer fold with the yarn stranded on the inside.

Strand the yarn across the slipped stitches firmly, as this helps to maintain the fold. Although the stitches of the inner foldline are slipped with the yarn stranded on the outside of the fabric, the strands will be hidden in the fold and won't be seen.

Securing the Pleat

The finished Pleat must be secured at the top edge to hold it in position. While it can be sewn into position after casting off, that tends to be far bulkier than using Joinery Decreases. In order to use the latter method, however, the Pleat must be folded into position while the stitches are still on the needle.

Securing a Pleat Folded to the Right

1. Working on the outside, knit across the row until there are the same number of stitches on the left needle before the first foldline as there are between the two foldlines, plus one. Slip these stitches for the underlay to a double-point needle.

2. Place the stitch of the inner foldline and the stitches of the foldback on a second double-point needle.

3. Fold the pleat into place with the left needle on the nearside of the two double-points and all three tips lined up. The stitch of the outer foldline will be the first on the near needle, on the right side of the Pleat. The stitch of the inner foldline will be the last on the center needle, at the left side of the Pleat.

4. Work across the top of the Pleat using Knit Three Together to join the stitches of the Pleat, taking one stitch from each of the three needles. Continue across the row.

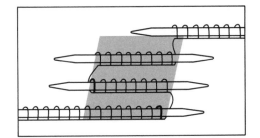

SECURING A PLEAT FOLDED TO THE RIGHT

Securing a Pleat Folded to the Left

1. Slip the stitches of the Pleat to the double-point needles just as described above.

2. Fold the Pleat into position with the left needle on the farside of the two double-points and all three tips lined up. The stitch of the outer foldline will be the last stitch on the near needle, on the left side of the Pleat, the stitch of the inner foldline will be the first stitch on the center needle, on the right side of the Pleat.

3. Work the double decreases and continue across the row.

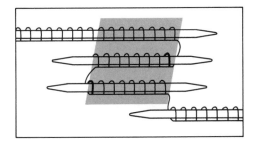

SECURING A PLEAT FOLDED TO THE LEFT

UNPRESSED PLEATS

You can, of course, form Unpressed Pleats by adding the extra width for the Pleat, but eliminating the foldlines. Fold the Pleat into position and secure it just as described above.

TAPERED PLEATS

If you wish to reduce the bulk at the top edge, Pleats can be tapered so that the fold at the top is either narrower or diminished entirely.

Plan the change in width using the information in Calculating Steps and Points (page 437). If you want the Pleat to disappear at the top, use both foldlines, but abandon the inner one when it is likely to become visible as the Pleats flatten out. Make the increases or decreases as unobtrusive as possible, and place them on either side of the inner foldline. The outer foldline should be continued to the top as a decorative element, even when it is no longer working to create a fold.

Tucks

A Tuck can be thought of either as a Pleat secured along one side, or as a flat Welt, and like the latter it can be horizontal or vertical. Remember there will be three layers of fabric, so this is not a technique to use with bulky yarn.

HORIZONTAL TUCK

Using your stitch gauge, calculate the number of rows required for the depth of the Tuck, double this figure, and add one more row for the foldline. Remember that the rows that make up the Tuck will not add length to the garment.

Work to the row where you wish the Tuck to be and then proceed as follows:

1. Work the Tuck, placing either a Purl or a Picot Foldline (page 202 or 203) on the center row.
2. When the Tuck is complete, pick up the Purl nubs in the row below the Tuck and use Joinery Decreases to secure the fold, just as for the Knit Below Welt, above.

If you think you will have difficulty identifying the correct Purl nubs to pick up, work the first row of the Tuck in a different-color yarn on a circular needle, then slide the stitches back to the other tip of the needle where you can pick up the original yarn and continue with the remainder of the rows of the Tuck. The running threads in the contrasting color will lie below the heads of the stitches, identifying them for pickup. Be-

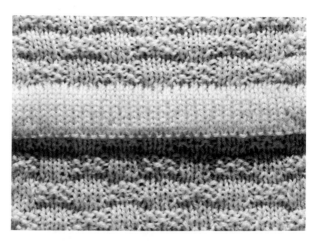

HORIZONTAL TUCK WITH PURL FOLDLINE

cause the Tuck folds down over this first row, the other color will not be seen in the finished fabric. Just as with the Welt, you can entirely eliminate the difficulties of picking up the stitches in the row below by using a Double Knit Tuck (page 241).

VERTICAL TUCK

Just as for a Pleat, determine the number of stitches necessary for the width of the Tuck, double this figure, and add two stitches for the inner and outer foldlines. The completed Tuck will not add width to the garment.

1. Work the Tuck exactly as for a Pleat, finishing it at the top to the right or left as the case may be.
2. To secure the Tuck along its length, sew the edge of the inner fold to the inside of the garment with a Running Thread Seam (page 365).

Because the Tuck is secured all along one side, if a ribbing or some other border is wanted at the bottom of the garment, this must be worked in the opposite direction on stitches picked up along the lower, outside edge after the Tuck is folded and sewn into place.

PARTIAL TUCK

This combines some of the features of a Tuck with some of the features of a Pleat. Work the Tuck just as outlined above, but in finishing, seam it on the inside only part way down. The portion that is treated as a Pleat will add width to the garment, the portion that is treated as a Tuck will not.

To make a Partial Horizontal Tuck place the stitches to either side on holders while you work the Tuck; when it has been secured, reactivate the stitches and go on as usual. This would, for instance, make an interesting pocket flap.

12
Openings

A variety of functional elements, such as buttons, pockets, and thumbs or fingers all require openings in the knitted fabric. For the most part, these openings call a great deal of attention to themselves, and it is important that they be done skillfully and smoothly. Since buttonholes cause a lot of people trouble, and because there are quite a variety, the greater part of this section will deal with them. Fortunately, many of the techniques used to make buttonholes are also those used for the other purposes, and it is relatively simple to explain how the principles used for the former apply to the latter.

Buttonholes

Buttonholes make me rather unhappy, I suppose because I am a perfectionist by nature and it is quite impossible to make a perfect buttonhole in a knitted fabric. Oh, we can make reasonable buttonholes, but they all look rather better when covered by the button than they do alone. The biggest problem is that a knitted fabric is so resilient that the buttonholes stretch out of shape and become large and unsightly, sometimes so much so they won't hold the button unless it is enormous and out of proportion to the garment, and that simply won't do. It's not a bad idea to avoid them entirely whenever possible, but then there are all the pleasures of a good cardigan sweater or vest to deal with, and so we must have them after all.

The problems buttonholes present are minimized if they are kept as small as possible. Whereas in a woven fabric, one would make the buttonhole slightly larger than the button, in knitting one makes it slightly smaller because of the stretch inherent to the fabric. Your stitch gauge also affects the size; when using the same number of stitches, what might be a small buttonhole in fine yarn will become a good-sized one in heavy yarn. While I have given you the instructions here for the larger buttonholes, I can't think of many situations where you would actually use them because they really do get too big. As a general rule, choose the smallest buttons that are appropriate to the style of the garment and make test buttonholes on a swatch to check the size opening that works best.

One of the difficulties with researching buttonholes is that so many knitters have found them unsatisfactory, and come up with so many clever attempts at a solution, that it took a good bit of time to go through all of the subtle little tricks and test how well each one of them worked compared to the others. After more buttonholes than I care to think about, here are the best of the lot, some of them quite respectable and sensible. I am going to give all the instructions as if you were working in Stockinette and starting on the Knit side. Regardless of what sort of stitch you are using, however, the buttonhole is treated as a separate case and the instructions are the same.

Eyelet Buttonholes

There are very small buttonholes, all of them quite simple to work. In fact, you need seek no farther, as one of them will do for pretty much anything you have in mind.

SMALL EYELET BUTTONHOLE

This is the easiest buttonhole to make, and it is quite nice. It is traditionally used for layette and children's garments, but is perfectly appropriate any time a small button will be used. It also works nicely as an opening for a drawstring.

- Use either the Left or Right Smooth Eyelet: SSK, YO; or YO K2tog.

Since an Eyelet makes a round opening rather than a slit, as is the case with the typical buttonhole, the button must be quite a bit larger than the opening in order to stay in place. For this reason, the technique is generally used only with the finer yarns and needles, and it is also why there is no point in using a Double Eyelet, as that just compounds the problem. If you want a really tiny opening, eliminate the Yarnover, and on the next row work an Open Running Thread Increase (page 71) adjacent to the decrease stitch.

If you are going to use this buttonhole on Single Rib, remove a Purl stitch with the decrease, so the opening is recessed between two columns of Knit.

NARROW EYELET BUTTONHOLE

Here is a new version of an Eyelet Buttonhole that changes its shape from round to narrow. It is more trouble to work than the Small Eyelet Buttonhole, although not much, and the result is so superior I am sure you will not mind. This is a very neat, quiet, and orderly little buttonhole. The technique can also be used in horizontal series to create openings through which to thread ribbon.

1. On the inside, work a Yarnover where you want the opening.
2. On the next row, work a Slip Pullover Decrease on the Yarnover strand and the preceding stitch; do not discard the strand. Then work a Knit Two Together Decrease on the strand and the next stitch.

In other words, the same Yarnover strand is worked with both adjacent stitches, first with a left decrease, then with a right decrease, so it is hidden on the inside of the fabric. While it is possible to work the Yarnover on an outside row and the decreases on an inside row, the latter are more difficult to do than those in the version given above.

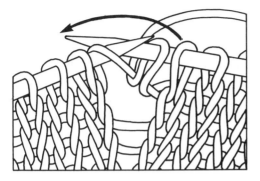

WORKING FIRST DECREASE OF NARROW EYELET
BUTTONHOLE

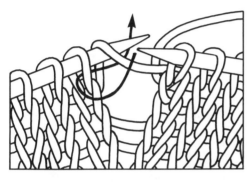

WORKING SECOND DECREASE OF NARROW EYELET
BUTTONHOLE

Notice that this buttonhole is made between two columns of stitches, rather than in one, which helps to keep it narrow, and because of the way the decreases are used, the columns of stitches on either side are uninterrupted. These two qualities combine to make it very unobtrusive.

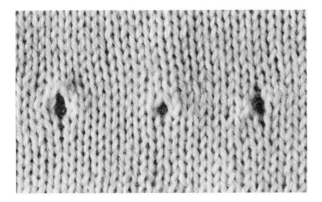

EYELET BUTTONHOLES/RIGHT: SMALL EYELETS/
CENTER: NARROW EYELET/LEFT: "THREE ROW"

Vertical Buttonholes

Here is a group of buttonholes ranging in size from three rows to as many as you wish, depending upon your stitch gauge and the desired effect. In appearance,

a vertical buttonhole is more successful than a horizontal one. The difficulty is with its behavior. In wear, the button exerts tension against the side of the buttonhole, which causes it to widen and enlarge. At its worst, the edge of the button band will take on a scalloped appearance and the button may pop out of the buttonhole. For this reason, except for the very small ones, these buttonholes should not be used on a tight-fitting garment.

There are times, however, when vertical buttonholes are the type that would fit the garment design best, and since they are more attractive than the horizontal buttonholes, you will want to use them anyhow. Some of the splaying problem can be overcome by backing the buttonhole band with some sort of woven facing. For information on this, see page 383.

THREE-ROW BUTTONHOLE

This variation lengthens the Eyelet Buttonhole without widening it.

1. Begin on the outside with a Yarnover in the correct position.
2. On the next row, slip the Yarnover, and then make another Yarnover. (There are now two Yarnover strands on the right needle, one from each row.)
3. On the final row, first work a Slip Pullover Decrease on the preceding stitch and *both* Yarnover strands; do not drop the strands from the left needle. Then work a Knit Two Together on the same strands and the following stitch.

Generally, a single Yarnover on the first row of the buttonhole is adequate. If you knit tightly, and want to enlarge the opening somewhat, use a Double Yarnover on the first row, a single on the second row, but otherwise work in the same way. The result will be somewhat looser and wider than the version given above.

FOUR-ROW BUTTONHOLE

Here is a way to carry the Yarnover another row, although at this point we are getting into rather large buttonholes, and I advise caution.

1. Beginning on the outside, work to the point where you wish to make the buttonhole, turn, and work back. Turn and work to the buttonhole again. (This makes three rows on one side of the buttonhole.)
2. Make a Yarnover to cross the gap and continue to the end of the row. Turn.
3. Work to the stitch before the buttonhole and work a Purl Together Decrease on that stitch and the Yarnover strand; discard the stitch, but retain the strand on the left needle. Turn and work to the end of the

row. (This makes three rows on the other side of the buttonhole, with the Yarnover strand caught up behind the stitches on rows two and three.)

4. On the final row, work back to the stitch before the buttonhole and do another Purl Together Decrease on that stitch and the Yarnover strand. Discard the strand and complete the row.

The decreases are worked so that the Yarnover strand is hidden on the inside of the garment. If you find that the buttonhole is constricted, use a Double Yarnover instead of a single. The same technique can be applied to a six-row buttonhole: Use a Double Yarnover, work five rows on the first side, five rows on the second, attaching the strand on the second, fourth and final sixth row.

If you are working in Stockinette, please keep in mind that it tends to curl toward the Purl side. The longer you make a vertical buttonhole, therefore, the more likely it is that you will begin to see evidence of the curl. It is possible to work the edges of the buttonhole in Garter Stitch Selvedge to help overcome this tendency, but actually the best way to avoid the curl is to work a smaller buttonhole.

Traditional Vertical Buttonhole

This method of working a vertical buttonhole is found in every book and can be made over any number of rows. Unfortunately, it requires breaking the yarn and, therefore, leaves two ends of yarn at the buttonhole (one of which can be used to reinforce the buttonhole, if you choose), and both must be hidden on the inside. I have developed another version that does not do this, below, but it can only be worked over an even number of rows. The basic principle used in both of them can be extended to working vertical pocket openings (see below).

Version One/Even-Number Rows

1. Work to the lower point of the buttonhole. Leave all of the stitches on the other side of the buttonhole in waiting. Turn and work a minimum of three rows back and forth along one side of the buttonhole, ending with the tips of the needles at the opening.
2. Pick up the yarn from a second ball and start it on the first stitch on the left needle. Work an even number of rows, one less than worked on the other side, ending with the tips of the needles at the opening.
3. Break off the second ball of yarn and complete the final row with the original yarn.

Version Two/Uneven-Number Rows

1. Work the first step just as outlined above but break off the yarn.
2. Leave the first side in waiting, reattach the yarn on the first stitch on the left needle, and work the second

side of the buttonhole the same number of rows as the first, ending at the selvedge.

3. Turn and work the final row directly across the top of the buttonhole without further ado.

Either way, there will be two ends of yarn hanging from the buttonhole, one at the bottom, one at the top. If one is to be used to reinforce the buttonhole, make sure to allow adequate length when you break it off. Even if you do not wish to reinforce the buttonhole, leave the ends at least long enough to thread through a wide-eyed sewing needle and work them invisibly into the fabric on the inside of the garment (see "Purl Duplicate Stitch," page 380).

Version Three/No Ends

Here is a new version with no ends at the buttonhole to worry about. In these instructions, when I refer to "right" and "left," it is as if you are looking at the outside of the fabric as you are knitting.

1. If you are not already working with a long double-point or circular needle, use one in your right hand and work across the row below the buttonhole. This should be an inside row.
2. On just that portion of the fabric to the right of the buttonhole, work two rows, ending at the right selvedge.
3. Break the yarn, then go to the first stitch at the left selvedge and reattach it. Work two rows to the left of the buttonhole.
4. Turn and work directly across the top of the buttonhole and complete the row.

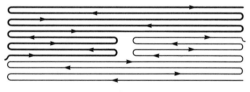

ROW PATTERN FOR TRADITIONAL VERTICAL BUTTONHOLE/VERSION THREE

As you can see, instead of two ends of yarn at the buttonhole, there will be one at each selvedge. This is a two-row buttonhole, but it is easy enough to work it over four rows; three is impossible. If the row below the buttonhole is an outside row, just work the left side of the buttonhole first, break the yarn, reattach it on the right, and then work that side. Unfortunately, there is no way to work it so there is just one end of yarn for reinforcing; this is an either/or situation.

Please note that the rows above and below the buttonhole are worked in opposite directions. This comes about because you are working on a double-point needle and can work in any direction you want (see the Slide, page 236), but it does have implications if you are working a complex stitch pattern from written instructions rather than charted ones, and it could cause some patterns to be more difficult to work. If necessary, chart your pattern (see page 459) and try this out on a swatch to see what will happen. You may very well decide that it's easier to deal with the ends at the buttonhole.

The principle used in working this buttonhole is also applicable to a Vertical or Sloped Pocket Opening (see page 228).

Horizontal Buttonholes

This is the most common type of buttonhole. Functionally, it is a better style than a vertical one because the button rides in the corner of the buttonhole and the pull it exerts causes less distortion of the fabric. Unfortunately, when worked in the way given in most books, the appearance of these buttonholes often leaves a great deal to be desired, but there are some tricks that can be used to make them satisfactory.

TRADITIONAL HORIZONTAL BUTTONHOLE

Here is the way a horizontal buttonhole is usually made. Frankly, I don't recommend that you use this buttonhole and include it only because it is so common I must mention it. It does introduce the basic idea at work here, and it is worth understanding so you grasp the underlying principle. The number of stitches involved, of course, depends upon your gauge and the size buttonhole appropriate to your garment design.

1. Knit to the point where you wish to make the buttonhole.
2. Use Pullover Cast-off to remove the number of stitches required for the size opening you desire.
3. Continue across the row, turn, and work back to the buttonhole.
4. Use Simple Cast-on to replace the number of stitches cast off. Continue with the work.

The buttonhole is simplicity itself to work, but when you examine the result you won't be particularly happy with it. There will be a gap at the lower right corner

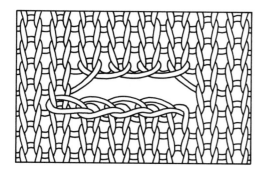

TRADITIONAL HORIZONTAL BUTTONHOLE

where the running thread stretches between the column of stitches to the right and the first cast-off stitch to the left, and the last cast-off stitch will cross the column of stitches to the left of the buttonhole. So while the cast-on stitches are centered in the top half of the buttonhole, the line of stitches in the bottom half of the buttonhole will look like they are one step to the left, giving the buttonhole a skewed appearance. In addition, it is difficult to work Simple Cast-on tightly enough to give a neat and firm edge, and since it does not resemble Pullover Cast-off, the top of the buttonhole will have a different appearance from the bottom, and the whole thing will be wide open. It can't be used without reinforcing the edges to pull things together (see page 223).

IMPROVED HORIZONTAL BUTTONHOLE

Here are the best tricks I could find or think of, all assembled into one technique. The result needs no reinforcement of any kind, is reasonably symmetrical and neat, and causes a minimum of distortion to the stitches on either side. The instructions are lengthy, but the technique is easy enough to do. Once you've gone through it a few times it will make sense and I'm sure you'll appreciate how much better your buttonholes will look.

1. On the outside, work to the point where the buttonhole is to begin. Take up an extra strand of the same yarn, fifteen to sixteen inches long. Allow an end on the extra strand, then, holding this yarn and the yarn you have been knitting with as one, bring the yarns to the nearside. With the right needle tip, reach around to the farside and slip one stitch so that it crosses to the left. Strand the yarns past the slipped stitch and return them to the farside between the needle tips and leave them hanging there.
2. Slip a second stitch in the same manner, then pull the first over the second and off the needle. Repeat with this crossed version of Slip Stitch Cast-off until you have removed the number of stitches required, but one. Slip the last stitch normally, pull the previous stitch over, then return the remaining slipped stitch to the left needle.
3. Use Half-Hitch Cast-on to replace the stitches cast off, carrying the separate strand of yarn on your thumb for the baseline, and the yarn you have been knitting with on your forefinger for the stitches (information on how to use Half-Hitch Cast-on within a fabric can be found on page 140). Pinch the end of the baseline strand against the fabric with your right hand to prevent it from pulling loose and cast on very firmly, particularly with the first stitch in order to draw the corner together.
4. When you have cast on the required number of stitches, pass the baseline strand to the farside, slip the first stitch left of the buttonhole to the right nee-

METHOD OF SLIPPING STITCH TO CAST-OFF FOR IMPROVED HORIZONTAL BUTTONHOLE

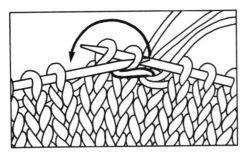

CASTING-OFF FOR IMPROVED HORIZONTAL BUTTONHOLE

PATH OF YARN FOR FINISHING CORNER OF IMPROVED HORIZONTAL BUTTONHOLE

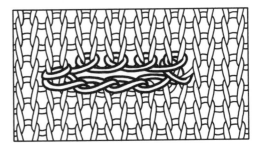

IMPROVED HORIZONTAL BUTTONHOLE

dle, pass the strand to the nearside, slip the stitch back to the left needle and pass the strand to the farside, thus wrapping it just as for a Wrapped Turning Point (page 176).

Pick up the yarn you have been knitting with and continue with the row. To finish the buttonhole:

1. Thread the end at the right corner into a tapestry needle, and bring it through to the nearside between the first two cast-on stitches, then down between the baseline strand and the running thread, as shown. Next pass the needle back to the farside under the running thread to the right of the first stitch. On the inside, hide the end with Purl Duplicate Stitch (page 380).
2. On the inside, thread the end at the other corner into the tapestry needle and hide it with Purl Duplicate Stitch as well.

There are many things to notice here. Because this uses a crossed Slip Stitch Cast-off, the stitches will be tight, giving them a much neater appearance than could be achieved with regular Pullover Cast-off. (You may want to use a smaller needle for this step.)

The two strands of yarn are laid under the first cast-off stitch so when the first stitch is cast on at the top of the buttonhole, the corner will be pulled together. The wrap around the stitch to the left matches the appearance of the last cast-off stitch, which encircles the base of the same stitch.

The method of working in the end at the left corner extends the cast-on edge to the corner and helps tighten it up.

CONTRAST-COLOR YARN BUTTONHOLE

This technique is used for horizontal buttonholes, as well as for pocket openings and thumb holes in mittens; it's very clever and easy to do.

1. At the point where you wish to make the opening, Knit the required number of stitches with a strand of yarn in a contrasting color.
2. Slip these stitches back to the left needle, one at a time.
3. Now work across the contrast-color stitches with your regular yarn and complete the row.

Continue with the knitting without further ado. You may wish to tighten up the contrast-color stitches to make sure they don't pull out, or even tie the two ends together loosely. After the garment section is completed, the stitches are freed by removing the contrast-color yarn and finished in whatever way is appropriate (finish-

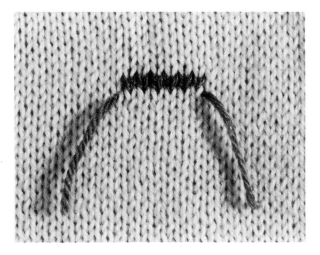

CONTRAST COLOR YARN OPENING

ing techniques for this as a buttonhole can be found on page 223, for a pocket on page 227, and for a thumb on page 229).

Edge and Border Buttonholes

There are a variety of ways to make buttonholes in the join between fabric and border. With any edging or border that is sewn into place, the spaces for the buttonholes can be skipped so they are left open. If you are using a corded edging, it can be sewn into place so as to form loops for the buttons. The same effect can be achieved with crochet by skipping a certain number of selvedge stitches and chaining across the top of the buttonhole, or you can work a buttonhole within a crochet edging.

Similarly, if you are picking up stitches along a selvedge to knit the border, skip sufficient selvedge stitches for the width of the buttonhole, casting on those stitches instead. It is traditional to use a Knit Cast-on for this, but it leaves a strand at the corner that is unattractive. You might want to try Half-Hitch Cast-on using an extra strand of yarn for the baseline. Although this requires hiding the ends of yarn, they can be used as reinforcement.

If you want to use Corded Cast-off on the picked-up stitches (page 155), work the cord without attaching it to the fabric for several rows, then begin attaching it again. If you begin attaching it on the next selvedge stitch, it will form a loop; if you skip a few selvedge stitches, it will form a slit buttonhole.

Finishing Techniques for Buttonholes

Some of the above buttonholes may be used just as they are when you have finished knitting, and with many of the others finishing is optional; but if the buttonhole is going to be subjected to rather hard wear, if the yarn used for the garment is particularly fragile, or if the fabric was worked with a loose tension, you might wish to finish the edges with one of the sewing techniques described here. This will reinforce the buttonhole so it will stand up to the abrasion and pull of the button better, and it reduces the resilience of the opening so it will be less likely to stretch out of shape. The Contrast-Color Yarn Opening, when used for a buttonhole, must be finished in a particular way, which is detailed below. All of these techniques are most successful when you use a finer yarn, or split your main yarn in order to reduce bulk (see page 363).

If the yarn is not plied, or if it is fuzzy or nubby, there is no point in attempting to use it for sewing a buttonhole. Fortunately, there are some good alternatives, but one must be a little more resourceful, a little more creative in a situation like this. If you cannot match the yarn, you can at least try to match the color. If you are working with a wool, or a wool-like yarn, the best choice would be a needlepoint or crewel embroidery yarn. If you are using any other fiber, you will want to look at either cotton or silk embroidery threads. All of these materials are plied and easily divided, and you will find a large range of colors to choose from.

If you cannot find a color that matches, you may have to consider using a contrast-color yarn on the principle that if someone hands you a lemon, it's best to make lemonade. While it is possible to use plain sewing thread, I think it is difficult to handle compared to the materials mentioned above; it tends to tangle and doesn't lie as smoothly around the edges of the buttonhole, although for a very tailored, sporty garment you might find buttonhole thread satisfactory.

Once you have selected an appropriate material, you will want to practice sewing a buttonhole on a test swatch until you have mastered it. Don't practice on your garment, or trick yourself into thinking that it looks easy and you don't have to bother with the test swatch. That route only leads to frustration and disappointment.

Attaching the Yarn

For the most part, hiding the ends on the inside of the fabric with Purl Duplicate Stitch (page 380) is adequate to secure typical knitting yarns when used for finishing an opening. Weave in the first end before you start sewing the opening; weave in the second when you are done.

However, if you are working with a smooth, slippery yarn, by all means, use a knot in addition to weaving in the ends. The knot described here is very minimal and will not show itself on the outside of the fabric.

1. Weave the ends in on the inside of the fabric with Duplicate Stitch, stopping at the bottom of a stitch.
2. Bring the needle up under the side of the last Duplicate Stitch (the one in the same yarn you are sewing

with) and draw it through until a small loop is formed.

3. Pass the needle down through the loop, tighten the loop first, then draw the remainder of the yarn through.

4. When you have finished sewing, make another knot on the inside on the closest strand of the same yarn, then hide the end with Duplicate Stitch as before.

Knotting the yarn to itself rather than to the strand within the fabric helps prevent the knot from peeking through to the outside and is essential if you are working with a contrast-color yarn.

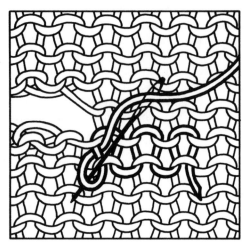

ATTACHING YARN FOR BUTTONHOLE WITH PURL DUPLICATE STITCH

OVERCAST STITCH

Any but the buttonhole done with contrast-color yarn can be finished with a simple Overcast Stitch. It will stabilize the buttonhole so it doesn't stretch out, but it will not reinforce it against hard wear. The technique works quite well on garments made with fuzzy yarns, where the sewn stitches will be obscured by the yarn, but it isn't attractive enough for garments done in smooth yarn, where the edges of the buttonhole will be fully visible. When working an Overcast Stitch, it is important to watch the tension carefully, as it is easy to draw the stitches up too tightly and reduce the size of the buttonhole.

1. Thread a wide-eyed sewing needle with a twelve- to fourteen-inch length of split or fine yarn, or embroidery thread. Secure the end of the yarn on the inside of the fabric.

2. Work once into each stitch and once under each running thread, inserting the needle from nearside to farside and bringing it out the center of the buttonhole.

3. When you have worked your way all around the buttonhole, bring the yarn to the inside, and hide the ends as described above.

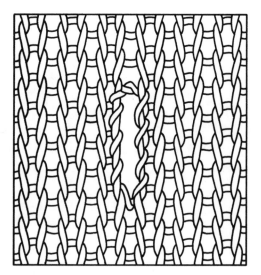

BUTTONHOLE WITH OVERCAST FINISH

BUTTONHOLE STITCH

Buttonhole Stitch works well to reinforce and stabilize the opening, but it has quite a commanding appearance and shouldn't be used when you want the buttonhole to pretend it isn't really there.

The instructions below are for the Traditional or the Improved Horizontal Buttonhole:

1. Thread a wide-eyed sewing needle with the length of yarn and attach it on the inside.

2. Bring the needle bearing the yarn through to the outside under the running thread at the lower right corner of the buttonhole.

3. Loop the yarn over your extended left forefinger, then insert the needle from nearside to farside under the first cast-off stitch, then up through the circle of yarn. Release the yarn from your forefinger and tighten the stitch firmly, making sure that the yarn comes off the stitch at the very edge of the buttonhole.

4. Continue in this way, under each stitch once or twice all the way around the buttonhole.

5. To tie the corner together and reinforce it, you may either work two or three Buttonhole Stitches, fanning them around the corner, or use a bar tack, two or three vertical strands.

6. When you have worked all the way around the buttonhole, make a simple knot around the beginning of the yarn, then hide the end on the inside as described above.

In various needlework books, you may find other ways of handling the needle and yarn as you work the stitch, but they all produce the same result, and this one is simple to describe and to do and keeps the yarn free from tangles. If you have another familiar way of working, by all means use it. If the yarn twists up as you work, periodically roll the needle between thumb and

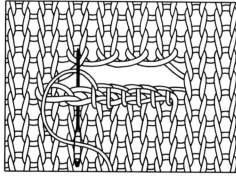

FINISHING WITH BUTTONHOLE STITCH

forefinger in the direction opposite to the twist to undo it, or let the needle dangle from the work long enough for it to unwind itself. The important thing about Buttonhole Stitch is not to use too many of them, as they will get bulky and start to distort the opening.

If you wish to use this stitch on the Contrast-Color Yarn Buttonhole, do so after the first round of sewing, which secures the stitches from unraveling (see below), and work a Buttonhole Stitch under each running thread and into each stitch so it encloses the first line of sewing.

When using Buttonhole Stitch on an Eyelet or a vertical buttonhole, you will be working into the sides rather than the tops of the stitches. Because of this there are several variables that must be taken into consideration. If you work into the inner half of the selvedge stitch, the Buttonhole Stitch will be more obvious; if you work into the outer half of the selvedge stitch, it will be somewhat hidden and less obvious. With some yarns or stitch patterns, it may be that working just once into each stitch will give too thin a look, whereas working twice will be just right; in some cases, the opposite may be true. No rules can be given for these things; you must determine for yourself what will work better given the design of the garment and the type of yarn that you are knitting with. Finally, as with working Buttonhole Stitch on a vertical buttonhole, you will want to decide whether to work several stitches around the corner or to wrap the yarn at the corner to form a bar.

Finishing Contrast-Color Buttonholes

The stitches surrounding the contrast-color yarn must be secured against unraveling before the strand is removed. The sewing requires two rounds, one to secure the stitches, one to give the opening a finished appearance.

To begin, thread a wide-eyed sewing needle with a twelve- to fourteen-inch length of your main yarn. A split yarn works best (see page 363) but is not necessary.

First Round

1. Hide the end on the inside, then bring the needle through to the outside under the running thread at the lower right corner of the buttonhole.

2. Working from right to left, draw the yarn through each stitch across the base of the buttonhole. Insert the needle from nearside to farside between two stitches, then from farside to nearside through the center of the stitch.

3. At the left corner, pass the needle under the running thread at the bottom and turn the work upside down.

4. Pass the needle under the running thread in the corner and pick up the stitches across the top in the same manner as you did the bottom. Bring the needle under the running thread in the other corner to complete the circle.

5. Once you have all the stitches threaded with yarn, remove the contrast-color yarn and turn the work right side up again.

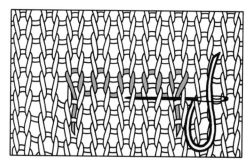

SEWING THE FIRST ROUND FOR A CONTRAST COLOR BUTTONHOLE

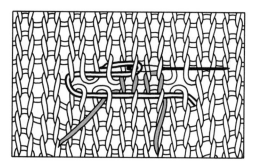

REMOVING THE CONTRAST COLOR

Second Round

1. Pass the tapestry needle from nearside to farside through the center of each stitch, under the strand that was threaded through them previously, and out the center of the buttonhole.

2. When you have sewn off all the stitches, bring the yarn to the inside and use a simple knot to attach it to the yarn where you started. Hide the ends.

The buttonhole is complete as it is, but it may also be further finished by using Buttonhole Stitch, above. If you plan to use Buttonhole Stitch, however, I recommend that you both sew off the stitches and work the Buttonhole Stitch with split yarn to reduce the bulk.

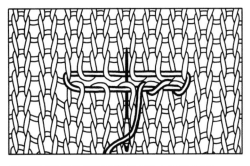

SEWING THE SECOND ROUND FOR A CONTRAST COLOR BUTTONHOLE

Other sewn cast-off techniques could be used with this type of buttonhole, and you may see them recommended in various books, but they tend to create a much bulkier edge than this version. If you are working buttonholes into Single Rib, a very attractive result can be obtained by using Invisible Cast-off for Single Rib. Unfortunately, although it may be attractive, it isn't terribly functional, as the edge created is very resilient and the buttonhole lacks stability. I have tested all the possibilities and am convinced that the method given above is superior.

CROCHET FINISH

The Contrast-Color Yarn Buttonhole can also be worked off using Single Crochet. The result is a rather assertive buttonhole outlined by a chain of crochet stitches. It is best to use a rather fine hook and a split yarn to reduce bulk.

1. Thread a sewing needle and pass it through the stitches on the first round, as above.
2. Set aside the sewing needle, remove the contrast-color yarn, and switch to the crochet hook.
3. Work Single Crochet around the edge instead of sewing the last round, making sure to include the strand from the first round in each stitch.

It is important to regulate the tension carefully so the buttonhole is neither constricted nor splayed out. Practice on a swatch until you can consistently achieve a result you are pleased with.

Machine-Sewn Buttonholes

Machine-made buttonholes are a subject of controversy among knitters. Many people object to the intrusion of machine work on a handmade garment and will not have them under any circumstances. Others are sufficiently dismayed with their knitted buttonholes that they are willing to compromise their principles on this matter. Still others don't give a thought to any controversy stemming from the industrial revolution and think machine buttonholes are so superior they wouldn't bother with those lumpy handmade ones. My own opinion is that I'm not fond of rigid rules of any sort, and I think you should do whatever you think will enhance the design of the garment.

A machine-made buttonhole, done badly, will be just as homely as a handmade one done badly, so here as usual things are much improved by a mastery of technique. If you do not have an excellent sewing machine and familiarity with making buttonholes, I do not recommend you try to do this at all. In that case, it is far wiser to plan from the outset to take your completed garment to a professional. The store where you bought your yarn may know of someone who does this sort of work, or your Yellow Pages should yield the name of a cleaners, a tailor, or, most likely, a dressmaker that can do buttonholes. You must then assure yourself that that person is familiar with making them on knitted fabric by asking to see samples of their work. Do all this *before* you begin your garment—if you cannot find someone whose skills match your notions of what is acceptable, given the work you will invest in the knitting, you will still have the option of knitting the buttonholes.

Should you decide to make your own sewn buttonholes, I must emphasize again the importance of practicing on a swatch of knitting that matches you garment—a strip one and a half to two inches wide and ten to twelve inches long will give you a good length to work on.

Before sewing, carefully mark the position of the buttonholes on the outside using short lengths of contrast-color yarn. Don't use sewing thread—it will disappear into the yarn and you won't be able to see it well enough when you are sewing. Mark the buttonhole at either end, but rather than marking it down the center, mark it along the sides, about the width of your presser foot. This way there is no chance of catching some of the contrast-color yarn into the buttonhole stitches where it will be very difficult to remove. A machine-sewn buttonhole will have no stretch, so the size should be calculated exactly as one would a buttonhole on a woven fabric. It is important to work out the correct length for your buttonhole on the test swatch before you begin on your garment.

The major difficulty with making a successful buttonhole by machine is that the presser foot has a tendency to stretch the fabric out. The fabric must be stabilized before the buttonhole is stitched, and special sewing techniques must be used in order to prevent this from happening. There are several ways to do this.

• It helps to work a line of very small straight stitches around the outside of the buttonhole prior to working the zigzag stitching. In order to do this, you will need some sort of special attachment foot that will "walk" or pull the fabric under the needle. Most modern machines will have an attachment of this kind; they are frequently recommended for leather and leather-like fabrics, or for fabrics that are slippery, but I find they help on knits as well.

- Another method of stabilizing the fabric is with a special interfacing, used for appliqué work and buttonholes, which pulls away from the completed stitching and aids the fabric in moving smoothly beneath the presser foot. Any tiny bits of interfacing that remain caught in the buttonhole stitches will wash out the first time the garment is laundered. To use, simply place a square of this interfacing beneath the buttonhole, baste it into place if you wish, and then sew.
- Alternatively, you could face the entire button band with a woven fabric prior to working the buttonholes.

Hand baste the facing to each buttonhole position to stabilize the stitches for oversewing.

The built-in or attached buttonhole maker on your machine may sew a fairly narrow bead on a knitted fabric. You might want to experiment with doing the buttonhole using the regular zigzag stitch rather than the special buttonhole stitch, or oversewing the buttonhole stitch with a wider zigzag stitch. It also helps to work the buttonhole over a cord. The cord stabilizes the buttonhole against stretching and helps to make the zigzag stitches smooth. Refer to your sewing machine manual for information on working corded buttonholes.

Other Openings

As I mentioned in the introduction, some of the simpler techniques used for buttonholes can also be used for other sorts of openings such as pockets and necklines.

Pocket Openings

There are quite a few interesting ways to make pockets in a knitted garment. There are patch pockets, horizontal, vertical, and diagonal pocket openings, and a variety of pocket linings and borders. For the most part they constitute a design problem and are therefore outside the scope of this book. An interesting pocket not described here is the Double Knit Pocket (page 243), which involves a previously unknown application of that technique. Other techniques used for pockets are scattered throughout the book and are simple enough. They include casting off, working foldlines, hems, and borders, calculating and working slopes, Joinery Decreases, picking up stitches, and sewing linings into place. Here are a few aspects of making openings in a fabric that are pertinent to pockets and not covered elsewhere.

CONTRAST-COLOR POCKET OPENING

The Contrast-Color Yarn Buttonhole described above can be expanded to form a horizontal pocket opening. When the garment section is completed, pick the stitches

up and then remove the contrast-color yarn. The pocket opening can then be finished in a variety of ways. You can cast off the stitches of the bottom edge without further ado, or work them up into a border or use a foldline with a mini-hem. The stitches on the top must then be worked down in the opposite direction to form a lining. Before beginning to work either border or lining, it is a good idea to immediately increase one or two stitches at each side so no gap appears at the corner of

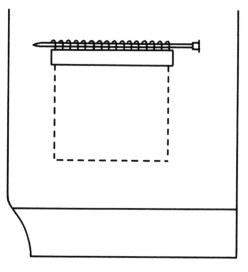

WORKING A POCKET BORDER ON STITCHES OF A CONTRAST COLOR OPENING

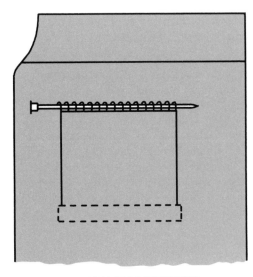

WORKING THE LINING FOR A HORIZONTAL POCKET OPENING

the opening. To finish, the border and lining are sewn into place with the method described on page 365.

Alternatively, you can work a full pocket that hangs free on the inside. While this is bulkier than other pockets, the garment does not get pulled out of shape when the pocket is full of hands or keys or goodies. Pick up the stitches around the opening on two double-point needles. Work a Purl or Picot Foldline (page 202) on the bottom set, then join the stitches into a round and work the pocket lining. (For knitting in the round on three needles, see page 112.) It is a good idea to work Vertical Foldlines (page 205) at the sides of the pocket to help it lie flat and smooth, and then use Joinery Cast-off at the bottom.

AFTERTHOUGHT POCKET

Elizabeth Zimmerman gave this technique a most appropriate name. This is the way to add a pocket to a completed garment if you didn't plan for it during designing, or were unsure of its proper placement. Actually, it can be done on any knitted fabric whenever and wherever you decide a pocket is suitable. The technique is related both to the Contrast-Color Pocket Opening, above, and to dividing a fabric and working in the opposite direction, which is covered thoroughly in that section (see page 192). For purposes of a pocket opening, only a portion of the fabric is divided.

1. Determine the row and width of the pocket opening, placing markers if necessary.
2. At the center of the opening, insert the tapestry needle or a knitting needle into a stitch and stretch it out until you can slip the point of a scissors into it and snip the yarn.
3. Begin to unravel the row of stitches, first toward one side of the opening, then toward the other. You may

pick up the stitches onto two double-point needles as you work or once all the stitches are freed. Make sure they are on the needle in the correct position.
4. Proceed to work a pocket such as described above in Contrast-Color Pocket Opening. When you are finished, hide the unraveled ends of yarn on the inside in the normal way.

The whole process is really quite simple once you overcome your fear of snipping that first stitch. I would advise great caution when attempting this on any fabric made in a complex stitch pattern or a color pattern. Place the opening on a plain row and pick up the stitches on the needles *before* you unravel the yarn.

VERTICAL AND SLOPED POCKET OPENINGS

These are made using an extension of the principles outlined above for the Traditional or the Improved Two-Yarn Buttonhole, where the fabric is divided and the two sides are worked separately for the length of the opening and then rejoined. While for a buttonhole there is no need to place inactivated stitches on a holder, when working a larger and more complex opening of this sort, it is much easier if you do so. In addition, it is necessary to knit a pocket lining as an extension to one side of the divided fabric, which is therefore called the lining side; the other side is referred to as the facing. In most cases, a pocket of this sort has a sloped opening, which is what is described here; the general principles can be readily applied to a vertical opening if that is what you want.

1. Make the proper calculations for the slope to determine the placement of the decreases (see page 441). If you are working in Stockinette, or any other pattern that curls, the opening must have a border or a small hem of some sort. Use your stitch gauge to determine the number of stitches required.
2. Divide the fabric, placing the stitches between the opening and the side seam on a holder. If you are using a border, cast on the extra stitches at the base of the opening on the facing side. Work the facing, sloping the edge according to your pattern, with the decreases placed in the fabric adjacent to the border, until the opening is the length required. Place the facing stitches on a holder.
3. On a separate pair of needles, cast on the same number of stitches for the width of the pocket lining as were removed at the slope, plus a minimum of one inch additional, and work to the depth required *below* the bottom point of the pocket opening.
4. With the stitches of the pocket lining on the right needle, continue with the same yarn and knit across the stitches on the holder to reactivate those stitches and join the side of the divided fabric to the pocket lining. Work side and lining together as one until the

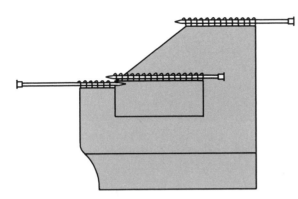

JOINING LINING TO SIDE STITCHES FOR SLOPED POCKET

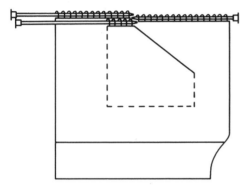

JOINING LINING TO FACING STITCHES AT TOP OF SLOPED POCKET

length matches that of the facing side, ending at the lining selvedge.

5. Reactivate the stitches of the facing section, working across the row toward the opening until there are the same number of stitches remaining on the left needle as there are *extra* pocket lining stitches. Hold the left needle bearing the facing stitches parallel with the left needle holding the lining stitches and use Joinery Decreases (page 64) to secure the top corner of the lining to the inside. Work across the row, thus rejoining the divided sides, and continue with the garment section. At your convenience, sew the sides and bottom of the pocket lining to the inside of the garment (see page 370).

Thumb and Finger Holes

I am very fond of hand-knitted mittens. They are one of a small, select group of seemingly ordinary and mundane things that, when done right, are transported into the realm of sentiment and art. In recognition of this truth, knitters who live anywhere it is cold have lavished their skill and effort on these otherwise practical items. There have been some glorious mittens and gloves in the world. To be sure, it is partly that they are small and

take relatively little time, giving knitters an opportunity to try out new patterns and color combinations, and display their talents. But at heart, they make a generous and comforting gift, as anyone lucky enough to receive a pair well knows. When done in good fine wool, as they should be, there is no better way to keep hands warm. Please don't make mittens in artificial fibers; there is no point, as their thermal qualities will be poor to nonexistent. And do please make them at a very fine gauge so the wind won't whistle through; six to ten stitches to the inch is the area to work in. For real warmth, they should not only be done in fine wool but in two fine wools, using a Stranded Color pattern (page 276) or an Inlay technique (page 279).

All of the various techniques that one might use to make mittens and gloves, and they are various, are discussed at length elsewhere. Here we must concentrate on the openings needed for thumbs and fingers. For making something this small, I strongly recommend either the Shetland Three Needle method (page 112) or Double Knit (page 233).

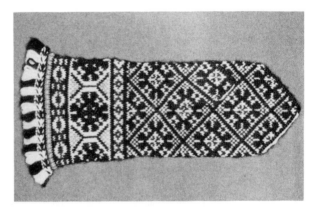

LATVIAN MITTEN, IN THE STYLE OF KURZEME

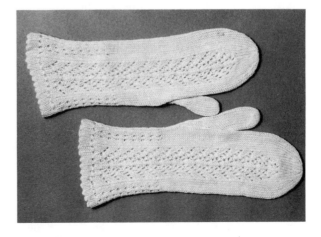

VICTORIAN CHILD'S LACE COTTON MITTENS

CONTRAST-COLOR THUMB OPENING

A thumb may be worked up from the palm or from the side of the hand, depending upon the wearer's preference. The simplest approach is to use the Contrast-Color Opening, then complete the mitten and return later to pick up the stitches around the opening to knit the thumb in the round. This produces an adequate fit, especially for a child's hand.

THUMB GUSSET

A more complex approach, but one that produces a better fit, is to work a Gusset between the wrist and the position of the thumb opening. A Gusset is a small triangle of stitches gradually introduced into the fabric with increases to provide additional width in one particular area for wearing ease. The number of stitches to add depends entirely on the measurement of the hand and the stitch gauge. Measure the circumference of the hand at the base of the thumb and again at the base of the fingers; the difference between the two is the amount to introduce with the Gusset. For the length of the Gusset, measure from wrist to base of thumb. Use your stitch gauge to work out the number of stitches and rows in the Gusset and the increase pattern. Similarly, ease is added between thumb and hand by the introduction of a diamond-shaped Gusset called a Fourchette (a French word for the crotch or fork of a tree branch).

1. Determine the position of the Gusset, either at the side or on the palm. As you work the mitten in the round, begin the increases either side of a single stitch and continue them in a line to each side of the Gusset. When the Gusset is complete, place those stitches on a holder.
2. Use Stranded Cast-on (for casting on within a fabric, see page 138) to add one-half to one inch of stitches across the thumb opening for the Fourchette and continue the mitten or glove in the round. Immediately begin decreasing to either side of these extra stitches until they are eliminated.
3. When it is time to work the thumb, pick up the thumb stitches and those along the cast-on edge of the Fourchette, removing the baseline, and join into a round. Immediately begin decreasing to either side of the Fourchette as on the hand.
4. Work the thumb to the length required and decrease to each side or all around until just a few stitches remain, at which point graft them together, draw the yarn through to the inside and hide with Purl Duplicate Stitch (page 380).

Mittens and gloves are frequently done with one color pattern on the back of the hand, another on the palm, and yet a third on the Gusset. This little triangle of fabric, therefore, not only serves a good fit, but offers

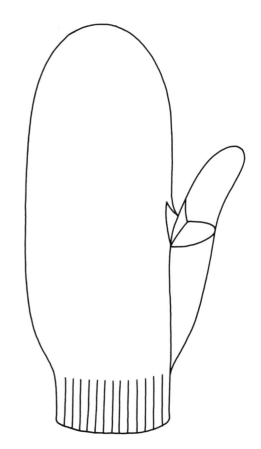

MITTEN WITH THUMB GUSSET AND FOURCHETTE

itself as a frame for further embellishment. A chart of a mitten pattern is shown on page 530.

FINGERS

Fingers are worked much like the thumb opening with a Gusset, described above. They also have tiny Fourchettes lying between each finger. Depending on the size of the hand, the Fourchette should be one-quarter to one-half inch wide, the exact number of stitches determined by your gauge.

1. At the base of the fingers, the stitches of what would otherwise be a mitten are divided into four groups, three of equal size and one larger for the forefinger, containing two to four additional stitches.
2. Place the forefinger stitches on needles, the others on a holder.
3. Cast on stitches for the Fourchette between the first and second fingers to close the round and begin to work. Gradually decrease the extra stitches to form the Fourchette. Work the correct length on the remaining stitches, then decrease and finish the finger as for a thumb, above.
4. Place the stitches for the next finger on the needles, pick up the stitches at the base of the Fourchette between the first and second fingers, work around,

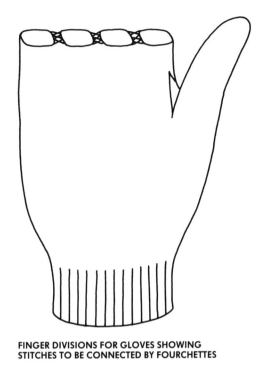

**FINGER DIVISIONS FOR GLOVES SHOWING
STITCHES TO BE CONNECTED BY FOURCHETTES**

and then cast on the same number between the second and third finger. Join into a round and work as before, decreasing the Fourchettes at each side.
5. Repeat step 4 for the third finger.
6. For the small finger, place the remaining stitches on the needle and pick up stitches at the base of the previous Fourchette, but cast on no additional stitches on the other side; work as for the forefinger.

Neckline Openings

There are several garment styles worked flat, but all in one piece, front, back and sometimes sleeves, so there is a minimum of sewing up. In these cases, the neckline openings are treated in much the same way one would a large buttonhole or a pocket opening.

Horizontal Neckline Openings

When working a garment design that calls for you to knit up the front half of the garment, over the top, and down the back, it is necessary to cast off stitches for the front of the neckline, work some shaping (or not, as the case may be) at the corners, and then cast on again. For a very long time it has been traditional to use Pullover Cast-off on the front and Knit Cast-on for the back, but I have never found that to be satisfactory because they don't match, and because I don't like the edge Knit Cast-on provides. It is far better to use one of the Finger Cast-on techniques (for information on how to do this

within a fabric, see page 140), as they generally produce much more attractive edges and the option of matching a cast-off edge to its cast-off partner on the other side of the opening.

Then, if you want to pick up the stitches around the neckline and work them into a border of some sort, place the front neckline stitches on a holder and use Stranded Cast-on for the back neckline. This allows you to pick up the stitches all the way around without having any selvedge turned to the inside except at the corners, where you may have done some shaping. An even simpler approach is to use a contrast-color yarn opening.

If you want to work a ribbed border on the front neckline, use Invisible Cast-off there, and then use Alternating Cast-on for the back neckline; the two will not only match, but you will have a beautifully resilient edge.

Vertical Neckline Openings

Another garment design that allows you to develop some interesting effects with stitch pattern is one that is knit from side to side. In this situation the neckline resembles a vertical buttonhole, although it may have more shaping than a simple slit. If the neckline will require no further finishing, you may wish to place the ends of yarn that result when you divide the work somewhere besides the neckline itself by using version three of the Traditional Vertical Buttonhole described above.

Cut Openings

Many traditional sweaters, especially in Scandinavia and Great Britain, were worked in the round to the shoulders and then openings were cut for the neck and arms or for the center front. Generally this was done because the knitting methods used were very fast in Knit but not as efficient in Purl, so people preferred to work in the round at all times. It may be that the technique was first used on felted garments, which would not unravel when they were cut. The development of the Steek (page 113) made it possible to use the concept on nonfelted fabrics because the edges could be knotted. Sewing machines can also be used to secure the edges against unraveling, eliminating the need for knots. The method is still used, although less so today, probably because people tend to use heavier yarns than they used to and a cut selvedge can be bulky. Details on how to machine-sew the openings before cutting can be found on page 115; information on seaming a cut opening is on page 369 and that for picking up stitches along a cut opening is on page 188.

13
Double Knit

This technique is a great deal of fun—actually, it will seem like magic the first time you do it—and it has many interesting and creative applications. Double Knitting allows you to knit two fabrics at the same time with one pair of needles (or a single circular one). Generally both fabrics will be done in plain Stockinette. They may be attached along all four sides or open on some of the sides, and in the more complex patterns they may also be linked to one another in the center. The two fabrics can be worked in the same or different colors, in two different color patterns, or with a color pattern on one side and a solid on the other.

The reversible quality of Double Knit makes it a good choice for blankets, scarves, hats, and vests. Because the fabrics are double thickness, they also have excellent thermal properties, even better than ones made with Stranded color patterns (see page 255), making them ideal for warm jackets and coats. There are also some interesting structural qualities that allow the technique to be used for hems, pockets, and casings, or to make items in the round without the use of double-point needles. It is even possible to use batting in chambers created with Double Knit to form a quilted effect.

When planning a project, keep in mind that a garment done in Double Knit will be twice as thick and will require at least twice the amount of yarn as the same size garment done in Single Knit. Because of the special structure of the fabric, both stitch gauge and yarn requirements must be calculated with special care (see page 429).

Basic Double Knit

Double-faced fabrics can be worked flat or in the round and with one or two yarns. Obviously two yarns would be needed to create color patterns; however, the methods of handling two yarns are also used for special purposes while making solid-color fabrics. Here we will only discuss the different approaches to making these fabrics; the application of the fundamental techniques to color work is discussed in detail starting on page 251, in the chapter "Working With Color."

Flat and Circular Fabrics

Needless to say, most Double Knit fabrics are worked flat so the pleasures of both faces can be appreciated. Nevertheless, not only are there many garments worked in the round that might do double duty if made reversible, but there are many applications of the Double Knit techniques in which reversibility is not the issue, and therefore you will want a good understanding of how to work either way.

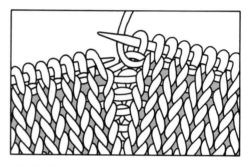

STANDING PAST STITCH OF FABRIC ON THE FARSIDE

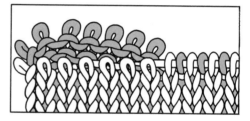

REMOVING NEEDLE REVEALS THE SEPARATE DOUBLE KNIT FABRIC FACES

DOUBLE KNIT WORKED FLAT

This creates a fabric that is attached on all sides, but one face is not attached to the other down the middle.

1. Use Half-Hitch Cast-on to place twice the number of stitches required for the width of the fabric on the needle.
2. Work every row as follows: *Yns, sl1, yfs, K1*, repeat from * to * across the row.
3. To cast off, see below.

Let's examine what is happening here. Double the number of stitches are cast on, with the odd number stitches allocated to one fabric, the even number stitches to the other. All of the stitches that are Knit in one row form the Stockinette face of the fabric on the nearside; all of the stitches that are slipped are those which belong to the fabric on the farside. When you turn the work and Knit the second row, you will slip the stitches that were Knit, and Knit the stitches that were slipped in the first row. Therefore, when you complete two rows of pattern, you will have knit just one row of each fabric.

In effect, you are knitting in the round and therefore need never Purl. The two fabrics will be joined on the bottom by the row of casting on, and on each side by the running threads that pass between one fabric and the other as you turn the work in the knitting, but they will be completely independent at the center.

Because you are working both fabrics with the Knit sides facing out and the Purl sides facing one another at the center, it is easy to know what to do with each stitch once you have the pattern established. As you look at the needle, the stitches of the fabric on the nearside will be Knit stitches and the stitches of the fabric on the farside Purl stitches, so all you have to do is Knit the Knit stitches and slip the Purl stitches.

Notice that the yarn is always stranded past the slipped stitches so it will lie between the two fabrics. When you slip a stitch of the fabric on the farside, the yarn is always stranded nearside; when you slip a stitch of the fabric on the nearside, the yarn is always stranded farside. This is one of the few times when you should strand the yarn past a slipped stitch fairly firmly. The stranded yarn is the running thread that passes between two stitches of one fabric, which while being worked are separated by a stitch from the other fabric and are therefore further apart than they should be. Once those stitches are off the needle, however, they fall into their correct relationship side by side, and the running thread should be the normal length. If it is not, the stitches will enlarge. You may find it necessary to work with a smaller needle than you normally would in order to get the gauge you want for the fabric.

Please note that the pattern given above calls for Half-Hitch Cast-on, and establishes a sequence where the first stitch of every row is slipped and the last stitch is Knit. Both these things are quite arbitrary. There are a variety of ways to cast on, discussed below, and you could as easily Knit the first stitch and slip the last. In addition, there will be times when you may be working on an uneven number of stitches instead of an even number and you will start and end the row in the same way. What is important is that you grasp the principle. Then you won't need the recipe, and all the variations on the theme will be yours to play with.

DOUBLE KNIT IN THE ROUND

Working a Double Knit fabric in the round is quite straightforward and requires only a minor modification of the basic pattern.

1. Cast on as described above.
2. Work the first round of the near fabric in Knit, slipping the stitches of the far fabric with yarn nearside, exactly as for Double Knit Worked Flat.
3. When you return to the starting point, Purl the stitches of the far fabric and slip the stitches of the near fabric with the yarn farside.
4. Continue in this way, always Knitting the near fabric and Purling the far fabric.

The Knit side of one fabric will always be facing you on the nearside, the Knit side of the other fabric will always be facing into the center of the circle, which is why you will Knit the stitches of one fabric and Purl the stitches of the other as you go round and round. When you slip a stitch of the fabric on the farside, the yarn is always stranded nearside; when you slip a stitch of the fabric on the nearside, the yarn is always stranded farside so they fall between the two fabrics. If you are using a single yarn for both fabrics, they will be joined only where the yarn switches from one fabric to the other at the end of each round.

When knitting a circular fabric, the yarn winds up in the same place at the end of every round. If you set the work aside at this point, you must look to see which stitches were last worked in order to determine whether to proceed on the near or far fabric. When doing color patterns (see page 254), the situation can be more prob-

lematic. A simple solution is to make a note to yourself. Another is to never stop at the end of a round; working the first few stitches of the next round will make it quite clear how to proceed when you pick the work up again. Alternatively, don't stop working until you have balanced the two fabrics so they have the same number of completed rows. If you do this consistently, you will know that you can always start with the near fabric.

Working with Two Yarns

As I mentioned above, even when working solid-color fabrics in Double Knit, there are reasons to use two supplies of yarn. One of these reasons is to separate the fabric at each side; the other is to speed up the work.

Separating the Sides

In order to separate the fabric at the selvedges you will need one supply of yarn for each face of the fabric; you can either use two balls or draw the yarn from both ends of a single center-pull ball.

1. With one yarn cast on as described for Double Knit Worked Flat, above, and continue as follows:
   Row 1: Knit the stitches of fabric A, slip the stitches of fabric B with the yarn nearside. Turn.
   Row 2: Purl the stitches of fabric A, slip the stitches of fabric B with the yarn farside. Turn.

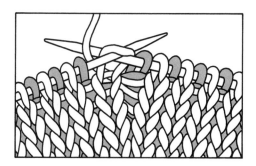

SEPARATING THE SIDES/WORKING WITH THE FIRST YARN: ROW 1 ABOVE/ROW 2 BELOW

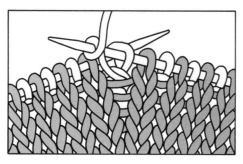

SEPARATING THE SIDES/WORKING WITH THE SECOND YARN: ROW 1 ABOVE/ROW 2 BELOW

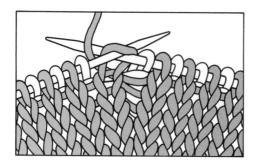

1. With yarn A, Knit the stitches of fabric A, slip the stitches of fabric B with the yarn nearside.
2. At the end of the row, drop yarn A, slide the stitches back to the right needle tip and pick up yarn B; do not turn the work.
3. Purl the stitches of fabric B, slip the stitches of fabric A with the yarn farside.
4. At the end of the row, both yarns are at the same place; turn the work and pick up yarn A.
5. Purl the stitches of fabric A, slip the stitches of fabric B with the yarn farside.
6. Repeat step 2 above.
7. Knit the stitches of fabric B, slip the stitches of fabric A with the yarn nearside. The yarns are again together.

These instructions use an ABAB sequence to handling the yarns; you can certainly work ABBA if you wish to.

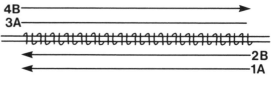

THE SLIDE TECHNIQUE FOR DOUBLE KNIT

2. Drop the first yarn and take up the second yarn.
   Row 3: Purl the stitches of fabric B, slip the stitches of fabric A with the yarn farside. Turn.
   Row 4: Knit the stitches of fabric B, slip the stitches of fabric A with the yarn nearside. Turn.
3. Repeat these four rows to length desired, always using one yarn for rows 1 and 2, the other yarn for rows 3 and 4.

Notice that you are working first two rows on one fabric, one in Knit, one in Purl, then two rows on the other. If you were to cast on the two fabrics separately, then intersperse their stitches on a single needle and work as described above, you would make two entirely unattached, flat fabrics. Now you may consider that a fairly empty exercise, and to some extent it is, but it appears later in a surprising way. What is most important for you to realize about this now is that you can work on either the outside or inside of each face, depending on what it is you want to accomplish and where the yarn you need to work with next is; that will be important in some applications, as is the following alternative.

THE SLIDE

With the above technique, you must work two rows on one fabric in order to return to the point where the second yarn is in waiting. If you prefer, and if you are working on a circular needle or double-point, you can work one row on each fabric, as follows:

Holding Two Yarns

If you are comfortable holding one yarn in each hand (page 257), or two yarns on one finger (page 256), as for Stranded Color Knitting you can speed up the process of making a Double Knit fabric. It is much like working a Double Knit fabric in the round, described above, but because you will be working with two yarns, one for each face, you can work every stitch across the row instead of slipping every other stitch. It produces a fabric just like that of Basic Double Knit.

Carry the yarn you will need for the Knit stitches on your left forefinger; carry the yarn you will need for the Purl stitches in your right hand, or on your right forefinger, and work as follows:

1. For a Knit stitch, hold both yarns on the farside, insert the right needle into the stitch to Knit, and catch up the left yarn for the new stitch in the usual fashion.
2. For a Purl stitch, bring both yarns to the nearside. Insert the right needle into the next stitch as to Purl, hold the left yarn well away from the needle and pass the right yarn between the left yarn and the needles to wrap it for the new stitch.

It is generally much easier to Purl with the Right-Hand, or Right-Finger, method than the Left-Finger method, but you may certainly hold the yarns in any manner that is comfortable and efficient for you. Notice that at the end of the row you will have completed one row on each fabric.

In order to join the sides, always maintain the same yarn in the same hand. In other words, the yarn in the left hand will be used first to Knit the stitches of fabric A and then those of fabric B; while the yarn in the right hand Purls the stitches of fabric B and then those of fabric A. In order to separate the two faces at each side, switch the yarns from one hand to the other at the end of the row.

Stitch Patterns for Double Knit

Typically, Double Knit fabrics have Stockinette facing out on both sides, but there is no technical reason for that limitation. At the very least, you can just as easily have Purl facing out on both sides, Knit facing out on one side, Purl on the other, or use any combination of Knit and Purl stitches that you wish, which means any Brocade pattern. There really isn't anything difficult about it; just keep in mind which fabric you are working on and where the stranded yarns must go in order to remain hidden. Let the columns of stitches guide you, and you won't go wrong.

Of the other techniques, Slip and Crossed Stitch will certainly work, as will a Bobble, but any that involve more than one stitch would be so difficult and complex to work out as to not be worth it. Also, see the information on using the Stranded Brocade technique in "Color Patterns in Double Knit," page 278.

Making Double Knit Fabrics

Before we go on to look at any of the variations or applications of these basic ways of working Double Knit fabrics, it is important for you to understand how to deal with the special requirements a fabric of this sort has in regard to casting on, casting off, and shaping.

Casting On

As you have seen, a Double Knit fabric requires twice the number of stitches as would normally be cast on for a given width. Half of these stitches are allocated to one fabric, half to the other, but they are all cast on at once. There are several casting-on techniques that work very well for Double Knit; all but one of them will be familiar to you from the chapter "Casting On."

Using Half-Hitch Cast-on

In the instructions above I suggested the use of Half-Hitch Cast-on. It provides an edge that is crisp and neat and that is, in addition, highly elastic, as the baseline zigzags back and forth between the stitches of one fabric and those of the other. Because there are twice as many stitches along the baseline as there would normally be for the width of the fabric, it is important to work this cast-on fairly tightly.

A "ribbed" version of Half-Hitch Cast-on also works very well. See page 129 for how to do Purled Half-Hitch Cast-on; once you know that, you can "Knit" one stitch on, then "Purl" the next. This version is tighter than the plain Half-Hitch Cast-on edge, yet provides excellent resilience. A stitch belonging to the near fabric should be cast on in Knit and one belonging to the far fabric cast on in Purl so the cast-on edge matches the stitches above them.

Double Knitting makes extensive use of color patterns, and for that purpose Half-Hitch Cast-on with a contrast-color baseline (page 129) produces an interesting effect. As you know, Half-Hitch Cast-on creates both the edge and the first row of stitches; so, as the two yarns are alternated stitch by stitch across the row, the first row of each fabric will be in a different color with a contrast-color edge.

Using Alternating Cast-on

A totally different look can be had with Alternating Cast-on, which creates a rounded edge that does not look cast on at all; it looks, rather, like a hem without a foldline. In fact, Alternating Cast-on has so much in common with the structure of Double Knit that they seem made for one another. Establish the sequence of casting on so the stitches brought up on the near side of the baseline will become the stitches of the near fabric.

Alternating Cast-on done with two yarns also lends itself admirably to color work in Double Knitting. As the two yarns are alternated stitch by stitch across the row, all the stitches coming up the nearside of the base-line will be in one color and all the stitches coming up the farside of the baseline will be in the other. Unlike Half-Hitch Cast-on done this way, there will be no con-trast-color edge.

Using Stranded Cast-on

This technique may be used in those situations in which you want to pick up stitches to work in the opposite direction. Keep in mind that a Double Knit fabric has twice the number of stitches required for the same width if done single thickness, so if you are changing from one to the other, you must reduce their number (see Double Knit to Single Knit, below).

Using Cable Cast-on

Although it is quite slow to do and has very little elas-ticity, Cable Cast-on provides a handsome, tailored edge for Double Knit fabrics. An even more interesting edge can be had with Knit/Purl Cable Cast-on. I quite like them both.

Using Picot Cast-on

This cast-on gives a more serrated edge, and the two sides look quite different. It can be done in two colors. I don't think it is quite as attractive as some of the alternatives, but it may provide just the touch you are looking for.

CIRCULAR CAST-ON

As you will see in the section below on applications (page 241), the technique of Double Knitting can be used to work Single Knit fabrics in the round on two straight needles. Here is a rather clever method of cast-ing on that makes that possible, as it leaves the two faces of the fabric unattached at the bottom edge.

1. Using a long double-point needle or a circular nee-dle, cast on the full number of stitches required for both fabrics. Half-Hitch Cast-on works well.
2. Slip half the stitches onto a second double-point nee-dle, then fold the first needle forward and alongside the second so the two are side by side. (The folded end of the cast-on edge should be to the left; the first

and last stitch cast on will be to the right, with the yarn coming off the first stitch on the far needle.)
3. Slide the two sets of stitches to the tips of the needles at the right.
4. Begin working in Double Knit, slipping the first stitch from the far needle and Knitting the first stitch from the near needle.
5. Continue in this manner until all of the stitches have been worked off and are interspersed on a single needle.

Selvedges

Because of the thickness of a Double Knit fabric, it is far better to avoid seams whenever you can. If a seam is necessary, it can be handled just like any other, or you can use overlapping selvedges to produce a smooth seam on both faces of the fabric.

On a Double Knit fabric, you must work as if you are making a Chain Selvedge, although this will actually produce a regular Stockinette Selvedge. As you know, when you have knit two rows of Double Knit, each fabric will be just one row longer. Therefore, if you were to work the selvedge stitches on every row, they would have twice as many rows as the Double Knit portion of the fabric and the edges would splay out. When you are ready to sew, decide which face of the fabric you wish to wear on the outside and use either a Selvedge or a Running Thread Seam. The selvedges will be visible on the inside of the garment.

If your fabric changes at some point from Single to Double Knit or vice versa, maintain your selvedge stitches separate regardless of what is going on in be-tween, but work Stockinette Selvedge along the single-thickness fabric and Chain Selvedge along the Double Knit.

If you prefer to have a seam that is not visible on either side of the garment, cast on two extra stitches at each side edge to form a wide selvedge worked single thickness. The two selvedge stitches at each side should be worked twice in succession, then skipped the next time you come to them so they don't have too many rows. When you sew up, these wide selvedges will be overlapped to offset the seams (the sewing method is described on page 369).

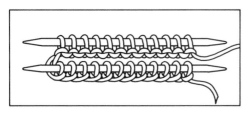

CIRCULAR CAST-ON FOR DOUBLE KNIT

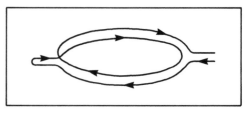

WORKING AN OVERLAPPING SELVEDGE

Shaping

A Double Knit fabric may be shaped with increases and decreases just as with a single-thickness fabric, but each fabric must be treated equally. If you make an increase on one, you must make a corresponding increase on the other, and the same with decreases.

To Increase

The Raised, or Slip Raised, Increase works the best, as it is so unobtrusive.

1. Work the increase on the correct stitch of the near fabric. (This places the original and the new stitch side by side between two stitches of the other fabric.)
2. On the return row, work the corresponding increase on the correct stitch of the other fabric, and slip the first increase pair. (Now there are two pairs of stitches side by side in the increase position, one pair for each fabric.)
3. On the next row, use a cable holder to reestablish the correct alternating sequence of stitches.

To Decrease

Use the right or left decrease, whichever is appropriate to the garment. Work to the point where the decrease must be made on the near fabric, and then proceed as follows:

1. Slip the right stitch of the decrease pair to the right needle, and slip the intervening stitch from the far fabric to a cable holder.
2. Return the first stitch slipped to the left needle, and slip the stitch from the cable holder to the right needle.
3. Work the decrease on the two stitches of the near fabric and continue across the row with Double Knit.
4. On the return row, the two stitches that must be decreased on the other fabric will already be side by side and can be worked together without further ado, restoring the correct sequence on the needle.

Single Knit to Double Knit

There may be times when you will wish to cast on and work a portion of fabric single thickness and then begin Double Knitting. All that is necessary is to increase in each stitch across the row in order to add the stitches necessary for the second fabric. Any increase technique will work, but some work better than others.

Using Slip Raised Increase

The variation on the Raised Increase that I have called Slip Raised Increase (page 69) produces the best result. (The regular Raised Increase badly distorts the row of stitches in which the increases are made and shouldn't be used for this purpose.) This technique places each

new stitch directly behind the original stitch where it belongs. It is easiest to work this increase on the Purl side, but it may be done on the Knit side if necessary.

When you increase in this way, the result will be slightly different depending upon whether or not you are using selvedge stitches. A Slip Raised Increase cannot be done on the first stitch of a row, as it simply comes undone. Therefore if you are not using selvedge stitches, increasing every stitch but the first results in an uneven number of stitches on the needle. If you are using selvedge stitches, they should not be increased, so work them normally and double all the others. This results in an even number of stitches on the needle. Whether you work on an odd or even number of stitches is really not important, but you will want to continue the original fabric on the same stitches so the continuity of the columns of stitches is unbroken. If necessary, modify the sequence of Knit and Slip Stitches given in Basic Double Knit in order to allow for this, working according to the principle rather than the pattern.

Other Increase Techniques

Probably the simplest way of switching from a single to a double fabric is to place a Running Thread Increase between each stitch; the result is reasonably satisfactory, and a good second choice. A related method would be to use a Yarnover, which will produce a row of Eyelets.

The "bars" of a Bar Increase will remain slightly visible on the face of the original fabric, and since it is slow to work, there really is nothing to recommend it in this situation.

Double Knit to Single Knit

If you are working in Double Knit and wish to revert to a single-thickness fabric, you must halve the number of stitches using one of two techniques.

JOINERY DECREASE

This method is very simple and appropriate for most purposes.

- Work a right decrease, either as to Knit or as to Purl, on every pair of stitches across the row. Make sure that the stitches of the near fabric are the left stitches of each decrease pair, regardless of which side you are working on.

The decrease pairs one stitch from each fabric. These pairs must be in the correct relationship so the columns of stitches on the fabric that is to be continued will be unbroken. If the sequence of stitches is not correct, the two stitches will be twisted around one another, with the stitch from the far fabric becoming the facing stitch of the decrease. If you are working on an uneven number of stitches, or you have the near fabric on the odd-numbered stitches, you can establish the correct relationship of the stitches in the decrease pairs by working the first stitch of the row by itself.

PULLOVER DECREASE

This method of decreasing has a rather specialized use in finishing a Double Knit Welt (page 241), but if you like the effect it creates, there is no reason not to use it under any circumstances. The stitches must be paired as for Joinery Decrease, above.

On the Outside: Insert the right needle into the second stitch on the left needle as to Purl and pull it over the first stitch and off the needle. Knit the remaining stitch of the pair.

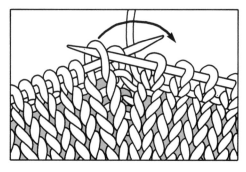

DOUBLE KNIT TO SINGLE KNIT/PULLOVER DECREASE

On the Inside: Each decrease pair must first be slipped to the right needle. With the left needle, reach around on the farside, pick up the second stitch on the right needle, and pull it over the first stitch and off the needle. Insert the left needle into the farside of the remaining stitch of the pair and Purl. Continue with the work single thickness.

What is happening is that the stitches of the outside fabric are pulled over the stitches of the inside fabric and the knitting continues on the latter.

If you have been working the two faces of the Double Knit fabric in contrasting colors, work the last row of each face in the color you plan to continue with, then work the row of decreases to change the fabric to Single Knit.

Ribbing and Double Knit Fabrics

Single Rib and Double Knit fabrics have a great deal in common, and it is simplicity itself to switch from one to the other. For the purposes of calculating widths, however, you must do a gauge on each stitch pattern; you cannot count on the number of stitches appropriate for the Double Knit to produce exactly the width you re-

quire for the rib. See Stitch Gauge for Ribbed Fabrics (page 424) and Stitch Gauge for Double Knits (page 427).

Casting Off Double Knit

Because of the number of stitches on the needle, a simple Pullover Cast-off will not work unless it is done very tightly on small needles, as the edge splays out and becomes unsightly. Fortunately, there are some very nice alternatives.

Using Joinery Cast-off

As you know, this technique combines a decrease with Pullover Cast-off (for more details, see page 150). It is the simplest, and best, method to use on a Double Knit fabric, for it produces an attractive edge and is easy to do. Joinery Cast-off is particularly suitable for Double Knit, as the edge will have only half the number of stitches as were on the needle, which is correct for the width of the fabric, and therefore there will be no splaying.

Just as when Joinery Decreases are used to change from a double- to a single-thickness fabric, the position of the stitches in the decrease pair is critical to the success of the technique when used in this situation. Regardless of whether you are working the cast-off with a Knit Two Together or a Purl Two Together prior to the Pullover, a stitch from the fabric on the nearside must be the left stitch of the decrease pair.

Using Invisible Cast-off

This cast-off, as you know, produces an edge identical to that of Alternating Cast-on. It is a very nice finish for any Double Knit edge that will show, such as on a scarf. Unfortunately, the technique has limitations that must be taken into consideration. There are some yarns that are not suitable for use with a sewn cast-off, and it does best on relatively narrow widths (please see page 160 for more details). Should you need to use it on a wide piece, and must resort to several lengths of yarn for the casting-off, you will have to knot the ends before locking them between the two fabric faces.

Using Single Knit Cast-off

There are times in Double Knitting where you will want to separate the two sets of stitches so the fabrics will not be joined at the top. In some cases, both sets of stitches are then cast off separately; in other cases, one set is cast off and the work continues on the other set with a single-thickness fabric.

Separating the Stitches: If it is a relatively short width of fabric and the yarn is well behaved, the simplest thing is to pull out the needle. The two fabrics will immediately separate and the stitches can be picked up on two double-point needles.

A safer approach is to leave the stitches on the needle, hold two double-point needles side by side in the right hand, and slip the stitches, the first to one needle, the next to the other across the row.

Casting Off: Once the stitches are separated, slide them to the end of the needle where the yarn comes off the first stitch and use Pullover Cast-off across one set of stitches.

If you are going to continue and also cast off the other set of stitches, proceed as follows:

• When one stitch remains of the first fabric, turn the work and cast off the second set in the same way, pulling the last stitch of the first fabric over the first stitch of the second fabric.

If you are not going to cast off the other set of stitches, secure the last cast-off stitch as follows:

• Enlarge the last stitch, pass the ball of yarn through it, and then tighten the stitch to form a knot, or
• Work the last stitch in a decrease with an adjacent stitch so it is hidden on the inside of the fabric, or
• Pull the last stitch over an adjacent stitch or the first stitch of the other fabric.

Applications: Hems, Welts and Casings

All of this has been quite abstract. Now that you have all the techniques necessary to make a garment out of a Double Knit fabric, let's turn our attention to some of the applications that are possible.

Horizontal Bands

There are any number of useful and interesting ways to make use of a band of Double Knit placed at the edge or inserted into an otherwise single-thickness fabric. The Double Knit section may be worked over as many rows as you wish before the original stitch count is restored. At its simplest, this concept can be used to create softly rounded horizontal bands. A band of this sort is rather subtle, but the concept is important and can be expanded in many interesting ways.

Rounded Edge for Single Rib

Alternating Cast-on gives a narrow rounded edge to Single Rib. If you add four rows of Double Knit above the cast-on edge and then continue on the same number of stitches in Single Rib, the edge will be even more rounded, although not as elastic as it would be otherwise.

Double Knit Hems

Double Knit is one of the easiest and nicest ways to do a hem at the lower edge of a garment.

1. Cast on and work Basic Double Knit to the depth required for the hem.
2. Use Joinery Decreases to reduce the stitch count by half.

3. Continue with the garment section on the normal number of stitches.

If you use a Half-Hitch Cast-on or a Cable Cast-on, the edge will be similar to that created by a Purl Foldline; one side of Picot Cast-on is even more pronounced. If you use Alternating Cast-on, there will be no foldline, just a rounded edge.

Double Knit Welts

Here is a clever trick that I quite like. Welts are normally done using the Knit Below technique (see page 29), but it is never that easy to reach down and pick up the correct stitch in the row below. There is a way around the difficulty.

1. Work in single thickness to the row where you wish to start the Welt and then use Slip Raised Increases on all stitches but the selvedges.
2. Work back and forth single thickness on *only* the original stitches, Knitting one row and Purling the other, always slipping the new stitches and the selvedge stitches until you have the required number of rows in the Welt according to your stitch gauge. The new stitches are never worked, even though they are interspersed on the needle as for a Double Knit fabric.
3. On the next row, begin to work the selvedge stitches again and return to the original stitch count using Pullover Decreases (page 64) rather than Joinery Decreases. Make sure you always pull an original stitch over a new stitch and continue the fabric on the new stitches.

What is happening here? You have picked up the stitches in the row below *before* you work the Welt! Pullover Decreases must be used to pull the Welt up tightly; if Joinery Decreases were used instead, the picked-up stitches would gain an extra row and the Welt would lose its corded appearance and flatten slightly.

If you have worked the fabric flat and wish to close the ends of the Welt when seaming, run the sewing needle through the edge stitches of the Welt and draw it up like a drawstring, then continue with the seam.

Also keep in mind that the Welt can be worked in a contrasting color. Because the new stitches made with the increases are those on which the main fabric will continue, work them in the main color. Then begin working the contrast-color yarn on the Welt stitches. Work the decreases that complete the Welt in the main color again.

Double Knit Tucks

A horizontal Tuck can be made on the same principle as a Welt. Increase and continue working just the original stitches. When half the rows have been done, work a Purl Foldline, then the other half of the required number of rows. Restore the stitch count with Pullover Decreases and continue the fabric single thickness.

Double Knit Casings

A band of Double Knit can serve as a casing for elastic or a drawstring if it is worked with a Two-Yarn Double Knit method, which leaves it open at each selvedge. It works best on an uneven number of stitches, with the outside fabric getting the extra stitch. Keep in mind that any knit casing for elastic can be bulky unless you keep gathering to a minimum, or use a finer or split yarn for the inner facing (for alternatives, see page 204 or 381). For a drawstring on a circular fabric, you will need an opening on the outside. This can be done by placing a simple Eyelet Buttonhole in the required position, as follows:

- Slip one stitch from the near fabric, slip the next stitch from the far fabric to a cable holder and hold on the farside, and return the first slipped stitch to the left needle. Yarnover. Slip the stitch from the cable holder to the right needle. Knit the next two stitches together.

Multiple Casings: An interesting overall fabric can be made using multiple casings, one on top of the other. There are three ways to do this.

- Work a casing to the depth desired. Work Joinery Decreases across the row and knit one or two rows on the single-thickness fabric according to the effect desired. Then use Slip Raised Increases to return to Double Knit and work another casing. Continue in this manner throughout, or
- An even simpler approach is to work one row of Single Rib on a smaller needle between each section of Double Knit without changing the number of stitches on the needle.

An alternate method requires no single-thickness rows between the casings. Instead, the stitches are pulled through one another, which interlocks the two fabrics across the row, ending one casing and beginning the next automatically. This is done using a Threaded Stitch technique as follows:

1. Work with pairs of stitches as for Joinery Decreases, with a stitch of the near fabric being the left stitch of each pair.
2. With the yarn on the nearside, insert the right needle into the second stitch on the left needle (a near stitch) as to Purl and pull it over the first stitch (a far stitch). Keep the stitch on the right needle just as if it had been slipped. Move the yarn to the farside and Knit the remaining stitch of the pair. Continue in this way across the row. Turn.
3. On the return row, slip the first stitch of each pair with the yarn nearside (the one previously worked)

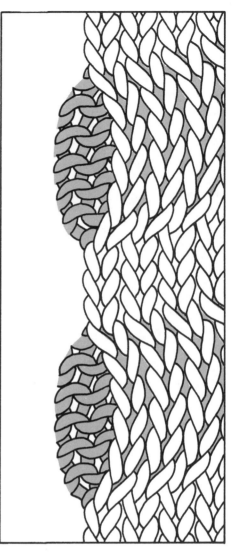

DOUBLE KNIT CASINGS/INCREASE-DECREASE METHOD

and Knit the other. Continue with Double Knit on the next casing.

Keep in mind that if Two-Yarn Double Knit is used, the casings can also be done in reversible colors, with the colors alternating from one side to the other along with the stitches. The technique can be combined with the Interlock method of creating vertical color reversal stripes to form a checkerboard pattern (see page 275).

Quilted Double Knit: A Double Knit casing can be stuffed with batting to create a more corded effect. If you work the Double Knit open at each selvedge the batting must be something like candle wicking or a bulky yarn that can be drawn through the width of the fabric without coming apart.

Alternatively, separate the two fabrics as for Open Cast-off, insert the batting, then hold the two needles side by side and join the stitches with Joinery Decreases to restore the original stitch count.

DOUBLE KNIT CASINGS/PULLING STITCHES OF ONE FACE THROUGH THE OTHER

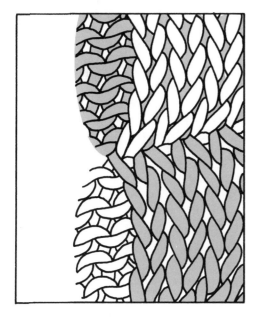

DOUBLE KNIT CASINGS/THREADED STITCH METHOD

QUILTED DOUBLE KNIT CASINGS

The concept of the Welt suggests the idea of adding an extra row or two to just the outside fabric so that it will puff out slightly more to exaggerate the effect. See also Double Knit Motifs (page 277).

Double Knit Yoke: The concept of a casing can be expanded in several useful ways. For instance, a thick yoke done in Double Knit can add a great deal of warmth and an interesting look to a sweater or jacket.

Increase at the lower line of the yoke and work as for Basic Double Knit. Use the decreases described above for any required neck shaping, and use Joinery Cast-off for the shoulders, which can be done as for Stepped Cast-off (see page 152) if desired.

Alternatively, when the yoke is complete, work Joinery Decreases to change from double to single thickness and then use Joinery Cast-off to join the front and back shoulders.

Double Knit Horizontal Pockets

There is no rule that says that a section of Double Knit must run from selvedge to selvedge, and once we realize that, it does not take an extraordinary leap of the imagination to get from casings and yokes to pockets, and quite the nicest pockets of all, I think. The instructions are given for working the pocket in a Stockinette fabric.

Work the garment section single thickness to the lower edge of the pocket. Place stitch markers on the needle on either side of the stitches of the pocket. Then work the increases as follows:

1. Knit across to the second marker. Turn.
2. Use Purl Slip Raised Increase on every stitch of the pocket. At the marker, turn. (The original stitches will form the pocket facing, the new stitches will form the lining.)
3. Knit the original pocket facing stitches, slipping the new, interspersed pocket lining stitches with the yarn nearside. At the second marker, begin plain Knit to the end of the row. Turn.
4. Purl to the first pocket marker. Purl the pocket lining stitches, and slip the pocket facing stitches with the yarn nearside. At the second marker, begin plain Purl to the end of the row.

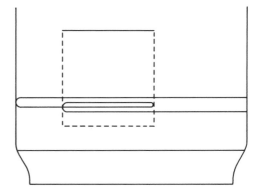

WORKING A DOUBLE KNIT HORIZONTAL POCKET

Work subsequent rows as follows:

1. Knit to the first marker, Knit the stitches of the pocket facing, slip the stitches of the pocket lining. At the second marker, turn.
2. Purl the stitches of the pocket lining, slip the stitches of the pocket facing. Turn at the marker.
3. Knit the stitches of the pocket facing, slip the stitches of the pocket lining. At the marker, Knit across the remaining stitches of the row. Turn.
4. Purl to the first marker. Purl the stitches of the pocket lining, slip the stitches of the pocket facing to the marker. At the second marker, Purl across the remaining stitches of the row.

When the pocket is as deep as you wish it to be, separate the two sets of pocket stitches as for Single Knit Cast-off, above, casting off the stitches of the pocket facing. Continue to work single thickness on the stitches each side of the pocket and on those that continue up from the pocket lining.

As you can see in the diagram, the stitches to each side of the pocket, those of the pocket facing, and those of the lining are all worked two rows by the end of step 4. Notice that the stitches of the pocket lining are worked so the Knit side of the lining faces in the same direction as the Knit face of the outside pocket, as when the pocket is complete they will continue into the rest of the garment.

A simple cast-off edge is not the best way to finish the top of the pocket because, unless the pocket is fairly narrow, the edge may curl to the outside. This can be overcome by adding an edge in crochet, which will not only stabilize it but can add a decorative note. Alternatively, once the stitches are separated, work those of the pocket facing up into a border and sew it into place at both sides.

Double Knit Sloped Pockets

Using the same general concept discussed above for a horizontal pocket, it is also possible to make a pocket with a sloped opening. The pocket described here opens to the left; reverse the instructions for a pocket that opens to the right.

Increase and work as described above to form the portion of the pocket lining below the lower point of the opening. Continue as follows:

1. Knit to the first marker. Knit the pocket facing stitches, slip the lining stitches. At the second marker, turn.
2. Purl the facing stitches, slip the lining stitches. At the first marker, turn.
3. Knit the lining stitches, slip the facing stitches. At the second marker, continue to Knit across the row. Turn.
4. Purl to the first marker, then Purl the lining stitches, slip the facing stitches. At the second marker, Purl to the end of the row.

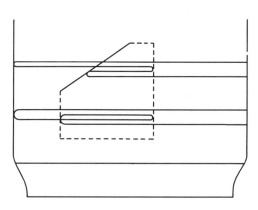

WORKING A DOUBLE KNIT SLOPED POCKET

It is necessary to work the decreases to form the slope at the very edge of the opening, otherwise you would have to constantly readjust the way the stitches are interspersed with one another. If you want a border, work some of the stitches at the open edge in Seed Stitch. You can extend the border to the left of the lining by using Slip Raised Increases to widen the facing between the lower and upper points of the opening. Use Joinery Decreases at the top to return to a Single Knit fabric. For more detail, see the discussion and illustration of traditional sloped pocket construction on page 228.

Double Knit Elbow Patches

Do you lean on your elbows? Would you like a little padding that helps to reinforce the sleeve against wear? You can work an elbow patch in Double Knit in much the same way as a Double Knit pocket.

Use Slip Raised Increases along the bottom line and begin to work the interspersed stitches as for a pocket. Place additional increases in a slope up each side until the Double Knit section is as wide as you want, continue for a while, then begin the decreases to restore Single Knit according to the same pattern.

If you want colorful patches, see the material on Double Knit Motifs in the section on Working with Color (page 277).

Joining with Double Knit

As you know, grafting is a sewing technique used to invisibly join two pieces of knitting. It is frequently used at shoulder lines or to finish off mittens or sock toes. Some people don't like to graft knitting, and find it difficult to get a good result with nice, even stitches. Double Knit provides an alternative, but you must be willing to knit from the top down, or from the toe up, as it were. The example given is for a sweater worked from shoulder to waist.

1. With needles several sizes smaller than you plan to use, place twice the number of stitches required for

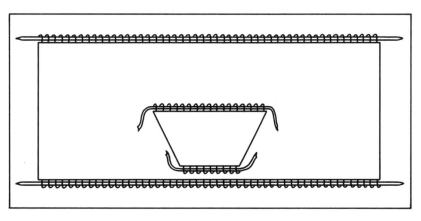

DOUBLE KNIT USED AS A SUBSTITUTE FOR A GRAFTED SHOULDER LINE

one shoulder on the needle with Alternating Cast-on, continue with Stranded Cast-on across the back of the neck, then switch back to Alternating Cast-on and add twice the number of stitches for the width of the other shoulder.

2. Switch to the correct-size needle, and using one ball of yarn, work two to four rows on just the stitches of the back, slipping the stitches of the two front shoulders (which are interspersed on the needle at each side), as you would to make a Welt, (see above). On the first row, make sure you are Knitting the stitches that come up the near side of the cast-on edge.

3. At you convenience, separate the interspersed stitches of the front shoulders from those of the back, placing one set on a holder.

4. Work down the front and back separately. At the underarm, cast on stitches at each side to shape the armhole and then join the front and back on a circular needle, and work in the round to the waist.

It is important that you use a very fine needle for the casting on so those stitches will not be enlarged. In order to pick up the stitches across the back of the neck to finish, split the baseline strand at the center, pull the ends out to each side, picking up the stitches as you do so. Slip all these stitches to a single needle, then pick up the stitches around the front neckline and work the border in the round.

The same concept can be used to work a sock from toe to top, or a mitten from fingertips to wrist. I'm not sure you'll think any of this is worth the trouble just to avoid grafting, but it's always fun to try some new approach to things, and some of you jaded knitters who are tired of doing the same old thing might want to give it a go.

Single Knit Fabrics Using Double Knit Techniques

In discussing the method of using two supplies of yarn in order to separate a Double Knit fabric at the sides, I mentioned that the approach could be used to make two separate flat fabrics. Well, two flat fabrics worked at the same time might assure you of having the same number of rows in each, but other than that it really isn't very interesting. However, the Double Knit technique can also be used very effectively to produce a single thickness fabric in the round using two straight needles, and as you will see, this turns out to be very useful indeed. Less useful, perhaps, but quite a lot of fun, are two circular fabrics done simultaneously. There isn't anything magical about it, but you'll feel like a wizard the first time you try it.

Circular Fabrics on Single Point Needles

Small items, like mittens, hats, and socks, that won't fit on even a small circular needle are normally handled with a set of double-point needles. I don't know about you, but I find it very awkward to knit in the round on double-point needles, and the smaller the object the more awkward things can get; it's all those points. Furthermore, with multiple needles, many knitters have trouble crossing the gap from one needle to the next without elongating the running thread between the last stitch on one needle and the first on the next, and this shows as an irregularity in the finished fabric. It is far easier to get a smooth fabric with the Double Knit technique, as the stitches are side by side and so there is no gap to cross. However, because adjacent stitches are separated by another stitch and this tends to elongate the running thread somewhat, you might want to reduce the size of the needle to get the gauge you want for the fabric.

You can certainly work a circular fabric of any size in this manner; however, it seems to me that it would hardly be worth it to do so. Circular needles are very comfortable to work with when making a fabric that has an adequate circumference to be accommodated on them. Really the only justification for using the Double Knit technique to make a Single Knit fabric is to avoid working with a set of double-point needles.

There are two methods of working a fabric in the round, one with the Knit side facing out and a somewhat faster method with the Purl side facing out, which nevertheless (the magic continues), requires no Purling.

Working on the Outside

1. Use Circular Cast-on (page 111) to place the required number of stitches on a single needle.
2. Work as for Basic Double Knit, shaping as necessary.
3. Finish with Joinery Cast-off.

With Circular Cast-on, the two fabrics will not be joined at the bottom. They will be joined at the sides, though not in the center, by Basic Double Knit. Joinery Cast-off closes the top. It sounds like a mitten or a hat to me.

When working mittens, you can use the Contrast-Color Yarn Opening (page 230) for the thumbhole without separating the stitches. When the body of the mitten is complete, pick up the thumb stitches and any that you need at each side to make the correct circumference, intersperse them on a single needle, and work as above. Work the fingers of a glove in exactly the same way.

This is also a good method to use for hats, and even for sleeves. For the latter, of course, you will want to separate the stitches either for casting off or to shape the sleeve cap. Color stripes and Stranded Color patterns will work just as well as they would done on circular needles. Do check from time to time to make sure you have not stranded wrong and bound the two faces together in the center! The wayward running thread should be quite obvious on the outside, but the quickest way to check is to insert your hand.

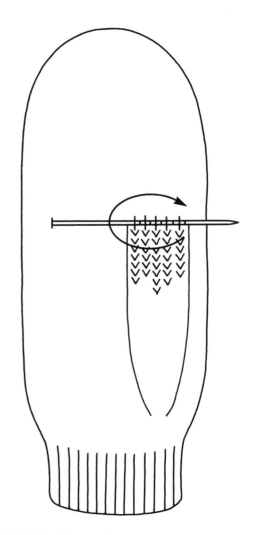

WORKING A MITTEN THUMB WITH DOUBLE KNIT

Working Inside Out

The normal way of working Double Knit is rather slow because you must constantly switch the yarn from one side to the other in order to strand it past the intervening stitch. When you are making a Single Knit fabric with the Double Knit method, working with the fabric inside out is far more efficient and speeds things up considerably.

- Use Circular Cast-on, intersperse the stitches on a single needle, and work as follows: *Sl1, K1*.

In this case you will Knit the stitches of the fabric on the farside while slipping the stitches of the fabric on the nearside. Also, because the fabric is inside out, all of the yarns are stranded on the outside rather than between the two fabrics, as they would be in the normal method. Therefore, it is not necessary to switch the yarn from one side to the other after every stitch, and this makes the work go much faster.

You must have at least one edge open in order to turn the fabric right side out again when the work is done. Use Circular Cast-on as described here, or use any cast-on suitable for Double Knit, work the fabric as above and finish with an Open Cast-off.

Working Two Circular Fabrics Simultaneously

. . . better known as the sock trick. Double Knit can be used to work two entirely separate, circular fabrics at the same time, most commonly a pair of socks. It looks, to the uninitiated, as if the knitter is making a single sock. However, when the last stitch has been worked, a second sock is pulled from within the first (most often before an audience and accompanied by a dramatic flourish). The technique is discussed among knitters with alternating awe and amusement, and in fact, since it is a complex exercise, the only real point in using it is to delight the children. If you know how to make socks, and understand Double Knit, you can be the magician.

1. Using a small-size double-point needle, cast on the stitches required for one sock, then distribute the stitches to three needles, join into a round, and work the ribbing.
2. Repeat with a second set of needles and a second ball of yarn for the other sock.
3. Place one set of stitches inside the other and transfer the stitches, alternating one stitch from each needle, to three larger size double-points, one-third of the interspersed pairs of stitches to each needle. The yarn for the inner fabric should come up through the center of the circle; the yarn for the outer fabric should be on the outside and you can work one yarn at a time or both simultaneously.
4. Begin working Stockinette so that the Knit side of both fabrics is facing you in one of the following ways.
   Using one yarn at a time:
   a. To work the outer fabric, *yfs, K1, yns, sl1*.
   b. At the end of the round, bring the outer yarn nearside, drop it and pick up the inner yarn.
   c. To work the inner fabric, *sl1, K1*.
   d. At the end of the round, leave the inner yarn on the farside.

Using both yarns:
   a. Hold the yarn for the outer fabric on the left forefinger; that for the inner fabric on the right forefinger.
   b. To work a stitch of the outer fabric, hold both yarns farside and Knit using the left yarn.
   c. To work the next stitch of the inner fabric, bring just the outer yarn nearside, Knit using the right yarn.
   d. Return the left yarn farside prior to working the next stitch of the outer fabric.
5. At the ankle, inactivate the instep stitches in the usual way and work the heel flap and the heel cup flat; it is easiest to do this if you use the Slide technique for the Short Rows, working one row at a time on each fabric.
6. To rejoin the round, pick up stitches along the selvedges of the heel flaps, one stitch from each fabric, alternating yarns as you alternate stitches to intersperse them on the needle. (Have the outer yarn nearside as you pick up an inner stitch; bring it back farside to pick up the next outer stitch.)
7. Work the Gusset, continue down the foot to the toe, and then do the toe decreases.
8. Separate the remaining interspersed stitches onto four needles—two for the inner sock, two for the outer—and graft first the inner toe, then the outer toe.

Do be careful to check the fabrics from time to time to make sure they remain separate; any error in the Double Knitting technique will bind the two together. Some people knit these socks from the toe up. Use Alternating Cast-on and intersperse the stitches after the toe shaping is complete. The flap and Gusset are worked in the same sequence, but while perfectly serviceable, they will be upside down. If you want to try this but dread the heel shaping, work tube socks.

In order to make all of this worthwhile, of course, you will need an audience that delights in things magical to witness the final dramatic moment when one sock becomes two. Aside from the theatrics, the only practical reason to work this way is to make sure you have exactly the same number of rows in each sock (or sleeve, for that matter).

PART THREE

DECORATIVE TECHNIQUES

14
Working with Color

The introduction of more than one color to a knitted fabric livens things up considerably, and the possibilities are limited only by your imagination and the materials you have to work with. There are color techniques simple enough for the beginning knitter and others that can challenge the expert. A great deal of color knitting is done as a Stockinette fabric, and with good reason. The smooth face of Stockinette allows the color scheme to be dominant and get all the attention, and it is so easy to do that the knitter can concentrate solely on working the pattern. However, there is no need to limit yourself to that, and in fact many techniques that appear in other guises in knitting take on a whole new dimension when color is used to highlight their characteristics.

If you have little or no experience at working with color and perhaps have avoided it because it seemed so time consuming and difficult, I would like to reassure you. The most important thing to keep in mind is that you cannot judge the difficulty of working a color pattern by its appearance, as there are some paradoxes here. For instance, the method of handling color that requires the most practiced skill is nevertheless often used to produce subtle, even plain effects. On the other hand, there is another method that is simplicity itself to do, yet it produces extremely complex patterns, such that everyone will believe you are being altogether too modest if you reply truthfully to their compliments by saying, "Oh, it was really very easy."

Simple Color Techniques

Let's start with a few truly elementary techniques, one that allows you to design your own yarn, so to speak, and the others having to do with making horizontal stripes. Simple they may be, but very effective when matched to a good sense of color and design.

Treating Multiple Yarns as One

One of the simplest ways to introduce color to a knitted fabric is to design your own yarn. If you knit with two or more yarns at once, treating them all as if they were one, the different colors and/or textures will blend together in the fabric producing a tweedy effect. Notice that I said "textures," for these need not be the same types of yarns. In addition to blending colors, you can combine smooth with fluffy or nubby, fine with heavy, or shiny with dull. In what would otherwise have been a plain, Stockinette pullover sweater, I combined a tie-dyed silk, a cotton bouclé, a fine, shiny rayon, and a threadlike strand of lurex, all held together and knitted as one.

When you are purchasing yarn, twist a few inches of the different yarns you are considering together and make several wraps close together around your finger to get an idea of the effect they will create when combined. Don't let the sum of your efforts turn into a yarn bulkier than is suitable for the type of garment you plan; this is an opportunity to use those superfine yarns you might otherwise avoid. Even sewing thread will show, randomly appearing and disappearing as it wraps around a carrier yarn.

Do not attempt to wind the yarns together into a single ball; they will wind onto the ball one way and take up into the knitting in another, and you will have a terrible tangle on your hands and a worse job undoing everything. Place each yarn in a separate bag or in something like a shoe box with a hole in the top, so you can unwind from each ball individually; don't bring them together until they are in your hand ready to form a stitch.

Horizontal Stripes

Another elementary way to add color is to do a few rows in one color, then a few in another. Even this simple approach can be used to produce quite a variety of effects.

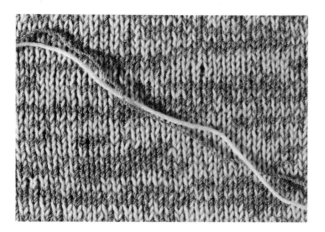

RANDOM PATTERN CREATED BY HOLDING TWO YARNS AS ONE

HORIZONTAL STRIPES

Wherever you want a stripe, just begin working with the new color in the same way you would if you were tying on a new ball of yarn in the same color (see page 352). Please note that there are certain details of doing even such a simple technique as this that will change depending upon whether you are working flat or in the round, and whether you are working an odd or even number of rows. The concepts discussed here are also applicable to more complex patterns that, like stripes, work different colors across an entire row.

Stripes on Single-Point Needles

If you are working on single-point needles, it will take two rows in the stripe color to bring you back to the side where the original yarn is hanging off the work. (If you were to work a pattern with an odd number of rows, you would find the original yarn at the wrong end of the needle when you needed it again.) When you have returned to the starting point, you may drop the second color, pick up the original again and continue.

Stripes on Double-Point Needles/The Slide

Stripes of any number of rows, odd or even, may be made on a flat fabric, but the work must be done on a pair of double-point needles or a circular needle in conjunction with a technique called the Slide.

For the sake of simplicity, I will give the instructions for a one-row stripe.

1. Work to the point where you wish to have the stripe, attach the second color yarn, and work across the row.
2. At the end of the row, do not turn the work.
3. Drop the second yarn, slide the stitches back to the point of the needle at the right, pick up the original yarn, and work across the row. (The same face of the fabric will be on the nearside after the Slide as before.)
4. At the end of these two rows, both yarns will again be on the same side. Turn the work and continue according to your pattern.

Once you realize that you can move the stitches to either end of the needle in order to bring a particular yarn into play, you will find you can apply the Slide technique in many situations where it may not even be suggested in a pattern, but it will either simplify working or suggest variations that might otherwise be impossible.

Keep in mind that Slides interrupt the normal sequence of Knit and Purl rows in a given stitch pattern, but as you know, Knit and Purl are simply two aspects of the same stitch and it doesn't matter which one you do, as long as you place the correct aspect of the stitch on the outside of the fabric. For ease in working in this manner, however, it is far better to convert a written stitch pattern to a charted one so that no confusion arises (see page 449).

Color Stripes Knitted in the Round

When knitting in the round, the same side of the work is always facing you, and you return to the same point at the end of every round. Therefore when changing colors, the yarn is right there where you want it, regardless of how many rows have intervened between one and the other. Most traditional color knitting is done in the round because the outside of the fabric where the pattern is developed is always facing the knitter, because the yarn changes are easy if working in one color at a time, and because it is easiest to do Double Stranding in Knit (see below). However, there are some decided disadvantages to knitting in the round that must also be taken into consideration (see page 115), and knitting stripes, or any pattern with a strong horizontal configuration, is one of them.

Vertical Stranding

When you have completed a section in one color, and it is time to bring the other color into play again, you may find the yarn some rows down. The best method of carrying the yarns up as you work depends upon the kind of fabric you are making.

When working a flat fabric to be seamed, it is possible to simply strand the yarn up the selvedge and begin working with it again, and this works reasonably well over short distances. If the distance between one stripe and the other is more than an inch, however, the strands may snag in wear, and it is best to attach them to the selvedge row by row by wrapping one yarn around the other every time they are both on the same side of the fabric. Just bring the working yarn under the one in waiting and continue with the knitting.

Regardless of whether or not you bind the strand to the selvedge, the stranded yarn should be carried up the side at an easy tension. At a color change, work the first stitch or two, then stretch the selvedge out to make sure it isn't constricted in any way. It is best to get in the habit of checking this, because the only way to correct it later is to work some yarn out of the stitches at either end of the strand, and that will tighten them up.

If you are knitting with more than two colors, the yarns stranded up the selvedge can get bulky. The solution is to work on double-point needles or a circular one so that you can use the Slide technique, attaching two yarns on one side, one yarn at the other.

On edges that will show, such as blankets and scarves, Vertical Stranding may not be the most attractive solution. In this case you might wish to work the first stitch of each row with both yarns held as one. This gives a very neat finish to the selvedges, and controlling the tension on a vertical strand is not an issue. The technique can, of course, be used when the selvedges will be seamed, but it adds more bulk to the seam than Vertical Stranding does, as the yarn is doubled back on itself with each stitch.

When working in the round, the yarns will be carried up at the juncture between one row and the next and so must be all in one place. The same basic technique of wrapping the working yarn around the one in waiting is used to attach them to the fabric so they cannot be snagged. In this case, it is even more important that care be taken with the tension of these strands so the fabric is not gathered up by the vertical strands.

If the second color constitutes a major section of the fabric, you may want to break off the original yarn and reattach it when you need it again so you don't have two balls of yarn hanging off the work. However, remember that later you will have two ends to hide at each color change, one from the yarn you have finished working with and the other from the one you are starting, and these will add more bulk to the selvedge than carrying one strand up will. (In some cases you can use these ends for seaming.)

Handling Ends

In some traditional methods of working color stripes, the yarn is broken off at the completion of each section and the new color started. The ends are then handled in one of two ways:

- They can be attached to the first few inches of stitches on the inside of the fabric using the Purl Inlay technique (see page 281). This eliminates any bulk in the selvedge but adds it to the fabric itself. Since there will be two ends of yarn to weave in every time one color stops and another begins (and in complex patterns there may be four), this adds up to a great deal of extra yarn trailing behind the stitches on one side of the selvedge or the juncture between one round and the next. Personally, I don't like what this does to the way the fabric feels and behaves; I'd much rather have a small amount of extra yarn in the selvedge than all those ends woven into the fabric.

- The other approach, used on true Shetland Fair Isle sweaters, which are knit in the round, is to just tie the ends together in a knot, cut the yarn off short, and leave it at that. This leaves a little fringe on the inside all the way up one side where a seam would otherwise have been, and all the way around the armholes, but no bulk in the fabric. Because these sweaters are worked in very fine yarn, the knots and fringe are so tiny and unobtrusive that one is not aware of them at all.

Color-Patterned Stripes

So far we have been looking at color effects that are created by working every stitch of a particular row in a single color. However, solid color stripes are just the beginning. Very elaborate patterns can be developed by working some of the stitches in a row in one color, others in a different color, with the pattern and the colors changing row by row. A color-patterned garment of this sort can look extremely complex, and the best ones can justifiably be called one of the highest forms of the knitter's art. In many ways, however, they look more challenging than they are.

Color-patterned stripes are almost always worked in plain Stockinette, although, as I discussed above, there is really no technical reason for that restriction; it seems based solely on custom. In addition, while many colors can be introduced, it is rare for there to be more than two colors used in any row, and the patterns are almost always charted, which makes them quite easy to follow (see page 486 for details on Charted Stitch Patterns). There are three different methods of handling the yarns

in order to create these types of patterns, and they all produce exactly the same kind of fabric. Their differences have primarily to do with the level of skill re-

FAIR ISLE STRANDED COLOR PATTERN (DETAIL)

TRADITIONAL FAIR ISLE OF THE 1920s

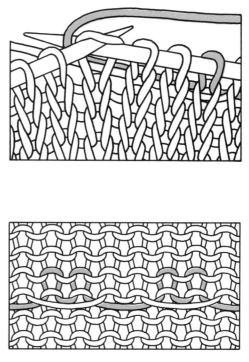

STRANDED YARNS ON INSIDE

quired and the speed and ease of working. A garment of this sort is never a "quicky knit" even for experienced knitters—they do take concentration and patience—but even a novice knitter can make one. I had a wonderful student once who used some color pattern of this sort on her very first garment with great success.

Stranding

In working color-patterned stripes, the color not immediately in use will be stranded on the inside of the fabric past the stitches being worked in the other color. The only real skill involved with stranding is control of tension, but that is critical. If you provide too much yarn, the stitches in the same color on either end of the strand will have a tendency to take up the extra and enlarge. If you don't provide enough yarn, the stitches the strand spans will bunch together, and the fabric may become constricted and lose its resilience. In order to prevent either of these things from happening, at every color change stretch out the entire group of stitches to be spanned on the right needle, then work the next stitch. This measures out precisely the amount of yarn the strand will require when the fabric has been dressed and is ready for wear.

Most patterns that depend on this technique will use relatively small blocks of color, so the yarn need not be stranded farther than about one inch. Technically, you can strand past any number of stitches you want to, but the longer the strands, the more difficult it becomes to tension them properly, and the more likely you will be to tangle your fingers up in them when you put the garment on. Some instruction books will have strict rules on the matter, advising you never to strand past more than four or five stitches, but as you know, this may be half an inch in some stitch gauges and one inch in another. Rules of that nature should always be scrutinized for what purpose they serve. To give you an extreme example of the inadequacy of that kind of guideline, Mary Thomas, in her book *Mary Thomas's Knitting Book,*[1] discusses a fragment of Arabian color knitting some thousand years old, which she says is worked in silk at an astonishing thirty-six stitches to the inch. (They certainly had both more patience and more time than we do today!) Needless to say, stranding every four stitches would be quite unnecessary as a strand of one-ninth inch would be difficult to snag if you tried.

It is quite simple to analyze a pattern in terms of the gauge you should be able to expect on the yarn and needles you plan to work with (see page 415). If according to your gauge the pattern has sections where the yarn would be stranded past more than about an inch, you may wish to select another pattern, or you can catch the strands against the fabric where they can't be snagged with a technique called weaving in (see page 258).

The strands that lie behind the stitches on the inside of the garment provide a great deal of added warmth while still providing all the benefits of a garment and pattern worked in fine yarn. The wonderful play of color and the warmth come at a price, however, for

1. New York: Dover Publications, Inc., 1972, p. 91.

INSIDE OF FABRIC IN STRANDED COLOR PATTERN

aside from the time they consume, a garment made with a Stranded pattern will require considerably more yarn than the same garment worked up plain. Please consult the material on page 429 for information on making an accurate assessment of how much of each color to purchase for your project; it is more complex to calculate the requirements for these kinds of patterns than for simple stripes.

I mentioned above that most Stranded knitting patterns use only two colors in a given row. It is technically possible to work with more colors, but each additional strand will add additional bulk to the fabric. With a fine yarn, this may be less of a consideration, especially if it is only on an occasional row, but it should certainly be avoided with the heavier-weight yarns. If a pattern really requires more than two colors, the best alternative is to combine stranding with the Intarsia method of working (see below), which allows the introduction of small, isolated bits of color, or Duplicate Stitch, an embroidery technique that can be used after the knitting is completed (see page 286).

And finally, one of the nicest ways to begin a fabric of Stranded Knitting is by using one of the techniques that allow casting on in two colors. Either Alternating Cast-on or Half-Hitch Cast-on can be used to great advantage in this way.

Now let's look at how to handle the two yarns as the pattern changes stitch by stitch across the row. All of the instructions presume that you are working in Stockinette, and begin on the Knit side.

Alternating Two Yarns

Here is a simple and very common way of working with both yarns at once. It is as easily done in Knit or Purl and can be used either for flat knitting on single-point needles or knitting in the round on double-point needles or a circular one. This is a precise way of working, allowing careful control of tension and great accuracy in following even a complex pattern, yet is simple enough even for a knitter unaccustomed to multicolor

knitting. Unfortunately, it is the slowest method, and I therefore recommend it only for those of you who have never done a color pattern or find you have trouble following patterns of this sort.

1. Work the required number of stitches with color A. When you come to a stitch which is to be worked in color B, drop color A, stretch the stitches just worked in color A out on the right needle to control the length of the color B strand, and begin to work the stitches in color B.
2. Continue in this way, alternating the colors according to the pattern across the row.

When working in Knit, the yarns will be stranded on the farside; when working in Purl, they will be stranded on the nearside so all strands lie on the inside of the garment.

Many people go to a great deal of trouble to wrap the yarns around one another every time a change from one color to the other is made. As this is done, the yarn going to the balls gets all wound together and must be untangled from time to time before the work can proceed. All of this is completely unnecessary when stranding, as you will see once you have tried Slip Stranding, described below; it isn't done there, and it needn't be done here, and only serves to make the whole thing even more tedious.

Slip Stranding

This technique may be used to knit either in the round or flat, but the latter must also be done on either a circular needle or a pair of double-point needles. The method requires no special skill, is considerably faster than Alternating Two Yarns, and allows precise control of tension. I highly recommend this way of working for any knitter who does color patterns only occasionally.

To Work a Flat Fabric

1. Knit across the row with color A, working only the background stitches, and slipping all the pattern stitches with the yarn stranded on the farside.
2. At the end of the row, drop color A, slide the stitches to the right, and attach color B.
3. With the same side of the fabric facing you, Knit across the row with color B, this time working all the pattern stitches and slipping all the background stitches. The yarn is again stranded on the farside. (At the end of these two rows of knitting, you will have complete one row of fabric.)
4. Turn the fabric to the other side and work in the same manner in Purl, once across with color A, once across with color B. The yarn will be stranded on the nearside.

Needless to say, there is no reason why you shouldn't work the pattern stitches first, the background stitches second.

To Work a Fabric in the Round

1. Knit one round with color A, working only the pattern stitches, and slipping all the background stitches with the yarn stranded on the farside.
2. Knit the next round with color B, working only the background stitches, and slipping all the pattern stitches, again with the yarn stranded on the farside. (At the end of two full rounds, one row of fabric will be complete.)

On the face of it, it would seem that having to manipulate all of the stitches twice in order to do a single row of fabric would be a very slow way of working. In fact, it goes along quite well, as the slipped stitches move from one needle to the next very rapidly. This method is considerably faster than Alternating Two Yarns.

The only real problem with working in this way is that, while using the first color on a row, it is sometimes difficult to tell where you are in the pattern if you are interrupted or your attention lapses. The color of the stitches on the right needle are rarely an accurate guide to what you have done because some of the stitches slipped may be the same color as those you have just knit. The only way to check the pattern is to look on the inside, where the strands will reveal exactly what has been knit and what has been slipped. When working with the second color of the row, the stitches on the right needle will show the pattern as it should be.

There are many patterns designed for this type of knitting in which the second row is an exact repeat of the first. This means that they can be worked on single-point needles, as two rows can be worked in one color, bringing you back to the yarn in waiting without need for Slides. In other words, at the end of four rows, two with the first color then two with the second, you will have completed two rows of fabric, the second an exact duplicate of the first (see Mosaic Patterns, page 263).

Double Stranding

By far the fastest way of doing Color-patterned stripes is to carry one yarn in each hand as you work across the row, making some of the stitches with the yarn held in the right hand, some with the yarn held in the left hand, depending upon the requirements of the pattern. This method is used by many traditional knitters in Great Britain and Europe, who can work even complex patterns with speed and ease.

In fact, the claims that are put forth regarding the speed that is possible with this method are made on the basis of what can be achieved by an expert. Keep in mind that most of the knitters who work this way usually learned it as children, knit frequently, and rarely do any other sort of knitting, so they have honed their skills with years and years of practice. The knitter who does a Stranded color-pattern garment only occasionally cannot hope to match the quality or the speed that can be

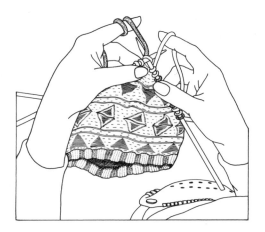

DOUBLE STRANDING

accomplished by practiced hands, and I think it would be unfair of me to raise expectations on the matter. Given that it is unlikely that you will be able to knit as fast as an expert anyway, and since quite precise control of tension is possible for even the occasional knitter with either Slip Stranding or Alternating Two Yarns, you may be much happier with what you produce using one of those methods instead. However, if you find yourself wanting to make color-patterned fabrics everytime you pick up the needles, then by all means have a go at this; it will be well worth your investment in time.

In order to work this way, of course, you must have some facility with both Left-Finger Knitting and either Right-Hand or Right-Finger Knitting (see pages 4–14). Practice the method you need to improve by itself before you try to use the two methods together. Few people ever become equally skilled with both hands, so the best result is obtained by carrying the yarn to be used most frequently in the hand that does the best. It is one thing to learn to make the stitches both ways, but it is control of the tension on the stranded yarns that is critical. Just as with any other Stranded color pattern, you must stretch the stitches out on the right needle at every color change in order to measure out the required length for the strand.

As an aid to speed, traditional knitters who use Double Stranding work in the round as much as possible, and many use a knitting belt (see page 5). The speed that can be gained in this way comes at a price, however, for there are some aspects of knitting in the round that are not ideal. One is that there is a slight distortion of the pattern where one row ends and the next begins, particularly with horizontal stripes such as these, although this is not serious if you are working with a fine enough yarn. Second, there is the problem of center front and armhole openings, for which there are several solutions, none of them entirely satisfactory but adequate to the task (see page 113 for a full discussion of knitting in the round). Fortunately, the method can also be used to make a flat fabric on single-point needles, working back and forth in Knit and Purl, and I recommend the effort be made to learn how to do so. You will undoubtedly find that the Purl rows are slower than the Knit rows, but I believe there are benefits that make it worthwhile to accept this slight compromise.

This method of handling two yarns is used almost exclusively for Stockinette patterns; color work that makes use of other stitch techniques is best done with the Slip Stranding method. There are some patterns that will not work when both yarns are carried across the row at the same time, and others that would simply be unnecessarily complicated or very awkward. One exception is the Stranded Brocade patterns (page 504).

On the face of it, there is nothing more to it than that, but the elegant simplicity of the method is deceptive, as it requires considerable practice before you can achieve a fabric you will take pride in. Despite its limitations, I don't wish to discourage you, however, for it can be really fun to work this way once you get the hang of it. Just don't make a big investment in your first few garments, and be forgiving of your early efforts; a smooth fabric made with gratifying speed will be the reward of patience and persistence.

Alternate Methods of Stranding

Knitters have left no stone unturned in their search for methods that would improve speed and reduce effort when working color patterns. Some people, rather than carry one yarn in each hand, wrap both yarns around the left forefinger, or one around the left forefinger, and one around the left middle finger, or ditto for fingers on the right hand. I find it quite hopeless to work in any of these ways because it is so difficult to maintain good tension control, particularly because the yarns get taken up into the fabric differentially and I find I must stop every few stitches and rewrap my fingers. It may be I didn't bring enough patience to the task, but I suspect the incentive wasn't there; I much prefer either Slip Stranding or Double Stranding and they serve me well enough that I admit I looked at these methods more as an academic exercise than as something I wished to put into use. But then my hands are not your hands, and you may do just fine with this.

If you are working with both strands on the left forefinger, it is relatively easy to scoop up whichever color you need next. If you have the yarns wrapped around the forefinger and middle finger of either hand, place the yarn that will be used the most on the forefinger when Knitting and on the middle finger when Purling so that yarn is always the one closest to the needle; the other is more awkward to handle. Because of the way the yarns must move through your fingers, the method works best on patterns with a regular alternation of colors, with each color being used on the same number of stitches. Although it is possible to work this way in Purl, it is more difficult and, in fact, the technique is really only used by knitters who work in the round and therefore only Knit.

Shaping a Stranded Pattern

With one exception, increases and decreases are no different when done in a color-patterned fabric than when done in a solid-colored one. However, you will want to concern yourself with another aspect of placement, and that is what effect the shaping unit has on the color pattern. For instance, if you are required to make a decrease in a position where two different color stitches are side by side, you may wish to choose a left or right decrease not so much for its appearance relative to the edge of the fabric, but in regard to which color stitch will become the facing stitch of the decrease and thus maintain the pattern most successfully.

Similarly, if an increase must be placed where the pattern requires the stitches to be different colors, there are three solutions. If you are using a Raised Increase, you can easily make one stitch in each color yarn. A more direct, and far simpler, approach is to knit a stitch with both yarns held as one. Wrap the yarns carefully so that the color sequence is correct on the two new stitches; on the next row, knit each of the yarns separately. And finally, some knitters use a Crossed Yarnover Increase to control the color of a new stitch.

Stranding for Warmth

Should you be interested in enhancing the thermal properties of a garment, but not terribly interested in going to the trouble of working a color pattern, either Slip Stranding or Double Stranding can be used to advantage. Work with two balls of the same yarn in the same color, or use a center-pull ball (see page 331), drawing one strand from the inside, and one strand from the outside, and alternate the yarns stitch by stitch throughout the fabric. This is a very nice way to add considerable warmth without forfeiting the advantages of a garment made in a relatively fine yarn.

Weaving In

Weaving in is a technique, used in conjunction with Double Stranding, that cures the problem of long strands, attaching them to the inside of the fabric so they can't be snagged. This is done by catching the yarn being stranded against the fabric with the running threads as you work stitches with the other yarn. Although there are other applications of the technique (see page 281), most commonly the strand is caught against the fabric at its midpoint, so that instead of one long strand there are two shorter ones.

Just as with regular stranding, care must be taken regarding tension when using this technique so the fabric is not constricted in any way. Also note that because the strands are wrapped around the running threads, it is possible for them to show through on the outside, particularly if the fabric was knitted at a loose tension,

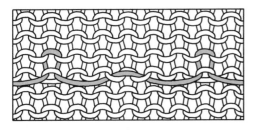

WEAVING IN

if the two yarns are in highly contrasting colors, or if the garment fits tightly and the fabric is stretched. Before you decide whether to use weaving in, dress the sample (see page 418) in order to get a realistic picture of how the finished fabric will look and behave.

BASIC WEAVING IN

In weaving in, the strand will get caught on either side of a stitch; to the right as you work the stitch with a weaving technique, to the left as you work the following stitch in the normal way. The way the two yarns are manipulated in order to accomplish this is different depending upon whether you will Knit or Purl the stitch, and whether it is the yarn held in the left or right hand that will be stranded. When the left strand is woven in, it will lie above the head of the discard stitch; when the right strand is woven in, it will lie below the head of the discard stitch. Only two of the required motions are in any way complicated, and you will see when you try it that once you grasp the concept on those two, they are in fact quite simple to execute. Hold the two yarns as for Double Stranding, one on the left forefinger, one on the right forefinger.

Knit Right Yarn/Left Yarn Woven

1. Insert the right needle into the stitch as to Knit.
2. Shift your finger so the left yarn leans against the farside of the right needle tip.
3. Pass the right yarn on the farside of the left yarn,

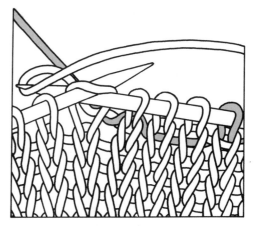

KNIT/LEFT YARN WOVEN/THE SECOND STITCH

wrap it around the needle in the usual way to Knit, and draw through a stitch.
4. Shift your finger in order to hold the left yarn out on the farside away from the needle tips in the normal way, passing the right yarn between the left yarn and the needle to Knit the next stitch.

Knit Left Yarn/Right Yarn Woven

1. Insert the right needle into the stitch as to Knit.
2. Wrap the right yarn around the tip of the needle as to Knit, then shift your finger in order to lay the left yarn over the tip of the right needle from nearside to farside just to the left of the other yarn.
3. Take the right yarn back off the needle, retracing the same path used to put it on; it will pass over the left yarn, which should remain on the needle.
4. Draw the left yarn through to form the new stitch.
5. Hold the right yarn in the normal position and Knit the next stitch with the left yarn.

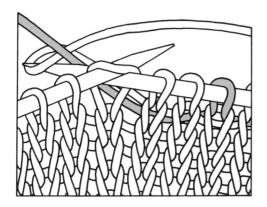

KNIT/LEFT YARN WOVEN/THE FIRST STITCH

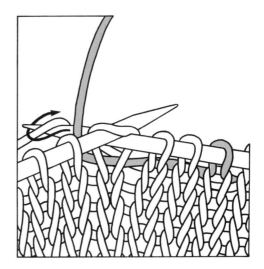

KNIT/RIGHT YARN WOVEN

Purl Right Yarn/Left Yarn Woven

1. Insert the right needle into the stitch as to Purl.
2. Shift your finger so the left yarn leans against the nearside of the right needle tip.
3. Pass the right yarn on the nearside of the left yarn, around the needle in the usual way to Purl, and draw through a stitch.
4. Shift your finger in order to hold the left yarn to the nearside away from the tip of the needle, pass the right yarn between the left yarn and the needle and Purl the next stitch.

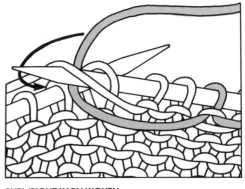

PURL/RIGHT YARN WOVEN

4. Draw the left yarn through to form the new stitch.
5. Hold the right yarn in the normal position away from the tips of the needles and Purl the next stitch with the left yarn.

Lattice Weaving

There is another method of weaving in that works reasonably well for those of you who use the Slip Stranding method of handling the yarns. The technique is the same as the Lattice Stitch technique (see page 27). As you work, strand the yarns in the usual way. On the next Purl row, at the midpoint of the strand, catch it up as follows:

- Slip the next stitch, then lift the strand up to the right needle. Insert the left needle into the farside of both strand and stitch and Purl.

Obviously it is easier to see what you are doing if you catch the strands on the Purl row, although those from the previous Purl row will be carried up two rows, those from the previous Knit row just one. Generally this will not be a problem. However, if you want to be more consistent and careful with the tension on the strands, you can also catch them up on a Knit row.

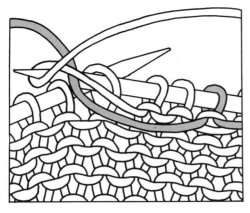

PURL/LEFT YARN WOVEN/THE FIRST STITCH

- With the right needle, reach down on the farside and lift the strand onto the left needle. Knit the next stitch and the strand together.

Alternating Two Yarns and Weaving In

Should you not be skilled at working with two hands, weaving in can also be done if you are working with the Alternating Two Yarns method.

- Set the working yarn down. Pick up the yarn in waiting with the right hand and tuck it between the left forefinger and needle. Pick up the working yarn again and make the next stitch. Release the stranded yarn from your left hand at your convenience.

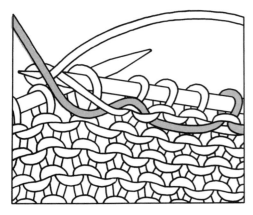

PURL/LEFT YARN WOVEN/THE SECOND STITCH

Purl Left Yarn/Right Yarn Woven

1. Insert the needle into the stitch as to Purl.
2. Wrap the right yarn under the needle from nearside to farside, then shift your finger in order to lay the left yarn over the needle from nearside to farside just to the left of the other yarn.
3. Take the right yarn back off the needle, retracing the path used to put it on; it will pass over the left yarn, which should remain on the needle.

This attaches the strand to one side of the stitch, which is sufficient to reduce the possibility of snagging. It requires several more steps to attach it on the other side of the stitch, and since that is unnecessary, why go to the trouble?

Color Stitch Patterns

While most color knitting is done in Stockinette, there are many beautiful effects possible when color is combined with other stitch techniques. In fact, any stitch pattern can be adapted for this purpose although some are much easier to handle than others. Success lies in understanding the relationship between the color changes and the structure of the stitch. Purl stripes are an easy place to start.

Color Patterns in Purl

As you know, when you work a Purl stitch, both the head of the discard stitch and the running threads passing into and out of that stitch will be discarded on the nearside. The Purl row is made up of two horizontal rows of nubs, those on top being the stitch heads, those on the bottom being the running threads. The trick here lies in controlling the color of the two stitch elements, as they can be the same or different.

BROKEN PURL STRIPES

With this version of a Purl Stripe, the color of the stitch elements is different. The effect is only seen on the first row of a color change.

- Take up a contrast color yarn and work so as to place Purl on the outside of the fabric. Notice that the new

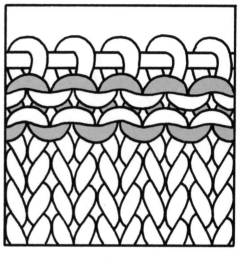

THE BROKEN PURL STRIPES

stitches on the needle and the running threads passing from one to the other are in the new color while the discarded stitch heads are in the previous color.

A Broken Purl stripe occurs at every color change, regardless of whether you are changing from background to stripe or from stripe to background. With two-row Purl stripes the effect is quite tweedy, as the stripe color appears in the running threads of the first row but in the stitch heads of the second row. When the stripe contains more than two rows of Purl, those in the center will all be solid color.

UNBROKEN PURL STRIPES

With this version of a Purl stripe, the heads of the discard stitches and the runnng threads will all be the same color.

1. Holding a contrast-color yarn, work so as to place Knit on the outside of the fabric. The discarded Knit stitches will be in the previous color, the new stitches in the color of the stripe.
2. On the next and all subsequent rows using that color, work so as to place Purl on the outside.
3. When the stripe is complete, hold the background color and again work so as to place Knit on the outside of the fabric. The discarded Knit stitches will

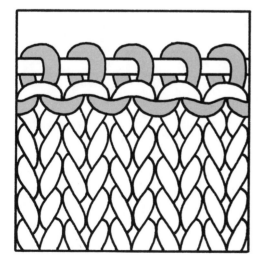

BROKEN PURL STRIPE

UNBROKEN PURL STRIPE

of working stripes, you will find that instead of stripes you will get various kinds of tweeds.

While most Brocade patterns are geometrics, Purl stitches can also be used to form fairly elaborate motifs such as flowers, stars, bows, or whatever, done against a background of plain Knit. We have not yet discussed the methods of working Intarsia patterns, isolated motifs done in contrasting color (see below), but in many old fabrics, Intarsia and Brocade were splendidly combined with the motifs done in contrast-color Purl stitches on the Knit ground.

be in the color of the stripe, the new stitches will be in the background color.

In other words, in order to get unbroken color in Purl stitches you must work the first row of any color change in Knit so as to place the broken color Purl row on the inside of the fabric.

Purl Brocade Patterns

The above rules for controlling the color of the stitch heads and the running threads apply whenever you are working Purl on the outside in a color pattern. When the elementary Brocade patterns such as Garter Stitch and Seed Stitch are combined with the simple methods

COLOR PATTERN WITH PURL AND BOBBIES

16TH CENTURY ITALIAN SILK TUNIC. PURL PATTERN OUTLINED WITH INTARSIA ON KNIT GROUND

Stripes in Ribbing

If you are adding a stripe to a section of ribbing there will, of course, be both Knit and Purl stitches on the outside of the fabric. If the first row of the stripe is worked in pattern, it will have a smooth color transition on the Knit columns and a broken color transition on the Purl columns. If instead you would prefer to have a smooth transition throughout, work every stitch of the first row of a stripe with Knit stitches on the outside of the fabric, then revert to the ribbing pattern on all subsequent rows. Amazingly enough, the row of Knit stitches will completely merge themselves with the columns of ribbing, and you will see no break in the pattern.

STRIPES IN RIBBING

Slip Stitch Color Patterns

In Slip Stranding, Slip Stitches are used simply as a means of handling two yarns; however, a Slip Stitch, for all its simplicity, is also one of the most versatile and multifaceted of stitch techniques, and all of its aspects are exploited in the creation of color pattern. Stranding a contrast-color running thread past the Slip Stitch on the outside of the fabric instead of the inside creates little horizontal flecks that can be built up into complex patterns.

There are many patterns that include stitches in one color that are slipped so they will be pulled into rows containing stitches in another color. Depending upon how the patterns are designed, the Slip Stitches may cause some distortion of the fabric, which can also be exploited. The most exaggerated examples of this sort are the "blister" patterns, in which the slipped stitches pull the rows together, puffing the intervening stitches out. Also, Elongated Slip Stitches may be coupled with the Drop Stitch technique to pull a contrast-color stitch up at an angle. Any stitch pattern in the Honeycomb (also known as Brioche) family will produce beautiful effects when done in more than one color, as they blur the strict horizontal line of the rows, pulling one color into the other.

Mosaic Patterns

Barbara Walker has defined and developed a category of Slip Stitch patterns that she calls Mosaics, and they are very interesting, versatile, and attractive. These patterns are basically two-row color stripes. Stitches from one stripe are slipped and drawn up into the contrast-color stripe above to form a pattern. Only one color is used at a time to work two rows, with the same stitches worked and the same ones slipped on both rows. The patterns may be worked in either Stockinette or Garter Stitch at the discretion of the knitter.

Any Mosaic pattern worked in Stockinette with the same yarn and needles and by the same hands will have the same stitch gauge. The same is true of those done in Garter Stitch. This makes it very easy to combine a variety of these patterns in a single fabric because there is no need to calculate a new gauge for each pattern or adjust the number of stitches on the needle. While Garter Stitch pattern gauges will not match Stockinette pattern gauges, changing from one to the other can create interesting effects, as it exploits the difference in the stitch gauges as well as the texture and appearance of the patterns themselves. Another nice aspect of these patterns is that there is no need to concern yourself with the stitch multiple in calculating the number of stitches to use for the width of the garment; you can work these

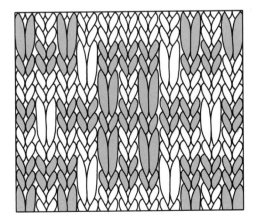

THE STRUCTURE OF A MOSAIC PATTERN

SCARAB, A MOSAIC PATTERN

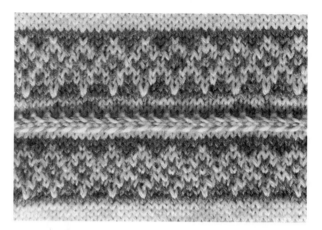

HERRINGBONE BRAID

patterns on any number of stitches, but you must use edge stitches to anchor the yarn at the end of each row. (For more information, see the section on charted Mosaic patterns, page 492.)

Horizontal Braids

Here is a decorative braid technique found in Northern and Eastern Europe. It is rather tedious to do, as the yarns get tangled up, and so they are most often found on small items such as mittens. Fortunately, only a few rows are required to obtain the effect, and it's worth trying, as the result is very charming. Actually, there is nothing new about this; all that is required is to wrap the yarns just as one would at a color change in Intarsia Knitting, below, or Braided Cast-on (page 134). In this case, however, there is a color change on every stitch, and the Purl rows, where the yarns are stranded, are used on the outside.

HERRINGBONE BRAID

The wrapped and stranded running threads will have a striped, corded appearance, which will slant either upward to the left or upward to the right, depending upon how the yarns are changed. The yarns can be changed one way on the first row and the other on the next to form a pair of cords striped in opposite directions one above the other, which creates a herringbone appearance.

Method One

- Set the yarn just worked down to the left, bring the yarn to be worked next over it and to the next stitch.

   If you are working in Purl, the braid will slant upward to the left on the outside; if you are working in Knit, the braid will slant upward to the right on the outside.

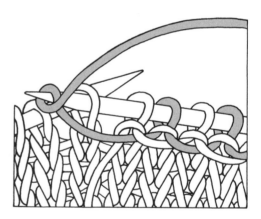

BRINGING ONE YARN OVER THE OTHER FOR A BRAID

Method Two

- Set the yarn just worked down to the right, bring the yarn to be worked next under it and to the next stitch.

   If you are working in Purl, the braid will slant upward to the right on the outside; if you are working in Knit, the braid will slant upward to the left on the outside.

   Please note that if you are working a flat fabric, you will work in the same way on both the Knit and Purl faces in order to create a Herringbone Braid. Setting a yarn down to the left and bringing the other over it to

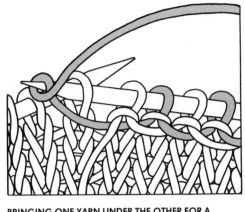

BRINGING ONE YARN UNDER THE OTHER FOR A BRAID

the next stitch is the easiest way to work, and doing it that way on both the Knit and Purl rows will create a braid with the yarns slanted up to the left on the first row and up to the right on the second row. It is a bit easier to start if you work the selvedge stitches at the beginning and end of each row with both yarns held as one, or at least interlock the two yarns at the beginning of every row.

If you are working in the round, you will be working Purl on every row, so in order to create a Herringbone Braid, you will have to bring the next yarn over on one row and under on the next. If you change the yarns the same way every row, the yarns will all slant in the same direction rather than alternating.

There will be a row of Purl nubs showing above each line of braid. If you have been working in a solid color, the nubs above the first row of braid will be all one color, those above the second and subsequent lines of braid will alternate color. If you want the first row to alternate also, work one row of braid on the *inside* of the fabric, then begin the braid proper on the outside. The appearance of the braid will change slightly if you always use the same color yarn for each stitch, making vertical stripes on the Knit side of the fabric, or alternate the colors, making a checkerboard pattern on the Knit side.

As you work across the first row, the two strands of yarn will begin to wrap around one another as if they were being plied into a single yarn. For a short stretch, this is not a problem. If they tangle up close to where you are working, force the plied section down closer to the two balls of yarn so you always have two separate yarns to work with. If you work the slant going one way on one row, and the other way on the next row, the yarns will ply together on the first row and magically unply themselves as you work the second row.

If you are working across a wide row the twist can make it impossible to continue—here is a clever way around the problem:

1. Allow the yarns to twist up until you get to the center

of the fabric. Spin the work around and around until you have undone the twist.

2. Now as you work to the end of the first row, the yarns will twist up again. As you work to the middle of the second row, they will untwist. From the center to the end of the second row they will then twist up again, and from the beginning to the center of the row after that, they will untwist. Then the cycle starts all over again.

Alternately, hang the work from the yarn, pull the two yarns apart and let it unspin itself.

TRIPLE HERRINGBONE BRAID

Most often, a Herringbone Braid is done with two colors, but a three-color braid is possible. The principle is the same and the working method similar. Work the selvedge stitches at each side with all three yarns, then work one stitch in each of the three colors.

TRIPLE HERRINGBONE BRAID

Method One

- As you work across the row, alternate the yarns. Always pick up the yarn farthest to the right, work the next stitch, then set that yarn down to the left of the other yarns.

  If you are working on the Purl side, the braid will slant upward to the left; if you are working on the Knit side, the braid will slant upward to the right.

Method Two

- As you work across the row, alternate the yarns. Always pick up the yarn farthest to the left, work the next stitch, then set that yarn down to the right of the other yarns.

  If you are working on the Purl side, the braid will slant upward to the right; if you are working on the Knit side, the braid will slant upward to the left.

Braided Knitting

In Sweden, the braid technique described above is used for entire fabrics. It is usually done in fine yarn and needles and used for making very thick, warm mittens, hats, sleeves, socks, etc.

The Purl face of the fabric, where the yarns are stranded, is sometimes used as the outside, or a cuff can be turned down to display the strands on the inside. These fabrics are always done with the strands sloping in the same direction row after row rather than alternating, as is typical for the braids. The Knit face of the fabric has a distinctive striated look as the stitches do not lie as flat as they do in a normal single yarn fabric, and when used on the outside, certain unique stitch techniques described below in Stranded Brocade can be used to create pattern.

As with the individual braids, two different colors can be used and if you always work a stitch using the same color yarn, the Knit face will have vertical stripes; if you always use the alternate color on a stitch, the Knit face will be in a checkerboard pattern. The inside, of course, will have row after row of striped braid and, again, either face of the fabric could be used on the outside.

The two strands of yarn will wind around one another as you work and they must be periodically unwound. While this is not a serious problem for a few rows of braid, when working an entire fabric, even a small one such as a mitten, the type of twist put on the yarn must be taken into consideration. If you work by taking each strand over the last, an S-twist yarn will gain twist, gradually getting thinner and kinking up. If you work by taking each strand under the last, an S-twist yarn will lose twist, getting fatter and looser. The opposite is true when working with a Z-twist yarn. It is far easier to work with the yarn losing twist than gaining it as it is bad enough that the two yarns ply together, let alone having both of them kink up!

However unorthodox, if you alternate, bringing the yarn under for one stitch, over for the next, the two yarns do not ply together, nor do they individually gain or lose twist; it is a much easier and faster way to work. The Knit side of the fabric will look much the same, but the strands on the inside will travel horizontally rather than slanting upward as is true with the braided method. You must, however, work the yarns consistently. When working a flat fabric on an even number of stitches, always start the row in the same way, with the yarn stranded over the other and ending with a yarn stranded under the other or vice versa. When doing a circular fabric, alternate how you start each round, once with a yarn stranded over the other, next with a yarn stranded under. If this is not done, the Stockinette face will exhibit a subtle vertical striping. The true braid fabric is denser and more windproof, but both are exceptionally warm.

INSIDE OF FABRIC SHOWING BRAIDED KNITTING ABOVE AND STRANDED KNITTING BELOW

In Sweden both yarns are held in the left hand, but I think the older, and perhaps more efficient method, is to use a modification of the Right-finger method. Wrap both yarns around the small finger for tension, then insert the middle finger between the two strands to separate them, or wear a Double Yarn Ring (see "Tools," page 333) on the middle finger. With the forefinger, pick up whichever strand is needed next to form a stitch. Alternatively, hold one yarn in each hand, although this will only produce the unbraided version.

SINGLE-COLOR STRANDED BROCADE

These stitch techniques, combining Purl stitches and strands on the outside, are only possible in Braid Knitting (although the illusion can be had with stitches slipped with the yarn nearside). In the single-color version, the two yarns are alternated stitch by stitch across the row until a pattern unit is wanted on the outside of the fabric, at which point, work as follows.

STRANDED BROCADE GLOVE FROM SWEDEN

DETAIL OF STRANDED BROCADE PATTERN

shapes, or scattered for spot motifs. When the pattern units are side by side, Yarn A remains on the nearside Purling every other stitch, Yarn B remains on the farside, Knitting every other stitch.

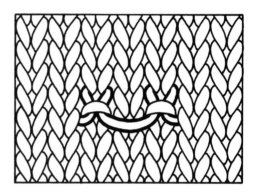

TWO PURL STRAND

Two Strand Purl

1. Bring Yarn A nearside and Knit one with Yarn B.
2. Purl one with Yarn A; leave the yarn on the nearside.
3. Knit one with Yarn B, bring Yarn A farside.

This pattern unit is often interspersed with the Two Purl Strand version in order to refine a pattern.

Two Purl Strand

1. Bring Yarn A nearside and Purl one.
2. Retain Yarn A on the nearside and Knit one with Yarn B.
3. Purl one with Yarn A and return it farside.

The basic pattern unit can be stacked vertically, sloped at an angle to form diagonals and diamond

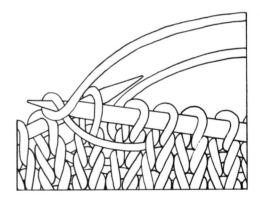

WORKING TWO STRAND PURL

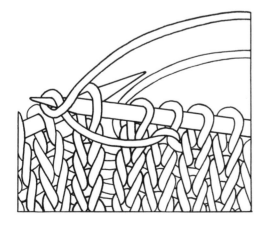

WORKING TWO PURL STRAND

TWO STRAND PURL

Double Strand Nub

• Work a stitch with two yarns held as one. When you encounter the double stitch on the next row, work it as Purl on the outside of the fabric.

Single Strand Nub

1. Bring Yarn A nearside and Knit one with Yarn B.
2. Bring Yarn A farside, Yarn B nearside and Knit with Yarn A.
3. Continue in this way, switching the two Yarns after every stitch as many times as desired.

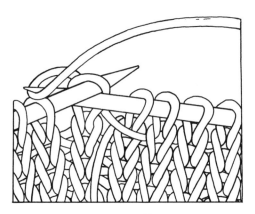

WORKING SINGLE STRAND NUBS

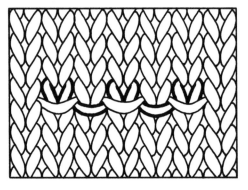

SINGLE STRAND NUBS

It is customary, and far easier, to work in the round as you can see the pattern develop, but these stitch patterns can also be done in flat knitting. The great advantage of the technique is that it produces a fabric with very fine stitches, giving a wealth of pattern detail, yet it is dense and warm due to the stranded yarns on the inside and the outside.

TWO-COLOR STRANDED BROCADE

While not at all traditional, Stranded Brocade techniques lend themselves for use with two colors. Introduce the contrast color in just the pattern area, either stranding the yarn on the inside between pattern areas, or using a separate supply for each area as for an Intarsia pattern.

• At a color change, bring the yarn to be stranded to the outside of the fabric. Work the intervening stitches with the other yarn and then bring the stranded yarn into the correct position to work the next stitches in that color.

STRANDED BROCADE PATTERN

Other Stitch Techniques

Purl is just one of the stitch techniques that can be used in conjunction with color to make texture and pattern more complex and more interesting. You can look at any pattern or technique with an eye to how it might look if color were added. For example, the rows of an entire stitch pattern repeat can be done in one color, with the next repeat done in another color. Simple tailored stitches like Crossed Stitch will set off a stripe done in a contrasting color against a background of Stockinette, or could be used to set up alternating bias in stripes of alternating colors.

True bias patterns, done with increases and decreases to create undulations or chevrons in the fabric, are even more interesting when color stripes are added, as the color will follow the rows of stitches as they change course. Variegated yarns, or multiple yarns held as one, are also particularly effective when used with these types of stitch patterns. Somewhat similar effects can be achieved by elongating groups of stitches that lie between color stripes or using Short Row sections (see pages 36 and 175).

Any pattern that contains one of the Knot family of techniques can be made even more dramatic if just the Knots are done in contrasting colors. Wrap, Pullover, Couching, and Threaded Stitch techniques can all bring horizontal strands of a contrast-color yarn to play on the surface of the fabric. Cluster stitch patterns are highly textured and easy to work as stripes. Finally, it is possible to alternate the colors stitch by stitch on one row and use Twist Stitches on the next, or to underlay a pattern of Cable Stitches with a contrast background.

Some of the most masterful examples of the interplay between color and stitch technique are the justly famous Bohus sweaters, those designed by Emma Jacobsen in Sweden between 1930 and 1960. Combining Knit, Purl, and Slip Stitches with subtle variations in color, she raised these otherwise simple garments out of the ordinary. If you ever see an example, study it carefully.

OLD SHALE WITH STRIPES

PICOT STRIPE/AN EMBOSSING PATTERN

DETAIL OF BOHUS PATTERN

Intarsia

Here is another approach to using color, where instead of working in stripes, either solid or patterned, the colors are placed in separate sections or motifs. Whereas Stranded Color patterns are relentlessly horizontal, Intarsia frees you from that strict geometry. On a large scale, a garment could, for instance, be designed with the right half of the front in one color and the left half in another; on a small scale, color could be used to define isolated motifs of various shapes scattered on the garment, or to do vertical stripes. In fact, you can approach the fabric in much the same way one would the creation of a woven tapestry and introduce new colors and new shapes wherever you wish.

The challenge here is that the sections of color are separated one from the other by so many stitches that stranding as discussed above is not practical. Instead,

individual portions of yarn must be used for each color section, which allows the use of as many colors in a row as you wish. While this makes things more challenging, it also offers unparalleled opportunities in design. This is knitting and painting joined.

A complex pattern, with many different colors in play, can look daunting when you see someone working on one, but in fact no special skill aside from patience is required, and only one yarn is worked with at a time. As with other color work, most of these fabrics are done in plain Stockinette, but when planning a project of this nature, I highly recommend that you keep in mind the creative possibilities that can be had by also using other stitch techniques. It is only tradition that dictates Stockinette, not technical necessity, and color, shape, and texture may do more to enhance a concept than color and shape alone.

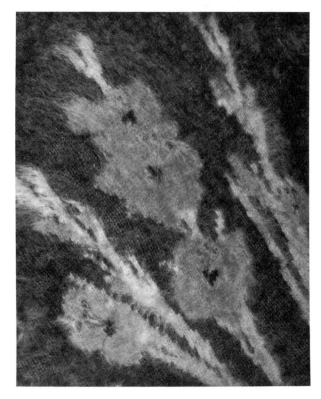

MASTERPIECE WOOL CARPET FROM ALSACE, 1781, 163 SQUARE CM

Intarsia Worked Flat

Intarsia work presents some special problems in handling the extra yarns required. They must be tied on carefully, numbers of them kept separate, untangled, and available to work with, and entwined with adjacent color areas so no gaps appear in the fabric.

Starting a Color

Unlike stripes, where the yarns are tied on at the edges, in Intarsia the yarns must be started within the fabric. When you are establishing the pattern and come to the first stitch to be worked in a new color, attach the new yarn to the existing yarn with the Temporary Knot described on page 126 and begin knitting without further ado. The knot will be removed prior to securing the two ends of yarn in finishing, and is used only so the first few stitches don't pull out or enlarge. To finish, thread an end onto a tapestry needle, knot it to a strand of the same yarn on the inside, and work it into the Purl nubs of the same color on the inside of the fabric (see page 379 for more details).

It is a temptation to use the weaving-in technique (page 281) to hide these ends of yarn while knitting, and many knitters do so. However, when the stranded yarn and the yarn used for the stitches are in strongly contrasting colors, or if the knitting is done at a loose tension, the woven-in strand is likely to show through on the outside. If the ends are woven in against stitches of the same color, as may be possible when you begin the motif, this will not be a problem. However, the motif may be too narrow to provide sufficient stitches of the same color to use, and even if there are enough stitches

as you begin the motif, there will obviously be no way to hide the one left at the end of the motif in the same way. The tapestry needle allows you to work the ends in vertically, if necessary, and hide them properly so they don't work loose. On the whole, I think it gives a far superior result, and is worth the bit of extra time it takes in finishing.

Interlocking

When changing from one color to another mid-row, under certain circumstances gaps will appear in the work unless the yarns are wrapped around one another to interlock them. The interlock is essential when the pattern produces vertical lines and the color changes between the same two stitch columns row after row, and also when the diagonal travels in the opposite direction than that in which you are knitting; in both these cases the yarn needed next will be below the left needle.

When the next yarn is below the left needle:

• Tuck the yarn last worked with between the needle

INTERLOCK

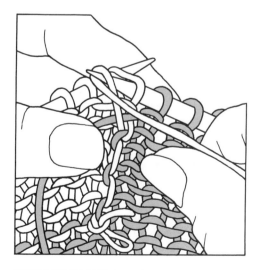

INTERLOCKING YARNS WHEN CHANGING COLORS

and either the left forefinger (when Knitting) or left thumb (when Purling). Pick up the next color with the right hand and begin to knit, releasing the yarn from the left finger at your convenience.

You need not interlock the yarns when the diagonal travels in the same direction in which you are knitting; the yarn needed next will be found below the right needle and will cross the other yarn automatically as it is brought into play. However, if the yarn is stranded any distance, it may help to bind it to the fabric.

When the next yarn is below the right needle:

• Pass the yarn to be used next over and then under the yarn last used.

Keep in mind that when working a pattern that is moving on a slope, the yarn may have to strand over several stitches and a row in order to be brought into play. Correct tension is just as important to these strands as it is with those on a Color-patterned Stripe where the strand lies horizontally. Stretch the fabric out slightly to make sure the strand has adequate length.

It is important to watch the tension on the stitches to either side of the interlock. When you pick up a yarn to use it again, get into the habit of checking the size of the stitch it emerges from and, if necessary, tighten up that stitch as you go to knit the next one. For those of you who knit with one of the finger-wrap methods, you may have particular trouble with the last stitch of a section on a Purl row. If you have that problem, try working just that stitch with a Purl Under and then Knit it farside on the next row.

Bobbins and Butterflies

When working Intarsia patterns where several motifs are scattered across the row, each requiring its own supply of yarn, it would be cumbersome to use a full ball of yarn for every section. One solution is to use yarn bobbins (see page 339), which hold just enough yarn for each motif and dangle off the fabric like so many Christmas tree ornaments until needed. The bobbins are available at most yarn suppliers and are usually made of plastic. Should you not wish to purchase them, or need some when the stores aren't open, you can make your own out of a small rectangle of cardboard, Styrofoam, or plastic, or even just use a Yarn Butterfly (page 125), but the ones made for the purpose are particularly handy, as they have a built-in lock to keep the yarn from unwinding until you want it to. You can cut a notch in your homemade bobbin, or use a rubber band to serve the same purpose.

The more bobbins there are hanging from the fabric, and the longer they are, the more likely they are to tangle up with one another to the point where they can be more hindrance than help. One very simple solution is to drop one on the nearside, the next on the farside as you work so that they are not side by side, all on the

BOBBINS ON THE INSIDE OF A FABRIC

inside of the fabric. Another approach is to just leave each length of yarn hanging at full length on the inside face of the work. At a color change, tuck the yarn last worked between left finger and needle, pick up the required color for the next stitch, and draw the full length of it free of the other yarns. You should have very little problem with tangles unless you are working with rather fuzzy yarns.

Regardless of whether you wind the yarn on a bobbin or let it hang free, it is always a question of how much yarn to allow for each motif so you will not run out before it is finished. The trick to use is a simple extrapolation from the method for calculating yarn requirements for a garment (page 428). Because an Intarsia pattern is not stranded, yarn requirements will be closer to that of a plain Stockinette fabric plus something for the interlocks.

You may have occasion to knit a fabric with large sections of color, in which case the bobbins are too small to hold an adequate supply of yarn, and Yarn Butterflies have turned into proper balls of yarn. Set each ball in its own box or basket, lined up at your feet, one after the other in the same sequence as they are attached to the inside of the fabric. As you turn the fabric row by row, turn clockwise at the end of every outside row, counterclockwise at the end of every inside row (or vice versa) to keep the yarns from twisting together.

Combining Intarsia and Stranding

Some interesting possibilities open up when these two techniques are combined. As you know, stranding adds bulk to a fabric, so the typical Color-patterned Stripe is worked with no more than two colors per row. However, other colors may also be added by stranding the yarn of the main colors past small sections of Intarsia. Just tie on a bit of yarn in the appropriate color wherever it is needed, interlocking as necessary with the yarns that are being stranded.

Casting Off for Intarsia

If your color pattern runs to a cast-off edge that will remain visible in the garment, you must take care to have these edge stitches match the colors in the fabric below. Each cast-off stitch will lean to the left on top of the adjacent stitch. Therefore, work the last stitch of each color section in the color of the following section; when it is then pulled over, it will match the stitch below.

CASTING OFF WHERE TWO COLORS MEET

Intarsia Worked in the Round

For the most part, Intarsia patterns are done only in flat knitting. If you think about it, you will quickly see why. As you work across a section of color, the yarn will move from the first stitch on the right side of the section to the last stitch on the left side of the section. Therefore, if you were working a circular fabric, when you began the next round you would find all the yarns still on the left side of each color section, opposite the point where you needed them to be. However, it is possible to do Intarsia patterns in the round with the help of a little trick called a Seam Stitch, but you must also work back and forth in Knit and Purl.

THE SEAM STITCH

1. Cast on the number of stitches required for the garment, plus one extra, and join into a round.
2. Knit one round, including the extra stitch. Turn to the Purl side.
3. Slip the extra stitch at the beginning of the row, then Purl one round, Purling the extra stitch at the end of the row. Turn to the Knit side.
4. Slip the extra stitch at the beginning of the row, then Knit one round, Knitting the extra stitch at the end of the row. Turn to the Purl side.

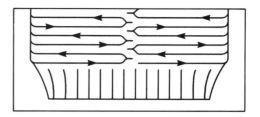

JOINING A ROUND WITH A SEAM STITCH

As you can see, this is halfway between knitting in the round and knitting flat. The Seam Stitch must only be worked once for every round; the way I have given it here, it is always slipped at the beginning of a row, and worked at the end, but you could do it the other way around, knitting it at the beginning and slipping it at the end. If you examine the result, you will see that a running thread enters this stitch from the left on one row and from the right on the next row. The Seam Stitch will look slightly different from the surrounding stitches, so you must take this into consideration when deciding whether it is worthwhile working this way.

Intarsia Sections

One can also add a portion of Intarsia or Slip-Stranded pattern to an otherwise solid-color fabric knitted in the round. The color section must include some background stitches in the same color as the main portion of the fabric in order to carry that yarn past the pattern. There is a charming example of a Dalmatian sock done this way in Mary Thomas's book.[1]

1. Place all the stitches for the color section on one double-point needle with all the other stitches distributed on the remaining needles or on a circular needle.
2. Work in the main, background color to the point where the color pattern begins. Work the color pattern, slipping any background stitches.

1. *Mary Thomas's Knitting Book* (New York: Dover Publications, Inc., 1972), p. 112.

3. Return to the right point of the needle and work the background stitches, slipping the pattern stitches. Continue to the end of the round.
4. When you come to the color section on the next round, the yarns for the patterns will all be on the left. Turn the work and Purl back in pattern, slipping all background stitches.
5. When the pattern section is complete, turn the work

again and Knit across the background stitches, slipping all pattern stitches. Continue to the end of the round.

In other words, for every two rounds of plain knitting you must work one row in Knit and one row in Purl on the pattern section so there will be an equal number of rows in each.

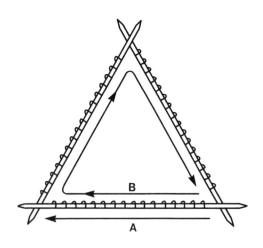

INTARSIA SECTION/FIRST ROUND

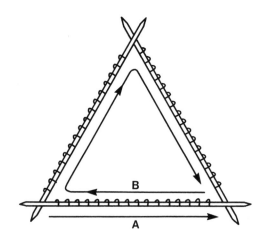

INTARSIA SECTION/SECOND ROUND

Color Patterns in Double Knit

The kinds of color patterns that can be used on a Double Knit fabric are limited only by your imagination. More than two colors may be used, and the color patterns may be the same on both faces of the fabric or entirely different. One face may be plain while the other has a color pattern that may use the same yarn as the first or two different ones. The patterns may be identical or color reversed—that is, the subordinate color in one fabric is the dominant color in the other.

There are four different methods of working a Double Knit color pattern, and each produces a fabric with different characteristics. In the first, the fabric is joined only at the edges, just like a Basic Double Knit fabric. In the second, the yarn weaves back and forth

between the two faces, which joins them in the center as well as at the edges. In the third type, Double Knit is combined with Single Rib in such a way that the fabric resembles the former more than the latter, but has some of the qualities of both. Jane F. Neighbors has developed many wonderful patterns done in these ways in her fine book *Reversible Two-Color Knitting*.[1] You may find her explanations of how the techniques work very difficult to follow, as I did, but you can skip all that and simply avail youself of the patterns, which are marvelous. The book is invaluable for those occasions when you are looking for a color pattern with no "wrong" side, and it should be next to Barbara Walker's volumes

1. New York: Charles Scribner's Sons, 1974.

COLOR REVERSAL PATTERN IN DOUBLE KNIT

Striping One Face

Let's take a look first at how to make a one-row stripe on just one face. Work on double-point needles or a circular one.

1. Knit fabric A stitches with the stripe color, slipping the stitches of fabric B.
2. Slide the stitches to the right needle tip and Purl fabric B with the main color, slipping the stitches of fabric A.
3. Turn, Knit the stitches of fabric B with the main color.
4. Turn, Knit the stitches of fabric A with the main color.

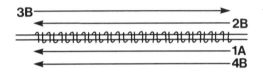

STRIPES IN DOUBLE KNIT USING THE SLIDE

This completes two rows on each fabric face, one stripe row and one plain row on fabric A, two plain rows on B.

For a two-row stripe, alter the process just slightly.

1. Knit fabric A with the stripe color, turn, Purl fabric A with the stripe color, turn.
2. Purl fabric B with the main color, turn, Knit fabric B with the main color.

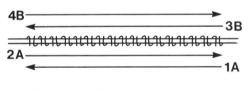

TWO ROW STRIPES IN DOUBLE KNIT

This should make it clear to you that you can work either face, regardless of which one is on the nearside, and turn or slide the stitches depending upon where the yarns are and what is required to achieve the effect.

Color-Reversal Stripes

For one-row color-reversal stripes, the above concepts are expanded slightly.

1. With the stripe color, Knit fabric A, slide.
2. With the plain color, Purl fabric B, turn.

on every knitter's bookshelf. And finally, there is a method of stranding the contrast-color yarn on the outside of the fabric in order to create pattern.

In the following instructions, I am going to assume that you are working the fabric flat; once you understand the principles, the adjustment to working in the round will be no problem.

Stripes in Double Knit

Even simple stripes are fun in a Double Knit pattern; you can stripe both sides the same, stripe one face and not the other, or do color reversals. Play with these ideas on a swatch and try to pay less attention to the recipe than to what it is you want to do. This is one of those areas in knitting where the instructions make something relatively easy seem quite complicated.

Matched stripes are very elementary; just work round and round with one color as many rows on each face as you want and then switch colors much as you would to add a stripe to any other fabric. Adding a stripe to one side introduces the idea of how to work to produce color pattern.

3. With the stripe color, Knit fabric B, slide.
4. With the plain color, Purl fabric A, turn.

For two-row stripes, work as above to the first turn, then with the stripe color Purl fabric A, slide; with the plain color Knit fabric B, turn.

Stranded Color Patterns

In this type of color pattern, both faces of the fabric are treated separately, and you work with just one color at a time in the same manner as for Stranded Color patterns on a single-thickness fabric (see page 255). Any color pattern that can be done with that method on a single-thickness fabric can be done on a double fabric.

STRANDED COLOR-REVERSAL PATTERNS

To give you an idea of how these patterns work, let's take an example in which the same color pattern stripe is worked on both fabrics with a color reversal—the background color of one fabric forms the pattern stitches of the other fabric. We will call the two fabrics A and B to distinguish them, and the two colors Red and Blue.

Row 1: Knit the background stitches of fabric A with Red, slipping the stitches of fabric B with the yarn nearside and the pattern stitches of fabric A with the yarn farside. Turn.

Row 2: Knit the pattern stitches of fabric B with Red, slipping the stitches of fabric A with the yarn nearside and the background stitches of fabric B with the yarn farside. Turn.

Row 3: Knit the pattern stitches of fabric A with Blue, slipping the stitches of fabric B with the yarn nearside and the background stitches of fabric A with the yarn farside. Turn.

Row 4: Knit the background stitches of fabric B with Blue, slipping the stitches of fabric A with the yarn nearside and the pattern stitches of fabric B with the yarn farside. Turn.

Repeat these four rows to create one row of pattern on each fabric.

What distinguishes this from plain Double Knit is that both the pattern stitches of the fabric being worked and the stitches of the other fabric are slipped. When you slip a stitch of the fabric being worked, strand the yarn past it loosely enough so the pattern is not distorted, just as with color patterns done single thickness. When you slip a stitch of the other fabric, strand the yarn fairly firmly so that stitches that are to be side by side on the same fabric are brought together and don't enlarge. In some patterns, both things will happen at once, in which case you must gauge the amount of yarn required as best you can. By the way, if you can keep

your wits about you, you can certainly work with one yarn held in each hand, as described on page 236.

All this is somewhat theoretical as a fabric with two faces joined only at the sides is not terribly successful unless it is a small item or the separated faces occupy a small portion of a larger fabric. Therefore, this method of working a stranded color pattern is most appropriately used when working a single-thickness circular fabric using the Double Knit technique (see page 245). Other methods of introducing color pattern on truly reversible fabrics produce more satisfying results.

Other Color Combinations

There are other color variations possible, as I mentioned above. You could make one fabric in a solid color, with that same yarn used for either the background or the pattern in the other fabric. Alternatively, three colors can be used, one shared by the two fabrics for the pattern stitches and two different colors for the respective backgrounds, or vice versa.

In the color-reversal pattern type given above, the two fabrics are tied together at the sides by the running threads as the yarns pass from one fabric to the other. If you were to use two colors on one fabric, and two different colors on the other fabric, they would not be joined at the sides. In that case, you would have to rely on selvedge stitches to bind the two fabrics together, but remember to work them only once for every pair of rows, alternately using a yarn from one fabric, then from the other.

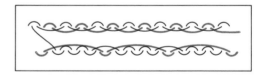

STRANDED DOUBLE KNIT

Interwoven Color Patterns

This next technique can only be used with two yarns in a color-reversal pattern. In other words, if a group of stitches on the near fabric is to be done in one color, the same group on the farside will be done in the other. In working these patterns, all of the stitches in the same color are done on one row, regardless of which fabric

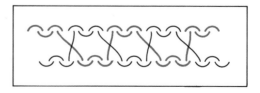

INTERWOVEN PATTERN STRUCTURE

they belong to. The yarn thus travels back and forth between the two fabrics, which weaves them together where they face one another down the center. The easiest way to grasp the concept is with a pattern of vertical stripes.

VERTICAL STRIPES

1. Cast on a multiple of eight stitches. The stitches are interspersed on the needle in the normal way for Double Knit.
2. With color A, Knit the first two stitches of the near fabric, alternately slipping the first two of the far fabric with the yarn nearside, then Purl the second two stitches of the far fabric, alternately slipping the second two of the near fabric with the yarn farside. Continue in the same way across the row. Slide.
3. Attach the other color and work all the stitches that were slipped, slipping those that were previously worked in the same way, Knitting those of the near fabric, Purling those of the far fabric.

As the yarn passes from one pair of stitches to the other, the running threads join the sides of each stripe to the sides of the adjacent stripes on the other fabric. The resulting fabric is a series of vertical tubes, and its structure is somewhat related to that produced by work-

ing horizontal Multiple Casings (page 242). The two can be combined for a checkerboard pattern. There are other patterns far more complex than a stripe where the connection between the two faces is not so straightforward, but the principle remains the same and the patterns are not difficult to understand or to do.

It is possible to work two rows in one color, then two rows in the other, but the running threads of the second color will ride over those of the first, which will give a very slight distortion to the fabric.

Double Knit Motifs

Some very interesting and charming fabrics can be created by making use of isolated color motifs done with the Interwoven Double Knit technique. These motifs can be scattered on a background of Double Knit, Single Knit, or on one of Single Rib, and can be left as is or padded for a trapunto effect.

A single motif of this sort can be introduced into any single-thickness fabric using a contrast-color yarn and doubling the necessary stitches with a Slip Raised Increase and returning to single thickness with Joinery Decreases. Use a tapestry needle to pull the ends of yarn to the inside of the motif to hide them.

If the motif is worked on a single-thickness fabric, it will form a perfect little pocket for padding. Just separate the stitches at the top of the motif, insert the padding, and intersperse the stitches back on the needle. Complete the motif, return to a single-thickness fabric, and continue. If the motif is worked on a Double Knit fabric, only the side will be joined by the interlock method of working. The top and bottom will not be, however, and you may need to interlock those stitches using the Threaded Stitch technique (described in detail in the section on Multiple Casings on page 242).

CHECKERBOARD/A VARIATION ON VERTICAL STRIPES IN INTERWOVEN DOUBLE KNIT

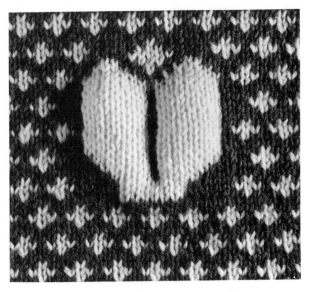

CROWN WITH FLEUR-DE-LYS/A PADDED DOUBLE KNIT MOTIF

Double Knit/Single Rib Combinations

When a Single Rib fabric is relaxed, the Knit stitches close over the Purls, creating the illusion of a fabric with Stockinette on both sides; as you know, Double Knit creates the reality. When the stitches are on the needle, it is difficult to tell at first glance which is being done, and it is only the manner of working that produces one fabric rather than the other. In fact there are some fascinating color patterns in which the line blurs between the two to the extent that the resulting fabric is really neither one nor the other.

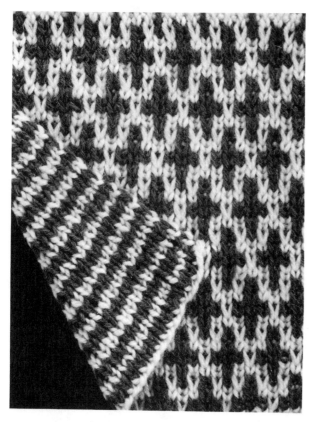

ACROSS AND ACROSS/A DOUBLE KNIT/SINGLE RIB COMBINATION

In this third, combination technique, some portions of the pattern are worked as for Single Rib, and some portions are worked in Double Knit. The Double Knit portions encourage the Single Rib ones to behave more like a double-faced fabric and less like a rib. These fabrics are not quite so thick as Double Knit nor so thin as Single Knit, they have a springiness halfway between Stockinette and a Rib, and the patterns are more efficient to work than a Stranded Double Knit pattern.

While they are more efficient to work, the fabric structure is by far the most complex of any double fabric. Some stitches may occupy more than one row (true Slip Stitches), and the row count of one fabric may not match the row count of the other. Many of these patterns are quite charming, but the stitches are not a consistent size and the fabric not as smooth as a true Double Knit. I refer you to Jane Neighbors' book for some happy and challenging knitting.

Double Knit Stranded Brocade

As I mentioned in the section on Stitch Pattern for Double Knit, color patterns can also be created using a variant on Stranded Brocade. The trick is to carry the yarn in use past a given stitch of the other fabric face on the outside rather than between the two fabrics. The instructions are for working one fabric with Stranded Brocade pattern, the other plain.

STRANDED PATTERN/ONE FACE

1. Work a row of fabric A in Stockinette in the normal manner for Double Knit; turn.
2. As you work fabric B, slip the stitches of fabric A that will form the pattern with the yarn stranded on the *outside* rather than between the two fabrics. Slip the stitches of fabric A that are to be the background with the yarn stranded in between the two fabrics in the normal way.
3. Work one row on each fabric plain, then repeat the two steps above for the next row of the pattern.

DOUBLE KNIT STRANDED BROCADE

The two fabrics are bound together into one double-thick fabric as the running threads travel around the stitches to form the pattern. It is particularly important that you watch the tension on these strands or the fabric will lose its resilience and begin to behave like a woven fabric. Notice that there is a shadow of the pattern on the solid-color face caused by the compression of the fabric wherever it is bound together; I find this quite attractive in its own subtle way. While there is no technical reason why you couldn't use Stranded Brocade on both faces for a color-reversal pattern, the compression and loss of resilience in the fabric is intensified.

15
Inlay

There are two techniques that can be used to lay a second yarn into a knitted fabric without that yarn being knitted itself. Because the strand is never knitted, the resilience of these fabrics is compromised even when tension is regulated carefully, and they will behave somewhat more like a woven than a knit. This can be a definite advantage in some cases where it is important to stabilize a fabric against stretching out, but the techniques can also be used to enhance the thermal properties of a garment, to reinforce areas of wear, or to incorporate a strand of elastic. Aside from all those very practical purposes, either technique has purely decorative possibilities when the second yarn is of a different color and/or texture.

The two methods used to lay a second yarn into the fabric in this way are quite simple, both in the working and in their respective structures. Purl Inlay requires that you use the Double Stranding method of handling two yarns, one in each hand. However, since only one of the yarns is used for knitting, even those of you who are not skilled at Double Stranding should be able to cope with this. Stitch Inlay can be done with either the Double Stranding of the Slip Stranding method of handling the yarns.

HORIZONTAL INLAY WITH RIBBON

Stitch Inlay

Stitch Inlay is generally done on a Stockinette fabric, with the second yarn stranded directly past certain stitches on the outside of the fabric to form the pattern, and past all the other stitches on the inside. There are horizontal and vertical versions, and both are simplicity itself to do.

HORIZONTAL STITCH INLAY HOLDING TWO YARNS

1. Hold the knitting yarn in the hand you normally use and the inlay yarn in the other.
2. Before working a stitch, move the inlay yarn between the needle tips to the inside of the fabric if you do not want it to show; move it to the outside of the fabric if you do want it to show.

Please note that if you hold the working yarn in the left hand, the inlay yarn will pass above the running threads and across the new stitch. If you hold the working yarn in the right hand, the inlay yarn will pass below the running threads and across the discard stitch.

Do be careful to maintain an easy tension on the stranded yarn so that it neither loops up nor draws in the fabric. You can strand the inlay yarn past more than one stitch on the outside of the fabric, but strands longer than one-half inch are liable to snag, which is something of a problem with these fabrics. (If you do get a snag, stretch the fabric horizontally and work it back in.)

HORIZONTAL STITCH INLAY HOLDING ONE YARN

If you have no facility with handling two yarns simultaneously, you can use the Slip Stranding method, working one row for the stitches, one row for the inlay pattern, as follows:

1. Using double points or a circular needle, work across the row, Knitting or Purling as required. If you are working flat, at the end of the row slide the stitches back to the right needle tip.
2. On the next row, take up the inlay yarn and slip every stitch, weaving the yarn past the stitches nearside or farside according to the pattern.
3. If you are using a circular fabric, use one round to work the stitches, one round to strand the weaving yarn.

The inlay yarn may be in the same or a contrast-color yarn. For added interest you could use a yarn in a different texture, narrow ribbon, or two different yarns held as one, and you can mix colors and textures row by row. It is a good idea to secure the beginning and end of the inlay strand on the inside with a knot to keep it from pulling free, but otherwise treat the ends normally. If you are going to have a lot of ends, handle them as the Shetlanders do color changes and tie pairs together with a Square Knot and cut them off short (see page 254). If that will be unacceptably bulky or produce too much fringe and you are working flat, you can secure them at the edge with a line of zigzag machine stitching done along the selvedge.

The patterns used for this technique are generally quite simple; most often the yarn is stranded past every other stitch on the outside of a Stockinette fabric, either in columns or staggered row by row, or stranded past the Knit stitches on a Seed Stitch ground, for instance. In effect, you are treating the Knitted fabric as if it were the warp of a woven fabric, and weaving books and handwoven fabrics are a source of inspiration for patterns that can be used with this technique. There is a pattern of this sort in charted form on page 499.

VERTICAL STITCH INLAY

Once you have the concept in mind, it doesn't take much of a step to get from horizontal inlay to vertical, and with that you can make not just vertical stripes, but inlay plaids.

1. Attach the supplies of yarn just as you would for Intarsia work, leaving the strands long or winding them into Butterflies or onto bobbins (see page 272).
2. As you work, leave the yarn hanging on the outside as you work the rows where you want it to show; bring the yarn between the needle tips and let it hang on the inside as you work the rows where it should be hidden.

You needn't start the inlay yarns at the bottom of the fabric; they can be introduced anywhere you please, just secure them as you would any Intarsia yarn. There is also no reason why you have to maintain a strict vertical. In order to make diagonals, bring the yarn through to the inside one stitch column to the right or left of the one it emerged from a row or two down. Here again, be careful of the tension so you neither get loops in the inlay yarn nor constrict the fabric.

Purl Inlay

This method of laying in a yarn relies on the weaving-in technique that is used for attaching strands to the inside of the fabric in Stranded Color work. In this situation, however, one yarn is used exclusively for the stitches and the other exclusively for the strands and the weaving is done on every stitch in a consistent way. Used in this way, the technique has many practical applications, discussed below, as well as the two decorative Purl patterns described here.

The patterns may be done with the strands always above the head of the stitch in one column and always below in the adjacent column, or they can be staggered so that if the strand is above on the stitch of one row, it will be below on the next stitch up. As the motions required when weaving in the left yarn are the simplest to do, carry the working yarn in your right hand, the stranding yarn in your left. When done on every stitch in this way, the weaving-in process is quite rhythmic and easy to maintain.

Purl Inlay Worked Flat

- For the regular pattern work on an uneven number of stitches.
- For the staggered pattern work on an even number of stitches.
- Begin each row with the stranded yarn held against the needle as you work a stitch, then hold it away for the next, alternating in this way stitch by stitch across the row.

REGULAR PATTERN IN PURL INLAY

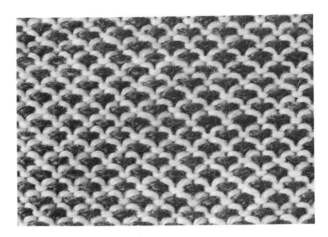

STAGGERED PATTERN IN PURL INLAY

When you begin with the weaving yarn held against the needle on an uneven number of stitches, the last stitch will be done in the same way as the first. Then, when you turn the work, you will begin the second row just like you did the first, making the pattern easy to remember.

Similarly, when you begin with the weaving yarn held against the needle on an even number of stitches, on the last stitch the yarn will be held away from the needle. Then, when you turn the work and begin the second row just like you did the first, the sequence will be staggered. In other words, you begin and work both patterns the same way, but the number of stitches on the needle, odd or even, will determine the pattern.

Purl Inlay Worked in the Round

- For the regular pattern, work on an even number of stitches.
- For the staggered pattern, work on an uneven number of stitches.
- Begin the first stitch of the first row with the weaving yarn held against the needle, hold it away for the next stitch, and continue to alternate stitch by stitch throughout the fabric.

When you are working in the round on an even number of stitches, and begin with the strand held against the needle, the last stitch of the row will be done with it held away. This means the first stitch will always be worked in the same way and the pattern will be regular.

When you are working on an uneven number of stitches, if the first stitch of the row is done with the stranded yarn held against the needle, the last one will be worked in the same way. This means the first stitch of the next row will be done with the yarn held away, and the last stitch of the next row will be done the same way. The first stitch of the third row will then be done with the yarn held against the needle, and so on, staggering the pattern.

PURL INLAY WITH FLEECE, OUTSIDE OF FABRIC

PURL INLAY WITH FLEECE, INSIDE OF FABRIC

Purl Inlay for Warmth

As you know, any Stranded pattern, whether woven in or not, provides a great deal of thermal benefit. When Purl Inlay is used for warmth, the strands would be worn on the inside and the woven yarn could be in the same color as the stitches, or in a much fluffier yarn for maximum warmth. If the woven yarn is the same as that used for the stitches, the simplest way to work is with a center-pull ball (see page 331), with the yarn to one hand coming off the outside of the ball, the yarn to the other hand coming out of the center. This way only one ball of yarn is hanging from the work.

Do keep in mind that you can achieve the same thermal benefit with true Double Stranding, without compromising the elasticity of the fabric (see page 258). You would only use Purl Inlay, therefore, when you not only wanted the warmth, but a relatively inelastic fabric, or when you did not want the second yarn to show in the stitches of the fabric.

Are you looking for real warmth? Try holding a narrow roll of unspun fleece, or a thick, softly spun fuzzy yarn as the weaving-in yarn.[1] The fleece can be woven in as described here, or, if you work with short lengths to avoid tangling the two yarns, the fleece and each running thread can be interlocked just as for a color change on Intarsia patterns.

Talk about warm!

Purl Inlay for Reinforcement

Just as Purl Inlay can be used to enhance the thermal properties of a garment, it can also be used to add strength. The technique is often used in this way to reinforce sock heels and the palms of mittens, and although I have never seen it mentioned, it could certainly be used at elbows. For these purposes, it would be best to use a fine yarn to reduce bulk, and perhaps one with added nylon for strength.

Hiding Ends of Yarn

The Purl Inlay technique can be used to hide the ends of yarn left when you must start a new ball of yarn, although I do not think that is the best way to handle them (see the discussion on page 379 for more information).

Purl Inlay for Markers

There are occasions in knitting, such as when it is necessary to pick up stitches within a fabric or to sew on a patch pocket, when it is helpful to mark the line along which you must work. This can be done with a tapestry needle and length of yarn, or it can be done with Purl Inlay. Select a strongly contrasting color in a smooth yarn or embroidery thread so it can be easily removed without fraying the stitches.

The marker is more securely held with Purl Inlay, but you can just as easily use Stitch Inlay, either horizontally or vertically, for this purpose.

Purl Inlay for Elastic

Whereas weaving in a yarn can reduce the resilience of a knitted fabric, weaving in elastic thread will definitely enhance it. Ribbing at waist or wrists can often pull out of shape with wear, particularly when knit in cotton or silk, which have little elasticity of their own. In these cases, it helps to weave in some fine elastic to help the garment hold its shape. The elastic can be added later (see page 380) or worked in during the knitting with the technique of weaving in.

There are two kinds of elastic marketed to knitters for these purposes. One is extremely fine, like a sewing thread, the other is more the weight of a fine yarn. Both can be used for the purpose, but it is somewhat more

---

1. From the charming book of mitten patterns, *Flying Geese & Partridge Feet, More Mittens from Up North and Down East,* by Robin Hansen, with Janetta Dexter (Camden, Me.: Down East Books, 1986).

difficult to regulate the tension of the very fine one; use it only with fine yarns. Neither should show on the outside in wear, except when the fabric is stretched out, but it is still wise to attempt to match the color of the elastic to that of the yarn as closely as possible. Good yarn stores increasingly have some selection, at least between light, medium, and dark colors.

Most commonly, elastic of this sort is added to ribbing, and herein lies the rub. Weaving in can only be done on the Purl side of a stitch. Therefore when working a rib, the elastic must be stranded past all of the Knit stitches that are to be on the inside of the garment, and can only be attached to the fabric on the Purl stitches. For this reason, Single Rib works somewhat better for this purpose than Double Rib, as it will only strand past one stitch each time instead of two.

Hold the elastic in the left hand, the knitting yarn in the right hand.

Weaving In Elastic on Single Rib

- When working on the outside, hold the elastic against the farside of the right needle tip as you work a Knit stitch. Then hold the elastic away on the farside, bring the knitting yarn to the nearside and Purl; return the yarn farside.
- When working on the inside, hold the elastic against the nearside of the needle as you work a Purl stitch. Then hold the elastic away on the nearside, bring the knitting yarn to the farside and Knit the next stitch; return the yarn nearside.

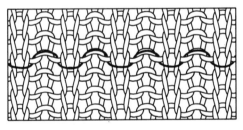

PURL INLAY FOR ELASTIC/SINGLE RIB

Weaving In Elastic on Double Rib

When weaving in elastic on Double Rib, the method of working is more or less the same, but because of the structure of Double Rib, the results are slightly different. The elastic must be stranded past every pair of Knit stitches on the inside face of the fabric, and it can only

be woven in on one of the Purl stitches. Let's see how this works.

If you weave the elastic above on the first Purl stitch and below on the second, the result will be that it actually strands directly past three stitches, the second Purl stitch and the next two Knit stitches. It is only caught against the inside of the fabric, then, on every fourth stitch.

If, however, you weave the elastic above on both Purl stitches, you will find that the elastic will be caught by the running threads that flank the two Purl stitches, but not by the one between them. In this way the elastic is caught against the fabric every other stitch, which is far better.

- When working on the outside of the fabric, hold the elastic against the farside of the needle as you work two Knit stitches. Then hold the elastic away on the farside, bring the knitting yarn to the nearside to Purl two stitches; return the yarn farside.
- When working on the inside of the fabric, hold the elastic against the nearside of the needle as you work two Purl stitches. Then hold the elastic away on the nearside, bring the knitting yarn to the farside, and Knit two stitches; return the yarn nearside.

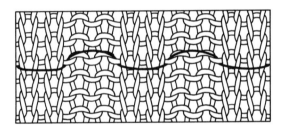

PURL INLAY FOR ELASTIC/DOUBLE RIB

Check your tension on the elastic from time to time; if you have not gone too far along, you can adjust it, either by stretching the elastic to pull it tighter behind the stitches, or by stretching out the knitting to draw in a bit more elastic. Also, don't try to knit with the elastic and the yarn held as one. First, unless the two colors match perfectly, you will see the elastic on the outside of the fabric, and second, it is very difficult to get the elastic to lie smoothly along the contour of the stitch; it is sometimes too light or too loose.

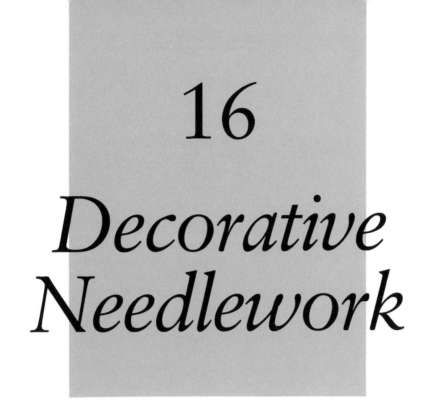

16

Decorative Needlework

Needlework of one sort or another is a quick way to add small amounts of color to a knitted fabric, and the variety of techniques offer many creative possibilities. Some of what can be done with stitchery must be carefully planned for prior to making the knitted fabric, some can easily be added as an afterthought, but all of them are quite easy to do.

Materials and Techniques

Any sort of yarn or embroidery-type thread can be used for needlework on a knitted fabric. You can certainly use knitting yarns for this purpose, but you might also want to consider cotton, linen, silk or metallic embroidery thread, or needlepoint or crewel embroidery yarns. All of these fray less than knitting yarn and so stand up better to being pulled repeatedly through the fabric, and the plied strands are easily separated so you have great flexibility regarding the thickness to be used. If you will be using a different yarn, choose one that has the same care requirements as the yarn used for the garment, and of course it must be colorfast.

Tying on Yarn and Hiding Ends

When attaching yarn for needlework, special care must be taken to hide the ends so they will not poke through or show behind any of the unadorned stitches. The solution is to secure the ends only on strands of the sewing yarn itself rather than on the yarn of the fabric.

1. Allow a twelve-inch end of yarn and bring the needle through to the outside. Hold the end of the yarn against the inside of the fabric with your fingers and begin working.
2. When you are done sewing, bring the needle through to the inside. Pass the needle under the nearest embroidery strand and draw it up to form a loop. Then pass the needle down through the loop, tighten the loop and pull the remainder of the yarn through to form a knot.
3. Wrap the end of yarn around a few of the other embroidery strands as neatly as possible, stretch out the fabric beneath the end to force it to take up some extra length for give, and cut it off.
4. Thread the end of yarn left where you started into the needle and knot and finish it as you did with the other.

These ends won't look as neat on the inside as ones hidden with Duplicate Stitch, but they will stay in place well enough and the tiny knots used will not show.

Embroidery Techniques

Virtually any of the basic embroidery stitches will work on a knitted fabric, but you must take into considera-tion that they will tend to thicken and weight down the fabric if done extensively. Generally speaking, therefore, it is best to use relatively small areas, particularly with stitchery that is itself dense.

DUPLICATE STITCH

This is just what it says it is. The embroidery yarn is drawn through the knitting so it lies on top of and exactly duplicates the Knit stitches. The type of pattern created in this way is very similar to what can be achieved with Intarsia, although it is generally used for smaller areas. In deciding which approach to take, keep

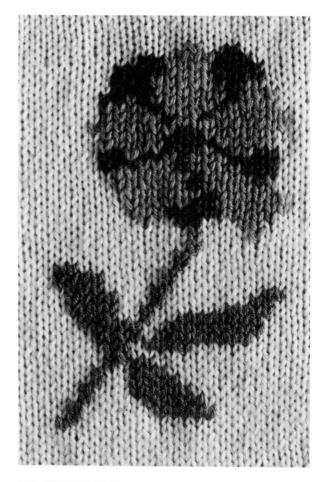

DUPLICATE STITCH FLOWER

in mind that Duplicate Stitch doubles the amount of yarn in the embroidered area, which makes the fabric thicker and somewhat stiffer. You may see this as an advantage or not, as the case may be. Typically, the yarn used for the embroidery is the same weight as that used for the fabric to ensure that the base stitches don't show through. That is not, however, an ironclad rule, and you may wish to use a thinner yarn that will create a tweedy look, or a fuzzier yarn for additional texture. A heavier yarn may add too much bulk.

When planning the design, keep in mind that a Knit stitch is wider than it is tall, and if you try to work the design from a pattern drawn on regular square graph paper, the result will be squat and distorted. The solution is the same as that used for charting Intarsia patterns (see page 486).

Embroidery is done from right to left on the outside of the fabric, beginning in the lower right corner of the area. You may work either horizontally along one row, or on a diagonal. When you have gone as far as you wish in one direction and want to work back on the stitches above, turn the fabric around in order to continue working from right to left. Fortunately, the stitches of a Stockinette fabric look exactly the same upside down as they do in the correct position, and the work will proceed in the same way except that the first and last steps must form half stitches. (For a full explanation of just why this is so, see page 190.) Work the stitches gently and with careful tension—too loose and you will have stitches that pull out of shape, too tight and you will constrict the fabric and expose the base stitches.

1. Thread a large-eyed, blunt sewing needle with a length of yarn and secure the yarn on the inside at the lower right hand corner of where the embroidery is to begin.
2. Bring the yarn to the outside at the center of the stitch *below* the first one to be duplicated.
3. Pass the needle from right to left behind both sides of the stitch above the one being duplicated.

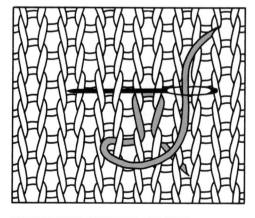

DUPLICATE STITCH/STEPS TWO AND THREE

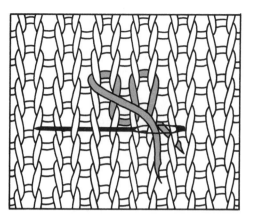

DUPLICATE STITCH/STEP FOUR

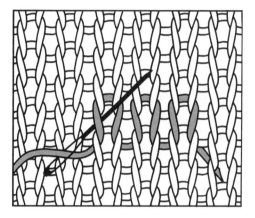

DUPLICATE STITCH/TURN AT LEFT SIDE

4. Insert the needle into the center of the same stitch below, then out the center of the stitch to the left below the one to be duplicated next.
5. Repeat this sequence for each stitch worked.

When you have worked as many stitches in the row as you require, you must turn the work upside down to work back, first securing the yarn at the lower corner of the last stitch in the following way:

• If the first stitch on the next row is immediately above, or to the right of the last stitch worked, bring the needle out to the left, passing it under then over the adjacent running thread, and then out the center of the stitch below the one to be worked next.
• If the first stitch is up to the left, pass the yarn around the running thread to the left of whatever stitch is below the one to be worked next and then out the center of that stitch.

When you have turned the fabric upside down, notice that the first and last movements on an upside-down row will form half stitches, otherwise the path of the yarn will be the same as on a right side up row. The half stitch that is worked at the beginning of an upside-down row can be a bit confusing. In order that there be no mistake about where to begin, you may want to bring the needle out at the base of the stitch to be worked next *before* turning the fabric around.

• When you turn the fabric right side up again, lock the yarn under the running thread to the right of the stitch below the next one to be worked.

Wrapping the yarn around the running thread prevents any distortion of the first and last stitches of the row as the yarn travels from one row to the next. The wrap will tuck itself in behind the head of the stitch, and will not be noticeable on the outside.

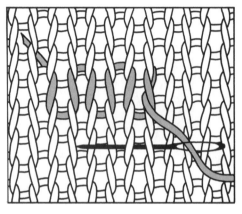

DUPLICATE STITCH/ROW TWO/STARTING
UPSIDE-DOWN ROW

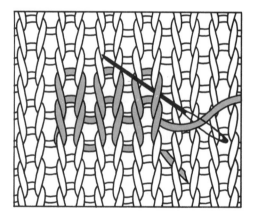

DUPLICATE STITCH/TURN AT RIGHT SIDE

Cross Stitch

Closely related to Duplicate Stitch in the way it makes use of the grid of the knitted fabric, Cross Stitch produces a nubbier, more embossed effect. As shown in the above illustration, the stitch is worked around the running threads. If you work around a single running thread on each side of the Knit stitch, the result is more dense. If you work around a pair of running threads on either side of the Knit stitch, the embroidery stitch will be slightly flatter and more expanded and will match the proportions of the knitted stitches better.

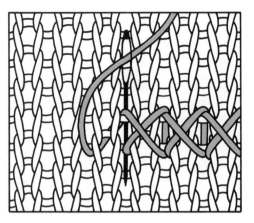

CROSS STITCH EMBROIDERY/STEP ONE

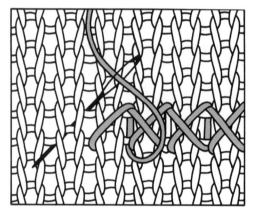

CROSS STITCH EMBROIDERY/STEP TWO

Stitched Ladders

Another aspect of embroidery, often called "insertion work," adapts very nicely to a knitted fabric, but must be planned for ahead of time. When done on a woven fabric, certain threads are snipped and pulled out of the fabric to open it up. The remaining threads are then pulled into a variety of configurations with embroidery stitches. Much the same thing can be achieved in a knitted fabric with the use of a Ladder to create an open column spanned by the running threads. The trick is to use controlled unraveling, dropping a stitch that will run no farther than you want it to.

Probably the simplest way to work is to introduce an extra stitch column with a Running Thread Increase. Work this stitch with the rest of the fabric the length desired, then drop the extra stitch and allow it to unravel to the base. A related method of working is to make a Yarnover in the position of the Ladder. On the next row, drop the previous Yarnover and make another. Continue in this way row by row until the Ladder is as long as you want it to be. And finally, it is possible to base the Ladder on an Eyelet (Knit two together, Yarnover). When the stitch is dropped, it will go no farther than the original Yarnover.

AN EMBROIDERED LADDER

EMBROIDERED GLOVES FOR A BRIDEGROOM, SWEDEN

The Ladder can be decorated with "needleweaving," a form of embroidery that pulls the running threads into various patterns, which can be found in any standard embroidery book. In this case, very fine thread or yarn used for the embroidery would allow the pattern of the running threads to be dominant, while a strongly contrasting color or highly textured yarn would stand out on a subtle background of the openwork and the Running Thread pattern.

Free Embroidery

A knitted fabric may, of course, be embroidered just like a woven one, and any book of basic embroidery stitches will provide you with a wealth of ideas. Embroidery of this sort allows the application of surface pattern with a very free line, in contrast to the strict gridlike nature of other means of using color in knitting. And as long as you are considering embroidery, give a thought to beads and sequins; with a little effort and attention to detail, a simple sweater can be dressed up to take you warm and cozy to the fanciest evening.

While the same type of yarn used for the knitting may also be used for the embroidery, generally a finer yarn is more suitable, as it will add less bulk and display the structure of the stitches better. Probably the most satisfactory result is obtained with silk or cotton embroidery thread or needlepoint yarn.

Needless to say, one cannot transfer a pattern to a knitted fabric as one would to a woven one. There are several approaches to solving the problem. The simplest is to outline the area to be embroidered with a contrast-color yarn marker and work more or less free hand. A more precise approach is to draw a grid that roughly matches your stitch gauge, then trace or transfer the embroidery pattern onto this grid and work with the pattern as a guide. The squares on the chart represent the Knit stitches, the horizontal line between two intersections represents the head of a stitch, and the vertical line between two intersections represents the space between stitches. You should exploit all of these aspects of the fabric to anchor your stitches and refine the embroidery.

Many fabric or craft stores carry a special tear-away fabric that can be used for this purpose. Transfer the embroidery pattern to the tear-away fabric and baste it to the outside of the knitted fabric. Embroider directly through both fabrics, making sure your needle passes completely through the knit in order to anchor the stitches securely. Be very careful with your tension; the stitches must be tightened down sufficiently to hold their shape but should in no way constrict the knitting. When you are finished, gently tear away the fabric bearing the design, and pluck out any little shreds caught in between the stitches; what you don't pull out will come out in washing.

Needlepoint and Counted Thread Work

If you are planning an embroidery pattern that is filled in rather than just an outline, you might want to use a fabric suitable for counted- or pulled-thread embroidery for the pattern. Draw the design on the fabric, baste it to the outside of the knit and stitch through both. When you are done with the stitchery, cut the fabric away from the pattern with a small, sharp scissors, being careful not to cut the embroidery threads. This leaves the fabric under the pattern, adding a certain amount of support.

Another, similar approach is to use netting or fine needlepoint mono-canvas. Transfer the design to the canvas, baste the canvas to the knitted fabric, and do the embroidery through both fabrics, making sure not to split any of the canvas threads with the needle. (If you are working over a fairly large area, baste within the area as well as around the perimeter, and remove the basting threads as you work.) When you are done, pull the individual threads of the canvas out from beneath the embroidered section. While the canvas grid somewhat inhibits the freedom of line you could achieve with the previous method, it does help to control tension and to produce a very smooth result, and the technique provides the opportunity of using the many stitches available for needlepoint.

Smocking

Smocking is a stitchery technique used to produce precisely controlled, decorative gathers that shape the garment without the need for a seam between the narrow portion and the full one. It is most commonly used on yokes and bodices, particularly on children's and wom-

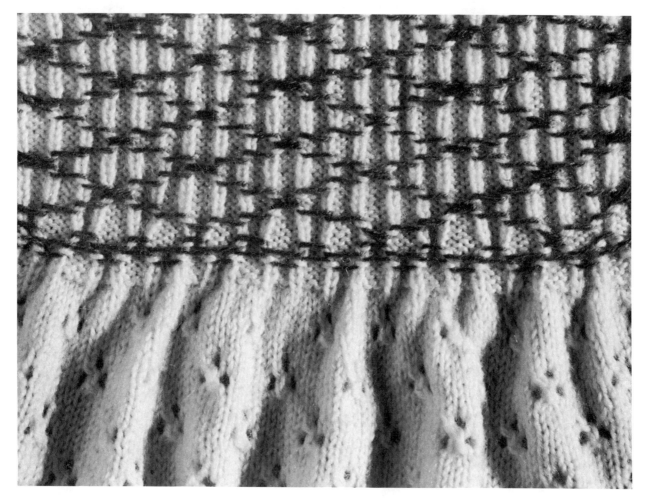

SMOCKING ON SINGLE RIB

en's clothing. There are always good books on the market that give detailed instructions for smocking on a woven fabric, and the basic principles are readily applied to a knitted fabric as well. It is important to keep in mind, however, that a knitted fabric is generally far bulkier than the types of fabrics most often used for smocking. For this reason, not only is it best to use the technique primarily on fine to medium knits, but it is necessary to reduce the amount of gathering to the minimum needed to achieve the effect. Careful calculations ahead of time are in order, and it is essential to try out the smocking in a fairly large swatch so the full effect of the gathering can be seen and felt.

One of the advantages of a knitted fabric for smocking is that the columns and rows of stitches provide perfect guides and there is no need to mark the fabric as one would with a woven fabric. While a Stockinette fabric smocks quite nicely, Single Rib is really ideal for this purpose, as it gathers the fabric without undue bulk. You may also place two or three rows of Purl between each Knit column if you wish. Of course, the more Knit ribs you have across the width, the more stitchery will be displayed and the nicer the effect will be, another advantage to be had with working in a fine yarn. Also note that smocking effects can be achieved with the use of certain stitch techniques such as Wrap, Couching, and Pullovers (see pages 55, 81, and 82).

Sewing on Beads or Sequins

If you are adding beads or sequins, just slip one on the needle and down against the fabric where you can secure it with the next stitch. You may decide to incorporate the beads into a pattern of decorative embroidery, or just use the beads to form a pattern. In the latter case, you will want to have as little of the sewing thread show on the outside of the fabric as possible; have the thread travel from one bead position to the next on the inside, being careful about tension.

You can also use a bead to secure a sequin. Pass the needle up through the sequin so the concave side faces out, then through the bead, then down through the hole of the sequin again and into the fabric.

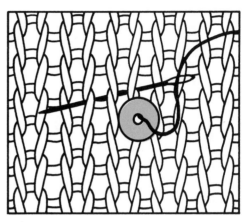

SEWING ON A SEQUIN

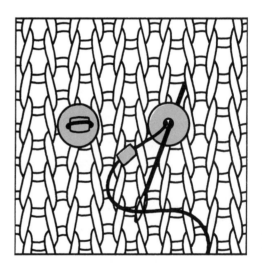

SEWING A SEQUIN ON WITH A BEAD

17
Beads and Sequins

Beads or sequins may certainly be embroidered onto a completed fabric as I discussed on page 291, but there is also a way to work them in simultaneously with the knitting. The advantage of this approach is that of quantity. Should you wish to decorate a large section of fabric, sewing them on could turn into a major project and a real chore. With the knitted-in method, you can decorate the entire garment in very little more time than it would take you to knit it plain. A beaded or sequined garment is one of the more elegant expressions of the knitter's art, and the trouble you go to to create one will be amply rewarded with satisfaction and praise. In addition, you will feel like you are getting away with something, because they are not all that difficult to do.

Some careful planning in design, appropriate materials, and a little patience in the work are what is needed; the skills required are modest and within reach of every knitter. Any pattern developed for Stranded or Intarsia color work can generally be adapted for this purpose. Beads or sequins will, of course, add pattern, a great deal of surface texture, and a decided gleam to the fabric regardless of whether they are in the same or different colors from the yarn. This is glamorous knitting.

Beads

These shiny little bits of glass, plastic, or metal are great fun to work with. They behave reasonably well and, while they will slow you down somewhat, I am sure you will feel the results are well worth the small amount of extra effort they require. Once you get the idea, you'll find yourself looking for opportunities to use them. They are very easy to add to garment patterns that don't call for them, and tuck very nicely into a wide variety of stitch patterns that would otherwise look quite sedate.

Materials

Before you embark on a project of this sort, it is not only necessary to know how to knit the beads into the fabric, but you must give some thought to the marriage of bead and yarn. The choice of appropriate materials and the method of stringing the beads onto the yarn are the first steps.

Yarns and Beads

Because knitted-in beads must be strung on the knitting yarn, which is then continuously pulled through the beads during the work, the opening in the bead must be large enough to accommodate the yarn, and the beads must be smooth so they do not fray the yarn either during the knitting or in wear. It is also important that the yarn be sufficiently strong to support the weight of the beads, and smooth so it will reasonably withstand any fraying that might occur. Strong silk, cotton, or linen yarns are excellent, those sold for crochet are particularly suitable, but beads can also be hung on any fairly fine, well-spun wool or wool-like yarn. Keep in mind that the heavier the collective weight of the beads, the more they will cause the garment to sag in wear, and this is exacerbated with inelastic yarns (see the information on page 420 for how to handle a tension sample when you must compensate for sagging). If you are planning to use relatively heavy beads, it is best to reduce their number.

Be sure that the beads can be subjected to the same sort of care required by the yarn and can be either washed or dry cleaned. A project of this sort will require a considerable investment of your time; do buy the finest-quality materials you can find and afford. Work a large sample swatch, not only to get a sense of how the work will progress, but for a clear idea of how the materials will behave together and what the resulting fabric will feel like.

Threading the Beads

Even if you are persuaded that the yarn will fit through the bead, the limitation in stringing one on the other is the eye of the threading needle, which must also pass through the bead. If you are working with beads that have fairly large openings, you may well be able to thread the yarn into a tapestry needle and transfer the beads directly to the yarn. However, if a needle with a small enough eye to pass through the bead is too small to accommodate the yarn, you must use an intermediary.

1. Test a variety of needle sizes until you find the largest one that will pass through the bead, then find a fairly strong or heavyweight thread that will pass through the eye of the needle doubled.
2. Cut about a twenty-inch length, double it, and thread the doubled ends through the needle, then pass the knitting yarn though the folded end of the thread.

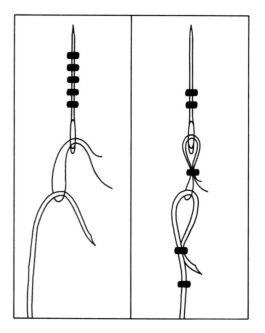

THREADING BEADS ONTO YARN

3. Insert the needle into a group of beads, slide them down from needle, to thread, to yarn. Alternatively, eliminate the needle, double a fine wire and pass the yarn through the folded end of the wire. Dental floss threaders also work very well (for those of you not familiar with orthodontia, they are used to thread the floss under the wires of the braces, and are available wherever ordinary dental supplies are sold).

Generally speaking, you must thread enough beads onto the yarn to complete the beading pattern before you commence the knitting. Should you find you did not string enough beads, there are two solutions. The simplest one is to break the yarn at the end of a row, thread on more beads, tie the yarn back on, and continue with the work. If you are close to the end of a ball of yarn, you can unwind the yarn from the ball, string the beads from the other end, and rewind the ball. Don't do this unless you are sure you can keep the unwound yarn from tangling up in the process.

Because the yarn is continually pulled through all of the beads strung on it, you may wish to reduce the possibility of fraying by stringing only enough beads for a limited number of rows, breaking the yarn, and restringing at the end of each small section. Of course, the disadvantage of this method is all those ends on the inside during finishing. However, this is really no different from what occurs with a multicolor pattern in unbeaded knitting, in which new yarns are constantly being tied on at the edges, and it is particularly appropriate when there will be quite a few rows of plain knitting between the beaded areas. Another technique that mitigates fraying is to use Stranded Beading (see below).

Beading Techniques

There are three areas in the knitted fabric where the beads may lie—on the running threads, on one side of the stitch, and on the head of the stitch. In most cases, the knitted fabric is worked at a fairly close tension to prevent the beads from slipping through to the inside; however, it is also possible to design a very open fabric with the beads positioned so they hang in the spaces. When the bead is on either the running thread or on the head of the stitch, the opening in the bead will be horizontal; when the bead is on the side of the stitch, the opening in the bead will be vertical. If your beads are not perfectly round, you may wish to choose one method over the other in order to have the beads positioned in just the way you want them.

RUNNING THREAD BEADING

This is by far the easiest way to bead, and the work moves along quite smoothly. In this method, each bead

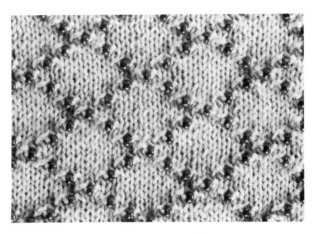

DIAMOND PATTERN IN RUNNING THREAD BEADING

rides on the running thread between two stitches. Now, as you know, the running threads lie on the Purl side of the fabric, so in order for the beads to show on the outside of the garment, a pair of Purl stitches must flank each bead. Therefore, the work is done either in Garter Stitch, Reverse Stockinette, or in a Brocade pattern.

• Work the stitch before the bead, bring the bead up the strand of yarn against the right needle, and work the stitch after the bead. (If you are working on the inside, you will Knit the stitches on either side of the bead, and the bead will be on the farside of the needle. If

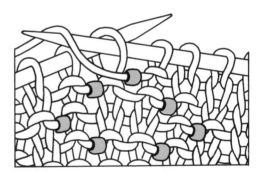

SETTING A BEAD ON THE RUNNING THREAD

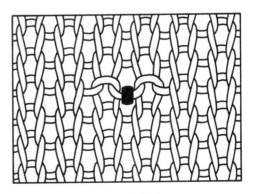

RUNNING THREAD BEAD IN FABRIC

you are working on the outside, you will Purl the stitches on either side of the bead, and the bead will be on the nearside of the needle.)

There really is nothing more to it than that; it takes patience rather than some esoteric skill. Do be careful with the tension on the running thread. The weight of the bead has a tendency to drag the yarn down; pull the bead up firmly against the fabric as you work the next stitch. As it is the beads will force the stitches apart; this is not the best method to use for a heavily beaded pattern as it distorts the fabric.

If you are planning to do Running Thread Beading from a pattern charted for color knitting, you will find yourself thrown off a bit. In a color knitting chart, each square represents a stitch. However, a running thread lies between two stitches, and as you know, there is always one less running thread in a row than there are stitches. In this case, therefore, each color square on the chart must be read as representing the space *between* stitches where a bead will go, and each vertical line at the intersections will then represent a stitch. Rather than having to make the constant mental adjustment necessary, it is best to rework the chart so it is correct for Running Thread Beading (see page 490).

While Running Thread Beading is typically done with just one bead inserted between each pair of stitches, this is not a hard and fast rule. If several beads are set on each running thread, the stitches on either side will spread apart to accommodate them. Actually, it is possible to use the number of beads on the running thread to shape the width of the fabric instead of doing so with increases and decreases. For this purpose, the beads are generally arranged in strict vertical columns, with the number of beads graduated in a carefully worked out progression that continues row by row from bottom to top. Once started, however, you must maintain the width by continuing to place beads in that position, row by row from bottom to top, or the fabric will force the beads out into a loop, see below.

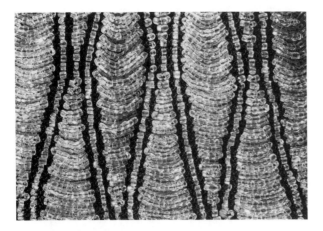

DETAIL OF HANDBAG WITH MULTIPLE BEADS ON THE RUNNING THREADS

SLIP STITCH BEADING

There are many stitch patterns that employ running threads stranded on the outside of the fabric past a Slip Stitch and these patterns can readily be adapted to beading. Because the strand is secured on the outside of the fabric by the Slip Stitch, there is no need to Purl the adjacent stitches. In addition, the strand is slightly elongated and can easily accommodate several beads instead of just one.

A SIMPLE SLIP STITCH BEADING PATTERN

STRANDED BROCADE BEADING

Stranded Brocade patterns also use strands on the outside of the fabric, but in this case two yarns are used, so only one of them would carry beads.

1. With the beading yarn, Purl the stitch before the one where the bead is to be placed and leave the yarn on the nearside of the work.
2. Knit the next stitch with the other yarn.
3. Bring one or more beads up to the needle, strand the beading yarn past the last stitch worked, and Purl the next stitch. Return the beading yarn to the farside and continue.

Because the running thread strands past another, intervening stitch, it is longer than normal and can carry several beads, depending upon their size.

LOOP BEADING

There are two ways to place a small loop of beads on the fabric. Please keep the weight of the beads in mind when using this technique. Either the beads should be tiny, or pattern areas should be small or widely scattered.

By far the simplest approach is to use Running

Thread Beading. Bring three to five beads up to the needle between two stitches and allow sufficient yarn to the running thread to form a loop. The weight of the beads hanging down will keep the stitches on either side the correct size even though the running thread is elongated.

The other approach is to use Knotted Loop Stitch (page 39), bringing the number of beads required up to the needle after the yarn is brought to the nearside, and before it is wrapped around the thumb.

Using an uneven number of beads will bring one to the bottom of the loop, which looks nicer. This suggests using a different bead in that position, either in a different color or perhaps slightly larger.

When beading with Stranded Brocade, it is also possible to use more beads than the length of the strand would normally accommodate, thus forcing the strand to loop down into a curve.

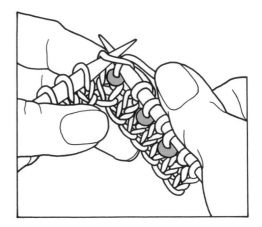

SETTING A BEAD ON A STITCH

CROSSED STITCH BEADING

With this technique, the bead rides on one side of the stitch. In order to do so, it must be pushed through the center of the discard stitch as the new stitch carrying the bead is made. The method is slower to do than Running Thread Beading, but it has some advantages because there is no need to use Purl stitches on the outside, and there is no need to alter a color chart in order to adapt it for beading. While the technique can be used on plain Stockinette, Crossed Stitch is generally used to prevent the bead from pushing through the center of the stitch to the inside.

Placing the Bead

1. Work to the position where you wish to set a bead, insert the needle either as to Knit or Purl as the case may be, and wrap the yarn around the needle tip.
2. Now bring the bead up the yarn to the needle, and as you bring the new stitch through the discard stitch, push the bead through with either left forefinger or thumb.
3. On the return row, each beaded stitch should be worked through the farside, the others worked plain. Have the bead on the nearside of the stitch as you Knit farside; have the bead on the farside of the stitch and insert the needle tip above it to Purl farside.

If your pattern allows, it is easiest to set the beads on a Purl row and cross the beaded stitches with a Knit farside, having them no closer than every other row. If the beads are set every row, it is best if they can be set every other stitch and staggered row by row.

If you are going to use this technique to set beads all over a fabric, you must take into consideration the be-

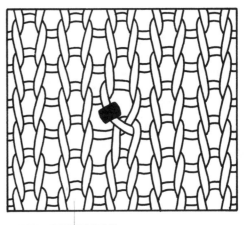

CROSSED STITCH BEADING

havior of Crossed Stitch and its tendency to go on the bias (see page 32). In that case, you will want to work as follows:

Balanced Crossed Stitch for Beading

1. On the outside, Knit into the farside of every stitch, wrapping the yarn over the needle.
2. On the inside, Purl the turned stitches in the normal way.

Work in this way consistently, regardless of whether a stitch is beaded or not. Here again, set the beads on the Purl rows, cross the beaded stitches on the Knit rows.

On the other hand, you may wish to exploit the bias as a design element, which will encourage the beads to move on the bias as well. Just don't let the bias happen inadvertently, when that is not the effect you wished to achieve.

Should you be working with a bead that is relatively large in relation to the stitch size, you may find that crossing the stitch is unnecessary, and eliminating the extra step will speed up the work. There is a tradeoff here, however, for as the stitch gets smaller in relation to the bead, it becomes more difficult to pass the bead through it. Try both methods on your swatch to test their relative merits, but keep in mind that the slight savings on working time may come at a price in quality.

I have encountered instructions for this type of beading that call for crossing the stitch through which the bead is pushed. In other words, the needle is inserted into the stitch farside and the bead is pushed through with the new stitch. As you know from the material on Crossed Stitch, it is the discard stitch that is crossed in this way, not the new stitch carrying the bead. Now the intention in crossing the stitch is to hold the bead in position on the outside of the fabric, and crossing the stitch below the bead obviously accomplishes nothing whatsoever. It is the stitch carrying the bead that must be crossed, and that must be done as described above.

STITCH HEAD BEADING

With this method, the bead is set on a plain stitch, then locked into position on the head of the stitch as it is discarded on the next row. While this requires the use of Purl on the outside of the fabric, the visual presence of the stitch is completely overshadowed by the bead.

1. As you work across the row, set the beads on the appropriate stitches according to your pattern, Knitting or Purling as required.
2. On the next row, when you encounter a stitch bearing a bead, push the bead to the nearside of the left needle with your forefinger, insert the tip of the needle into the stitch beneath the bead and either Knit or Purl. Work in Purl if you are on an outside row, in Knit if you are on an inside row.
3. As you move the yarn to work the next stitch, bring it under the bead to the left.

The point is to set the bead at the very center of the Purl nub, where it will be held between the sides of the new stitch and the two flanking running threads. This is an excellent method to use as the beads cannot slip through to the inside of the fabric, and there is no need

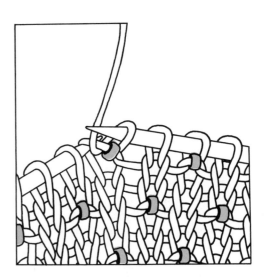

STITCH HEAD BEADING/SECURING THE BEAD

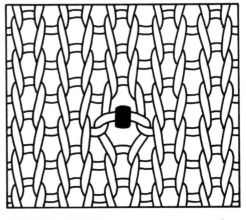

STITCH HEAD BEADING

to concern yourself with bias. Any Brocade pattern can be used for this method of beading, but remember you must set the bead on the stitch in the row prior to the one in which it will be Purled. In some patterns you may have to set a bead on a new stitch and simultaneously secure one from the previous row. (There is an example of a charted pattern of this sort on page 491.)

BEADING ON YARNOVERS

A Yarnover is no more than an elongated running thread, but it is also treated as a stitch. We can, therefore, place a bead on the Yarnover, secure it with the technique used for Stitch Head Beading and have it hang framed in the resulting Eyelet for a very charming effect. And a Half Double or Double Eyelet can be host to two beads.

1. Bring the bead or beads into position against the needle and work the Yarnover in the normal way.

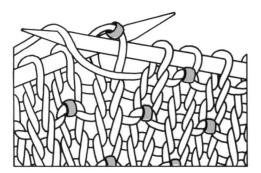

STITCH HEAD BEADING/PURL

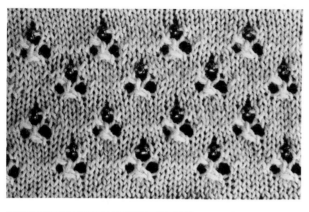

YARNOVER BEADING IN AN EYELET PATTERN

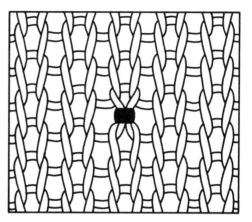

HOOK BEADING

2. On the return row, work into the strand to the right of the bead, then bring the yarn under the bead as you go to work the next stitch.

STRANDED BEADING

Should you want to combine beading with a Stranded color pattern (see above), use two yarns and string the beads on the one for the pattern. Use the Crossed Stitch or Stitch Head technique, stranding the beaded yarn past the plain stitches to those that must be beaded. The method would also work for Stranded Brocade patterns. You can use either Double Stranding or the Slip Stranding method of working with the yarns.

If you would like to use beads that are considerably smaller than can be accommodated on your yarn, or you would like to reduce fraying when working with a delicate yarn, you can string the beads on a separate fine yarn, stranding it past the plain stitches and holding the two yarns as one when it is time to set a bead. In Running Thread Beading, this would be the two flanking stitches; in Crossed Stitch or Stitch Head Beading, just the one carrying the bead. When the two yarns are in the same color, the beading yarn will not really show, especially if you have used Crossed Stitch Beading. If the two yarns are in different colors, those stitches where they are used together will have a tweedy appearance, which is particularly effective if the beading yarn is something shiny like a silk, rayon, or metallic. Actually, you can hold the two yarns as one for every stitch, and just bring up a bead whenever you want one.

HOOK BEADING

If the opening in the bead is large enough to accommodate a small crochet hook, there is a way of knitting in beads that avoids the necessity of stringing them on the yarn. It is a particularly good approach if you are con-

CERAMIC BEADS ON LINEN WALL HANGING, HOOK BEADING TECHNIQUE

cerned about the strength of the yarn in relation to the bead, or if the center of the bead is too big for the yarn and flops around. Both because it is only appropriate for rather large beads and because it is a slow way of working, this is not the method to use for a heavily beaded pattern.

• Insert the hook into a bead, hook the next stitch off the left needle, pull it through the bead, and return it to the needle in the correct position.

In this case, both sides of the stitch come through the center of the bead and the bead rides at the base of the stitch. The method is slow to work because you must set the needle down and pick up the hook each time, but if you are placing only the occasional bead, it won't make much difference.

Beaded Patterns

Now that we have discussed all the different methods of setting beads into the fabric, let us look at some of the ways to handle working a beaded pattern. In selecting patterns to use for beading, it is important to consider the weight of the garment and the depth of your patience; it is not necessary to use a great many beads to create a stunning effect. If you want to use them all over the fabric, space them out at a maximum of every other stitch and every other row. Alternatively, work some areas beaded and some plain.

Stripe Beading

At its simplest, the beads can be worked in stripes, with a bead set every stitch or every other stitch. For all the ease of working in this way, many delightful patterns can be created.

Rows of beads may alternate with rows of plain knitting, or the stripes may be fully beaded. The beads may be the same color as the yarn, or a different one. The color of the beads may change stripe by stripe, the yarn behind the beads may change color with the beads themselves remaining the same, or both may change.

Geometric Beading

Beads can also be worked into Fair Isle–type patterns using two different approaches. The most direct way of working is, instead of using a contrast-yarn, set a bead on every pattern stitch, and work the background stitches plain.

More interesting effects can be achieved with Stranded Beading in which two different-colored yarns are used, with the beads strung on the pattern yarn while the background yarn is worked plain. Of course, once you have two yarns, they may be in different textures as well as different colors, and given that the beads may be in yet a third color, the patterns can become quite complex.

If the beads are a different color from the pattern stitches, the color of the yarn behind the beads will be more effectively displayed if you use Running Thread Beading. However, because of the stranding, you cannot place a bead at a color change (the bead would just slide along the strand on the inside of the garment); instead it must always be placed between two pattern stitches. If this is a problem in terms of your design, try either Crossed Stitch or Stitch Head Beading to see if enough of the pattern color shows through behind the beads.

Fully Beaded Geometric Patterns

In the above approach to working Fair Isle patterns, the beads are used only for the pattern stitches. However, it is also possible to use beads for both pattern and background stitches. In this case, a single yarn is used with the different-color beads strung onto the yarn in a precise order according to the pattern chart.

When stringing beads for a pattern of this sort, keep in mind that the first bead strung will be the last bead worked, so you must commence stringing at the top of the chart and work down. Also remember that a chart reads from right to left on one row, and from left to right on the next when doing a flat fabric. Depending upon which row you start the beading on, and whether there are an odd or even number of rows, you may start stringing the pattern at either the top left- or top right-hand corner. Work this out carefully so you are absolutely sure which squares on the chart represent the first and last beads. If you are knitting in the round, it is much simpler, as you always begin stringing at the top left-hand corner, and end in the bottom right-hand corner.

Do the work at a time when you will not be interrupted, and check the sequence of beads on the yarn frequently so you will discover any errors before you go too far. Once the pattern of beads is established on the yarn, you will not be able to correct it in the knitting unless you break the yarn. For greater accuracy, you may find it far better to string several small sections, rather than attempting to string everything at once. Heavy beading of this sort requires a fine strong yarn of silk, linen, or cotton.

Intarsia Beading

Just as the Stranded Color technique suggests itself for use with beading, so does that of Intarsia. There are two approaches. In the first, an Intarsia pattern can be defined entirely with the beads, while a single-color yarn is used for the garment. In the second, the Intarsia pattern is both beaded and knit with a contrast-color yarn.

For the former approach, when you come to the row where the Intarsia pattern is to start, break the yarn, string the required number of beads, reattach the yarn, and begin to knit. Set the beads according to the pattern.

For the latter method, the beads of each pattern section are threaded onto separate strands of contrast color yarn. Bobbins don't work in this situation; instead, knot the end of the yarn around a button or large bead to act as a base, then string the beads. Once you tie on the yarn carrying the beads, just let it hang down off the inside of the work until it is needed. The work should rest in your lap to support the weight of the beads.

Regardless of which approach you use, a beaded Intarsia section can also have an internal color pattern. Work the pattern out carefully on a small chart and string the beads accordingly, as described for the Fair Isle patterns above.

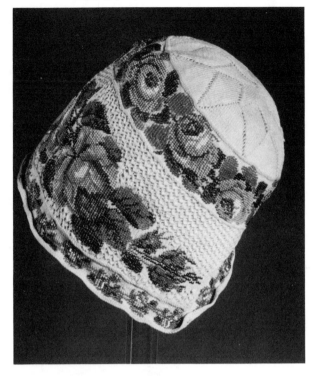

VICTORIAN BABY BONNET WITH INTARSIA BEADING AND MEDALLION CROWN
RIGHT: DETAIL OF BEADED BONNET

Sequins and Paillettes

Although similar to beads in the way they can be used to create design on a knitted garment, because of their shape sequins and paillettes present some special problems in handling. Working with sequins is easy enough, but I will be perfectly frank in telling you that it requires great patience. A beautifully made, fully sequined hand-knit garment is a treasure that should be treated with great respect and deserves all the admiration it garners. I have met one woman who knits them regularly; I suspect the rest of us would count it a great achievement to make one in a lifetime. Nevertheless, the necessary skills are easily acquired, the materials are inexpensive, and even a small section of a garment can be decorated with sequins, which will dress it up immeasurably and give you a

chance to try this out. After trying it on a small scale, you may be inspired to make that once-in-a-lifetime evening sweater or jacket that you could wear with such pride. Do it in a classic style with timeless colors and it will never go out of style.

Paillettes are a much enlarged version of a sequin, and are much easier to work with. While certainly dressy, however, they tend more toward the playful than the elegant.

Sequins

A sequin is a small, round, slightly concave, faceted disk with a hole in the center. Made of plastic, they are light in weight, and therefore there is no need to compensate for any sagging in the finished garment. Sequins are generally sold strung on double heavy thread that is knotted into a circle and are purchased by the strand, a thousand sequins per strand.

Because the opening in the center of the sequin is so small, there are limitations on the size yarn that can be used, and fraying is a problem. Use a yarn no heavier than sport weight, or string the sequins on a fine yarn and carry it together with a heavier one as discussed above in Beading. If only certain sections of the garment are to have sequins, don't string them until it is necessary to begin each pattern section. Break the yarn and reattach it once you have done so.

A sequined garment must be cold blocked (see page 394). Heat will discolor the sequins and steam will melt them. Please handle with care.

Stringing Sequins

The sequins must be transferred from the string on which they come to the yarn in the same manner as for beads.

- The concave side of the sequin will be facing the doubled, folded end of the string; the convex side will be facing the two ends. Pass the end of the yarn through the doubled end of the string and then slip the sequins in small groups off the string onto the yarn.

Should you run out of yarn before you use up all the sequins strung on it, or should the yarn have a knot, you will have to rethread the sequins before they can be transferred back onto the new supply of yarn as follows:

1. Break the yarn bearing the sequins and knot the end on the convex side.
2. Use a fine sewing needle and an intermediary thread, or a folded wire (see page 294), and rethread the sequins onto a doubled length of fine, strong cord such as the one they came on. The folded end of the cord should be closest to the needle, the cut ends farthest away. Knot the cut ends around a button to keep the sequins from slipping off the other end as you work.
3. Pull the yarn down tightly on either side of a group of sequins and insert the needle on the concave side, keeping it above the yarn as much as possible. With the sequins on the needle, remove the yarn and then transfer the sequins to the thread. Repeat until all sequins have been threaded.

This is a bit of a nuisance to do and is to be avoided as much as possible. Check your yarn carefully for flaws before you string the sequins; if necessary, rewind it so you can examine the entire length before you begin. It also helps to try to string the correct number of sequins so you don't run out of yarn before you use them all up. If necessary, push the sequins together and measure the length; divide this figure into 1,000 to get an idea of how many sequins there are per inch. Determine from

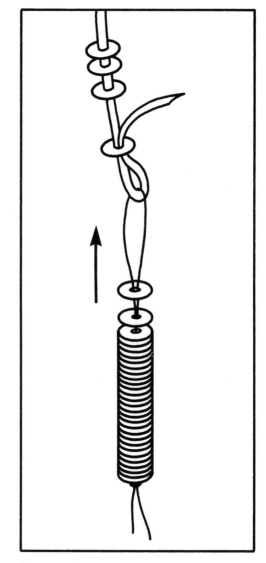

STRINGING SEQUINS

your pattern how many sequins you will need per row and how many rows you require. Use your stitches per yard figure (see page 428) to determine how much yarn is needed. With these few simple calculations you should be able to determine the correct quantities of both materials.

Setting the Sequins

Sequins are set on a stitch, quite like what is described above in Stitch Beading. None of the other methods for setting beads will work because the yarn must pass from the center of the sequin to the edge. A stitch head is too small to accommodate half the sequin, and although it is possible to set one on a running thread, the sequin tends to tilt out, perpendicular to the surface of the garment.

While it is relatively easy to slide a bead up to the needle, sequins don't cooperate so readily; they are all nested together, and it can be a challenge to separate one from the pack.

1. Bring a small group of sequins up the yarn to within about five or six inches from the needle.
2. With the thumb of your left hand, push the group of sequins flat against the strand of yarn. This forces them to separate slightly. Press the flattened sequins between thumb and forefinger and push them apart further.
3. Separate the three or four sequins closest to the needle from the group, flattening them as necessary to do so, and string them about one inch apart.
4. Bring a single sequin up to within about one-quarter inch of the needle. Insert the needle into the next stitch and wrap the yarn as to Knit. Reach the left forefinger over and flip the sequin through the stitch as you draw through the yarn.

You will learn to gauge how far away from the needle to place the sequin prior to forming the stitch. If it is too far away, it will miss the stitch entirely; if it is too close, it can be a struggle to force it up the yarn and through the stitch. Passing it through the stitch itself is really not a problem if it is placed properly. Do be careful to bring up only one sequin at a time; the difference between one and three sequins is fairly obvious, but the difference between one and two is frustratingly subtle. Flatten the sequin against the yarn; if there are two, you will see the edge of the first just back from the rim of the second.

Sequin Fabrics

Sequins are traditionally set on a background of Stockinette Crossed Stitch. Most books will tell you to set a sequin and then Knit the next stitch through the farside. The return row is worked in plain Purl. The reasons given for this method of working are that it ostensibly prevents the sequins from flipping up or pushing through to the farside of the fabric. Actually, it doesn't work very well to prevent either problem.

When you work the stitches on either side of the sequin through the farside, you are actually crossing the discard stitch. Crossing the adjacent stitches in the row below has absolutely no effect on the stitches bearing the sequins. I'm not sure how this tradition evolved, but it may have been the result of directions that were not accurately passed on, because crossing the stitch bearing the sequin does help, although it too is not the best way to work, as it turns a time-consuming task into one that is unbearably tedious. Fortunately, there is an alternative, and it is simplicity itself.

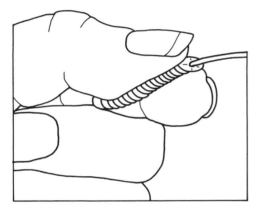

SEPARATING SEQUINS

SEQUINED SEED STITCH

The sequins should be set on every other stitch of every other row and staggered row by row so if they are on the even number stitches of one row, they will be on the odd number stitches on the next.

1. Set the sequins on an outside row, Knitting every stitch.

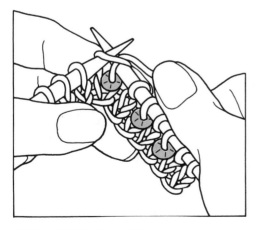

SETTING SEQUINS ON A STITCH

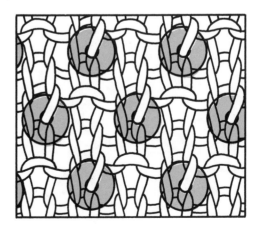

SEQUIN SEED STITCH

2. On the inside, Purl every stitch bearing a sequin. Knit all the others.

The Purl nubs on either side of the sequins prevent them from pushing through to the inside and work against their tendency to flip up. This produces a flat fabric that requires no blocking—a real boon since sequins cannot be steamed—and the sequined surface remains smooth and regular. If you are doing just a small section, or you are truly a glutton for punishment, the sequins can certainly be set every row, on the odd stitches of one row, the even stitches of the next. On outside rows, set a sequin as you Purl a stitch, Knit a stitch bearing a sequin. On inside rows, set a sequin as you Knit a stitch, Purl a stitch bearing a sequin. If the sequins occupy a small section rather than going from edge to edge, and the remainder of the fabric is to be worked in Stockinette, do place a Purl stitch on the outside before the first and after the last sequin.

Sequin Patterns

Sequins can be set all over the entire fabric on a similar- or different-color yarn. They can be set in stripes alternating plain and sequined, or where either the color of the sequins or that of the background yarn alternates, or both.

Intarsia patterns done with sequins are particularly stunning. Just as with beading, the yarn can be the same as the remainder of the garment with the shape of the motif defined solely by the sequins, or both a contrast-color yarn and the sequins can be used to do so.

Geometric patterns can also be formed with sequins. Brocade and color knitting patterns are an excellent source of design ideas but will require reworking to indicate Purl stitches and the placement of the sequins. An example of a pattern of this sort is shown in charted form on page 490. Unlike beading, however, don't attempt also to strand two different-color yarns, because in this case the Purl stitches will complicate the color effects. Also, while technically possible, it would be an excessively tedious job to string different color sequins in order to form both pattern and background.

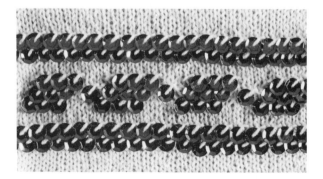

GEOMETRIC SEQUIN PATTERN

PAILLETTES

Paillettes are larger than sequins. They are flat and unfaceted, generally made of clear or variously colored plastic, and the hole is placed close to the edge. Traditionally, these were sewn on to a completed fabric, but recently some are appearing on the market with a larger hole, and they can be knitted in. Because of the material of which they are made, any garment bearing paillettes will, of course, have to be cold blocked (see page 394).

Setting Paillettes

The paillettes can be strung on the yarn and set on the running thread in the same manner as for sequins. However, because the running thread is horizontal, they tend to tilt out from the surface of the fabric somewhat. Paillettes are too large to push through the stitch as you would with sequins; however, if you are working with a relatively fine yarn and small needles, it is possible to set them on the stitch in the following way:

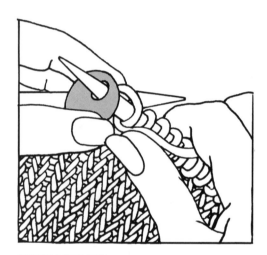

SETTING A PAILLETTE

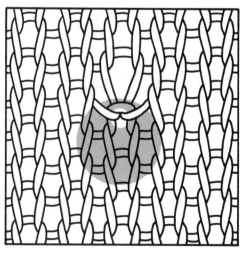

PAILLETTE

1. Do not string the paillettes on the yarn. Knit to where you want to set the paillette, and bring the yarn to the nearside.
2. Pick up a paillette and place the hole against the first stitch on the left needle.
3. Insert the needle through the stitch and through the hole in the paillette, wrap the yarn as to Purl and draw the new stitch through.

This pulls the entire stitch through the hole of the paillette. Because it is done as Purl, the running threads that pass on the outside of the fabric into and out of the new stitch will cross over the edge of the paillette in a slight V shape, holding it flat against the fabric. You can also set the paillette as you Knit a stitch, but it won't be held as firmly against the fabric.

Paillettes are generally placed so they will slightly overlap one another, the ones above covering the holes in the ones below. It will depend upon your stitch gauge how many stitches or rows should be placed in between; you might want to try things out on your swatch in a few different ways to judge the effect.

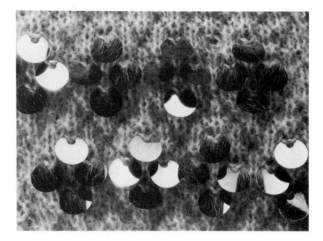

GEOMETRIC PATTERN WITH PAILLETTES ON MOHAIR

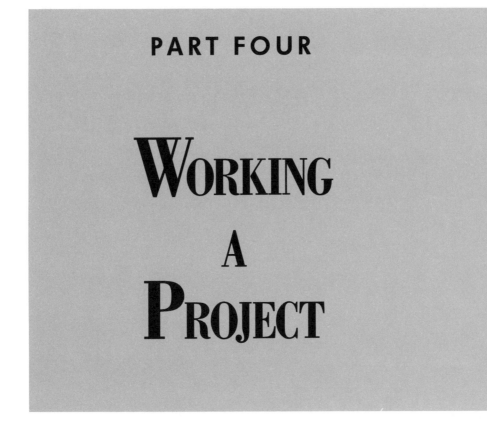

PART FOUR

WORKING A PROJECT

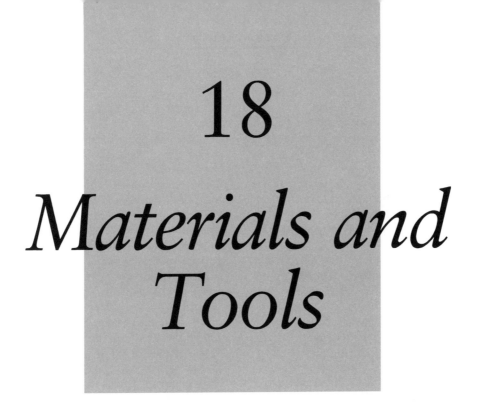

18
Materials and Tools

Knitting seems a simple craft. It requires very little in the way of materials, no more than some yarn, some needles, and a few elementary techniques that are quite easy to learn. As the size of this book testifies, however, the apparent simplicity of knitting is somewhat misleading. Just as a deeper knowledge of the techniques and methods expands the possibilities and produces superior results, so it is with an understanding of the tools and materials. You cannot know how a garment will turn out if you are not familiar with the properties of the materials you are working with.

The following discussion will provide you with detailed information on the various fibers used in knitting yarns, how the different types of yarns are made, and what effect their respective characteristics have on a knitted fabric. This information is of particular importance for those who enjoy designing their own knitted garments; however, knitters who work from commercial patterns will also find that it helps them make more informed choices. Just because the picture in the pattern looks good doesn't mean you are going to be satisfied with the way the garment turns out. It is worth your while to learn to judge when the recommended materials are worthy of your efforts and appropriate for what you have in mind. An exquisitely styled garment can be ruined by the wrong yarn: a beautiful yarn can be wasted in a design that fails to exploit, or works against, its best features.

You will have a great deal of time to contemplate the yarn you have purchased as every inch of it will pass slowly through your hands. Good materials are a joy to work with and make garments that are a joy to wear year after year; it is worth buying the best you can possibly afford. Knowledgeable consumers stimulate manufacturers to produce higher-quality products. If the mills and shopkeepers think that knitters care little and know less about the quality of the fibers and yarns they use, and are interested only in color and fluff, that is what they will give us.

The kinds of yarns available for knitting have become astonishingly varied, and new ones appear on the market every season. On the positive side, the number of choices has stimulated creativity and provided much more scope for individual expression. On the other hand, new and untried yarns present certain problems, as their qualities and characteristics are an unknown. Even a good-sized tension sample may not reveal exactly how a yarn will behave when worked into a garment nor how well it will hold up to wear and cleaning. However, if you know something about the structure of a yarn and the fiber it contains, it is far more likely that you will use the yarn appropriately and be satisfied with the results.

The classic yarns tend to be trusted friends, and there are great advantages to developing a familiarity with a limited number of them. Knowing what to expect, you can concentrate on the designing and knitting, confident that your efforts will produce a garment that is just what you expected it to be. This is no more a constraint on creativity than it is for an artist to use the same type of paint and canvas throughout a lifetime of work.

There are manufacturers that have a reverence for the natural fibers and pride themselves on the quality of the yarns they produce. These companies typically have a few lines of dependable, consistent, basic yarns that have been marketed successfully for many years. It is important that knitters learn who they are and favor them with business so those kinds of yarns will continue to be produced. Furthermore, if you have always been pleased with the quality of the classic yarns from a particular manufacturer, you are more likely to know you can trust the quality of the novelty yarns they produce as well.

Hand spinners frequently work with high-quality or exotic fibers and produce their yarns with loving care. If you are interested in yarn of that sort, seek out the spinners in your area and patronize them; they may be willing to spin (and even dye) a yarn to your specifications. Yarn stores that cater to weavers often know who the spinners are. There may be a spinners' guild in your area, or you may find them at a local craft show or state fair.

Finally, while the tools needed for knitting are simple and inexpensive, this does not mean that any old thing will do. Good-quality needles and accessories can make the knitting more satisfying and less fatiguing to do. I will discuss the components in turn: first the fibers that make the yarns, then the yarns that make the garments, and finally the tools that help make it all happen.

Fibers

There are three main classifications into which the fibers fall: protein, vegetable, and synthetic. The protein fibers are provided by animals, most commonly the sheep and the silkworm, but also various members of the goat and camel families. The commonly used vegetable fibers, derived from plants, are cotton, linen, and less often, ramie. The synthetic fibers are primarily products of the petroleum and gas reserves of the Earth. Many people have trouble classifying rayon; it is made from cellulose, a component of all plant life, but it was developed in laboratories by textile chemists and is manufactured much like other synthetic fibers.

Protein and vegetable fibers are now often referred to as "natural" fibers to distinguish them from the synthetic fibers introduced after 1940. The natural fibers, in this case including rayon, are all taken from renewable resources: animals and plants that, when well cared for, replenish themselves year after year. The synthetics are made from raw materials that, while certainly natural in origin, are nonrenewable and were developed at a time when there was little concern for possible shortages, whether from depletion or politics. Because of the growing concern about these limited resources, textile chemists are at work trying to synthesize other fibers from various plant or animal products such as milk and seaweed, much as they once did with rayon, although few are yet on the market.

You will find in the discussion that follows that I have a bias toward the natural fibers. This does not entirely derive from any ecological concerns I might have, serious as they are, nor do I have any prejudice against human artifice—it can be clever and wonderful. It is rather a critical judgment based on the characteristics of the fibers in question and their suitability for knitting. While the synthetic fibers all have some uniquely desirable qualities, in most cases when these fibers are intended for use in knitting yarns, the manufacturers attempt to mimic the feel and behavior of a natural fiber. To my way of thinking they are, at best, only partially successful, and it is far better to work with the real thing; humans have yet to match what Mother Nature has already done for us so beautifully.

Synthetic fibers have been successfully marketed on the basis of being easy to care for and economical. The former claim is only marginally justifiable, as we shall see. They are considerably cheaper to produce than the more labor-intensive natural fibers (although this could conceivably change if there were serious petroleum shortages in the future). However, I hope to persuade you that buying them is really a false economy, as the performance, wearability, and comfort of the natural fibers is so superior that the amount saved is not worth it. If economy is a major concern, it is better to wait for sales or make one less item during the year in order to afford the real thing; I think you will be happier with your investment.

It seems to me the only valid reason for the use of synthetic fibers in knitting yarns is to take advantage of whatever unique characteristics they offer that are not available in a natural fiber, and for that purpose they have their place, if a greatly reduced one, primarily with the novelty yarns.

Protein Fibers

Any fiber produced by an animal, whether hair, down, fleece or fur, is a protein fiber, meaning its chemical composition is primarily protein, much like that found in human hair or fingernails. There are many animals not represented on the list of those who contribute to yarn because their hair is not conducive to spinning or is too short or coarse to be useful.

Technically, the Wool Products Labeling Act of the United States Federal Trade Commission defines wool as "the fiber from the fleece of the sheep or lamb or hair of the Angora or Cashmere goat (and may include the so-called specialty fibers from the hair of the camel, alpaca, llama, and vicuña)." However, when people think of wool, they think of sheep's wool, and that is how I will use the term here; to distinguish the others, I will refer to them as specialty wools. Furthermore, because of wool's preeminent position in knitting, I will discuss it at some length but will be more brief with the others, as they share many characteristics, and we need discuss only in what ways they differ.

Wool

The wool fiber comes from the domesticated sheep, whose covering of thick hair is called a "fleece." There are many different breeds of sheep, some of them now obscure but true descendents of ancient stock, many more the result of selective breeding programs that have gone on since Roman times. Some breeds produce a short, tightly crimped fine wool used primarily for woolens; others have longer, shaggier fleeces that produce the long-staple fibers preferred for worsteds (for the difference between the two, see page 323). Finally, there are breeds with long, coarse coats good for such things as rug yarn.

Certain breeds, the Merino and the Rambouillet in particular, produce extremely high quality fleeces. The Merino, which originated in Spain, sets the standard, and other sheep are commonly rated by the percentage of Merino blood they have. After the defeat of the Spanish Armada, Elizabeth I acquired these sheep, previously never allowed out of Spain, and used them to establish the English wool industry, which in turn helped finance the expansion of the British Empire. Elizabeth's sheep have descendents in Australia and New Zealand that now produce most of the world's wool; more than 75 percent of the sheep there are Merino.

Fleece color ranges from white through all shades of gray and brown to black. White wool is preferred, as it can be dyed any color, but the natural colors are appreciated, particularly by hand spinners. In order to protect the fleece from damage as it grows, the better-quality herds are sometimes kept in roofed pens, or in enclosed pasture where underbrush is kept out, and they may be further protected with fleece coats. Fleeces treated with such care are, of course, of particularly high quality.

There are three ways the fibers can be removed from the sheep. The oldest method is "rooing," running hands through the fleece to pull out loose hair. Actually, very old breeds of sheep used to shed, and wool was collected both by rooing and by "wool gathering," picking up the wool where it caught on fences and bushes; given how we use the word today, the activity was obviously a pleasant one.

The old Shetland lace yarn was collected by rooing from the necks and backs of the sheep. The fiber was so delicate that it was not carded, just straightened gently by hand or with a comb and then spun into a two-ply yarn with the fineness of human hair. Sarah Don, in her

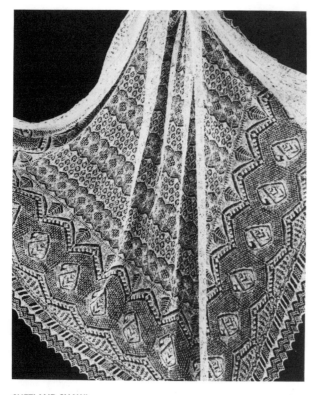

SHETLAND SHAWL

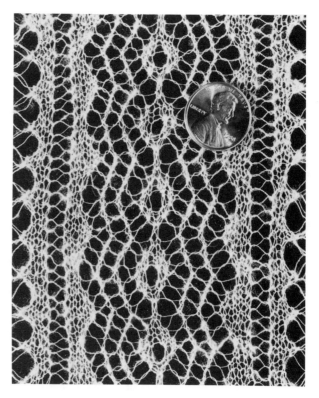

DETAIL OF SHETLAND SHAWL

book *The Art of Shetland Lace*,[1] tells us that a Mrs. Peterson of Unst, one of the last lace knitters, took a year to spin two ounces of yarn and another year to knit that two ounces into a six-foot-square gossamer shawl! Needless to say, this is an act of reverence for the fiber and the craft and rarely done.

To give you an idea of how fine this yarn was, two ounces of normal two-ply woolen fingering yarn is usually spun out to two to three hundred yards. Two ounces of Shetland lace wool can be spun out to an astonishing six thousand yards![2]

Most sheep are sheared in the springtime. The fleece is removed in one piece and weighs an average of ten pounds (one Merino ram produced a record fifty pounds). Fleece sheared from animals under seven or eight months of age is called "lamb's wool" and is softer and finer. The fleeces are graded for color, fineness, length, and crimp (the amount of natural elastic curl in the fiber) and then sorted, or divided into sections of different quality. The best wool comes from the shoulders, sides, and backs, as this receives the least wear and tear while on the sheep. As a general rule, the longer the staple the coarser and more lustrous it is. Kemp is hard, straight, shiny hair found mixed in some fleeces. It does not dye or spin well and must be removed; breeding programs attempt to eliminate it.

The wool fiber is light in weight, ranges from 1 to

18 inches in length and anywhere from 8 to 70 microns (a micron = .00004 inch); good Merino is around 15 microns. The Bradford wool "count" is a number representing a relationship between fineness and micron diameter, and the higher the number the finer the wool. The Merino count falls between 60 and 90 while the count for most wool used in knitting yarns lies somewhere between 40 and 60.

Before it can be spun into yarn, the wool is usually scoured or cleaned in a detergent bath. This also removes the natural oil called lanolin that, while on the sheep, softens the fibers and acts as a water-repellent. The lanolin is collected and sold as a by-product for use in cosmetics and in various industrial applications. If the wool still contains vegetable matter after scouring, it may be cleaned further with carbonization or freezing. Either process destroys or breaks down any remaining vegetable matter, which can then be combed or shaken out.

The poorest-quality wool is of three types. Reprocessed wool has been previously spun and woven into fabric, and reused wool is taken from garments that have been previously worn. Fabric scraps are cleaned and picked apart in a process called "garnetting," which returns them to a fibrous state, although in poor condition. Wool of this sort is referred to as "shoddy." If the yarn you are considering purchasing is very cheap, fiber

1. London: Bell & Hyman Ltd., 1980, 1986.
2. Helen Bennett, *Scottish Knitting*. Shire Album #164. (Aylesbury, Bucks, England: Shire Publications Ltd., 1986.)

lengths are very short, and it is not marked new or virgin wool, you may be in the presence of shoddy; it is not worth the time you would put into it. So-called ragg yarn sometimes contains one ply of shoddy with two ply of woolen. "Pulled" wool is chemically removed from a sheepskin. It is less elastic and does not dye well but may be blended with other wool in cheap products.

The wool fiber has a complex structure. On the outside is the epicuticle, a membrane that forms a water-repellent but vapor-permeable sheath somewhat like a wax coating. This membrane is responsible for two of wool's remarkable characteristics. Because the epicuticle is water repellent, a wool garment will float for a while, only absorbing water gradually; light rain tends to bead up, and water-borne spills will sit on the surface and can be wiped away.

On the other hand, the epicuticle will allow water vapor to pass through it and be absorbed into the fiber. This means the fiber "breathes," not only responding to the humidity in the air, but absorbing and evaporating moisture from the body, thus keeping the wearer dry. Wool can hold up to 30 percent of its weight in moisture before it begins to feel damp because the epicuticle itself remains dry. The moisture content also prevents the buildup of static electricity; because it is not "charged," wool does not attract lint and soil.

Beneath the epicuticle lies the cuticle, a hard protein substance called "keratin" that is similar to that of human fingernails. The cuticle is covered with rectangular scales, anywhere from 600 to 3,000 per inch, attached to the fiber shaft only at their base; the higher the number of scales, the higher the quality of the wool. These scales trap warm air and help one fiber cling to another. This makes wool easy to spin and means that even softly spun wool yarns will hold together.

Within the cuticle lies the cortex, packed with fibrous, spindle-shaped cells that provide elasticity, resilience, and strength and are responsible for the natural crimp, or curl, of wool. The crimp gives wool its "loft," creating air pockets between one fiber and another in the yarn where additional heat is trapped; as much as 60 to 80 percent of the volume of wool fabrics may consist of air. What all this adds up to are garments that are exceptionally warm for their weight.

The resilience of the fibrils means that high-quality wool fibers can stretch and bend without breaking, making them very durable, and the fabrics will return to normal after being stretched or wrinkled. The fibrils respond to the application of moist heat by rearranging their molecular structure. This rearrangement is not permanent, however, as they are quite content to alter themselves again if you require. It is thus that wool takes a "set," stretching out somewhat, contracting somewhat, holding a crease or releasing wrinkles as you wish. On the other hand, if you become warm and damp, your wool garment may rearrange itself in ways not entirely to your liking; see the discussion on dressing

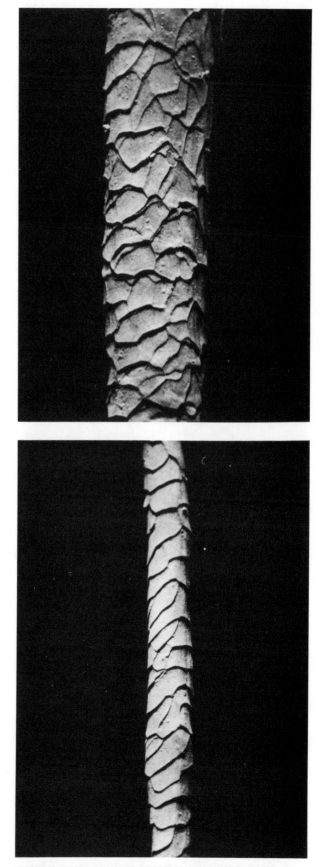

ELECTRON MICROGRAPH OF COARSE AND FINE WOOL FIBERS

(page 387) and that on weighted gauge (page 420). Wool held under copious steam and first stretched, then released, will shrink by as much as two-thirds; it disintegrates at 212° F., and dry heat is damaging. Wool is also somewhat weaker wet than dry and should be handled gently when washed.

Wool takes dye extremely well and fast, partly because of its absorptive quality, which allows the dye to thoroughly penetrate the fiber, and partly because of its molecular structure, which offers places for the dye to permanently attach itself.

The scales and the elastic cortex play a dual role in the ability of the wool fiber to "felt," or shrink and mat together. (See page 400 for a more detailed discussion of how this occurs. While most of us do not want our nice wool garments to shrink, felted wool is actually a very remarkable textile with unique, highly desirable characteristics.) Correct hand washing will prevent felting, and more often now you will encounter wool yarns that are labeled "machine washable." This means that the fibers have been treated to prevent them from felting. There are two processes used to accomplish this.

The older method of creating a washable wool involves a chlorination process that blunts or burns off the scales, making it difficult for felting to take place. Unfortunately, the process also makes the wool harsh and weak. Newer processes involve coating the fibers with one or another type of resin to glue the scales down. The label of a wool yarn treated in this way will be marked "machine washable" or "Superwash," the latter a trademark of the International Wool Secretariat in London. The IWS is an international marketing and research organization formed and supported by the world's major wool producers; the branch in the United States is called The Wool Bureau. In order to use the Superwash symbol on a label, a manufacturer must submit the product to the IWS for testing and certification that the process used meets their standards for shrinkage control.

It is something of a question what other characteristics of the fiber are changed by this process, but The Wool Bureau maintains that none of its other valuable attributes are affected. Critics contend that wool treated in this way feels slick and denatured and that it is not as warm. The resin coating makes the fiber smooth and lustrous and a bit harder to spin, and gives it slightly less loft. As the scales and the loft are two of the ways heat is trapped in fiber and yarn, respectively, it does make sense that resin-coated wool might be somewhat less warm. On the other hand, many people prefer these wools not just because they are washable and often have a lovely sheen, but precisely because they are so smooth and therefore more comfortable to wear. The resin coating also interferes with the absorption of the usual dyes; however, this is being overcome with new processes. Check the fastness of these yarns before you commit yourself to a project (see below).

Let's talk about allergies. According to the medical literature, a true allergy to wool is extremely rare. People have worn wool for millennia without complaint, so isn't it somewhat suspicious that, with the development of synthetic fibers, all of a sudden there is this new phenomenon of being allergic to wool when hardly anyone was before that time? There is no doubt that a coarse, hairy wool worn next to the skin will be itchy and irritating, but wool ranges from coarse to fine, and the kind used in a garment must be appropriate for how the garment will be worn. I have a set of machine-knitted wool long underwear that is the smoothest, softest, and coziest thing I could possibly wear on a cold day.

People who think they are allergic to wool may be responding to the microscopic bits of vegetable matter that can be left behind by the typical scouring process. In other words, it may not be an allergy to wool, but to timothy grass or some such thing. The cruder or more "natural" a yarn looks, the more likely this is to be a factor. Worsted and washable wools tend to be quite clean because of the extra processing they undergo. (Some mill should pick up on the idea that carbonized fleece makes "hypoallergenic" wool; this could be a strong selling point with those consumers who might otherwise buy synthetic fibers.) On the other hand, people with eczema-like conditions are likely to be more comfortable in a wool garment than in a synthetic, because the former keeps the skin warm and dry and the latter does not.

I am especially troubled by people who do not put wool on their babies or young children. Children are no more allergic to wool than any adult, nor will wearing wool when they are young make them become allergic; certainly the tender young should have the benefits of the softest wool next to their skin. Many people also think that caring for wool children's garments is too much trouble, but please read the chapter on washing knits, starting on page 387, for information on just how easy it is. Wool does not attract soil and does not absorb spills quickly, it sheds soil easily during washing, and the new washable wools make things even easier. What could be better for a child's garment? Please do not hesitate to knit wonderful wool things for the children in your life—nothing will keep them warmer and cozier.

Finally, wool is naturally flame retardant, to such an extent that it is used for clothing worn by fire fighters and for the blankets they use to smother flames. Wool shrinks from flame, burns very slowly, and self-extinguishes, making it very safe for you and for your little lambs.

Specialty Wools

Mohair: The all-white Angora goat probably originated in the Himalayas, but it came to fame as a producer of wool in Ankara, Turkey, whence its name. Turkey and the United States are the major producers of mohair, and most U.S. production is in Texas. The goats are sheared twice a year, and the fiber is between 4 and 12 inches long with a diameter of 20 to 60 microns. Just as young sheep give us lamb's wool, young goats give us kid mohair, the finest and softest grade.

It is odd that what we think of as the airiest, softest, fuzziest knitting wool of them all comes from a fiber that is actually smooth and very strong. Mohair has considerably fewer scales than wool, making it a slick fiber with high luster that does not felt easily. Because of this smoothness it is usually spun tightly in order to hold the fibers in the yarn. Few mills in the United States are set up to handle its special requirements, and 95 percent is exported for spinning and then reimported as yarn. Smooth mohair yarns are used in weaving; for knitting the yarns are usually brushed to lift the fiber ends.

Mohair is resistant to damage from abrasion, is extremely hard wearing, sheds soil easily, and dyes beautifully. It makes such durable fabrics that before cheaper synthetics came on the market, it was favored for upholstery that received heavy use, such as in theaters and railroads. It is, however, slightly more sensitive to chemicals than wool; wash in a mild, pH-neutral detergent.

The cortex of mohair contains air pockets, making the fiber very light in weight, with excellent insulating properties. In addition, mohair yarns are typically worked up into fluffy, loosely knitted fabrics that trap and hold warm air, making these garments both weightless and very warm.

Cashmere: The Cashmere goat also originates in the Himalayas, taking its name from the province of Kashmir in northern India; the finest cashmere today comes from Mongolia and northern China. The goat has two coats, the "beard," the coarse, hairy outer coat, and an undercoat of fine wool down, both combed from the goat when the animal sheds and then separated. One goat produces only a few ounces of down each year, which, along with the fiber's feather-light softness, is the reason it is so expensive.

The down fibers are 1 to 3½ inches long and average 14 microns (somewhat finer than Merino wool); it is usually tan to brown in color, and most is bleached before it is dyed. Cashmere has fewer scales than sheep's wool, giving it a silky feel and resistance to felting. The fiber will wet faster and, due to its fineness, it is more fragile to abrasion and susceptible to alkalis than wool; wash carefully. Cashmere is only suitable for gently worn garments. Because of its delicate nature and its expense, it is most often found blended with wool or silk.

Technically, many other goats and some other animals produce down of similar fineness to that of the Himalayan goat and may be substituted for true cashmere without the consumer's being aware of the difference.

Camel: The wool-producing Bactrian camel, the one

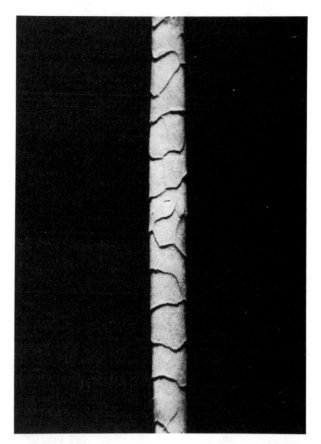

CASHMERE FIBER

with two humps, is native to the high desert steppes of central Asia and must endure extremes of heat and cold. The wool was traditionally collected as the animal shed great clumps of hair in the spring. On the caravans, the last camel bore the baskets in which the hair of the entire herd was collected.

The outer coat of coarse hair is up to 15 inches long, the undercoat of wool down is 1 to 5 inches in length, and the two must be separated by combing. Camel down averages 20 microns in diameter, only slightly less fine than Merino wool. Because the resemblance is so close, sheep's wool is sometimes used as an unlabeled substitution for the more expensive camel wool. The distinctive "camel color" is an integral part of the fiber and cannot be bleached; it is usually sold undyed or dyed darker. The fiber is very lightweight and has excellent insulating properties but, like the other downy fibers, it is fragile.

Vicuña: The graceful, lovely, long-necked vicuña is the smallest member of the South American branch of the camel family, and lives at altitudes of sixteen thousand feet in Peru. The animal is intractably wild, and the only way to obtain the hair is by killing it. It is now protected by the Peruvian government, and very limited quantities of its extraordinarily fine down, 2 inches in length and averaging 13 microns, are ever on the market. Vicuña is the finest of any of the wool fibers; on the

Bradford count (see page 312), most knitting yarns fall between 40 and 60, the very finest Merino rates in the 80s—vicuña is 120 to 130.

Guanaco: Another South American camel, the guanaco, more recently domesticated, has a fleece of beautiful, warm beige, but the fiber is not produced in any quantity.

Llama: The llama, tallest of the South American group at about five feet, remains the chief beast of burden in the high Andean plateau. It has a thick, coarse outer coat and a soft undercoat that is indistinguishable from alpaca. Because of the need to separate the two types of fiber, the llama is less attractive as a commercial producer of wool. The llama is being established in the United States, and there is interest in commercial development of the wool.

Alpaca: The South American alpaca is rapidly becoming an important producer of specialty wool fiber. An animal that was indispensable to the Incas, the alpaca has a shorter neck and heavier body than the llama and produces an extraordinary fleece. It is sheared twice a year (the unsheared hair can grow to 30 inches) and comes in a rich array of fifteen basic colors and many shades between; the fleece contains no kemp and little waste. Alpaca has few scales and averages 8 to 12 inches in length and 27 microns, slightly less fine than mohair,

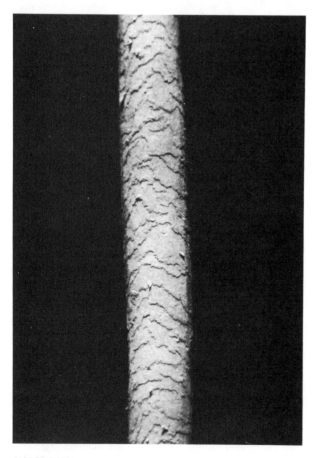

ALPACA FIBER

which it resembles in some respects. Like mohair, alpaca requires special spinning equipment and is usually made up as worsted yarn; these yarns do not felt easily, nor do they pill.

Alpaca is sleek, lustrous, and stronger than wool (although the dark colors are slightly weaker), and it has similar moisture and vapor properties. Unlike most fine wool, it has a medulla, a hollow core at the center of the cortex that traps air, making it somewhat warmer than wool. It also is denser than wool, with less crimp and elasticity, giving garments made of it a silky, almost heavy drape. Drop should be carefully taken into consideration when designing an alpaca garment (see page 420).

Angora: The fiber we call "angora" is produced by a domesticated rabbit, of which there are three main varieties: English, French, and German. The latter two countries are the main commercial producers of angora yarn, although the fiber comes from many different countries. In this country, there are hand spinners who raise their own rabbits and produce limited quantities of high-quality angora yarn. The rabbit may be either combed or clipped to obtain the fur, which contains both down and stiffer guard hairs.

The fiber is very fine, 13 to 15 microns, 1 to 4 inches in length, smooth and inelastic with a silky hand. Considered by many to be warmer than wool, it has the same absorbency, and it will felt. Angora yarns have a reputation for shedding; however, the handspun angora yarns are not as guilty of this. Hand spinners use only the long staple and spin the yarn more tightly so the fiber is firmly held in the yarn. Angora is usually spun unblended, but an angora/silk combination is very attractive, with less fluff and a beautiful sheen. When blended with wool, the fluff is lost, but angora can be plied with wool very successfully.

Angora sweaters are usually worked up on large needles to allow room for the yarn to fully expand. Because the fiber has no elasticity, plan the dimensions of any garment carefully; the combinations with silk or wool provide more resilience. The fabric is incredibly soft and fluffy and very warm for its minimal weight. It should be cleaned as for any other fine protein fiber. The cold air-fluff cycle on an automatic dryer can be used to loft an angora garment after it has been packed away.

Qiviut: Oomingmak, "the bearded one," erroneously but commonly called the musk ox, is native to the Arctic; it is about half the size of an American bison. Programs began in the 1950s to domesticate this wild creature, and it has turned out to be hardy, affectionate, intelligent, and playful. Under their shaggy outer coat grows an extraordinary down fiber known as "qiviut" (*kiv*-ee-uht). In the spring, the animal sheds six to seven pounds of down that can be pulled out from under the outer coat in large sheets. The fiber closely resembles cashmere but is a soft pale gray; it dyes well and does not shrink. During the 1970s, a hand-knitting cottage industry using qiviut wool was established in the remote, scattered native American villages of Alaska. The Musk Ox Producers Cooperative sends the fiber out for spinning into very fine yarn, distributes the yarn to the Eskimo women, and then sells the knitted lace garments they produce. The fiber is still very scarce; only about six hundred pounds a year are produced. No yarn is available on the commercial market.

Silk

This glorious fiber was used in China long before it was first mentioned in written records over four thousand years ago. Sericulture, the production of silk from domesticated moths, spread to Japan and India around A.D. 300 and from there to the rest of the world. The finest silk produced today still comes from its earliest homelands, particularly Japan.

Silk is given to us by two species of moth, one domesticated, one wild. The life cycle is brief. The moth lays four to six hundred eggs and then dies; the larvae hatch and feed on carefully selected chopped mulberry leaves for about a month as they grow into caterpillars. When it is time for the metamorphosis from caterpillar to moth, the insect begins to spin its cocoon, moving its head in a figure eight while secreting two continuous protein filaments called "fibrin" that are encased in sericin, a gummy substance. After two or three days of work, the result is a silk cocoon about the size of a peanut shell. The largest cocoons are set aside to hatch into moths and continue the cycle; the others are heated to kill the chrysalis and then washed in warm soapy water to soften the sericin and release the filaments.

The silk filaments, averaging 800 yards long, are unreeled from the cocoon and twisted with others directly into yarn. Damaged cocoons and those from which the moth has emerged contain broken filaments that are cut into staple lengths and handled much like any other short fiber; this is the silk used in knitting yarns. If the sericin is not removed from the filaments, it is referred to as raw silk. The fiber color depends on the diet, and while white is preferred for dyeing, there is natural yellow and green silk. Wild silk, known as "tussah," is brown in color and both coarser and stronger than domestic silk.

The silk filament is very smooth, translucent, and lustrous, about 10 microns in diameter (finer than any wool) and exceptionally strong. Silk shares many characteristics with wool. It has nearly the same ability to absorb moisture and retain heat, but it is slightly lighter in weight and pills less. The fiber is elastic, although it recovers more slowly than wool, and will neither shrink nor stretch appreciably, making knitted silk garments quite stable. Silk resists mildew and moths, but is susceptible to perspiration. The fiber is weaker wet than dry, and is damaged by dry heat and alkalis. Dry clean or wash like wool with a pH-neutral detergent, and use

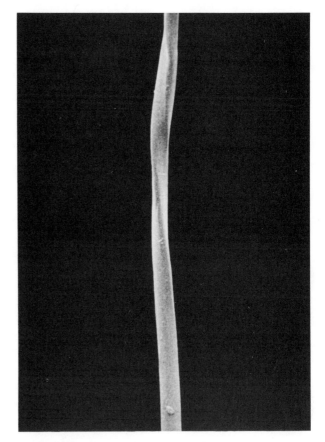

SILK FILAMENT

steam and a moderate iron temperature. Silk burns reluctantly and will self-extinguish. Silk and wool make a beautiful blend in yarns. The former provides a smooth sheen, the latter greater elasticity.

Vegetable Fibers

Quite conveniently, while protein fibers retain heat and keep us warm, vegetable fibers conduct heat away from the body and keep us cool. Mother Nature has provided us with summer and winter garb, with sweaters all year around.

However, while wool is perfection itself for knitting, the vegetable fibers present some challenges. Because of its inherently flexible structure, any knitted garment is liable to sag from its own weight, giving up something in width as it gains in length. Wool, being relatively lightweight and elastic, works against this tendency, helping to support the garment. The vegetable fibers are heavier and lack elasticity and, therefore, contribute to the problem.

For this reason, thin or softly spun yarns are more successful than dense, thick ones; smaller-scale garments, better than overly large ones. Heavily embossed stitch patterns will add to the weight, so it is better to select something smoother or more open. It is quite hopeless to expect ribbed waists and wrists to provide any elasticity; while ribbing can be used as a border pattern, it will not draw in unless elastic is added on the inside. Do not ask these yarns to do what they cannot readily do.

Cotton

The earliest known place of cultivation of the cotton plant is India, and the oldest fragment of cotten textile dates to about 3,000 B.C. Some of these ancient textiles were spun of fibers from a species of cotton so fine the fabrics were transparent, and their qualities have never been duplicated. Fine Indian cotton was one of the rare commodities Columbus was seeking on his voyage, and it is interesting to know that he found the people of South America wearing it. It is speculated that cotton migrated with the earliest Americans from Asia, which would make cotton cultivation a very old practice indeed. The plant grows best in hot climates, and the southern United States, South America, Egypt, China, and the Soviet Union are the major producing areas. More cotton is used in the world than any other fiber.

The cotton plant produces first a flower, then a pod containing a mass of cotton fibers surrounding the seeds. When the pod opens, the cotton is picked and passed through a cotton gin that removes the seeds and short fibers, called "linters." The cotton fiber has a hollow core called the "lumen," surrounded by concentric layers of cellulose laid down somewhat like the rings of a tree, but with a spiral or twisted pattern that gives it some elasticity. The living fiber is like a hollow tube, but once picked it wilts, flattening and curling up. This natural curl gives the fiber its soft loft and comfortable feel. The cotton fiber varies in length and color depending upon the type of plant and the growing conditions; the whiter the color and the longer the fiber, the higher the quality (there is a relatively rare, naturally brown cotton that some crafts people prize for its unique color).

Cotton is a heavy fiber, has little elasticity, and it stretches. This behavior must be compensated for not just with the size and scale of the garment, but through the method used to determine your stitch gauge (see page 415). Contrary to common belief, however, cotton does not actually shrink. It does exhibit what is known as relaxation shrinkage, meaning that while it will stretch as you knit with it and it will stretch in wear, washing will restore it once again, although its ability to do so will lessen with time.

The fiber absorbs moisture readily and conducts heat away from the body, making it comfortable in a hot climate but not in a cold one. Not only does it not insulate well, but once wet it is slow to dry and tends to cling—if you are wet and cold in cotton, you can quickly become dangerously wet and cold; change clothes as quickly as possible. On the other hand, if you want to cool off on a really hot day, wear wet cotton; as it slowly evaporates, you will fell refreshed.

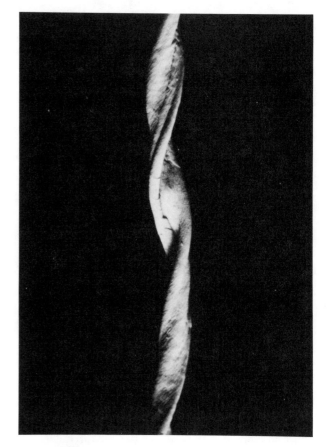

COTTON FIBER

Cotton is weaker than silk or linen, stronger than rayon or wool, and stronger wet than it is dry. "Mercerized" cotton has been treated with an alkali that causes the fiber to swell and straighten, making it stronger and more lustrous. Cotton sheds soil and stains well, can be machine washed with soap or detergent, and can be bleached if necessary (chlorine bleach should be properly diluted and the fabric neutralized afterwards; see page 388). Machine drying will assist relaxation shrinkage, restoring the shape of a stretched-out garment, but the abrasion is hard on the softer cottons (see page 391). Cotton is susceptible to mildew if stored damp and makes an excellent meal for silverfish, particularly if soiled.

Linen

Linen is produced from the stalk of the flax plant, which grows in cool, temperate climates with good rainfall. Fragments of linen textiles survive from Egypt and Europe that are some six to seven thousand years old. Aside from wool, which it predates as a textile fiber, linen was the most important fabric in western Europe until the arrival of imported cotton. Linen is more labor intensive than cotton, even when production is mechanized, making it more costly, but it is extremely durable.

The plant is pulled out of the ground, the seeds and leaves are removed, and then the stalk is "retted," or

LINEN FIBER

not as acute as it is with cotton yarns. Made into a garment that takes these characteristics into consideration, linen is a beautiful fiber to knit with. While woven linen wrinkles badly, this is not a consideration with knitted fabrics. Yarns made of long-staple linen are smooth, lustrous, and will not pill. Those spun from shorter lengths will be softer, fuzzier, and less strong, much like a carded cotton.

Linen can be safely dry cleaned but is easily washed, and since it is even stronger wet than when dry, you need not fuss over it. It is damaged by acids but not by alkalis, meaning strong detergents and soaps are quite safe, as is properly diluted chlorine bleach, as long as it is used infrequently and the fabric neutralized afterward (see page 388). The fiber tolerates hot dryers and iron temperatures, but will burn if exposed to flame. If stored damp, linen is susceptable to mildew but not to insects or rot. Avoid repeated creasing of the fabric, which will cause wear lines and break the fibers.

Ramie

Ramie comes from a tall, leafy plant of the nettle family that grows in semitropical areas. A white fiber, ramie is similar in many respects to linen and is fine, strong, and lustrous. It is absorbent and takes dye well, and is particularly appreciated in tropical climates for its resistence to mildew. Until recently, ramie was too labor intensive to be produced in economical quantities and little was imported into the United States, but this is changing. In knitting yarns, ramie is most often used as a substitute for the more expensive linen, and is sometimes found in blends with silk and cotton or with linen itself.

Rayon

Rayon was developed in the nineteenth century and was the first manufactured fiber. It is made from cellulose derived from wood pulp or cotton linters. The cellulose is subjected to various chemical baths and aging processes that turn it from a blotterlike sheet of paper into a thick solution resembling honey, which is then formed into filaments as for any other synthetic (see below). There are many different types of rayon, but the most common is viscose. (Acetate and triacetate fibers are also made from cellulose, but have very different properties and are rarely found in hand knitting yarns.)

Rayon is quite absorbent and dries quickly, making it comfortable to wear in hot weather. It is about as heavy as cotton and, like it, has poor elasticity. The fiber stretches, but will recover somewhat with laundering, especially if dried in an automatic dryer. Rayon is damaged by both alkalis and acids; it is not a strong fiber and is even weaker when wet. It should be handled carefully when laundered in a mild pH-balanced detergent; if bleaching is necessary, use an oxygen rather than a chlorine bleach. These fabrics are susceptible to mildew, bacteria, and insects; store them clean and dry.

exposed to the action of moisture and bacteria or to chemicals that rot and break down the bark. Next the stalk is crushed and beaten in order to remove the woody portions of the stem and free the valuable fibers. These fibers range from 5 to 20 inches or more in length; they are smooth and lustrous and naturally cream or tan in color. Because linen is beautiful in its natural state, it is often left undyed, but it takes color very well.

Linen is the strongest of all the fibers discussed here, natural or synthetic, and it gets smoother, softer, and more lustrous with age and proper care; actually, new linen is not as nice as old linen. (Many woven linen garments today are not in fashion long enough for them to age well, so the full benefits never become apparent. You can get a sense of what is possible with these fabrics only if you have an old treasured linen nightgown, or fine linen sheets, towels, or tablecloths.)

Linen is even more comfortable than cotton in a hot climate. It not only absorbs moisture but dries more quickly, wicking excess moisture along the fiber shaft where it can evaporate, conducting heat away from the body.

Like cotton, linen is a heavy fiber and even less elastic; it will, however, neither shrink nor stretch appreciably. This means that while its weight will contribute to drop, the fiber itself does not stretch, so the problem is

Rayons are constantly being improved, and the newer ones have increased strength and elasticity. In knitting yarns, it is most often found blended with cotton or linen; the rayon reduces the price and gains strength from the other fiber, and because the feel and behavior of rayon is so similar to cotton, these blends are quite successful. It is also found in many blended synthetic novelty yarns as a substitute for the more expensive cotton.

Synthetic Fibers

The list of synthetic fibers produced is long, and textile chemists are working constantly to improve their characteristics, and new variations appear on the market yearly.

Synthetic fibers begin as a liquid or molten chemical soup of some sort. The solution is forced through a device called a spinneret, which resembles a shower head, and as the fluid emerges from the spinneret it congeals into long, continuous strands called filaments. This is very like what the silkworm has been doing all along. When first made, synthetic filament yarns are very smooth, almost slippery. Manufacturers have developed a variety of techniques for changing the shape of the filaments in cross-section, adding crimp or texturizing the surface to give them characteristics that mimic those of the natural fibers or that create some other desirable quality.

There are five main types of synthetic fibers: nylons, polyesters, acrylics, olefins, and elastomerics, with many variations on these themes. A limited number of them are used in knitting yarns, and these all have certain general characteristics in common.

Synthetic fibers are hydrophobic, or water-resistant. This means water remains on the surface of the fiber rather than being absorbed into it, as is the case with natural fibers. This quality has several positive and negative aspects. One the one hand, the fibers dry quickly after wetting, and they resist water-based stains. This is the basis of the "wash and wear" claim. On the other hand, they have an affinity for oil- and grease-based stains. These are very difficult to remove, because the oil or grease penetrates the fiber where water cannot get in to help remove it, and therefore the stains must be treated with special grease solvents. Synthetics also tend to absorb odors such as perspiration, which can become impossible to remove.

The hydrophobic quality is also responsible for making garments of synthetic fibers feel clammy because they neither absorb moisture nor do most of them wick it away from the body. When fibers absorb moisture from the body, this moisture contains heat. Wool traps the moisture and the heat, keeping us both warm and dry. Vegetable fibers absorb the moisture and heat and evaporate it, keeping us cool and dry. Synthetic fibers do neither. Although some heat is held in the air

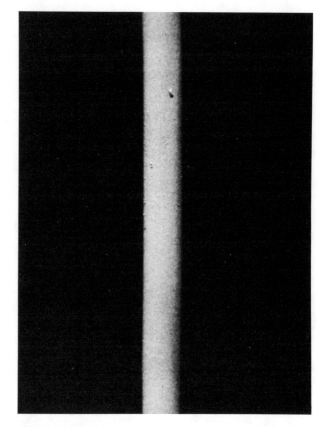

POLYESTER FILAMENT

pockets that lie between one fiber and another within the yarn and within the structure of the fabric itself, the fiber itself does not insulate.

The lack of absorbency also causes synthetics to build up static electricity, a problem more serious when selecting carpeting than yarn, perhaps, but a factor to keep in mind. In addition to the possibility of shock, static electricity attracts and holds lint and soil in a fabric.

Synthetic fibers are generally lightweight, very strong, and resilient, and fabrics made of them are therefore durable and retain their shape well. Unfortunately, they also pill badly because the tangled fiber ends are so strong they don't release from the surface easily. None of these fibers are of any interest to mildew or moths.

Finally, most synthetic fibers are thermoplastic, meaning they are very sensitive to heat. Some will actually melt at relatively low temperatures, and most will take a permanent shape, such as a fold or pleat, when sufficient heat and pressure is applied. When exposed to flame, these fabrics will melt, and the molten chemicals can cause serious burns; be extremely careful when wearing synthetic garments and consider carefully whether you want your children to wear them at all!

On that unhappy note, let us talk about how the individual fibers differ from one another and what role they play in knitting yarns.

Nylon

Nylon was invented right before World War II but was not available on a wide scale until the war had ended. It has, of course, lent its name to one of the most justifiably popular products on the market, women's nylon stockings, which caused a sensation when they were introduced. The family to which nylon belongs is the polyamide, a word you may see on some yarn labels. There are several different types of nylon, each one stressing certain characteristics over the others, but aside from the common nylon we are all familiar with, the other polyamide fibers are used primarily in industry.

Nylon fibers are lightweight, very strong, abrasion resistant, and elastic. They do not stretch out of shape and will shrink only at high temperatures; a too-hot iron can cause the fiber to soften or melt. The fiber is very easy to wash, and any detergent is safe, but some dry-cleaning solvents are harmful. Light-colored nylon can pick up dyes from other fabrics, giving it a yellow or a gray cast; it is best washed alone or with other white fabrics.

In knitting yarns, nylon is most often combined with natural fibers in order to gain the advantages of its strength and elasticity. Since very little of it is required to accomplish this goal, and because its other characteristics are not particularly desirable, you will rarely see a yarn containing more than 10 to 20 percent nylon, at which level it is very unobtrusive but effective.

It is at its most useful combined with wool in sock yarns, and is so strong the wool will wear away long before the nylon is affected. Small quantities of pure nylon yarn used to be sold for the express purpose of being knitted up along with a wool yarn on just the heels and toes, which made it possible to turn any wool yarn into a good, long-wearing sock. Since few of us make socks any longer, sock nylon has become very difficult to find; in fact, it is becoming difficult to find good sock yarn, for that matter.

Polyester

Polyester of one sort or another has become the most common synthetic fiber since its introduction in the early 1950s. Like nylon, it is made in many different variations with a wide range of applications.

These fibers are relatively strong and elastic, although less so than nylon, and have excellent resilience. They are medium in weight, roughly equivalent to wool. These factors mean that garments containing polyester hold their shape without sagging through repeated wearings.

Because of its economy, polyester is frequently blended with natural fibers, particularly cotton. Most of these blends contain no more than 40 percent polyester to allow the characteristics of the natural fiber to dominate; the polyester adds strength, less weight, and greater resilience. Modifications of the shape and surface of polyester are bringing it closer to feeling like silk and wool, although it shares few of their other admirable qualities.

While the fiber is nonabsorbent, it will wick moisture away from the body, making it somewhat more comfortable to wear than most other synthetics. Polyester can be dry cleaned, machine washed in any normal detergent, and machine dried at low heat. These fabrics will shrink at high heat; if you are steaming a garment made with a yarn containing polyester, reduce the iron heat to low.

Metallics

Gold and silver were, once upon a time, woven into priceless fabrics meant to adorn the favored few. In fact, they were quite impractical, as they were heavy and the thin metals tarnished and broke. Glitter is no longer reserved for the elite; it is now democratically and economically available to all, and we have the advantage of its being lightweight, reasonably durable, and permanently shiny.

In order to create metallic fibers or yarns, sheets of aluminum are coated with an adhesive, sandwiched between layers of polyester, and heat set. The aluminum gives the appearance of silver, or various colors can be added to the adhesive to simulate gold or any other natural or fantastic metal that might be thought desirable. Another version uses metal deposited on a polyester film and sealed with a resin. With either method, the resulting fabric is cut into filaments, which can be texturized. They are not particularly strong or soft and so are usually combined with yarns of other fibers. All of these types of yarns are heat-sensitive; read the label carefully for care instructions.

Acrylics

Since their introduction in the 1950s, acrylics of one kind or another have become the most common synthetics used in knitting yarns. The fiber is not particularly elastic, but it is resilient, has a soft hand, and is very lightweight and lofty. Because it can be made into yarns that to some extent mimic the feel and appearance of wool, if not its behavior, acrylics are primarily marketed as an economical and nonallergenic alternative to wool (for wool "allergy," see page 314). There are a wide variety of pure acrylic yarns on the market, and it is found blended with wool or other natural fibers to reduce their cost.

However, an acrylic garment is by no means as warm or comfortable as a comparable garment made in wool. While the loft of these yarns will trap some body heat, none is absorbed into the fiber, nor will moisture be carried away. This means you will be reasonably warm only as long as you don't exert yourself. Acrylics do offer high loft without weight and a variety of textures that cannot be achieved with natural fibers. These characteristics are often effectively exploited in the novelty yarns.

Acrylics can be dry cleaned, laundered, and bleached, but are subject to the usual problems with grease stains and odors. They are moderately strong fibers, but less so when wet. Furthermore, they are quite heat sensitive and will shrink if not washed and dried carefully according to label instructions; they will also shrink if steamed. Those that are crimp set may stretch out if not laid flat to dry.

Acrylics, unless specifically marked "flame retardant," will ignite and burn readily, and as they burn they melt; the molten chemicals cause serious burns and can ignite other substances. (A closely related fiber, modacrylic, most often used in pile and fake-fur type fabrics, is fire retardant and self-extinguishing. It is this type of acrylic that is found in children's sleepwear.)

Olefins

There are two main types of olefin fibers, polypropylene and polyethylene, both made from gases. The latter is found in packaging materials and such like, and does not interest us.

Polypropylene, an exceptionally strong, very lightweight, inexpensive, and abrasion-resistant fiber, is found in industrial textiles, indoor-outdoor carpeting, and upholstery. More recently, it has appeared in machine-knitted undergarments and light sweaters designed for active sports, for which its wicking ability is appreciated. It is not used in hand knitting yarns.

Polypropylene pills with a vengeance, builds up static electricity, attracts and holds lint and hairs tenaciously, and has a great affinity for grease and oil stains and for perspiration and other odors; it melts at relatively low temperatures and is altogether unpleasant to deal with and to wear. If you want long underwear, wool is best and silk is nice; they are easy to care for and will stay beautiful, fresh, and clean for a long, long time (although both are harmed by perspiration if it is allowed to remain in the garment).

Spandex

This is the one situation where the synthetic fiber is superior to the natural one, rubber. Spandex will stretch just as far as rubber, but it is stronger and less prone to deterioration. It can be machine washed and dried, but should not be bleached; hot water will yellow white Spandex.

In yarns, Spandex most often serves as a core and is wrapped with one or more other yarns. These highly elastic yarns are used for stretch fabrics such as undergarments, swimming suits, and other active wear. Most good knitting stores carry a small supply of fine Spandex yarns in a few colors for working into ribbings at waist and wrists to preserve elasticity (see page 380).

Some attempts have been made to use Spandex in knitting yarns, usually as a core wrapped with yarn in some other fiber. This has not been found successful in hand knitting, as it is extremely difficult to control the tension, and the feel of the yarns is not particularly satisfying.

Yarns

Regardless of what sort of fiber is used, the process of turning fiber into yarn is much the same. However, slight differences in how any fiber is handled throughout the stages of this process produce distinctively different yarns, both in appearance and behavior.

Spinning

Before any natural fiber can be formed into a yarn, the separate fibers, called "staple," are usually smoothed out so there are fewer tangles. This process, referred to as "carding," is much like brushing your hair. Hand spinners use carding paddles mounted with leather or rubber and studded with a great many fine bent wires; they look like giant dog brushes. A bunch of fibers is laid on the wires between two paddles, which are drawn in opposite directions until the fibers are relatively smooth and straight. In manufacturing, the process is basically the same, but with huge spinning drums substituted for the paddles.

For certain types of yarn, carding is followed by combing. This process further aligns the fibers so they are parallel and removes lengths shorter than two or three inches. The combed fibers are referred to as "top" and the shorter ones are called "noil." The shorter staple combed out of linen is called "tow"; the longer staple, 10 to 30 inches in length, is called "line." Combed wool is used for spinning the smoother, more tightly twisted yarns called "worsted"; the shorter lengths are spun into softer, less tightly twisted yarns called "woolen." A similar distinction exists for carded and combed cotton and for other fibers. Noils retrieved from combing are usually blended back into carded yarns.

Silk is reeled directly out of the cocoons in long, continuous strands called "filaments" and may be twisted into yarn without further ado. Short fibers and those from damaged cocoons, known as "frisons," are handled like a worsted or a woolen and referred to as "spun" silk; this is the type used in knitting yarns. Like silk, manufactured fibers are produced in the form of long, continuous filaments; technically no carding or combing is necessary before spinning, but generally the mill cuts the filaments into whatever staple lengths are thought suitable for the type of yarn wanted and then spins it as they would a natural fiber.

In commercial yarn production, the carded bundle of fibers is elongated and drawn out into what is called a "sliver" and then given a slight twist that thins it down into the form known as a "roving." A roving is like a thick, very soft rope of fibers from which true yarn is spun. You can, however, knit directly with a fine roving; Icelandic yarn is of this type. Different types of fibers and/or colors may be blended together as they are carded or when they are drawn into the sliver. To produce combed, worsted-type yarns, a complex drawing-out process is used to further blend and align the fibers and refine the sliver before it is twisted into a roving.

Hand spinners roll short staple off the paddle in the direction in which it is carded into a little cigar shape they call a "rolag," from which the fibers are spun directly. Long staple fibers are rolled off the paddle from side to side, combed, then folded over the forefinger and drawn out from the center as they are spun into the yarn. Semiworsted is long-staple wool that is spun like worsted but not combed. Short, downy fibers may be spun directly out of a gently amalgamated mass without carding. Most linen knitting yarns are made from relatively short staple and spun like a carded or combed cotton. For line, a hank of fiber called the "strick" is tied to the distaff, a pole on the spinning wheel. The fiber ends are drawn out of the strick into the yarn a few at a time during spinning. The fiber spun from linen when it is wet is smoother than that spun dry.

In manufacturing there are a variety of ways that yarn can be spun depending upon the fiber, the staple length, and the type of yarn desired. The equipment needed for handling carded or combed yarns is different, but basically the machines were designed to mimic hand-spinning techniques. Two common methods are ring spinning and the newer open-end spinning. In the former the fibers are drawn out of the roving by rollers and then twisted by the ring spinner onto the bobbin; this is closest to the hand-spinning method. With the latter, fibers are pulled out of the sliver (no roving is needed) into the spinners by a current of air. While this is faster and more economical and produces uniform yarn, the yarn is of lower strength, and the method cannot be used for fine yarns.

Recently I have heard knitters talk of yarn having a "nap" or "direction." What they seem to mean by this is that the yarn is supposedly smoother and fewer ends will be raised when it is pulled through your fingers one way than when it is pulled the other way. People who manufacture yarn do not recognize the distinction, and there is no physical reason for the yarn to display this characteristic with the spinning techniques they use. After all, every fiber has two ends, and it is just as likely for one end to be sticking out of the yarn as for the other end to do so.

Hand spinners, however, claim that worsted and other long-staple yarns have a "direction" because they draw the fibers out from the center of the fiber mass, something the mills do not do. In other words, the folded ends of the fibers are pulled into the yarn first, the tips and cut ends last. Since there are, therefore, half as many ends in one direction as in the other, the yarn will rough up somewhat more if you run it through your fingers in the direction opposite to which it was spun. If you are purchasing a hand-spun worsted or other relatively long-staple yarn, you might want to ask the spinner if it makes a difference which end of the ball to start with, or check the yarn to see if you can discern which is the smoothest direction. With woolens and other yarns containing short-staple fibers that are less aligned, it does not matter which way you draw the yarn through your fingers; this is true whether the yarn is hand spun or not.

The amount of twist gives the yarn unique characteristics. If it is twisted firmly, the yarn will be fine, smooth, and strong and it will reflect more light, giving it a lustrous quality. Given high twist, the yarn will become thinner and will "crepe," or kink up, and have a pebbly, rough surface. If it is twisted gently, the yarn will be softer and thicker, somewhat less durable, and more muted in color.

When the yarn is twisted to the right as it is spun, it is referred to as "Z-twist"; when twisted to the left, "S-twist." The resulting strand is called a "single" or a "ply."

Ply Yarn

In order to form true yarn, two or more singles are twisted together to form what is called a "plied" yarn; this adds strength as well as dimension. If the singles were given a Z-twist as they were spun, they will be plied together with an S-twist, or vice versa. The con-

FOUR-PLY S-TWIST YARN

NOVELTY YARNS

trary twist of the singles and the plies holds the yarn together so it will not unply.

Many people mistakenly believe that the number of plies in the yarn is a designation of its thickness, but this is not true. A four-ply yarn made of very fine singles will be considerably thinner than a two-ply yarn made of thicker, softly spun singles; the former is typical of worsteds, the latter of woolens. Classic woolen knitting yarns are traditionally made up in two- and three-ply versions to produce two different thicknesses suitable for light- to medium-weight sweaters. However, not all manufacturers, nor consumers, agree on what is meant by light- or medium-weight sweaters, so there is considerable variation. With the wider variety of yarns on the market now, the number of plies is not particularly useful as a guide to how thick a yarn is. Therefore, when you encounter a term of this kind, treat it as specific to the brand of yarn indicated.

Occasionally you will now see cord or cable yarns on the market. These are made up of several plied yarns. In other words, a mill might start with two very fine Z-twist singles combined in an S-twist yarn and then finished with four of these two-ply yarns brought together with a Z-twist. Because cords contain extremely fine

singles, the fibers are closely held in the yarn, making it smooth and strong. Most cord yarns are in cotton, but wool versions are appearing on the market that are more loosely plied and very plush.

Straight, smooth yarns where all plies are of the same uniform type are referred to as "simple," or "classic," yarns. What are called "novelty," or "complex," yarns come in many different forms. It is impossible to cover all the possibilities that exist because they are highly individual, and new variations take their turn on the market every year; there are, however, some common types.

One way of adding texture to a simple yarn is to rough up the ends. Mohair, for instance, is a long, smooth fiber spun on the worsted system with a firm twist to help it hold together. For knitting yarns, it is plied into a very fine yarn and then the surface is brushed to raise the ends, giving it the familiar hairy look.

Most novelty yarns, however, are made up of singles with different characteristics. "Slub" yarns are made up of one normal single and one that was spun unevenly. When the two are plied together, the loosely spun sections form soft, thickened bumps on the yarn. If one single is more tightly twisted than the other, the former will curl up around the latter; "bouclé" yarns are of this type. In so-called spot, or nub, yarns one ply is intermittently bunched up tightly in sections around the other as the two are plied. "Gimp" is made up of one thin and one thick ply.

Two singles may be held together by a third, "binder" yarn. I have seen yarn that was basically a thin roving wrapped with a very fine binder yarn to hold it together and others that consist of a core yarn wrapped with two binder yarns in a double-helix pattern.

Chenille yarns are not spun, but cut from a specially woven fabric. Ribbon yarns may be woven narrow, but many synthetic ribbons are cut strips with heat-melted edges.

Dyes

It is beyond the scope of this book to go into all the different dye types and methods that are used, nor is such a highly technical discussion really necessary. However, some general information is useful.

Natural fibers may be "stock" or "top" dyed, meaning they are dyed before spinning. This process requires careful handling and gives excellent penetration, fastness, and even color. It is most often used in the production of tweed and heather yarns (a wool yarn dyed in this way may be marked "dyed in the wool"). For artificial fibers, color may be introduced to the liquid chemical mixture prior to extruding the filaments; this is called "solution" dyeing. Whether the fiber is natural or artificial, it is far more common and economical for the mills to dye yarn rather than fiber, as this allows them greater flexibility in responding to changing fashions in color. Some novelty yarns are made up of yarn singles dyed different colors and plied together.

For the knitter, it matters less how the yarn was dyed than that it is colorfast. Some dyes may fade in sunlight, in water, in dry-cleaning solutions, or with exposure to perspiration. Reputable manufacturers indicate on the label if the yarn is colorfast under all or some of those conditions. If the label is marked "dry clean only," it may be because the dye used is not fast in water. In the absence of information on the label, there are certain tests you can conduct at home.

To test for colorfastness to sunlight, knit a sample swatch of fabric and tape it to a sunny window, or, in good weather, set it outside for a day or two. Compare it to a sample not similarly exposed to see if there has been any change.

To check for colorfastness to water, place a small sample in a jar filled with warm water and a small amount of the detergent you plan to use for laundering. Shake the jar vigorously, allow it to sit for half an hour, then shake it vigorously again. Remove the sample, allow the water to settle, and check it for color. If you are working a multicolored pattern, use two samples in the bath, one light, one dark. After agitation, check the light sample for color change.

Some excess dye may very well come out in the first few washings without serious loss of color in the yarn; however, you will want to know if this will continue. Therefore, repeat the test one or two more times and then check the sample against a ball of yarn to see how much color change has occurred. If it is significant and the last wash water still shows evidence of color loss, you must decide whether you want the chronic expense of dry cleaning; otherwise, return the unused yarn to the store and select something else. Modern dyes are quite effective, and there is really no excuse for knitting yarns that are not colorfast.

If you are planning to machine-wash a garment, you may also want to check the fabric for "crocking," which is color loss due to abrasion. Take a clean, white rag and rub it vigorously over the surface of the sample, then check the rag for color transfer; wet the rag and repeat the test. This is particularly important for any garment you plan to machine-wash and dry.

Yarn Characteristics

As I discussed above, it is very important that you select a fiber suitable for the garment you have in mind, but how the yarn is spun also imparts very important characteristics that you will want to take into consideration.

The main distinction in classic yarns is between the carded, woolen-type yarns and the combed, worsted type. The latter tend to be more expensive because they use only the long staple and there are more steps in manufacturing. However, knitters should not necessarily consider a worsted or combed yarn superior to a woolen or carded one, although that is sometimes thought to be the case. Both have a valued place in knitting, and it is more appropriate to focus on whether the yarn suits the project you have in mind.

Most important is the "hand"—how the yarn feels. You will want a fine, soft fiber and a thinner yarn if you plan a garment that will be worn indoors and close to the skin. For an outdoor, sporty garment, something thicker and coarser may be perfectly acceptable or even more appropriate. Both carded and combed yarns may be either coarse or soft, depending upon the grade of fiber used and how it was spun.

Combed worsted-type yarns contain relatively long fibers. Since there are fewer ends, the yarns will pill less and, when an inherently soft fiber is used, they are smooth and comfortable against the skin. This smoothness also means that these yarns display stitch techniques clearly and produce crisp details in color patterns. Combed yarns are usually spun with a moderate to high twist, which compresses the fibers, producing yarn that is fine and relatively dense. This imparts greater elasticity, strength, and resistence to abrasion and soil. Yarns of this type are, therefore, an excellent choice for hard-wearing, outdoor garments. Firmly spun yarns work best when knit at a fairly close stitch gauge, as they loft less than yarns spun more softly. The resulting garment will be somewhat heavier and more windproof than one worked up in a more softly spun yarn at a looser tension. Finally, long staple fibers tend to have more luster, which is enhanced by a tighter twist. This means that in addition to being strong and durable, worsted-type yarns can also be very elegant.

Carded or woolen-type yarns contain a mixture of different fiber lengths that are less well aligned and are spun with a low to moderate twist. This makes them softer, fuzzier, and less strong than the worsted-type yarns. Yarns made mainly of short staple are fuzzy and sometimes irregular in appearance and tend to be weak. Downy fibers, such as cashmere, make relatively fragile yarns; because of this, and their high cost, they are frequently blended with another fiber for reasons of both economy and strength.

More softly spun yarns have a much wider range of acceptable needle sizes that can be used, as they will loft into the stitches in a relatively loosely knit fabric or compress down into a more firmly knit one. Stitch techniques and color patterns will be somewhat blurred and less distinct, but quite satisfactory. The softer twist leaves more space between fibers, meaning these yarns tend to be somewhat warmer and cozier than the typical worsted type. Unfortunately, because of all the ends, they pill more, and sensitive individuals may find them a bit more irritating against the skin if the yarn was not made of a soft fiber. Because the fibers are short and not held as tightly in the yarn, carded, woolen-type yarns are more susceptible to abrasion and soil and are, therefore, less suitable for hard wear.

Crepe and bouclé yarns are usually quite fine, strong yarns, with a subtly textured, pebbly surface and a quiet, dull appearance. Because of the tight spin, they do not pill and tend to be more elastic. For these reasons, they have been traditionally favored for knitted dresses, suits, and blouselike sweaters that have a very nice drape and good shape retention. Wool crepe yarns are comfortable even in warm weather. As people are less accustomed to working with fine needles today, these yarns are frequently knit together with a thicker yarn to add color and texture rather than being worked alone.

Few of the novelty yarns do justice to stitch techniques, which are obscured by pronounced texture. However, these yarns are often well displayed when Purl stitches are used on the outside, as the nubs heighten the textural effect. Moderately textured yarns are excellent for beginning knitters. They conceal irregular tension and minor errors, they are usually intended to be worked up on larger needles, and the lack of any necessity for stitch pattern makes a project go quickly and with gratifying results. Mohair and angora are also worked on large needles to give them room in the stitches to fluff out as much as possible. Novelty yarns can be effective when used for bold color patterns, but not for those that are finely detailed.

There is no difference in the behavior of the S- and Z-twist yarns in hand knitting. Although it is probably somewhat more common to find knitting yarns with an S-twist, this is apparently due more to the type of equipment the mills have than to any effect it has in the knitting. There are several aspects of twist, however, that must be taken into consideration.

When knitting with any plied yarn, it is possible to add twist or remove it, depending upon the method of working. As you work, you may notice that the yarn begins to kink up on itself or, conversely, it will thicken and the plies begin to separate. In order to prevent this when you are knitting flat, turn the needle tip away from you at, say, the end of every outside row and toward you at the end of every inside row; as long as you are consistent, the yarn will remain balanced. When working in the round with an S-twist yarn, the direction of your work will add twist; with a Z-twist yarn, it will begin to unply. Periodically give the needle a few turns in the direction opposite to which you are working, or push the stitches back from the needle tips and allow the fabric to hang from the ball of yarn; it should spin itself back into balance again.

I have seen people add a great deal of twist and get into a terrible tangle when working a Stranded color pattern because they are not only knitting in the round, but have the mistaken notion that it is necessary to wrap the yarns around one another at every color change. Wrapping the yarns is only necessary in Intarsia patterns, not in Stranded patterns.

What is called "singles" yarn (one ply) is sometimes available in shops that cater to weavers. Knitters would be advised to avoid these yarns, as when used for knitting the resulting fabric can go on the bias in the direction of the yarn twist. One can, however, hold one S-twist single and one Z-twist single and knit them together as if they were a plied yarn; one will counteract the bias of the other.

Icelandic-type yarn, which is really a loosely spun single or a fine roving, could perhaps cause some bias in the fabric if it is not handled correctly as described above, but there is so little twist in it that it usually isn't a problem. Rovings are weak, however, and may come apart unless they are handled gently. Once knitted, the fabric structure helps to hold the fibers together, but these are not yarns for hard wear, and they will pill and abrade. Because of their loft, they are very warm and cozy.

There are various woven ribbons sold for knitting, usually in silk, rayon, polyester or acetate or some combination thereof. When ribbon was first introduced for knitting in the 1940s, it was sold on spools. Patterns specified that it should be drawn off and carefully

RIBBON KNIT

wrapped flat around the needle for every stitch so the ribbon lay as smoothly as possible in the fabric. A variety of stitch patterns were used, but the most common was Balanced Crossed Stitch. In order to display the sheen that is the primary desirable characteristic of these "yarns," they were worked on large needles and the fabric was carefully steam pressed flat in finishing, giving the stitches an overlapping, scaly appearance; in synthetic fabrics, the stitches could be permanently heat set. In many cases the garments were lined, and most often they were dry cleaned. A fine ribbon-knit garment is a painstaking creation with a unique and beautiful surface texture and drape. Most people today knit with ribbon as they would with any other yarn, allowing it to crumple into the stitch, and the effect is quite different.

Yarn Labels

It is worth your while to read labels carefully before you buy, but you must also learn to read them critically. As a general rule, the less a label has to say, the more questionable is the quality of the yarn. Many yarn manufacturers now provide considerably more information than was formerly the case, for which they must be commended.

The label, of course, tells us where the yarn was made and who made it. Actually, it may tell us who has designed and marketed it, but not necessarily what mill manufactured it, and one mill may sell to several different labels. The kind of fiber (or in blends, what percentage of each fiber was used) should be indicated. I have seen labels marked "cashmere/wool" on the front only to discover in small print on the back that the proportions are 80 percent wool and 20 percent cashmere. The truth has been served, but when one sees something like that, it is difficult to trust the manufacturer about any other claims they might make. If you shop at a reputable store, you will rarely encounter things like that; if you see them, complain.

Labels do not always give the knitter much information about the quality of the yarn. Fortunately, when a yarn does contain high-quality materials, the manufacturer generally wants you to know about it, as this is a good selling point with knowledgeable consumers. For instance, a label may mention that a yarn is worsted wool or combed or mercerized cotton because these are distinctive types and are more expensive to produce. A manufacturer will always draw attention to the presence of the finer and more precious fibers, such as Merino wool, lamb's wool, kid mohair, alpaca, or cashmere.

The Woolmark, a trademark of the International Wool Secretariat (see page 314) indicates that a product contains 100 percent virgin wool and has passed their "international standards of quality. . . . These tests include color fastness, fiber content and level of workmanship." In order to receive permission to use the

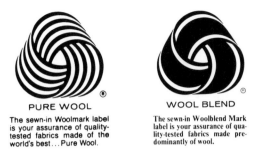

PURE WOOL
The sewn-in Woolmark label is your assurance of quality-tested fabrics made of the world's best . . . Pure Wool.

WOOL BLEND
The sewn-in Woolblend Mark label is your assurance of quality-tested fabrics made predominantly of wool.

THE WOOLMARK AND WOOLBLEND SYMBOLS

Woolmark symbol on a label, a manufacturer must submit the product to the IWS for testing. The Woolblend symbol works the same way for products that contain at least 60 percent wool. These marks protect the consumer from unlabeled substitutions and guarantee a reasonable standard of quality—meaning they are fit for the use intended. You are unlikely to find the Woolmark on a shabby knitting yarn.

A label may also point out that the fiber comes from a country with a reputation for producing excellent material. However, even those justly famed for mohair, silk, or wool, for example, also produce poorer grades of these fibers, which may find their way into the knitting yarns you purchase. Some labels, for example, trumpet that the yarn contains "pure virgin wool," however, this only means the wool is new, not that it is soft or of a high quality.

Unfortunately, price is not an accurate measure of the quality of a yarn either. A high price may instead indicate a high-fashion novelty or designer yarn, a large advertising budget, a fancy store in a high-rent neighborhood, or an import, but the quality of the yarn itself may be average or poor. Your only assurance of quality, therefore, is the reputation of the yarn manufacturer, the store you patronize, and your own experience with both. Ask questions and use your hands to confirm the label's claim; you are the ultimate arbiter of whether or not the yarn is appropriate for what you want to make.

On the back of the label, you will often find suggested needle sizes and sometimes the average number of stitches per inch to expect in Stockinette. Unfortunately, this latter information is problematic, for several reasons. First, American manufacturers suggest needle sizes that produce a much looser fabric than is customary in Europe, so you must take into consideration where the yarn is from and guess what sort of fabric they had in mind. Second, you must decide whether the needle sizes given are British, European, or American (see the chart on page 336). And finally, you may not be able to produce that gauge with the needle size suggested or you may not be working in Stockinette, in which case the information is irrelevant.

The labels will also have a color number and, most often, a dye-lot number. On some wools only the color

INTERNATIONAL CARE SYMBOLS

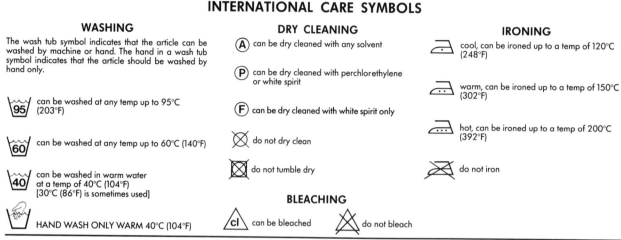

WASHING

The wash tub symbol indicates that the article can be washed by machine or hand. The hand in a wash tub symbol indicates that the article should be washed by hand only.

95 — can be washed at any temp up to 95°C (203°F)

60 — can be washed at any temp up to 60°C (140°F)

40 — can be washed in warm water at a temp of 40°C (104°F) [30°C (86°F) is sometimes used]

HAND WASH ONLY WARM 40°C (104°F)

DRY CLEANING

(A) can be dry cleaned with any solvent

(P) can be dry cleaned with perchlorethylene or white spirit

(F) can be dry cleaned with white spirit only

do not dry clean

do not tumble dry

BLEACHING

Cl can be bleached

do not bleach

IRONING

cool, can be ironed up to a temp of 120°C (248°F)

warm, can be ironed up to a temp of 150°C (302°F)

hot, can be ironed up to a temp of 200°C (392°F)

do not iron

CARE SYMBOLS

number, or perhaps just a name, will be present if the yarn is not dyed and the color range is supplied by the animal who grew the fiber. The color number is most useful when you are mail-ordering or when you must discuss the yarn with the store or the manufacturer.

The dye-lot number is essential. It designates all the yarn dyed at the same time and, therefore, guarantees that the color of each ball of yarn bearing that number will match all other balls similarly labeled. It is very important that you use yarn all of the same dye lot for any solid-color project. The differences between one dye lot and another will generally not be apparent to the eye when looking at the balls of yarn, but will be obvious once the two yarns are worked up side by side in the fabric. For this reason you must check the label on every ball you want to purchase to make sure the dye lot numbers match. Be especially careful if labels are missing or have come off, particularly if more than one dye lot is present in the store's stock, as you have no way of knowing at that point what you are dealing with. Ask the shopkeeper for a fresh supply from a box in storage if you have any doubt. If you are dealing with a multi-colored pattern, dye lot is not critical as long as yarns of the same color but different lots are always well separated by other colors.

Finally, a good label will indicate the care requirements and whether the yarn is colorfast. This information may be written out or provided in the form of a set of internationally recognized symbols. In addition to the symbols, some labels will provide detailed information on how to clean a garment knitted with that yarn. Further, wool labels will indicate if the yarn has been moth-proofed (if it has not been, you might want to ask your dry cleaner to mothproof the finished garment). If the wool is labeled washable or "Superwash" (see page 314), it has been treated to prevent shrinkage during laundering; these yarns can be machine washed and dried.

Many manufacturers suggest the most conservative approach to cleaning a garment knitted of their yarn because they want to avoid dealing with complaints that arise out of mishandling. If you understand the nature of the fiber you are dealing with and how it should be handled, you may want to override the instructions; see page 387 for my recommendations on the subject, and do test whatever method you wish to use on a sample swatch.

Weight and Yardage

Yarn is sold by weight. Most European yarns are sold in 50-gram balls (1¾ ounces), while American yarns are usually 2 ounces (56.7 grams), but there is considerable variation; skeined yarn is almost always sold in larger quantities. This system is most unfortunate, as what a knitter really needs to buy is yardage. It is not how much the yarn weighs that counts, but how much of it is taken up by each stitch and how many stitches it takes to make the garment. Furthermore, there is no really accurate way to calculate the amount of yarn to buy based on weight, while the method based on yardage is very precise (see page 428). This discrepancy between how the yarn is sold and what the knitter requires has led to a great deal of guessing and frustration when it comes to purchasing yarn.

I have seen various charts that suggest so many ounces for a man's sweater, so many for a woman's, etc. Given the number of yarns on the market today and the wide variety of garment styles, these approaches are quite obsolete and were only suitable when people worked repeatedly with the same yarn and garment styles time after time. Two yarns of the same fiber and weight may have different yardages due to the way they were spun. Conversely, different fibers may have the same yardage but considerably different weights due to their inherent density; for example, cotton fibers weigh more than wool fibers. Finally, every stitch pattern absorbs a different amount of yarn.

Instructors may suggest that you weigh an existing sweater similar to the one you want to make to determine how much yarn to purchase. Aside from the problems discussed above, this might work reasonably well for synthetic fibers, but natural fibers respond to humidity changes in their environment, and as they take in or give off moisture, the weight may vary. This is particularly true of wool, which is often manufactured under controlled humidity (meaning the weight on the label is only really accurate while the yarn is at the mill). The weight of a wool garment can change by as much as 30 percent. Weigh it on a dry day and you will think you need twenty ounces of yarn to make a garment like it; weigh it on a damp day and it will tell you to buy twenty-six ounces. Therefore, the only time you can use weight as a guide to how much yarn to buy is when the second garment will be identical to the first; not just also in wool, but made in the same size, stitch pattern, and brand of wool.

Most yarn labels show both the weight and the length of yarn in each ball, sometimes in both grams/meters and ounces/yards, and this is much appreciated. However, it would be far better for knitters if the manufacturers would package and sell yarn by standard lengths and let the weights come out willy-nilly instead of the other way around. I would much rather deal with balls of yarn that are 100 yards, 200 yards, 300 yards, and so forth, than some at 168 and some at 223! Having yarn packaged in even-number yard or meter lengths would not only make yarn requirement calculations easier for designers, it would make it much easier for the average knitter to substitute one yarn for another in a pattern and vastly simplify price comparisons for all concerned. (It would also be much appreciated if each ball contained more yardage so we had fewer ends to deal with.)

Yarn Substitution

If you want to substitute one yarn for another in a commercial pattern, it is important that you select an alternate yarn of the same fiber and type. In other words, substitute neither a worsted for a woolen nor a cotton for an acrylic. The most accurate way of comparing two yarns for this purpose is to use the relationship between the weight and yardage.

One woolen yarn, for instance, spun so as to produce 160 yards per 50-gram ball, will be thinner than another woolen spun so as to produce only 120 yards per 50-gram ball; the same amount of fiber didn't go as far because the yarn was fatter. When there is more than a 20 percent difference in the yardage for two balls of the same weight, the yarns will take up into the fabric differently; a substitution of that sort is not wise. Ideally, the two figures should be the same.

There is greater difficulty for the consumer in comparing two yarns that are sold with differnt weights. In this case, divide the yardage by the weight for both balls. It does not matter if you divide grams into yards or ounces into yards, as long as you calculate both yarns the same way. This will give you decimal numbers something like 3.2 and 2.4. If these ratios differ for the two balls by more than .5, select another yarn.

To find the amount of yarn to purchase, calculate the total yardage the pattern calls for by multiplying yards per ball by the number of balls required (it would be helpful if the patterns provided this figure). Then divide the total yardage by the number of yards per ball in the alternate yarn to find the number of balls of yarn to purchase. Buy an extra just in case. If the yardage is not indicated on the yarn, ask the shopkeeper; frequently the information is available on the yarn sample cards shopkeepers receive from the manufacturer for ordering purposes.

You may find yourself in the situation of trying to substitute one yarn that is available to you for another you know only by its description in a pattern book. If the book does not provide yardage figures for the yarn suggested, your best guide to finding an appropriate substitute is to use the stitch gauge the pattern calls for. Find a yarn you think will produce a comparable gauge, buy one ball, and try it out.

Yarn Names and Sizes

Manufacturers and pattern magazines frequently use a variety of traditional terms when referring to a size or type of knitting yarn. Unfortunately, few of these terms reveal anything useful to the uninitiated, and some of them are quaint or obsolete; rarely are they very descriptive of the real characteristics of the yarns.

Fingering is a fine yarn used today only for gloves, mittens, stockings, and baby clothes, but previously it was used for any sort of light garment; it may be a woolen or a worsted-type yarn. The term "worsted weight" is often used to mean a medium yarn, but as you know, worsted really means a particular type of wool yarn and not a yarn size. What Americans call "sport" yarn is somewhat thicker than fingering and is roughly equivalent to what the British refer to as "jumper-weight" (by which they mean sweater-weight). It comes in two- and three-ply versions that are either firmly or softly spun. What the British call "double-knitting" yarn is roughly equivalent to what Americans call "Germantown," a medium-thick, somewhat softly spun worsted.

"Shetland" has come to be a generic term for yarns that resemble in some way the traditional yarn of Shetland and usually means a heather blend rather than a yarn size. Traditional Shetland was once a fine, somewhat hairy two-ply worsted yarn made of the wool of the native sheep, a distinct breed. It is now made, even there, in a variety of thicknesses much like other jumper-weight yarns. You may also come across the term "fisherman" or "Aran" used to refer to a medium-thick yarn typically used for the Aran sweater style. Both "bulky" and "chunky" are used when referring to thick yarns intended for large needles. The custom of dealing in yarn by weight is the source for referring to yarn as "heavy" or "light" when what is really meant is that the yarn is thick or thin.

All of these different names and others like them simply confuse the issue. Fortunately, more manufacturers, shops, and pattern magazines are referring to the various yarn sizes simply as "very fine," "fine," "medium," "bulky," and "extra bulky," which are far more appropriate. It would, however, also be useful if these very general terms could be combined with others that would indicate the amount of texture the yarn had, such as "classic" or "smooth" for the traditional smooth yarns, "soft-spun" for a loosely spun yarn, "novelty" for one that has a different ply or is irregular in some way, "textured" or "fleecy" for one that is hairy, etc. A yarn might then be described as "medium/smooth worsted" or "fine/soft-spun combed cotton," for instance. This would be particularly helpful for those who are mail-ordering yarn and for when it is necessary to substitute a yarn for that called for in a commercial pattern.

Windings

Yarn is sold wound into many different configurations, and you may find it useful to know the various names and how to put yarn into whatever form you find convenient.

A "skein" or "hank" refers to yarn wound into a coil or large circle. In order to keep the strands from tangling, the skein is tied, folded in half, then twisted, and the free ends are pulled through the folded end to secure the bundle. It is up to the knitter to wind the yarn out of the skein into a ball to work from. You can hang the skein on a hook, a chair back, or an umbrella swift, or even sling it over your chest like the ribbon for a general's medals and knit directly from the skein. You cannot, however, draw the yarn out of a skein as simply, easily, and quickly as you can draw the yarn out of a ball, and you risk tangles; unloop the yarn from the skein rather than pull it out.

A ball of yarn is just what it suggests—nice, round, and baseball sized, and suggestive of home because manufacturers do not wind yarn into this form; the shape presents packaging problems and the balls don't stay put in the store. If you are working with balled yarn, it is best to put it in a basket or bag as you work, because it won't stay put for you either. Winding a ball of yarn is a simple, peaceful procedure, to be valued as an opportunity for daydreaming or conversation, depending upon whether you are alone or have help. There is something to be said for prolonging the opera-

WINDING YARN FROM SKEIN INTO BALL

tion, therefore, but for those of us who are always in a hurry, manual yarn-winding devices do the same job in minutes (see page 340).

To wind by hand, place the skein on an umbrella swift (page 340), the back of a chair, or the outstretched arms of a friend. First make a fat Yarn Butterfly (page 125), take it off your fingers, fold it in half, and begin winding the yarn over the butterfly, your thumb and two or three fingers. Having your fingers in there as you wrap guarantees that you will not make the ball too tight. Every few wraps, withdraw your fingers, rotate the growing ball to distribute the yarn evenly and let your fingers get caught up again; each new wrap should go in a different place.

The most important thing is not to wind the ball tightly. In a tightly wound ball, the yarn is at tension and will stretch out. Left in that state for a long time it may permanently lose its resilience. If not too much time has elapsed, stretched fibers will recover somewhat when washed and shrink back to nearly normal condition, the degree varying from fiber to fiber. When this occurs, it will affect the fabric you make and must be taken into consideration in planning. As you know, it is important to wash your tension sample before calculating the gauge (see page 418). When you wash a sample knit up with stretched yarn, as it recovers the stitches will become smaller and the fabric firmer. You may find that it needs to be worked on a larger-size needle than you expected. To avoid these problems, wind yarn so the ball is squeezably soft; keep checking on it as you work. If you have yarn that was too tightly balled and left for any length of time, it is best to return it to skein form and wash it and then rewind it gently before use.

If you want to wind yarn into a skein, you must use a niddy-noddy (page 340) or an umbrella swift, a pair of chair backs, or a friend's outstretched arms. You might have occasion to do this when you want to recycle yarn (see below).

The manufacturers have several other forms they

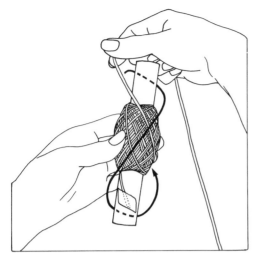

WINDING A CENTER-PULL SKEIN

prefer to the homemade ball. One is a center-pull skein. These are not really skeins at all (but then no more are the other forms they use balls, although they are referred to as such). The yarn is wound into a cylindrical shape anywhere from four to twelve inches in length, depending on how fine the yarn is and how smoothly the skein is wound, with a label passing around the middle. Both ends of the yarn are accessible, but it is easiest to draw the yarn out of the center of the skein, as this way it will not tumble around as you knit.

To wind a center-pull skein by hand, use a rod of some sort like a pencil or a dowel. Secure the end of the yarn to one end of the rod with a bit of tape, then wrap a core of yarn around the center of the rod to get started and begin winding in a figure eight—across to the left and under, back across the top to the right and under. As you wind, walk the fingers holding the rod over the wound yarn to gradually rotate it. When the yarn is completely wound, release the first end and pull the rod out. If you use a relatively thick rod, the ball will soften down a bit when it is withdrawn—good insurance against winding too tightly.

Manufacturers also wind yarn in a center-pull ball, a smaller, rounder version of the center-pull skein and used in the same way. When the yarn wound in this way is very soft and delicate, the label passes through the center of the ball, which may collapse down almost into a doughnut shape. More substantial yarns will stand up on their own a bit and take on more of a real ball shape. When the yarn is smooth and firm, such as a cotton or linen, it may be wound on a cardboard core and the label will pass around the outside; in this case, the yarn can only be drawn from the outside.

The center-pull ball is the form the home manual yarn winder will produce. The easiest way to work when using this device is to draw the yarn off an umbrella swift, but here again a chair back or a friend's arms will do quite nicely. If you use the yarn winder to draw the yarn off directly, the forces necessary to spin

the swift place tension on the yarn and the ball will be much too tight. It is far better if you alternately draw a supply of yarn off the skein and then wind, allowing the yarn to slip through your hand to provide an even, more gentle tension. You can also wind a center-pull ball by hand by keeping the first end free as you wind in the usual way.

Finally, yarn may be sold wound on a cone. This is the form preferred by machine knitters, for whom a long continuous length of yarn that feeds without interruption is important. The cones are, of course, not very portable, a quality hand knitters appreciate in their yarns. However, if you are knitting at home, there is no reason not to work with coned yarns. The coned form does not wander away, the yarn feeds easily and always stays neat to the last yard, and because it is continuous you will have fewer ends to hide in finishing. Most coned yarns are relatively fine, as this is what machine knitters prefer, and are usually sold mail-order in large quantities by weight. There are some knitting stores that carry coned yarns, but they are not generally available to hand knitters.

Recycling Yarn

During World War II, commodities of all kinds were scarce. People were encouraged to make their own clothing to aid the war effort, or did so out of necessity. While yarn was more available than ready-to-wear sweaters, it was still scarce and costly, and knitting instruction books contained information on how to recycle yarn from worn, outgrown, or out-of-style garments. This is undoubtedly a very old practice, as throughout most of human history textiles were precious things, not the casual disposables we have today.

While economic constraints may still encourage some knitters to go to the trouble of recycling an entire garment, and you might be tempted to recycle a well-loved yarn from an unfashionable garment, more often than not it is done today because of a serious error, or because a project did not work out satisfactorily and was abandoned halfway through. In a situation of this sort, it may be that the dye lot needed or the yarn itself is no longer available, and unless you recycle the used yarn, even the unused portion may be a loss.

If you are recycling the yarn from a finished garment, take the garment apart in a sequence opposite to the manner in which it was put together. First you must rip out any fabric worked on picked-up stitches such as neckline ribbing and center front borders, and then undo all seams. (Here is where a garment worked in the round with sleeves knit from shoulder down has a definite advantage.) Use a tapestry needle to find the yarn ends and assist in pulling out the seams; cut the yarn off from time to time to keep it short. Once the garment sections are separated, begin to unravel (see page 355).

Yarn that has been knit up into a fabric for any length of time needs to be washed before it is reused. This is done to help remove any stretching that occurred during knitting or wear, to restore resilience and loft, and to remove the kinks so it will knit up again smoothly. Because the yarn needs to be skeined for washing, you might want to wind it directly into that form as you unravel. Either enlist the help of a friend (the one with the outstretched arms) or seat yourself next to your umbrella swift, and as you pull the yarn out of the fabric, wind it onto the swift. If you find it easier, you can unravel the yarn with your yarn winder, then skein it out of the ball onto the swift.

Tie the skein in two places and wash it as you would a knitted garment. If you have several, do a few at a time so they are not crowded in the basin. Wash cotton or linen in hot water to help remove any stretch; wool, of course, should be washed in tepid water. Hang the wet skeins in the shower or over the bathtub to drain. It is a good idea to shift each skein on its hanger from time to time as it dries so it doesn't get a crimp in one spot.

If washing does not remove the kinks from the yarn, and frequently it does not, there are two approaches to take. You can weight the wet skein, removing the weight when the yarn is just damp dry to let it recover from being stretched. Alternatively, you can steam and stretch the skein after it has dried. This is easy to do with any vegetable fiber and works well with wool, but you must handle it very carefully. Tie one side of the skein to the ironing board. Pull the skein gently in the opposite direction, just enough to remove the kinks, and apply copious steam until you see the kinks relax. Hold the skein at steady tension until it dries. (Do not continue to steam wool after you release the tension; the molecular changes that occur under these conditions may actually cause the wool to shrink.) You do not have to worry about cotton or linen as you do this because they do not shrink (see pages 318 and 319).

When the yarn is dry, wind it into balls and knit it up again. If only a portion of your yarn supply has been recycled, try to use the recycled yarn for ribbings or for separate sections like the sleeves. If you work new and recycled yarn side by side in the same fabric section, you may see a difference, particularly in delicate, softly spun, or highly textured yarns such as mohair, because there will be some inevitable loss of fiber during ripping.

CONVERSION CHARTS

Here are some numbers you may find useful:

MULTIPLY BY	TO CONVERT	TO		
2.54	inches	centimeters	0.3937	1 yard = 0.91 meter
30.48	feet	centimeters	0.0328	1 meter = 1.09 yards
0.9144	yards	meters	0.000621	2 ounces = 56.7 grams
6.452	sq. inches	sq. centimeters	0.155	50 grams = 1.75 ounces
28.35	ounces	grams	0.0352	1 inch = 2.54 centimeters
0.4536	pounds	kilograms	2.2045	2 centimeters = 0.79 inches
	TO FIND	MULTIPLY	BY	5 centimeters = 1.97 inches

YARN BALL TYPES

Tools

Every craft needs its tools and needs them to be efficient in a way that not only gives good results but eases the work. The process of knitting makes few demands, really no more than needles and a supply of yarn. The needles, well cared for, can last a lifetime, yet are very inexpensive. In addition to needles, of course, there are a variety of other tools that are convenient in one way or another, but none of them, except for the needles, are essential. Nevertheless, these gadgets are fun and useful and will be discussed in turn.

Knitting Needles

When you think about it, a knitting needle is a marvel of efficiency, an old and simple tool that is still perfectly suited to its task. Oh, there have been improvements over the centuries, needles that are stronger, rustproof, lighter in weight, more precisely sized, and so on, but it would be difficult to imagine any improvement on the concept.

What is wanted from a knitting needle? Ideally, it should be light in weight to prevent fatigue, strong enough to resist bending out of shape, and with a well-tapered tip that inserts into the stitches easily but not so pointed that it will split the yarn. It should be polished to a very fine smoothness so it offers no resistance to the yarn, yet its surface should not reflect light, as this can tire the eyes. The material of which it is made should resist the abrasion of one needle rubbing against the other. And finally, while needles of any dimension are useful, it is generally best to have a set of needles in precisely calibrated circumferences in order to achieve the gauge you want.

Types of Needles

Needles come in three basic forms: single-point, double-point, and circular. All will do the job, and to a great extent the choice among them rests entirely with personal preference. However, a critical look reveals certain advantages or disadvantages to using one or the other for certain types of work, and most knitters have collections containing all three types.

Single-Points: The most basic needles today are the single-points, straight needles used for flat knitting that were first developed in the nineteenth century. These have a point at one end and a cap at the other to prevent the stitches from slipping off. They are sold in pairs, in

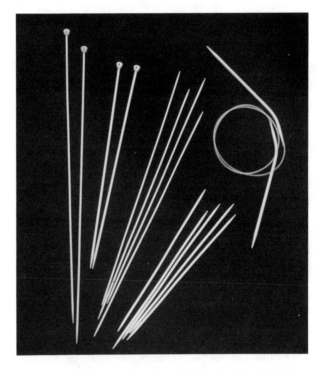

KNITTING NEEDLES/SINGLE POINT, DOUBLE POINT AND CIRCULAR

a full range of sizes and usually in ten- and fourteen-inch lengths; although I have seen shorter ones, they are not commonly available. Single-point needles became popular with the advent of amateur knitting and the more complex garments styled to meet the demands of fashion that are easier to shape in flat sections. Single-points serve this purpose well but for one minor flaw.

When knitting on fourteen-inch straight needles, any slight manipulation of the point causes the capped end of the needle to move in a rather wide arc. This often-unnoticed larger motion causes great fatigue as the knitter repeatedly lifts and lowers the weight of the fabric hanging from the needle in order to make each stitch. Because of this I do not recommend these needles at all. The job they were designed to do can be much more easily accomplished with a circular needle; the weight of the fabric will be distributed evenly around the center cable, and no wider motion created (see below). If you knit for a while on a long straight needle and then switch to a circular, you will immediately feel the difference, and once you are aware of it, I am sure you will never go back to the straight ones.

There is a new version of the long straight needle on the market. The tip is the correct diameter for the size, but the shaft is narrower to facilitate moving the stitches along the needle. It is a good idea, as far as it goes, but does not solve the problem inherent to the length of these needles, as discussed above.

Short single-point needles are another story, because as the needle grows shorter the movement of the head diminishes and ceases to be a problem. These needles are just right for making narrow widths, such as scarves, and for gauge samples, the latter being what I use them for the most. I want to point out, however, that even though needles produced by different manufacturers may be marked with the same sizes, there can be slight but important differences in their actual diameters (see chart page 336). In addition, using needles made of different materials can change the tension with which you knit. Therefore, if you plan to knit your gauge sample on a short straight needle and the garment on a circular needle, use the same brand for both.

The Circular Needle: The circular needle, called "twin pins" in Britain, consists of two needle tips joined by a length of fine nylon cable. These are also sold in a full range of sizes and in sixteen-, twenty-four-, twenty-nine-, and thirty-six-inch lengths, and can be used for either flat or circular knitting. Since their invention shortly after World War I, they have supplanted double-point needles (see below) for all but small items that must be worked in the round, and they are gradually replacing the long single-points for flat knitting as well.

Circular needles are really quite wonderful. Because the work is drawn into a circle, the weight of the fabric is supported in the lap, relieving you of its weight and cutting down on fatigue. Further, the needle tip narrows as it moves toward the cable and the cable is narrower still, which encourages the stitches to move along as you work; this, too, reduces fatigue and speeds things along. When you are not knitting, the fabric can be pushed back from the tips onto the cable, which then acts as a stitch holder. A circular needle is lightweight and flexible, and it is, of course, impossible to lose a needle, as you have only one to worry about and that is always engaged. You can nicely fit into even the narrowest chair (read airline seat) and still manage to knit, and you create a far less threatening picture to anyone sitting nearby who, should you be using long straight needles, might worry about getting poked.

The choice of which length to use depends on what you are working on. For flat knitting you can knit the smallest item on even a thirty-six-inch circular needle should that be all you have, but the twenty-four-inch length is optimum, and it will comfortably hold flat fabric sections even for a large man's garment. For knitting in the round, the fabric circumference must be about two inches larger than the length of the circular needle. You can, therefore, think of the four lengths available as appropriate for, respectively, children's,

young adult's, women's, and men's sizes. However, the twenty-nine-inch length will also accommodate the usual men's sizes, so there is no real need to invest in the thirty-six-inch length. That length is useful, however, for doing knitted throws and blankets. The sixteen-inch length is somewhat problematic, as there is so little of the tip that it is difficult to gain a purchase for your hands, but some people prefer them to working on a set of double-points, which must otherwise be used for circumferences smaller than eighteen inches (see below).

The hybrid "jumper" needles are circular needles cut in half with stops put on the ends of the cables; in other words, they are two separate single-point needles with metal tips and cables instead of shafts. They apparently were intended to provide some of the benefits of circular needles for those who prefer straight ones for knitting. They are lighter weight and do eliminate the problem caused by the motion of the long straight needles. Unfortunately, the cable ends can flip about disconcertingly; they always seem to be jumping off in some unexpected direction when you move the work (perhaps that is where they acquired their name). They really don't present enough advantages to compete with a circular needle.

Double-Points: The oldest form of needles are the straight double-points, originally used for all knitting, now reserved for small items knit in the round. They are, as the name reveals, pointed at both ends and are sold in sets of four or five, in a full range of sizes, usually

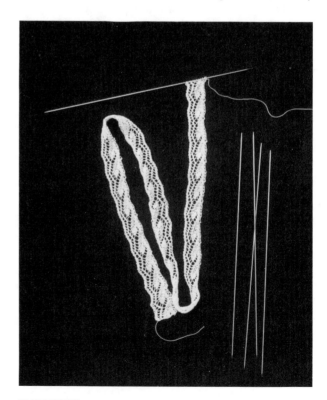

LACE NEEDLES

ten to twelve inches in length, which is adequate for the socks and mittens for which they are generally used today. The double-points still used in Shetland are up to sixteen inches long. Those sold for lace work are shorter and very fine, less than two millimeters in diameter and six to eight inches long.

Double-point needles can be used to knit any size garment, flat or circular. The knitters of Shetland frequently work in the round with just three needles, two for the stitches and one to work with, and so prefer long needles, as two must be adequate to hold an entire sweater. That seems to be a unique approach; it is the custom most other places to use four or five, although any number may be employed in order to coordinate the length of the needles and the fabric circumference required. For flat knitting, tip protectors can be used to convert them to single-points. The most comfortable and efficient method of working with double-points is to use a knitting belt (see below).

Needle Materials

The original knitting needles were made of whatever materials lay at hand, generally bone, ivory, or wood. Beautifully crafted needles in smooth, hard woods are still made, and many people prefer them for their quiet performance and aesthetic satisfaction. Bamboo needles have long been used in Asia and are now commonly found in the United States and Europe. Attractive in the same way wooden needles are, bamboo is also light-weight and has great tensile strength.

For all of their attractiveness, however, there are problems with wooden or bamboo needles. While bamboo is very light in weight, some of the wooden needles can be heavy. More important is the fact that these materials, no matter how highly polished they seem, create friction with the yarn. Some are varnished to give a smoother surface, but this can wear off; the better bamboo needles are impregnated with a resin rather than just coated. Because of the friction, it can be tiring to work with these needles, particularly if you knit tightly. If you doubt me, do a test: knit for ten or fifteen minutes with the wood or bamboo needle and then switch to a metal one and note the ease with which the needles move along the shaft; it is surprising how much effort that constant motion can add up to in the course of even an hour's work. If, however, you generally work at a very loose tension or you are using a slippery yarn, a needle that holds on to the stitches somewhat can prove an advantage.

Many people like plastic needles for their quiet, warm feel and for their economy; I have heard knitters with arthritis say that they appreciate them for their light weight (although they should be well served by knitting on circular needles instead of straight needles, as that makes the most difference in terms of weight). There are two kinds of plastic used. The older, more expensive type of plastic, called "rhodolite" or "celluloid," is hard and durable and frequently has a marbled appearance that is quite attractive. There are needles imported from Europe made in this type of plastic that are stiffened with a metal core to prevent them from being deformed. They have a rather nice heft and warm feel to them, and they are very quiet to knit with, although the tips are somewhat rounded, making them more difficult to insert into a stitch, particularly for those who knit tightly.

The nylon needles commonly sold in the United States are featherweight and very flexible; actually, whenever I have used them, which is not often, I kept thinking of spaghetti. They seem fine for simple knitting at average or loose tension, but with a firmer tension or complex stitch techniques, I find the tip is just too limp to do its job. The circular versions do have the advantage of being in a single continuous length, eliminating the sometimes problematic join between the needle tip and the cable (see below).

The most common metal used for needles today is aluminum, as it is inexpensive, lightweight (even in the larger-size needles often used today), and reasonably strong. In order to reduce glare, they are anodized or coated; the American needles usually come in various colors, the European ones in a neutral gray. These coatings will wear off the tips with time, but this does not affect the performance of the needles.

The older style double-point needles used in Europe and Britain are made of nickel-plated steel, which is stronger and somewhat heavier, but as they are only done in relatively small sizes, the weight is inconsequential. These needles are smooth, with a good point on the tips, making them fast and effortless to knit with. Fine-steel lace needles are uncoated and must be protected from rust; they are only available in sizes of 2mm or less (American sizes 0 to 0000).[3]

Finally, there are some chrome needles on the market, the shafts of which are coated with brightly colored paint. On the whole these are excellent needles, very smooth and strong with a good point. However, the highly reflective surface of the tip can strain the eyes, and the painted coating adds a subtle dimension to the needles that restricts the smooth movement of the stitches, particularly for those who knit tightly. If you have some of these needles I strongly suggest you remove the paints with nail polish remover (protect the caps as you do so—it will melt the plastic), and work in indirect light to cut down on glare.

Circular needles are made in all of the above mate-

---

3. According to the Bishop of Leicester in his book *The History of Handknitting,* the development of the technology for drawing steel wire, which occurred during the Renaissance, was a very important factor in the spread of knitting after that time, as it made the essential tools cheaper and more readily available.

rials, including bamboo but not wood. Some of them have straight tips, while others have a slight bend in the shaft between the tip and the cable. Aside from all the considerations listed above regarding what makes for a good needle, with the circular needle it is critical that the join between the needle shaft and the cable be both smooth, so the stitches don't snag as they are brought up from cable to tip, and strong, so the tip doesn't separate from the cable. Most contemporary needle manufacturers have solved these problems, and they are excellent tools to work with. Plastic circular needles are made of a continuous length of extruded nylon, so no join exists.

There are sets of circular needles on the market that contain separate needle tips that can be screwed onto cables of various lengths, allowing you to create any combination of needle size and length you require. The initial investment is a rather serious one; however, the sets are compact and come in a storage case, which makes them nice for traveling. Unfortunately, there are quite a few little pieces that can get lost, the smaller-size needles are not included, and I have heard it said that

the join between needle and cable is not as smooth as it should be; I have not worked with these.

Comparative Needle Sizes

There are three different methods of sizing needles, the metric system used in Europe, the British system, and the American system, each using a series of numbers (and often diameters) that has no relation to the others. Increasingly, British and European needles sold on the American market have the American size on the needle and both that size and the metric equivalent on the package.

Unfortunately, there are still idiosyncracies, and a needle made by one manufacturer may be a slightly different metric dimension than one made by another, even though they bear the same size number, as you can see in the accompanying chart. For this reason, it is important that you use the same brand needles for every aspect of a given project in order to maintain a consistent gauge. Having some discrepancies between the sizes of one manufacturer and another does give you a way of subtly adjusting gauge, as the size increments between two different brands are sometimes smaller than within the same brand. For instance, if you were to find a 3.25 produced too tight a gauge and a 3.5 a bit too loose, there is that odd 3.3 to work with. (The needles checked were Bernat/Aero, Boye, Clover, Inox, Leisure Arts, and Phildar.)

Other Tools

There are a miscellany of other small tools that are useful for the knitter to own. They represent a minor investment compared to that involved in acquiring a good range of needle sizes and types, and while none of them are essential, most are useful; at the very least, you will want to know which of the array you will see displayed at the shops are really worth having.

Needle Size Gauge

If you work frequently with sets of double-point needles or circular needles, a needle size gauge is an essential tool. Straight needles generally have the size marked on the caps, so there can be no doubt about what they are, but double-points or circular needles are not marked, and once out of the package you cannot be sure what size a needle is unless you measure it with the gauge. You should get in the habit of checking the size every time you start a new project. Not only might you inadvertently store a needle in the wrong package and thereby mistake the size, but you might have the unhappy experience, as I did, of purchasing a needle in the wrong size package (I confess it took me altogether too long to figure out why my garment was turning out larger than expected).

The gauges are made of metal, are usually rectangular or circular in shape, and contain holes marked

Needle Sizes
(All Bernat/Aero and Clover except noted)

Metric	American	British
1.25	0000	16
1.50	000	15
1.75	00	14
2	0	
2.25	1	13
2.3	1 [1]	
2.75	2	12
2.8	2 [1]	
3		11
3.125	3 [4]	
3.25	3	10
3.3	3 [1]	
3.5	4	
3.75	5	9
3.8	5 [1]	
4	6 [2]	8
4.25	6	
4.5	7	7
5	8	6
5.25	9 [4]	
5.5	9	5
5.75	10 [4]	
6	10	4
6.5	10.5	3
7	10.5 [3]	2
7.5		1
8	11	0
9	13	00
10	15	000

[1] Leisure Arts   [2] Inox   [3] Phildar   [4] Boye

with the various sizes in which you can measure your needles.

Tip Protectors

If you are working with straight needles, it is very helpful to use tip protectors, small rubber caps that fit on the needle tips and prevent the stitches from falling off when you store your work away. This is particularly important when the width of the fabric is large in relation to the length of the needle. You can, of course, use rubber bands, wrapping one tightly around each needle tip, but don't plan to use them for any length of time, as they can deteriorate and stain the needle or the stitches.

Knitting Belt or Stick

The nineteenth-century English production knitters are probably responsible for the development of the fastest,

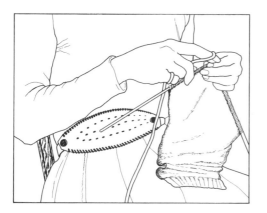

KNITTING BELT

most efficient, and least fatiguing method of knitting, in which the yarn is carried on the right forefinger and the right needle is held by a knitting belt or stick. These latter devices are rarely seen today, although they are still commonly used in Shetland.

The knitting belt is a leather pouch stuffed with horsehair, pierced with holes and attached to a belt. One dons the belt, placing the pouch at the right waist or hip, inserts one tip of a double-point needle into a hole in the pouch and begins to knit. The pouch holds the needle in any convenient position, depending upon the hole selected and the angle at which one pushes the needle into the horsehair. There is no need whatsoever for the right hand to support the weight of the needle or growing fabric, and this frees the right forefinger to act solely as a shuttle, cutting down on fatigue and speeding the work.

The knitting stick acts on the same principle. The stick has a hole in one end for the needle, and the shaft can be inserted into a belt or the waist of one's skirt or pants. The sticks were often charmingly carved and quite attractive but had the disadvantage of accepting only one size needle or at best a very narrow range of sizes. Since they were typically used by knitters who always worked with the same needles and yarn, and made the same style garments time after time, this was no disadvantage to them but limits the concept today. The knitting belt is far more versatile, although it, too, has the contemporary disadvantage of accepting only double-point needles in a relatively fine and narrow range of sizes, about 2 to 3.5 mm or smaller.

Knitters familiar with the concept but lacking a knitting belt or a lovingly carved knitting stick used various

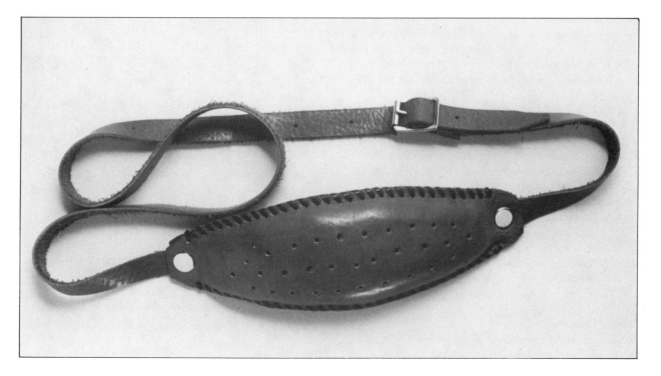

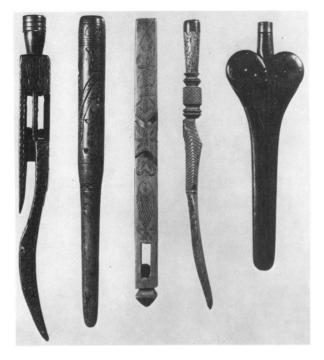

KNITTING STICKS

other devices to accomplish the same task. One of the more charming of these substitutions was a bunch of feathers bound tightly together like a feather duster and tied to the waist, feathers to the rear and quills to the fore, with the knitting needle stuck securely into the quills.

Cable Stitch Holders

In order to work a cable stitch pattern of any kind, it is necessary to have a cable stitch holder, a very small double-point needle used to hold the stitches as they are transferred to their new position. The holders generally come in three sizes, for fine, medium, and heavy-weight yarns, and there are three different designs on the market.

One is a tiny straight needle about three inches in length. The second is the same except it has a dip in the center where the stitches can ride; this helps to keep the stitches from coming off the holder as you work the others off the main needle. You can take the stitches from needle to holder on the left tip, then either knit the stitches directly off the right tip of the holder or return them from the left tip to the left needle for knitting. The third type is bent something like a fish hook, with one tip shorter than the other; these hold the stitches more securely than the type with the dip in the center. The stitches are taken from needle to holder and back again with the short tip or knit directly off the longer tip.

Crochet Hooks

The short, hooked needles used for crochet are also of use to knitters, primarily for finishing exposed edges

with various decorative borders. There are also methods of casting on, casting off, and sewing up which employ a crochet hook, discussed elsewhere in the pertinent sections. The hooks are sold in attractively cased sets, or you may buy just the sizes you think you will use most often. They are available in aluminum and steel, the former lighter in weight, the latter smoother and favored for fine yarns.

Sewing Needles

In order to finish your project, you will need a yarn sewing needle. These are used for sewing up seams in flat knitting, for hiding ends, and for grafting.

This type of needle is often called a "yarn" or "tapestry" needle, being the same as that used for needlepoint. It is about two inches long and has a blunt tip and an eye large enough to accommodate yarn. I have also come across one that has a slightly flattened, bent tip that helps to scoop up a strand or lift a stitch off a needle, and which I think works very well. There are plastic versions, usually with a ball point, the reason for which totally escapes me; I find them annoying to use.

Unfortunately, it is harder to find smaller needles suitable for work with fine yarns and needle sizes; although they are available, you may have to search a bit to find them. If your knitting store does not carry any, you can usually find one in a package of mixed-purpose sewing needles at a fabric store, or you can buy a petit-point needle at a shop that specializes in needlepoint supplies.

By the way, do not attempt to thread the end of the yarn through the needle eye. Instead, fold the yarn end over the needle, pinch the yarn down tightly around the eye, then slide it off the needle and push the folded, pinched end through the eye.

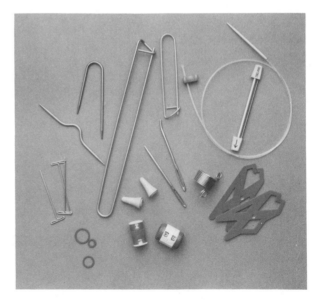

KNITTING TOOLS

Stitch Holders

As you work a project, it is sometimes necessary to place a group of stitches on hold. The simplest and most economical way to deal with this is to use a length of yarn, string, or embroidery thread in a contrasting color to make the stitches easy to see. It is, however, far more convenient to use one of the various types of stitch holders sold for this purpose. These holders are rigid, like a miniature knitting needle, which makes it much easier to transfer the stitches back from holder to needle.

There are various styles of holders sold, many of them a variation on a safety pin. A true safety pin is not a good choice, as the yarn can snag in the turn at one end or on the head at the other. The pin-type holders designed for knitting are smooth and will not snag the stitches, although I have found that stitches can work their way off. There is another type sold with a tiny needle on the bottom for the stitches, and a spring-held cap that snaps over the tip; this type holds the stitches quite securely.

Finally, there is a stitch holder sold that resembles a jumper needle. It has a cable, one small tip about two inches long, and a cap at the other end of the cable that has a hole for the needle tip so it can be locked in a closed circle. These are especially convenient for holding fabric worked in the round or for circular necklines, for instance. Unfortunately, the tip does not always stay in the cap securely, and I have had them open up. I find it safer to use a cable needle or a few double-points with tip protectors as a stitch holder.

Counters

As you know, I strongly recommend that a count be kept of the rows you work so the garment is the correct length. You really need no more than a pencil and paper, using either hatch marks in groups of five, or making a check or dot next to the rows on a garment chart.

If you prefer, however, there are several devices sold for this purpose. The most common one is barrel shaped, with a hole through the center so it can be slipped onto a straight knitting needle. There are little windows that display numbers riding on two dials, and it will count up to 99. Unfortunately, these devices, when used as intended, make the head of the needle even heavier, and lifting the additional weight stitch by stitch adds up to a considerable amount of extra work for the knitter; I don't recommend using them in that way. Further, they don't work at all when working in the round. However, if you have one, consider running a strand of yarn through the counter and hanging it from the fabric; it will always be available but the weight will rest in you lap, and it can then be used for working in the round as well.

There is another type that sits next to the knitter and uses pegs in holes on a little plastic platform something like a cribbage board. These have never recommended themselves to me—the pegs can fall out or get lost, and there isn't always convenient chair or table space near me when I knit on which to set the thing.

Devices for Measuring Stitch Gauge

In checking over the gadgets available to knitters on display at the stores, you will undoubtedly come across a metal or plastic gauge with a window in the center that is intended to measure stitch gauge. If you have not done so already, please read the section on Stitch Gauge, starting on page 415, for why I do not recommend that method of determining gauge. All you need to measure gauge is an ordinary ruler or measuring tape.

Marker Rings

These are little colored metal or plastic rings that can be slipped onto the knitting needle between two stitches to mark the end of a round or to mark off pattern repeats as an aid in keeping your place. They are sold in small and large sizes or in packages of mixed sizes so they will fit on any needle you might use. They are inexpensive, lightweight, and very handy.

If you have no commercial ring markers available, you can cut a drinking straw into thin rounds or make a Slip Knot on a short length of contrast-color yarn and use that (see page 349 for other tips on keeping track of things as you work).

Bobbins

Plastic bobbins are designed for holding the small supplies of yarn used when working an Intarsia pattern. While you could use a Yarn Butterfly (page 125), the bobbins are more convenient because they have a lock that prevents the yarn from unwinding until you want it to. On the other hand, if you are working a project that requires a great many bobbins, they can tangle up with one another; for an alternative way of working, see page 272.

When working a flat garment that will be seamed, it is a good idea to also allow sufficient yarn for sewing up when you calculate the amount of yarn tail you need for casting on (see page 140). This seaming yarn can be wound into a Yarn Butterfly, but a bobbin works quite nicely for this purpose, and the yarn stays neater while you work.

Double Yarn Ring

This device, rarely seen in the United States, is used by some left-finger knitters for working Stranded color patterns. Worn on the left forefinger, it is a coiled metal ring with two eyes through which the yarns are fed. The eyes keep the yarns separated, allowing the knitter to scoop up whichever color yarn is needed for the next stitch of the pattern. The device works quite smoothly for Knit but is awkward for Purl, so it is most useful when working in the round.

It is also possible to use the ring on the right forefinger, although it is not quite as efficient to do so, and even less so for Purl. Nevertheless, it works reasonably well, and some of you may find it speeds the work.

There is another version of this type of tool, which resembles a plastic thimble with tiny pegs that are intended to separate as many as four yarns. The one I have seen is not adjustable for different-size fingers, and the yarn does not stay between the pegs as it should.

Ball Holders

Not all that long ago, most yarn was sold in skeins, and the knitter was required to wind it into a ball. Since these balls could escape across the floor, under the chair, and into the paws of your cat, it used to be more common to see various ball holders on the market, plastic containers with a hole in the lid to feed the yarn through. Today most mills wind the yarn for us into various shapes that tend to stay put (see page 331), and ball holders are following skeins into obscurity.

When working Stranded color patterns, it is a challenge to keep the different yarns all nicely separate and untangled. At one time there were wooden stands with several upright pegs that held the different balls of yarn; a more contemporary version is a clear plastic container with several compartments, although they are hard to come by. If you do color patterns frequently, you might want to acquire something of this sort. A less aesthetically satisfying but perfectly satisfactory alternative is using shoe boxes with holes punched in the lids.

Swifts and Niddy-Noddies

A swift is a large wooden or metal umbrella-like device that clamps on to a table edge. It serves to hold a skein as you wind the yarn out of it and into a ball. It consists of the clamp, a center pole, and then six or eight arms that fold up compactly and can be extended to hold skeins of virtually any size. The umbrella-like portion spins on the pole as you unwind the yarn. Most knitting yarns today come already balled, but some of the more traditional yarns, yarns from smaller mills, from hand spinners, or from artisan dyers, are still available in skein form, in which case the swift is a very handy tool to have. You can, of course, use the tried-and-true alternative of a chair back or that friend's outstretched arms, the latter being the most companionable method.

Should you ever be in a position to recycle yarn (see page 331), you will want to skein and wash it before knitting with it again. The traditional tool for hand winding a skein is a niddy-noddy—isn't that a nice word?—which consists of three poles set at various angles to one another. You move the niddy-noddy to catch up the yarn first on the end of one pole, then on another. Most of them wind a skein about a yard in diameter.

In the absence of one of these charming, old-fashioned tools, you can certainly use the umbrella swift to make a skein. Lift the arms until they measure the diameter you want, attach the yarn to one arm and then push the arms to set them spinning and winding up the yarn.

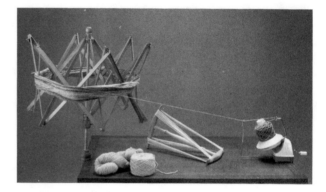

SWIFT, NIDDY-NODDY AND BALL WINDER

Manual Yarn Winder

A yarn winder is just what it says it is, a device for winding a ball of yarn. They are very handy if you work with skeined yarn or occasionally find yourself recycling or rewinding balls of yarn. There are simple and complex variations. The former simply winds a ball of yarn of the type that allows you to work with the yarn coming off the outside or from the center of the ball, or both, as the case may be. The latter will do the same job, but is also capable of combining two yarns. These combined yarns are not truly plied, as no counter-twist is put on the separate yarns before they are brought together; it simply wraps them around one another as it winds them together into a ball. This latter function is really somewhat frivolous, as there is no need to combine yarns until you hold them to knit with. However, if you enjoy combining yarns—and it is an easy way to make a highly textured and unique garment—you might prefer to deal with one ball of yarn rather than two, and that type of winder may be preferable.

Regardless of which one you have, be careful about the tension you place on the yarn as you feed it into the winder. For reasons discussed on page 329, it is not a good idea to wind any ball of yarn tightly.

19

Starting and Carrying Out a Project

Knowing how to work the stitches and how to shape the fabric are certainly the most essential aspects of making a hand-knit garment. However, regardless of your skills in these matters, there are several other ingredients, ones far more modest and perhaps less interesting, that make the difference between a garment that looks amateurish and one that looks polished and professional.

Of course, it does no good to make a garment that does not suit you or one made of poor or inappropriate materials; you will not be satisfied with it, nor will you garner many compliments for it. The section on selecting a pattern and yarn will be useful in this regard. In the section "Working Tips" you will find various methods of working more carefully and accurately, and of handling the addition of new supplies of yarn, all of which will make your work go more smoothly and produce a more beautifully finished garment. And finally, all of us make mistakes, but a skilled knitter knows how to eliminate the problems without leaving a trace; do read the section on correcting errors.

Selecting a Pattern and Yarn

For many of us, the look and feel of a certain yarn, a charming pattern spotted in a magazine, or just the urge to have some knitting in hand is what gets a project going. Unfortunately, we should hold all these impulses in check long enough to give some serious consideration to what it is we are about to embark upon, for most garments involve a respectable investment of time and money, especially the former.

Whether you are designing your own garment or planning to use a commercial pattern, the first step is to decide on a style that is appropriate for the person, for the season, and for the use it will be put to. If you are knitting for yourself, or course, things are a bit easier, but I'm sure I'm not the only one who has knit something lovely only to discover it didn't suit me at all. If you are knitting for someone else, you must be particularly careful or you may be hurt to realize that the garment is never worn.

If the garment is for yourself, first analyze exactly what you need in your wardrobe. Is there a beautiful skirt or handsome pair of slacks that needs a pullover, a lovely blouse that would look just right with a cardigan, or a jacket that is crying out for a scarf or a vest? If this is where you start, you will solve many problems at once, for it not only establishes the type of garment, but may very well decide the color. Take the item with you to the shop so you are sure the knitting pattern and the yarn color and texture are all just right.

If you are knitting for someone else, of course, the safest thing is to ask them what they would like. When you are planning a surprise, however, you must do a bit of detective work. Be alert to what that person wears. Is their style casual or formal? Are there certain sports or activities that suggest an idea? Be very attentive to the colors they like and look good in, and keep in mind that your favorites may be something that person would never dream of wearing. Some people enjoy dramatic, contrasting color combinations, others a quieter, monochromatic palette; youth may prefer bright colors, age those with more subtlety.

If you are looking at commercial patterns, take an extremely critical look. The pictures are always of very attractive, carefully posed models, but few of us look like models, nor will we always stand around in attractive poses. Many patterns will provide a schematic drawing, a small line drawing of the finished garment

with the dimensions of key areas. The schematic drawing will tell you how much ease (the difference between your body measurements and the garment measurements) is built in, what the depth of the armhole and width of the sleeve is, and what the finished length will be, and it will point up details of the garment that you may miss with all the distractions built into the photograph. You might want to compare the pattern measurements with those of a sweater already in your wardrobe that fits correctly.

Analyze key garment pattern elements for whether or not they will be flattering. Cap sleeves and sleeveless garments enhance only the prettiest arms. Yokes emphasize the bustline and broaden shoulders. Open or round necklines and small collars can make a short neck look longer, while cowls and turtlenecks, ruffles and large collars are best for those with long necks. Consider where the garment falls against waist or hips and whether it should be a blouson style to add softness or something with straight lines that trims the figure. Vertical lines, either those of the garment or the stitch pattern, are slimming and add height, while horizontal lines do the opposite. Short jackets and vests are best on those who are small, although the latter are nice for any figure when worn under a longer jacket.

Also keep in mind the general figure type you are knitting for. A bold stitch or color pattern or an oversize garment can work well for those of medium build, but may upstage a small person and exaggerate the proportions of a large one. Bulky, nubby, or fuzzy yarns will add stature, smooth ones are more slimming. The best approach is to use as a model some other favorite garment that has always worked well in your wardrobe, that you frequently receive compliments on, or that makes you feel particularly good when you wear it. If you're looking for something new, go to the store and try on different sweaters. When you find a style that is attractive on you, measure it and then see if you can find a similar pattern, or design one of your own.

If you are planning to use a commercial pattern, read some of the garment instructions to see whether you think your skills are equal to the project. Look at the stitch gauge and the type and amounts of yarn called for to get a better sense of what kind of fabric it will be. If the stitch gauge is low and the yarn heavy, it will be a quick, bulky sweater. If the gauge is low and the yarn medium, it will be loosely knit. If the gauge is high, the garment will be fine and lightweight. Check what sort of yarn is called for, and keep in mind that some, like angora and mohair, require special handling, while others, like silk, lamb's wool, and cashmere, or fancy designer yarns or those that are artisan dyed, can be quite expensive. Also consider what kind of care the yarn will require. The natural fibers can be washed or dry cleaned, but many new blended yarns require dry cleaning only, and this is an ongoing expense you may want to take into consideration.

If the yarn represents a serious investment, you might want to buy the pattern you are interested in and just one ball of yarn, take them home, and do the tension sample. This will give you a much better sense of what the fabric will be like, and how difficult the stitch pattern is. It will also give you time to think, away from all the seductions of the yarn shop. You can hold the

swatch you make up against clothes already in your closet to see if it is a good color, think about the pattern in relation to garments you might want to wear it with, and compare the measurements given in the schematic to measurements of other sweaters that you know fit well. After all of this sober reflection, you may decide the whole idea was a mistake. Don't think of your time or money as wasted, think instead of all the time and effort you have saved. Go back and try again—you're likely to make a much better selection the second time.

While it is certainly practical to start with a clear idea of what kind of garment you want to make, there are a great many projects that start, either by whim or by necessity, with the yarn. If you go into a store and find a yarn you really like before you have any idea what to make, the shopkeeper should be able to direct you to a selection of commercial patterns that use any yarn you select, or a similar one for which it can be substituted.

PATTERN IN BULKY, MEDIUM AND FINE YARNS

In some stores, if you bring in a schematic drawing of a design you want to make in a yarn they carry, they will be able to help you develop a pattern for it. Ask if the shop has a swatch knit up in that yarn so you can get an idea of what it will look like. If they don't, perhaps they would let you sit down right then and there and knit one for them; short of that, it is wise to take a single ball home to try it out before you commit yourself to a project. If you are a beginning knitter, it is a good idea to consider yarns that are fuzzy, nubby, or variegated in color because they will kindly obscure any little irregularities in your tension.

When you are designing your own garment, you will want to choose a garment style that is appropriate for the yarn. Don't use a fragile yarn for a sporty pullover, or a rough yarn for something worn against the skin. If you are going to wear a sweater inside the house or at the office, you will want a lighter-weight yarn than if you want something warm and sturdy to throw on when you take the dogs for their walk. If you want something for wear under a jacket, don't make it too bulky. As a rule, garments made with fine- to medium-weight yarns are far more versatile and comfortable to wear than those made with heavy yarns.

Bulky yarns have come to be popular because they allow you to make something rather quickly; this comes, however, at a price. If you work these yarns up at even a moderately firm tension, you will have a heavy, very warm garment suitable only for outdoor wear. If you knit at a loose tension, the wind will whistle through the fabric so it will no longer be effective outside, yet it may be too warm inside, and the garment may snag or sag out of shape. Also keep in mind that stitch patterns will be on a bold scale, frequently with a highly embossed surface texture, and color patterns that require stranding will considerably increase the bulk and warmth of a garment even further. Therefore, when working with these yarns, it is particularly important to select stitch patterns that will be in proportion with the garment, and it may be best to concentrate your selection on those that have relatively fewer stitches and rows in the repeat, and to avoid Stranded color patterns entirely.

Medium-weight yarns are excellent for most purposes and can be worn comfortably indoors when the heat is turned down, outdoors on a cool day, or under a jacket on a cold one. Nearly any stitch pattern can be used to good effect, although those based on Eyelets will leave very large holes. Intarsia patterns and color stripe patterns will do very well, but Stranded color patterns, including Mosaic patterns, while certainly beautiful in medium-weight yarns, make very warm garments and should be reserved for sporty, outdoor wear.

When you work with a finer yarn, you need only consider whether the pattern suits the yarn and the design of the garment because any of them will work. In

BRITISH FISHERMAN'S GANSEY

PATTERN IN THREE GAUGES

addition, the number of pattern repeats that cover the surface of the fabric will be much higher than the same patterns used with a bulky yarn, giving a subtle, richly textured look to the garment rather than a chunky or bold one. The old British guernseys were knit with a fine, tightly spun five-ply worsted wool on needles sometimes as small as 1.5 mm, and were expected to keep hard-working fishermen very warm, some of them lasting twenty years or so.[1] They are still knit today, but more often on bigger 2.25 mm needles (American size 0), which gives a gauge of about nine stitches and ten rows to the inch. It generally took the equally hard-working fisherman's wife about one week to knit a sweater of this kind—in her spare time.

Stranded color patterns are also at their very best when knit with fine yarn. Those beautiful Shetland Fair Isle sweaters are done in a very fine two-ply yarn at a gauge of at least eight stitches to the inch. They are

lightweight and supple, and although stranded, are not too warm to wear indoors with the heat turned down a bit.

Many people today seem afraid of working with fine yarns—partly because they want something that will knit up more quickly, partly because they seem to be daunted by the size of the needles and the stitches. I would like to reassure you. Knitting is knitting, after all, and working with small-size needles is no different from working with larger ones. They will feel strange in your hands at first, but once you have knit with them for a while, changing to a large needle will feel just as strange. It is possible to work out exactly how many stitches you will need to knit a particular garment (see page 428) and therefore to estimate that when working a fine yarn in Stockinette with a gauge of 8sts/10rows, the garment will have about 30 percent more stitches than when done in medium yarn at a gauge of 6sts/8rows, 60 per-

1. Mary Wright, *Cornish Guernseys & Knit Frocks* (Alison Hodge/Ethnographics, Ltd., 1979), p. 19.

cent more than a heavy yarn with a gauge of 5sts/7rows, and 75 percent more than a bulky yarn done at 4sts/ 5rows. What this means in more concrete terms is that if you are accustomed to using medium-weight to heavyweight yarns, making a similar garment with a fine yarn is more or less the equivalent of knitting a sweater and a half, instead of one sweater. Now that doesn't sound too painful, does it? Needless to say, if you are going to expend the extra time and effort to make a garment in a fine gauge, you will want to choose a classic, timeless style that will never look dated; it will give you years and years of pleasure.

When you are designing your own garment, you will want to select not only a suitable style and yarn, but an appropriate stitch pattern. The drape, weight, and texture of the fabric are just as important aspects of garment design as color or shape, and it is essential to match the characteristics of the stitch pattern to the type of garment you will make. Some stitch patterns are sporty, some delicate, some very tailored. There are those that work up dense, others are very open or soft and fluffy. A dense pattern might be just right for outerwear such as a jacket or hat, a soft one will have good thermal properties, and a more open fabric is better for summer or fancy evening wear. In addition, some patterns will only show themselves to advantage when done in a smooth yarn and are completely obscured by a fuzzy one, whereas others may enhance the qualities of a variegated or highly textured yarn.

Part of the process of deciding whether a particular stitch pattern works on the yarn you have chosen is to select the correct gauge for it. There are no hard and fast rules about what gauge to use; however, for most purposes you would not want to knit so tightly that the fabric is stiff, nor so loosely that it will snag or become shapeless. Remember that openwork patterns are far more refined and hold their shape better if done on very small needles, and dense patterns require relatively large needles to prevent them from getting stiff. Make up three small swatches of the stitch pattern and yarn, using a different needle size on each to make a good comparison before you decide. Then make your tension sample with the needle size that gave the best result. As you know, I recommend using a tension sample or gauge swatch of about six inches square, and one of the decided advantages of doing so is that it will give you a really good sense of the way the stitch pattern looks, how the fabric drapes, and how it will feel against your skin.

While it is always more fun to go to the yarn store and revel in the lovely colors and textures, you may already have a supply of yarn at home that you bought for a project you abandoned, and feel it would be economical, sensible, practical, and altogether righteous of you to do something about it at last. Every knitter has yarn like that; some of us have quite a lot of it. I know knitters who have reconciled themselves to the nagging presence of this sort of thing and have given up any hope of ever working their way through all the yarn they have and plan to be buried with it, but those are extreme cases. Usually what happens is that you impulsively buy a pattern and some yarn, and get started full of enthusiasm. Then a big project comes up at work, or your son's graduation is suddenly closer than you thought, and your knitting sits by your chair for several months and then gets put in the closet. When you take it out again, you may wonder what you ever saw in it. The worst losses are when you no longer like the yarn. The only choices at that point are to think of someone who would like it and give the yarn to them, or knit something for them. If that fails, give the yarn to a retirement home, a nursing home, or a charity resale store. Far better for it to find a good home and appreciative hands than to fill that lonely corner in your closet.

If it is the pattern you no longer like, the situation can be salvaged. Rip out the part of the first project you did complete, then skein, wash, and rewind the yarn (see page 331). Reserve this yarn for ribbing, collars, pocket linings, etc., because yarn that has been used may have a subtly different look from yarn that has not been. Calculate the yardage so you know exactly what you have to work with. Go back to the yarn store and explain your problem and see if they can direct you to an alternative pattern, or help you to design a pattern of your own. If you are concerned about having enough yarn, select a pattern that is on a smaller scale than the original, or uses a stitch pattern that absorbs less yarn. If you want to be sure, use the calculations for determining yarn requirements on page 428. If you do not have enough yarn for what you have in mind, consider adding another yarn of a different color or type. Sometimes just making all the ribbings at waist, wrists and neckline in another color will assure that there is enough of the original yarn for the body. Perhaps adding stripes or a contrast-color yoke will do it. If all else fails, change the size and make something for someone smaller.

Working Tips

Once you have selected a pattern and yarn, you will no doubt be very eager to get right to work. Please be patient. There are some important preliminary steps it is essential for you to take. This section contains general suggestions about what you must do to get started on the right foot and to carry out the project in a satisfactory way, and includes material on measuring and counting, and tying on additional yarn that you should be familiar with before you start.

Getting Started

First, make sure that you have any tools that will be required—the correct size and length needles, stitch holders and markers, measuring tape, and something to keep the project in as you work on it. Use a metal gauge to check the size of each circular needle (see page 336) because they are not marked. I wasted more time than I still care to think about knitting something that persisted in turning out too big until I discovered that the needle was one size larger than I thought it was—it had been sold to me in the wrong package.

If you are working from a commercial pattern, the next step is to read the instructions through from beginning to end so you know exactly what to expect. (Further details on reading stitch and garment patterns can be found on page 407.) Next, it is a good idea to read the material in this book on any special techniques used in the garment pattern. Some patterns leave the choice of which particular form of a technique to use up to the knitter. In that case, the material here will help you decide which is the best method to use. Even when a particular technique is specified, it may not be ideal and you may very well find that you wish to make some changes, selecting a different method of casting on, a better buttonhole, or neater shoulder line than that suggested. As long as you do nothing to alter the stitch gauge or basic shape, these sorts of changes are easy to do and may very will improve the quality of the garment considerably. Try any techniques you are not familiar with on a swatch so you will be comfortable with them when it comes time to work them in the garment.

If you are working from a commercial pattern in a magazine, it is a good idea to rewrite it in larger print to make it easier to read. This also gives you the opportunity to incorporate any changes so there is no confusion about what to do, and so you need not rely on your memory should you set the project aside for a while. If you have access to a photocopier that does enlargements, that can be a simple way to make a written pattern more readable. However, I highly recommend that you work from a pattern in charted form. Charting helps you to learn a pattern very well before you start, so when you actually take up your knitting, the work will go far more smoothly. In addition, a pattern in charted form is infintely easier to follow than written instructions, making even the most complicated aspect of the directions clear. (The details of how to convert any written stitch or garment pattern to a chart can be found on page 422.)

Regardless of whether you are working from written or charted instructions, make several photocopies. File one away in case anything happens to the one you are working from. Place the one you work from in a plastic sleeve to keep it neat and clean. If you want to make marks on the chart to mark off rows as you work, make extra copies for each armhole and each sleeve so you can use it just for that purpose.

Tension Sample and Gauge

The next step is to do your tension sample. In the section on "Stitch Gauge," I have gone on at length about the absolute necessity of a properly done tension sample, but at the expense of appearing to be a nag, I will repeat myself here. Don't skip this step! You risk serious disappointment and a great deal of wasted time if you persuade yourself that it isn't necessary; it is.

Actually, before you make your tension sample, I would like to urge you to play for a while first. Many knitters dutifully make up a tension sample, get their gauge, and start to work, only to find that they are no longer knitting at the same tension and the fabric is the wrong size. If you are tense and nervous, you will undoubtedly knit more tightly than if you are relaxed and at ease. This is a problem that affects beginning knitters, or those who have not knit for a while, far more than experienced ones, who have settled into a fairly consistent way of working.

However, whether you are experienced or not, your tension may very well be different when you are familiar with a stitch pattern than when you are learning that pattern. You may also knit at a different tension when you are first handling a new yarn. Therefore, I highly recommend that you thoroughly familiarize yourself with the particular combination of needles, yarn, and pattern *before* you make your tension sample for gauge.

Practiced hands are more relaxed hands, and they will produce a more consistent fabric. Cast on enough stitches for about six inches of fabric and knit until you know the pattern and the way the yarn and needles behave.

Just as you did with garment techniques, look up any stitch techniques you are unfamiliar with in this book so you understand them thoroughly before you begin. The fastest way to learn a pattern is to pay attention to the relationship between the row you are working on and the one below. Before you make the next stitch, take a good look at the stitch below the left needle. After a while, you will know when you work a particular technique or set of stitches that they belong on stitches that look a certain way. This visual memory of the structure of the pattern will become so automatic that if anything goes wrong it just won't "feel right," and you'll stop yourself. And when you have that kind of intimate knowledge of a stitch pattern, it will take you only a moment to set things right and get going again.

Once you are thoroughly comfortable with your pattern and materials, then make your tension sample for gauge as described on page 418. The completed sample should be saved, at least for the duration of the project. In the event that things don't turn out the way you expected them to, the tension sample is a key element in figuring out what is going wrong. I write the "vital statistics"—garment size and amount of yarn required, the name of the stitch pattern and the gauge on one side of a large index card, and I staple the tension sample and a yarn label to the other side. These tension samples are very useful as you plan other projects because they give you an idea of how different yarns and stitch patterns behave. The yarn label is nice to have for any details it provides about the yardage, fiber content, dye lot and care requirements, and should you wish to use that yarn again, you will have a record of the name and manufacturer.

Caring for Work in Progress

I mentioned above that you will need some sort of a container to keep all your assembled materials together. A lined basket is ideal because it decorates the floor next to your favorite chair, and the lining prevents anything from being snagged, but even a shopping bag will do. Shops sell knitting bags of various kinds, or you can make something if you don't find one to your taste. I like to have both a large basket where everything is together and a smaller, portable bag that is just large enough for the portion that I am working on. That way my knitting is always ready to go and keep me company in a waiting room or at a meeting.

Plastic zipper bags from the stationer's, or even heavy-duty zip-lock bags from the grocery store, are nice for all the little things you carry along—wipes, measuring tape, markers, pen or pencil, stitch counter, tapestry needle, crochet hook, cable holders, and needle guards. Or, you might want to make yourself a nice zippered bag that matches your knitting bag.

It is *not* a good idea to store yarn in plastic, especially if it is a natural fiber. These fibers will stay in better condition and have a longer life if they have air circulating around them. As temperature and humidity change, natural fibers constantly absorb and give off moisture. If you keep your knitting in a plastic bag, you might reach for it one hot day and find the inside of the bag dripping wet from moisture given off by the yarn, and if there is any soil in the yarn or in the bag, things can begin to grow fairly quickly. If the yarn is very dry when it is sealed in a bag, and it is left there for any length of time, it can become brittle and lose its resilience. Many yarns are now treated to protect them permanently against moths, but if the label does not specify this, it is not a bad idea to tuck a mothball or two in with the yarn. Moths dine in the dark; if you keep your yarns out in the light and air they will be safe. Just avoid direct sunlight, which can bleach some dyes.

Try to keep your work clean. Wash your hands before you pick it up, especially if it is a light-colored or delicate yarn. I keep little packages of wipes in my knitting bag so I can clean my hands even when it is not convenient to go and wash. Another excellent way to keep the work clean is to have it in a nice, old pillowcase. Take the pillowcase out of your bag or basket, open it up, and leave it spread out on your lap. It makes a clean surface for you to rest the work on as you knit, and will protect your clothing from lint. To put your work away, just pick the pillowcase up around the knitting and tuck it safely away in your bag again. It is far easier to wash the pillowcase than to wash the knitting.

When you must stop knitting and set your work aside for a while, try not to stop mid-row. If you are working in the round and everywhere is the middle of a row, or you must stop immediately, be careful that the gap between the two needle tips doesn't stretch out, because this may show up in the finished fabric as an unsightly irregularity. There are a few things you can do to prevent this.

- If you are working on circular needles, every time you stop knitting, push the stitches off the needle and onto the cable. Because the cable is thin, any tension placed on the running thread at the gap will draw some yarn out of the adjacent stitches, which will then be recovered when you push the stitches back onto the needle.
- If you are working on straight needles, fold the fabric so the needles are side by side, and holding them as one, wrap some of the yarn around the needle tips before you put it away.
- If you notice that the gap has stretched out, you can repair things later by working yarn out of the running

thread and into any stitches that look constricted. The running thread at the gap runs between the first stitch on the left needle and the stitch *below* the one on the right needle. Therefore, if things are stretched out, the problem is likely to be constricted stitches to the right; tension can pull yarn out of them, but it is difficult to pull it out of stitches still on the needle.

Setting Markers

Markers are frequently used in knitting to identify where something is or should be done, or as an aid to counting or measuring.

Stitch Markers

Yarn shops sell metal or plastic ring markers that ride on the needle between two stitches and are slipped from one needle to the other every time you encounter them so they are carried up row by row as you knit. (I have a friend who cuts narrow slices from plastic drinking straws to serve as ring markers; they are soft, lightweight, and, needless to say, very inexpensive.) They are generally used to identify the beginning of a row in circular knitting or the position where a certain stitch technique must be worked or a different stitch pattern started, and they can even be used to mark off every stitch repeat on a complex pattern. Safety pins of various sizes can be quite useful, serving to identify individual stitches rather than being carried up row by row as with ring markers. Any function performed by a ring marker or a safety pin can be accomplished with a bit of contrast-color yarn just as easily. To make a yarn marker, cut a four- to six-inch length of yarn and work as follows:

- If you wish to use the marker between two stitches, make a Slip Knot in the middle of the yarn and place it on the needle. This can be carried up row by row just like a ring marker.
- If you wish to leave it in the fabric to mark the position of a particular stitch, use the marker yarn to work a Running Thread Increase. Insert the left needle into the nearside of this "stitch," wrap both ends of marker yarn around the needle, and Knit. Now pull both ends through the discarded stitch and gently tighten the knot thus formed around the running thread.

The only difference between a ring marker and a yarn marker used to mark a position in the row is that the latter is softer under your hands. However, there are pros and cons to using either a safety pin or a yarn marker as a stitch marker. The safety pin is certainly quicker, but it can split or snag a stitch. With the yarn marker you take the chance of distorting the stitch, and those on either side, when you remove it; use a smooth, fine yarn or embroidery thread that will pull out easily and leave no lint behind.

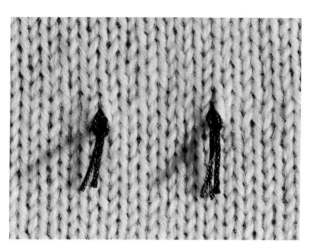

STITCH MARKERS

Marking and Counting a Cast-on Edge

It is very important that you cast on the correct number of stitches, but it can be a real nuisance to have to keep recounting them every time your attention lapses for a moment, and it can be tedious to make a last accurate count before you begin to work, especially when there are a lot of stitches involved. If you mark the stitches as you cast on, you only have to count once. Ring markers are certainly easy to use for this purpose, but they can distort the cast-on edge; therefore, it is best to use a contrast-color length of yarn instead.

To Mark a Finger Cast-on

1. Make a Slip Knot at the end of a length of contrast-color yarn slightly longer than the fabric will be wide, and place it on the needle.
2. Make a Slip Knot in the yarn to be used for casting on, place it on the needle, and begin.
3. As you cast on, after every tenth stitch pass the extra yarn either from farside to nearside or vice versa, so it passes under the needle tip and over the two strands being used for casting on.

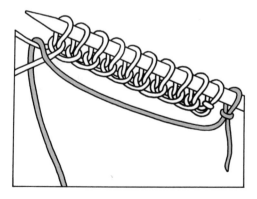

MARKING FINGER CAST-ON

When you are done, you need only count up by tens to make sure you have cast on the correct number of stitches. You may either pull the entire strand out all at once or release the yarn as you work the first row of knitting. An added advantage to casting on this way comes when you are working in the round, because wherever the cast-on edge is twisted over the needle, the contrast-color yarn will betray it.

To Mark a Knit Cast-on

• Pass the marking yarn under the tip of the needle, nearside or farside, after you make a new stitch, but before you transfer that new stitch to the left needle.

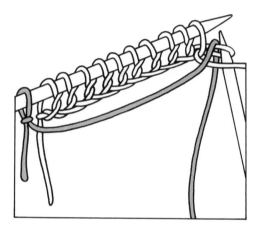

MARKING KNIT CAST-ON

Marking Rows

I am a firm believer in counting rows as you go. Yarn shops sell counters of various sorts; try several kinds until you find one you like to use. If you are not working from a chart and you don't have a counter, you can use groups of five hatch marks on a pad of paper. Simple counting of this sort is best for keeping track of long stretches, but at critical portions of the pattern, particularly where shaping takes place, I prefer to make a small pencil mark on the chart next to each completed row so there is no question about where I am and what I need to do next. Not only does this keep count of the rows, but it draws your eye to the point on the chart where you are working. Many people prefer to keep track of a pattern of increases or decreases by marking each one on the fabric itself with a safety pin or a yarn marker; it's far easier to count these than it is to find and count each shaping technique.

If you are counting or measuring rows from a particular point in the fabric, mark the row you must count up from so you know exactly where it is. There are a variety of ways to do this. At the point from which you

will have to count, use an Inlay technique (page 282) and a short length of embroidery thread in a contrasting color to mark five or ten stitches of the row. If you are concerned that it might pull out, allow a length sufficient to loop the ends together into a knot. You can also place a pin or yarn marker at every fifth or tenth row as a way of counting rows over a long stretch. Alternatively, use the same principle discussed for marking a cast-on edge and use a length of yarn, laying it back and forth between the needles every fifth or tenth row (see page 280).

If, however, you forgot to do that, you will have to find the correct row you must start counting from in some other way. If you are working with a distinctive stitch pattern, you may be able to identify the row that way, and it is easy enough if you must count up from where a stitch pattern changes. If you must count up from armhole to shoulder, or count the rows of a sleeve cap, it can be more difficult because of the curved edge.

To Mark a Row Near a Curved Edge

1. Thread a length of embroidery thread into a blunt tapestry needle. Identify the row of stitches that lie directly below the short edge cast-off for the under-arm.
2. On Knit stitches, insert the needle under the right side of every other stitch, across the row. On Purl stitches, work under the running threads. Work your way across until you are at a column of stitches still on the needle. You can then count up or measure from this marker.

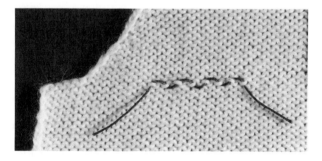

MARKING A ROW NEAR A CURVED EDGE

Marking Stitch Columns

If you wish to mark a column of stitches in order to count or measure from some point to a side edge, or between two columns of stitches, lay in a length of yarn as described above for keeping track of how many rows have been knit. This type of marker can also be inserted with a tapestry needle, running it up under every other running thread, row by row.

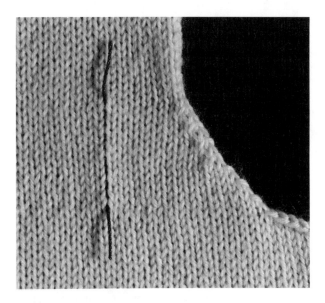

MARKING A STITCH COLUMN

Counting Stitches and Rows

It is easy enough to count the stitches on the needle, but it takes a little more concentration to count them in the fabric. However, you will find you have no trouble doing so if you really know what a stitch looks like, or are truly familiar with the structure and appearance of the stitch pattern you are using.

Actually, counting the stitches is simplicity itself—it's losing your place a few times that gets frustrating. Put the fabric down flat on a hard surface and in a good light. I find it helpful to use a needle tip as a pointer, and stick it into the center of each stitch as I count. If I pause for a moment, I leave the needle in the stitch so I can't lose my place. If you are counting over a wide stretch, thread a tapestry needle with embroidery thread, use the needle tip as a pointer, and count off groups of ten stitches. Run the needle under the right side of the first stitch of every group as you go. When you're all the way across, add up the tens for your final count and remove the thread.

If you are working with a stitch pattern, you may find it far easier to count according to stitch repeats than to worry about where each stitch is. Alternatively, count on a plain row rather than one with complex stitch techniques in it.

Counting rows is much the same—do it by stitch pattern row repeats if you can. If you must count rows on a Stockinette fabric, the easiest way to do so is on the Purl side, because the nubs are nice and visible. Here again, using a knitting needle as a pointer helps, or you can use the embroidery-thread marker idea. The latter works very well on the Purl side of the fabric because it is so easy to run the needle up under the stitch heads.

Measuring

Measuring a knitted fabric is not a very good way to determine if it is the correct length or width. First, knitting is resilient and inherently difficult to measure very accurately. Second, the measurements of an undressed fabric frequently do not at all resemble those of the same fabric when dressed (see page 418 for more information). For this reason, I strongly recommend that you determine the correct number of stitches and rows to work for a given width and length from an accurately and carefully made stitch gauge, then cast on accordingly and keep a careful count of the rows as you work, or count them to see if you have the correct number. (If a pattern suggests that you work to a certain length, see page 417 for how to convert measurements to an equivalent number of stitches or rows.)

Measuring Undressed Length and Width

There are times when measuring offers a useful, if crude, method of knowing how you are getting along. You might, for instance, prefer to measure until you're close to your goal, and then do an accurate row count when the time comes, or check the width not long after you start to see that things are roughly what they should be. For this purpose, it is important that you work with a gauge taken from an undressed tension sample, because this resembles the fabric while you are working on it. This gauge can be used to translate your measurement into a figure close to what your actual row count is (see "Stitch Gauge Ratios," page 422).

To Measure Length

1. Lay the fabric down on a flat surface with the stitches spread out on the needle so the fabric is in a perfectly relaxed state.
2. Use a firm tape measure or a hard ruler and butt the end up against the needle then measure down to where you have marked a row.

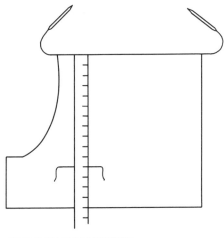

MEASURING FROM A MARKER

While measuring length is only marginally helpful, it is a very good idea to measure the width of your fabric after you have worked a few inches. This way if something is wrong you will find out sooner than later. Here again, you must measure and compare to the undressed gauge.

To Measure Width

1. In order to measure the width, it is necessary for the fabric to expand and lie flat in a natural way. If the fabric is not too wide, let the stitches ride on the cable between the points of a long circular needle. Otherwise, take them off the needle with Stranded Cast-off (page 156) and a length of smooth cord or embroidery thread that will act as a stitch holder.
2. Measure on the inside, an inch or two above the cast-on edge, and use a hard ruler to overcome any curl at the edge.

If you are making a garment with a ribbed waist or cuffs, you will have to knit several inches above the ribbing in order to get to a point where you can measure fabric that is not gathered. Stretch the ribbing out until the gathers disappear, and pin it to a padded surface such as an ironing board. Once it is secured, smooth the section above the ribbing flat and measure as described above.

Measuring for Fabric Worked on Picked-up Stitches

A border worked on picked-up stitches is a problematic area in knitting, and many people get disappointing results. However, there are a few simple steps you can take that will virtually guarantee a happy outcome.

• It is not a good idea to determine the width of the new section of fabric by measuring the edge along which you will pick up the stitches. Instead, take the measurement you need from a full-scale pattern draft, or at least from the schematic drawing of the pattern. If you are improvising and don't have a pattern, at the very least clean and dress the garment section first and then measure as described above.
• Always do a stitch gauge for any border pattern. Frequently people do not bother with this, especially for a ribbing, counting on the elasticity of those patterns to accommodate themselves to any edge. This is generally shortsighted. (Detailed information on the special characteristics of stitch gauge for ribbing can be found on page 424.)
• If you are working a center front border but not using ribbing, keep in mind that most stitch patterns stretch horizontally more than they do vertically; Garter Stitch is an exception. Therefore, when working a border on picked-up stitches, either select a stitch pattern that is fairly stable widthwise, or reduce the width of the border fabric by 5 or 10 percent by re-gauging or reducing the stitch count, and steam or

stretch it to fit when you clean the garment (see page 394). This will help prevent it from stretching out in wear.
• Finally, work out a careful pick-up pattern (see page 444), so you will have the correct number of stitches evenly spaced along the edge.

Tying On Yarn

When you have exhausted the yarn in one ball, you must tie on another in order to continue. Believe it or not, this simple necessity is fraught with controversy. Knitting instructions frequently have "nevers" and "shoulds" sprinkled about, often in regard to tying on yarn. Some books will admonish you to never tie a knot, and others will tell you just how to go about doing so. Some instructors will scornfully tell you that you must never under any circumstances tie the yarn on at the selvedge, while you will hear from others that that is the only reasonable place to do so. Who to believe? Use your common sense. Armed with the information below, you can dance right past all the nevers and shoulds and do what works best for the particular project you are working on.

It seems to me that the important thing is that there should be no evidence on the outside of the fabric of what you have done, and any selvedges or joins on the inside of the garment should be as smooth and neat as possible. Given that, there are some situations where knots work and some where they don't, and there are some occasions where you must tie the yarn on within the fabric and others where you shouldn't or can't. While this discussion focuses on how and where to start a new supply of yarn, it is inextricably linked to the discussion on how to hide the ends of yarn left when you do so, and that can be found on page 379.

If you are working a fabric in the round, you will, of course, have no choice but to tie the yarn on somewhere within the fabric. This is also true if you are tying on a supply of yarn for an Intarsia pattern, regardless of whether you are working flat or in the round. In addition, there will be times when you must tie on yarn within the fabric for openings such as buttonholes or pockets, or for embroidery, etc. There are perfectly satisfactory ways to handle these situations, with no evidence of the join showing on the outside, and others that are commonly used but don't work as well.

When you run out of yarn in the middle of a fabric, the break between the previous supply and the new one will occur at a running thread. If you are working in Stockinette, the running thread, and therefore the break, will be on the inside of the fabric. Nevertheless, any knot placed on the running thread will poke through slightly to the outside and show itself, particularly if the fabric is stretched out or is loosely knit. If you are working a pattern based on Reverse Stockinette, the running threads will be on the outside of the fabric and there is no place to hide a knot, even if it would stay hidden. Nevertheless, the two strands of yarn must be joined somehow, and if a knot isn't a good idea, what then?

First of all, knots aren't all that important because it takes very little to secure yarn in a knitted fabric. Actually, the difficult job is to undo things; it really isn't easy to work a yarn back out of the fabric once it has been woven in, and it isn't likely to work free in wear if it is properly placed. Instead of a knot, the ends of the yarn can be woven in with some of the stitches where they will sit happily throughout the life of the garment.

DOUBLE YARN TIE-ON

One of the most common methods of starting a new supply is to knit with the old and new yarn simultaneously for three or four stitches.

1. When you have about twelve inches of yarn left, pick up the new yarn, allow an end of just a few inches and hold the new yarn and the end of the previous yarn together.
2. Knit three or four stitches, drop the end of the previous yarn and continue with the new yarn.
3. At your convenience, cut off the two ends of yarn about a quarter to a half inch from the fabric.

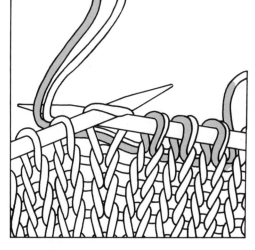

DOUBLE YARN TIE-ON

This automatically weaves in the two ends of yarn, no later finishing is required, and it can be used whether Knit or Purl is the primary stitch on the outside. More important, the woven-in ends have the exact contour, and therefore the same elasticity, as a stitch. This means that no matter how the fabric is stretched in wear, the ends are unlikely to pull out. This is especially important if you are working with a slippery yarn, but it's a nice quality under any circumstances. For all its nice

simplicity, however, the method has a few drawbacks that you will want to take into consideration.

- Because you are temporarily knitting with a yarn that is twice as thick as normal, these few stitches will be somewhat enlarged and the fabric will be thickened. If you are using a nubby or fuzzy yarn, or a highly textured stitch pattern, this is inconsequential, and your eye will never pick out the change. You can overcome the enlargement somewhat by working the stitches of the tie with a very firm tension or by using Splicing (see below). However, if you are using a very smooth yarn and a smooth stitch pattern, you will see the irregularity in the fabric.
- Because the two yarns will twist around one another as you knit with them, some of each yarn will be on the outside face of the stitches. (You can see what I am talking about best if you try to use this method at a color change, as the stitches with doubled yarn will have a tweedy look and both colors will be in evidence.) Because of this, if an end works free of the stitch, it is likely to pop through on the outside, which is why you shouldn't cut the ends off close to the fabric—you'll just have to put up with those fuzzy little ends on the inside for security. The end is even more likely to work its way out of a stitch if you are knitting at a loose tension.

SPLICING

When using the above method of tying on a new yarn, it is possible to avoid enlarging the stitches if you splice the old and new yarns together.

1. Split the ends of both yarns back about twelve inches and remove one or two ply from each. When there is more than two ply, you might want to cut each one at a different length in order to blend the two yarns more subtly.
2. Place the thinned yarns side by side, with the ends going in opposite directions, and wrap one about the other to reconstitute the yarn at normal thickness, then begin to knit.

This is a bit of a nuisance to do, but it does reduce the bulk of the join and therefore may be worth your while if you are working with a heavy yarn. Unfortunately, it is hard to control where the broken-off ply of the new yarn will fall. That of the previous yarn will be at a running thread, but the new one may wind up within a stitch where there is a good possibility that it will work its way free and show as a bit of fuzzy yarn on the outside of the fabric, particularly if you have worked at a loose tension. I don't see any way around this, which is why I generally don't recommend splicing. If that happens, it is probably best to pull the end of the ply through to the inside and leave it there; it's unlikely to go much further.

DUPLICATE STITCH TIE-ON

Here is the method of starting within the fabric that I prefer. It produces a join that is a nearly identical, but improved, version of the Double Yarn Tie-on, above.

1. When you have about twelve inches of yarn left, stop. Allow the same length end on the new yarn, and tie the new yarn to the end of the previous yarn with a Temporary Knot (page 126), as shown. Slide the knot up firmly against the last stitch worked and begin to knit. (The knot is necessary to hold the stitches on either side of the join at the proper tension so they don't enlarge.)
2. During finishing, undo the knot, interlock the two yarn ends, and weave them in with Duplicate Stitch as shown on page 380.

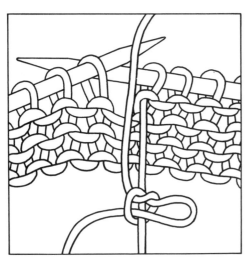

TEMPORARY TIE-ON

It is obviously more trouble to weave yarns in during finishing than to just knit with the two of them, so you may wonder why I prefer this when knitting with both yarns is so simple. First, because you never knit with more than one yarn, the stitches will not be enlarged as they are with the previous method. Although the fabric will feel thicker if you run it through your fingers, just as it would if you had knit with both yarns, it will at least not look thicker. Second, the woven-in end sits like the shadow of each stitch on the inside face only, so while it has the contour and elasticity of the stitches, it is not possible for the end to pop through on the outside.

And finally, because this is done during finishing rather than while knitting, you can choose which

stitches to weave in on. In some patterns, the row above or below may provide a better hiding place than the one the join actually occurred on. For instance, this method can be used on an openwork fabric if you position the join in or near a small section of solid fabric. Also use this if you are tying on yarn for a color change for a section of Intarsia and weave the ends in only on stitches of the same color. And by all means, use this if you are working a flat fabric that will not be seamed, because this gives a far more satisfactory result than any method used to hide the ends along a selvedge.

This is also the best method to use to hide the ends when you have reattached yarn at a pocket opening or neckline after the fabric has been separated.

INLAY TIE-ON

Here is a more specialized method, frequently used in Stranded color work.

1. Leave ends of twelve inches on both yarns, drop the previous yarn, pick up the new, and work one or two stitches.
2. Now pick up both ends of yarn in your left hand, hold the new yarn in your right hand, and use Purl Inlay on one or two inches' worth of stitches (see page 281).

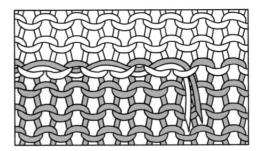

INLAY TIE-ON

This is also very simple to do, but has two problems. The yarn is woven in just along the running threads, so the end doesn't have the inherent elasticity it has when woven in with the shape of a stitch; therefore, when the fabric is stretched, the end can pull out slightly. If you have woven in a sufficient length, it won't come out entirely, although the very end might work free and pop through to the outside. An end worked in this way is also more visible and less neat on the inside, and if that face of the fabric will show at all, you would be better off with some other method. While this does not distort any of the stitches, it does thicken the fabric, particularly in a heavy yarn, because both ends are woven in behind the same stitches.

This method is most often used when doing

Stranded color work where weaving in is also used to attach long floats to the fabric. When contrast-color yarn is wrapped around the running threads, whether it is a strand or the ends of yarn, it will show slightly on the outside. You may or may not find this objectionable, and in a busy color pattern it may be lost to the eye, but if you have otherwise not used weaving in, a pair of woven-in ends of yarn peeking through in the middle of things is going to draw attention to itself.

Tying On Yarn at an Edge

Although the method I recommend above is quite successful, I still prefer to attach yarn at the side edge when knitting a flat fabric that will be seamed, if for no other reason than to avoid thickening the fabric itself.

1. Before you start to knit, use your stitches-per-inch calculation to determine the length of yarn you will need to knit across one row (see page 428). When you have less than that amount, break the yarn, leaving a twelve-inch end.
2. Tie the new yarn on to the old one with a Temporary Knot, just as you would within a fabric, pushing the knot up against the selvedge.
3. After you have seamed the edge, untie the knot, interlock the ends, and weave them in along the selvedge as shown on page 379.

This method adds a negligible amount of bulk to a selvedge, and since there is going to be some somewhere, I'd rather have it in a selvedge than in the fabric itself. If you are going to seam one edge and pick up stitches along the other for a border, tie on the yarn at the edge that will be seamed, as the hidden end will show at the join between the main fabric and the border. You will not waste very much yarn by tying it on one row earlier if necessary, and the result will be more satisfactory. If you are planning a garment in a very open lace pattern, you might want to consider knitting it flat just so you have a seam in which to hide the ends of yarn.

Ripping

First console yourself—it happens to everybody. It usually doesn't take as much time as you think it will, and once you've done it a few times, it isn't difficult at all. It's essential, however, that you understand the structure of the basic stitch, and that of your particular stitch pattern. The methods of working given here are intended to minimize any missing stitches or having any run down.

Ripping Back Stitches

When an error has occurred in the row you are currently working on, rip the stitches out one by one much as you knit them.

To Unravel a Knit Stitch

1. Insert the tip of the left needle into the stitch below the first stitch on the right needle from nearside to farside so the left side of the stitch is on the farside of the needle.
2. Drop the stitch above off the right needle and pull the yarn to unravel that stitch.

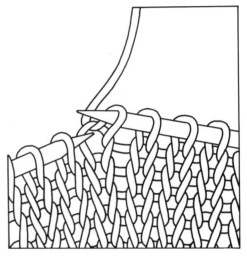

UNRAVELING KNIT STITCHES

To Unravel a Purl Stitch

- Insert the left needle up under the Purl nub below the right needle, then drop and unravel the stitch above.

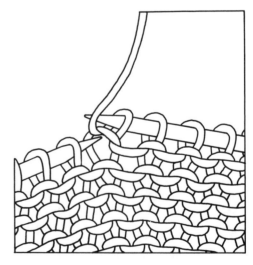

UNRAVELING PURL STITCHES

Continue in this way, stitch by stitch, until you have worked back to the problem. If you have trouble inserting the needle, pull up on the yarn so you can see where it comes through the stitch below.

If you are ripping back past stitch techniques, you must be particularly careful to make sure that each stitch freed is on the needle in the correct position. Any stitches that were turned, such as for a Pullover or a Left Decrease, must be returned to their correct positions. Any stitches that were slipped directly should be slipped back without change. If any stitches were twisted or cabled or worked into a decrease, you may have to drop the stitch off the needle first, then unravel the yarn and pick up the freed stitches in their correct positions. As you work stitches of this kind again, look at each one carefully to see that it is as it should be.

Unknitting

When you are ripping out fragile yarns like mohair and angora, or those which are highly textured, you must be particularly careful to avoid fraying. If not handled correctly, the ripped section of yarn will be visibly different from the rest and will have to be abandoned. Most of these yarns are costly, and you will want to avoid throwing some away. Even the relatively gentle process of ripping back stitch by stitch can sometimes be damaging, particularly with certain stitch techniques. If you find that the yarn snags as you rip it out, try the following method instead.

1. Insert the left needle into the stitch below the right needle as described above.
2. Remove the right needle from the stitch above and reinsert it into the stitch now on the left needle either as to Knit or as to Purl, depending upon how the stitch being ripped was formed.
3. Unwrap the yarn of the new stitch, reversing the motion used for Knit or Purl, then remove the right needle from the stitch.

Having both needles inserted into the stitch opens it up, allowing the yarn to be pulled through with less stress and abrasion.

Ripping Back Rows

This can be painful, but it is generally worth it. You may be tempted to persuade yourself that the mistake you found won't really show, but I can promise you—your eye will seek it out every time you wear the garment and it will remain a nagging disappointment. I have found the best approach is to get the pain over with quickly. If you put it away at that point, you may never pick the project up again—I know of countless people who have done just that. The minute you find the mistake, rip things out right then and there. Once it's ripped out, immediately knit a few rows—console yourself with the knowledge that the process of knitting is just as gratifying as the results—and you'll be surprised at how quickly you forget what happened.

1. Mark the row above the mistake with a pin so you know exactly where to rip down to and pull the stitches off the needle.

2. Hold the fabric down against your lap with one hand and pull up on the yarn with the other. When you have a few yards of yarn, stop ripping and wind it on the ball so it doesn't get tangled. (If the yarn is fragile, rip very gently, disentangling it with your fingers from any stitch it gets caught on rather than pulling on the yarn. It may help to insert a knitting needle into the stitch and unknit it as above.)
3. When you come to the pin, remove it, rip to the end of the row, and stop.
4. Take up a needle a few sizes smaller than the one you were knitting with and hold it in your left hand. (A smaller needle makes it easier to pick up the stitches and is less likely to cause runs in adjacent stitches not yet on the needle.)
5. Hold the fabric in your right hand and work much as if you were unraveling stitches still on the needle. Insert the needle into the stitch below the first free loop in the correct manner, with the right side of the stitch on the nearside of the needle, and then pull the yarn to unravel the stitch above. Continue in this way across the row. If there are any complex stitch techniques, you may have to pull the yarn free of the stitches first, and then carefully pick them up on the needle.

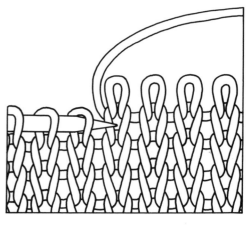

UNRAVELING ROWS

If any stitches run down before you can pick them up, get them on the needle just the way they are and continue. If this has only happened once or twice, and you are an experienced knitter, you will be able to begin knitting again and just fix those stitches when you come to them (see correcting runs, below). If the pattern is complex and there were quite a few stitches that you know have problems, or if you are at all unsure of yourself, the safest thing to do is to get all the stitches safely on the needle and then rip down one more row stitch by stitch, as described above. You must get to the point where every stitch is in the shape it should be. Do count the stitches on the needle carefully before you start to knit again with the correct-size needle in your right hand. If the yarn is badly damaged by being ripped out, you may have to discard it and use fresh yarn to reknit with.

Picking Up Before You Rip

Here is another approach, which works well on relatively plain stitch patterns and makes it impossible to miss a stitch or have one run down.

1. Determine which row has the mistake in it. Use a circular needle several sizes smaller than the one you had been knitting with.
2. Work from right to left, inserting the needle into the right side of each stitch in the row below the one where the error occurs. You may work on either the inside or the outside (see "Picking Up Within the Fabric," page 198). Be careful to pick up each selvedge stitch as well.
3. When you have all the stitches on the needle, then and only then rip out the stitches above.

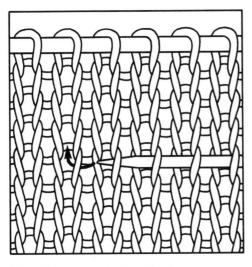

PICKING UP STITCHES BEFORE YOU RIP

Obviously, this won't work on patterns employing Twist or Cable Stitches, although it can be used on a plain row of an otherwise complex pattern. With the circular needle, it doesn't matter whether the yarn winds up on the right or left side after you rip, because you can just slide the stitches to where the yarn comes off the first stitch and begin to knit again.

Dropped Stitches and Runs

If the needle has pulled out of a group of stitches accidentally, generally they won't go anywhere if you handle the fabric carefully. When the stitches first come off, they are frequently lined up sideways, just as they were on the needle, and you can sometimes slip them right back on again. If they've been off for a while, or the fabric has been moved, they will gradually turn "shoulder to shoulder." As you pick them up again, insert the needle through the center of the stitch from farside to nearside so the right side of the stitch is on the nearside of the needle.

If you think the stitches might run down, get them on the needle any old way, and worry about whether or not they are turned once they are secure again. If you think some are not on right, slip them back and forth between the two needles, checking each one until you are sure they are as they should be. If a stitch has run down, get it on the needle as it is and work it back up later. Count the stitches on the needle to make sure you have the correct number.

Once you've handled this situation a few times, it won't seem quite the frightening event it does the first time.

Correcting Short Runs

When you have stitches off the needle for any reason, one may run down a row or two before you can pick it back up, or you may have dropped it off as you were knitting. Once you have it back on the needle, a stitch in this condition will look exactly like a slipped stitch with a running thread stranding past it for every row it ran down. When the stitch has only run a row or two, it is easy enough to work it back up in pattern with the knitting needles.

To Place a Knit Stitch on the Nearside

1. Have the stitch on the nearside and its running thread on the farside.
2. Pick up the stitch on the left needle in the correct position, with the right side of the stitch on the nearside of the needle. Then pick up the running thread in the same way and place it on the left needle to the right of the stitch.
3. Insert the right needle tip into the nearside of the stitch and pull it over the running thread and off the needle.

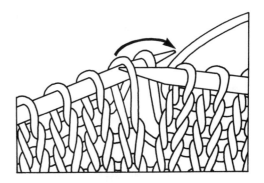

CORRECTING A DROPPED KNIT STITCH

To Place a Purl Stitch on the Nearside

1. Have the stitch on the farside, the running thread on the nearside.
2. Pick up the stitch on the right needle in the correct position, then pick up the running thread in the same way and place it on the right needle to the left of the stitch.
3. Insert the left needle tip into the farside of the stitch and pull it over the running thread and off the needle to the nearside.

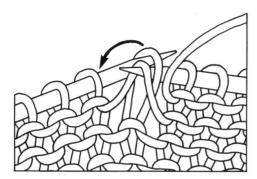

CORRECTING A DROPPED PURL STITCH

If the stitch has run down more than one row, you must repeat this process for each running thread, starting with the lowest one and working your way up. Do be careful not to miss any of the threads or get them out of sequence, and always make sure to place the right side of both stitch and running thread on the nearside of the needle. If you find it easier, you may also use a crochet hook.

Correcting Long Runs

If a stitch has run down several rows before you discover the problem, it will leave a ladder as evidence of its travels, and all you have to do is follow the ladder down to where the wayward stitch can be found. For the moment, secure it from wandering any further by fastening a safety pin through it, or pick it up on a cable needle and tuck the ends of the needle into the fabric so it won't slip out. Knit over to where the lost stitch column is, and either push the other stitches well back from both needle tips or place tip protectors on so no other stitches jump off while you're not looking. Take up a crochet hook the same size as the needles you are using and work as follows:

For a Knit Stitch on the Outside

• With the outside of the fabric facing you, insert the hook into the stitch from nearside to farside, catch the lowest running thread and draw it through the stitch. Repeat as necessary.

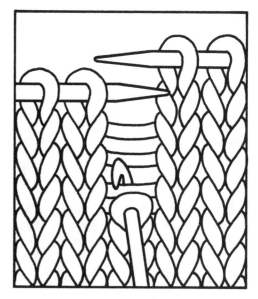

CORRECTING A RUN WITH A CROCHET HOOK

For a Purl Stitch on the Outside

• With the inside of the fabric facing you, repeat as above.

It is particularly difficult to do this successfully if you are working with an inelastic yarn, as the fabric doesn't recover well. Once the run is repaired, you may have to ease yarn out of some stitches and into others with the tip of the needle to get things looking as if nothing happened.

Runs to Increases and Decreases

A stitch column originating on an increase technique can run no farther than that point. If the increase was a

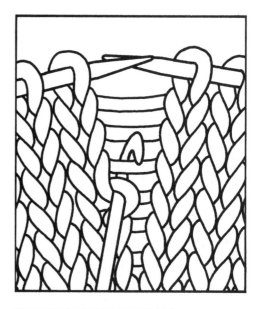

CORRECTING A RUN TO AN INCREASE

Yarnover, the running thread at the base of the ladder will be the Yarnover strand. Pull the second running thread under the bottom one to form the first stitch. If some other increase was involved, you will have to study the structure of that particular technique and use a crochet hook to bring the first available running thread through whichever adjacent stitch the increase was originally made on.

If a stitch runs in a column that contains a decrease technique, the run will affect two stitch columns below the point of the decrease. You will know this has occurred if the ladder abruptly widens. You can either work the stitches up one at a time or simultaneously (see "Reworking Partial Sections," below). Reconstruct the decrease with either needles or crochet hook and then continue to work the remaining stitch up to the current row.

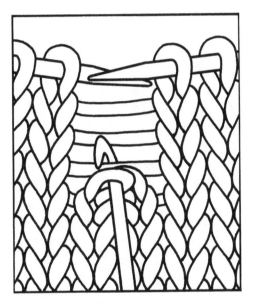

CORRECTING A RUN TO A DECREASE

Correcting a Run Within the Fabric

If you have continued to work several rows after the stitch dropped off the needle, the ladder will start somewhere within the fabric instead of directly below the needle. When this happens, there will not be sufficient yarn in the running threads above the dropped stitch to form new stitches in those rows, and if you attempt to work the stitch back up to the needle, you will have to pull yarn for each new stitch out of the adjacent ones, distorting them considerably. The best way to correct a situation like this is to rip all the rows down to the point where the stitch dropped off the needle, work the stitch up from the bottom of the ladder to the needle, and rework.

If you are not willing to go to all that trouble, and

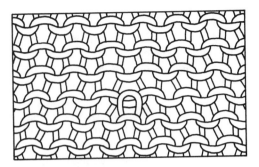

DROPPED STITCH WITHIN FABRIC

willing to compromise on the finished appearance, work as follows:

1. Work the stitch up to the top of the ladder and temporarily secure it on the inside with a cable needle or safety pin.
2. Take up a tapestry needle and a strand of yarn, the same used to knit the fabric, and starting five or six stitches away, work the end of the yarn in with Duplicate Stitch as described on page 380.
3. When you come to the dropped stitch, run the yarn through the dropped stitch from nearside to farside, then up under the head of the stitch to the left.
4. Duplicate the stitch above.
5. Pass the needle down through the same stitch head below, then through the dropped stitch again from farside to nearside.
6. Work the other end into the stitches to the left as before.

This gives as subtle a fix as possible, and if you take care it won't be very noticeable, particularly if the stitch pattern or yarn provides other distractions for the eye.

DUPLICATE STITCH CORRECTION FOR DROPPED STITCH

Reworking Partial Sections

If you thoroughly understand your stitch pattern, you should be able to rip down a group of stitches to correct an error and knit them back up again. This is not the task for an inexperienced knitter, and even those who are confident of their skills should only take it on after carefully weighing the options. If the alternative is to rip out a large number of rows of challenging knitting, this may be worth the effort. But since this approach is a considerable amount of work itself, don't tackle it unless you really need to. Unless it is done with great care, the finished appearance of the repair may not be worth the time you invest in it, and ripping would be a better choice. I reworked a Cable that had a mistake in it halfway down the front of a sweater for my son and it turned out beautifully—I can't even tell you any more where it was—but I must say it was an awful lot of work, and I probably would have enjoyed reknitting the front a great deal more than fussing with that one Cable for as long as I did. You may want to mark off the pertinent section on a copy of your stitch chart so you are quite sure of exactly what you must do at every step of the way.

1. Drop whatever group of stitches are involved off the needle and rip them down to the point where there is a problem.
2. Work with a pair of short double-point needles the same size as the ones you are knitting with, and pick up the stitches at the base of the run.
3. In order to "knit" each stitch, work as described above for correcting runs. The running thread should be placed on the left needle to the right of a stitch for any Knit technique, and on the right needle to the left of a stitch for any Purl technique.
4. Work back and forth across each little "row"; there is no need to turn the work, but do be careful that both stitch and running thread are in the correct position.
5. When you have worked back up to the current row, slip the stitches to the regular needle.

Because the running threads get pulled on as you work the stitches back up, you will find that the stitches on either side of the reworked section have probably tightened up, there may be a gap at each side of the section, and the reworked stitches themselves may be irregular or enlarged, particularly if you are working with an inelastic yarn. Examine the fabric carefully so

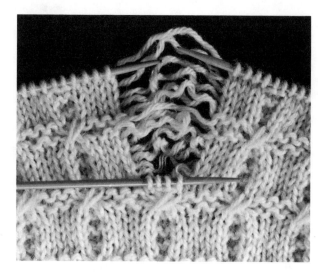

REWORKING A PARTIAL SECTION

you know what the appearance and size of a normal stitch is. Take up a free needle and gradually work the yarn out of the enlarged stitches and over to those which are too tight. It takes patience and going over things a few times, but usually you can get it to look as if those are perfectly normal stitches knit in their proper place like all the others.

Removing an Error with Grafting

There is an alternative approach to dealing with a serious error that would require extensive ripping. Here again, you must be confident of your skills to try the correction. The solution can also be used to repair a hole in the fabric.

1. Snip a stitch at the center of the problem area and open the fabric as many stitches to each side as necessary (see "Afterthought Pocket," page 228).
2. Pick up the freed stitches above and below the opening on relatively fine double-point needles.
3. Thread a tapestry needle with a length of matching yarn and graft the stitches (page 371), correcting the error as you do so.

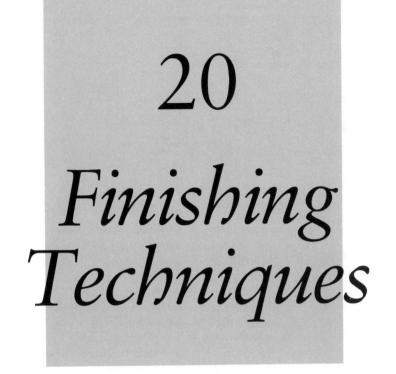

20
Finishing Techniques

When you have finished knitting the last stitch, there is still work to do before the garment is ready to wear. Any necessary seams must be sewn up and all the ends of yarn hidden away. There may be elastic to weave in, a zipper to set in place, or a lining to sew in. These are generally the most difficult tasks for any knitter—most of us, with good reason, like the knitting much better than the sewing up, and after all those patient hours we are suddenly in a hurry. Unfortunately, a poor and hasty finishing job can often ruin what would otherwise have been a splendid piece of work. Slow down, take the time to do the job well, and you will be amply rewarded.

Seams

Seams are an aspect of knitting that arouse some controversy. There are those who argue against them entirely, contending that they are a stiff intrusion in an otherwise resilient fabric. It is quite true that wherever a seam is placed the fabric will have a relatively firm and inelastic line and a ridge on the inside created by the selvedges. However, it is also true that this may be either good or bad, depending upon the use to which the fabric will be put.

For instance, if you are making a shawl and wish to attach a border, a seam would definitely be out of place. It will both interfere with the drape and soft give of the fabric and be unsightly on the inside. Actually, in almost every situation where you are dealing with a border, it is probably best to pick up the stitches instead of using a seam. Also, a sock or a mitten knit in the round will obviously be far more comfortable than one that is seamed. On the other hand, seaming a shoulder line is a definite advantage because it helps to support the garment and prevent the armhole from being pulled down by the weight of the sleeve.

Whether or not to place a seam down the length of a sleeve or down the sides of a sweater is less clear cut. There is really no need for a seam in a sleeve; however, many people dislike working on the small double-point needles that are necessary to avoid one, so most sleeves are knit up flat and have a seam whether it is good for them or not. Without a side seam, a sweater takes on something of the shape of a barrel; adding a seam straightens the side and adds definition and contour to the design lines. Because this affects only the finished appearance, it is a matter of personal taste and not a technical question of which method is superior.

Frankly, I think the seam dialogue falls more properly into the realm of the Great Argument, flat knitting vs. round. People who argue against seams are really arguing for knitting in the round, partly because they dislike the process of sewing up, and/or are unhappy with the seams they do sew, and partly because they dislike to Purl. I dislike compromising a design for the lack of a basic skill, and strongly suggest that you both learn to Purl and learn to sew up properly. Then you can decide whether to knit in the round or flat on the basis of which method will enhance the garment in some way.

Nevertheless, the decision as to whether to work flat or in the round affects only certain seams, not others. Those others also have some options as to how they may be handled. By far the most common situation in which the tops of two fabrics must be joined is along a shoulder line. Traditionally the slope is done with Stepped Cast-off (page 152) and the seam with Backstitch (page 383). If what you want is a thick ridge on top of your shoulder, that works very well indeed. I think you will be much happier if you slope the shoulder with Short Rows (page 175) and join the two fabrics with Joinery Cast-off (page 153). This offers excellent support, columns of stitches that are perfectly lined up, and a neat join that is not at all bulky; it is altogether preferable to any sort of seam, and quicker and easier to do. A shoulder line may also be grafted (page 371), although grafting is as resilient as the fabric and therefore offers no support for the line of the garment.

Sleeves must also be attached to the garment in some way, and while the bulk of a side seam will not really be felt in wear, a heavy seam around the armhole can be irritating. Obviously, in medium- to fine-weight yarns, any seam will also be slight and not a problem, but in heavier yarns and denser fabrics it can be. In these situations, if you are familiar with working on double-point needles, you might want to consider picking up the stitches around the armhole and working the sleeve in the round from shoulder to wrist. This way of working, however, while simple enough when the shape of armhole and sleeve are themselves simple, will require some expertise if what you want is a cap sleeve (for more information, see page 197). If you are knitting a garment flat, join just the shoulders, pick up the stitches for the sleeve around the armhole, and work flat to the wrist. Seam the sleeve and the side of the garment continuously. And finally, there are ways of working an entirely seamless sweater from the top down including sleeves (see Barbara Walker's book *Knitting From the Top*[1]).

If you have decided to use a seam on certain portions of the garment, there are other questions that must be addressed during the planning process. Any garment that must be seamed along side edges should have selvedge stitches in addition to the stitches required for the width of the fabric. If you do not provide a selvedge

1. New York:Scribner's, 1972.

stitch at each side edge, one stitch of the fabric itself will be absorbed into the seam. While this is not a big problem when you are working in Stockinette in a relatively fine yarn, in other situations it is more serious (see page 168).

Sewing a seam has quite a bit in common with picking up stitches; the latter is, after all, simply a different method of joining one fabric to another. Where picking up stitches creates a single selvedge turned to the inside, sewing generally creates two, but otherwise they are very similar. Before you read this material, therefore, I think it would be worth your while to be thoroughly familiar with that on both selvedges and picking up stitches; much of what I say here will refer to information found in those sections (pages 163–168 and 183–200).

In all these techniques, there are two factors to consider. One is the outer appearance of the seam and whether the two fabrics are smoothly joined with no gaps and no evidence of the sewing thread. The other is whether or not the seam is bulky, which depends upon how much of the selvedge stitch is turned to the inside. These two factors have an unfortunate relationship—the closer and smoother the seam is on the outside, the bulkier it will be, and if you reduce the bulk, you will reveal more of the seam. Nevertheless, there are some very nice seams here that I think you will find quite satisfactory.

Yarns for Seams

Most people sew up a garment using the same yarn they knit with. This is rarely a very good idea. First, while you may want a seam, there is no advantage to a bulky seam, so at the very least, the yarn should have one or two of its ply split off to make it thinner if it is amenable to such treatment. Second, knitting yarns will generally fray when they are used for sewing, and the longer the seam the more serious the problem will be; some are simply unsuitable at the outset, particularly if they are fuzzy or highly textured. In these cases it is far better to select an alternative yarn. Embroidery thread of cotton, silk, or wool or needlepoint wool are excellent choices. For any of these, there is a vast array of colors to choose from and, therefore, the hope of making a good match with your garment. With all of them the plys can easily be separated so you can achieve a suitable weight, and they are designed to withstand fraying better than knitting yarns will do.

However, if you are working with a nice, smooth, well-behaved yarn of good strength, there is no reason not to use it for sewing up. Allow sufficient length of yarn for sewing either before casting on or after casting off, depending on where you want to start a seam, and tie it into a Yarn Butterfly (page 125) until you are ready to use it. The advantage of doing so is that instead of having to hide the end of yarn left from casting on or

off, and the end left when you start to seam up, you will have no ends to hide and no knot at all! Much better, yes?

Yarn from a Butterfly can still be split if you wish, but don't do so right away. Sew about an inch of the seam, then remove one or two ply and continue. This keeps the ply that is cut off from fraying out of any stitches along the edge.

As a general rule, the yarn for seaming should be one and a half times the length of the seam, plus any additional required for hiding the ends. A generous length passed through the needle allows a comfortable margin for error. If the seam is long, it may be best to use two shorter lengths to avoid fraying.

Attaching the Yarn

If you have not used a Yarn Butterfly, it is important to start the sewing yarn in an unobtrusive way.

First, there is no rule that says that you must start from the bottom and work up. If possible, always start at a point that will itself be hidden in a seam. (For instance, start a sleeve or a side seam at the armhole and work down.)

Second, secure the sewing yarn with a knot; knots may be controversial in other areas of knitting, but in the case of a seam they are entirely appropriate. The following knot looks quite a bit like a cast-on or cast-off stitch, so it is an excellent way to start the yarn for sewing a seam if you are using the same yarn you knit with.

1. Insert the needle up through the center of the corner edge stitch, then back down through the center of the same stitch and draw it through to form a loop. Tighten the loop down until it is about half an inch long, leaving a twelve-inch end of yarn.
2. Now bring the needle up through the center of the edge stitch at the corner of the other fabric, then back up through the loop.

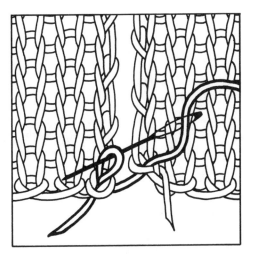

ATTACHING YARN FOR A SEAM

3. Pull on the end to tighten the loop down, then draw the remaining length of yarn through the knot.

Use the same knot at the other end of the seam and hide the ends in the selvedge as described on page 379.

Don't try to pull the yarn through and tighten the knot at the same time, you will get in a tangle; when making a sewing knot, always tighten the loop, then draw the yarn through.

If you are using yarn from a Butterfly, wound from the same yarn you cast on or cast off with, there will be no end to hide at the beginning; just make the knot, sew the seam, and hide the one end when you are done.

When are using a separate strand to sew with, it would seem to be easy enough to hide the end of yarn at the beginning before making the first knot, but usually that doesn't work out well. Because the ends are generally hidden in the selvedge along a seam, if the end is worked into the selvedge before you start to sew, it can make it harder for you to see where you are going. It takes just a minute to hide it later.

In those cases when you are sewing up with a different yarn than you knit with, it would be inappropriate to have the knot showing at the edge, in which case, attach it as described above to a single selvedge stitch just above the corner, then bring the needle out at the corner to start sewing.

Seam Techniques

There are a surprising number of ways to sew up a knitted fabric. Many books present the different methods as more or less equal, the choice seemingly only one of preference. In fact, they all have quite different characteristics, and it is worth your while to know what these are so you can make an informed choice. In the discussion of the basic methods, I am going to assume that they are being done on a Stockinette Selvedge. For information on working other selvedges, and other sorts of edges, see below.

OVERCASTING

This is a very elementary method of sewing. It is done from right to left along the edge, with the two outside faces of the fabrics placed together.

1. If you are working along a side edge, insert the needle from nearside to farside beneath both sides of one selvedge stitch on each fabric (into the space between the running threads). If you are working along a top or bottom edge, insert the needle under the entire cast-on or cast-off edge.
2. Bring the yarn over the edge and repeat the step above.

Worked as described here, the entire edge of both fabrics is included in the seam. The same technique can

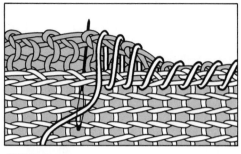

OVERCAST SEAM

be used to work under just the inner portion of either the selvedge or the cast-on or cast-off edge stitch so only half the selvedge is included, or just the outer half so none of it is.

This method of sewing does not lock the two sides of the fabric firmly together. Because the yarn passes around the selvedge stitches, the fabric can open on it like the pages of a spiral-bound book, revealing the sewing thread in the seam. In addition, when worked around a full selvedge, it will add considerable bulk. While this type of seam has a long and venerable history in knitting, and you will find it in many instruction books, I think you can safely ignore it; there are far better alternatives.

BACKSTITCH SEAM

This method produces an extremely strong, rigid seam. Because the intention is for it to be sturdy, it is always done so the full selvedge is turned inside. The seam is worked from right to left along the edge, with the outside faces of the fabrics together.

1. To sew a side edge, insert the needle from nearside to farside under the first pair of selvedge stitches at the corner, one on each fabric.
2. Skip the next pair and insert the needle from farside to nearside under the pair of selvedge stitches two to the left.
3. Insert the needle from nearside to farside under the pair of selvedge stitches to the right.

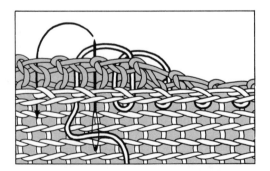

BACKSTITCH SEAM

4. Repeat the last two steps the length of the seam.

To sew a top or bottom edge, work under the entire cast-on or cast-off edge stitches in the same way.

As you can see in the accompanying illustration, the seaming yarn constantly doubles back on itself, and this adds bulk to the seam. Do not attempt to run the needle through to the farside and back to the nearside all in one motion. This makes it impossible to pass the needle carefully under the stitches, and the result will be rows of fabric that are not lined up properly, stitches from the fabric caught into the selvedge, or part of a selvedge left on the outside.

Most books recommend this way of sewing up because it produces a very rigid, strong seam; however, there is almost no situation I can think of where a seam of that sort is really necessary. Remember that the tree that does not bend will break in the storm. Besides, seams in knitted fabrics are rarely under much stress because the fabric itself is so resilient. I am afraid this is another one of those venerable artifacts of knitting which continues to be used only because it has always been used, and that isn't a very good argument for doing anything. I sewed all my seams this way while I was growing up and always thought they were ugly, but I knew no other way to work; well, there are other ways, and very nice ones, too.

CROCHETED SEAM

If you are handy with the crochet hook, here is another way to join two fabrics.

1. Work across the edge to be seamed from right to left with the outside faces of the two fabrics together.
2. Insert the crochet hook beneath one full selvedge stitch on each fabric (between the running threads), or between the stitches that lie along a cast-on or cast-off edge. Draw through a loop.
3. Insert the hook in the same manner under the pair of selvedge stitches to the left. Draw the loop through the fabric and the loop already on the needle. Repeat this last step the length of the seam.

In other words, run a chain of Single Crochet along the selvedge.

This is another seam that is found in virtually every instruction book, but it is very bulky, even bulkier than a Backstitch Seam; therefore, I see no reason to use it, except for two purposes. First, it is excellent as a basting stitch. If you would like to temporarily sew a garment up to see if it fits properly, by all means use a Crochet Seam because it zips right off again. You can then make any necessary alterations, and when you are ready, sew up with a good Selvedge or Running Thread Seam (see below). Second, with a Crochet Seam the length of yarn is not drawn through for each stitch, so the technique is also a reasonable compromise if you couldn't find an acceptable substitute and must sew up with a fragile yarn.

There is another Crochet Seam used to attach a border worked in the same direction as the main fabric. The column of selvedge stitches on the border is first unraveled from top to bottom and then a chain of Single Crochet is worked that joins the selvedge stitches of one fabric to the loops of yarn released from those of the other. The chain of crochet stitches will be on the outside of the garment. It is very difficult to do this smoothly and neatly, and the join is slightly ridged. I think you will find it far easier to use Picking Up and Joining (see page 193), and you will get a much better result.

RUNNING THREAD SEAM

This is most often called Invisible Seam, but as you will see below, it is not really the only one that can legitimately claim that title, so I have had to give it another name. It produces a very successful seam for side edges, with the columns of stitches lying closely together, shoulder to shoulder. In addition, it is easy to do in a neat way, with all the rows of each fabric perfectly lined up. It is as strong a seam as you could ever need; since, however, it does turn the full selvedge to the inside, it will be bulky in the heavier yarns.

Work on the outside, with the edges to be seamed lying side by side.

1. Pass the needle up under the running thread that lies between the selvedge stitch and the first stitch of the fabric. Repeat with the running stitch of the same row on the other fabric.
2. Continue in this way, alternating back and forth between the two fabrics, each time drawing the yarn under a single running thread.
3. Work three or four stitches in this way, drawing the

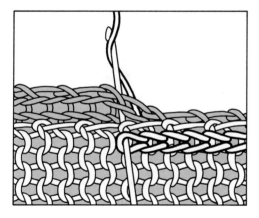

CROCHET SEAM

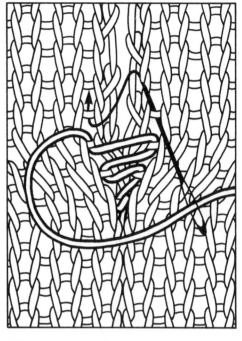

RUNNING THREAD SEAM

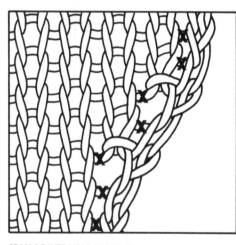

SEAM POINTS NEAR INCREASES

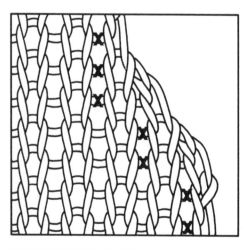

SEAM POINTS NEAR DECREASES

yarn through loosely each time, then tighten the yarn all at once, just enough to pull the two sides of the fabric together without gathering up the seam.

For most fabrics, you will want to work under every single running thread, each pair consisting of one from the same row in both fabrics. On fine yarns, the seam will be adequately joined if you work under two running threads at a time on each side. You must, however, be careful to line the rows up perfectly, as errors will begin to gather one fabric in relation to the other.

If you have worked increases or decreases on the column of selvedge stitches, you will have to pick up a running thread within the fabric, turning the increase to the inside, and then jog back out to the edge. Study the accompanying diagrams for the method of working around the problem.

SELVEDGE SEAM

This method of sewing up produces a very, very nice side seam. It is virtually invisible on the outside of the fabric, and while it is otherwise just as strong and neat, it produces a selvedge that is considerably less bulky than the Running Thread Seam described above, making it a particularly good choice for heavy yarns. Also, it can be used for Reverse Stockinette, a pattern for which Running Thread Seam does not work very well. The two columns of stitches adjacent to the seam are slightly farther apart, but subtly so, and in fact it looks somewhat more natural than the Running Thread Seam, which almost pulls the stitch columns too closely together.

Work from right to left across the edge with the outsides of the fabrics facing one another.

1. On the near fabric, insert the needle under the inner half of the selvedge from farside to nearside. Then insert the needle under the inner half of the selvedge stitch to the left from nearside to farside.
2. On the far fabric, insert the needle from nearside to farside under the inner half of the selvedge opposite

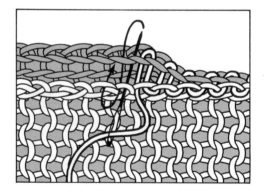

SELVEDGE SEAM

the first of the pair of step 1, above. Insert the needle under the inner half of the selvedge stitch to the left from farside to nearside.

3. Repeat these two steps the length of the seam. (The first stitch of each subsequent pair should already contain a sewing thread—in other words, you will eventually work through each stitch twice.)

What is happening here is that you will be passing the yarn around the head of each selvedge stitch instead of through the side of the stitch or adjacent to it. In doing so, less of the selvedge is turned inside, but the seam is still smooth and firm and will not stretch out or show any gaps. Speaking of gaps, it is possible, but not a particularly good idea, to use this sewing method on a Chain Selvedge.

Do be careful to pass the needle through so the yarn passes around the head of the stitch on the inside; if you work in the other direction, the seaming yarn will be visible on the outside. Please study the accompanying diagram so you will understand exactly what path the yarn must take.

If you prefer, you can work with the fabrics side by side, outside facing up.

1. Pass the needle through the center of the first selvedge stitch from fabric toward seam, and through the selvedge stitch above from seam toward fabric.
2. Repeat on the other side with the pair of selvedge stitches in the same rows.
3. Continue as above, always inserting the needle first into the last stitch of the previous pair.

COMBINATION SEAM

If you need to pull the stitch columns slightly closer together, you can work under the running thread on one

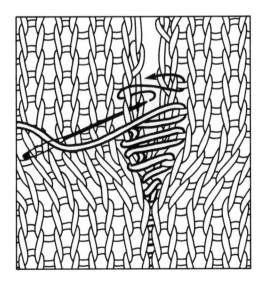

COMBINATION SEAM

fabric and around the head of the selvedge stitch on the other fabric. Work with the outside of the fabrics facing up and the edges to be seamed side by side.

Machine-Sewn Seams

Many machine knitters do all seams on an interlock machine, and technically there is no reason why you can't use them on a hand-knitted fabric as well. The problem is that they do not sew a seam as precisely as you can by hand. The fabric is not necessarily lined up row by row or stitch column to stitch column as with the hand seaming methods given here, and it is extremely difficult not to leave a bit of selvedge stitch on the outside, or include part of the first column of stitches on the fabric within the seam, producing an uneven line on the outside. In order to prevent this, baste the seam carefully with a length of contrast-color yarn, which will serve as a guide and hold the fabric in position, but be careful not to catch that yarn in the seam; it would then be difficult to remove.

Seaming Other Edges

Stockinette is not the only selvedge you might want to seam, nor are side edges the only ones you might need to join.

Seaming Chain Selvedge: A Running Thread Seam works quite well for a Chain Selvedge if it is handled correctly. Because each selvedge stitch spans two rows, in some cases gaps can appear in the seam if you use a single seam stitch adjacent to each selvedge stitch. In order to prevent this, keep in mind that while there is only one selvedge stitch, there will be the full complement of running threads. Unfortunately, they lie closely together in pairs, and it is not always easy to separate one from the other in order to seam under each one. However, this may not always be necessary; the method of handling a seam of this sort depends upon the fabric you have knit.

If you are working with a very fine yarn and a closely knit fabric, the larger stitches of the Chain Selvedge make it much easier to see where you are going, and sewing up under the pair of running threads adjacent to each selvedge stitch will generally be adequate to pull the two edges together without any gaps. When the yarn is fine but the fabric loosely knit, it is better to work under individual running threads, making two seam stitches alternately next to each selvedge stitch.

When you are working with a heavy yarn, the Chain Selvedge is an excellent way to reduce the bulk of a seam. In this case it is generally sufficient to make one seam stitch next to each selvedge stitch, but if you find that that approach leaves gaps, you know you have the option of working the seam more tightly by sewing under each running thread individually.

Seaming Reverse Stockinette

In a Reverse Stockinette fabric, the running threads are, of course, on the outside. For this purpose, therefore, the Running Thread Seam is problematic. If you draw the seaming yarn up gently, more in the way you would for grafting (see page 371), the edges will be butted up against one another and the join will be reasonably successful, as the nubbiness of the fabric tends to hide the seam. A much more successful result is obtained with the Selvedge Seam.

Turning the Selvedges Outside

If you use a Running Thread Seam, but work on the inside, or Purl side of the fabric, the two columns of selvedge stitches will be turned side by side on the outside of the fabric forming a ridge that is quite handsome. Either the Stockinette or the Chain Selvedge will work, but the latter is particularly attractive. It produces a novelty seam that you may find adds just the right touch to a sporty garment or one with more innovative styling.

SELVEDGE SEAMED TO OUTSIDE

SEAMING GARTER STITCH

Garter Stitch fabrics are generally joined with a very flat seam that butts the two edges up against one another. When you work this way, the seaming thread will show a bit and there may be slight gaps, but most of these sins are covered by the general nubbiness and elasticity of the fabric.

1. Examine the edge of the fabric and you will see a little knot at the edge of every Purl row. Work into the strand of this knot that sort of wraps around the edge. It looks almost like the last stitch head on the right side, and the first running thread on the left side.
2. Work back and forth between the fabrics, running the needle under the strand on one side, then under its mate on the other side, just as for a Running Thread Seam.
3. Draw the yarn through loosely stitch by stitch, then tighten it up after you have worked four or five stitches.

The difficulty lies in drawing the fabrics together closely enough to hide the seam without drawing it so tightly that it gathers up.

Alternatively, you can use a Running Thread Seam with a Garter Stitch edge, and because Garter Stitch is so compressed, it is sufficient to work into every other row—that is, just the Purl rows—and in any case, the running thread for the intervening Knit rows is on the other side. Remember that the running threads are the nubs in the lower half of a Purl row; you want to work into the one that passes to the selvedge stitch. This seam

SEAMING GARTER STITCH FABRIC

will be nubby on the inside, but not too bulky in a medium to fine yarn.

Seaming Turned-Back Cuffs

When seaming turned-back cuffs, you must work from the cast-on edge to just past the foldline on the inside, then turn the fabrics over and continue to seam from the outside. Do the same if you are seaming a hat and want the ribbing to fold back for added warmth around the ears.

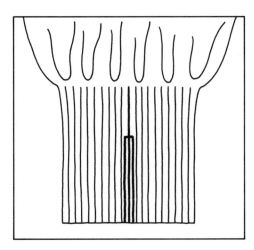

SEAMING A TURNED BACK CUFF

Seaming Cut or Knotted Edges

In the chapter on constructing a fabric we discussed the various methods of forming vertical openings in fabric knit in the round. One, the Steek, leaves a knotted edge. For the other, the stitches are secured with machine sewing and then cut open. In either case, the Running Thread Seam is the method to choose when you must seam these edges to one another or to a normal selvedge. Simply work into the column of running threads within the fabric, adjacent to the knots or the line of machine stitching; the knots or cut edge will be turned to the inside.

Similarly, you can pick up stitches along a cut edge in order to add a border to a center front opening or to knit a sleeve from shoulder to wrist. Insert the needle between the same running threads you would use for seaming.

Seaming Unlike Fabrics

When sewing up the side edges of two pieces of fabric with a Running Thread Seam or a Selvedge Seam, the rows are automatically lined up so there is no need to pin the fabrics together. Do be careful not to miss any running threads or selvedge stitches, however, or it will go crooked. However, if you are sewing together fabrics worked in different stitch patterns with different row gauges, or when you are joining a sloped to a straight edge, you must adopt one of the following approaches because one side will have fewer selvedge stitches and running threads than the other side, so you cannot do a one-to-one match.

- Lay the fabrics down on a hard surface and use safety pins to link them side by side at one-inch intervals. Work back and forth into whatever selvedge stitches or running threads are available as best you can, relying on the spacing of the pins to guide you and to keep the fabric lined up correctly.
- If you wish to be more precise, use Calculating Steps and Points (page 444) and the row count of each fabric, just as you would to work out a pickup pattern, to determine which running threads along one selvedge you may have to skip in order to line things up properly.

In these situations, because you will either need to skip some selvedge stitches on one fabric or work under more than one on the other in order to blend the two together, it is best to use the Combination Seam. If you skip a stitch on a Selvedge Seam, it may poke through on the outside and be visible. Therefore, use the Running Thread Seam method on the side where you may have to work occasionally under two at a time in order to line things up, and the Selvedge Seam method on the side where you will work into every one. This is the method I recommend for setting in a sleeve, and it is very easy to do if you work flat. It produces a smooth seam and a reasonably fine selvedge.

Seaming Double Knits

Because of the bulk, it is far better to work a Double Knit fabric without seams if possible. If a seam is necessary, you can use a single selvedge stitch at each edge and sew up with either Running Thread or Selvedge Seam. This will show on the inside.

Jane Neighbors, in her *Reversible Two-Color Knitting*[1], recommends the use of an overlapped selvedge to reduce bulk, and the result is a seamless appearance on both sides of the fabric. (Information on

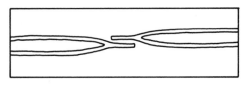

OVERLAPPED SEAM FOR DOUBLE KNIT

1. New York: Charles Scribner's Sons, 1974.

how to knit the selvedge stitches can be found on page 238.) When you are ready to sew, overlap the two selvedges and use a Combination Seam on each face of the fabric. Work into the selvedge stitches of the overlap and into the running threads between the other flap and the fabric itself.

Seaming Wide Selvedges

In some areas of the world, there were certain traditional sweater designs that were seamed with wide selvedges, more like what one would do in sewing a woven fabric. To some extent this does distribute the bulk of the selvedge away from the seam, but it is still heavy and quite unnecessary, given that there are much more successful ways to seam. A wide selvedge was also sometimes worked at the top of a sleeve when set into a cut armhole opening. After seaming the sleeve into place, the selvedge was sewn down on the inside where it served as a facing, covering the cut edges.

Seaming Top and Bottom Edges

Don't. There is no good way to sew these edges without producing bulky and unsatisfactory seams and, fortunately, there is no need to do so. It is far better to leave the stitches at the top on the needle or release a cast-on edge (see page 190) and use Joinery Cast-off (page 153). In order to join a top or bottom edge to a selvedge, see "Grafting to a Selvedge," below. Whenever possible, pick up stitches so no join is necessary (see page 183).

Occasionally a garment is designed with the stitch columns running horizontally instead of vertically. This is generally done as a way of turning a vertical stitch pattern on its side, or a horizontal one upright, or perhaps just for the novelty of it. Regardless of the reasons, it typically leaves you with two side seams to sew up that have cast-on and cast-off edges. While it is possible to release the two edges and graft them together, that's a fairly long seam to graft, and a lot more tedious job to do well than it is to sew a seam. Here's an alternative, and although this is here in the seams department, it's actually a way to avoid them.

Whatever shape your particular pattern takes, at the point where you must add stitches for the side edge, use Stranded Cast-on (see "Finger Cast-on at Side Edge," page 140). When you have worked across the width of the garment, place the stitches of the other side edge on a holder. When you are ready to seam the sweater, intersperse the stitches of the two edges to be seamed on a single double-point or a circular needle and use Joinery Cast-off (page 153). The result will be side seams with half the bulk (one cast-off edge instead of two) in the selvedge.

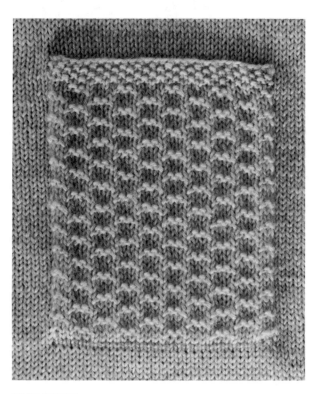

PATCH POCKET

Seams Within a Fabric

It is less common to sew anything within the fabric, except for the occasional pocket or hem, but here, as always, the right technique produces a better result.

Sewing in Pockets

The best approach for attaching a patch pocket to the outside of a fabric is to pick up the stitches for the base of the pocket (see "Picking Up Within the Fabric," page 198). This avoids the necessity of seaming along a cast-on edge. Increase one stitch at each side for selvedges. When you have knit the pocket and cast off, sew the sides down with Running Thread Seam, working under the running threads adjacent to the selvedge stitches on the pocket, and under the running threads between two columns of stitches on the fabric. (You may find it easiest to mark the columns of stitches at each side with a contrast-color yarn before you start so you sew the pocket down straight and true.) This turns the selvedge stitch of the pocket to the inside and creates a very smooth join.

When sewing a pocket lining into place on the inside of the fabric, work into the running threads of pocket and fabric, but draw the yarn up very gently as for grafting. It is especially important to mark the sewing line in this case as it is more difficult to see where to sew next on the inside than on the outside.

Hems

In most books, the recommended method for sewing up a hem is with a simple Overcast Stitch worked under the baseline of the edge and into the running threads of the fabric.

Although certainly adequate, and simple to do, I don't think this is the best technique to use because it can so easily compromise the elasticity of the fabric, and because it tends to cause a slight indentation along the sewing line that is visible on the outside of the garment. It is far better to use a grafting stitch (see page 377.)

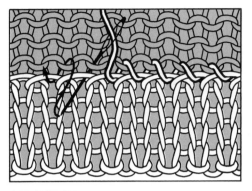

OVERCAST HEM

Grafting

Grafting, also known as Kitchener Stitch, creates a horizontal, stitch-to-stitch join between two pieces of knitted fabric without either casting off or seaming. It is a sewing technique that exactly duplicates the structure and appearance of the Knit or Purl stitches. In order to decide whether, or when, grafting is preferable to a seam, one must be familiar with the advantages and disadvantages of each approach.

As we discussed in the last section, a knitted fabric will have considerably less resilience along the line of a sewn seam than it otherwise would. This is not necessarily a negative condition, however, for the seam works to support the lines of the garment and add definition to the design. This might be particularly important, for instance, along a shoulder line, where the seam will prevent the fabric from stretching out due to the weight of a sleeve. There are other situations, however, where the lack of resilience along a seam would detract from the design or from the way the garment behaved while being worn.

The most common use for grafting is to rejoin two portions of knitting that have been separated for alterations (see page 192) or to join together the toe of a sock so there is no seam to rub. It is also used in certain shawl designs in which sections are worked in different directions due to the demands of the stitch patterns, and then certain portions are joined together with grafting in order to maintain full resilience throughout the assembled fabric. There are other situations, however, in

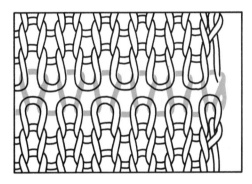

ROW OF GRAFTED STITCHES

which a variation on the technique behaves more like a true seam, albeit a resilient one.

General Technique

There are many useful applications for this technique, but as with all other aspects of knitting, one must understand the possibilities and limitations in order to use it appropriately and to full advantage.

Before I go on to a discussion of how to actually do the grafting, therefore, let's take a look at what happens when two fabrics are grafted together.

There are aspects of grafting that share much in common with those encountered when one knits in the opposite direction. Therefore, for a deeper understanding of what is happening here, please read the material on page 190. You will find this material easier to understand once you have done so.

Lining Up the Fabrics

The sections of knitting being grafted together may be in two different positions in regard to one another, top to bottom, or top to top.

In the first case, such as when a fabric has been divided for alterations and must be rejoined, the top of one section is grafted to the bottom of the other. The stitches at the top of one section and the running threads at the bottom of the other section must be picked up, each one in the proper position with the right side of the stitch on the nearside of the needle; it is important to check their position carefully so none of them cross during the grafting process. There will be one less running thread "stitch" on one needle than there are regular stitches on the other needle, but this is as it should be. (You have read "Picking Up and Knitting in the Opposite Direction," pages 190–193, haven't you?) When grafted, the running threads will nest between the stitches and the columns of stitches from both fabrics will line up perfectly, just as they would if they had been worked in the normal way.

In the second case, such as at a shoulder line or a sock toe, the top of one section is grafted to the top of another. The two sets of stitches are therefore "head to head," rather than in the normal position of head to base, and the needles will each bear an equal number of stitches. However, when turned upside down, one set of stitches must function as running threads and fit between the stitches of the other fabric. This means there is one stitch too many, resulting in an offset at each side. This is somewhat compensated for by the way the grafting sequence is begun and ended, but while the slight jog this creates along the side would be hidden in a seam, it will be visible in something like a scarf or blanket, particularly in a bulky yarn. It also has serious implications when working in any stitch pattern but Stockinette.

Because Stockinette is the same right side up as it is upside down, the offset is only visible at the edges. With any other stitch patterns, however, particularly ones that have strong vertical lines, the offset will be in evidence all the way across the fabric. In these situations it is better to avoid grafting entirely or, if it is essential, to introduce several rows of plain work on either side of the join in order to trick the eye into not seeing the offset.

Also, keep in mind that grafting creates the appearance of Knit and Purl stitches. If you have worked the fabric in some more complex stitch pattern, consider whether a row of Knit, for instance, will look appropriate when interjected between two portions of the other pattern. Technically, of course, it is possible to use a sewing needle and yarn to weave the duplicate of any

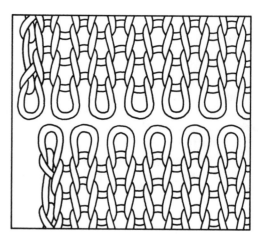

A TOP-TO-TOP GRAFT

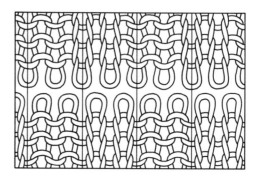

STITCH COLUMN OFFSET IN VERTICAL PATTERNS

stitch done on knitting needles, but in practice this exercise would generally become so complex as to not be worth it at all.

Yarns for Grafting

Grafting is a sewing technique, and therefore the entire length of the yarn being used must be pulled through each stitch, which causes it to fray. For this reason, the technique may not work at all with many slubbed, nubby, or fuzzy yarns, or with any yarn that is particularly delicate. Even yarns that are rather smooth and strong will start to thin out, and the appearance of the stitches grafted at the beginning of the row will be different from those done toward the end. These changes will be negligible when the grafting is done over relatively short distances, but when it is necessary to graft any fabric that is fairly wide, it may be necessary to use several shorter lengths of yarn rather than one long one. While this necessitates hiding the ends of yarn on the inside of the garment, which is not ideal, that may be the compromise that makes the difference between using the technique or not.

Most commonly, grafting is done with yarn that comes off one of the sets of stitches to be joined, but if for some reason the length is insufficient, or should you wish to, a separate strand of yarn may be used, either the same yarn or a different yarn or color. In order to calculate the correct length needed, (see "Calculating Stitches per Yard", page 428). When you have separated a fabric to shorten it, ripping one row will provide a perfectly measured length of yarn.

Holding the Work

There are two methods of supporting the work while grafting. The two sections of fabric to be joined may be placed on a table top, with the outside of the fabric facing up and the two sets of stitches lined up, one above the other. Alternatively, the two needles may be held side by side, with the inside faces of the fabric together, the outsides facing out nearside and farside. Try both approaches and see which one works best for you. When you work on a table, it is easier to see what you are doing, but I think once you are familiar with grafting the other method is a bit faster, and that is the one I prefer. Therefore, in the instructions below, I am going to refer to the near needle and the far needle, as if you were holding the needles side by side in order to graft. If you have the work on a table instead, the near needle would be the lower one, the far needle the upper one. Regardless of which way you choose to work, the points of the knitting needles must both be facing to the right (if necessary, either work one more row on one section or rip back a row in order to accomplish this).

I recommend that the stitches remain on the needle while they are being worked. Many people drop just those few stitches being immediately worked on from the needle, and that is in some ways easier. Then, however, it is also easy to have a stitch run down or to split a stitch with the sewing needle, particularly if the fabric is worked at a firm tension or the stitches are small. In addition, the tips of the needles obscure the stitches that you are trying to work on. All in all, I think it makes more sense to keep each stitch on the needle until it is completely grafted, and that is the manner of working for which the instructions below have been written.

The Grafting Patterns

As the Stockinette grafting pattern is the most common one used, I will write the steps out in some detail to make the manner of working clear, and then I will provide a brief pattern so you will have it to refer to while working if you need it. With the others I will simply give the formulas; they all start and end in the same way.

In each of the grafting patterns given below, there will be a preliminary step that begins any sequence in the correct way and also corrects for the problem of the half stitch at the edges in a top-to-top join.

If you are working with the yarn that comes off the first stitch on the far needle, insert the sewing needle into the first stitch on the near needle according to the pattern and draw the yarn through. Move the needle from right to left around and under the grafting yarn where it passes between the two needles and then insert it into the first stitch on the far needle according to the grafting pattern.

If you are working with the yarn that comes off the first stitch on the near needle, work in the same way, but pass the grafting yarn around the yarn that is hanging off the first stitch on the far needle.

STOCKINETTE GRAFTING PATTERN

This is by far the most common method of grafting. Pay attention to what is happening as you work and you will soon make sense of it; it is not at all difficult to do. To begin, then, thread the yarn coming off one of the needles through a blunt, wide-eyed sewing needle. Hold the two sections of fabric, insides together, in the left hand, with the tips of both needles facing to the right.

Preliminary Step

1. Pass the sewing needle through the first stitch on the near needle as to Purl, and draw the yarn through.
2. Pass the needle around the strand at the edge, and then through the first stitch on the far needle as to Knit. Draw the yarn through. Both stitches should remain on the knitting needles.

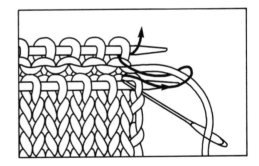

STOCKINETTE GRAFTING/PRELIMINARY STEP

The Grafting Sequence

1. Near needle: Insert the sewing needle into the first stitch as to Knit, drop this stitch from the needle, and draw the yarn through. Insert the sewing needle into the next stitch as to Purl and draw the yarn through, leaving the stitch on the knitting needle.
2. Far needle: Insert the sewing needle into the first stitch as to Purl, drop this stitch from the needle, and draw the yarn through. Insert the sewing needle into

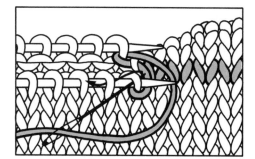

GRAFTING STITCHES ON THE NEAR NEEDLE

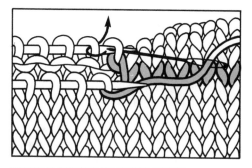

GRAFTING STITCHES ON THE FAR NEEDLE

the next stitch as to Knit and draw the yarn through, leaving the stitch on the knitting needle.

Abbreviated Pattern

Preliminary: Near/Purl, far/Knit.
1. Near: Knit/drop, Purl.
2. Far: Purl/drop, Knit.

As you work, keep the yarn for the grafted stitches off the knitting needles, bringing it under the near needle tip as you switch from one set of stitches to the other. It is much easier to draw the yarn through the stitch the second time if it has already been dropped from the knitting needle. Therefore, insert the tapestry needle into the stitch in the correct way, slip it off the knitting needle, and then draw the yarn through.

Notice that the needle passes through two stitches on the lower needle, then two on the upper, back and forth in this manner across the row, and that the yarn must be drawn through each stitch twice. When the second pass in one stitch has been completed, it is dropped from the knitting needle and the first pass through the adjacent stitch is made. Then the work shifts to the set of stitches on the other needle where this pattern is repeated. The first stitch on the needle, therefore, will always have a single grafting strand passing through it when the two-stitch sequence on that needle begins. If it doesn't, you will know that you have either missed a step or dropped a stitch from the needle, and you will have to retrace the path of the yarn to see where you have gone wrong.

Moving the sewing needle horizontally between one

stitch and the next on the same fabric will create a running thread nub. If you get the nubs in the right place, the sides of the grafted stitches, which lie between the two fabrics, will position themselves. Whether the nub winds up on the inside or outside of the fabric, and whether the discarded stitch becomes a Knit or a Purl, is determined by the manner in which you insert the sewing needle into the stitches. Do not make the mistake of thinking that inserting the sewing needle into a stitch "as to Purl" will produce a Purl stitch; as a matter of fact, in order to form a Knit stitch on the nearside, the first pass through a stitch is as to Purl, the second as to Knit.

Moving the sewing needle between one set of stitches and the other will form one side of the new stitch. You will find that part much more straightforward; however, it is on this step that you must carefully regulate the tension so each grafted stitch is a consistent size, both with its fellows and with the stitches in the sections of fabric that are being joined. Because you do not have a knitting needle to maintain a regular stitch size, you must do this by eye. It is best to check what you have done every three or four stitches and, if necessary, work some of the yarn to the left or right to even out the stitches.

Ending the Grafting Row

Regardless of whether you are grafting top to top or top to bottom, you can end the sequence in the same way, although the appearance will be different; in the latter case, one full stitch will end the sequence, and in the former it will be a half stitch.

• When you have completed the second pass through the last stitch on the needle, bring the needle through the side of the last grafted stitch from farside to nearside, then down through the loop of sewing yarn at the edge; tighten the yarn down to form a knot to secure the stitches and weave the end into the selvedge (see page 379).

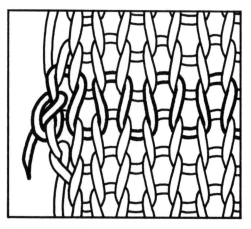

LAST STITCH ON TOP-TO-BOTTOM GRAFT

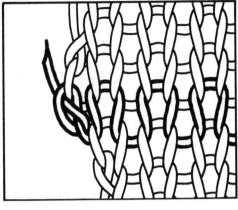

LAST STITCH ON TOP-TO-TOP GRAFT

REVERSE STOCKINETTE GRAFTING

Since Reverse Stockinette Stitch is just the Purl side of a Stockinette fabric, the simplest thing to do, therefore, is to work exactly as above for Stockinette Grafting, with the two sections of fabric lined up in the same way, with the Purl faces together.

GARTER STITCH GRAFTING

The sequence given here is appropriate when there is a row of Purl below the stitches on the near needle, and a row of Knit below the stitches on the far needle.

Preliminary step: Near/Purl, far/Purl.
1. Near: Knit/drop, Purl.
2. Far: Knit/drop, Purl.

SINGLE RIB GRAFTING

In this case there will be four steps, two for the Knit stitches on each needle and two for the Purl stitches. I am going to assume that the first stitch of the Single Rib sequence is a Knit. Remember, this will line up properly only when grafting the top of one section of fabric to the bottom of another.

Preliminary step: Near/Purl, far/Knit.
1. Near: Knit/drop, Knit.
2. Far: Purl/drop, Purl.
3. Near: Purl/drop, Purl.
4. Far: Knit/drop, Knit.

DOUBLE RIB GRAFTING

As with Single Rib, this can be done successfully only when grafting the top of one section to the bottom of

another. Here we must have eight steps: one for each needle when the two stitches to be worked on are both Knit; a pair for when they are a Knit stitch, then a Purl stitch; a pair for when they are both Purl; and a pair for when they are a Purl stitch, then a Knit stitch. I will assume that the Double Rib sequence starts with a pair of Knit stitches.

Preliminary step: Near/Purl, far/Knit.
1. Near on two Knit: Knit/drop, Purl.
2. Far on two Knit: Purl/drop, Knit
3. Near on one Knit, one Purl: Knit/drop, Knit.
4. Far on one Knit, one Purl: Purl/drop, Purl.
5. Near on two Purl: Purl/drop, Knit.
6. Far on two Purl: Knit/drop, Purl.
7. Near on one Purl, one Knit: Purl/drop, Purl.
8. Far on one Purl, one Knit: Knit/drop, Knit.

Grafting Ribs off Four Needles

There is an alternate method of grafting any Rib pattern that you may come across in some books. It involves slipping all the Knit stitches of one fabric to one double-point needle, all the Purl stitches to another. The same thing is done with the other fabric so that there are a total of four needles. Place the two fabrics on a table with one set of needles above the other. Graft together the Knit stitches on one side, turn the fabrics over, and graft together the Knit stitches on the other side.

The problem with this, aside from all those needles, is that it effectively turns a single fabric into a Double Knit one, so it will be only half as wide at the edge. I think the technique is awkward to do, the result is not satisfactory, and the whole thing is not worth the bother.

Grafting the Exceptions

Should you have occasion to graft a fabric where the pattern is something other than Stockinette, Garter Stitch, or a Single or Double Rib, here are the instructions, broken down so you know what to do with a Knit stitch or a Purl stitch wherever it happens to fall. In these instructions, "first pass" means the first time the yarn is drawn through a particular stitch and "second pass" is the second time the yarn is drawn through that same stitch. As you know from the general principles on grafting, between the first and second pass a pair of stitches on the other needle will be worked in whatever way is appropriate for them. Because the stitches on the far needle cannot be seen as you work, you may want to chart the patterns of both fabrics as a guide.

Near Knit stitch:
• First pass as to Purl.
• Second pass as to Knit.
Far Knit stitch:
• First pass as to Knit.

• Second pass as to Purl.

Near Purl stitch:
• First pass as to Knit.
• Second pass as to Purl.

Far Purl stitch:
• First pass as to Purl.
• Second pass as to Knit.

Grafting for Seams and Hems

Grafting is traditionally used to link two sets of free stitches with another intervening row of stitches woven into place with a tapestry needle and yarn. However, the technique of duplicating the form of a knitted stitch with a sewing needle and yarn affords some options in areas typically handled with other sewing methods, and in most cases the technique produces a far more resilient and satisfying join than if handled with a more conventional seam.

Grafting to a Cast-off Edge

I mentioned above that grafting offers no support to the line of a garment, particularly when used at the shoulder. Here is a way to achieve the appearance of a grafted join, with the support provided by a cast-off edge.

Cast off the stitches of one shoulder, leave the stitches of the other on the needle. Place the outside of the two fabrics face up, with the cast-off edge above the needle bearing the stitches and the tip of the needle pointing to the right, and work as follows:

1. Thread the yarn into a tapestry needle and pass the needle from farside to nearside through the center of the first stitch above the cast-off edge.
2. Insert the sewing needle into the first stitch on the knitting needle from right to left, as to Purl.
3. Pass the yarn from nearside to farside through the center of the same stitch above, then from farside to nearside through the stitch to the left.
4. Insert the sewing needle into the first stitch on the knitting needle from left to right as to Knit; drop the stitch from the needle.
5. Repeat the last three steps until all of the stitches have been joined.

On the outside, the fabrics will have the seamless appearance of grafting; on the inside, the single line of cast-off stitches will support the shoulder line. Work in exactly the same manner to join free stitches to a cast-on edge. The technique can be used on two cast-off edges or a cast-off and a cast-on edge, grafting above one and below the other, but while the appearance is quite good, the seam itself is wide and stiff and has little to recommend it.

Grafting to a Selvedge

There are several situations in which you might find it necessary to graft free stitches to a selvedge. If you want to work a hemmed center front border on picked-up stitches, for instance, the bulk of a join of this sort is considerably reduced by eliminating the cast-off edge entirely and grafting the last row of stitches into place on the inside of the garment. This approach is also useful should you find a border pattern you like that you think would be more attractive if knitted up separately and attached at the top edge instead of working it up from picked-up stitches.

Because the number of stitches in the border is unlikely to match the number of rows along the edge, to make a perfectly smooth join you will have to develop a pattern using Calculating Steps and Points (page 437) in order to coordinate the two just as you would for picking up stitches.

There are two different ways to work, depending upon whether you must graft to the outside or the inside of the fabric.

Working on the Outside: In order to graft the top edge of a border to a selvedge, work with the border below the selvedge and the outside of both fabrics facing up.

1. Graft the stitches of the border off the needle in the normal way, working all in Knit or in a combination of Knit and Purl if you wish to blend the grafting with the border pattern (for detailed grafting patterns, see page 373).
2. On the fabric, work under the running threads that lie between the selvedge and the first column of

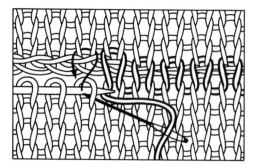

GRAFTING TO A CAST-OFF EDGE

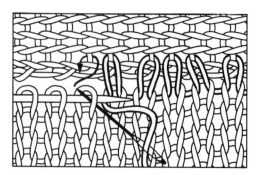

GRAFTING TO A SELVEDGE ON THE OUTSIDE

stitches within the fabric just as for Running Thread Seam (page 365), if necessary skipping one from time to time according to the pattern you worked out to space the border stitches along the edge.

This turns the selvedge to the inside of the garment and produces a result virtually identical to picking up the stitches and working in the other direction.

Working on the Inside: Use this version if you are planning to work a hemmed border on stitches picked up along a selvedge. Pick up the stitches, spacing them along the edge according to your pattern, work the border facing, the foldline if one is desired, and the turnback. Fold the border into position on the inside of the fabric, then graft as follows:

1. Pass the sewing needle into the first stitch from right to left as to Purl.
2. Pass the needle up under the side of the selvedge stitch directly above the stitch and then back down under the side of the selvedge stitch to the left.
3. Pass the needle into the first stitch as to Knit and drop it from the needle.

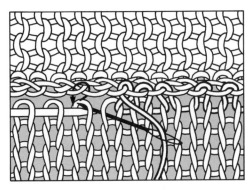

GRAFTING TO A SELVEDGE ON THE INSIDE

If necessary, mark the columns of stitches in the border with a contrast-color thread (page 349) in order to line the stitches up correctly so the border will not be skewed. If you find this method adds too much bulk to the join, graft the stitches off the needle but use a simple Overcast Stitch into the selvedge.

Grafting Two Selvedges

Grafting two selvedges together is really no different from using a Running Thread or Selvedge Seam with the yarn drawn up loosely to form stitches. Experiment with the effect this creates in your particular yarn and fabric; I have found that grafting into the running threads adjacent to each selvedge on the outside of a Stockinette fabric does not produce a particularly attractive result; the Reverse Running Thread Seam is much more attractive. In any case, it does not produce

a particularly resilient join, because while the grafting stitches are structurally capable of resilience, the selvedge stitches are not. Look on this as a decorative possibility, not a method of achieving an elastic seam.

Grafting a Hem

Sewing down a hem on the inside of a garment, whether a typical one at the bottom edge or that of a hemmed neckline border, is generally done with Overcasting (page 364); however, the result is much more satisfying, both in terms of appearance and behavior, if you use a grafting technique.

If you are planning to fold a hem up from the bottom edge, use Stranded Cast-on so you can easily free the stitches for grafting. If you are folding a hem down, such as for a waistline or a border at a neckline, either leave the stitches on the needle or use Stranded Cast-off. (When working a circular neckline on double-point needles, you must either pick up the stitches on the inside or use Stranded Cast-off, because it is nearly impossible to pull a set of needles through a neck opening.)

In both these situations, you will be grafting on the inside of the fabric, which, more often than not, will be in Purl. Determine exactly which row within the fabric you want to graft into; if necessary, mark the row with a yarn marker (page 349). Similarly, in order to line the columns of stitches up accurately so the hem will not be skewed, run several yarn markers, spaced along the width, down a column of stitches from the edge to the row you will attach it to.

Break the yarn you have been knitting with and thread it through a tapestry needle. Have the fabric above the needle bearing the stitches and work as follows:

1. Pass the sewing needle through the first stitch on the needle from right to left as to Purl.
2. Pass the sewing needle under a running thread within

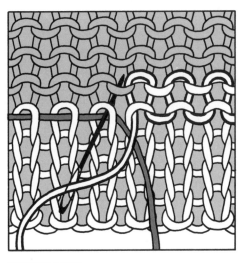

GRAFTING A HEM

the fabric, then down under the running thread to the left. The yarn should follow the contour of the intervening stitch head.

3. Pass the sewing needle through the first stitch on the needle from left to right as to Knit; drop the stitch from the needle.

4. Continue in this way until all of the stitches have been worked off the knitting needle.

This is quite straightforward when working a plain hem at a bottom edge. In that case, graft the first stitch on the edge to the selvedge stitch on the row you will be grafting to. If the garment was seamed, attach the first free stitch to the seam.

If the hem was worked in the round, graft the stitches off the needle in the same direction as you have been working. This may require that you work with the free stitches above the fabric you are grafting into instead of the other way around. The principles are the same, but you will have to modify the grafting pattern slightly. (Detailed grafting instructions for any situation can be found on page 373.)

One of the more attractive ways to finish a circular neckline opening is with a hemmed, ribbed border knit in the round. Grafting the last row of this neckline into position helps to preserve the elasticity of the opening, preventing both a constricted opening that is hard to pass the head through and one that splays out with wear. For best results, I also recommend that you use a very fine needle in order to make the ribbing more elastic, and calculate the stitch gauge and pickup pattern carefully (see page 444).

Grafting a Patch Pocket

The same general idea can be applied to attaching something like the base of a patch pocket to the outside of a fabric. Actually, I think it far simpler to pick up the stitches for the pocket within the fabric, knit it up, and then just sew down the sides. Nevertheless, there is an advantage to working this way. If you cast on the stitches for the pocket and then sew it down as described here, it will behave just like the grafted shoulder line discussed above; the cast-on edge will provide some stability to the pocket, preventing it from sagging or stretching out in wear.

1. With a contrast-color length of embroidery thread,

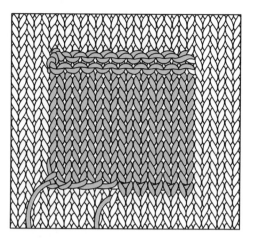

GRAFTING A PATCH POCKET

mark the row of stitches below the pocket for placement.

2. Attach the sewing yarn on the inside and bring it through to the outside at the top right corner. Turn the fabric upside down and sew up the first side of the pocket with Running Thread Seam (page 365).

3. Turn the fabric right side up again. Bring the needle out through the center of a stitch in the fabric at the bottom right corner of the pocket.

4. Pass the needle behind both sides of a pocket stitch, just above the cast-on edge.

5. Pass the needle from outside to inside through the center of the stitch below, then from inside to outside through the center of the stitch to the left.

6. Repeat these last two steps across the base of the pocket.

7. Use Running Thread Seam to attach the other side of the pocket.

Both the selvedges and the cast-on edge will be turned inside the pocket, but the pocket itself will look almost seamlessly joined to the fabric. It's a very nice effect.

Alternatively, use Stranded Cast-on for the pocket. On the first row increase one stitch each side for selvedges. To attach, sew the sides with Running Thread Seam, free the stitches of the bottom edge, and graft them into place. Work in much the same way when attaching a pocket lining to the inside of the fabric.

Miscellaneous Finishing Techniques

Here are all those little housekeeping details that one must do before the garment is presentable and ready to wear. I know how difficult it is to restrain yourself at this point; after all the time and effort, you are no doubt impatient to wear your creation. But you must at least hide all the little tail ends of yarn, and in some cases there are buttons to sew on or buttonholes to face, etc., before it is really truly finished.

Hiding Ends of Yarn

Whenever you start or finish knitting, tie on a new supply of yarn, or change colors, you will leave an end of yarn that must be hidden on the inside of the fabric during finishing. Actually, it doesn't have to be hidden, but it does make the inside of the garment look neater. Those gorgeous Shetland Fair Isle sweaters have hundreds of tiny knots on the inside where the color changes occurred, and the yarn ends are just cut off about half an inch long and left like a little fringe. Because the yarn used is so fine, you hardly notice they are there. So much for those who say never tie a knot and aways hide the ends. However, this is really a local tradition, not generally followed in other parts of the world, and since most people today don't work with such fine yarn, knots and ends have become a real presence that cries out for attention.

As a general rule, I recommend that yarn be tied on and the ends hidden at the selvedge whenever possible. When done mid-row, even the best of the methods for starting a new supply of yarn and hiding the ends will thicken the fabric at that point, although the change will otherwise be invisible if handled correctly. However, if you are knitting in the round, there will be no selvedge available, and there are occasions such as tying on yarn for Intarsia, for embroidery, to finish a buttonhole or sew on a pocket that require a technique for attaching yarn within the fabric rather than to an edge. (For more information, see below.)

Hiding Ends at the Edge

Ends of yarn left at the corner of a cast-on or cast-off edge, or when a new supply has been tied on at the edge of the fabric, should be hidden in the selvedge itself after any seam has been sewn.

1. Untie any knot made on the ends of yarn. Wrap the two ends around one another once to interlock them, and tighten up the selvedge stitches that they emerge from if necessary.

2. Thread the lower end into a tapestry needle, and use Overcasting (page 364) to weave it down along the outer half of the selvedge stitches about one and a half to two inches. Remove the needle, stretch the seam out as far as it will go and cut the end off close.

3. Thread the other end into the needle and work it up along the selvedge in the same way.

Always work the ends in two different directions to keep the selvedge from getting too bulky.

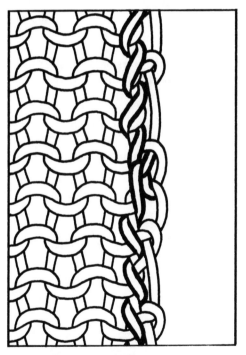

ENDS WORKED INTO A SELVEDGE

Hiding Ends Within the Fabric

The most common method of hiding ends of yarn on the inside of the fabric is to thread the end into a tapestry needle and use the equivalent of Overcast Stitch to wind it around the running threads or heads of the stitches in one row for an inch or two. There are real problems with this. First, the end has no elasticity, so when the fabric is stretched out it can work its way free and sometimes poke through to the outside. Second, because it is wrapped around the running threads, it may be visible on any fabric worked at a loose tension or in an openwork pattern. And finally, with some patterns you may not even have Purl nubs available on the inside, and if you try to weave the end into the sides of the Knit stitches, it will definitely show on the outside.

By far the best method for hiding any ends left within the fabric is to use the equivalent of Duplicate Stitch (page 286), the same stitch used for embroidery. While in that case the stitch is intended to be highly decorative, here it is used as camouflage. The advantage of this method is that the end takes on the exact contour of a stitch, which gives it the same resilience and elasticity that the fabric has. This means that it won't pull free when the fabric is stretched out, and because the end lies completely on the inside of the fabric, even if the very end did work free, it wouldn't be able to pop through on the outside.

As you know, when tying on a new supply of yarn, the break occurs between two stitches. When working in Stockinette, this means the two yarn ends will be on the inside of the fabric where the running thread would have been, and they will be woven in on Purl stitches. When working in Reverse Stockinette, the two yarn ends will be on the outside and must be drawn through to the inside to be secured where they will be woven in on Knit stitches. When working on a fabric with mixed stitches, always arrange to have the break occur between two Knit stitches whenever possible.

To begin, undo any knot used when tying on the yarn. Examine the outside of the fabric to see that the stitches on either side of the break are the size they should be and adjust them if necessary. Then proceed as follows:

PURL DUPLICATE STITCH

1. Thread one end into a tapestry needle. Interlock the two yarns by wrapping them around one another once, gently so as not to disturb the size of the stitches.

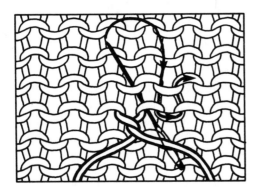

WORKING IN ENDS WITH PURL DUPLICATE STITCH

2. After interlocking the yarns, insert the needle up through the same head of the stitch the end emerged from and weave it back in the direction it came from.
3. Following the contour of the stitch, pass the needle up through the running thread in the row above and down through the next running thread in the same row.
4. Pass the needle down through the head of the same stitch you started with in the row below, then up through the head of the adjacent stitch.
5. Finally, pass it up through the running thread last used in the row above and then continue the sequence for as many stitches as necessary.

KNIT DUPLICATE STITCH

1. If the yarns are on the outside of the fabric, draw them through to the inside. Thread the tapestry needle, but do not interlock the two yarns. Weave them in the direction opposite to that from which they came.
2. Bring the needle out through the center of the stitch to the right or left in the row below the break.
3. Pass the needle behind the two sides of a stitch in the row above.
4. Insert the needle into the center of the same stitch below, then out the center of the adjacent stitch in the same row. Repeat as necessary.

If you are working with Garter Stitch, follow the path of the yarn, working Knit below and Purl above, or vice versa. If you are working on a complex stitch pattern, it is best to hide the end along a plain row; otherwise, you must simply try to follow the path of the yarn in the adjacent stitches as best you can. If you really understand the structure of the stitches, working Duplicate Stitch is very easy.

When you are working with contrast-color yarn, hide the ends behind stitches of the same color. This may require that you work the end into some stitches vertically or on a slope rather than horizontally. This causes no problems, as long as you are careful to follow the contour of the stitches as much as possible, and don't skip any, leaving strands between them.

Should you be working with a slippery yarn, you may need a knot to hold the stitches on either side of the break in position. Use the knot described for attaching embroidery thread on page 286, knotting the end to itself in as unobtrusive a position as possible and then hiding the ends as described above.

Sewing in Elastic

While knitted fabrics are generally very resilient, nevertheless there are occasions when it is necessary to sew in some elastic. Knitted ribbings are not adequate to support the weight of a skirt from the waist, for instance, and ribbings in some yarns may lack the elasticity required for waists and cuffs or become permanently stretched out with wear.

Threading in Elastic

The method of weaving in elastic while you knit is described on page 281. If you did not do that and find later that a ribbed edge is not holding, you can add some elastic thread with a tapestry needle. Many knitting shops now sell the type of elastic used in several colors, which helps it to blend in and not show through on the outside. Decide how wide you want the ribbing to be in its relaxed state.

1. Knot the elastic to a seam, or pass it around a stitch head and knot it to itself, leaving sufficient end to hide later.
2. Pass the needle up under the stitch head in each Purl column, then strand past the Knit stitches. Pull the elastic through after every few stitches.
3. When you get to the end, measure the ribbing and ease the elastic in until it is the correct width.

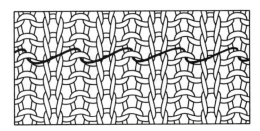

THREADING IN ELASTIC ON SINGLE RIB

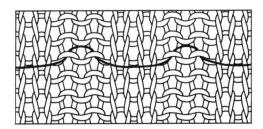

THREADING IN ELASTIC ON DOUBLE RIB

This hides the elastic quite well, so it can hardly be seen even with the ribbing stretched open, especially if you have managed to find an elastic that is fairly close in color to your yarn.

You may find it adequate to weave the elastic in only on the top row of the ribbing, right below where the stitch pattern changes for the main section of the fabric. If you want the elastic throughout the ribbing, run it in on every other row, or in a fine yarn on every third or fourth row.

Sewn Thread Casing

A sewn thread casing is the least bulky method of attaching flat elastic on the inside, but it is relatively fragile and should be used for the narrower widths of elastic and on garments that are on the delicate side. The elastic may be attached on the inside of any stitch pattern, but ribbing is ideal because it pregathers the fabric. Use a fairly strong, doubled thread or embroidery thread, matched in color to the knit.

1. Measure the elastic carefully, allowing for any overlap. Pin or baste the elastic into position on the inside of the fabric.
2. Working from left to right, pass the needle up under a Purl nub or a running thread just above the top edge of the elastic. Repeat with a nub at the bottom edge, one or two columns to the right. Continue in this way, one stitch at the bottom, one at the top.
3. When you are done, adjust the elastic and try the garment on for fit. If the elastic is in a circle, sew the overlap securely. If it is flat, attach it securely at both sides, preferably to a seam.

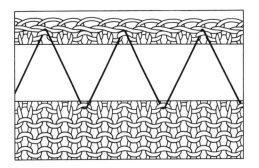

SEWN THREAD CASING FOR ELASTIC

Worked in this manner, the threads enclose the elastic, which can freely move within the casing. If you want to attach the elastic so it cannot move, work as described above, but in each case pass the needle through both stitch and elastic. In this case, exact fit must be determined first and any overlap sewn together.

Crocheted Casing

This works much like the one above, in which the elastic can move within the casing, but it is considerably stronger. It is also slightly bulkier, but far less so than any woven (see below) or knitted casing (see page 204) would be.

1. Work a Single Crochet into a Knit stitch at the top edge of the elastic.
2. Work a Single Crochet chain the width of the elastic, then make another Single Crochet into a stitch of the fabric slightly to the right at the bottom edge of the elastic. Repeat.

This can be done ahead of time and the elastic inserted later as it would be for a woven casing, or you can work over the elastic as described above for a sewn thread casing.

Woven Casings

A woven casing for elastic is very nice when the elastic would otherwise be next to your skin. However, keep in mind that it will also be gathered up by the elastic and will add a certain amount of bulk. For this reason, select a very fine weight fabric. Sewing techniques are the same as when attaching any other woven fabric (see below).

Sewing Wovens to Knits

Whether you are attaching a lining, backing buttons or buttonholes with ribbon, attaching a facing or a casing, or sewing in a zipper, the hand sewing methods and thread used are precisely those you would use when sewing any of these things to a woven fabric.

Any woven fabric that you intend to sew to a knit should be preshrunk first, and the knit should be cleaned and dressed. Preshrink a facing by dunking it in a hot basin of water and ironing it dry. If you are dealing with a lining, either wash it before cutting it out, or have your cleaners steam it well.

Always cut the woven according to your pattern, not according to a measurement you have taken from the knitted fabric. (For reasons why this is so, see page 418.) For a full lining, allow generous ease pleats down both front and back and at the hem to allow both for movement and the resilience of the knitted fabric. Pin the woven into position, easing the knit in or stretching it out slightly to fit.

HEMSTITCH

This can be used to attach linings and facings of any kind. Fold down and press the edge of the woven fabric. Knot the thread onto the woven under the folded edge and proceed as follows:

1. Pass the needle under a strand of the knit fabric from right to left directly beneath the stitch made in the woven edge.
2. Pass the needle up through the woven, very close to the folded edge, about one-quarter inch away from the last stitch.
3. Repeat these two steps.

In the lighter-weight fabrics, use a single strand of thread: If you are working with a heavy fabric and facing, you may want to double the thread. Working this way hides the thread that passes from one stitch to the next, which not only produces a nearly invisible hem, but prevents the threads from being snagged in wear.

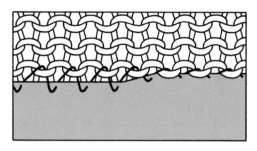

HEMSTITCH

CATCHSTITCH

This is an excellent method of sewing any woven fabric to a knit because it is flexible, and therefore much less likely to break; it is, however, fully visible. If necessary, finish the edge of the woven first.

1. Working from left to right with the woven edge up, attach the thread to the inner side of the woven and bring it through to the outside.
2. Take a stitch from right to left into the knit about one-quarter inch to the right.
3. Take a stitch from right to left into the woven about one-quarter inch to the right. Repeat.

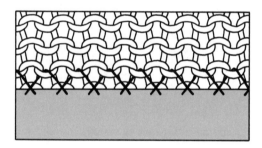

CATCHSTITCH

BLINDSTITCH

This is done just like Catchstitch, but under the edge of the woven where it can't be seen. If necessary, finish the edge of the woven first.

- Work from left to right with the woven edge up. Fold the edge down slightly and work as for Catchstitch.

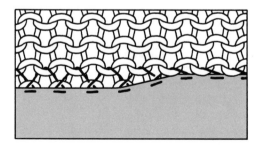

BLINDSTITCH

BACKSTITCH

This creates a very firm and inelastic attachment between two fabrics, which makes this an excellent choice for attaching zippers. It is also good if you need to sew in a woven tape to stabilize the fabric, such as to correct a sagging shoulder or neckline.

If you are using this to attach a zipper, the edge of the fabric should be finished with a firm, attractive edge stitch or a row or two of crochet. Pin or baste the zipper into position with the edge of the fabric positioned slightly back from the center of the teeth. Always work on the outside, using a single strong sewing thread carefully matched in color to the knitted fabric. It is best to work the sewing around the running threads between two columns of stitches, or around the head of a stitch if sewing along a row. Attach the thread on the inside and bring the needle through to the outside.

- Insert the needle down one step to the right, then up two steps to the left.

Continue in this way, using your fingers to guide the sewing on the inside to keep it as straight and neat as possible. Be careful to go all the way through knit and zipper each time.

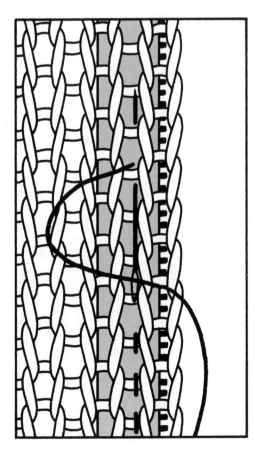

BACKSTITCH

If you prefer to baste the edges together before sewing in the zipper, use a contrast-color yarn for the basting and a simple overcast stitch (page 364). Overcasting will butt the two edges together so they will lie perfectly flat, and the contrast-color yarn will make the join visible so you can position the zipper correctly.

Use Hemstitch to attach the edge of the zipper tape to the inside of the fabric for a nice finish. If you are putting the zipper into a center front opening, the tape is likely to show on the inside when the garment is worn open. This can be unattractive, and if you want to cover it, knit a narrow strip of bias with split yarn (see page 172) and sew one side to the zipper tape fairly close to the teeth, and the other side to the fabric to completely cover the tape.

Buttons and Buttonholes

Because of the flexibility of a knitted fabric, most buttons and buttonholes require some support.

Sewing on Buttons

A button can be sewn onto a knit in the same way it would be sewn onto any woven fabric. You can use the yarn you knit with, or a color-matched embroidery thread or strong sewing thread. If you want it to be stronger, and take the strain of wear off the knitted fabric, sew the decorative button on the outside, and a very small inconspicuous button underneath it on the inside, passing the needle through both buttons and knotting the thread off between the two. Alternatively, cut out a small square of felt, color-matched as closely as possible to the knitted fabric, and sew it on the inside of the fabric under the button. On heavy knits, it is a good idea to use a button with a shank or make a thread shank to accommodate the fabric around the buttonhole.

Faced Buttonholes

Sewing a grosgrain ribbon facing behind buttonholes and buttons helps to support the line of the garment and stabilize the fabric. The grosgrain can be sewn to the fabric with Hemstitch (page 382). The buttons should be sewn through both knit and facing. For the buttonholes, the facing will have to be cut open and attached to the opening in the knit.

Slashed Opening

1. Sew the grosgrain to the inside of the buttonhole band.
2. Slash the ribbon from the inner edge to the outer point of the buttonhole.
3. Turn the two slashed edges under to form a V-shaped opening and sew it neatly to the fabric with Hemstitch, securing it firmly where it meets the point of the buttonhole.

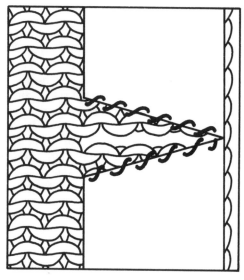

SLASHED BUTTONHOLE LINING

The advantage to this is that the ribbon will reinforce the point of the buttonhole where it takes the strain, while the slash allows resiliency to the rest of it so the button can pass through.

Machine Sewn Opening

1. Baste the facing into place, and carefully mark the position of the buttonholes.
2. Remove the facing and work machine-sewn buttonholes.
3. Then permanently attach the facing and use Hemstitch to attach the facing buttonhole to the inner edge of the buttonhole in the knit.

Hand Sewn Opening

1. Mark the openings as above.

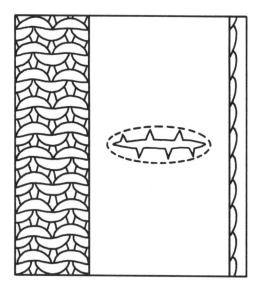

REINFORCING STITCHES ON BUTTONHOLE FACING

2. With tiny reinforcing stitches, sew around what will be the edge of the buttonhole on the facing.
3. Slit the buttonhole open within the sewing and notch several times between cut edge and sewn stitches.
4. Turn the cut edge under and sew the hemmed opening to the knit.

Edgings

To a great extent, knitted fabrics can be pre-finished by selecting the proper type of stitches to be placed near edges. Ribbings and flat, noncurling stitch patterns such as Seed Stitch are obvious choices, and there are a variety of decorative selvedges that can be used on side edges (see page 165). In addition, there are many beautiful stitch patterns knit narrow and long that can be worked up separately and sewn on, or attached during the knitting with the method described on page 193. There are also many beautiful crocheted edgings found in the stitch pattern books.

There is one minimal and unobtrusive edging you are unlikely to find elsewhere, and since it is so useful, I will include it here. It is particularly good for finishing a selvedge that didn't turn out neatly, particularly along a zipper.

SINGLE-CROCHET TURNED EDGE

1. Fold the column of selvedge stitches toward the inside of the fabric.
2. Working from right to left, insert the hook between two running threads adjacent to the selvedge and then through the center of the selvedge stitch underneath. Hook the yarn and draw through a loop.
3. Insert the hook between two running threads and a

SINGLE CROCHET EDGE

selvedge stitch to the left, hook the yarn and draw the loop through the fabric and the loop already on the needle.

Repeat this last step the length of the selvedge, adjusting the size of the stitches carefully so they are even and so as not to draw up the fabric. If you have used Stockinette Selvedge, work between every pair of running threads; if you used Chain, between every other pair.

Fringe

Fringe can make a nice finishing touch for shawls, scarves, blankets, and pillow covers. Elementary fringes are very easy to make and to attach, and there are also a wide variety of decorative knotting patterns for more elaborate fringes that are available in knit or crochet stitch pattern books, or in any elementary book on macrame.

When you intend to use a fringe, plan ahead and use a method of casting on or casting off that will make it easy to pull the fringe through (see the glossary on page

533), on a side edge, use Chain Selvedge (page 164), or crochet a border that will accommodate fringe. The fringe must be wrapped around a gauge to measure off the length. Gauges for this purpose (and for making pompoms) are available in most knitting shops, and include instructions for their use.

Attaching Fringe

1. In order to attach the fringe, insert a large crochet hook through the edge and pull the folded end through, forming a loop.
2. Reach the hook down and draw all the ends through the loop, then pull the ends down to tighten the knot against the edge.

Knitted-in Fringe: A knitted-in fringe can be done along the side edges of a fabric.

1. Cast on one or two additional inches of fabric on the side where you want to have the fringe. Work these stitches in plain Stockinette the entire length of the fabric.
2. Before casting off, drop these extra stitches from the needle and unravel them from top to bottom. Cut the looped ends and tie each pair of strands together to keep the first few stitches within the fabric from enlarging.

And finally, you can knit a separate border covered with Knotted Loop Stitch (page 39), and sew it to the edges of the fabric wherever you like.

KNOTTED FRINGE ON FAIR ISLE SCARF

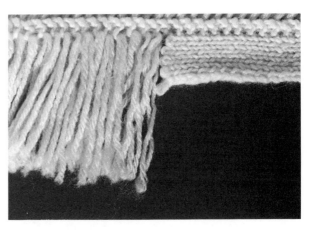

PARTIALLY UNRAVELED KNITTED-IN FRINGE

21

Cleaning and Dressing a Knitted Garment

As careful as you may have been while knitting a fabric, it has been much handled in the process and will need to be freshened up for wear. Given that you have put so much planning, time and effort into making the garment, you will also want to give careful thought to how it should be cleaned.

There are several different methods that can be used to clean a knitted fabric, and the choice depends primarily on what fiber was used. In addition, various combinations of stitch pattern and type of garment require different approaches to drying and giving the fabric a finished, ready-to-wear look. The process, regardless of which particular method is chosen, is referred to as "dressing" the fabric and, while different in the particulars, is the general equivalent of cleaning and pressing a woven fabric.

Washing vs. Dry Cleaning

In deciding whether a garment should be washed or dry cleaned, first and foremost you must consider the type of fiber you are working with. The yarn label should provide you with the manufacturer's recommendations on this subject. Please check the section in "Materials and Tools" for instructions on how to handle various fibers used in knitting yarns and, if you see nothing to indicate otherwise, by all means wash a sample swatch just to see what will happen. Many yarn labels specify dry cleaning not because the fiber cannot be washed, but because the manufacturer is concerned that you will not wash it properly; they want to play it safe and protect the yarn shops, and themselves, from complaints.

As a general rule, I think garments that are properly washed turn out much fresher, and the fiber will have a longer, healthier life, than when they are given chemical baths. However, there are times when it is appropriate or desirable to dry-clean a garment instead of washing it. If you are concerned about the stability of the dyes, particularly in a multicolored garment, dry cleaning is probably your best choice. This is something you should discover when you dress the tension sample. You may also want to choose dry cleaning if a garment is badly soiled or stained. And, of course, there will be times when you do not have the facilities or the time to hand wash.

If you must dry-clean a garment, please find a reputable cleaning establishment that has its own plant and changes the chemicals frequently. (You can check on them by sending something washable to the cleaners. When it comes home, immediately wash it by hand—dirty water tells a sad tale.) Ask your cleaners how often they filter the chemicals and on which day of the week they are likely to be the freshest and then bring your fine garments in on a day when you can expect the best results.

Home Cleaning Materials

There are a somewhat overwhelming number of choices when it comes to cleaning products, some sold to the general consumer for day-to-day laundry chores, some sold specifically to knitters. Advertisements offer no rational means of making a decision as to what is suitable for hand-knitted garments, but some knowledge about fibers and what effect various cleaning ingredients have will help a great deal.

Detergents and Soaps

Until recently I had believed, on no evidence but that of tradition, that a mild soap was the gentlest way to handle any delicate fabric, especially my precious sweaters. After considerable research on the question, I have been disabused of that idea. In fact, soap is generally highly alkaline, and alkalis are extremely damaging to any protein fiber such as wool and silk. (Alkaline substances are the opposite of acidic substances as measured on what is called a pH scale, with 7.0 being neutral; numbers below 7 are acidic, those above 7 are alkaline.) For protein fibers, therefore, a mild liquid detergent is a much better choice.

The label on the bottle of a liquid detergent can often help you decide whether it is mild enough to use; as a general rule, select one that has the fewest ingredients.

The most important ingredients in detergents are the surfactants, used to help release the soil from the fabric and prevent it from redepositing. Anionic surfactants do this with a negative charge, working like tiny magnets that attach themselves to the soil; nonionic surfactants, which are not charged, are more effective with oil stains. In both cases they float the soil off the garment. Many mild detergents will contain both types, and these ingredients will have no adverse effect on the fibers.

Water that contains relatively large amounts of calcium and magnesium, naturally occurring minerals, is referred to as "hard" water. These minerals bind with the soap or detergent, meaning that more detergent must be used in order to accomplish the cleaning, as some is absorbed by the water itself before it can act on the soil. For this reason, many detergents contain some form of water softener such as phosphate or washing soda, both of which are alkaline. Therefore, if you know that your water is hard, it is best to pretreat the water system so you don't have to use stronger detergents.

Substances in detergents called "whiteners" or "brighteners" are deposited in the fabric and affect the way they reflect light; they do not clean and are not necessary for fine garments. Suds are not a factor in cleaning; in fact, a low-suds detergent is preferable because it is easier to rinse out. Some detergents are scented, but, personally, I would rather have my garments smell clean than to have them smell of cheap perfume.

There are a few alternatives to the common liquid detergents. If you are traveling and have no mild detergent available, you can use your own shampoo—after all, your hair is a fine protein fiber, and most of the better ones are pH balanced (be careful, however, because inexpensive shampoos can be harsh, and baby shampoo, of all things, is strongly alkaline and shouldn't be used). There are also some detergent products sold specifically for delicate fabrics, knitted ones included. Woolite and Wool Tone are two that have been on the market for a long time. The former is pH balanced and quite safe and gentle; the latter, however, is rather alkaline, and both are far more expensive than liquid dishwashing detergents.

Museum conservation departments use a product called Orvus for cleaning the precious textiles in their care. Orvus is pH neutral and has a single surfactant, sodium laurel sulfate, and no other additives. When the protection of fragile dyes is important, as it is in textile conservation, Orvus is used as a low-moisture suds that is worked into the fabric and then blotted out, or the fabric is placed on a screen and a pure water rinse is poured through to prevent the dyes from running into one another. However, it can be used like any other detergent, and if you can find it, it is an excellent product to use for washing any of your delicate garments and it is quite inexpensive.

While alkalis can damage the protein fibers, they actually strengthen cotton and linen fibers and will not harm any of the artificial fibers, such as nylon, polyester, or acrylic, meaning these can be washed in any detergent or in soap. Certain kinds of rayon, such as viscose, are more susceptible to damage from strong alkalis than others, but generally are not harmed by household detergents or mild soap.

If you want to check the safety of a product you use, pH test strips are available at pharmacists and are quite inexpensive.

Stain and Spot Removers

Any pre-wash spotting should be done with care. Test the product you plan to use on a seam to make sure it will not affect the color.

If you are using a liquid solvent, place the spot face down on an absorbent surface such as an old towel or a rag, and pour the solvent through from the inside. Gently push the soiled area down into the towel with your fingers to help it soak up the solvent and released stain.

Spot removers that dry to a powder can be difficult to remove from the fibers—shake as much of the residue off as possible, then use a terry towel or a very soft bristle brush on the remainder.

Laundry pre-wash spotting agents are generally safe, but the colorfastness of the fabric should always be tested. In some cases it may be safer to soak the entire garment rather than to treat just the spot. For details on types of stains and removal techniques, see pages 395–397.

With proper care, your fine sweaters should never need bleaching; however, for fibers that gradually yellow with age, or for serious stains, you may need to resort to some kind of bleach. Bleaches oxidize, or whiten, the coloring matter in stains but do not actually remove the stain itself; this must be done with detergent. Chlorine bleach should *never* be used on protein fibers, but when reasonably diluted is safe for cotton, rayon and linen, although any residue remaining in the fabric can cause damage over time. After bleaching, rinse the fabric thoroughly and give it a final mild acidic rinse (see below), to restore the pH. Oxygen bleaches are milder and safer for all delicate fabrics. For instance, to remove heavy stains from cotton or linen fabrics, use a twenty-four-hour soak in an oxygen bleach, followed by a twenty-four-hour soak in a detergent. Hydrogen peroxide, properly diluted, is a safe bleach for protein fibers.

If you have saved your tension sample, or still have some yarn and can knit up another one, it is best to try one approach or another on the sample before you risk the garment.

Neutralizers and Softeners

Any delicate fabric that has been subjected to harsh cleansing agents could do with a bit of neutralizing. This is especially true of silk and wool, but it isn't a bad idea for any fiber. The opposite of alkali being acid, a bit of vinegar in the rinse water is a tried and true recipe for restoring a balanced pH. A teaspoon in a small basin, a tablespoon in a large basin of rinse water should be sufficient. The odor will evaporate by the time the garment dries.

Fabric softeners deposit a waxy substance on the fibers that cuts down on static electricity, softens and gives loft to napped fabrics, and causes woven fabrics to be smoother and require less ironing; they remove some of the harshness from fabrics that are not tumbled in a dryer. Used in moderation in the final rinse water, they can do wonders for a yarn that is not naturally soft, making it much more comfortable against the skin. It's my impression it also gives the yarn a certain gleam. These products can build up in a fiber, however, so they should be used infrequently.

Washing

There are a lot of people today who shun anything that isn't wash and wear. Believe me when I say I understand the competing demands of work, family, friends, self, and the domestic chores and how far down on the list the latter can fall. Nevertheless, I think too much is made of the small task that washing a sweater represents; somehow it has been magnified in people's minds, and it really isn't that bad at all. It's a bit like baking bread; you deal with it lovingly from time to time and ignore it between times.

If it is a garment that is expected to have a short but serviceable life and is amenable to that sort of treatment, by all means, throw it in the washer and dryer. If, on the other hand, you are dealing with something out of the ordinary, treat it well and it will give you many years of gratifying wear. And given that material objects reflect their histories, taking on a patina of affection or an air of shabby neglect as the case may be, your beautiful knitted garments will age gracefully if you commune with them regularly at the wash basin. I am especially grieved by people who will not treat children's sweaters with the same respect as their own, making them of inferior materials because they expect stains and machine washing; how is a child to feel special or come to respect what is beautifully made?

Speaking of materials, people have also gotten it into their minds that wool is particularly difficult to care for. Nothing could be further from the truth. It is not only easy to handle but it gives up stains and soil quite readily. This is not the case with the artificial fibers, which cling to stains and, worse, odors, which become impossible to remove.

Water Temperature

Knitted fabrics should be washed in warm water. A little warmth lets the fibers relax and helps to release and dissolve the soil. Body temperature is fine for any fiber (test it with the inside of your wrist the way mothers test the milk in a baby's bottle; if it makes you uncomfortable, it will make your garment uncomfortable).

However, with certain stains this may not be true and either hot or cold water is more suitable (see page 395). While it is quite obvious that cold water won't adversely affect fabrics, many people are anxious about using hot water, particularly for wool. Wool fabrics can felt, although this is harder to do than you think (see page 401). It requires not just heat and moisture, but agitation as well—without the latter, you are quite safe; use a tepid rinse rather than a cold one to avoid shocking the fibers.

Cotton, linen, and rayon all can be safely washed in hot water. Surprisingly enough, cotton fibers do not actually shrink. However, the fiber is easily stretched as it is being woven or knitted, and will stretch in wear, and it lacks the elasticity to recover. When washed, the fabric will exhibit what is called "relaxation" shrinkage, meaning it shrinks back to its normal condition as it dries, restoring a stretched-out garment to size (more evidence of why you should dress your sample before calculating the stitch gauge). Cotton and linen are stronger wet than dry, while rayon is weaker and should be handled gently; it too will exhibit relaxation shrinkage as it dries.

Hand Washing

Use a basin large enough to comfortably hold the garment, and add warm water and about a teaspoonful of mild liquid detergent. Add the fabric, push it into the water until it is fully immersed, and allow it to soak twenty or thirty minutes.

Most soils will be released from the fabric without

any activity on your part. Some are water soluble, and the remainder will be lifted off by the action of the detergent. It is perfectly all right to slosh the garment up and down in the bath gently to help the soapy water move through it and penetrate thoroughly, but do not rub or wring it at any time. Rubbing will simply fray the yarn and cause pilling or felting, and it may drive the soil into the yarn rather than eliminating it; wringing will stretch the fibers. The amount of detergent you put in the basin will have a finite capacity to dissolve soil, so if the garment is very dirty, it is better to follow the first washing with a second one using a fresh supply of detergent.

When the garment has soaked long enough, do not remove it from the water, just let the water out of the basin; this is much easier on both you and the garment. Water is very heavy, and a knitted garment can hold a great deal of it. If you lift it out of the basin in this condition, you risk stretching the fibers and straining the seams. This is particularly true of garments made of wool or rayon, as these fibers are weaker wet than dry. Gently push the garment against the side or bottom of the basin to force some of the soap and water out, then plug the basin and refill it with cool water. Repeat as necessary until the water runs clear.

If you wish, use a small amount of vinegar or fabric softener in the final rinse. Push the garment against the sink again, and let it drain for up to an hour before you attempt to move it.

If you have access to a washing machine, I highly recommend that you put the wet sweater into the machine, set it to a gentle spin cycle, and allow the machine to centrifuge out most of the water. If it is a heavy garment, you might want to balance the load by putting a towel on the opposite side of the tub. Believe me, this will not hurt even the most precious and delicate fabric; it is simply pressed against the side of the tub while the water is extracted. This will considerably shorten the drying time.

If you do not have access to a washing machine, allow the garment to drain, then roll it up in a large, heavy towel and press on the roll with your full weight. This will wick a great deal of moisture out of the garment and into the towel. If necessary, repeat with a second towel.

Machine Washing

Cotton, linen, and most rayons will stand up reasonably well to machine washing. It is not a good idea for most silk yarns, particularly the smooth ones, and should be avoided with any wool unless the label is clearly marked "superwash" or "machine washable." This means the fiber has been treated with resins to prevent any possibility of felting (see page 314).

Nevertheless, agitating a knitted garment with other clothing is abrasive, and you will find the garment pills and fades more than one washed by hand. At the very least, wash it by itself, using the gentle cycle and a mild liquid detergent.

Drying

After washing, most knitting books recommend "blocking," a method of stretching a wet fabric out to smooth it and give it the dimensions called for in the pattern. There seems to be a certain ritual mystique about this process, and quite frankly I think too much is made of it; there are actually very few times when true blocking is required. Let me explain why I say that.

Knitting forces the yarn into a series of relatively fixed loops that have a wave form. The resilience and springiness of the fabric is due to the fact that these loops can be stretched and then will recover. While the size of the loops is fixed by the size of the knitting needle, if the fabric is stretched widthwise, the stitches will give up something in length, if it is stretched lengthwise, they will give up something in width.

In addition, different yarns will have different amounts of stretch and resilience, depending upon the fiber of which the yarn is made and the type and amount of twist given the yarn when it is spun. Finally, each stitch pattern imparts an inherent structure to the fabric that gives it unique characteristics such as density, resilience, or spread in one or more dimensions. In most cases, a stitch pattern is rather compressed just after knitting. When the fabric is damp, either because it has been washed or steamed, it will relax and can be stretched to open it up and maximize the appearance and special qualities of the stitch pattern. If it is allowed to dry in this stretched condition, the fabric will be more or less set until the next time it is cleaned.

Many people erroneously believe that they can block a fabric out in order to adjust the overall size of the garment, counting on this process to correct problems with the fit. There is also a popular misconception that blocking a sweater is in some way permanent. In fact, cleaning a knitted fabric has some analogy with what happens when human hair is washed and set to give it curl.

First, as you no doubt are aware, wetting the hair removes any trace of a previous set, and the same is true of a knitted fabric. And, just as warmth and moisture will cause a hairdo to fall, so with a sweater; the more artificial the set, the more tenuous it is. Given this, it is a hopeless task to try to compress a too-big sweater or stretch out one that is too small; a little body warmth and the weight of the garment itself will quickly overcome your best efforts—particularly in light of the fact that the hanging weight of the garment will cause it to lengthen at the expense of width (see page 420).

This means that the dimensions of the garment lying flat are quite different from those it has in wear. While smoothing out the surface of the fabric obviously will have some effect on the overall dimensions, the size and shape of the garment is determined in the knitting, not

with washing and blocking. The most successful garment, therefore, is one that was made according to a carefully done stitch gauge and is the right size in a natural, relaxed state. Every time the garment is cleaned it must be smoothed and shaped again, but in a simple way, much as you would a woven.

The origin of blocking lies in the days before steam irons—a heavy dry iron, even with the help of a press cloth, is an obviously unsuitable tool for finishing a knitted fabric, and some other method needed to be used. Instead, knits were either pinned into shape and left to dry or they were put on a stretcher. A stretcher is an adjustable wooden drying frame, still used in Shetland and probably other parts of the world. Some were in the shape of squares or rectangles for use with shawls and scarves. The fabric would be stretched out and tied to pegs or holes set evenly all around the frame. Others had adjustable bars that could be inserted inside the body and arms of a sweater. There were also flat board frames for socks and gloves. This worked well for the simple shapes of traditional garments; however, when knitting was taken up by fashion, no simple stretcher frame worked for all styles, so garments were pinned out to dry instead.

Since the advent of steam irons, blocking with pins or stretchers is no longer necessary unless the fiber can-

SHETLAND SHAWL ON STRETCHER FRAME

not tolerate steam and the stitch pattern must be stretched open beyond what can be done by hand. A situation when both of these things are true is quite rare. Once dry, most garments can be dressed simply and easily with just steam. But tradition dies hard, and many knitters today go to a great deal of trouble not only to measure and pin out a garment just the way their grandmothers did, but then when they are dry, they steam them. The steam immediately relaxes the fibers and erases the dimensions so painstakingly achieved with the pins. Pinning out was the most tedious aspect of washing a handknit; aren't you glad you don't have to do that any more?

Air Drying

When air drying a knitted garment of any kind of fiber, laying it flat both protects the seams from strain and prevents the fiber from stretching out. Work as follows:

1. Spread a dry towel out on a flat surface and lay the garment on top. (If necessary, use a large sheet of plastic to protect the surface below from dampness.)
2. Once or twice while it is drying, change the wet towel for a dry one and turn the garment over to expose the other surface.
3. When the garment is just damp, use a tape measure

and smooth it out to its correct dimensions and leave it undisturbed until it is thoroughly dry.

You will find many books that recommend that the garment be placed between heavy towels; some even recommend that you use damp towels. It takes long enough for the knitting to dry without all those wet towels around it, and I've never been able to understand what purpose they are supposed to serve.

Various sweater-drying racks are available and are a minor and worthwhile investment. These racks have a plastic or fabric mesh secured in a frame that can be suspended over a bath tub; in some the frame has short legs so it can be set on the floor or placed on a table. The mesh allows air to pass through the garment and thus speeds drying time considerably, and there are no damp towels to deal with.

It is worth knowing that the position of the fabric while it is wet is of no real importance, as any set you manage to impart to it occurs in the relatively brief period when it passes from damp to dry. This means that even if something cannot be steam finished or must be pinned out, you needn't bother with smoothing it out to the correct shape until it is barely damp. This allows you to change towels and turn it over to speed the drying process.

Further, the dimensions the garment has while

FAIR ISLE SWEATER STRETCHED OUT TO DRY IN THE 1920s

drying are not really all that important as long as the fiber can be steamed. If it can be steamed, the surface can be smoothed and the dimensions refined at that point, see "Steam Dressing" below.

Cold Blocking

If the garment can't be steamed, or it can but you don't have access to a steam iron, smoothing out the surface and shaping the garment to the correct dimensions before it dries is generally sufficient to give it a nice, finished look. There is really no need to use pins.

However, remember that the dimensions in wear are different from those flat, so do not give the garment the pattern dimensions. If you have worked from a commercial pattern you must improvise a bit here, but you are safe if you just stretch the garment out so it is somewhat wider and shorter than what the pattern calls for. If you have designed the garment yourself, you should have the data on both the flat and weighted gauges. To find the measurements to use as it dries, divide the number of stitches in the width of the fabric by the flat stitch gauge; do the same with the row gauge for the length. Write these dimensions down and save them to use every time you clean the garment.

For fabrics with a stitch pattern that must be stretched open, but made in fibers that cannot tolerate steam, work as follows:

1. Improvise some drying surface into which you can insert pins. Cork or fiber board padded and covered with toweling works well. Use rust-proof steel T-pins.

2. Pin the four corners of each garment section to the correct dimensions, then set pins all the way around the edge at one- or two-inch intervals. Try to keep the edge from scalloping as much as possible. If the edge is supposed to scallop, however, set the pins to emphasize this.

3. Leave the garment undisturbed until it is completely dry.

Keep in mind that this imparts a relatively tenuous "set" and that the fabric in wear will not be as open as it is when pinned out. For lace fabrics of cotton or linen, sizing will preserve the appearance (see below).

Machine Drying

Garments of cotton, linen, and rayon can be put in a dryer; however, the abrasion of other garments and the sides of the dryer itself can fuzz the surface and cause fading, particularly of dark colors. On the other hand, the dryer will promote relaxation shrinkage in these fibers and helps to soften the fabric. For the best of both worlds, let the garment air-dry until just barely damp, turn it inside out to protect the outside surface, and then finish it in the dryer. Dry heat will damage protein fibers, so mechanical drying should never be used on silk or wool.

Steaming

Steam is wonderful for most yarn fibers and should, when possible, be used after every washing. It softens and fluffs up the yarn and takes away some of the hardness you may feel after a garment has been washed and dried—the same hardness you feel in a shirt hung up to dry. While the fabric is damp with steam you can smooth out the surface to display the stitch pattern, straighten the edges, and give the garment the dimensions it should have.

Do be careful, however—some fibers that can be washed cannot be steamed; be extremely cautious about metallic yarns, and never steam sequins or plastic beads —they will melt! Read the yarn label and test the tension sample to see how it responds.

Because steam is produced by irons, I want to take pains to point out that a knitted garment is *not* ironed.

There is never any reason to "press" a knit—this will only flatten the yarn and the stitch pattern, and any excess heat may damage it irreparably. Therefore, *never* let the iron rest on the garment. Hold the iron so it just skims over the surface—it need not even touch it; all that is required is for the steam to penetrate. (A steam appliance is excellent because there is no hot soleplate, and therefore no mistake can be made.)

Steam Dressing

Work on a surface large enough to lay the garment out flat. An ironing board will do, but it is not ideal because it will only accommodate small sections at a time, and the weight of the remainder hanging off the board may stretch things out in unintended ways. Far better to set heavy towels on a counter, the carpet, or on a table protected by plastic. Toweling is nice because the surface allows both the fibers and stitch pattern elements to puff out nicely. If you don't have a large enough towel, use a folded sheet.

Turn the garment inside out, lay it on the towel and work as follows:

1. Steam one garment section at a time, avoiding any folds such as at the shoulders and on the sides of the body and the sleeves.
2. While the fabric is warm and damp with steam, shape it, using your measuring tape to check the dimensions (remember to use the flat dimensions, not the pattern dimensions). Smooth the fabric, straighten the edges, and make sure everything is square and true. Apply more steam as necessary until the fabric is in the shape you want it to be. Leave that section undisturbed and allow it to thoroughly dry before you move it.
3. When you have finished all the sections on one side, turn the garment over and repeat on the other side.
4. Turn the garment right side out again. Using a seam roll or a rolled towel, apply steam and then press and smooth each seam with your fingertips or the heel of your hand. Steam and smooth out the length of the sleeve to eliminate any foldline. As before, allow each section to dry before it is moved.
5. Lay the garment flat again and check the stitch pattern and dimensions. Apply steam to any areas that need a final touchup or any adjustments, and allow to dry.

Steam Blocking

If you are dealing with a fabric that must be stretched open with blocking, but can tolerate steam, lay the fabric on a surface you can insert pins into. Have the fabric right side up so you can see the stitch pattern and set the pins at an angle out from the edges of the fabric so they will not interfere with bringing the iron close enough to provide sufficient steam, then work just as

described above. Do not remove the pins until the fabric is completely dry.

If you are dealing with a garment that has an embossed surface texture, turn it inside out and pin it out to the correct dimensions. If the fabric is single thickness, pin it face down on top of a thick towel. Working this way allows the embossed pattern elements to puff out more.

Sizing

If you are dressing a cotton or linen knitted lace medallion, table cloth, or curtain, you may want to size it to help preserve its shape. This is the only occasion I can think of where it is permissible to press a knitted fabric.

The traditional method of sizing a fabric of this sort relied on the cold-blocking process described above. Starch was dissolved in cold water and added to the final rinse water. The item was stretched and pinned into place and left to dry. Today, spray starch makes the job considerably easier; work as follows:

1. There is no need to cold-block the item, just wash it and smooth it out to dry, in which case you will have to dampen it for pressing, or squeeze the wet fabric in towels until it is damp dry and starch immediately.
2. If the item is large enough to accommodate the iron between the pins needed for stretching, pin it out on a padded board, spray it with starch if you wish, and press gently. Work in sections, allowing each area to dry thoroughly before moving the fabric and repinning. If the item is small, eliminate the pins and press, stretching it out as you work.

Starch not only stiffens the fabric, which displays the stitch pattern, but it coats the fibers, protecting them from soil and making them easier to clean. Old-fashioned starches are vegetable products and can attract insects in storage; if you are planning to store lace textiles that you customarily starch, wash them first. The newer spray starches are more often resins of one kind or another and don't present this problem.

Stain Removal

There are four kinds of stains: nongrease, grease, a combination of these elements, and miscellaneous. Whatever method of stain removal is recommended, test it first on your tension sample or on a seam to make sure it will not affect the color or fabric

any way. Stain removal for knitted garments should never involve rubbing, as this will damage the yarn and mat the fabric. If you are in doubt, or if the label recommends against washing, take the garment to a dry cleaner.

Any stain is best dealt with as quickly as possible; those set by age or heat become difficult or impossible to remove. In many cases, a stain will sit on the surface of the fabric, and if you act quickly, much of it can be carefully blotted up into an absorbent paper towel or rag before it penetrates the garment. The general rule is cold water for nongrease stains, hot water for grease ones.

Nongrease Stains

Common nongrease stains include alcohol, antiperspirant, blood, tea, coffee, egg, fruits, vegetables, juice, wine, milk, and soft drinks. Some of these stains—particularly blood, fruit juice, and wine—are permanently set by heat.

If blotting does not remove the stain, immediately run cool water through the fabric from the side opposite where the stain occurred to force it back out the way it came in. Alternatively, hold absorbent toweling against the stain and sponge cold water through; some people recommend using cold carbonated water. If the stain persists, gently press in liquid detergent or, for nonprotein fibers, a paste of powdered detergent, then let sit for a while and rinse again. If necessary, soak the entire garment, protein fibers in cold water with liquid detergent, vegetable fibers in a solution of oxygen bleach followed with a detergent wash.

Grease Stains

Common grease stains include butter, margarine, lard, cooking oils, meat fats, furniture polish, floor wax, automobile grease or oil.

To remove these types of stains from a protein fiber, gently press liquid detergent into the stain and then rinse with warm water; repeat as necessary. For a vegetable fiber, use a paste of powdered detergent. Pour the rinse water directly through the fabric from the opposite side as described above.

If your normal detergent does not work, you might try one of the soap-type liquid spot removers on the market. These can be harsh and may affect dye; try some on your tension sample or on a seam before applying it to the garment. If something like this must be used on a protein fiber, be careful to handle the fabric gently and wash and neutralize it after the stain has been successfully removed (see page 389).

As discussed in the section on fibers, synthetics absorb grease and oil but resist the penetration of water; therefore, these types of stains can only be removed with a grease solvent. The solvents are made from various petroleum products, some of which are combustible and all of which produce toxic fumes (trichloroethylene will also dissolve some acetates and polyesters); it may be best to rely on your dry cleaner. However, if you want to act quickly and have solvent in the house, test a seam first and then, if no damage occurs, place the stain face down on absorbent paper or a rag and pour a small amount of solvent through from the opposite side to force the stain out. Press the stain against the paper with your fingers to help it wick out of the fabric. Repeat as necessary, constantly using a clean section of toweling. Once the stain is removed, launder the garment normally to remove any traces of solvent.

Combination Stains

Combination stains contain both greasy and nongreasy elements and include gravy, mayonnaise, cosmetics, crayons, and anything containing cream or chocolate. Use the cold-water method for the nongreasy portion first, followed by the hot-water method to remove the greasy part. Do not use hot water until or unless the nongrease stain is entirely removed.

Miscellaneous Stains

There are other stains that don't fit so neatly into the above categories.

Ink

Ink is devilish to remove, but alcohol sometimes works. For nonprotein fibers the best hope is an ammonia/detergent paste followed with a cool rinse.

Fingernail Polish

For fingernail polish, use polish remove either by blotting or pouring a small amount through the fabric from the opposite side into an absorbent rag.

Grass Stains

Grass stains can best be sponged out with alcohol, but check the fabric first for color fastness; if dye is not stable to alcohol, use the method described above for nongrease stains.

Mildew

Mildew can be difficult or impossible to remove; wool is not particularly susceptible, but it will attack cotton and linen if they are stored damp. Sometimes leaving the detergent-soaked fabric in the sun will bleach out the stains, but if this is not successful, try a twenty-four-hour soak in an oxygen bleach.

Paints

Water-based paints will usually wash out with detergent. For oil-based paints, first use paint remover. This will remove the pigment but may leave a greasy residue, which should be treated as for other grease stains.

Wax

For wax, sandwich the stain between thick paper towels and apply a warm iron; this will melt the wax into the paper, but a greasy residue will remain in the fabric that must be removed with one of the described methods.

Storage

Knitted garments tend to be highly seasonal and, therefore, spend some portion of every year in storage. Please put them away clean. Any soil left in the garment will attract insects, damage dye, and weaken the fibers. Speaking of insects, if the garment is made of a protein fiber, include some mothballs. It is not a good policy to store fine garments in plastic. If the fabric is slightly damp, you invite mildew and rot; if it is dry, you invite fiber breakage and deterioration.

I think it is an excellent idea to fold the garment differently every time you put it away to prevent the formation of wear lines and fiber breakage along the folds. For long-term storage pad the inside of the garment with tissue and lay it as flat as possible.

As a general rule, it is not advisable to hang knitted garments because the hanging weight will strain shoulder seams and cause the fibers to stretch out. If the garment is lightweight and made of a nice elastic fiber like wool, however, it will not suffer from being hung on a padded hanger. An acquaintance of mine who knits her entire wardrobe, including coats and suits, hangs these heavy garments before finishing with linings, etc., to make sure they have stretched as much as possible. They can then be left on hangers just as a garment of woven fabric would be. This is also true of fulled fabrics or those knitted in flat, inelastic stitch patterns.

22
Fulled (Felted) Knits

The phenomenon of felting has been appreciated and exploited for thousands of years to make nonwoven cloth from animal hair. From the old yurts and saddle blankets to contemporary industrial applications, it is one of the most versatile fabrics known to man, and very easy to make. Felt will not ravel when cut and can be shaped over forms with heat and moisture. A felted fabric is wind, water, and flame resistant; it cushions against shock and vibration; it is an excellent heat and sound insulator, and is extremely durable. Fulling, or the felting of a woven or knitted cloth, is also an old tradition, not much seen today in knitting but still deserving of our interest and attention. It is ideal for mittens, hats, slippers, heavy socks or boot liners, and sturdy hard-wearing jackets or vests. And for all its practicality, it can be a very beautiful fabric.

The difference between a fulled and an ordinary knitted fabric rests entirely with the planning and finishing stages; the knitting itself is done in the ordinary way, and there are no special techniques required. Plain Stockinette is ideal, as most stitch patterns will lose definition and clarity, but by all means consider the use of color.

Felting

Felting, or fulling, is done in exactly the same way today as it was thousands of years ago, and while the conditions are precisely controlled, it is done in basically the same way in a modern factory as it still is on the steppes of Central Asia.

There are four stages in the felting process. In the first preparatory stage, the wool is carded and combed into batts, fluffy blankets of wool fibers layered perpendicularly. The second stage is called "hardening," or felting proper, in which heat, moisture, pressure and/or agitation are used to force the fibers into an entangled and permanently linked fabric. The third stage, fulling, is a continuation of the felting process under more controlled conditions, and is used to refine the qualities of the fabric. The last stage is finishing, in which various techniques can be used to treat the surface of the completed fabric to give it a particular appearance.

When weaving or knitting is substituted for the first and second stages, the felting process is called fulling.

Fibers for Felting

Sheep's wool is the finest material for felting because of certain chemical and structural properties unique to that fiber. Other wool fibers such as camel, goat, alpaca, etc., will also felt, but are generally considered too costly for that sort of treatment and produce fabrics with unique characteristics. For instance, camel's hair makes a rather fragile felt, while alpaca produces one that is very compact and hard. Fur hairs are also felted, particularly for hats, but must be specially treated with chemicals in order to be used for this purpose.

There is a full discussion of the structure and properties of wool fibers starting on page 311, but for our purposes here, what is important is the behavior of these fibers under certain conditions. The protein molecules making up the wool fiber are called "keratin," and these molecules have a helical or spiral form that gives wool its curl. At the center of the fiber shaft there is a cortex made up of elastic, longitudinal bundles of relatively soft keratin called "fibrils." These bundles are surrounded by a cuticle of hardened keratin in the form of overlapping scales that have the root end secured and the tip free. The fibrils in the cortex are stretched slightly and held in position by the cuticle. If the cuticle is softened, the stretched cortex can relax and the fiber will gain additional crimp, or curl. It will also crimp slightly if it is mechanically pulled from root to tip and released.

Heat, moisture, and alkalis soften the cuticle and break some of the molecular linkages, allowing the fibrils to crimp further. When these are combined with agitation and pressure, the elastic, crimped fibers entangle to the point where the scales interlock with one another permanently. The felting characteristics of sheep's wool are so strong that only 20 to 25 percent needs to be present in any fiber blend in order for felting to occur. Once the fibers have felted, they can never be restored to their original condition.

Traditional Felting

In Central Asia, felting is most often done with plain hot water, while in Europe it has traditionally been done with soap and sometimes with alternating baths of hot and cold water. Since felt is successfuly made in Central Asia without either of these two things, they are obviously not necessary. Whether or not they speed up the process or improve the result is a question I could not resolve with certainty, but there seems to be some merit in their use.

The hot and cold baths are apparently intended to "shock" the fiber, which may encourage it to crimp as it alternates between relaxing and shrinking. However, this is not used in commercial felt production. Soap is an alkali, and as I mentioned above, alkalis break down and soften the cortex, allowing shrinkage to occur more readily. In addition, any soap or detergent is what's called a "wetting agent"; it breaks down the surface tension of the water, making it more "slippery." Soapy water will, therefore, penetrate the fabric more deeply and lubricate the fibers so they can move and entangle. It will also dissolve any grease or soil remaining in the wool, both of which prevent thorough wetting and impede felting. If you use soapy water during the felting, add some vinegar to the last rinse water to restore the normal pH to the fabric (see page 389).

In true felt making, the batt of fibers must be held in position at least until preliminary felting has occurred and the loose fibers have been transformed into a fabric that will hold together. The fibers are either placed on a cloth, and then rolled up and tied, or sandwiched between two cloths, the whole basted together into a bundle. Once the batt is secured, it is kept saturated with hot water while it is pounded, beaten, and rolled to promote felting. In peasant societies that make felt, this is a community effort accompanied by songs and feasting.

Fulling

In this situation we must transform a knitting yarn into a garment instead of forming the batt, but that done, the process is otherwise nearly identical. It is, however, necessary to take into consideration the selection of appropriate materials and the special requirements of working out a pattern for a garment that will be fulled.

Selection of Yarns for Fulling

The degree to which any wool fiber will felt depends upon the breed of the animal, its health, the length of the fiber, and whether or not it was sheared or pulled. Since the labels on knitting yarns rarely indicate what kind of sheep produced the wool, to say nothing of what it might have eaten, finding a good yarn for fulling is rather a hit or miss operation. Because the wool fibers must be able to move during the felting process, for knitters, the amount of twist put in the yarn during spinning and plying is also a factor.

As a general rule, yarns labeled "worsted" have longer fibers and are spun with a tighter twist, making them less suitable for fulling. Those marked "woolen" generally have shorter fibers and are more loosely spun, making them better candidates. Very loosely spun yarns such as the Lopi type are a good choice. Needless to say, machine-washable wool yarns will not felt, precisely because they have been chemically treated to prevent that possibility (see page 314). If there are spinners or felt makers in your area, you might consult with them for a yarn recommendation.

Planning a Fulled Garment

As usual with any knitting project, planning a fulled garment starts with the tension sample, which should be fulled in precisely the same way that you plan to full the garment itself. The sample should be made larger than usual to allow for shrinkage (it will shrink more in length than in width), and should be measured from edge to edge in the usual way before and after fulling. Do remember to write down the number of stitches and rows in the sample, because you may have trouble counting them later.

SAMPLE FOR FULLING/BEFORE

SAMPLE FOR FULLING/AFTER

In deciding on needle size, keep in mind that it is important for the fibers to move during fulling, so a loosely knit fabric will full more than a tightly knit one; therefore, use fairly large needles for the size of the yarn. You might want to knit and full two or three samples, each with a different-size needle, to see which size works best.

If this is your first trial of a particular yarn, you might also want to make several samples on each size needle, fulling them in slightly different ways or for different lengths of time to see how they will behave. Keep an accurate record of exactly what you do during fulling so you can re-create the conditions that produce the effect you are after when it comes time to full the garment itself. Once the sample is dry, and you are satisfied with its appearance, measure it and calculate your stitch gauge in the usual way.

In planning the garment, it is a good idea to use simple shapes and allow generous ease. Remember a fulled fabric is stiffer and heavier than a supple, resilient knit. You will have to decide for yourself whether to full unassembled garment sections, or an assembled garment or one knit in the round. There are problems associated with either approach. With the latter, you will have to baste some sheeting or muslin to the inside of the garment to separate the two sides and prevent them from felting to one another. With the former, you will have to make sure each piece fulls in the same way.

Given that a fulled, knitted fabric will not ravel when cut, and that exact control of shrinkage during the felting process is difficult, you may want to knit up a big rectangle, full it, then cut out the garment pieces and sew them together. This guarantees a precise fit.

Traditional Hand Fulling

This is the old-fashioned way to full, and it allows more precise control of the finished product. As you work, you can feel how well the fabric is fulling, make sure it fulls evenly, measure it whenever you want to check progress, and stop at just the right moment. It is also fun, but fairly strenuous work—pick a day when you feel energetic and enlist some amusing companions to help you. The basic instructions for fulling are really very simple.

Select a hard, flat surface that drains reasonably well. For small items, a flat-bottomed sink or sink drain will do; for larger ones try the bathtub, a cellar floor with a drain, or, on a nice day, your driveway or patio. If you are dealing with a garment rather than a flat piece of fabric, baste some muslin or old sheeting between the layers so they will not felt to one another.

It is obviously not necessary to tie a knitted fabric into a bundle or roll, but it nevertheless offers some advantages in fulling. When the fabric is rolled or bundled, it is held securely in position, and the friction and pressure can then be systematically distributed over the entire surface. When it is not bundled in some way, particularly when dealing with large fabrics, it can be very difficult to work evenly on a heavy, sodden fabric that bunches up and slips away from you at every turn.

If you are going to use the roll idea, lay the fabric down on the cloth, saturate it thoroughly with hot, soapy water, then roll it up in the cloth and tie it. (I have seen dental floss recommended for tying and plastic mosquito netting for the wrapping cloth.) Don't roll it too tightly or the fibers won't be able to move.

Pour on more hot water, then lean on it with your full weight, and roll it back and forth, somewhat as if you were kneading very heavy bread dough. It helps to have several pairs of hands here, but at the very least shift your hands to a new position on the roll every time you press and roll. Add more water as you feel necessary to keep it well saturated.

The fibers will shrink and crimp parallel to the direction of the roll; therefore, after a period of time, unroll the bundle, place the fabric perpendicular to its original position, check on your progress, rewrap it, and continue rolling. If you want, walk or stomp on the bundle, beat it with a stick, or pound the roll itself on the ground—vibrations encourage the felting.

If you are going to use the bundle idea, lay the fabric down on one cloth, saturate it, then cover it with the other cloth and "quilt" the whole together through all three layers in several horizontal and vertical rows, using very large basting stitches. Leave the edges free so you can check your progress.

Saturate the bundle again and use whatever means you have available to apply pressure and agitation. A heavy rolling pin is ideal because it can be used to both roll and beat the fabric, but you can use a large mallet, a rug beater, or your feet—stomp on it, dance on it, have your kids jump up and down or roll around on it. Some people use a tub and an old-fashioned washboard, but I've found it more difficult to handle a heavy wet fabric that way. Use your imagination and have fun!

Keep working the fabric over until it shrinks and felts as much as you want or it is willing or able to do. When you have felted it enough, pour some more hot water on it, leave it to soak, and sit down to rest. Once you have recovered sufficiently, thoroughly rinse the fabric with cold water, then roll it in towels or use the spin-dry cycle of your washing machine to extract as much moisture as possible. The fabric should still have some residual stretch, so smooth it out, measure it, stretch and pull it into shape, pin it out if necessary, and leave it to dry in the usual way (see page 391).

Machine Fulling

The modern washer and dryer are great labor-saving devices, not only for the weekly laundry, but for fulling as well. The only drawback is that it is somewhat more difficult to control the process, but with frequent check-

FULLED, EMBROIDERED SLIPPERS FROM SWEDEN

ing it works reasonably well, particularly on simple garments where sizing is not critical.

Hot, soapy water and the agitation of the washing machine will only achieve a moderate amount of fulling by themselves. It helps considerably to throw in some heavy clothing like sheets, towels, or jeans along with the fabric to be fulled—the friction and increased agitation will encourage results. Don't use too much water; the fabric should be crowded.

Keep a close eye on things and when the garment being fulled is approaching the right size and density, use the rinse and spin cycles and then put it in the dryer with the other clothing. Check the fabric at regular, timed intervals to make sure it doesn't shrink too much, gradually shortening the time between inspections to make sure the process does not go too far. When it has the size and appearance you are after, lay it flat to finish drying in the air.

Finishing

There are a variety of traditional ways to finish the surfaces of fulled fabrics. Experiment on your swatch before you work on the garment.

For a highly textured look, brush the surface with a teasel, a metal clothing brush, or a dog brush. Alternatively, for a very smooth look, hold a pair of scissors parallel to the surface and cut off all the fuzz, being very careful not to cut the fabric itself. This is difficult to do smoothly and well. In some places the surface fuzz is removed from felt by singeing it, which depends for its success on the natural flame-retardant properties of wool. Needless to say, this approach should be handled with great caution.

A steam iron is an excellent tool to use in finishing a fulled fabric. First, because fabrics fulled in the washer and dryer may felt somewhat unevenly, the steam iron can be used to correct any problems. In fact, it can be used all by itself to full a fabric, although that would only be practical for relatively small items. Second, the iron can be used to create a very smooth surface and to flatten the fabric and make it more compact.

1. Lay the fabric flat on a hard, padded surface.
2. Cover the fabric with a damp cloth and press it firmly with a hot iron. When all you want is to flatten and smooth the surface, use a lift and press motion.
3. If you slide the iron over the fabric, you will encourage additional shrinkage and felting. Use this motion to correct any uneven areas.

Under no circumstances use the iron in the presence of quantities of water—you may be in for a shock. If you want to encourage further felting, work with the fabric damp; if you are just touching up or finishing the surface, work with the fabric dry and use a damp press cloth. And while the more steam there is, the better, it also increases the likelihood of scalding burns, so work carefully and keep your hand away until the steam has dissipated.

Before the fabric has fulled as far as it will go, it can also be shaped. Lay the fabric over a pressing form and use the steam iron and a press cloth to continue the fulling. This is particularly nice for hats, but can also be used to shape the top of a sleeve cap, for instance, and should be used to give a smooth look to seam lines and to smooth out any foldlines created during fulling that might otherwise set into the garment.

Finally, fulled fabrics take well to embroidery. Because they are firm and inelastic with a relatively smooth surface, you can embroider on them much as you would on any woven fabric. They can also be painted with fabric dyes, although penetration may be minimal if the felt is very dense.

PART FIVE

Reading and Designing Patterns

23
Reading Written Garment and Stitch Patterns

S hould the instructions for even a simple pattern be written out entirely in English, it would take up an inordinate amount of space. Instead, most knitting instructions are written in "knitter's English," a combination of knitting jargon and abbreviations. Not only do these terms and abbreviations conveniently compact the information in a small space, but they considerably speed up writing a pattern or making notes, especially for stitch patterns. They are not, however, particularly easy to read or to follow as you work.

In many places in the world, it is far more common to knit from two charts, one a system of symbols on graph paper that conveys the instructions for the stitch pattern, the other a diagram of the garment pattern, and written instructions are kept to a minimum. Many people find these charted patterns much easier to follow, and the method of reading and writing them is discussed in full in the next section.

However, that is not to say that written instructions don't have their place. First and foremost, there are many written patterns, both old and new, and even if you prefer to knit from a chart, you must be able to read the pattern in order to convert it to charted form. Second, even charted patterns will have some written instructions, and since there are many occasions when it is important to be able to make written notes of various kinds, familiarity with the methods and forms of writing a pattern will be essential to you. This material contains first what I hope is a simple, lucid, pared-down glossary of abbreviations, followed by a detailed explanation of how to read stitch and garment patterns. You will find that the terms used primarily for garment patterns are really quite straightforward, no more than shortened forms of familiar words—it is only the context in which they are found that will be different. Both the abbreviations and the form of a stitch pattern, however, tend to be more esoteric and somewhat less standardized.

Abbreviations

Unfortunately, there are no conventions regarding what sort of abbreviations to use even for terms that may be the same, and frequently the terms themselves will be different. Nevertheless, most pattern books will provide a key to the system they use, and most systems are more similar to one another than they are different, which makes the mental adjustments you must make relatively easy.

These are the abbreviations I like to use; if you have a preference for some others that are familiar to you, by all means use them. I have combed every book for the most common terms, and many are perfectly serviceable and so obvious that there is no question of their value. Others reflect the idiosyncrasies of a small region or a particular writer and are less useful. In some cases, I have introduced a new term that I think has greater descriptive power, precision, or generality, or because material discussed elsewhere in the book demanded it. When writing a stitch pattern, there is no need for every esoteric technique to have its own abbreviation; that way only engenders confusion. Therefore, those given here are the most basic, essential ones, but as you will see they can all be combined with one another to convey more complex information, so the list has richer possibilities than its length indicates.

In practice, the abbreviations may or may not be capitalized, and the decision as to whether to do so is rather arbitrary. Most often, somewhat the same rules as English punctuation apply, so the first word of a "sentence," and any letter that stands alone is generally capitalized. Frequently, an abbreviation representing more than one word will have both letters capitalized, as in LH for Left Hand. This is conventional rather than systematic, and many others do not follow that form.

Glossary of Abbreviations

alt	alternate
approx	approximately
B	Bobble
beg	beginning
bel	below
C	Cable
cc	contrast(ing) color
c. off	cast off
c. on	cast on
cont	continue
cm	centimeter
cr	cross
dbl	double
dec	decrease
dis	discard
dpn	double-point needle
dr	drop
fol	following
fs	farside
h	hand
in	inch
inc	increase
incl	include/inclusive
ins	inside
k	Knit
kw	knitwise
l	left
m	meter
mc	main color
mm	millimeter
mult	multiple
n	needle
ns	nearside
o	over
outs	outside
p	Purl
p	pull or pass (always lower case and never used alone; see discussion below)
patt	pattern
pw	purlwise
r	right
rem	remaining
rep	repeat
ret	return
rnd	round
rth	running thread
sl	slip
st/sts	stitch/stitches
str	strand
t	turn
tog	together
tw	twist
u	under
wr	wrap
y	yarn
yd	yard
...	repeat material between asterisks
(...)	repeat material between parentheses
#	number
*	reference to key or note
#/#	designates number of stitches in a Cable

Written Garment Patterns

For the most part, garment pattern instructions are written in a plain, albeit very terse English, whatever abbreviations are used are quite straightforward, and generally all commercial patterns follow much the same format. The patterns are generally divided into sections, the first ones dealing with the preliminaries, the middle ones with the actual pattern instructions, and the last on finishing details.

Size and Materials

First, the pattern will provide basic information on garment size and the materials needed. Most patterns will include instructions for several sizes, which may be given as a chest measurement in inches and/or centimeters, occasionally as small, medium, and large, and for children sometimes as a range of ages. This information will look something like "To fit 38 (40, 42, 44)." All subsequent information for each size will occupy the same position inside or outside the parentheses; follow only those instructions pertinent to the size you are knitting and ignore the others. Before you start to work, you might want to circle all the numbers in the entire pattern that are correct for your size, or mark them with a transparent color marker.

Whether or not a schematic drawing of the pattern is shown, most instructions will include the finished measurements for the width and length of the main pattern pieces. These will be written to correspond to the sizes, such as "Width at underarm 41 (43, 45, 47) inches." These figures also tell you how much ease (the difference between the body measurement and the garment measurement) is built into the design.

Tools and materials will be specified, including the type, color, and amount of yarn to purchase, the correct size needles, and any additional items, such as markers or cable needles, and the number of buttons if needed. The yarn requirements will be different depending upon the size, and this will also be indicated with parentheses, such as "9 (10, 11, 12) 2-oz skeins of XYZ wool, color #123."

Stitch Pattern

Some patterns provide the detailed instructions for working the stitch pattern in written form; information on reading patterns of this sort can be found below.

Most European, Japanese, and, increasingly now, American patterns are provided in charted form; information on working from charts can be found starting on page 449.

Stitch Gauge

Next will come the information on the stitch gauge. In order for the garment to come out the correct size, *you must knit to the gauge specified*. The stitch gauge for every fabric is unique and depends upon a particular combination of hands, needle size, yarn, and stitch pattern. Before you begin to knit the garment, you must knit a sample, or tension swatch, of the fabric to make sure you produce the same gauge with the same yarn and same stitch pattern that the designer did. The gauge will be given as a certain number of stitches and rows per whatever measurement was used as the basis for designing the pattern. Usually this measurement will be one that will allow even numbers, so one may say 13 stitches and 17 rows every 2 inches, another might say 18 stitches and 25 rows to 5 centimeters.

The pattern book or magazine will describe the size and method of handling and measuring the swatch and calculating stitch gauge that they recommend. However, I do not think the methods generally used in commercial patterns are a very accurate way to determine stitch gauge, and suggest that you read the material on page 417 for an alternative. As long as your gauge matches that given, it does not matter how you obtain it, so you can substitute the method given here for that called for in any pattern.

You may encounter a pattern that instructs you to take a stitch gauge from a swatch worked in Stockinette even though this is not the stitch pattern used for the garment. This is sometimes done when the garment contains several different stitch patterns. A gauge was made for each and every stitch pattern in order to work out the pattern, but rather than have you match every one of them, the designer has used the same yarn and needles to also obtain a gauge in Stockinette, and it is assumed that if you can match that gauge, your general method of knitting will match the gauges the designer obtained on the other patterns as well. This is admittedly rough, but probably works well enough in most circumstances.

The needle size given in any pattern is a recommendation only. It is the needle size used by the designer to obtain the gauge given, but your hands are not the designer's hands, and you may not be able to match the gauge on the same needle size. If you find your gauge does not match, you will have to knit another one, with either smaller or larger needles, until you achieve a swatch that does. If there are fewer stitches and rows per inch than required in the gauge you make, this means your stitches are too large, and you will have to use a smaller needle to try to make a match; if there are more stitches and rows per inch, your stitches are too small, and you will have to use a larger needle to try to make a match.

Unfortunately, this is a rather crude method of having things come out right, and you may find yourself with a gauge that is too small on one size needle and too big on the next size needle. Nevertheless, unless you wish to rewrite the pattern, you have no choice but to come as close as you possibly can. There are slight variations in the same sizes of different brands of needles (see the discussion on needles on page 336), and needles made in different materials may change the way you knit, thus altering the gauge. It is risky to try to knit on one needle or the other trying to force yourself to work at a tighter or looser tension; that is difficult to maintain in a consistent way throughout an entire project. If you find yourself with this sort of a dilemma, use the calculations on page 417 to work out what the overall width and length of the garment will be if you go ahead and use a stitch gauge that is slightly off. If the garment is loose fitting and without a great deal of detail, it may be that making it a bit larger or smaller will not be a serious problem. In fact, I suspect many patterns are designed with generous ease allowances and simple styling because commercial pattern makers are aware that people have trouble with stitch gauge.

The Pattern

Following all these preliminaries, you will finally get to the actual pattern, which will generally be divided into sections, with individual instructions for the front, back, sleeves, etc. Included will be the correct-size needle to use for each section (you must substitute the size you need to use to match the gauge), how many stitches to cast on, and how many rows or inches to work in pattern before any change occurs. These instructions will be given in the same form that the size and yarn requirements were, reading something like "Using Size 5 needle, cast on 70 (74, 78, 82) stitches." The appropriate number of stitches for the garment you are making will be in the same position within the parentheses as the size was.

Most often, the garment starts with a ribbed edge of some sort on a small needle. If you must use a different-size needle from that recommended in the pattern for the body of the garment in order to match the gauge, also adjust the size of the needle used for ribbing accordingly. When the ribbing is the correct length, the next instructions will generally require you to change to the larger needle and a different stitch pattern for the body of the garment.

You may also be required to increase the number of stitches at this point. When shaping techniques are distributed across the width of the fabric, the instruction will read something like "Increase in every 7th stitch across row," which means work six stitches in pattern and make an increase on the seventh stitch, work another six stitches and another increase, etc. If the instructions read something like "Increase 10 stitches evenly across row," you will have to make your own calculations regarding which stitch to place the increases on (see page 437 for more details). Any time the number of stitches on the needle changes, the pattern should provide the new total for each size in the same form as the casting-on instructions.

The same format is used for the rows or inches, such as "Knit until piece measures 8 (10, 12, 14) in.," or "cont in patt 0 (4, 8, 12) rows" or "work even to row 32 (34, 36, 38)." All of these mean basically the same thing, that is, you are to continue on the same number of stitches, working the same stitch pattern until the fabric is a certain length. The zero indicates that only the three larger sizes continue for the number of rows specified; for the smallest size, you are to go on to the next instruction directly.

Following this will come the instructions for the method of working the armhole shaping. Shaping that occurs at the edges of the fabric is generally distributed over several rows. You may be told to cast off several stitches at the beginning of the next two rows, which will indent each side edge sharply for the underarm. Then, in order to continue the curve more gently, a pattern will be provided, such as "Dec 1 st each end every other row twice, every 4th row twice, every 6th row once." This means there will be a decrease on the first and last stitch of, say, row 56 and row 58 (that's "every other row twice"), then again on rows 62 and 66 ("every 4th row twice"), and finally on row 72 (six rows later). Increase patterns, such as for shaping a sleeve, will follow the same form.

Once the armholes are the correct length, you may be instructed to slope the shoulder line. The instructions for this will look something like "At each armhole edge, cast off 6 sts 3 (1, 0, 0) times, 8 sts 1 (3, 1, 0) times, 8 sts 0 (0, 3, 4) times." For the sake of example, let us first imagine that you are working the front of a cardigan sweater so only one shoulder is involved. As you know, you can only cast off at the beginning of a row, not at the end, so these stitches will be removed every other row. For the smallest size, that means six stitches will be cast off each time on, say, rows 128, 130, and 132, and the last eight stitches on row 134. (For more information regarding the best method of sloping shoulders, see page 178.)

Many knitters find these kinds of instructions difficult to follow, particularly when you must shape both shoulders and neckline simultaneously. This is the area of a pattern where working from written instructions can be especially frustrating and where a charted garment pattern is so useful. Regardless of what form your instructions are in, it is best to find some method of maintaining an accurate record of exactly what you have done so you don't lose your place. Many people make the mistake of thinking that counting the stitches on the needle will tell them what they need to know. For instance, if you think you should have fifty-six stitches on the needle, but count fifty-eight, you won't know whether you are not on the row you thought you were, or whether you forgot to decrease when you should have in some previous row. Experienced knitters know how to count rows in the fabric and recognize where the shaping techniques are, but doing so takes more time than keeping track as you work. Read the material on page 351 before you start for suggestions on keeping track of your progress.

Finishing

And finally, there will be a section on finishing details that may include the pattern for picking up and knitting the stitches for a collar or placket, and any hemming, seaming, and other finishing instructions.

Written Stitch Patterns

Whereas a garment pattern provides detailed instructions for how to shape the fabric into body and sleeves, etc., stitch patterns tell you how to handle each stitch in order to produce a particular surface texture. Written stitch patterns are far more formulaic than garment patterns. Indeed, there is a resemblance to mathematical notation because the intention is to convey a complex set of instructions in as clear and compact a way as possible. For someone new to knitting, the first exposure to a pattern can be intimidating, but they are really quite simple once you are familiar with the abbreviations and understand how the patterns are organized.

Combining Abbreviations

First, it is customary to combine several basic abbreviations into larger terms in order to describe a single step or technique. Very simple, common examples might be yo for "Yarnover," slst for "Slip Stitch," or psso for "Pull Slip Stitch over."

Frequently, the abbreviations are also combined with a number designating how often a technique should be worked, such as K2 for "Knit two stitches." A number may also be used to indicate how many stitches or rows are involved in the particular step, as with K2tog for "Knit two together," Sl2kw for "Slip two stitches knitwise," or K1bel for "Knit into the stitch one row below." Some patterns use the word "twice," as in "Yarnover twice" for a Double Yarnover, but that can easily be replaced by Yo2, which is more compact.

Special Cases

Whenever an unusual technique is involved, one not covered by any standard abbreviation, nor easily described by some combination of other abbreviations, the author will generally describe in plain English how the technique must be worked and then assign the technique a simple term to be used within the pattern. A pattern might, for instance, call for a certain type of Twist Stitch, describe it in words at the beginning, and then use just LT or Tw within the actual instructions.

This may present problems with some techniques such as the Cables—first, because there are so many varieties, and second, because several varieties may be used within one pattern. In hopes of solving this problem, I would like to suggest a system of notation that adequately describes any sort of cable you might want to work. The term LC2/2 would indicate that you should work a Left Cable "two over two"—in other words, two stitches drawn to the left on the outside past two others. The term RC3/2 translates Right Cable "three over two," where three stitches should be drawn to the right over two others.

Punctuation

In a series of instructions, the terms for each separate technique are generally separated by commas. An example would be "K2, p3, yo, k2tog, p3, k2," which means "Knit two stitches, Purl the next three, make a Yarnover and then a right decrease, Purl three more, and finally Knit two." When a single technique is made up of several different steps, each step is separated only by a space, as in "K1, sl1kw k1 psso, p2." The center term is a form of left decrease, so the abbreviation Ldec would also suffice, with the method of working it left to the knitter. (In some books you will find this decrease abbreviated SKP for Slip, Knit, Pullover; I find that too closely resembles SSK and SSP and may generate errors, so I prefer Sl P instead.)

I sometimes separate the steps of a complex technique with backslashes instead of spaces; this provides somewhat more of a visual cue that they all belong together. For instance, you might want to specify the steps in a pullover technique, writing "Sl1kw/k2/psso," for Slip one stitch knitwise, Knit the next two stitches, pass the Slip Stitch over the two stitches.

Repetitions

When a technique or group of techniques must be repeated a certain number of times before continuing with the remainder of the instructions, the term or group is generally enclosed in parentheses. In most patterns a statement of this sort looks like "K1, (k2, p3) 2 times, k1," which translates "K1, k2, p3, k2, p3, k1." Another example is "P1, (k2tog, yo) twice, P1." Written the long way, this would be "P1 k2tog, yo, k2tog, yo, p1." For these kinds of statements, I prefer to borrow from algebra and write them "K1, 2(k2, p3), k1" and "P1, 2(k2tog, yo), p1." This is more compact and informs you directly what to expect.

Similarly, the entire stitch pattern repeat, that section of the stitch pattern exclusive of edge stitches which is to be repeated again and again across the row, is set apart by asterisks. A pattern might read "K1 *p2, 2(k1fs, p2) k5, 2(p2, k1fs) p2* k1." The k1 at either end of the phrase is either a selvedge or an edge stitch (for a discussion of the difference between the two, see below), so you work a Knit one, then begin the repeat at the first asterisk. Work the pair of Purl stitches, then the sequence within the first parentheses twice, the center five Knit, the sequence within the second parentheses twice, and when you have worked the last pair of Purl stitches and come to the second asterisk, you must start the repeat all over again with the first p2, cycling again and again in this way within the asterisks until you run out of stitches on the row and have only the last stitch to Knit. Many patterns will say something like ". . . repeat from*" within an instruction of this sort; others might say "repeat from * to * across the row." All of

that is rather redundant, as the asterisks are quite sufficient on their own once you understand their meaning, and I don't think anyone has much trouble with it; I invite you to leave the explanations out.

Row repeats may also be provided, sometimes no more than a note saying "repeat row 1–6" of a six-row pattern, but occasionally one or two rows within a pattern may be repeated several times before the remainder of the rows are worked. This is equivalent to the parentheses around a few stitch terms and is usually indicated by having all the pertinent row numbers adjacent to a single line of instructions. Sometimes rows in different areas of the pattern are identical, and the pattern will say on row 4, for instance, "repeat row 2." In any instructions I use in this book, I eliminate the word "repeat" and write simply "Row 4: Row 2" to mean the same thing. These sorts of instructions are quite self-evident, but I mention them for those who are utterly unfamiliar with patterns, and for the sake of completeness.

Edge and Selvedge Stitches

A functional selvedge stitch is one that is added to those required for the width of the fabric and then incorporated into a seam. It does not contribute to the finished width of the garment and is not used on unseamed fabrics or those knitted in the round. A decorative selvedge consists of one or two columns of stitches worked in one of several special stitch techniques that provide a finished edge to an unseamed fabric. A selvedge stitch, regardless of what form it takes, is technically not part of a stitch pattern.

An edge stitch, on the other hand, is part of a stitch pattern, but not part of the repeat, being worked only at the beginning and/or end of a row and within the selvedges if they are present. It is used to balance a pattern at both sides, to keep complex stitch techniques away from the side edge or seam, or to fill in around staggered pattern elements. In the pattern instructions, the edge stitches are those that precede or follow the asterisks enclosing the repeat. In the instruction "*K3, sl1* k1," the k1 is worked only once, after the last repeat of the row; if selvedge stitches are used, one would be placed before the first k3, the other after the final k1 of the pattern. For more information on the role of edge stitches in patterns, see page 461.

There are some patterns in which the edge stitches at the end of the row are worked as a slight variation on the last term of the repeat. For instance, an instruction might read "K3 *p3, k7, p3, k5* end last repeat k3." Some people are confused by this, unsure whether the three stitches to be Knit should be there in addition to the final k5, or as a substitute for them; they are a substitute. It would be far more accurate to write the phrase "K3 *p3, k7, p3, k5* end k3 instead of k5," but that is lengthy. The notation I use on my own patterns is "... p3, k5* −k5 +k3," which means the same thing but is both very precise and very compact.

When a selvedge stitch is required for a commercial garment pattern, it is often included as part of the stitch pattern without being identified as such, in which case it will look like an edge stitch. This is not a problem when the stitch pattern is used for the specific purpose for which it was designed, but it may not be appropriate in another context. Before using any stitch pattern for a design of your own, therefore, first familiarize yourself with the pattern so you understand the role each stitch plays. You may find it necessary to add or eliminate edge or selvedge stitches in order to have the pattern work for the purpose you have in mind. By far the easiest way to do this is with stitch charting (see page 449); also, see below on coordinating stitch repeats and garment width.

Starting on Inside or Outside Rows

On a flat pattern, it is usually specified whether the first row is an inside or an outside row, although many instructions will refer to this as the right or wrong side. The way the pattern begins may or may not be appropriate to the type of casting on you have used, and may or may not be important, but you cannot tell that for certain until you either work a sample swatch or chart the pattern. (For more information on this and what adjustments can be made, see page 127).

Pattern Scale

If you want to get a sense of the scale of a pattern before you begin working from a commercial pattern, the stitches per inch from the gauge provided and the number of stitches in a repeat will tell you how wide each repeat is going to be, while the rows per inch from the gauge and the number of rows in the pattern will tell you how tall the repeat will be (see the information on page 342 regarding the relationship between gauge and stitch pattern). If you are taking the pattern from a stitch pattern book and designing your own garment, you can still get a rough idea of scale from the stitch- and row-repeat figures if a stitch gauge is listed on the yarn label. Even though any gauge provided will be for Stockinette, it will give you a general idea of what to expect, but you must also consider whether the pattern you want to use is one that compresses or expands in some way (see page 418).

Coordinating Pattern Repeat and Fabric Width

Your gauge determines how many stitches are required for a given width of fabric (see page 417), and you may or may not be able to fit an even number of stitch pattern repeats into that width. Stitch pattern books will often specify that a pattern requires something like "a multiple of 8 stitches, plus 3." The multiple refers to the stitch repeat, and the number added on at the end refers to any edge stitches. As I mentioned above, first determine what role the edge stitches play and decide whether or not they are appropriate to what you have in mind.

To find how many repeats can be accommodated within the width you need, subtract any edge stitches required by the stitch pattern from the overall number of stitches, then divide the answer by the stitch pattern multiple. Any remainder represents the number of stitches required for the width in addition to those in the repeats. It is generally not a good idea to simply add on enough stitches to accommodate another repeat as this will, of course, add to the width of the garment; instead fill in at each side with a partial stitch repeat or with some other plain or textured pattern. Of course, if the repeat is small and the fit generous, you may prefer to adjust the size and either add or remove a few stitches so the repeats divide evenly. These problems are much easier to solve if both stitch and garment patterns have been charted; for more information on coordinating stitch and garment patterns, see page 511.

24

Stitch Gauge

This is a Very Important Discussion that should be read by every knitter, beginner to advanced. I want to encourage the former to accept the necessity of a stitch gauge and learn to do one correctly, and I would like to encourage the latter to learn a new method of making a gauge that I think is a great improvement in accuracy.

A stitch gauge is a measurement of the number of stitches and rows per inch or centimeter in a knitted fabric. The gauge is obtained from a small swatch, or tension sample, that should be handled in exactly the same manner as the fabric of the garment. The gauge is used to determine the overall number of stitches and rows required for the width and length of the fabric and thus determines the size and shape of the garment. If you are working from a commercial pattern, the gauge will be specified, and you must knit so the fabric you produce matches it precisely.

There is absolutely nothing more important to success in knitting than an accurate stitch gauge. I'm going to repeat that. *There is absolutely nothing more important to success in knitting than an accurate stitch gauge*—and nothing in knitting seems to give people more trouble. Without an accurate stitch gauge to work from, it is highly unlikely that the finished garment will turn out to be the correct size. Knitting anything is a considerable investment of time and money, and having it turn out wrong can be a crushing disappointment. I have heard countless sad stories told of projects that were a total loss, all because of problems with the stitch gauge. What is worse, I am sure there are a great many people who like to knit, but who have given up entirely because there were too many of these disappointments.

There are always those who think they can get away with not doing a gauge at all. This despite the exhortations in every pattern in every knitting magazine, and from every instructor in every knitting store to carefully make a gauge. I suppose it seems like a waste of effort to make a "useless" little swatch, and it is all too tempting to tell yourself that, if you just use the yarn and needles recommended in the pattern, it will all come out close enough. Whatever the argument, this is an extremely shortsighted course of action. Every time you find yourself about to follow that line of reasoning, I want you to consider how you will feel about putting all that work into a garment that does not fit; I can promise you that that is exactly what will happen.

There are other exuberant types who would like to believe that creativity is everything and all the numbers and planning and measuring is just so much bother and restriction. I do not know how to persuade against the inclinations of temperament; I can only say that knitting is not really amenable to that sort of an approach. All of the appeal, beauty, and charm that can be evident in a knitted garment are the result of disciplined skill and knowledge and precisely worked out details.

The most unfortunate disappointments, however, are those which befall the well-intentioned people who *have* gone to the trouble of making a stitch gauge. And this is because the methods recommended in most books for making and measuring a swatch for the purposes of gauge are, for a variety of reasons, not very successful.

Something this important should not be so fraught with problems. Let's take a look at what is at work here and see if things can't be improved.

Basic Methods of Calculating Stitch Gauge

The following methods of calculating stitch gauge are very accurate. One method is suitable for when you are working from a commercial pattern, the other for when you are designing your own garment. The fundamental concepts detailed here apply to anything you might have occasion to knit, although some aspects need to be varied when dealing with certain special fabrics, and those are discussed in the section that follows this one.

The Variables

For any given gauge, there are four variables: the hands, the needles, the yarn, and the stitch pattern. *If you change any one of these variables, the stitch gauge will also change.*

This means that you cannot work on someone else's knitting nor have them work on yours, because everyone's hands impart subtle differences to the tension of the yarn and thus the size of the stitches; the difference will be visible. Along with the tension placed on the yarn, the size of the needle determines the size of the stitch, a larger-size needle producing larger stitches and a smaller-size needle, smaller stitches. The dimension, weight, and behavior of the yarn also affects stitch size, with thick yarns generally producing fewer stitches and rows per inch than fine ones. In addition, each stitch or color pattern produces a unique gauge—some dense and compressed, some widened or lengthened, some, such as lace, doing both. And finally, even with the same hands, yarn, stitch pattern, and needle size, if you use needles made by a different manufacturer for the garment instead of those you used for the sample, the gauge may change, particularly if the needles are made of a different material!

Therefore, the swatch from which the gauge is taken must be made in precisely the same way that the fabric will be. If the pattern calls for any changes in needle size, type of yarn, or stitch pattern, each new configuration requires a separate swatch and a separate gauge.

System of Measurement and Calculation

Throughout the United States and in the United Kingdom, knitting measurements and calculations have traditionally been done with the imperial system using inches and yards. Half-hearted efforts are being made to adopt the metric system of centimeters and meters, which knitters use in many other areas of the world, but these sorts of changes are not easy for adults. This has posed a problem for me, because I would like to accommodate both camps when discussing these matters. Unfortunately, having to write "inch/centimeter" or "yard/meter" every time tends to clutter things up and makes any formulas appear to be more formidable than they are.

Both systems offer some advantages and disadvantages, and I have been unable to make an arguable case for using one instead of the other. For instance, when you use inches and yards, you must convert any fractional measurements to decimals. Now, no one would pretend that these conversions are fun to do, although with time it becomes quite automatic and it affects only some of the calculations. On the other hand, despite my intellectual appreciation for the clarity and simplicity of the metric system, I find a centimeter, and especially millimeters, just a little too small to function accurately and well for the purposes of measuring a knitted fabric and obtaining a stitch gauge. The smallest practical unit is 2 cm.

I am also one of those who think in inches and yards, and so I have decided that for the most part I will write in inches and yards as well. The formulas presented here are all quite clear in themselves, and will be further explained at every step, so I do not think you will have trouble substituting the metric system for the imperial system if that is what you wish to use. When it is simple to do so, I will use both so that metric people will know that I at least have them in mind.

How Stitch Gauge Is Used

Before we go on to the discussion of exactly how to make a tension sample and get a stitch gauge, I think it would be wise to pause and explain more concretely just what a stitch gauge is and how it is used in knitting. I mentioned above that a gauge tells us how many stitches and rows there are in every inch of a particular fabric. In commercial patterns, this may be written something like "5 stitches and 7 rows per inch," or "13 sts/15 rows = 2 in," the latter seemingly used as a way of avoiding decimal numbers. In my own system of notation the latter would be written "G = 6.5/7.5," with stitches always written first and rows second, and always with a unit of one inch.

These two figures are then used with some simple mathematical formulas to determine both the overall

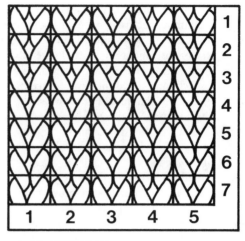

A STOCKINETTE GAUGE

width and length of a fabric, and the position of any shaping techniques such as increases or decreases. The basic concept is best understood in relationship to simple width and length.

Stitches per Inch × Width of Fabric = Number of Stitches

Rows per Inch × Length of Fabric = Number of Rows

There may be times when you already have the number of stitches or rows and want instead to know what the gauge is, or what the width or length of the fabric will be.

Number of Stitches ÷ Stitches per Inch = Width of Fabric

Number of Stitches ÷ Width of Fabric = Stitches per Inch

The same formulas can be used for rows and length.

Now that you know how they are used, let us see how a gauge is obtained.

The Tension Sample

The method of determining stitch gauge that I recommend is quite different from what is found in most books or in commercial patterns. Commonly, instructions will tell you to make a swatch of about 4in/10cm, place pins 2in/5cm apart in both dimensions and then count the stitches between the pins.

There are several problems with this approach. First, some pattern books do not instruct you to block the tension sample, and, as we shall see, this can make a crucial difference. Second, it is not easy to set the pins straight and in the correct position. Third, it can be difficult to count the stitches and rows accurately, particularly in a complex pattern or when using a yarn that is highly textured or dark in color. Fourth, there is no way to be very precise about any partial stitch that falls within the area; it may be a half, a third, or even a quarter of a stitch, and this difficulty is exacerbated by any complex stitch techniques. Fifth, any slight errors you make in trying to do all this will be multiplied when the resulting gauge is used to calculate the number of stitches for the width and length of the fabric. That adds up to a lot of problems.

With the method recommended here you don't have to set pins, and it does not matter how complex the stitch pattern is or whether the yarn obscures the stitches because you don't count stitches, you use the number of stitches cast on, the number of rows worked, and the full width and length of the sample for the calculations used to get the gauge. Any partial stitches per inch are therefore automatically included in the measurement.

Making the Sample

The larger the sample, the smaller the margin of error there will be in measuring; however, it may certainly be sized in relation to the fabric you are planning. As a general rule, make the sample roughly square, with a width no smaller than 15 to 20 percent of the widest measurement of your garment. In other words, for a sweater with a 40-inch circumference, make a 6-inch sample. For a child's sweater with a 20-inch circumference, one of 3 to 4 inches will do. I don't recommend a sample smaller than 2 inches no matter what you are making, nor do I think one much larger than 6 inches is necessary.

As long as the sample is large enough in proportion to your garment, exact size is not important, but you will want to cast on enough stitches to accommodate an even number of stitch pattern repeats; a minimum of two repeats in both the horizontal and vertical dimension is necessary. In adjusting the size of the sample to accommodate the stitch pattern, always make it larger if necessary rather than smaller. If you are going to use short needles for the sample and longer ones for the garment, use the same brand needle for both. Once you decide on the size sample you need, you must calculate the number of stitches required, as follows:

- If you are using a commercial pattern, first multiply the stitch gauge provided by the sample width you need to get a rough idea of how many stitches to cast on. Divide by your stitch pattern multiple; if it does not divide evenly, add enough stitches to the number for the sample until it does. If the stitch pattern is charted, the repeat should be marked off and numbered. If you are working from written instructions, the repeat consists of the number of stitches between the asterisks in one line of the instructions. Once you have the number of stitches that can be divided evenly

by the repeat, add any edge stitches that may be necessary (the stitches outside the asterisks). For more information on repeats and edge stitches, see page 412.

- When you are designing your own garment, you are likely to start by "shopping" for a stitch pattern and needle size to use, trying several before you settle on the combination that is suitable for your design. During this process, you will want to use small, preliminary samples of just a repeat or two, or about a two-inch square, in order to save time. If you wish, use the guidelines on the yarn label regarding needle size and average gauge for Stockinette to decide how many stitches to cast on for these samples, although your results will be different. Do not attempt to use these preliminary samples for stitch gauge—they will not be accurate—but you can use them to get an idea of how many stitches to cast on for the larger tension sample.

- Use a fully expandable method of casting on and casting off so the top and bottom edges are not restricted in any way; Stranded Cast-on and Stranded Cast-off are ideal. Do not use selvedge stitches.

- Keep an accurate record of the number of stitches and rows you work on the sample, and save this information. I make it a habit to tie a number of knots, equivalent to the size needle used, on one of the ends of yarn at the corner of the sample.

Dressing the Sample

After a knitted garment is assembled, it must be cleaned and made ready for wear. In addition to removing any soil, the warmth and moisture of the cleaning process allows the fibers to relax and the fabric can then be smoothed out so that the rows and columns of stitches lie straight and even and the stitch pattern is fully displayed. This is a process I refer to as dressing the fabric. The steps in this process are designed to give the garment its final wearable finish (see pages 387–397), and are similar in some respects to the process of washing and pressing a fine garment of woven fabric.

When a knitted fabric is dressed, the overall dimensions will change as the surface is smoothed. Some stitch patterns are quite compressed and irregular right after they have been knitted up, while others lie relatively flat and smooth, but when dressed, all of them will expand and change their proportions to some extent. This has very important implications for stitch gauge. If you were to use an undressed sample as the basis for determining the stitch gauge, you would find that while the garment was the correct size before it was dressed, it might be considerably larger afterward. For this reason, a stitch gauge should *always* be taken from a dressed sample, one that has been handled in every respect just as you will handle the finished garment every time you clean it.

For the same reason, any measurements you attempt to make of the fabric while you are working may have

A GAUGE SAMPLE BEFORE DRESSING

THE SAME SAMPLE, AFTER DRESSING

little relationship to what the finished garment will or should measure. Unfortunately, many commercial patterns suggest just this sort of thing, telling the knitter to work until the piece measures so many inches or centimeters. These sorts of measurements are simply not accurate.

To give you an example of just how misleading an instruction like this can be, let's assume you are using a pattern that opens up somewhat, and the gauge taken from the dressed sample is 5.5 rows to the inch while the gauge taken from the undressed sample was 6 rows to the inch. If you measure the depth of the armhole as you work and find that it is 8 inches, the undressed fabric will contain about 8 × 6 = 48 rows. However, when you wash and dress the finished garment, you will discover that the armhole has changed, and instead of the 8 inches you expected, it now measures 48 ÷ 5.5 = 8.7 inches.

You can see from this example how far off you might be if you relied on a measurement taken from work in progress. Obviously, it is far better to work a certain number of rows determined by a gauge taken from a dressed sample to achieve the correct length. When a pattern does call for working to a measurement, use the stitch gauge to convert it to rows, and then keep an accurate count as you work.

However, a gauge taken from an undressed sample has its uses, precisely *because* its gauge matches that of the fabric while you are knitting. If you have lost count, or doubt the count you have kept, measuring the fabric and comparing it to the undressed gauge can give you a realistic sense of your progress, although it should not be substituted for an accurate row count, which will have to be taken from the fabric eventually. An undressed gauge is also particularly useful as you work things like scarves, blankets, and hats where precision is not really required, although no pattern, even for such a simple garment, should be planned on the basis of an undressed gauge. And it should be used to check the width of the fabric after you have worked a few inches so you do not go too far wrong if something is amiss in your calculations.

For an undressed gauge, follow the same method of measurement and calculation described below for the dressed version. It only takes a moment to do, and if you write the gauge down somewhere on your pattern, you will have it if you need it. You can convert an undressed measurement to a dressed one by using the formula given below in Stitch Gauge Ratios.

Dressing the sample is not done just to obtain the gauge. Because you must clean the sample in exactly the same way as you will clean the finished garment, it will give you a good sense of how the fiber is going to behave with handling. It is far better to discover any problems with the yarn before you knit the garment than after. The manufacturer should provide care instructions on the label of the yarn; if no label exists, the store should be able to tell you how to handle it. If the store can't tell you, it may be a good idea to select something else, but if you are determined, you will have to experiment. Complete information on dressing a knitted fabric can be found starting on page 387, and detailed information on the characteristics of particular fibers on page 310.

If the label recommends against washing, you must still clean and block the swatch. Take your tiny little swatch to the dry cleaners and ask them to handle it according to the instructions; if necessary, show them the label. I know this seems excessive, but it can be very important. You will, after all, have to clean the finished garment according to those instructions, and I should think you would want to know what will happen before you invest your time in its construction. I found out the hard way what a good idea this can be when I knit the garment first and then took it to the cleaners. The yarn was a beautiful, narrow ribbon with a bit of sheen to it, but when it came home again all the sheen was gone. If I had known that ahead of time, I would never have used the yarn.

If you have handled the yarn according to the instructions and notice color bleeding, or a change in texture or sheen, by all means return the intact balls of yarn to the store and get a refund or select a different yarn. It is far better to have wasted a ball of yarn, time on the sample, and an extra trip to the store than to be disappointed in a garment that will require so much care and effort to make. Tell the owner of the store exactly why you are returning the yarn. Stores depend upon customer satisfaction, and they won't want to carry a brand that produces complaints.

Measuring the Sample

There are two methods of measuring for gauge—one suitable for work with commercial patterns, and the Weighted Sample Method for use when developing your own design. The first is simple and direct and the only method most knitters need concern themselves with. However, keep in mind that there is an adjustment necessary when designing and learn that method if and when the time comes that you require it.

Flat Method
Lay the dressed sample down on a hard surface, and measure with a ruler (not a fabric or plastic tape measure, which can stretch and be inaccurate).

1. Set the ruler down horizontally across the middle of the sample, lining it up evenly with a row of stitches, and note the measurement to one-eighth of an inch.
2. Do the same thing for the vertical measurement, lining the ruler up with a column of stitches.

If the sample has a tendency to curl, turn it over and measure on the inside, using the ruler to flatten the fab-

ric; however, be careful not to stretch the sample in any way.

If the edge scallops, it is most likely to go in on one side and go out in the same place on the other side, so as long as you measure from one side to the next, it doesn't matter. If the fabric goes out on both sides, then goes in on both sides, measure both and average the two figures.

Do not underestimate the importance of eighths of an inch in these measurements; an error can cause a difference of nearly an inch in the garment width. I frequently measure the sample two or three times to make sure I have not stretched it or misread anything; if it is the same each time, I can be sure I have it right.

Basic Weighted Method
In addition to the change in the dimensions of a fabric that takes place when it is dressed, most knitted garments will show evidence of "drop," a lengthening of the garment due to the hanging weight of the fabric in wear. Drop not only changes the length of the fabric, but as it lengthens it will narrow, and therefore the gauge of the fabric lying flat is quite different from the gauge of the same fabric in wear. The amount of drop evident in a garment is variable, depending upon the stitch pattern, the type of yarn, the density of the fabric, and the size of the garment. If you are developing a pattern for your own design, drop must be taken into consideration to achieve a good fit.

To give you an idea of just how important the phenomenon of drop can be, I will give you an actual example, the sleeve of a cotton sweater. On the table, the dressed sleeve measured precisely what the pattern called for in length and width. However, when the sleeve was held up, hanging as it would be from the shoulder of the garment, it gained nearly two inches in length! Returned to the table, it recovered the measurement the pattern called for. If you have been frustrated by garments that seem to "grow," drop is one of the major factors in what is at work. The other factor is that fibers themselves will stretch slightly as the garment is repeatedly worn. This is more of a problem with inelastic fibers such as cotton and silk than it is with wool, which is quite elastic, but they will all recover when cleaned. Drop, on the other hand, is due to a change in the *proportions* of the stitches; in other words, the gauge changes. This must be compensated for in the design process by measuring a dressed sample that is weighted to duplicate the condition the fabric will be in while it is being worn.

1. Insert a fine gauge knitting needle through the top edge of the sample. If you have used Stranded Cast-off, insert it into the stitches; if you used Pullover Cast-off, weave it through one strand of a cast-off stitch every half-inch or so.
2. Do the same with a second needle on the cast-on

edge. Smooth the stitches of the two edges out on the needles so the sample is neither stretched nor compressed.

3. Run string or a stand of yarn through the label of one of the balls of yarn you plan to use for the garment and tie the two ends to the bottom needle on either side of the sample.

4. Pick up the top needle and allow the sample to hang down weighted by the ball of yarn.

5. Using a hard ruler, measure horizontally across the middle of the sample, lining it up evenly with a row of stitches, and note the measurement to one-eighth of an inch.

6. Do the same thing for the vertical measurement, lining the ruler up with a column of stitches.

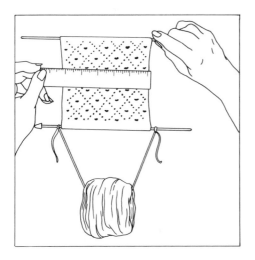

WEIGHTED SAMPLE METHOD FOR MEASURING GAUGE

If the sides of the sample curl slightly, hang the sample from something (a skirt hanger will do) in order to free your hands, and flatten the sample gently against the ruler with your fingers as you measure.

If you are planning to work the garment from side to side, insert the needles into the selvedge stitches and weight the sample in the other dimension.

When working an adult-sized sweater, one fifty-gram ball for a six-inch sample is sufficient for most purposes. However, if the fabric you plan to make is particularly dense or the garment is long, tie a second ball onto the first; if the garment is short, the fabric is relatively light or the sample is narrower, use whatever remains of the ball you used for the sample. When planning a garment that is small, like a child's sweater, for instance, just hanging the sample with the weight of the needle will make some difference in gauge. If you are working with balls of yarn that weigh more or less than fifty grams, use another ball of yarn that does weigh that much.

Precise Weighted Method

Should you want to be more precise, use the information given below in Additional Data From the Sample and work as follows:

1. Determine the number of square inches that would be in a strip of fabric as wide as your sample and as long as your garment, exclusive of ribbing.

2. Calculate the number of yards of yarn that would be required to knit that much fabric.

3. Divide the yardage on the yarn label by the weight of the ball and multiply this figure times the yardage requirement for the strip. This figure is the weight of the strip.

A ball of yarn is, of course, not the only thing you can use as a weight; if you need more or less than fifty grams, use your kitchen scale to find something that weighs the amount you require.

Do keep in mind that this gauge is only appropriate when weight is a factor; for a short sleeve, for ribbings, for collars of various sorts, it would be more accurate to use a gauge taken from a flat sample, or one that is hung but not weighted. Also, the effect of drop is more evident at the top of the garment than at the bottom. Therefore, if you are using a different stitch pattern on the yoke, you might want to weight that gauge sample more than the one for the section between waist and armhole. For a precision fit, therefore, you may find you have occasion to use several different gauges in a single garment. Once you have the concept in mind, you will find that it is quite easy to apply it to different situations.

If you are designing a commercial pattern, use the gauge adjusted for drop to develop the pattern, but ask the knitter working from the pattern to match the gauge obtained by measuring the same sample dressed and lying flat. This produces a drop-adjusted garment that will fit much better, while preserving the simpler method of obtaining gauge for the knitter. For those who might want to alter the pattern, however, you should inform them of what the weighted gauge is.

Calculating the Gauge

In the following material, you will find several methods of calculating a stitch gauge, depending upon the type of fabric you are working with. The standard method, discussed first, works for nearly all stitch patterns. However, there are some specialized fabrics that require some modification in the sample or the method of calculation in order to take their unique characteristics into consideration. These will be discussed in turn.

Standard Stitch Gauge

Once you have your two measurements, it is time to figure the gauge. I highly recommend a pocket calculator—they are fast, accurate, and painless. If you have measured in inches and the figure contains a fraction, you must first convert this to a decimal. Rounded-off but adequate conversions for eighths are as follows:

$\frac{1}{8} = .1$
$\frac{1}{4} = .25$
$\frac{3}{8} = .4$
$\frac{1}{2} = .5$
$\frac{5}{8} = .6$
$\frac{3}{4} = .75$
$\frac{7}{8} = .9$

If you are using centimeters, measure the tenths as best you can.

Number of Stitches ÷ Measured Width = Stitch Gauge

Number of Rows ÷ Measured Length = Row Gauge

In other words, divide the number of stitches used in the sample by the decimal measurement of the width to obtain the stitch gauge. Divide the number of rows used in the sample by the decimal measurement of the length to obtain the row gauge. If you are using the metric system, because the smallest practical unit is 2 cm, either divide the number of rows or stitches by *half* the measured width, or multiply the answer by 2 in order to get a gauge for every two centimeters (don't do any rounding off during this calculation; let your calculator worry about hundredths or thousandths).

Rounding Off

You must be very careful about rounding off the first answer obtained. Keep in mind that this figure will be multiplied by the circumference of your garment. Therefore, you may round the resulting numbers to the nearest tenth, but *do not drop the tenths*. In other words, if you get a number like 5.73, use 5.7 for the gauge. If you get 5.7852, use 5.8 for the gauge.

If you have any doubt about the importance of those tiny tenths of an inch, let me give you an example. Say that you did the above calculations and got a gauge of 5.7 stitches per inch. If you plan to make a 40-inch sweater, according to this gauge you will need 228 stitches. If, however, you persuade yourself that three-tenths of a stitch doesn't amount to much and that working with a gauge of 6 stitches to the inch will make all the calculations easier, you will cast on 240 stitches instead. Your garment will turn out to be slightly more than 42 inches around instead of the 40 you expected! If you thought 5.5 would do well enough, you would cast on 220 stitches and get a sweater 38.5 inches around. The larger the sweater, the more an error of this sort will compound, and I'm sure you would like to avoid surprises of this nature.

Commercial Pattern Gauges

The gauges in commercial patterns are often given as so many stitches per several inches or centimeters, such as 13 stitches and 15 rows every 2in/5cm. This can be translated to 6.5 stitches/7.5 rows per inch in order to coordinate the gauge given with the one you obtain using the method recommended here. For the centimeters, you will have to first divide each figure given by 5 and multiply the answer by 2, or calculate your own gauge according to a 5cm unit.

If you are working from a commercial pattern, it is absolutely essential to the success of your project that you match the gauge specified in the instructions. The needle size given is the one the designer used; however, using the same yarn and stitch pattern, you may very well produce a different gauge with that size needle. This means you may have to do several tension samples, each on a different-size needle until you get the gauge right (See page 409).

Stitch Gauge Ratios

There may be times when you will want to convert the number of stitches required for a given width with one stitch gauge, to the same width using another gauge. If, for instance, you want to use a garment pattern but change the stitch pattern or type of yarn, you will have to completely recalculate the number of stitches and rows used throughout. Similarly, when you change from one stitch pattern to another within a garment (see below) it is necessary to calculate how many stitches to increase or decrease in order to maintain the width of the fabric. Here is a simple ratio method that you can use to make these recalculations quite easy.

New Stitch Gauge ÷ Original Stitch Gauge = Stitch Gauge Ratio

New Row Gauge ÷ Original Row Gauge = Row Gauge Ratio

Stitch Gauge Ratio × Original Number of Stitches = New Number of Stitches

Row Gauge Ratio × Original Number of Rows = New Number of Rows

In other words, if you have been using a G = 5/7 for a 20-inch-wide fabric, you will have 100 stitches on the needle. If you then want to switch to a new pattern that gets G = 6/8, you must adjust the number of stitches. 6 ÷ 5 = 1.2 and 1.2 × 100 = 120 stitches.

The ratio method of recalculating is particularly useful when converting a written pattern in those areas of the garment where the fabric width is changing, such as at the armholes, or when the pattern tells you to work a certain number of rows and then work some technique. Whenever the pattern deals in measurements, of course, it is much more direct to simply multiply the figure given by your stitch gauge.

Regauging

Most knitters are not familiar with this term, but they are familiar with the phenomenon. Every time you switch from a Rib pattern on a small needle to a main pattern on a larger needle, you regauge the fabric. Regauging is defined as changing the width of the fabric without changing the number of stitches on the needle. This can be done either by changing the needle size, changing the stitch pattern, changing the yarn, or all three.

For decorative purposes, regauging is used to produce Ruching (see page 78), but it can also be used in a

highly controlled way to shape a garment. For instance, you can curve the armholes of a sweater by switching to a stitch pattern such as Rib and regauging instead of removing additional stitches above the underarm by decreasing. This application of regauging will require a separate stitch gauge for the new pattern in order to be accurate.

Regauging is also particularly useful for collars and hems of all kinds, but particularly for hemmed necklines and turned-back cuffs. For instance, you can work the inner portion of the cuff on a needle one size smaller than the outer portion, or grade the dimensions of a collar by progressively switching to larger and larger needles as you work out from neckline to collar edge, or vice versa. No separate tension sample is required for this use of the technique, because sizing is not as critical.

Saving Your Samples

I strongly recommend that you save all your knitted samples along with each one's vital statistics. I write all the data on a large index card and then staple the sample and the yarn label to the card for permanent reference. The information gained from a sample is not only useful in planning, but you will find it invaluable should your pattern be inaccurate and require reworking, and collectively they form a useful library for future ideas.

Frequently in planning a design, I will try several different stitch patterns in a particular yarn before settling on the one I want to use, or conversely, several different yarns to find the one that best displays the stitch pattern I want to use. If any of the rejects are nonetheless interesting, I will work up and save samples for them as well. These samples tell you a great deal about the interrelationship between yarn, stitch, and color, gradually providing a body of knowledge about what combinations are the most successful. Should I ever want to use the yarn or stitch pattern again, I've got something to start with.

Gauge for Special Patterns and Fabrics

There are a variety of situations that present problems when it comes to making a tension sample and calculating the gauge for which the basic methods described above will not work. Ribbing is a special case, as is any fabric made with more than one stitch pattern. Then there are certain types of unusual fabrics, such as Double Knit and those that are to be fulled, that require unique approaches. Even circular fabrics make demands that cannot be adequately met by the usual flat sample method.

Gauge for Ribbed Fabrics

Ribbed stitch patterns can be used in two different ways. They may be used like any other pattern for their decorative value, or because of their inherent elasticity, they may be elected to serve more functional purposes.

If you are using a Rib pattern for decorative purposes, treat the sample as you would any other stitch pattern, stretching it slightly to display its characteristics when you dress it. Calculate the stitch gauge in the normal way as described above.

Rib patterns chosen for their elasticity are commonly used at the waists, wrists, and necklines of sweaters. Unfortunately, it is all too common to see an otherwise beautiful knitted garment spoiled by a poorly done ribbing that has sagged out of shape. This occurs because it has become the norm in knitting instructions to suggest that any Rib pattern be worked on the same number of stitches as the body of the sweater, but on needles two sizes smaller. There is really no justification for believing that the gauge for any stitch pattern, on whatever number of stitches you happen to be using, will also produce a ribbing that fits. I don't know how the idea got started, or even less how it was perpetuated, but I would like to see it discarded. There are two steps to perfect ribbing.

- First, the smaller the needle in relation to the yarn, the more elastic the ribbing will be. It is my experience that you really cannot use a needle too small when you want the ribbing to be elastic; I have worked a medium yarn on size 0 and produced a beautiful, highly elastic Rib. A Rib of that sort consumes time and yarn, but I think you will be very pleased with the results. At the very least, try to go down at least three or four sizes instead of the usual two.
- Second, no matter how elastic the ribbing is, it still won't fit if it is not the correct width. The number of stitches required for the pattern used on the body of the fabric might very well produce a ribbing too tight at the waist or too loose at the hips, no matter what size needle you use. The only way to have a ribbing fit properly is to plan it the same way you would any other stitch pattern and do a proper gauge. I am sure you will be much happier with the results you get if you take the time to make one.

Ribbing does have special requirements for obtaining a correct gauge, however, precisely because it is intended to be elastic. In most cases, what is wanted is ribbing that will hug the body, and in order for it to do that it should be neither stretched to its maximum nor completely relaxed when in wear.

Making a Ribbed Sample

1. It is particularly important to allow completely unrestrained edges, so use Stranded Cast-on and Stranded Cast-off.
2. Make the sample 10 to 15 percent as wide as the largest measurement required and two inches long, but no smaller than two inches square.
3. Wash the sample, squeeze it gently in a towel and pat it flat, and leave it to dry in a completely relaxed state.
4. When it is dry, you may steam it gently to relax and soften the fibers, if you wish, but do not stretch it out in any way.

Measuring a Ribbed Sample

There are two gauges necessary for ribbing, the Relaxed Gauge and the Average Gauge, and the choice of which one to use depends upon the purpose the ribbing will serve (see page 21).

Relaxed Gauge: The Relaxed Gauge is made just like a normal one. Measure the sample in the center from edge to edge in both dimensions. Write these figures down and calculate the gauge as described above.

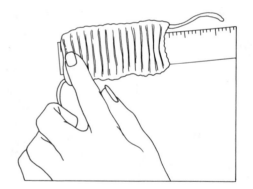

RELAXED MEASUREMENT FOR AVERAGE GAUGE

Average Gauge: In order to compute the Average Gauge, we must next measure the sample when it is stretched out as far as it will go.

1. Take the sample and hold the left edge against the left edge of a ruler, then take hold of the opposite

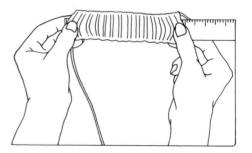

MEASURING STRETCHED WIDTH FOR AVERAGE GAUGE

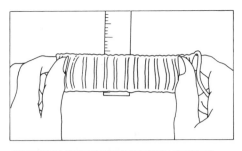

MEASURING STRETCHED LENGTH FOR AVERAGE GAUGE

edge and stretch the sample along the ruler as far as it will go and note the measurement. (You did use Stranded Cast-on and Stranded Cast-off, didn't you?)

2. Then take the side edges in both hands, stretch the sample as far as it will go again, and lay it down on top of the ruler to measure the length of the sample while it is being stretched. Write these figures down and calculate the Stretched Gauge.

Now, let's take these two gauges and average them.

Relaxed Stitch Gauge + Stretched Stitch Gauge ÷ 2 = Average Stitch Gauge

Relaxed Row Gauge + Stretched Row Gauge ÷ 2 = Average Row Gauge

Details of how to use Ribbed Gauges for calculating widths of various garment sections can be found on page 435.

Coordinating More Than One Stitch Pattern

If you would like to use different stitch patterns in vertical or horizontal stripes or in sections, each with its own unique gauge, careful planning is required to insure that the various patterns are compatible and the fabric is smooth and has the correct dimensions. Let's look at combining vertical panels first.

Samples for Vertical Panels

In designing a garment of this type, most often a few major patterns are selected whose widths are determined by the number of stitches required by the repeat. Narrower, plainer panels, or those with small stitch repeat counts, are then used to fill in between or alongside the dominant panels. The only way to adjust the width of the fabric, therefore, is to add, eliminate, or substitute panels of other patterns, to add or eliminate repeats within a panel, or to use a partial repeat of a pattern at each side (see page 412). This is easiest to handle when dealing with fairly large sections of pattern.

When the individual panels are relatively narrow, the easiest approach to working out the fabric width is

to group the narrower patterns in one or two tension samples in the same configuration they will have in the fabric. The grouped patterns can then be treated as if they were a single pattern. This works particularly well when you will be repeating a set of patterns across a garment, or using mirror images of the set on either side. After dressing the sample, measure the width of the sample and multiply it by the number of times that particular set of patterns will be used in the fabric. If there is a panel used just once, it is best to make a separate sample of it, even if it is somewhat narrow; measure it and add the width to the others.

Once you have the sum of the widths of the main patterns, subtract that figure from the width required for the garment to see how much must be added with a small-repeat, filler pattern of some kind. Do a separate sample at least two inches wide for the filler pattern and obtain a stitch gauge that you can use to determine exactly how many additional stitches are required.

When you are planning to use relatively wide sections of different patterns, say one pattern on each side of the center front, and another down the middle, do a separate tension sample for every pattern used, calculate the gauge, and work out the number of stitches required for each section width. Do make these samples large enough for an accurate gauge; they should be in proportion to the amount of the pattern to be used in the garment, but no smaller than two inches.

The row gauge is more problematic. Regardless of how many rows per inch a particular stitch pattern provides, when used with panels of other stitches it will be forced to accommodate itself to its neighbors because they are all worked at the same time. In other words, if you are using one pattern that normally gives six rows

GAUGE SAMPLE FOR A VERTICAL PANEL

A TRADITIONAL ARAN WITH MULTIPLE PATTERNS

used in larger panels, use whatever width seems appropriate for the individual samples, *but use the same number of rows in all of them* and then dress and weight them the same way. If you find a large discrepancy between the row gauges of the two patterns, it would be best to select an alternative combination; if the discrepancy is small, your calculations will probably be accurate enough if you use the average of the two gauges to work out the number of rows to use in the pattern. If the different stitch patterns occupy large sections of fabric, such as half the front, for instance, you might want to consider using an occasional Short Row (see page 175) to help the two patterns fit together better.

Samples for Horizontal Panels

Similar dynamics are at work when dealing with horizontal bands of pattern, but it is far easier to coordinate them. Because each stitch pattern will require a different number of stitches for a given width of fabric, should you continue from one to the next on the constant number of stitches, one pattern may pucker in relation to the other. Here again, relatively narrow bands of pattern with small discrepancies in gauge can generally be eased together in dressing. In this case, group the patterns in a gauge sample in the same way as described for vertical panels, and calculate a single combined gauge. You will be able to see immediately how well they work together, and if they are incompatible, either select a different pattern or work as described below.

A far more accurate way to combine patterns in horizontal bands is to do a separate gauge for each stitch pattern to be used and then increase or decrease the number of stitches on the needle when changing from one pattern to the next. Multiply the width you require by the gauge for each pattern and use the information in Calculating Steps and Points (page 437) to determine how to distribute the increase or decrease techniques evenly across the fabric. In planning your pattern, you will also want to know exactly how much length each section of pattern will contribute to the garment, or conversely, how many rows are needed to make the horizontal band a given length; for this you will use the row gauge in the normal way.

Gauge for Other Special Fabrics

Here is a miscellany of situations where some special consideration must be given to how to make a sample and/or calculate the gauge because of the unique structure of pattern or fabric.

Circular Fabrics

If you work every row from right to left on the outside of the fabric as you do when knitting in the round, your stitch gauge will be different than if you work one row

per inch and a second pattern that gives eight rows per inch, when you have worked six rows of both patterns, one will have produced an inch of fabric but the other will not have. Because they must live side by side, one will have to compress slightly and the other stretch a bit; this is what happens when you group separate patterns in a sample as described above. Knitted fabrics are so resilient that this is not generally a problem, and dressing the fabric will ease the different patterns together. If there is too great a discrepancy, however, you may find one will pucker or gather up in relation to its neighbors; in that case it would be best to choose some other combination of patterns.

In order to coordinate the lengths of stitch patterns

on the outside, the next on the inside as when knitting flat. This makes obtaining an accurate stitch gauge for circular knitting somewhat problematic, because the gauge sample is small and normally knitted flat.

I have seen it suggested that the best sample for circular knitting is one also knitted in the round. Unfortunately that is not really a solution. You must work either a small circumference on double-point needles or a large one on a circular needle. In the former case, given the same hands, yarn, and stitch pattern, double-point needles will generally produce a gauge different from one produced by circular needles of the same size because they change the way you hold the work. In the latter case, you would have to spend an inordinate amount of time to find out what you need to know. In addition, you can't measure edge to edge on a circular fabric, so the more accurate system for finding gauge described here couldn't be used. The solution is to work as follows:

1. Knit the gauge sample on the circular needle you plan to use.
2. Work from right to left on the outside, break the yarn off at the end of every row, slide the stitches to the right point, reattach the yarn and knit the next row.
3. Secure the edges against unraveling by tying pairs of yarns together all the way up both sides.

What you will have is a flat gauge sample, knitted just the way you will work for a circular garment.

Although I said above that you shouldn't knit in the round on straight double points in order to obtain gauge for a larger fabric to be worked on circular needles, it is possible to use the type of sample described here for small objects done on a set of double points. Any difference in gauge or error in measurement from the small sample will be multiplied in a large fabric. However, generally anything knitted on straight double points is

quite small and any slight difference in gauge between the sample and the actual fabric will be inconsequential.

Double Knits

The stitch gauge for a Double Knit fabric requires a somewhat different approach than for any other kind of pattern. Actually, getting the stitch figure for the gauge is quite straightforward, but the row figure must be handled in a special way. And both figures will, of course, be very large because you will be making two fabrics simultaneously.

1. Make the sample exactly as described above, but make sure you work it with full pattern repeats even if that means the swatch is slightly larger than usual.
2. Wash, dress, and measure the sample like any other.
3. For stitches per inch, divide the total number of stitches cast on by the measurement of the width in the normal way.

Don't attempt to count rows on these fabrics, because many contain Slip Stitches and some do not even have the same number of rows on each face. You also can't use the number of rows provided in a written pattern, because the number of "rows worked" is not the same as the number of actual rows in the fabric, which also means there is no point trying to keep count as you work. The only way to obtain an accurate count is from a chart of the pattern (see page 504). For each face of the fabric, count the rows in one repeat on the chart and multiply by the number of full repeats used in the sample, then add the answers together. Use this figure with the length measurement of the sample to get the rows per inch figure for the gauge.

In general, planning and counting by repeats is the easiest way to deal with the length of these fabrics, but you must understand what is at work well enough to deal with any calculations that have to do with partial repeats.

Color Patterns

Different color patterns have just as individually distinctive gauges as stitch patterns do. However, if you are using many different types of geometric figures in a Stranded color pattern, as long as you are consistent in the way you strand the yarn, they will all give the same gauge. If you are using several different types of Mosaic patterns in a fabric, the same is true as long as they are worked in the same way. But you cannot switch from solid-color fabric to color-patterned fabric, from Stranded to Intarsia, or from Garter Stitch Mosaic to Stockinette Mosaic without changing the gauge.

Beaded and Sequined Fabrics

Knit the beads or sequins in pattern on the sample just as you will on the finished fabric, because they will affect the gauge. While glass beads are not affected by

GAUGE SAMPLE FOR CIRCULAR KNITTING

steam, sequins will melt, so the sample, as the garment, must be cold blocked (see page 394). Keep in mind that these materials, beads in particular, can be heavy and will exacerbate the problem of drop. In order to get an accurate gauge, you must include the weight of the beads in your calculations of how much to weight the sample for gauge (see page 540).

Fulled Knitting

In order to do a stitch gauge for a fulled fabric make a square sample at least 20 percent as wide as the largest garment measurement. Write down the number of stitches and rows used. Then full the sample exactly as you will the garment (see page 401). Measure the fulled sample and calculate the gauge in the normal way.

Additional Data from the Sample

O f special interest to designers is the fact that a sample swatch can be used to make fairly precise calculations of the amount of yarn required for a project, as well as a rough idea of the amount of time it will take to knit it. These figures are as unique as stitch gauges and subject to the same variables. For those of you who are knitting for the market, this can be crucial information in planning your investment. Some of these calculations are also of use to the general knitter, who should at least glance over this material to see what it offers.

Calculating Yardage Requirements

Whether you are purchasing yarn for a project or using yarn you already have, it is important to determine fairly accurately whether you will have an adequate amount to finish the garment. This is particularly important when it is necessary to match the dye lot on all the yarn, as you cannot count on the yarn store having extra on hand should you run out, particularly if you take longer to finish the garment than you anticipated. Certainly you can purchase more than you require and, as long as the yarn was not on sale, most stores will give you credit for what you return within a reasonable period of time. If you are using yarn you already own there is, of course, no choice but to design something for which the supply is sufficient.

If you begin to suspect that you have miscalculated, an undercurrent of anxiety will spoil what would have been contented hours of knitting. There are few things more disappointing in knitting than getting more than halfway on a beautiful piece of work and discovering you haven't enough yarn to finish and that all your efforts have been wasted. There is no need for this if you will take a little time to make the following calculations as you work up your tension sample.

Stitches per Yard

First we need the number of stitches each yard or meter of yarn will produce.

1. As you work your tension sample, at the beginning of a row, tie a knot in the yarn one yard from where it comes off the first stitch at the beginning of a row.
2. Knit in pattern until you reach the knot, keeping track of how many rows you work.

Number of Rows × Number of Stitches per Row + Number of Stitches in Partial Row = Number of Stitches per Yard

Plain stitches absorb a different amount of yarn from those worked with special techniques, so if one yard doesn't include some elements of the pattern, tie the knot at two yards, or even five, and work in the same manner.

Number of Stitches ÷ Number of Yards = Stitches per Yard

This is a very useful figure to have as you work, because you will then always know whether or not you will make it across the row with the end of a ball of yarn. All you have to do is measure the remaining yarn to see whether it will produce more or fewer stitches than you have on the needle.

Yards per Square Inch

Next we need to find out how many stitches are in every square inch of the fabric. Calculate your stitch gauge and then work as follows:

Stitches per Inch × Rows per Inch = Stitches per Square Inch

Stitches per Square Inch ÷ Stitches per Yard = Yards per Square Inch

If the answers are decimal figures, round the number out to tenths, but do not drop the tenths.

Yarn Usage on Color Samples

In a Stranded color pattern, the yarn is taken up both by stitches and by the strands, and as the pattern changes, the amount of each color absorbed is continually changing as well. It is far too complicated to try to calculate the amount of each color used in each different pattern. Instead, what we can do is to get a figure for the average amount of each color yarn needed for a square inch of fabric. For this purpose, the tension sample should include one example of each pattern you plan to include so it is as representative as possible of the fabric you will make for the garment.

1. Cast on for the sample, measure off five yards on each color yarn, and tie a temporary knot in each one.
2. As you work in pattern, when you come to these first knots, undo them, then measure off five more yards and tie the knots again.
3. Continue in this way throughout the entire tension sample, keeping careful track of how many knots you have tied on each color so that at the end you will know exactly how much yarn of each color was used.
4. Block and measure the sample for gauge and calculate yardage as follows:

Sample Length × Sample Width = Total Square Inches of Sample

Total Yards Used for Each Color ÷ Total Square Inches of Sample = Total Yards of Each Color per Square Inch

This is also the method to use for Mosaic patterns and for Double Knit color patterns.

Calculating Garment Yardage Requirements

In order to find out how many balls of yarn to buy, you must determine the overall number of square inches required for the particular garment you want to make and then use this figure with the figure for yards per square inch to find out total yardage requirements.

Square Inches of Fabric

To find the total square inches of fabric in a given garment pattern, use the measurements from a schematic drawing (see page 513). There are two approaches: the approximate method, good for most purposes, and the precise method, for when it is essential to know exactly what to expect.

Approximate Method

Length × Maximum Circumference = Square Inches of Body

Length × Maximum Width = Square Inches of Sleeve

Body + 2 Sleeves = Total Square Inches of Fabric

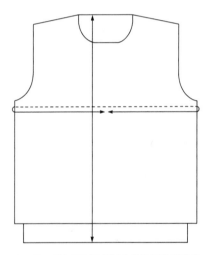

BODICE MEASUREMENT FOR APPROXIMATING SQUARE INCHES OF FABRIC

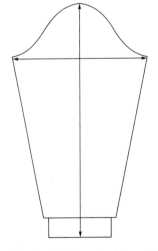

SLEEVE MEASUREMENT FOR APPROXIMATING SQUARE INCHES OF FABRIC

If there is a large collar or any other additional features that will require a substantial amount of yarn, calculate the square inches for those sections in the same way and add them in. If any sections are made with different stitch patterns, those must be calculated separately. This is particularly true of areas of ribbing, because they are real yarn-eaters.

Precise Method: The above calculations provide a generous estimate because nothing was deducted for areas removed by shaping. Generally speaking, it is best not to subtract those areas, because this allows for extra yarn just in case you miscalculate or any yarn gets worn or damaged if you should have to rip. There are times when the amount of yarn is already fixed, however, and it is crucial to know whether you have the correct amount; then you will want to make a more precise estimate.

In order to calculate the actual area of the sleeves, treat the caps and the body of the sleeve separately. Imagine turning one cap and one sleeve upside down and placing them adjacent to their counterparts from the second sleeve as shown in the illustration below. What you get are two trapezoids, and the area of a trapezoid is width times length.

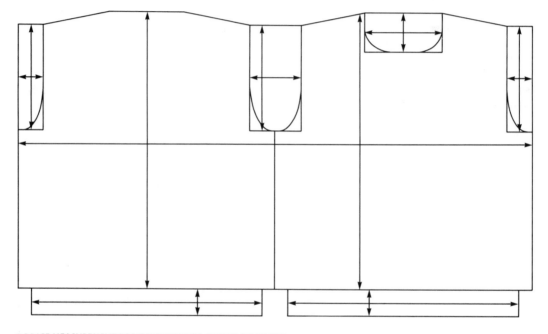

BODICE MEASUREMENT FOR EXACT SQUARE INCHES OF FABRIC

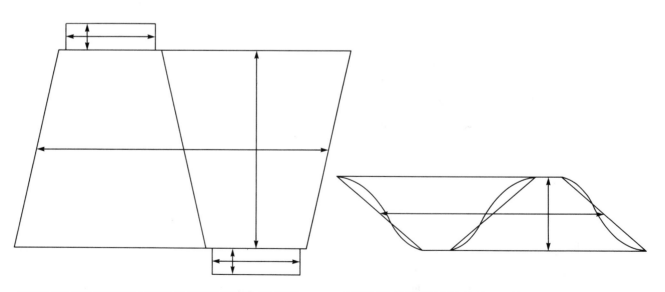

SLEEVE ARM MEASUREMENT FOR EXACT SQUARE INCHES OF FABRIC   SLEEVE CAP MEASUREMENT FOR EXACT SQUARE INCHES OF FABRIC

(Width of Cuff + Width of Sleeve at Armhole) × Length = Area of Sleeves

(Width of Cap at Top Center + Width of Cap at Armhole) × Length = Area of Sleeve Caps

Square off the areas of a circular neckline and the armholes and multiply length times width; remember there are four armholes, one each side, back and front. A V neckline is half of the length times the width. Subtract the areas of neckline and armholes from the approximate square-inch figure for the body.

Yardage Requirements for Garment

Now we put the data together to get the answer we want, the number of yards needed for the garment.

Square Inches of Fabric × Yards per Square Inch = Yards of Yarn Required for Garment

If you are using large areas of different patterns, calculate the requirements for each pattern separately and then add those figures together for the total for the garment. If you are working with many patterns such as for an Aran, work with an average Yards per Square Inch figure. If you are working an Intarsia pattern, you will have to calculate as best you can what percentage of the fabric is allocated to each color. For Stranded-color patterns, multiply the figure for each color times the total square inches of fabric.

Stripes are generally done with each color reappearing in a regular sequence making up a vertical pattern repeat. The simplest approach is to find the yardage required for the garment as if the fabric were a solid color. Then determine the percentage of each color used in a single repeat of the pattern and use those figures to get the amount required in each color.

Count the total rows in a single repeat. Count the number of rows of each color used.

Rows of Color A ÷ Rows in Repeat = Percentage of Color A.

Total Yardage × Percentage of Color A = Yards of Color A Required.
Repeat for each color.

Yardage to Buy

The label should indicate how many yards or meters of yarn are contained in each skein or ball, and with that and the information above, you will know exactly how much yarn to buy.

Yards Required ÷ Yards per Ball or Skein = Number of Balls or Skeins Required

If you are measuring yards and the yarn label gives meters, or vice versa, the conversion figures are:

1 yard = 91.4 centimeters, 1 meter = 39.4 inches

If the label does not provide a length figure, your yarn store should have this information, but if it isn't available, there is a way to obtain it.

The simplest method depends upon having a yarn swift or a niddy noddy. The former is an umbrella-like device that is used to hold a skein of yarn. It expands to fit any diameter, and spins on its axis so the yarn can be wound off the skein and into a ball. The latter is a device for winding a measured skein from a ball. Both are pictured on page 340. If you have one or the other, it makes it quite simple to determine the yards in a skein.

Measuring a Skein: If you are working with a swift and want to know the yardage in a ball of yarn, raise it up until it measures one or two yards around where the yarn will ride. Attach the yarn and spin the swift to wind the yarn out of the ball into a skein. Count the number of strands that encircle the swift and multiply by the circumference of the skein if larger than one; this is the number of yards in the ball of yarn. Rewind it into a ball to work from.

If you are working from a skein, place it on the swift, count the number of strands, then measure the circumference and calculate the yardage. A niddy noddy will only work to wind a skein, and they generally make a two-yard circumference. If you don't have a swift or niddy noddy, you can still make the ball into a skein, wrapping it around a chair back or a friend's outstretched arms, if necessary.

These measurements are somewhat imprecise because, as the amount of yarn builds up on the skein, the circumference of the last strand on the outside will be slightly larger than the one closest to the center. Also, the number of yards in each ball or skein of the same kind of yarn usually varies somewhat. Nevertheless, the number is certainly accurate enough to serve the purpose.

Stitches per Minute

If you would like to know how long it will take you to knit a particular garment, you will need a calculation of stitches per minute plus the total number of stitches the pattern requires. As you know, you will work at different speeds depending upon the type of pattern you are using, so for more accuracy you should make a separate calculation for each area of fabric made in a different stitch pattern. As you work your tension sample(s), therefore, set a timer for five minutes and continue to work in pattern until the bell rings. Keep track of how much you knit during this time.

Number of Rows × Number of Stitches per Row + Number of Stitches in Partial Row = Number of Stitches Knit in 5 Minutes

Stitches in 5 Minutes ÷ 5 = Stitches per Minute × 60 = Stitches per Hour, or

Stitches in 5 Minutes × 12 = Stitches per Hour

Stitches per Square Inch × Square Inches of Fabric = Stitches per Garment

Stitches per Garment ÷ Stitches per Hour = Hours of Work

Don't faint the first time you see these figures; they are generally larger than you expected, or perhaps wanted to know about. Some of the nicest things we do in life are those we might never have tried if someone had told us exactly what would be required.

Remember, this figure is an approximation. The five minutes of knitting that you time will include a certain amount for turning at the end of rows, pulling yarn out of the ball and shifting stitches up and down the needles, so it is a relatively accurate estimate of the time it takes to actually knit that particular stitch pattern. However, it does not include planning, ripping, counting stitches or rows, interruptions, finishing, or getting slowed down by a really good episode of your favorite soap opera, all of which may be included in the time taken to knit an actual garment.

25
Calculations Used in Pattern Making and Alterations

In the section on Stitch Gauge, I introduced the basic calculations that use the gauge to translate width or length measurements into the number of stitches or rows required to produce a fabric of the correct size. As you know, for any given stitch gauge, the length of the fabric is determined by how many rows it contains, and the width is determined by how many stitches each row contains. Changing the length of a fabric is quite straightforward; obviously you continue to knit to lengthen the fabric, and rip out rows to shorten it.

Changing the width, however, is far more complex, although it begins with a simple enough premise. If you increase the number of stitches on the needle, the fabric will widen. If you decrease the number of stitches on the needle, the fabric will narrow. This can be done using either casting-on, casting-off, or increase or decrease techniques to change the number of stitches on the needle, or by regauging (see page 423).

While the size of the fabric is determined by how many stitches are used, the shape of the fabric is determined by the position of these shaping techniques. The shaping techniques can be placed near the edge of the fabric or within it, and the change in size can be abrupt or gradual. Depending upon placement, you can expand or contract the width of a flat fabric in a straight line, at an angle, or in a curve, and you can make three-dimensional fabrics in the shape of cones, domes, pyramids, and more fanciful forms that may or may not have geometric names. The most common shaping

TRADITIONAL STUFFED DOLLS FROM SWITZERLAND

of a fabric, of course, is that designed to make it comfortably fit the human body, so things like necklines, armholes, sloped shoulders, and sleeve caps are of primary interest. The basic principles, however, can be applied to any shape, conventional or otherwise and the techniques used are discussed in "Contouring the Fabric," page 169.

By far the easiest and fastest way to develop a pattern for virtually any shape is to chart it, and the method of doing so is discussed in full in the section "Schematic Drawings and Garment Pattern Charts" (page 511). Nevertheless, I feel obliged to provide the mathematical approach for those times when you don't have graph paper available, and for those of you who prefer to work from written instructions.

Obviously, this material is of greatest interest to those who plan to design their own garments, and is necessary for any alterations, but the principles are so fundamental to the way patterns are organized that I think everyone who knits should become familiar with them. You needn't absorb all the information at once. Tackle the easiest concepts first and learn just what is immediately useful to you. For the most part, only simple mathematics is required for any of this, but some of the more advanced calculations will require some understanding of a little elementary geometry; all of this will be explained in a step-by-step way that will make it easy even if you have forgotten what math you learned in school. While none of the formulas are difficult, I heartily recommend the use of a calculator to make things as quick and painless as possible.

Because the calculations are based upon the gauge, you will more often than not be working with decimal numbers, although to simplify the explanations here I have used whole numbers. *When your gauge includes a decimal, use it in all the calculations: do not round it off*. In the end, however, when you come to the number of stitches on the needle or rows to knit, you will by necessity have to round out any decimal answers—after all, you must knit whole stitches and whole rows. In these situations, the general rule is to round up if you are dealing with a fine yarn, round down for a bulky one. That is not a hard and fast rule, however, and you must let your sense of things guide you. Due to stitch-pattern constraints, you may also have to decide, on the same basis, whether to go up or down in order to have an even or an odd number of stitches.

Calculating Width

In the last chapter I covered the simple calculations used to find the number of stitches and rows required to produce a given length or width. Here I will add the elementary formula for changing width abruptly and then, of more interest, go on to discuss the specialized approach to calculating stitch requirements for ribbings.

Changing Width Abruptly

If you wish to change an existing fabric width in a straight line from the edge, either by casting on so it is wider or casting off so it is narrower, the number of stitches to add or subtract is determined in the same way as for simple width.

Fabric Width to Add × Stitches per Inch = Number of Stitches to Add

Fabric Width to Subtract × Stitches per Inch = Number of Stitches to Subtract

Calculations for Ribbing

The correct width of a ribbed fabric is obtained much like that of any other, a simple multiplication of the measurement required times the number of stitches per inch in the gauge. However, as you know from the section on Stitch Gauge, there are two gauges used for ribbings, a Relaxed Gauge and an Average Gauge (see page 424). Following you will find some general guidelines regarding which of these gauges to use depending upon the function the ribbing must serve.

Wrists and Waists

The Average Gauge is ideal when you are planning the number of stitches for the width of ribbed fabric at wrists and waistlines. To give you an example of how this works, say that the measurement of the wrist is 7 inches, and that:

Relaxed Gauge = 8 stitches per inch

Stretched Gauge = 4 stitches per inch

Average Gauge = 6 stitches per inch

Cast-on 6 stitches per inch × 7 inches = 42 stitches for the cuff

Relaxed cuff will measure 42 stitches ÷ 8 stitches per inch = 5.2 inches

Stretched cuff will measure 42 stitches ÷ 4 stitches per inch = 10.5 inches

The cuff will obviously have plenty of give to allow the hand through, and enough grip to hold its shape around the wrist. It's a tight grip when new, but it will ease up slightly with wear and be just right.

For ribbing at hip or waistline, measure the body where the ribbing will actually ride—don't use the waist measurement if that isn't where you intend the ribbing to be worn. Use the information in "Horizontal Steps and Points," below, to work out the pattern to use for changing from the number of stitches required for the ribbing to the number required for the stitch pattern used on the fabric of the bodice.

Round Necklines and Armholes

In the case of a ribbed border for a round neckline or armhole opening, either form of the gauge might be used. If you look at a full-scale pattern draft of a neckline opening, for instance, you will notice that the mea-

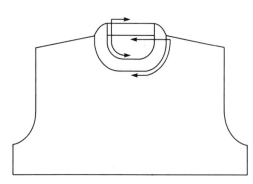

MEASUREMENTS FOR A ROUND NECKLINE

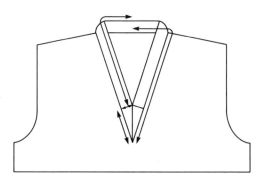

MEASUREMENTS FOR A V-NECKLINE

surement of the outer edge, where the border meets the neck, is smaller than that of the garment edge, where it is joined to the border. What is wanted is a ribbing that is fully relaxed at the outer edge, but slightly stretched at the join. This will allow the head to pass through the opening unrestrained, while the tension created at the join will help to support the neckline and guarantee that the ribbing will lie flat without sagging. In effect, this is a form of regauging (see page 423).

To find how many stitches to pick up and work for the border, you may multiply the Relaxed Gauge times the measurement of the outer edge of the ribbing, or the Average Gauge times the measurement of the garment edge where the stitches will be picked up. The results are very close, whichever approach you choose, although for the typical one-inch border the Average Gauge method will ask for slightly fewer stitches than the Relaxed Gauge.

Use the number of stitches required, the measurement of the garment edge and the formulas provided in "Calculating Steps and Points" (below) to develop a pattern for spacing the stitches evenly around the opening. Once your ribbing is complete, you may have to apply some steam to help the ribbing relax at the join so it doesn't gather the garment edge, but you can be sure that your neckline will never sag out of shape.

V Necklines

A V neckline is slightly more complex, because the stitches at the point must be taken out with a Miter, while the remainder of the ribbing should be calculated as described above.

1. On your pattern draft, draw a line parallel to the neck edge of the garment at a distance equal to the depth of the planned ribbing. Extend the center line of the garment to meet this line.
2. Draw a line perpendicular to the neck edge from the upper point of the Miter. The stitches between this perpendicular line and the lower point of the Miter will be removed with decreases.
3. Measure the length of the ribbing edge from center back to upper Miter point, then add to that figure

the measurement of the length from the perpendicular line to the lower point of the Miter on the garment edge and multiply the answer times 2.
4. Multiply that figure times the Relaxed Gauge to obtain the number of stitches to pick up around the opening.

Alternatively, measure the garment edge and multiply times the Average Gauge. See below for information on how to calculate the Miter. You can work in the same way for armhole openings if you want to use a Miter at the underarm.

Yokes and Ribbed Stitch Patterns

When a Rib pattern is used primarily for its decorative qualities, treat it as for any other stitch pattern, using the Relaxed Gauge times the width. Also use the Relaxed Gauge when ribbing is used on a Yoke to gather the fabric below.

Center Front Borders

A ribbed border on a center front opening done on picked-up stitches is used primarily for its ability to lie flat. Although some resilience helps to support the edge in wear, there is no need to severely reduce the size of the needle as you might in a situation where elasticity was the prime virtue of the stitch pattern. Also, for this reason, Average Gauge is not appropriate because you do not want the length of the border at the edge to be smaller than the length at the join between the border and the garment.

The simplest method, therefore, is to use the Relaxed Gauge and reduce the number of stitches by no more than 5 or 10 percent in order to provide some support and compensate for any stretching that might occur in wear. The method of calculating a pickup pattern is found below.

Sometimes the bottom side edge of a ribbed border will pull up into a curve. If you plan the relationship between border and garment carefully you are less likely to encounter the problem, but there is another solution I have seen. After picking up the stitches for the border, cast on two extra stitches at the bottom edge and work them together with the ribbing. In finishing, hem these two columns of stitches to the inside of the border.

Average Gauge for Non-Ribs

The Average Gauge concept can be applied to non-Rib stitch patterns when planning any garment that is intended to cling. A familiar example that springs to mind is that of the leg portion of a sock, where there is a great discrepancy between the measurement of ankle and calf. If you use the Average Gauge times the calf measurement to calculate the number of stitches required, the fabric will cling at that point and relax as it descends to the ankle, and there may then be no need to use decreases for shaping purposes. (Of course, a ribbed sock calculated with the Average Gauge will stay up even better.)

Calculating Steps and Points

The method of developing the pattern for distributing the shaping techniques within or at the edge of a fabric is called Calculating Steps and Points. This is a set of relatively simple formulas that are used to determine the exact position of each technique and how many stitches or rows lie between one technique and another. A step may be either a group of stitches or a group of rows, and a point may be a place where you turn the work, or the location of a shaping technique.

As you know from the discussion on Slope and Bias (pages 170–174), if you distribute shaping units across the width of the fabric it will gather, whereas if you distribute them along a side edge you will create slopes or curves. The angle of any slope is determined by how quickly the stitch count changes.

On the garment pattern, for every slope the number of stitches that are either added or subtracted forms the base of a triangle, and the number of rows over which the shaping units are distributed forms the side of the triangle. As you knit, the angle of the slope really takes care of itself; all you generally need to know is what number of stitches you are starting with, the number you want to wind up with, and how many rows lie in between.

When the number of stitches to be removed or added is no more than one stitch at each side per row, this is considered a gradual slope and is handled with increase or decrease techniques. When the number of stitches is greater than that, this is considered an acute slope, and it must be handled with casting on or casting off.

Horizontal Steps and Points

This is actually another method of changing the width abruptly, but it involves distributing the shaping techniques across the width of the fabric instead of placing them at the edges. The new section of fabric will puff out if you add stitches and gather in if you remove stitches.

Here are two schematic drawings of a typical pattern for horizontal steps and points. The xs are the points where a shaping technique is placed and the dashes represent the stitches of each step. Notice that, in a horizontal pattern for a flat fabric, there is one more step than there are points, but in the same pattern for a

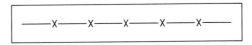

HORIZONTAL STEPS AND POINTS IN FLAT FABRIC

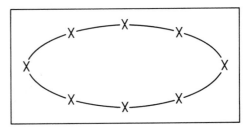

HORIZONTAL STEPS AND POINTS IN CIRCULAR FABRIC

circular fabric, there are equal numbers of steps and points.

I am going to take you through the process of calculating exactly where to place each increase in order to widen a hypothetical flat fabric. At the end of the section, I will give you the formulas in a step-by-step fashion as you will have them to refer to when you want to work out a pattern of your own.

Distributing Increases Across a Flat Fabric

Imagine that you are working a flat fabric 20 inches wide with a gauge of 5 stitches per inch and the pattern calls for adding 2 inches to the width with Raised Increases. Work as follows:

1. To find the number of stitches on the needle:

   20 inches × 5 stitches per inch = 100 stitches

2. To find the number of stitches to add:

   5 stitches per inch × 2 inches = 10 stitches

3. Each stitch on which an increase is placed represents a point, and we need one more step than points for a flat fabric, so there will be 10 points and 11 steps.

4. To find the number of stitches to distribute to the steps, separate out the 10 stitches that will have an increase technique worked on them:

   100 stitches − 10 increases = 90 stitches in the steps

5. Next, to find how many stitches will be in each step:

   Stitches Allocated to Steps ÷ Number of Steps = Number of Stitches per Step

In many cases, the number of steps does not divide into the stitches evenly and some stitches will be left over. Unfortunately, in working these sorts of things out on a calculator, it will persist in giving you decimal answers instead of a number with a remainder, which is what we need. To convert decimals to remainders:

1. Take the whole number in whatever answer you get and multiply it by the number you divided with.

   90 stitches ÷ 11 steps = 8.18 stitches per step

   11 steps × 8 stitches per step = 88 stitches

2. The difference between that answer and the number you are dividing into is the remainder:

   90 stitches − 88 stitches = remainder 2

Any remainder stitches must be distributed, one to a step, until they are all accounted for. In this case, there are 11 steps so far that have 8 stitches each, but there are 2 stitches with no place to go. Thus, there will have to be two steps somewhere with an extra stitch. Work as follows:

1. Subtract the remainder from the total number of steps to find how many steps have x number of stitches.

   11 steps − 2 steps with an extra stitch = 9 steps that continue at 8 stitches each

2. The remainder then equals the number of steps that have x + 1 stitches each.

   2 steps will then have 9 stitches each

The decision as to exactly which steps to put the extra stitches in is a matter of where you think they will fit the best or be the easiest to handle. They can be placed in the steps at the beginning and the end of the row, in those at the center, or interspersed among the others. Now let's write a pattern.

We have 9 steps with 8 stitches each and 2 steps with 9 stitches each. We can place one extra stitch in the first step and one in the last, so the first step is a k9. There is a point with an increase between each step, so next comes inc1, and then a k8, another inc1, another k8, and so on, nine times. Let's write that compactly as 9(inc1, k8). Then there has to be one more increase before the last k9. The pattern then looks like:

K9, 9(inc1, k8) inc1, k9

Do you want to check your work?

2 steps with 9 stitches each = 18 stitches

9 steps with 8 stitches each = 72 stitches

9 + 1 increase = 10 stitches doubled = 20 and

18 + 72 + 20 = 110 stitches.

If we had used Yarnover or Running Thread Increases, which lie between stitches, we would still have 10 points and 11 steps, but no stitches allocated to the points. The calculations would be:

100 stitches ÷ 11 steps = 9 stitches per step, remainder 1

11 steps − 1 remainder stitch = 10 steps with 9 stitches and 1 step with 10 stitches, or k10, 10(inc1, k9)

If we needed to decrease, we would have to subtract 2 stitches for each point, and the calculations would be:

100 stitches − 20 decrease stitches = 80 stitches allocated to steps

80 stitches ÷ 11 steps = 7 stitches per step, remainder 3

*11 steps − 3 remainder stitches = 8 steps with 7 stitches and 3 steps with 8 stitches, or
2(k8, k2tog), 8(k7, k2tog), k8*

Formulas for Horizontal Steps and Points

So that you have them in compact form when you need to work out a pattern, here are the formulas for dealing with any type of horizontal distribution of shaping units.

Horizontal Distribution of Shaping Units

1. Width of Fabric × Stitch Gauge = Number of Stitches on Needle
2. Change in Width × Stitch Gauge = Number of Stitches to Increase or Decrease
3. Number of Increases or Decreases = Points
4. Number of Steps:

   For Flat Fabric, Number of Steps = Points + 1

   For Circular Fabric, Steps = Points

5. Stitches Allocated to Steps:

   Stitches on Needle − 1 for each Stitch Increase

   Stitches on Needle − 0 for each Between-Stitch Increase

   Stitches on Needle − 2 for each Decrease

   Stitches Allocated to Steps ÷ Number of Steps = Stitches per Step

Dealing With Remainders

If you obtain a decimal number in calculating number of stitches per step,

1. Whole Number in Stitches per Step × Number of Steps = Number of Stitches that Divide Evenly
2. Number of Stitches Distributed to Steps − Number that Divide Evenly = Remainder
3. Number of Steps − Number of Stitches in Remainder = Steps with x Stitches
4. Number of Stitches in Remainder = Steps with x + 1 Stitches

Acute Slopes

As I mentioned above, acute slopes are created with casting on and casting off rather than with increases or

decreases. Short Rows are another form of an acute slope and make use of the same calculations.

Cast-off Slope

A common example of an acute slope is that of a shoulder line. In the drawing shown here, you can see the method of measuring. Use the width of the fabric at the point where the slope begins. The length is a vertical measurement from the row where the slope begins to the row where it ends. The method of measuring and the calculations used are basically the same for casting on rather than casting off, such as when adding stitches at a side edge for a dolman sleeve. Let us go through the steps for working out the pattern for a simple shoulder slope.

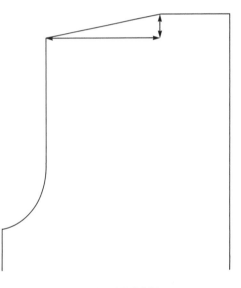

MEASURING FOR A SHOULDER SLOPE

As you know, casting off can only be done at the beginning of a row, so you must cast off and continue to knit to the end of that row. According to the recommended method of sloping a shoulder, on the next row you must knit back to the cast-off stitches, work a decrease on the last two stitches, then turn, slip, and cast off again, etc. The steps are the groups of cast-off stitches and the points are the decreases on the intervening row. A shoulder slope is always worked over an uneven number of rows because it starts and ends with steps, so there will be one more step than there are points. For each point, we will subtract only the single stitch removed by the decrease as the new stitch worked on the decrease pair is included in the next cast-off step.

A Shoulder Slope: Imagine that you are developing a pattern for a garment in which the width of the fabric at the shoulder line is 4.5 inches and the length over which it must slope is 1 inch and G = 6/8.

1. First we must find the number of stitches and rows involved in the slope:

   6 stitches × 4.5 inches = 27 stitches to be removed over 8 rows

2. Now we must find the number of steps and points:

   8 rows ÷ 2 rows between each point = 4 points + 1 = 5 steps

3. Next we separate the stitches of the steps and points. We must remove one stitch per point, so:

   27 stitches − 4 points = 23 stitches allocated to steps

4. Then find how many stitches there will be in each step:

   23 stitches ÷ 5 steps = 4 stitches per step, remainder 3

5. Use the same method of distributing remainder stitches as described for Horizontal Steps and Points:

   5 steps − remainder 3 = 2 steps with 4 stitches each, and 3 steps with 5 stitches each

Now we must write the pattern, including the decreases on the intervening rows. You can write the whole thing out as Shoulder Slope: 4-1-4-1-5-1-5-1-5, or abbreviate it as 2(4), 3(5). In the former case, the ones are the decreases and the other numbers represent the stitches cast off on each step; in the latter, the decreases at the points are understood and only the stitches in each step are indicated.

Cast-on Slope

The most common use for a slope of this sort is to add the stitches for a sleeve worked as one with the bodice of a sweater; however, you might also find it useful for shaping an edge at the bottom of a fabric. For the best method of casting on for the former situation, see "Finger Cast-on at Side Edge" (page 140).

In casting on a slope, each step will contain cast-on stitches, and at each turning point a stitch is slipped to make the transition smooth. Because the Slip Stitch is one of the newly added stitches, it need not be separated out to find the number of stitches to distribute to the steps. Therefore, work exactly as for an Acute Cast-off Slope, above, but eliminate step 5 and divide the full number of stitches to be cast on by the number of steps.

Short Row Slopes

Short Rows are used to create Acute Slopes. In this case, however, the steps consist of stitches that are either being activated or inactivated, and the points become the turning points of the rows where you would wrap and slip the stitches on either side. Use the formula for an Acute Cast-on Slope as there is no need to subtract out stitches at the points. However, the pattern you will write from the results will look different.

Calculation for Decreasing Short Rows: When working Decreasing Short Rows, what you need to know is the stitch count on each row that you knit approaching a turning point so you can count across and turn in the right place. Let's take as an example the same shoulder described above where 27 stitches must be sloped over 8 rows. Since there is no need to subtract out any stitches for the points, the calculations are simpler.

For 8 rows there are 4 points and 5 steps.

27 stitches ÷ 5 steps = 5 stitches per step, remainder 2

5 steps − 2 remainder = 3 steps with 5 stitches each, 2 steps with 6 stitches each, or, 6-5-5-5-6

Pattern for Decreasing Short Rows: Successively subtract steps from the total number of stitches in order to know how many to knit on each row approaching a turning point:

27 active stitches − 6 stitches in step 1 = 21 stitches worked in row 1

21 active stitches − 5 stitches in step 2 = 16 stitches worked in row 2

Continue in this way until you account for all the stitches.

The pattern can then be written: 27-21-16-11-6. Since you slip one active stitch after wrapping at the turning point, you will work one less stitch on the return row. In other words, you would Knit 27, wrap, slip, and turn, and Purl 26, etc.

Pattern for Increasing Short Rows: The calculations for Increasing Short Rows are the same; however, the pattern is again different. Keep in mind that you must work across the previous turning point in order to reactivate the stitches of the next step. Therefore, the first stitch of every step has been wrapped and must be handled accordingly. It helps to know when that will occur; therefore, in this case you must successively add the number of stitches in each step and indicate both how many stitches will be worked before you come to a Wrapped Stitch and how many are in the next step.

1. The first step is 6 stitches, wrap and turn.
2. Next time work the 6 stitches of the first step, work the Wrapped Stitch and the 4 remaining stitches of the second step, then wrap and turn.
3. Next time work 11 stitches (the first two steps) and

5 stitches of the third step (the first stitch of which will be wrapped), etc.

4. Continue in this way until you have accounted for all the stitches.

Write the sequence: 6-6/5-11/5-16/5-21/6-27. After the first step, the number to the left of the slash is the total of the two numbers in the previous pair and represents the number of stitches before the next Wrapped Stitch. The number to the right is the number of stitches in the next step, including the Wrapped Stitch, which is counted as 1.

Formula for Acute Slopes

1. Length Measurement × Row Gauge = Number of Rows in Pattern
2. If this is a decimal number, round up or down to an even number; if this is an uneven number, subtract 1.
3. Number of Rows ÷ 2 = Number of Points
4. Number of Points + 1 = Number of Steps
5. When casting off: Number of Stitches − Number of Points = Stitches Allocated to Steps (Eliminate this step when casting on or using Short Rows.)
6. Stitches Allocated to Steps ÷ Number of Steps = Stitches per Step
7. Distribute remainder stitches in usual way.

Gradual Slopes

Gradual slopes are very common in knitting. For instance, they are used to widen a sleeve between wrist and armhole or a bodice from waist to armhole. Here again, the number of stitches to add or subtract forms the base of a triangle, the height being the number of rows over which the slope travels; distribute the shaping units correctly and the slope takes care of itself. In these cases, the steps consist of rows and the points are those particular rows where a decrease is worked and the relationship of the steps and points can be more variable.

V Neckline

The shaping for a V neckline opening provides a good example of a gradual slope, as you can see in the adjacent drawing. Let's use G = 5/7, and assume that the neckline requires that we remove 15 stitches in 56 rows.

Since this type of pattern starts with a decrease point and ends with a step, we will have an equal number of steps and points. There is no need to separate out the rows on which a decrease is worked, as it is easiest to write these patterns with the decrease placed at the end of every step. However, since this type of slope calls for starting with a decrease, we must subtract one row from the total for that first point and then distribute the remaining rows to the steps.

56 − 1 row for initial decrease = 55 rows distributed to steps

55 rows ÷ 15 steps = 3 rows per step, remainder 10

15 steps − remainder 10 = 5 steps with 3 rows each and 10 steps with 4 rows each

The smoothest slope would be created by interspersing the three-row steps with the four-row steps, and while that is easy enough to do on a chart, it would make written instructions somewhat complex. To simplify, we will place the smaller steps together at the beginning. Remember we must start with a decrease point and end with a step that has no decrease. Therefore, after dividing the fabric at the center front, the pattern would read:

1. First we have a decrease:
   Decrease 1 stitch at neck edge
2. Then we have 5 steps with 3 rows each:
   then 1 stitch at neck edge every 3rd row 5 times,
3. Next 10 steps with 4 rows each, but there is no decrease at the end of the last step, so remove that step from the next part of the instruction:
   every 4th row 9 times,
4. And the last step:
   work 4 more rows plain.

In my notation I would write "Neck Decreases: Dec R1, then ev 3R 5x, ev 4R 9x + 4R."

Do you want to check your formula to see if it is right?

1 time + 5 times + 9 times = 15 points

1 row at the beginning, 5 steps x 3 rows = 15 rows, 9 steps × 4 rows = 36 rows and 4 rows at the end:
1 + 15 + 36 + 4 = 56 rows

Pocket Slopes

A pocket opening is another example of a gradual slope, but because the decreases will start and end the sequence, there will be one more point than there are steps. Say that 10 stitches were to be decreased over 29 rows. This means there would be 10 points and 9 steps.

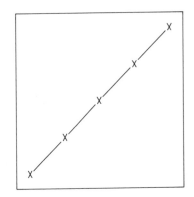

STEPS AND POINTS ON A GRADUAL SLOPE

Here again, we must subtract one row for the first point:

29 rows − 1 row for initial decrease = 28 rows

28 rows ÷ 9 steps = 3 rows per step, remainder 1

9 steps − 1 remainder = 8 steps with 3 rows each, and 1 step with 4 rows

The pattern instructions would read "Decrease 1 stitch at pocket edge (that's the first point), then 1 stitch every 3rd row 8 times, every 4th row once," or "Pocket slope: Dec R1, then ev 3R 8x, ev 4R 1x."

Increase Slopes

The formula is much the same if you are using increases instead of decreases, such as to shape a sleeve from wrist to underarm, but those sequences usually begin and end with steps, so there would be one more step than points. Remember, however, that the points fall on the last row of a step, so when a step ends the sequence, it does not contain a decrease.

Miters

When two sections of fabric are set at an angle to one another, this is called a Miter. For a Single Miter, a slope is worked at the side edge of each section and they are then seamed together. For a Double Miter, the slope is worked within the fabric, pulling the two sections into an angle.

The most common Miter seen in knitting is at the point of a V neckline, but they are also found at two corners for a square neckline, at the center front hemline of a cardigan or jacket, or to form the corners of a border for a blanket or shawl.

Many people assume that any Miter is just a matter of working decreases every other row. This works reasonably well for Garter Stitch and most Rib patterns, as they are resilient and forgiving, but no simple formula like that is accurate for all situations. Each Miter involves a unique combination of stitch gauge, degree of angle, and length of slope, and I think you will be much more satisfied with the results when you take the small amount of time required to work out a pattern, which is developed in exactly the same way as that of any other slope.

To Measure for the Miter

1. On your pattern draft, measure the width of the fabric at the lower point of the miter and multiply times the stitch gauge.
2. Measure the width of the fabric at the upper point of the miter and multiply times the stitch gauge.
3. Subtract the smaller number of stitches from the larger. The result is the number of stitches that must be added or removed, or the points. Even for a Dou-

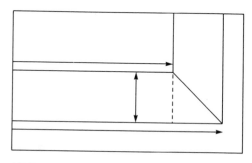

MEASURING FOR A MITER

ble Miter, it is only nescessary to calculate one slope, but you must use double decreases at each point to remove a stitch on each side of the slope.

4. Measure the depth of the mitred section of fabric and multiply times the row gauge.

Your calculations will always be more accurate if you measure the full width of the fabric before and after the change in order to determine the number of stitches to add or remove. Nevertheless, for the sake of brevity, in the following example we'll multiply the gauge directly by the amount to be removed.

Calculating the Miter

Say that you plan to use decreases to make a Double Miter at the corner of a border for a shawl. Two inches of fabric must be removed on each side of the slope, and the depth of the border is 3 inches with G = 5/7.

The number of points equals the number of shaping units. The number of steps may vary depending upon how the pattern works out; you have some flexibility in deciding whether to start or end the sequence with steps or points. Let's assume that the sequence starts with a step and ends with a point and therefore steps and points are equal.

2 inches × 5 stitches per inch = 10 stitches removed each side of the slope with double decreases

3 inches × 7 rows per inch = 21 rows

21 rows ÷ 10 steps = 2 rows per step, remainder 1

You may elect to place the remaining row at the beginning or end of the sequence or eliminate it. The Miter pattern calls for double decreases worked every other row, but obviously you could also use single decreases worked every row. If the border were only one and one-half inches deep that would be 10 rows and you would then use double decreases on every row.

If the border were 2 inches, however:

2 inches × 7 rows per inch = 14 rows

14 rows ÷ 10 steps = 1 row per step, remainder 4

10 steps − remainder 4 = 6 decreases worked every row, 4 decreases worked every other row

The pattern would be "Work a double decrease every row 6 times, then every other row 4 times."

Slopes in Medallions

Flat fabrics worked in the round are knit either from the center out to the edges, or from the edges in toward the center. Each round must be incrementally smaller or larger than the last, and the pattern must be precisely worked out so the fabric indeed lies flat. The outer edge of the fabric may be circular, square, or some kind of polygon, depending upon the position of the shaping techniques. The lines of shaping units are, in effect, multiple Miters and the method of working out the patterns is very similar.

- The number of stitches to be increased or decreased is from 3 or 4 at the center to the number of stitches that according to the gauge will be needed for the measurement of the perimeter.
- The number of rows over which the shaping techniques will be distributed is a measurement from the center, perpendicular to the edge as shown.
- The shaping units may be placed in straight lines, slopes, or curves, or distributed evenly throughout, depending upon what will assist in creating the desired shape and what will enhance the stitch pattern.

As an example, let us take a square, worked from the center to the edge starting on 4 stitches. Each edge measures 6 inches, the measurement from the center to the edge is 3 inches, and G = 5/7.

6 inches × 5 stitches per inch = 30 stitches × 4 sides = 120 stitches

120 − 4 cast-on stitches = 116 stitches to increase

116 stitches ÷ 4 slopes = 29 increases on each slope

3 inches × 7 rows per inch = 21 rows

There are more increases than there are rows, so it will be necessary to use double increases. However, there are an uneven number of increases on each slope. Let's subtract out 1 as single increase worked on the first round; that leaves 28 increases and 20 rows. Then 28 increases ÷ 2 = 14 double increases. The increases will start immediately but probably shouldn't run out to the very last row, so let's have an equal number of steps and points.

20 rows ÷ 14 steps = 1 row per step, remainder 6

14 steps − remainder 6 = 8 steps with 2 rows, 6 steps with 1 row

The simplest pattern would read "Work one double increase every other row 8x, then every row 6x." To make the slope as smooth as possible, however, you might want to intersperse the different-size steps with one another. Here again this would be much easier to work out on a chart. Rather than counting the changing number of stitches between the points, place markers at the slopes.

Polygonal figures are created by increasing the number of slopes. Curved and spiraled Miter lines can be worked out by shifting the shaping techniques one stitch to the right or left on each subsequent point instead of

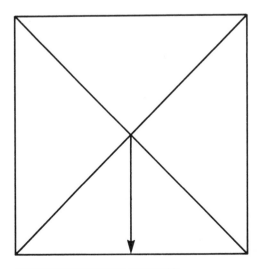

MEASURING FOR SQUARE MEDALLION

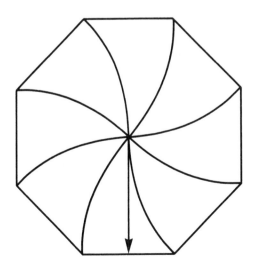

MEASUREMENT FOR POLYGON MEDALLION

placing them in straight lines. For a circle, the shaping units are distributed horizontally at intervals, combining the method used for gathering a fabric and that for creating a curve.

Formula for Gradual Slopes

1. Number of Stitches to be Added or Removed = Points
2. Number of Steps:
   If sequence begins and ends with points: Steps = Points − 1
   If sequence begins with a point: Steps = Points
   If sequence begins and ends with steps: Steps = Points + 1
3. When sequence begins with a point:
   Number of Rows − 1 Initial Point = Rows to Distribute to Steps
4. Number of Rows ÷ Number of Steps = Rows per Step
5. Handle Remainders as described in Horizontal Steps and Points
6. To write the pattern:
   If sequence starts with point, write alone at beginning
   If sequence ends with a step, separate in pattern as it contains no decrease

Calculating a Pick-up Pattern

Whether you are planning to pick up stitches along a straight edge or a curve, the method of developing the pattern is the same. Let's look at picking up stitches along a selvedge for something like a center front border.

Picking Up on a Selvedge

First you must have an accurate measurement of the length of the edge along which you will pick up the stitches. For accuracy, take this measurement from a full-scale pattern draft, rather than from the fabric.

Length of Edge × Border Stitch Gauge = Number of Stitches to Pick Up

Second, you will have to determine how many selvedge stitches there are along the edge. Regardless of

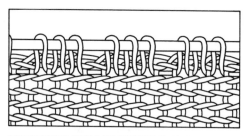

DISTRIBUTING PICKED UP STITCHES ALONG AN EDGE

whether the edge is straight, sloped, or curved, the number of selvedge stitches is equal to the number of rows in the length of fabric if you have used a Stockinette Selvedge, half that number if you have used a Chain Selvedge.

If the number of stitches to be picked up is larger than the number in the selvedge, you will have to work more than once into certain of the stitches. If the number is smaller, you will have to skip some of the selvedge stitches. Whether there will be increases or skips, these are the points of the pattern.

Stitches to Pick Up − Stitches in Selvedge = Stitches to Increase

or

Stitches in Selvedge − Stitches to Pick Up = Stitches to Skip

Stitches to Increase or Skip = Number of Points

What we need to know next is exactly which stitches to work into normally and which to either increase on or skip. In either case, this involves a single stitch.

Stitches in Selvedge − Points = Stitches Allocated to Steps

You will want to start and end the sequence with a step, so there will be one more step than points.

Stitches Allocated to Steps ÷ Number of Steps = Stitches per Step

If there is a remainder, distribute those stitches across the steps as evenly as possible; it is best to intersperse them rather than to have them all in one position. You will then have a pattern that reads something like "Working into every stitch along the edge, *pick up 4 sts, work an increase on the 5th*, repeat across the full length of the edge," or " . . . *pick up into every st 6x, skip 1 st, pick up into every st 5x, skip 1 st* . . . ," or "Pick Up: 6-1-5-1. . . . "

If for some reason you do not know the number of rows in the length of fabric along which you must pick up, you can mark the edge off into one-inch segments (for more information, see page 189). In this case, divide the number of inches into the number of stitches you need to pick up. Distribute any remainder across the steps as described above.

Picking Up Along a Slope

Necklines, center front openings, and armholes all contain slopes. Picking up stitches along a slope is very little different than picking up along a vertical edge.

First measure the slope on a full-scale pattern draft.

Multiply the length of the slope times your border stitch gauge to find how many stitches to pick up.

Work out the pick-up pattern exactly as for a vertical edge, above.

As I mentioned above, the number of Stockinette Selvedge stitches along the slope equals the number of rows that lie between the bottom and top of the sloped edge; there will be half as many Chain Selvedge Stitches.

If you are picking up for a V neckline, the center back stitches will be on holders. Use the method described above in Calculations for Ribbing to measure the neckline and find the number of stitches required. To find the number of stitches to pick up along each slope, subtract the stitches on hold and divide the remainder by 2.

Picking Up Around an Opening

Picking up stitches around a circular opening such as a neckline is very common. The stitches at the center front and center back should be on holders and therefore present no problems. Calculate the number of stitches according to the method described above for ribbings. Once you have the number of stitches you require, subtract out the total number of stitches on holders, then divide the remainder by 2 to find the number to pick up at each side. Work out the pattern for distributing these stitches evenly along the selvedge in the manner described above for Picking Up on a Slope.

If you are picking up around an armhole, the stitches at the base may be cast off or on a holder, and the number of selvedge stitches will equal or be one-half of the number of rows that lie between the base of the armhole and the shoulder. The measurement of the edge should be taken from a full-scale pattern draft if it is sloped.

Calculating a Curve

A curve is no more than a series of small slopes, with the angle of the slopes continually changing. Each slope must be calculated separately, just as described above, with so many stitches being removed or added over so many rows. In other words, if you decrease one stitch every row for a while, then one every other row, then one every third row, the slopes for each of those segments will be different. In knitting, the resilience of the fabric smooths this series of short straight lines into a nice curve.

These are never easy calculations to work out, and generally it takes some fooling around to get things right. As with slopes, charting offers a far easier, much more direct way to develop a pattern for any curve (see page 522), but should you be caught without graph paper, here is how to work the pattern out mathematically; once the principle is understood, it goes reasonably well.

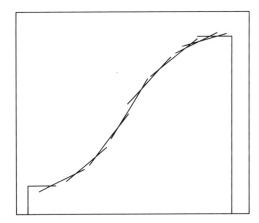

MULTIPLE SLOPES CREATE A CURVE

Standard Curved Edge

Say, for example, that instead of working a sleeve cap in a triangle shape, you wanted to give it a bit of a curve, more like the natural shape of the body. You must use a full-scale draft of at least one vertical half of the pattern.

1. On the center vertical line, measure off 1-inch intervals.
2. Draw a horizontal line from each mark to the curve. Measure the lines and use the stitch gauge to calculate the number of stitches you will need to have on the needle at each interval. Write the numbers down on the lines.
3. Subtract the number of stitches on one line from those on the previous line. This equals the number of stitches that must be removed between those two lines.

Because we are dealing only with how many stitches must actually be on the needle at each interval, we eliminate the problem of partial stitches entirely. However, we may still have partial rows; let's get rid of them, too.

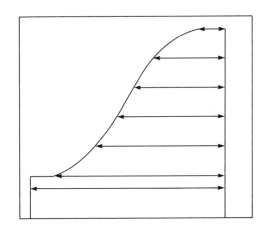

DRAWING FOR CALCULATING A CURVE

The intervals are the equivalent of steps, and all that is necessary is to distribute the rows evenly.

Say that your row gauge is 7.4 and you want to decrease a certain number of stitches over 5 inches.

7.4 rows per inch x 5 inches = 37 rows

37 rows ÷ 5 inches = 7 rows per interval, remainder 2

5 intervals − remainder 2 = 3 intervals with 7 rows, 2 intervals with 8 rows

Let us say that for this pattern we need to remove four stitches in the first interval, three stitches in the following one, two stitches in each of the next two, and one in the last. In order to curve the sleeve, we must develop a separate pattern for the unique slope of each interval; let's assume that steps and points are equal, and as with any slope, the last row of a step contains a shaping unit.

1. In the first interval we have 7 rows and 4 points (the decreases).

   7 rows ÷ 4 = 1 row per step, remainder 3

   4 steps − remainder 3 = 1 step with one row, 3 steps with two rows

   Write this "Decrease row 1, then every 2nd row 3x."

2. In the second interval:

   7 rows ÷ 3 steps = 2 rows per step, remainder 1

   3 steps − remainder 1 = 2 steps with 2 rows, 1 step with 3 rows

   Write this "Decrease every 2nd row 2x, every 3rd row 1x."

3. In the third interval:

   7 rows ÷ 2 steps = 3 rows per step, remainder 1

   2 steps − remainder 1 = 1 step with 3 rows, 1 step with 4 rows

   Write this "Decrease every 3rd row 1x, every 4th row 1x."

4. In the fourth interval:

   8 rows ÷ 2 steps = 4 rows per step

   Write this "Decrease every 4th row 2x."

5. In the fifth interval:

   8 rows ÷ 1 step

   Write this "Decrease every 8 rows 1x."

   How do you turn this into a pattern?

Combine all the similar pattern elements from each interval. For instance, the first and the second intervals both have decreases worked every two rows, three in the first, and two in the second. The pattern should then start "Decrease once R1, then once every 2 rows 5x, . . ."

Similarly, the second and third interval both have patterns for decreasing every three rows, once in each interval. This becomes ". . . once every 3 rows 2x, . . ."

Then the third and the fourth intervals have patterns for decreasing every four rows, once in the third, twice in the fourth. Change this to ". . . once every 4 rows 3x, . . ." and finish it off ". . . once every 8 rows 1x."

In my own notation system, I would write this "Decrease R1, 1 ev 2R 5x, 1 ev 3R 2x, 1 ev 4R 3x, 1 ev 8R 1x."

Three-Dimensional Shapes

Better known as hats, mitten tips, and sock toes, but who knows . . . just for fun, let's make a four-sided pyramid.

Pyramid

The sides of a pyramid are triangles joined in the round by mitered corners. If you know the dimensions at the base of the pyramid and how high you want it to be, with the help of the square-root sign on your calculator, or a full-scale pattern draft, you can work out the pattern.

1. The length of the fabric is a measurement from the center at the base of one side to the tip. Since the fabric itself slopes in on each face, this is actually the hypotenuse, or slope of a second triangle lying within the pyramid.
2. The base of the second triangle is the measurement from the center of the opening at the bottom of the pyramid to the edge.
3. The height of the second triangle is a measurement from the center of the opening to the tip.
4. Draw the triangle full scale and measure the slope directly, or work it out mathematically, as follows: The formula for finding the length of the slope, and therefore the length of the fabric is:

$$a^2 + b^2 = c^2$$

where a = base, b = height, c = hypotenuse (slope).

Once you find the length of the fabric from base to

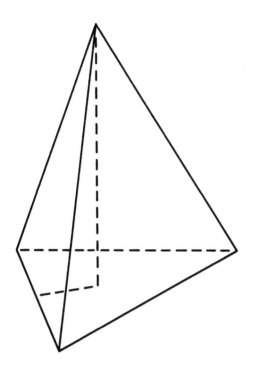

MEASUREMENTS FOR A PYRAMID SHAPE

1. Multiply the circumference times the Average Gauge for the ribbing to determine how many stitches to cast on.
2. Multiply the regular stitch pattern gauge times the circumference to find the number of stitches with which to start the body of the hat.

So far so good. The number of rows in the fabric is determined by a measurement of the curved surface from edge to tip, and this must be taken from a full-scale drawing of the hat. In order to draw this figure, we need some help from a pocket calculator and the formula for a circle.

First we must find the radius, the measurement from the center of the base circle to the edge.

Circumference ÷ 3.14 (Pi) = Diameter

Diameter ÷ 2 = Radius

Next, make a full-scale drawing of one quarter of the hat.

1. Draw a horizontal line on a piece of paper equal to the radius.
2. Draw another line the height of the hat at a right angle to the first.
3. Draw a nice, shapely curve from the point of one line to the point of the other. This is the contour of the hat, as shown in the display below. (The curve may take any shape you wish, from that of a true dome, to one which is nearly vertical at first, then curves in more sharply.)

tip, you can determine the number of rows required. Then take half the measurement of the base of the first triangle (the amount to be removed by the slope) and calculate the steps and points for the four Miters just as you would if the fabric were a flat medallion.

Calculating a Dome

Better known as a hat. A dome is a series of ever-smaller circles, one on top of the other. In order to make any hat, you start with the measurement of the circumference of the head, which is the base circle.

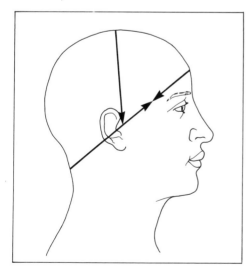

MEASURING FOR A HAT

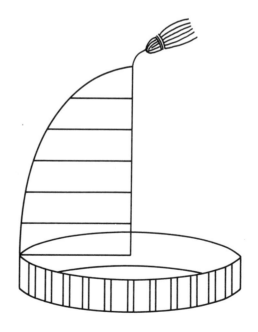

DRAWING FOR CALCULATING A HAT

4. With a tape measure, find the length of the curved line and multiply it times the rows per inch from your gauge to find how many rows of fabric you will need to knit.

Now it is necessary to develop a pattern of decreases in order to create that curve. The whole process is very similar to the calculations given above for the curve of a sleeve cap, except that the shaping techniques must be distributed horizontally all the way around each interval instead of being just at the edge.

- Along the vertical line, mark off one-inch segments and draw lines parallel to the base from each mark to the vertical line. (Each one of these lines represents a new radius for the progressively smaller circumference of the hat.)

In order to find out just how much smaller each one of those circles is, and therefore how many stitches must be on the needle at that point, we use the same formula, but turn it around slightly.

Radius × *2* = *Diameter*

Diameter × *3.14* = *Circumference*

Circumference × *Stitches per Inch* = *Stitches on Needle*

Repeat the procedure for each radius, writing the numbers down on the lines. In order to find how many stitches are removed each inch, subtract the number of stitches on the second line from the first, subtract the third line from the second, etc.

Use Horizontal Steps and Points to distribute the decreases within the fabric. The simplest approach is to distribute them across one row, then knit the remaining rows of the interval plain. Alternatively, divide the decreases over several rows of the interval.

And you thought hats were simple! You could simplify things by charting the curve (see page 522). That produces a pattern of decreases in four Miter lines, a style found in many hats.

26

Stitch and Color Pattern Charts

A stitch or color chart is a graphic representation of what should be done to each stitch of the fabric in order to achieve the desired pattern. The pattern is diagrammed on graph paper and every square of the chart represents one stitch. The pattern can be read row by row from the bottom up, just as one knits, with every square indicating clearly what should be done to the stitch it represents. For a stitch chart, each of the basic stitch techniques is assigned a unique symbol. Some color charts are colored in, with others letters or a few symbols may be used to indicate which yarn to use for each stitch.

These diagrams are not only easier to follow than written instructions, but provide a picture of the structure and finished appearance of the fabric. A well-done chart will help you to make sense of a pattern before you ever pick up yarn and needles, and as a result you will find that you can learn even a complex pattern very quickly.

Stitch Charting Symbols

Before we go on to discuss the actual stitch charts, I must first give you a glossary of the symbols that will be used. Unfortunately, just as with stitch abbreviations, there are no established conventions regarding which symbols to use in charting, and you will encounter quite a variety. No doubt each system seems vividly clear to its originator, as the one I offer here does to me. In the hope of not adding to the problem, for the most part I have retained commonly used symbols, although some may be from one system, some from another. Wherever I thought versatility or clarity would be served, however, I have developed a new symbol. In all cases, my criterion has been to choose those that are simple, resemble in some way the stitch they represent, and are also sufficiently dissimilar one from the other to avoid confusion. I have made no attempt to develop a symbol for every possible knitting technique, nor is that a desirable goal, as it would tax the memory in much the same way the Chinese character set does. What is required instead is a simple, flexible set of symbols more like an alphabet. Therefore, symbols have been assigned to only the most basic and common techniques; more esoteric maneuvers are indicated in the charts by combining all or part of several of these basic symbols to convey a sense of what is required. Even when you have never encountered one of these hybrid symbols before, you should be able to "sound it out" as you do a new word.

The point of the matter must be kept in mind, however, and that is that the symbols must be clear to you, the knitter. Therefore, I have included some alternative symbols where appropriate, both to give you a choice and/or because the alternate is commonly found in other charting systems you may have occasion to use. The important thing to grasp here, then, is not so much the particulars as the concept; learn how charting works and then use whichever symbols work for you, or make up some of your own.

In addition to refining the symbols, I have tried to solve some inconsistencies and limitations evident in other methods of using them and develop a system that is capable of describing any stitch pattern whatsoever. Charting is by definition an abstraction, but I have attempted to be very concrete here and make it somewhat less so, and to that end my model is the knitted fabric itself. Certainly it is not possible to get rigid squares on a piece of paper to look exactly like the flexible grid of a knitted fabric, but we can come very close indeed. While there is quite a bit that is new here, those of you familiar with more traditional charts will not find the change so radical that it looks strange. The discussion systematically covers every type of problem a stitch pattern can present when you attempt to chart it, compares different methods of solving some of these problems, and introduces methods of charting certain types of patterns not previously done.

My hope is that you will find these ideas useful and that they will enable you to readily understand any chart you might encounter, as well as to write charts of your own that are aesthetically satisfying and easy to work from.

Basic Stitches and Techniques

Knit: In many patterns, the most efficient symbol for the Knit stitch is none at all. This way, only those squares that represent stitches that should *not* be Knit contain a symbol. This adds clarity to the chart, drawing your eye to the pattern stitches and making them easy to read. It also saves a considerable amount of writing. This works particularly well for any Rib or Brocade pattern, and many lace stitches. There are situations, however, when this approach may not be sufficiently precise or unambiguous.

Knit: While using a symbol for Knit tends to clutter the chart up a bit, in many of the more complex patterns it becomes essential to indicate clearly what happens to each and every stitch. When writing a pattern, it is frequently useful to at least use this symbol in the rough draft as a way of counting out stitches and keeping your place; it can frequently be omitted in the final draft from which you will work. Also, whenever a pattern creates bias, the symbol can be set at an angle to indicate the direction in which the stitches will be pulled (see also Hatch Marks, below).

Purl: This symbol is used on its own to indicate that a plain Purl stitch must be worked on the outside of the fabric. It can also be used in conjunction with any other symbol to indicate that the Purl version of that particular technique should be worked on the outside.

Purl: Many people prefer to use a dash, and it is quicker to write; it does, however, take up more space, and therefore, while it can be used, it doesn't work as well in conjunction with another symbol. Because of this, I sometimes use them both, the dash for a plain Purl stitch, the dot when it is the Purl version of another technique. If you find this confusing, use the dot, as it works in every situation.

Left Crossed Stitch: This tiny hatch mark on a sloped Knit symbol indicates that the stitch must be worked through the farside. The same hatch mark used in conjunction with any other symbol instructs you to work that technique so it will cross.

Right Crossed Stitch: There are two methods of forming a Right Crossed Stitch, both producing the identical result. In one version all the steps are completed at one time; in the other, a preparatory step must be taken on the previous row. However, because other symbols may occupy the square below this sign, and because the preparatory step is temporary, no symbol can be used for it; the method of working must be understood.

Multiple Wrap Elongation: This symbol indicates that the yarn should be wrapped an extra time or two in order to elongate the stitch. The symbol must be written on the top line of the square to indicate that this affects the new stitch, not the discard stitch.

Needle Elongation: When a larger needle must be used in order to enlarge the stitches, the row number of

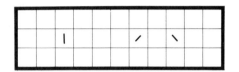

KNIT

BIAS

PURL

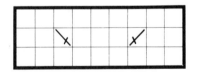

CROSSED STITCH

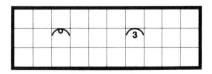

MULTIPLE WRAP ELONGATION

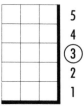

NEEDLE ELONGATION

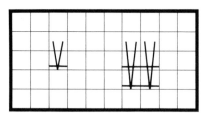

SLIP STITCH

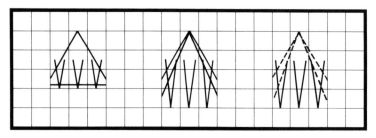

CROSSED SLIP STITCH

SLIP STITCH/YARN STRANDED OUTSIDE

LATTICE

either the written or charted instructions should be circled.

Slip Stitch: The general rule for reading this symbol is that you slip a stitch for the first time when you encounter the square containing the bottom of the symbol, and continue to slip it on each subsequent row, finally working the stitch when you encounter the square containing the top of the symbol. If the top of the symbol is open, it should be Knit; if the top of the symbol is dotted, it should be Purled. This is not the traditional way of using the Slip Stitch symbol in a chart (for a complete discussion, see page 462).

In some patterns, a Slip Stitch may be involved in a decrease or in a Cable or Twist Stitch technique. In these cases, the symbol may have to be placed at an angle or share part of a square with another symbol (for examples, see page 466).

Crossed Slip Stitch: Whenever instructions call for a Slip Stitch to be worked farside, the result will be a Left Cross. For a Right Cross, generally the stitch is first slipped knitwise to turn it on the needle and then worked normally, either on the same or a subsequent row.

Slip Stitch/Yarn Stranded Outside: The horizontal bar across the base of a Slip Stitch symbol indicates that the yarn is to be stranded past the stitch on the outside of the fabric. The strand may pass one or several stitches, and there may be additional strands passing the same stitches on later rows.

Lattice: The first symbol here shows a basic Lattice technique, where a strand passed on the outside of several Slip Stitches is picked up on a later row and worked together with a stitch. In order to convey what is happening, the strand is generally shown both where it was originally passed on the outside of the Slip Stitches, and again where it is caught up by the stitch above. If you feel it would be clear to you what to do if only the finished appearance was shown, you may certainly eliminate the line drawn across the bottom of the Slip Stitch symbols.

The second symbol indicates a Multiple Lattice, with more than one strand caught up, and the third, with the dotted line, is an Inside Lattice, where the strand lies on the inside of the fabric.

Honeycomb/Knit Below: This is a new symbol, intended to serve both methods of making this stitch technique. It was designed to look as much as possible like the stitch does in an actual fabric, and makes explicit the identity of the two methods and the technique's relationship to a Slip Stitch. The "tails" at each side of the Slip Stitch symbol represent the strands caught up with the stitch.

If you are working as for Knit Below, when you come to the square that contains the lower portion of the symbol, you may Knit or Purl, whichever is convenient, as these stitches will unravel once the technique itself is worked at the point when you encounter the square containing the top of the symbol.

If you are working as for Honeycomb, work the Yarnover/Slip Stitch when you encounter the lower portion of the symbol and work the decrease that joins the two when you encounter the top portion of the symbol. (For more information on how the symbol is used in charting, see page 481).

Knit Below: These are the more common symbols for this technique. Unfortunately, neither resemble the fabric, and the arrow is used in several other ways in charting and therefore has enough to do already. Nevertheless, here they are just so you will recognize them.

Ladder: The stitches represented by the squares through which the arrow passes can be handled in whatever way is convenient. Since they will eventually be unraveled, it doesn't matter whether they are Knit or Purl as long as they are worked.

Cable Stitches: In her book *Charted Knitting Designs*[1], Barbara Walker has worked out a very sensible system for indicating all of the Cable techniques. The parallel sloping lines indicate the path of the facing stitches of each cable unit, passing from the base of the squares where the stitches originate to the top of the squares they will occupy when the technique is completed. The two smaller lines slanting in the opposite direction indicate the origin and destination of the backing stitches. The vertical lines that extend up and down from the cross indicate the path of the columns of Knit stitches that extend up to and out of the Cable. These lines are optional but generally add visual clarity to a charted pattern. Despite the variety of Cable techniques, all of them can be charted using simple variations on this one symbol.

Mixed Cables: If the backing stitches are to be Purled, the lines indicating the backing stitches are replaced by a symbol for Purl. Although they are rare, there are patterns that use Purl stitches on the facing stitches, and the Purl dot placed in the appropriate square within the sloping lines makes this clear.

Cable Stitch/Alternate: These are two other commonly used symbols for the Cable technique. They are quite clear as to what to do, but neither of them are capable of producing as vivid a picture of the pattern as the symbol above, nor can they indicate whether some of the Cable stitches should be Purled. Nevertheless, they are quicker to write, and you may find them useful when you are doing a rough draft of a pattern.

Twist Stitch: While the working method and the path of the yarn may often be different from that of a Cable, the Twist Stitch is so closely related, and in many cases the resulting appearance is so similar, that it makes sense to use the same symbol. However, because there are so many methods of making a Twist Stitch (see page 46), it may be necessary to key the symbol to some

1. New York: Charles Scribner's Sons, 1972.

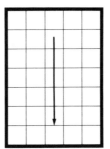

HONEYCOMB/KNIT BELOW

KNIT BELOW

LADDER

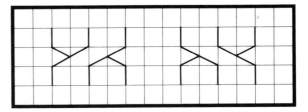

CABLE STITCHES

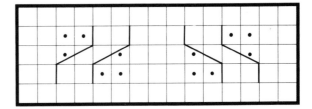

MIXED CABLES

CABLE STITCH/ALTERNATE

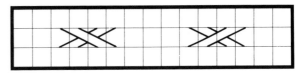

CABLE STITCH/ALTERNATE

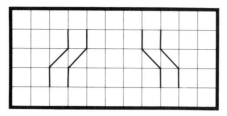

TWIST STITCH

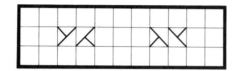

TWIST STITCH

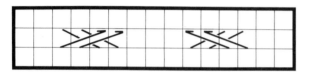

THREADED STITCH

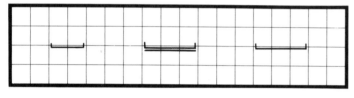

WRAP

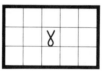

LOOP STITCH

STRANDED BROCADE

STRANDED BROCADE

written instructions that specify the particular technique to be used.

The vertical lines extending up and down from the Twist are optional and are generally seen only when the technique is being used to cause a column of Knit stitches to "travel" across the fabric. The hatch marks for the backing stitch are also optional and are usually abandoned in a pattern of the type just mentioned, where they tend to clutter things up.

Twist Stitch: The alternate Cable symbol works quite well for certain applications of the Twist Stitch, particularly in an allover pattern or in conjunction with some other technique. It is quicker to write and certainly adequate to work from, but it rarely conveys a good picture of the pattern.

Threaded Stitch: This is very similar in principle to the way a Cable Stitch is handled, except a single hooked line is used to indicate each facing stitch and a straight line each backing stitch. Because only half of the facing stitch remains on the outside, this resembles the resulting fabric quite well.

Wrap: The number of Wraps can be indicated by the number of lines drawn below the hooked one, or a small number can be used. The symbol is placed at the bottom of the square, as the Wrap includes the base of the discard stitches.

Loop Stitch: Easy to recognize and simple to use, this little symbol works nicely for those situations when a stitch pattern uses Loops only in certain areas; for an overall pattern, of course, you really don't need a chart at all.

Stranded Brocade: The first symbol represents the basic pattern unit, a strand flanked by two Purl stitches. The second represents the half-unit, two strands flanking a Purl stitch. The last two represent the Double and Single Strand Nubs.

Increase and Decrease Symbols

In many charting systems, a single symbol serves for any increase and another for any decrease, and it is left to the knitter to determine the particular technique to be used. However, the various techniques confer such unique characteristics to a fabric that I prefer to have specific symbols for each of them. As a general rule, an increase symbol expands pointing up to the squares the new stitches will occupy, while a decrease symbol is confined to a single square.

Bar Increase: If the barred, "Purl" portion of the symbol lies to the left, the technique must be worked on the outside of the fabric; if it lies to the right, the technique must be worked on the inside.

Rib Increase: The dotted portion of the symbol indicates the position of the Purl stitch of the pair. See also the appearance of this increase when used on a Yarnover, below.

Raised Increase: The sloping line indicates whether the raised stitch should be on the right or left side. For a Double Raised Increase, sloping lines will be on both sides.

If you are using a Raised Increase in a Rib or Brocade pattern, you may want to discard one or the other of the stitches as a Purl. Use the Purl dot below the sloped arm to indicate that the raised stitch should be Purled, next to the vertical arm to indicate that the stitch on the needle should be, and between the two if they both should be.

The Slip Raised Increase combines the two symbols, making the technique quite clear.

Running Thread Increase: This increase can be written sloping to either the left or the right, depending upon the effect it causes in the fabric or on what makes the pattern easy to read.

For the Purl version, dot the symbol.

The Crossed version employs the little hatch marks already seen in Crossed Stitch, above.

Yarnover: This is a new, alternate symbol for the Yarnover, which I highly recommend for reasons that are explained in detail on page 469. When you encounter the square containing the bottom of the symbol, you should pass the yarn over the needle to form the Yarnover. When you encounter the square containing the top of the symbol, you must work it as Knit on the outside; if it is dotted, work it as Purl on the outside.

Yarnover: This is the traditional symbol, which conventionally occupies a single square and indicates only that you should pass the yarn over the needle. It resembles the fabric less, but is still convenient in certain types of patterns.

Multiple Yarnovers: The symbol should be written differently depending on the function the Yarnover must perform. If just one stitch will be formed on the Double or Triple Yarnover, any extra wraps are being

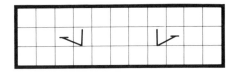

BAR INCREASE

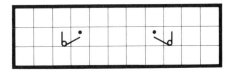

RIB INCREASE

RAISED INCREASE

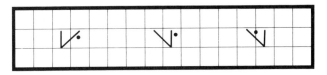

PURL RAISED INCREASE

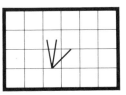

SLIP RAISED INCREASE

RUNNING THREAD INCREASE

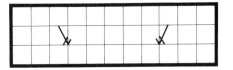

CROSSED RUNNING THREAD INCREASE

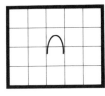

YARNOVER

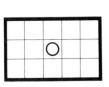

YARNOVER

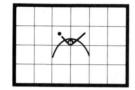

MULTIPLE YARNOVERS

RIB INCREASE AND MULTIPLE YARNOVER

SPECIALIZED YARNOVERS

MULTIPLE YARNOVER INCREASE

RIGHT AND LEFT DECREASE

RIGHT AND LEFT DECREASE/PURLED

RIGHT AND LEFT DECREASE/CROSSED

DOUBLE DECREASES

used as an elongation technique. A single symbol should therefore occupy just one square.

If the Yarnover will have two or three stitches placed on it in the next row, the symbol should span each square to be occupied by a new stitch. Generally a Rib Increase will be used on the next row, as shown.

Specialized Yarnovers: There are many occasions when the Yarnover is used in a special way and no stitch will be formed on it in the following row. In these cases, a tiny version of the symbol may occupy a square with another symbol or lie on the intersection between two squares—in short, whatever position makes the operation to be performed clear to you. If the Yarnover is used just as an elongation device and dropped on the subsequent row, the small bar over the symbol makes this clear.

There are a very few occasions, most often in Pullover techniques, where a Yarnover symbol must share a square with some other symbol representing a stitch that it will replace. In these cases, use the partial Yarnover symbol shown here; the one arching to the left indicates that it was made prior to the stitch in the square, the one arching to the right, after it.

Multiple Yarnover Increase: And finally, the Yarnover at the center of a double increase.

Right and Left Decrease: These are quite self-explanatory; the sloping line indicates the slant of the decrease, whether to the right or to the left. If the decrease is to be Purled, place a dot within the symbol; if it is to be crossed, use the hatch mark from Crossed Stitch.

Double Decreases: As with the single versions, the symbol slants in the direction the decrease should take. It is, of course, possible to use the center symbol for any double decrease as it is easy to write; in that case, key the symbol to a note that details the precise technique to be used.

Multiple Increase or Decrease: For the increase, the lines expand to touch the squares occupied by the new stitches. The decrease symbol occupies a single square with a number indicating how many stitches must be worked together. There are some few patterns where squares are available and the decrease symbol may be expanded, if you wish. Where important, a key should be used to indicate the precise technique to be used.

Hatch Mark: Whenever balanced increases and decreases are used on the same row but separated from one another, bias is created in the intervening stitches. As mentioned above, the direction of the bias can be indicated by slanting the symbol for the Knit stitch in the appropriate direction. Alternatively, this tiny hatch mark placed on an intersection can point from the square where the stitch was to the square it will occupy in the row above. (For further details on how to use this symbol, see page 478.)

Chain Nub: This technique is rarely seen and so hardly deserves a symbol of its own, but it is difficult to use any combination of other symbols to convey the sense of what is required.

Bobble: Because there are different ways to make a Bobble, the symbol should be keyed to written instructions or a mini-chart. Use the same principle for a Nub or a Knot.

Embossing: In this case, a multiple increase is not compensated for until several rows later. When just a few stitches are involved, or the pattern is very simple, a single symbol within the box can be read as applying to all the extra stitches. If the pattern is complex, it will require the use of a mini-chart or an expanded chart including blank spaces (see page 475).

Pullover: The basic symbol is the hooked line, used in every case. It should be placed at the top of the square, as the Pullover will encircle the base of the new stitches. If the hooked end lies to the left, the technique is to be worked on the outside of the fabric; if it lies to the right, it will be worked on the inside. The latter situation may or may not cause problems if you are working in the round (see page 485).

The first three variations on the basic symbol indicate Stitch Pullovers; notice that the hooked line originates within the square. The first Pullover is made with a new stitch, the second with a stitch slipped purlwise, the third with a stitch slipped knitwise.

The next three variations show the hook originating on a line, indicating an Increase Pullover. The first Pullover is done with a Yarnover, the second with a Running Thread Increase, the third with the running thread itself.

Alternate Pullover: There are some charting systems that use an arrow to indicate a Pullover. The symbol adequately indicates the operation to be performed, but does not resemble the appearance of the fabric. In addition, I find the arrow takes up so much space in the squares that it crowds the other symbols, making the chart hard to read.

Couching: This symbol makes it clear which stitch the Couching strand is attached to and whether it originates between two stitches or within one. The optional small mark below the symbol on the dividing line indicates the point at which the strand should be drawn through and placed on the needle.

MULTIPLE INCREASE OR DECREASE

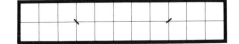

HATCH MARKS

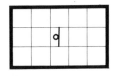

CHAIN NUB

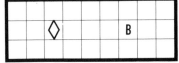

BOBBLE

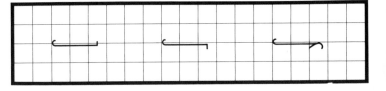

EMBOSSING

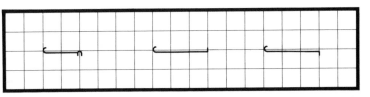

PULLOVERS

PULLOVERS

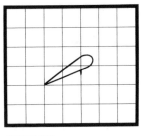

ALTERNATE PULLOVER

COUCHING

BEAD

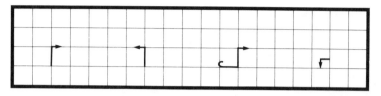

SHORT ROW

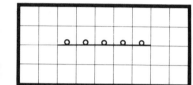

CAST-ON

CAST-OFF

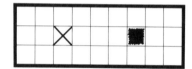

NO STITCH

STITCHES ON HOLD

ATTACH YARN

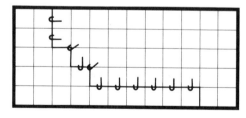

PICKUP POINT

OPENING

Miscellaneous Symbols

And finally, a few symbols used in charting that are not stitch techniques.

Bead: The first symbol is used in a Running Thread Bead chart and it is always placed on the line dividing two squares; the second is used for Stitch Head Beading (for more information see page 490). Other beading methods make use of standard color charts.

Short Row: The right and left arrow symbols instruct you to stop, turn, and work back in the other direction.

The arrow may be used in conjunction with the Wrap symbol when the gap at the turning point should be closed.

The downward arrow indicates that the Short Row section is finished and the work should continue on the remaining stitches.

Cast-on: There are a few patterns that require that stitches be cast on within the fabric rather than increased, but this symbol is primarily useful for garment pattern drafting.

Cast-off: As with Cast-on, above.

No Stitch: When the stitch count in a pattern changes row by row, there may be times when a square on the chart has no corresponding stitch in the fabric. In these situations, when a symbol for the Knit stitch is being used, leave the square empty to indicate that it should be skipped. When empty squares are being used as the symbol for Knit stitches, use an X or shade the square.

Stitches On Hold: This is a symbol used in garment pattern charts to indicate which stitches should be inactivated and placed on a holder.

Attach Yarn: Used to indicate where yarn should be reattached to the work.

Pickup Point: Indicates the precise place in which to pick up each stitch along an edge.

Opening: May be used to identify the position of any sort of opening, from a buttonhole to a pocket.

Reading and Writing Stitch Charts

Here you will find a sampling of stitch charts, along with detailed explanations of how to read them and how to translate written instructions into charted form. I have made no attempt to provide charts that exploit every possible symbol, and fortunately that is not necessary, as the ones included nicely demonstrate the full range of possibilities and constraints that are at work here. Whenever there are several different ways that a pattern could be charted, I compare them so you will be able to see for yourself what the advantages and disadvantages might be of one approach over another. As always, it is the general concept that is important for you to grasp and you must then decide for yourself which of the possible ways to chart a pattern is the easiest for you to work from.

Reading Charts

Here is a chart for Lozenge, a simple Knit and Purl Brocade pattern that will serve nicely to illustrate many of the basic principles. Brocade patterns are particularly well suited to the type of chart in which a dot is used for the Purl stitches and an empty square for the Knit stitches.

Lozenge: To work flat:

Row 1: *P1, k4*
Row 2, 3: *P3, k2*
Row 4: *P1, k4*
Row 5: *K4, p1*
Row 6, 7: *K2, p3*
Row 8: *K4, p1*

To work round:

Row 1: *P1, k4*
Row 2: *P2, k3*
Row 3: *P3, k2*
Row 4: *P4, k1*
Row 5: *K4, p1*
Row 6: *K3, p2*
Row 7: *K2, p3*
Row 8: *K1, p4*

You will notice that while there are two sets of written instructions, there is only one chart. One of the great benefits of a chart is that it will serve you equally well whether you plan to knit flat or in the round. No more consternation at finding a pretty pattern written up for flat work when you really want to make something in the round, or vice versa. Not only that, but charts speak

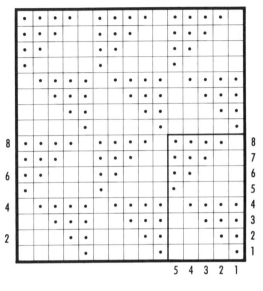

LOZENGE

an international language; once the concept of charting is understood, you can follow a pattern as easily in a Japanese knitting book as one from Germany or Italy, even when the symbols differ.

LOZENGE PATTERN

Working in the Round

While one chart serves both types of knitting, it must be written and read in a slightly different manner for flat or round knitting. The first and most important thing to realize is that the chart represents the stitch pattern only

---

459

as it is seen on the *outside* of the fabric. If you are knitting in the round, you will read the chart just as you knit, from the bottom up and from right to left, row by row. As you work across the row, if a square on the chart contains the symbol for a Knit stitch, you will work a Knit stitch; if it calls for a Purl stitch, you will work a Purl stitch.

Working Flat

Things are somewhat more complicated if you are knitting the fabric flat, because while you will be working one row on the outside, the next row on the inside, the chart shows only the appearance of the outside rows. As a result, the chart must be read from right to left on all outside rows, but from left to right on all inside rows (imagine that the knitting remains in position, but you walk around on the other side of it). Outside rows are quite straightforward, and you will Knit wherever a Knit symbol appears and Purl wherever a Purl symbol appears. However, on every inside row where the chart indicates that a Purl stitch should appear on the outside of the fabric, you must of course Knit that stitch on the inside, and where a Knit stitch appears, you must Purl. It's a bit like working through a mental mirror, but after a while it becomes quite automatic and you won't have to give it much thought.

Using the Knit Symbol

Here is the same chart written with the dash for Purl and the written symbol for Knit. I think you will agree the first version provides a much clearer picture of the pattern and is therefore easier to work from. I recommend that you write charts in that way whenever possible; however, the method shown here is not only very common, but you should be familiar with it because, as you will see, in some of the more complex charts specificity requires the use of a symbol for Knit.

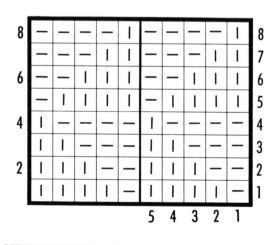

LOZENGE WITH KNIT SYMBOL

Relation Between Square and Stitch

Before we go any further, I would like to point out a fundamental organizing principle of stitch charting that is important for you to keep in mind. Each square on a chart must do double duty. It should provide both instruction as to what must be done to the next neutral stitch on the left needle and a graphic picture of the result, which in the fabric will be the newly discarded stitch lying directly below the new stitch on the right needle. Therefore, as you read or write a chart, imagine your right knitting needle lying on the line directly above the row of squares that you have just completed; your left needle lies above the squares of the row below, on top of the ones you will knit next.

With this concept in mind, the chart will provide you with important visual clues as to whether you are in the right place at any moment, and it also has special significance for certain techniques, such as Slip Stitch, Ladders, and Couching, where a stitch or a strand must be carried over several rows or stitches. A good chart should make these situations clear, both in terms of what to do to a particular stitch in a particular row and what its overall role in the pattern will be when its part has been fully played.

Numbering System

The columns of stitches making up a single horizontal repeat of the pattern are numbered across the bottom of the chart. When you have knit across one set of these stitches, either from right to left or left to right, repeat the unit again and again as many times as necessary across the width of the fabric.

For knitters working in the round, each row is numbered up the right side, starting with one at the first row at the bottom of the chart. In addition, every other row is numbered on the left side of the chart to guide those working flat. These numbers define a single vertical repeat of the pattern. When you complete the last row of a set, begin again with the first, as many times as necessary for the length of the fabric.

As you know, in flat knitting a pattern may commence on either an inside or an outside row. If you are to begin the stitch pattern on the inside, the rows will be marked on the left with odd numbers, beginning with one on the first row. If you are to begin on an outside row, the numbers on the left side will be even, starting with two on the second row, as they are here. (Actually this pattern is reversible, and it doesn't matter where you start.) Many patterns do not provide the left numbers, but I recommend you add them to any chart you may use. They help to locate you so you don't have to stop and try to remember how you started and which are inside and which are outside rows.

Stitch and Row Repeats

A good chart should include two or three stitch repeats horizontally and two or three vertically, as the one given here does, in order to provide a complete picture of how the motifs of the pattern fit together. The extra repeats are used only for planning purposes, discussed in more detail below; the actual knitting is done with reference just to the single repeat, which is enclosed by the darker lines within the chart. Many charts do not include these inner lines defining the repeat—in fact, they are not necessary as long as the stitches and rows of the repeat are numbered—but if you like them, add them on.

Edge and Selvedge Stitches

Before we go any further, it is necessary to make a distinction between selvedge stitches and edge stitches; they must not be confused with one another, although many patterns are ambiguous about this.

When a fabric is seamed, one stitch at the side edge is absorbed and winds up on the inside of the garment. A selvedge stitch is designed to perform this function, being added to the side of the fabric in addition to any stitches required for the width so no pattern stitches are eliminated and the correct width of the fabric is maintained despite seaming. On unseamed fabrics, selvedge stitches worked in one of several special stitch techniques may be added at the side edge to form a decorative border. Neither of these forms of the selvedge stitch are part of a stitch pattern.

Unlike selvedges, edge stitches are an integral part of the stitch pattern, but they lie outside the repeat itself, and may or may not be optional. Depending upon the function of the edge stitches in the pattern, they are sometimes eliminated when knitting in the round or when seaming. Patterns may use one stitch at each side of the repeat in order to have a plain stitch at the edge rather than a complex one; in other cases, several stitches may be required on one side or the other of the repeat either to balance it, because pattern elements are staggered, or to accommodate the pattern to a width of fabric which does not allow a full repeat at each side.

A chart therefore contains three kinds of stitches. One group is made up of edge stitches, which are worked only at the beginning or end of rows. A second group is the stitch repeat, which is worked as many times as necessary across the row. The third group is made up of copies of the stitch repeat, which are included only to reveal the relationship of pattern elements and not used at all to work from; after working the repeat as many times as possible, you will skip over the others to whatever edge stitches are required. In the charts shown here, no selvedge stitches are used; it is understood that you will add them for any edge to be seamed.

A written stitch pattern will frequently instruct you to cast on a "multiple of x stitches, plus x." The first half of that notation refers to the stitch repeat, or multiple, those columns of stitches numbered along the base of the chart. Unfortunately, the second half of the instruction, if it exists, may refer to either edge or selvedge stitches, and the only way to discover the function of the "plus x" stitches in a pattern is to work up a sample or to chart it. Information on using the multiple to coordinate stitch pattern and garment width can be found on page 413.

Writing a Chart

Writing a chart, transcribing written instructions to charted form, is very little different from reading one.

If the instructions were intended for working in the round, you will write the symbols into the squares just as you would work, stitch by stitch, row by row, always from right to left. The chart is then ready to read for either knitting flat or in the round as described above.

If the written instructions were intended for working flat, you will write outside rows from right to left, just as they are given. The inside rows will be written from left to right just as you will work, but you must, of course, transpose every instruction to its opposite so the chart shows only what the stitches will look like on the outside of the fabric.

If the written instructions specify that the pattern should start on an outside row, begin the chart in the bottom right-hand corner of the graph paper. If they specify starting with an inside row, begin in the bottom left-hand corner. This assures sufficient space for the pattern repeats. Write out the first row of the pattern with several repeats, then draw the lines and add the numbers at the bottom and two sides. When you have charted several vertical repeats, add the top line and then draw the interior lines around a single repeat, if you wish.

I recommend that you use graph paper of about four or five squares to an inch. Squares of that size are easy to write into, and with the chart next to you the symbols will be large enough to read as you knit. Even when a chart is provided in a commercial pattern, you might want to rewrite it in larger form to make it easier to work from, especially when it is in a magazine that does not lie flat and open. This also gives you the opportunity to make any changes in the chart, should you wish to do so. Work in pencil until you have the chart in finished form, and then either overwrite with a pen or make a new copy in ink. It is a good idea to write any explanatory comments regarding particular techniques that are problematic alongside the chart. Should you have any lengthy interruption in your work, these notes will be an invaluable aid to your memory. Slip the finished chart into a plastic sleeve so it stays in good shape for the duration of your project. When you are done, you may wish to file it, along with your sample and a yarn label, for future reference.

Charting Inside Rows

As I discussed above, charts customarily show only outside rows regardless of whether you are working flat or in the round. If the written pattern was designed for flat knitting, technically you could write one row of outside symbols and one row of inside symbols, just as given in the written instructions, but you would lose the visual clues that the charts provide about the appearance of the fabric, and it would no longer be suitable for knitting in the round. If you really find it difficult to work a flat fabric with only the information about the outside face available, chart the pattern as described above, then make a secondary chart to the left of the first that shows just the inside rows. The chart below shows what that would look like.

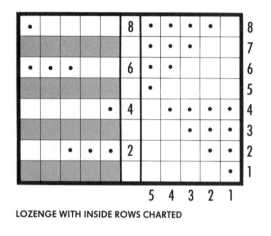

LOZENGE WITH INSIDE ROWS CHARTED

As you can see, every inside row has been transposed. The even-numbered rows in the main chart that would be read from left to right have been written on the same row in the second chart but from right to left, with all Knit symbols changed to Purl and all Purl symbols changed to Knit so they look as they will on the inside. Once done, every row can be read from right to left, just as you knit, outside rows from the right chart, inside rows from the left chart.

Most simple patterns such as this one are so quickly learned that you will probably not refer to the chart at all after one or two repeats, so it is highly unlikely that you would go to the trouble of making a double chart for something like this. However, simple as it is, it serves well to illustrate the principle, and should you find that you are making too many mistakes in working from a more complex chart, the concept may provide a solution to the problem you are having.

Stitch Techniques

With the general principles firmly in mind, let us now look at a variety of charts that illustrate the types of problems you might encounter in trying to convert written instructions to charted form.

Slip Stitch Charts

Here is a drawing of fabric being worked in a pattern with a grid superimposed on it so you can compare it with two charts, the first using the Slip Stitch symbol in the way I recommend, the second using it in a way common to other systems.

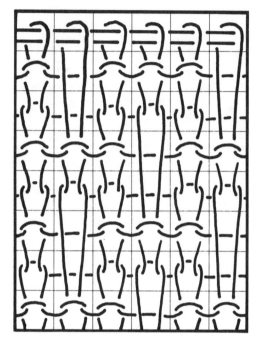

STRUCTURE OF THREE AND ONE STITCH

THREE AND ONE PATTERN

Three and One Stitch

Preparatory row (inside): Knit
Row 1: *K3, sl1yfs*, k1
Row 2: K1 *sl1yns, k3*
Row 3: *K1, sl1yfs, k2*, k1
Row 4: K1, *k2, sl1yns, k1*
Final row: Knit

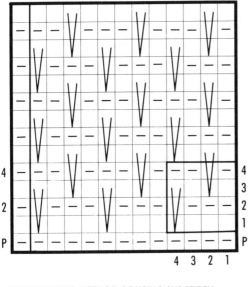

RECOMMENDED METHOD OF USING SLIP STITCH
SYMBOL

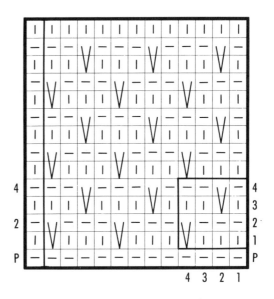

TRADITIONAL METHOD OF USING SLIP STITCH
SYMBOL

In this particular pattern, the stitch slipped in row 1 of column 4 is slipped again on the next row, and then finally Knit in row 3. In the first chart, when you encounter the square containing the bottom of the symbol, you are to slip the stitch in that column for the first time and continue to do so on each subsequent row until you come to the square containing the top of the symbol, at which point the Slip Stitch should be Knit. Notice that a single Purl stitch lies between the top of one Slip Stitch and the bottom of the next. This method of using the symbol precisely matches the fabric in both structure and appearance, indicating exactly how many rows the Slip Stitch spans and when the stitch is worked and discarded.

In the second chart of the same pattern, the Slip Stitch symbol only spans two rows, and on the row where the slipped stitch is finally worked, the pertinent square contains the symbol for Knit, meaning "Knit the slipped stitch." Thus what looks like two stitches, a Knit and a Purl, lie between the top of one Slip Stitch symbol and the bottom of the next. However, if you were to look at the fabric, you would find only the Purl stitch, because in this case the Knit symbol does not represent a separate stitch in that position, just an instruction to Knit and discard the Slip Stitch there. This can lead to confusion if you compare fabric to chart and causes many people to think they must be doing something wrong.

One of the advantages of using a symbol for Knit comes into play in transcribing a pattern using Slip Stitches. Because it may not be immediately obvious from the written instructions how far up the Slip Stitch will be carried, it is nice to leave the squares they occupy temporarily empty, only filling them in when you come to the row in which the stitch is finally worked. This

requires the use of a symbol for Knit so no ambiguity develops as you write. If, however, you prefer working from the other type of chart, use the Knit symbol for a rough draft, then rewrite the pattern without it.

The version of Three and One Stitch shown here was designed for an unseamed, flat fabric. If you were going to use the fabric on a pattern to be seamed, you would eliminate the edge stitch and add two selvedge stitches, one on each side, so when the fabrics were joined the sequence of stitches would be consistent. If you did not eliminate the edge stitch, there would be two columns of Garter Stitch side by side on either side of the join. For the same reason, the edge stitch should be eliminated if you plan to work the pattern in the round. If you were to use this pattern on the body of a sweater knit in the round, and then switch to working the upper bodice flat, you would want to retain three stitches of those you might otherwise cast off at the underarm, one to restore the edge stitch and two as selvedge stitches that will later be absorbed in the seams joining sleeves to armholes.

The chart for Three and One also has a preparatory and a final row, the equivalent of edge stitches in the other dimension; you will see these on some patterns, the former far more commonly than the latter. A preparatory row generally provides a baseline of plain stitches before the pattern commences, as it does here, or functions to prepare plain stitches to receive certain techniques on the next row and is never worked again. The final row here indicates only that no new stitches should be slipped beneath the cast-off edge. You will also notice that while row 1 is worked in exactly the same way on each repeat, it looks different the first time because there are no Slip Stitches being completed in that initial row.

Cable and Twist Stitches
The Cable stitch pattern shown next contains enough of that technique's wonderful variety to convey all the basic principles involved.

Close Braid Cable
  LC 2/1: Sl2sts to dpn, hold nearside, p1, k2 from dpn
  RC 2/1: Sl1st to dpn, hold farside, k2, p1 from dpn
  RC 2/2: Sl2sts to dpn, hold farside, k2, k2 from dpn
  LC 2/2: Sl2sts to dpn, hold nearside, k2, k2 from dpn

CLOSE BRAID CABLE

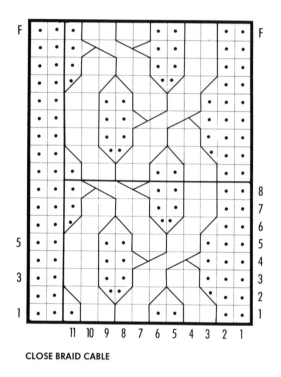

CLOSE BRAID CABLE

The pattern contains 2/1 and 2/2 Cable units going both left and right. Notice that the 2/1 Cables call for the facing stitches to be in Knit and the backing stitch to be in Purl. The first example is the Left Cross in Row 2, where stitches 3 and 4 are held nearside, stitch 5 is drawn across to column 3 and Purled, then 3 and 4 are drawn over to columns 4 and 5 and Knit.

Charts for these patterns generally use the dot for Purl and a blank square for Knit so the path of the stitches can be clearly seen. The vertical lines drawn between one Cable and the next are optional and serve only to define the columns of Knit stitches. There is no necessity to draw these lines, and some charts do not, but as you can see, it provides such a clear picture of the pattern that it is a nice touch. They should be ignored as you knit, as they do not convey an instruction of any sort.

Because it is a vertical panel pattern, no additional stitch repeat is necessary (although it could certainly be used that way), but two row repeats are given so the relationship between the top of one repeat and the bottom of the next can be seen clearly. Once the pattern is charted, it becomes evident that you could start on row 3, 5, or 7 as easily as on row 1, which might be necessary in some situations in order to balance the pattern on the fabric or in relation to other patterns (see "Coordinating Stitch and Garment Patterns," page 525).

Two edge stitches are included here to balance the pattern. If the Cable is to be used as a repeat across the width of a fabric to be seamed, selvedge stitches are optional. If they are used, the edge stitches will have to be eliminated or you would wind up with a four-stitch column of Purl, two stitches on either side of the seam. The same holds true if you are working in the round. If selvedge stitches are not used, one Purl stitch at the beginning and end of the rows will be eliminated, leaving a two-stitch column of Purl between two cables, which would look as it should, but the width of the fabric would be reduced.

Twist Stitch Medallion: Here is an example of a Twist Stitch pattern that causes columns of stitches to "travel" across the face of the fabric just like a Cable does.

Row 1:   *K3, p1, k3*
Row 2:   *P3, k1, p3*
Row 3:   *K1, RT, p1, LT, k1*
Row 4:   *P2, k3, p2*
Row 5:   *RT, p3, LT*
Row 6:   *P1, k5, p1*
Row 7:   *K1, p5, k1*
Row 8:   Row 6
Row 9:   *LT, p3, RT*
Row 10:   Row 4
Row 11: *K1, LT, p1, RT, k1*
Row 12:   Row 2

TWIST STITCH MEDALLION

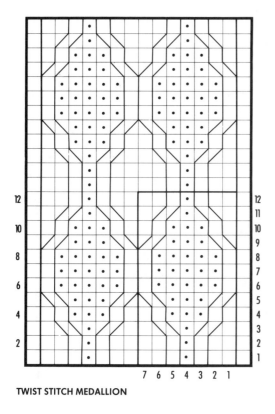

TWIST STITCH MEDALLION

Because a Twist Stitch rarely contains more than two stitches, in this chart I have eliminated the little hatch marks that refer to the backing stitches. The symbol is quite clear without them when the vertical lines are used to show how the columns of Knit travel between one Twist and the next. This pattern requires edge stitches on both sides in order to maintain its appearance.

For contrast, I include a chart of just one motif of the pattern done with the written symbol for Knit, the dash for Purl, and the alternate symbol for the Cable. To my mind it is visually cluttered and hard to decipher. Simplicity is the ideal.

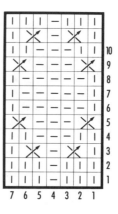

ALTERNATE CHART FOR TWIST STITCH MEDALLION

Bias Twist Fabric: Here are two charts for another type of Twist Stitch pattern, which allow comparison between the recommended Cable symbol and the alternate.

The one using the Cable symbol is a bit cluttered but looks very much like what the fabric will. However, the arrow symbol is quick and easy to write, and because the chart is of such a simple pattern, easy enough to read. If you are writing a pattern of this sort only for your own use, or as a rough draft just to see how it works, you might want to use the arrows.

Notice that because the pattern elements are staggered on each pair of rows, the lines defining the stitch repeat must jog. This necessitates an extra edge stitch at the beginning and end of row 4. In a written pattern, row 2 would read *Rtw* and row 4 would read *K1* *RTw* *k1*.

Combining Symbols

Twilled Stripe uses an interesting technique that combines a Slip Stitch and a Twist Stitch. There is no particular symbol for this technique, nor need there be, as it is rarely seen, but standard ones used in an adaptive way serve very well to convey exactly what is required, particularly when keyed to a note, as illustrated here.

Twilled Stripe: Left Slip Twist: Knit the second stitch farside, Slip the first stitch and then discard the second.

I have provided only a single stitch repeat for space considerations, but you can see that the pattern could be used either as a single column with other stitch patterns, or as a repeat for an allover vertical stripe effect, in which case you would eliminate the two edge stitches.

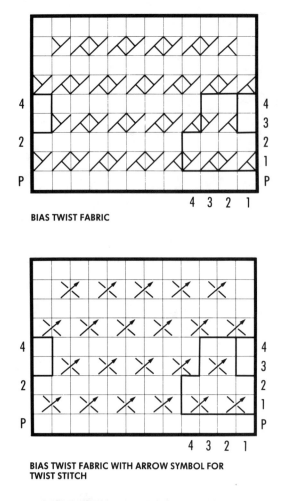

BIAS TWIST FABRIC

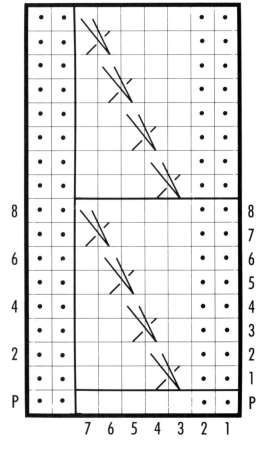

BIAS TWIST FABRIC WITH ARROW SYMBOL FOR TWIST STITCH

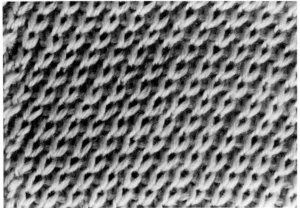

BIAS TWIST FABRIC

TWILLED STRIPE

English Diamond Quilting: In this pattern, the Slip Stitch is carried over five rows and then cabled. The first chart, which uses just an arrow to show how the Slip Stitch is to be cabled, is the simplest and easiest to write and to read, and simplicity is always a great virtue.

In the second, the Slip Stitch symbol rides up into the Cable symbol; it reads well enough but is a bit busy. Neither of these resemble the appearance of the finished fabric.

In the third chart, the Slip Stitch symbols slope just

TWILLED STRIPE

ENGLISH DIAMOND QUILTING

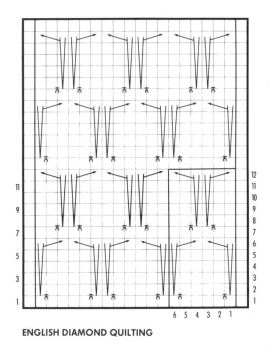

ENGLISH DIAMOND QUILTING

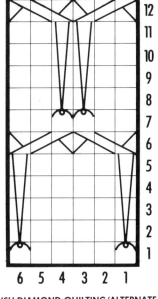

ENGLISH DIAMOND QUILTING/ALTERNATE SYMBOL

as they will in the fabric, but one must understand that in all rows prior to the Cable technique, these stitches are actually being slipped in the empty columns 2 and 7, while all the other stitches are being Knit. With an explanatory note adjacent to the chart, it would be perfectly clear what to do.

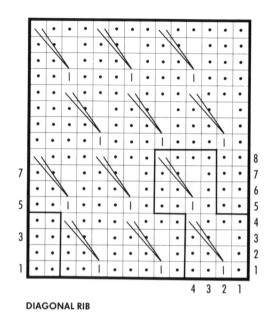

DIAGONAL RIB

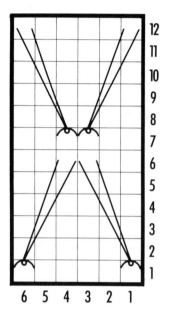

ENGLISH DIAMOND QUILTING/ALTERNATE SYMBOL

As an added bit of information, notice that in the first chart a Yarnover is made on row 1 and dropped on row 2; this is an elongation device for the Slip Stitch, to help it stretch as far as it needs to go. In the second chart, the Slip Stitch is elongated with a Double Wrap on the stitch below instead. This serves the same purpose but provides slightly more yarn than the first method; it depends on your materials and tension which will produce the better-looking fabric.

Diagonal Rib: Here is an illustration of an alternative method of handling this sort of problem, and in this case, no Cable symbol of any kind is used. Is it clear to you what is at work? The pattern uses cabled Slip Stitches on a Purl ground to create a diagonal rib. The stitch in column 1 is slipped on rows 2 and 3, then cabled past two Purled background stitches on row 4.

You will encounter these and other variations on the theme in charts you come across, and should be able to recognize that they all convey the same type of information. When charting your own pattern, you will have to decide whether it is more helpful to have precise instructions for each and every square as you work or whether you prefer to see the overall effect.

DIAGONAL RIB

Charts Containing Increase and Decrease Symbols

As you know, increase and decrease techniques frequently cause the columns of stitches to shift into new positions. If an increase and a decrease are paired side by side, they will cause no change, and all the adjacent columns of stitches will remain vertical. If an increase and a decrease are paired but separated by other stitches, they will cause bias in the direction of the decrease. If an increase and a decrease are paired but separated by rows, they will not only cause bias but a temporary change in the stitch count on the needle.

Because the stitches start to shift about, the relationship of some of the symbols to those above and below is less straightforward. As one knits, reference is constantly being made to the appearance of the stitches directly below the left needle as a check to see that a given technique is being worked in the correct position. One goal in writing these charts, therefore, is to find ways to maintain the symbol for each stitch directly above the symbol for the stitch it will be worked on, or when that is not possible, to indicate clearly the direction of the shift. Having the symbols lined up in this way on the chart both helps you to keep your place and makes the chart look as much like the fabric as possible.

In charts containing increases and decreases, the most common convention is to have all of these symbols occupy a single square regardless of how many stitches may be added or removed. Yarnover and Running Thread Increases are also given squares of their own, despite the fact that they are inserted between two stitches. However inconsistent this may be, it works reasonably well to knit from, particularly with the lace patterns for which it was primarily devised, although it frequently does not match the structure or appearance of the fabric. In comparing all the possible ways of conveying the technical and visual information a chart should contain, more often than not the most successful version was one where the symbol for every type of increase was expanded somewhat to touch the squares it affects, while the decrease symbols were confined to a single square. This is true because of what actually happens in the fabric.

Decreases

When you encounter a decrease symbol on a chart, you must work two or more stitches together and discard them all in one position, so it makes sense to have the symbol itself in just one square. The arms of the symbol point down toward the columns of stitches that will be joined, making it quite clear which stitches are involved and what the effect in the fabric will be. The top of the symbol points up at the square that will be occupied by the single new stitch when it is discarded in the row above.

Stitch Increases

An increase is just the opposite, and the symbol must instruct you to make several new, neutral stitches, while only one will be discarded. Therefore, the base of the increase symbol representing the discard stitch should occupy the square in the column of stitches the technique will be worked on. The arms extending up representing new stitches should point toward the squares they affect in the row above. In doing so, they necessarily cross over adjacent squares, which are generally available by virtue of the fact that decreases somewhere else have freed them up by removing a comparable number of stitches. While this must not be construed to suggest that the new stitches exist on that row of the fabric, it does match the change wrought on the discard stitch and very effectively sets up the bias that begins to take place in the fabric. A Raised Stitch Increase, for instance, brings a stitch up into the discard row that wasn't there before, and a Bar Increase makes it look as if a second stitch exists.

Between-Stitch Increases

The Running Thread Increase and the Yarnover are special cases because they are inserted between two columns of stitches. Keep in mind that generally the squares tell us what to do to the next stitch on the left needle and what the discard stitch will look like within the fabric. With these two techniques, we are not being asked to do anything to an existing stitch, yet we must put a symbol somewhere to instruct us what to do. When a new stitch is worked on a running thread, the strand is discarded in that position, so the square is legitimately occupied. With a Yarnover, however, a strand, the equivalent of a new stitch, is placed on the right needle, but nothing whatsoever is discarded. The square must serve to tell us instead that there is a hole in the fabric. The strand itself will not be discarded until the next row, and will therefore occupy the square above the one where we were instructed to make the Yarnover.

Most charting systems insert the Yarnover symbol in the position where you must pass the yarn over the needle and place some other symbol in the square above to indicate how the strand should be worked and discarded on the next row. Unfortunately, this makes it look as if there is an extra stitch above the strand, and leaves the hole smaller on the chart than it is in the fabric. The new symbol that I have devised for Yarnover works on exactly the same principle as the Slip Stitch discussed above, spanning the rows involved. When you encounter the square containing the bottom of this symbol, you are to understand that you must pass the yarn over the needle; when you encounter the top of the symbol, you will know that you are to work into a Yarnover strand rather than a normal stitch, and that it is discarded in that position.

However, there are instances when this new Yarnover symbol does not work well. This is particularly true in those mesh patterns where Yarnovers are worked in the same position on every row and it is impossible to write the symbol into two squares. Also, there are some lace patterns with a great many Yarnovers set fairly closely together, and these can look cluttered with the symbol that covers two squares. Use whichever one suits you. As long as you keep in mind the true relationship between the symbol and the structure in the fabric, the traditional symbol works very well. If you prefer to have the chart look more realistic, or have it clear just which stitches are normal ones and which are Yarnovers as you work, then by all means use the new symbol.

Let's look at how all of this theory works in practice.

Paired Increases and Decreases

Many Lace patterns, and all of the Eyelet patterns, make use of increases and decreases that are paired, one next to the other.

Elfin Lace: Here is a drawing of a fabric worked in an Eyelet pattern with single and double decreases and Yarnover increases placed side by side, each balancing the other so that no bias is created. A grid has been superimposed on the fabric to help you compare it with the two charts provided, one that uses the traditional Yarnover symbol, the other the symbol I recommend. I think you will agree that the chart with the new symbol more correctly matches both what is occurring as you knit, and what happens within the fabric.

Also notice that this is another example of a chart in which the stitch-repeat lines must jog because the

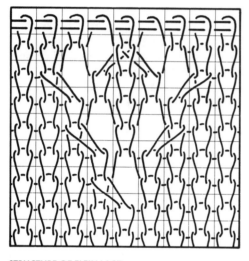

STRUCTURE OF ELFIN LACE

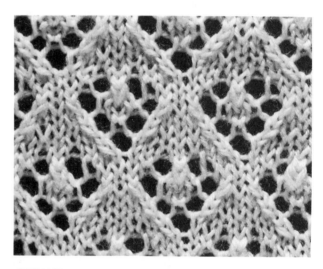

ELFIN LACE

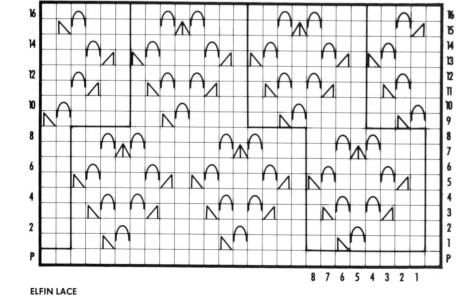

ELFIN LACE

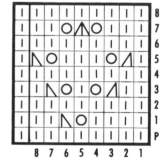

ELFIN LACE USING TRADITIONAL YARNOVER SYMBOL

pattern elements are staggered. Because of this offset, the left half of a motif is used to fill in as edge stitches, which begin rows 9 through 16, and the right half of a motif ends these rows. There are also two edge stitches necessary on the left side of rows 1 through 8, which help accommodate the half motif above them so the pattern begins and ends in a balanced way.

All the technical questions aside, probably the most important thing to notice here is just how simple a chart makes a lace pattern look, and in fact this lovely lace is very easy to do. I'm sure many people avoid lace knitting only because the written instructions look so daunting, and that is in most cases very misleading. If charts do nothing more than persuade people that lace is within their abilities, they will have earned their keep.

Bias Patterns

Now let's look at several stitch patterns in which the increases and decreases are separated by intervening stitches, creating bias.

Track of the Turtle: The first chart has Yarnovers and decreases separated by four stitches that will travel first to the left, then to the right, always leaning toward the decreases. The stitches at each side are also affected by the shaping units, and will be pulled into a soft curve,

first pushed away by the Yarnovers and then pulled back in by the converging line of decreases.

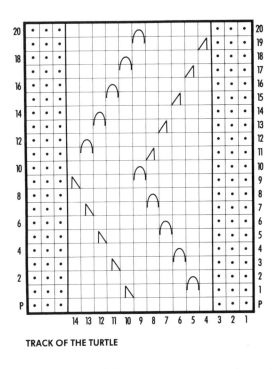

TRACK OF THE TURTLE

TRACK OF THE TURTLE

Chevron Fantastic: Next is a stitch pattern that contains bias, but which uses increases other than a Yarnover. This is a very nice, tailored pattern that could be dressed up, if you wish, by changing the Multiple Raised Stitch Increase shown to a Multiple Yarnover Increase. The decrease can be worked right, left, or center, but while there would be negligible difference between the first two, the latter would change the appearance of the pattern considerably.

Slip Chevron: Here is a related pattern, which I designed with a fancy Multiple Running Thread Increase just so you can see how clear even a complex instruction

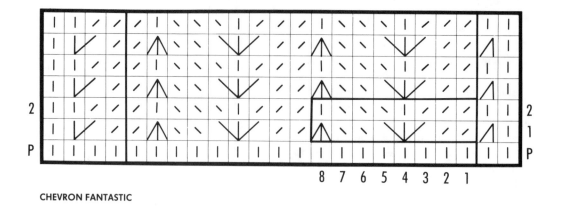

CHEVRON FANTASTIC

CHEVRON FANTASTIC

can be. Very small changes in arrangement or technique often result in strikingly different effects, and knowing this should inspire you to design your own patterns.

Changing Stitch Counts

When you transcribe a pattern in which the stitch count changes row by row, you will encounter some anomalies that make the instructions difficult to chart, and the chart difficult to decipher. You may have to write it in several different versions until it really makes sense and looks good. In some cases, the solution to the problem lies in an unorthodox use of a conventional symbol.

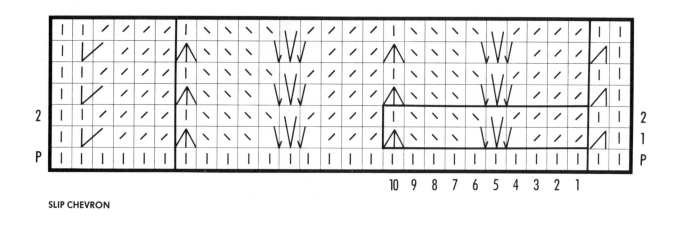

SLIP CHEVRON

SLIP CHEVRON

More often than not, however, it rests on the use of blank squares, squares that contain no symbol at all, that indicate precisely where stitches are temporarily missing.

Pique Lace: The first draft of this pattern is a direct transcription from the written instructions, done the traditional way with circles for the Yarnover. As you can see, things don't line up in a recognizable way. When you make the initial chart of something like this, and a row winds up shorter or longer than the one below, you will know the stitch count has changed, although you must make sure you haven't left anything out or added something that shouldn't be there; keep checking accuracy as you work. When this occurs, always place the first symbol of the next row directly above the last one of the row below, letting the edges go where they will. The four blank squares at the end of rows 6 and 7 tell you that there are two stitches missing in each of those rows, throwing off the relationship to all of the stitches on the rows above and below.

PIQUE LACE

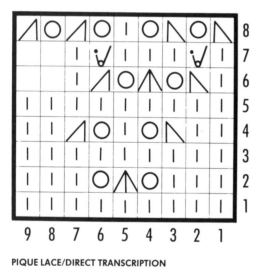

PIQUE LACE/DIRECT TRANSCRIPTION

In order to get the chart to make more sense, you must analyze what has happened so you can rewrite it with the symbol for each stitch above the one of the stitch it will be worked on. As you begin to rewrite the chart, for each stitch ask yourself where the stitch is in the row below that this one must be worked on. Notice that in row 6 four stitches are removed with a double and two single decreases. These four stitches are replaced by two single Yarnovers, which then have increases worked on them in the next row to restore the stitch count. The second chart has been rewritten with the new symbol for Yarnover, each expanded over the two squares of the stitches it replaces. Now the pattern makes visual as well as technical sense. Edge stitches have been added so the pattern can be used either as a repeat or as a column.

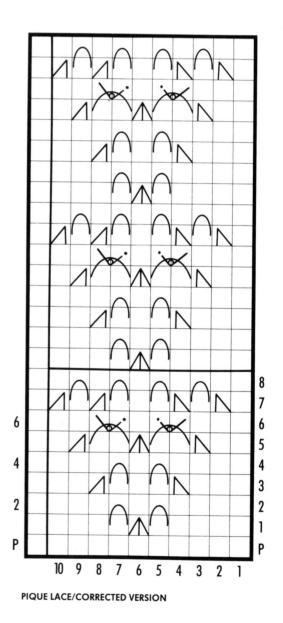

PIQUE LACE/CORRECTED VERSION

Embossed Patterns

With these types of patterns, the stitch count on any given row can change radically. The solution to the problems this presents lies with the placement of the blank squares representing stitches that are temporarily missing. There are two approaches to consider, the choice being a matter of what seems to work best for you.

Crown Embossed Rosebud: Here is a pretty pattern where the stitch count changes with a vengeance. The instructions call for casting on just eight stitches for each repeat; however, notice that the number of squares used in the chart is determined by the largest number of stitches in any row of the pattern, the count between rows 4 and 6. In a situation like this where the embossed motif is dominant and the background completely subordinate, blank squares can be used to indicate precisely how and where those changes occur.

Yo5 = Elongated Yarnover/wrap five times
YOinc5 = Multiple Yarnover Increase five stitches

Row 1: K3, p2, k3
Row 2: P3, sl next st to dpn, hold ns, k1, yo5, k1 from dpn, p3
Row 3: K3, p1, YOinc5, p1, k3
Row 4: P3, 6(k1, yo), k1, p3

Row 5: K3, p13, k3
Row 6: P3, k13, p3
Row 7: K3, p2tog, p9, SSP, k3
Row 8: P3, SSK, k7, k2tog, p3
Row 9: K3, p2tog, p5, SSP, k3
Row 10: P3, SSK, k3, k2tog, p3
Row 11: K3, p2tog, p1, SSP, k3
Row 12: P3, k1, k2tog, p3

In this first version of the chart, the blank squares necessitated by the missing stitches are placed between the motif and the background, thus maintaining every stitch symbol above the one it will be worked into. As you work from the chart, simply ignore the blank squares, skipping past them to read the next symbol to the left or right. Because your eye must travel over these distances, you may find it easier to read the chart if you place a ruler beneath the row you are currently working on.

Drawn as it is, the chart does not convey the information that the motif is actually resting on a background of Purl stitches. The only blank square still within the pattern is the one at the base of the motif, and this is necessitated by the fact that the pattern changes from an even to an odd number of stitches.

The increase at the base of the motif is an unusual one and provides another example of how charting sym-

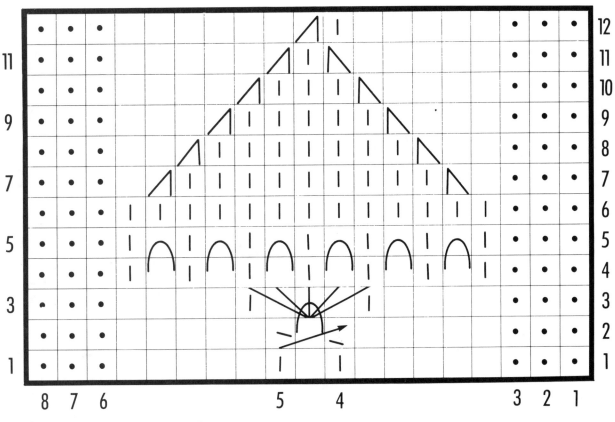

CROWN EMBOSSED ROSEBUD/VERSION ONE

bols can be used to define a technique for which no symbol exists. This is a combination of a 1/1 Right Cable with a Yarnover at the center. The regular Cable symbol would leave no room for the Yarnover symbol, so I have replaced it with the arrows that are sometimes used for Twist Stitch. In the next row, five stitches are worked on the strand using a Multiple Yarnover Increase. I find the symbol clear and explicit as it stands, but it is always wise in the case of esoteric techniques like this to key the symbol to a note giving written instructions.

I think this next version of the same pattern is a far more accurate picture of what is happening as you knit. The blank squares now lie between the pattern and the perimeter of the chart and the background stitches follow the contours of the motif. While this version is far more accurate visually than the one above, still it looks like the Purl background shifts, when in reality it stays pretty much in position while the motif puffs out with the extra stitches. Perfection escapes us, as it is wont to do; nevertheless, I think this would be the easier to work from and looks the most like the fabric will.

If you wanted to treat this vertical panel pattern as a repeat, it would consist of the first five stitches. Stitches 6 through 8 would then become edge stitches, used only at the left side of the fabric to balance things off.

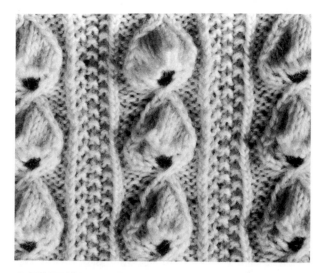

CROWN EMBOSSED ROSEBUD

Where the embossed motif is one element among many, the above solutions to the problem of change in the stitch count do not work as well; a more successful alternative is to use a mini-chart, shown in the following example.

Teardrop Pendant: Here is a bold pattern containing an embossed motif set on a background of Seed Stitch, the whole outlined with Twist and Crossed

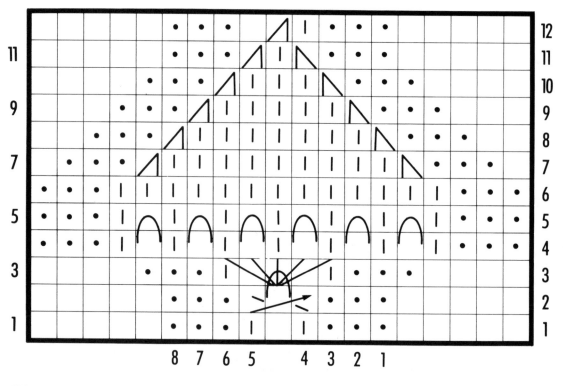

CROWN EMBOSSED ROSEBUD/VERSION TWO

stitches. In the first version, the blank squares are set between the motif and the background, which makes the pattern visually disjointed, and you must constantly shift your eyes from one side to the other as you work. In a pattern such as this it is not possible to set the blank squares out at the perimeter without distorting the background, which is complex in its own right.

The second version makes use of a mini-chart below, showing just the pattern for the embossed motif and a box within the chart that indicates where the motif is positioned. The motif is an easy pattern to learn when you see it set out this way, and once learned you need only refer to the main chart as you work. In addition, with the pattern for the motif set to one side in this manner, the pattern for the background falls into place and the whole becomes visually clear.

The general rule governing these situations is that if the motif is simple and the background complex, set the motif to one side. If they are both complex, or just the motif is, retain the motif within the pattern and use blank squares.

Exchange Motifs

Exchange Motifs are filled with stitches that shift back and forth, and because of this they are often the most difficult patterns of all to chart. Here is a wonderful example, which also includes some Eyelets and Bobbles.

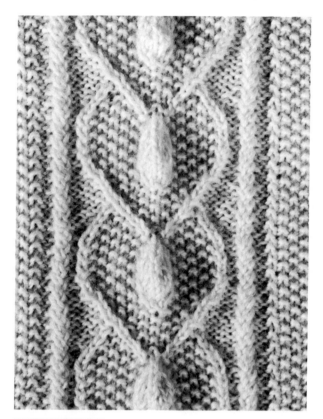

TEARDROP PENDANT

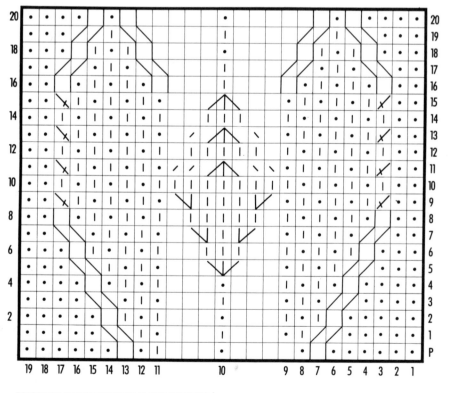

TEARDROP PENDANT USING BLANK SQUARES

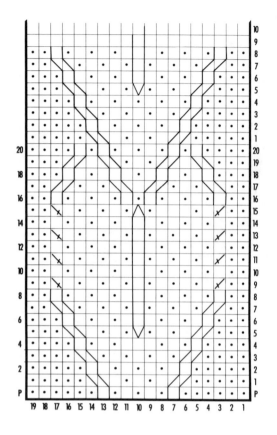

Row 9: *P1, k3, LDec2, k3, p1, k1, 2(yo, k1) *p1
Row 10: Row 4
Row 11: *P1, k2, LDec2, k2, p1, k2, yo, k1, yo, k2, *p1
Row 12: Row 2
Row 13: *P1, k1, LDec2, k1, p1, k3, yo, k1, yo, k3, *p1
Row 14: K1, *p4, YOinc5, p4, k1, p3, k1*
Row 15: *P1, k3, p1, k4, p5, k4,* p1
Row 16: K1, *p4, p5tog, p4, k1, p3, k1*

Charting a pattern of this sort is always a two- or three-step process. The first chart is a direct transcription from the written instructions, done without regard to whether or not a symbol for a stitch is above that of the one it will be worked on. As you can see, while this chart is technically correct, it makes very little sense visually.

The box contains a five-stitch Bobble worked over three rows (shown above). The specific instructions can be contained in a mini-chart, but if it is simple, as this one is, it is possible to use a single symbol in one square of the box to refer to how all of the extra stitches in that position should be worked.

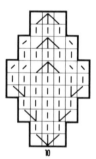

TEARDROP PENDANT WITH MINI-CHART

Mist Drops

LDec2 = Left Double Decrease/sl2kw, k1, p2sso
YOinc 5 = Multiple Yarnover Increase five stitches

Row 1: *P1, k1, 2(yo, k1), p1 k3, LDec2, k3,* p1
Row 2: K1, *p7, k1, p5, k1*
Row 3: *P1, k2, yo, k1, yo, k2, p1, k2, LDec2, k2,* p1
Row 4: K1, *p5, k1, p7, k1*
Row 5: *P1, k3, yo, k1, yo, k3, p1, k1, LDec2, k1,* p1
Row 6: K1, *p3, k1, p4, YOinc5, p4, k1*
Row 7: *P1, k4, p5, k4, p1, k3,* p1
Row 8: K1, *p3, k1, p4, p5tog, p4, k1

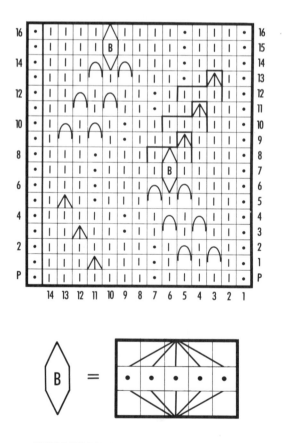

MIST DROPS/DIRECT TRANSCRIPTION WITH MINI-CHART

Once you have the direct transcription, analyze it for exactly how the increase or decrease techniques cause stitches to shift. Working from the top down, figure out which stitches are supposed to be on top of each other, encircling some groups as I have here if necessary to make things clear. In patterns of this type, usually there will be staggered motifs of some sort separated by a few background stitches. Most often the motif consists of a few rows of paired increases and then a few rows of paired decreases, which flank a pivot column of stitches at the center. I have outlined those stitches on the chart to help you learn to identify them.

On another piece of paper, copy out the stitches of just the motif, working out from the pivot stitch to either side. A chart in progress is shown to give you an idea of how that is done. As you recopy the motif, you might want to use hatch marks on each square affected by bias to show exactly where a particular stitch will travel to in the row above. Once the motif is complete, fill in the background stitches. It should then make sense how the other motifs fit alongside the first, and you can write them into their proper places in turn. Be careful on any row where the stitch count changes; this may

simply scallop the edge, which is no problem as the blank spaces will be at the perimeter, but it might indicate an embossing effect within the pattern, in which case you will have to use empty squares within. When this occurs, most often it will fall between motifs or between a motif and its background.

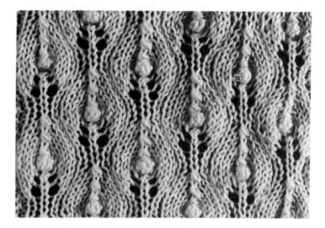

MIST DROPS

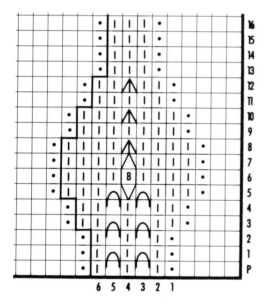

MIST DROPS/INTERMEDIATE CHART

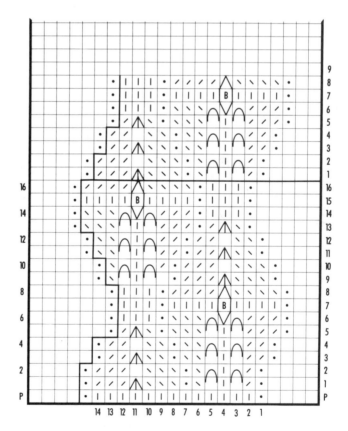

MIST DROPS/CORRECTED CHART

Straightening a Scalloped Edge

What if you didn't want the edges of the fabric to scallop? All you would have to do is fill the blank squares that lie between the stitch pattern and the perimeter of the chart with edge stitches consisting of either a half motif or plain Knit. In some stitch patterns employing multiple increases or decreases, you may be required to substitute a technique that removes or adds only half as many stitches.

Here are two versions of Berry Stitch that nicely illustrate that sort of change. In the first version, the edges scallop, but in the second the scallop has been filled in by single increases and decreases. Charts make it easy to see how to alter patterns in this way. Notice also that I have arbitrarily expanded the symbols for the decreases as well, just because I like the way it looks in a cluster pattern such as this.

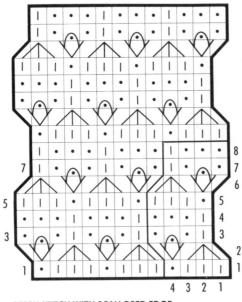

BERRY STITCH WITH SCALLOPED EDGE

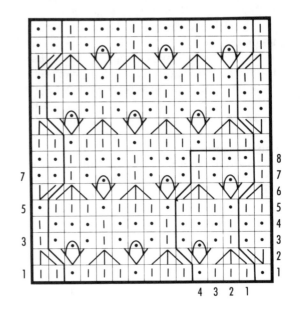

BERRY STITCH WITH STRAIGHT EDGE

BERRY STITCH

Honeycomb Patterns

Let's turn our attention now to charts for the Honeycomb-type patterns. These patterns can be done using either of two entirely different techniques, the Knit Below or a Slip Stitch/Yarnover worked together on the next row (see pages 29 and 85). The two methods look so different in a written pattern that it is difficult to tell that they produce the identical stitch. Conventional charting systems typically use one of two symbols for the Knit Below technique, the one shown here in the first example, or a downward pointing arrow. Previously, no symbol existed for the other method of working.

Honeycomb Rib

Prep: Purl
Subsequent rows: K2 *k1bel, k1*

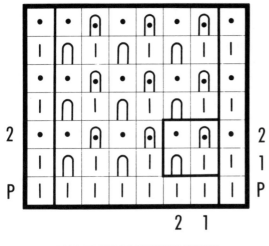

HONEYCOMB RIB WITH TRADITIONAL SYMBOL

This is very clear, very easy to read, but it conveys absolutely nothing of what the fabric will look like.

Here is the exact same pattern, rewritten for the alternate method and using the new Honeycomb symbol in the chart. The chart can now be used for either method of making the stitch, and also has a clear relationship to the structure and appearance of the fabric.

Yon = yarn over needle

Prep: K1 *yns sl1 yon, k1* k1
Subsequent rows: K1 *yns sl1 yon, k2tog* k1
Final: K1 *p1, k2tog*k1

If you are using the latter method, work the Yarnover/Slip Stitch when you come to the bottom of the symbol and work the decrease that joins them when you come to the top of the symbol on the next row. Should you wish to use this chart for the former method, when you come to the square containing the base of the sym-

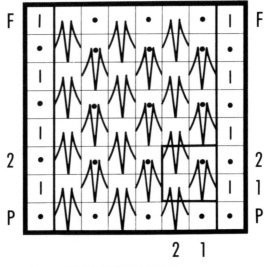

HONEYCOMB RIB WITH NEW SYMBOL

HONEYCOMB RIB

bol you would Knit or Purl a stitch (it doesn't matter which), then use the Knit Below technique when you encounter the top of the symbol in the next row.

It is possible to use the traditional Yarnover, Slip Stitch and Decrease symbols to chart a Honeycomb pattern, but as you can see in the small example given, it is extremely cluttered and hard to read.

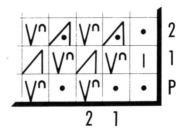

HONEYCOMB RIB WITH OTHER SYMBOLS

There are a few Honeycomb patterns in which the Knit Below method cannot be used, and which require either a modification of the symbol or a reliance on a combination of conventional symbols for each step.

In this chart for a pattern of that type, you will notice that the Slip Stitches, which were made at the same time as the Yarnover, are knitted alone on the next row, while the Yarnover is slipped in turn. The decrease joins the Yarnover strand with the stitch made on the Slip Stitch.

Waffle Brioche

Slyo = slip the yarnover

Prep: K2 *yns sl1 yon, k1*
Row 1: *K2, slyo* k2
Row 2: K1 *yns sl1 yon, k2tog* k1
Row 3: K1 *k2, slyo* k1
Row 4: K1 *k2tog, yns sl1 yon* k1
Two final rows:
Row 1: Repeat Row 1
Row 2: K1 *k1, k2tog* k1

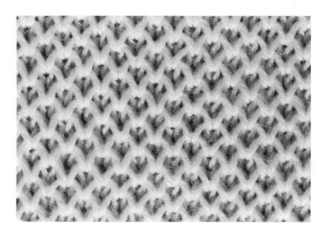

WAFFLE BRIOCHE

stitch and how the two should be handled in the decrease that joins them. Because of the complexity of the technique, it would be helpful to include some written instructions that describe what is required.

The second chart of the same pattern contains the conventional symbols. This makes each step perfectly clear, although the chart is very busy and it does not resemble the fabric.

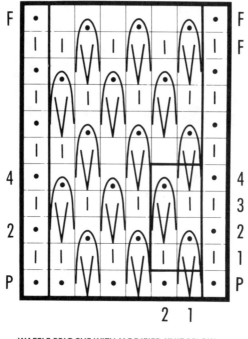

WAFFLE BRIOCHE WITH MODIFIED KNIT BELOW SYMBOL

In order to use the Honeycomb symbol to show what must be done, instead of the two little "tails" representing just the sides of the Yarnover strand, the full Yarnover symbol is used, stretching from the square where it originates to where it is finally discarded. A Knit or Purl symbol within the top of the Yarnover symbol is used to indicate the presence of the other

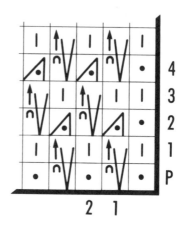

WAFFLE BRIOCHE WITH OTHER SYMBOLS

Pullover Patterns

Last but not least in the category of increase/decrease patterns are those that use the Pullover techniques. These are generally far simpler patterns than those looked at above, but there are quite a variety of techniques that create much the same effect, and the arrangement of symbols used to describe them can be fairly complex. There are two basic types of Pullover. In one a stitch is used for the Pullover, which is then compensated for by an increase that may be placed within the Pullover, before or after it, or even on the next row. In the other, some kind of increase is used for the Pullover, which therefore balances itself off. For space considerations, most of the examples given will be small partial charts showing just the technique rather than whole stitch patterns. The important thing to notice is that the Pullover symbol lies *above* the discard stitches, at the base of the new stitches, as this is what will occur in the fabric. Note that in the abbreviations used, psso (pull Slip Stitch over), p1o3, or some similar notation = pull one stitch over three others.

Stitch Pullovers: The large chart is Small Quilted Cross Stitch, which uses a Slip Stitch Pullover replaced on the same row with a Rib Increase (. . . sl1 Ribinc k1 p1o3 . . .).

SMALL QUILTED CROSS STITCH

SMALL QUILTED CROSS STITCH

In the group of small charts, the first has a Running Thread Increase preceding a Pullover done with a stitch slipped purlwise (. . . RThinc, sl1 k2 psso . . .).

RUNNING THREAD PULLOVER

The next shows a Yarnover Increase replacing a Pullover done with a new stitch. The Yarnover symbol arches over the stitch below, which indicates clearly both where it originates and that it replaces the stitch that had been in the column (. . . yo, k3 p1o2 . . .).

STITCH PULLOVER

The next example also shows a Yarnover replacing a Stitch Pullover, but this time it is the last of the group encircled by the stitch (. . . k2 yo p1o2 . . .). In a pattern where the Yarnover lies to the left but is not included in the Pullover, the hook would lie under the Yarnover symbol.

STITCH PULLOVER

And finally, an example in which the Pullover stitch is slipped knitwise and the compensating Yarnover doesn't occur until the next row (1: . . . sl1kw k2 psso . . . 2: . . . p2, yo . . .).

SLIP STITCH PULLOVER

Increase Pullovers: The large chart shows Diagonal Scallop, a pattern in which the Running Thread is lifted onto the needle and used as a Pullover (. . . RThinc k2 p1o2 . . .).

The first small chart indicates a Running Thread Increase (. . . RThinc k2 p1o2 . . .); in the second one, a Yarnover is used (. . . yo k3 p1o3 . . .).

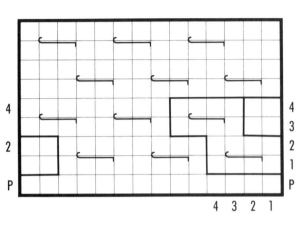

DIAGONAL SCALLOP

RUNNING THREAD INCREASE PULLOVER

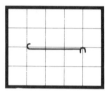

YARNOVER PULLOVER

DIAGONAL SCALLOP

When attempting to transcribe written instructions to charted form, you will find that the Increase Pullovers are the simplest to deal with; the challenge lies with the Stitch Pullovers, because stitch columns may shift. Keep in mind the distinction between new and discard stitches, pay particular attention to where each new stitch must be placed, and be willing to use the symbols creatively. Once you get the general idea of how several symbols can be combined to convey the particular technique required, you should have no trouble reading or writing any of these charts.

If you are working in the round, you may encounter problems, although not unsurmountable ones, with those few stitch patterns which call for a Pullover on the inside of the fabric. The chart of Open Star Stitch is of this type; you can see that the hook portion of the symbol lies to the right instead of to the left. If you analyze this pattern, you will see that it was written the way it is so it can be worked flat entirely in Knit, and I can't see that it would make much difference if you simply turned the entire Pullover unit around for a circular version. If the pattern had called for a Slip Stitch Pullover instead, you could pull a stitch from the left needle over and then knit the encircled stitches, working the appropriate increase before or after as called for.

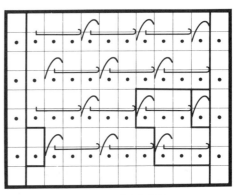

OPEN STAR/CHART FOR FLAT KNITTING

OPEN STAR PATTERN UNIT TURNED FOR CIRCULAR KNITTING

Stranded Brocade Patterns

Stranded Brocade charting is discussed in the section on color charts (page 504), because even though these patterns can be done in a solid color, the technique used is the same as that for handling two yarns.

OPEN STAR

Charting Color Patterns

Most color knitting charts that you will encounter are for Stranded and Intarsia patterns, although these are not the only methods of handling color in a knitted fabric. The principles upon which these charts are based are so matter of fact they require little explanation; nevertheless, it is important to make them explicit in order to understand how to read and write charts for more complex techniques.

Stranded and Intarsia Color Charts

In any standard color chart, such as the one shown here, one square on the graph paper represents one stitch, just as in stitch pattern charts, and they are read in the same way, from the bottom up and from right to left on outside rows, left to right on inside rows. However, there the similarities end.

On a stitch pattern chart, as I mentioned before,

each row contains information about what to do to the neutral stitches on the left needle and what the result will look like when these stitches are discarded. If you check your work to see if you have done the right thing, you will look at the stitches lying beneath the right needle. However, Stranded or Intarsia patterns are generally done exclusively in Stockinette, and information about what to do to the stitches is quite unimportant. The information you do need from the chart is what color yarn to hold as you work a given stitch. Therefore, on these charts each row conveys information about what color the *new, neutral stitches* on the right needle will be, and that is where you will look to check your work. To put it another way, whereas with a stitch pattern chart you must imagine your left needle above the row you are reading, in this case, imagine your right needle on the row you are reading. As you will see, this is an important distinction between the two types of charts.

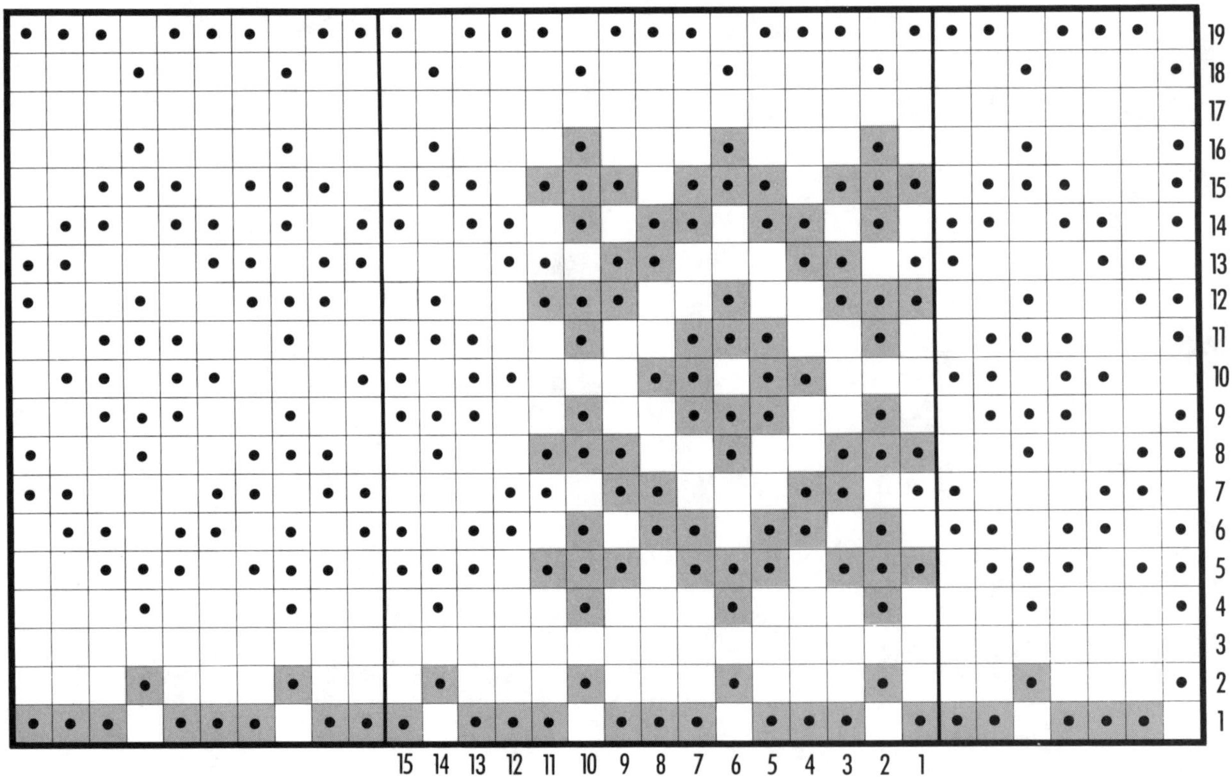

TYPICAL CHART FOR STRANDED COLOR PATTERN

Because no stitch symbols are required for these charts, the squares contain only information about what color to use. The background color is usually indicated by empty squares and the contrast-color stitches by either a darkened square or, if more than one pattern color is being used in addition to the background color, by symbols of some sort, such as A and B, or something like a dot for one and an x for the other. If a commercial pattern is printed in black and white, you may wish to fill in the squares with colors similar to those with which you will actually knit in order to get a better idea of how the pattern will look. Coloring the pattern gives you the opportunity to play with a variety of color combinations other than what might be suggested. You will find that even so small a change as making a dark background light often produces a striking difference in many patterns. And when a chart is written for only two colors, you may of course introduce others at will.

Reading and Writing Stranded Charts

As you know, there are several methods of handling more than one color yarn while knitting a Stranded pattern, but a color chart works equally well for any of them. A row on the chart matches a row of the fabric, and whether you alternate the colors as you work across the row, or employ Slip Stranding and use one at a time, makes no real difference. If you are knitting in the round

and alternating colors, you read each row of the chart once from right to left working some stitches in one color, some in the other according to the pattern. If you are using Slip Stranding, you must read each row of the chart from right to left twice, once for each color.

If you are knitting flat and alternating colors, you will, of course, read one row from right to left, the next row from left to right. If you are knitting flat and using Slip Stranding, however, there are two different ways of working, one that employs the Slide technique (page 236) and one that does not. If you use slides, you will read each row of the chart twice in the same direction, once for each color. This is called an ABAB color change pattern (first color A, slide, than color B, turn, etc.). If you attach the yarns at opposite sides of the fabric, however, the color change pattern is ABBA, or right to left with the first color, left to right with the second color, then right to left with the second, and left to right with the first.

The size graph paper you use for a color pattern is of little consequence, but to get some sense of scale, you may wish to use a grid that is close in size to that of your stitch gauge in at least one dimension. However, do keep in mind the discrepancy between the appearance of a pattern charted in squares and a fabric made up of rectangular stitches. These patterns will always look shorter in the fabric than they do on paper, which is of negligible importance when doing geometric

STRANDED PATTERNS IN THREE COLORS

Stranded patterns, but a serious consideration when planning an Intarsia pattern.

Charting Intarsia Patterns

The difference between the proportions of a charted Intarsia design and the result in the fabric can be considerable. If you were to just draw the motif directly onto the graph paper the way you wanted it to look, you would be grievously disappointed with the result.

For instance, say you wanted a motif to be 5 inches wide and 3 inches high in the fabric and your stitch gauge was 6.2 stitches per inch and 8.3 rows per inch. If you were to draw the motif on 5-square-per-inch graph paper, you would have a pattern that was 5 x 5 = 25 squares wide and 5 x 3 = 15 squares high. If you work directly from the pattern on this square grid, the result in your fabric would be 25 squares ÷ 6.2 squares per inch = 4 inches wide and 15 squares ÷ 8.3 rows per inch = 1.8 inches high, which isn't exactly what you had in mind.

PRELIMINARY DRAWING FOR INTARSIA PATTERN

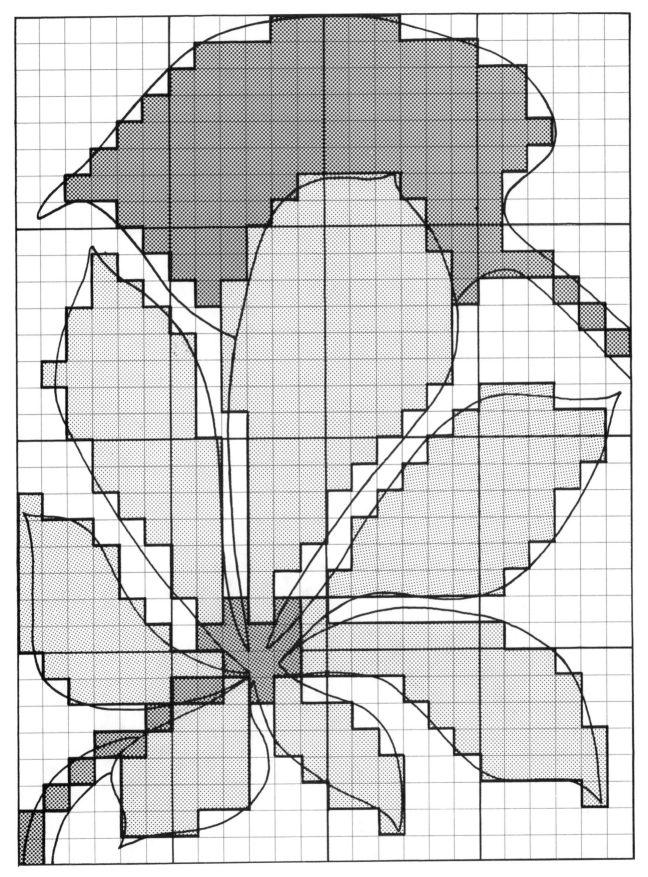

CHART FOR AN INTARSIA PATTERN

In order to correct for this difference, work as follows:

1. Draw the design first on plain paper with the proportions just as you wish them to be in the garment and then draw lines closely around the design to frame it.

2. Measure the height and width of the design and use your stitch gauge to determine the overall number of stitches and rows that will be required to make it that size.

3. On graph paper draw a perimeter for the design, *not* according to the actual measurements, but one that includes the correct number of stitches and rows. While it is not necessary, if you have it available, use graph paper that is close in scale to one of the dimensions of your gauge.

4. Redraw the design within this perimeter; if necessary, draw a grid on top of your original drawing to guide you in deliberately distorting the pattern.

You may come across what is called "knitter's" graph paper, which is often recommended for this purpose and for garment charting. It has a grid of five inches and seven rows per inch, this supposedly being the most common stitch gauge for a Stockinette fabric. Personally, I have never had occasion to knit anything that had that exact gauge, so I don't understand the value of this product. Every project you make will have its own unique gauge, and the grid on this special graph paper will, therefore, be no more suitable for determin-

ing the correct number of stitches and rows to knit for your design than a square grid would be.

Intarsia patterns are most often worked out on a charted garment pattern so the relationship between pattern elements, and between the pattern elements and the shape of the garment section, can be clearly seen. Remember that the garment pattern will be distorted in precisely the same way as the surface pattern, so they will be compatible. (For information on charting garment patterns, see page 511.)

Bead and Sequin Charts

Any chart done for Stranded color knitting can be used for Crossed Stitch Beading without modification, as the beads are set on the new stitch. However, while it is possible to use those charts directly for the other forms of beading, it is often easier to work from a chart especially designed either for Stitch Head Beading or for Running Thread Beading.

Running Thread Beading Charts

In order to use a standard chart for the latter method, you must make a mental shift and read the squares as if they were the intersections where the beads will lie, and the vertical lines dividing them as if they were the stitches. However, if you find that shift causes too much mental wear and tear, it really doesn't take much to convert a standard chart for this purpose and mark the bead positions on the intersections of the lines. This

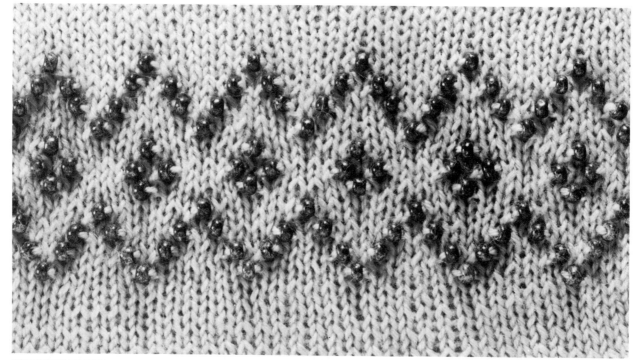

STITCH HEAD BEADING

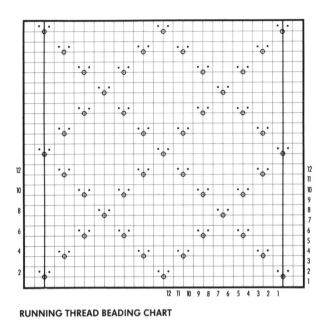

RUNNING THREAD BEADING CHART

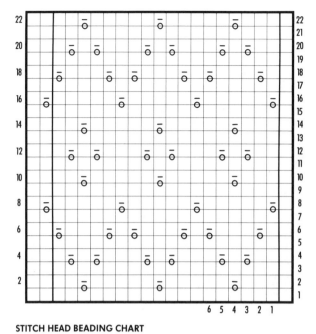

STITCH HEAD BEADING CHART

frees the squares so those stitches which must be in Purl can be marked accordingly.

You will recall that, in order to place the running thread carrying the bead on the outside of the fabric, this method requires flanking Purl stitches with the bead resting on the running thread between the two Purl nubs. Notice on the chart, therefore, that the dot indicating the bead is placed on the line dividing the two Purl stitches.

Stitch Head Beading Charts

Stitch Head Beading is much more straightforward, and generally any Brocade pattern can be used as the basis for a beaded design using this technique. However, because the bead must be set on a stitch in one row and Purled on the next row, and you may have occasion to work a beaded stitch at the same time as you set another bead, it can be helpful to convert a normal Brocade chart for this purpose. As you can see in the adjacent chart, the bead symbols have been placed below each Purl symbol, on the line dividing two squares. When you see a symbol at the top of a square, this indicates that a bead is to be set. Conversely, when you see a symbol at the bottom of a square, you will know you must work a stitch bearing a bead.

Sequins

Standard color charts are generally not useful for sequins because they are typically set, at minimum, every other stitch and staggered row by row. Nevertheless it is quite easy to adapt a color pattern for sequins by using the bead symbol in a way appropriate for this purpose.

Here are two charts, one the original color chart, the second showing the adaptation of the pattern for use with sequins. Notice that just as for Stitch Head Beading, the symbol lies on the line dividing two squares, indicating that the sequin is set on a stitch on one row and the new stitch bearing the sequin is then worked on the next row. On the same row, when the stitches bearing the sequins are worked as Knit on the outside, the stitches that flank each sequin are worked as Purl to hold them in place.

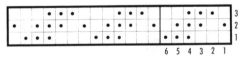

STRANDED COLOR CHART FOR SEQUIN ADAPTION

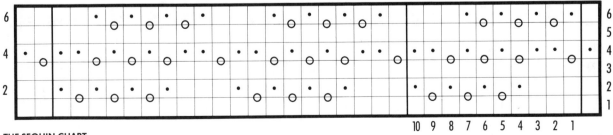

THE SEQUIN CHART

In charting a pattern of this kind, first set the sequin symbols in position on the chart in the same configuration as the dots of the color pattern, but spaced every other row, then place the Purl symbols on either side. Fill in any remaining empty squares with Knit symbols or leave them blank, as here. Select a color pattern that is relatively small in scale because it will double in size when used for sequins. Conversely, if you want a dramatic effect, select a large one and watch it take on truly grand and sparkling dimensions.

Color Stitch Pattern Charts

Patterns that employ both color and stitch technique are somewhat more challenging to chart than plain color ones, but like them their benefits are considerable compared to working from written instructions. There are two types of color-stitch pattern charts. One charting system was created by Barbara Walker for the Mosaic patterns that she defined and developed. The other is more general and can be used for any type of pattern, including the Mosaics.

Mosaic Pattern Charts

A Mosaic pattern is worked in much the same way as when Slip Stranding a regular color pattern; however, the structure of the fabric is quite different, and therefore the chart must contain different information.

Mosaics are really made up of alternating two-row, solid-color stripes that include some stitches that are slipped. Since the stitches slipped are always in the color you are not working with, contrasting notes of one color are pulled into areas of the other, and this is what creates the patterns. In other words, these patterns employ true Slip Stitches, not stitches that are temporarily slipped only as a means of handling different-color yarns.

Since the second row of every stripe in a Mosaic pattern is always identical to the first, one row of a Mosaic chart contains the information for working two rows of fabric, that is, *two passes* across the stitches with just *one yarn*. Therefore, as you can see on the chart below, each row is numbered twice, with the odd numbers on the right, the even on the left.

Reading the chart is very simple.

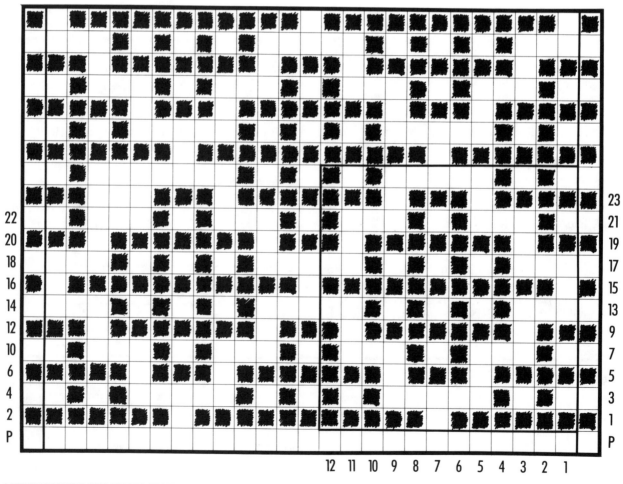

LATTICE MOSAIC/A TRADITIONAL CHART

1. If you are using the color represented by the black squares, read a row of the chart from right to left, working a stitch for every black square and slipping a stitch for every white one.

2. Then, with the same yarn, make a second pass across the stitches that is an exact duplicate of the first—same stitches worked, same stitches slipped, same row on the chart, reading left to right for a flat fabric, right to left for a circular one.

3. When these two rows are completed, pick up the second color yarn and work the next row on the chart in the same way, this time knitting a stitch for every white square, slipping a stitch for every black square and working two rows of fabric.

The colors always alternate in this manner, two rows with the yarn represented by the black squares, then two rows with the yarn represented by the white squares. Needless to say you may select a light-colored yarn for the black squares and a dark one for the light (as a matter of fact these patterns invite color-reversal effects).

It does not matter whether you adhere to the stitch multiple in calculating the number of stitches to use for the width of your garment, but you must begin and end each row with a stitch in the color being used. For this reason, there are always selvedge stitches on these charts, and you will notice that they alternate colors, with the color designated the one you must use to knit that pair of rows. Walker's patterns always start with a black square for the edge stitch of the first row, so you would cast on and knit one row with the color represented by the white squares and then pick up the color represented by the black squares to begin working the first rows of the pattern. If you are knitting in the round, the selvedge stitches must be eliminated, but the information they contain about what color yarn to use for each pair of rows remains valid.

While I have said that each pair of rows is the same, this refers only to which stitches are worked and which are slipped. However, as you know, these patterns may be done in either Stockinette or Garter Stitch. The chart itself contains no information as to how to work the stitches—this is left entirely to your discretion. Actually, you have a great deal of flexibility—you may work certain rows of a repeat with Purl on the outside and the remainder in Knit, you may alternate Stockinette and Garter Stitch on each row repeat, or on each stitch repeat, or both. (For more information on combining patterns and the effect this has on stitch gauge, see page 425.)

In order to transcribe the written instructions for a Mosaic pattern into charted form, on any row worked with the dark-color yarn, fill in one square for every stitch *worked* and leave all the others blank. On any row worked with the light-color yarn, fill in a square for every stitch *slipped* and leave those to be knit blank.

A Mosaic chart is very easy to work from, but it provides visual information only about the interplay of color in the pattern. If you want to see what the structure of the fabric is, or be more precise about which stitches are to be in Knit and which are to be in Purl, you must use an alternate method of charting, which is described below.

Writing Other Color Stitch Charts

Mosaics are by no means the only color patterns that employ stitch techniques, nor do Mosaics exhaust the potential of the Slip Stitch in this regard. In order to chart these patterns, it is necessary to merge the functions of a stitch pattern chart with those of a color chart. This is not as hard as it seems, as long as you keep in mind that there are two separate transactions going on as you work. The first is that a new stitch is being formed on the right needle. The second is that a stitch on the left needle will be given a particular stitch form as it is discarded into the fabric.

The new stitches formed on the right needle are neutral, that is, they have no stitch form—they are neither Knit nor Purl nor any other kind of stitch. What is being determined is their color, which will be that of the yarn you are using to knit with.

The neutral stitches on the left needle are those which were created on the row below, and will therefore be in whatever color you used to knit with on that row. In other words, if on the last row you knit with the blue yarn, the stitches on the left needle will be blue. If you are now knitting with a red yarn, the stitches on the right needle will be red. As you work into the blue stitches on the left needle, you will give them their stitch form; they will become blue Knit stitches or blue Purl stitches, etc., as they are discarded into the fabric, and at the same time a new, neutral red stitch will be formed above them on the needle.

On a stitch chart, the square tells you what to do to the stitch on the left needle in order to give it the required form; it refers only to the discard stitches. On a color chart, the square tells you what color to make the next new stitch on the right needle; it refers only to the new, neutral stitches. The challenge here is to create a chart that will tell us how to handle both stitches at once. The solution works best for any non-Stranded pattern, those in which a single yarn is used to work across a given row. For patterns that combine stranding and stitch techniques, see below.

Charting the Stitches

1. Transcribe the stitch techniques first in the standard way, ignoring all references to color. This tells us what to do to the stitches on the left needle.

2. Mark the row numbers on each side in the color to be used when working that row. This tells us what color the new stitches are to be.

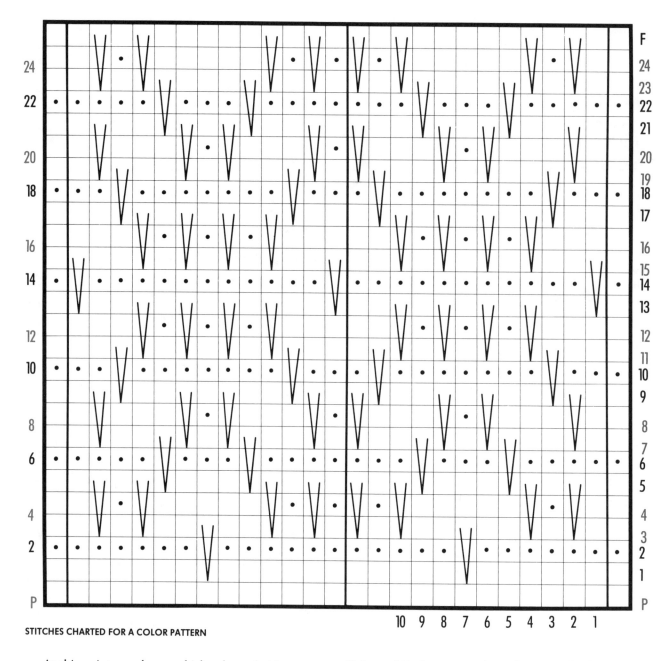

STITCHES CHARTED FOR A COLOR PATTERN

At this point, you know which color to hold as you knit a given row and what to do to each stitch. You could leave it at that and the chart would work just fine, but as you can see on the example shown, you still wouldn't have any graphic representation of the color aspect of the pattern.

Charting the Colors

• On any given row of the chart, each square containing a symbol for a stitch that is worked and discarded must be filled in with the color indicated by the *previous* row number.

Remember, if the current row number is red, you will be making new, neutral stitches in red, but those

Knits and Purls you are discarding into the fabric will be in blue if that is what color yarn you held as you knit the row below.

Next is the same chart as it looks when colored. Do you recognize the Mosaic pattern shown above? The two charts are made from the identical stitch pattern. There is also a fragment of the knitted fabric with a grid superimposed on it shown next to the chart so you can compare the two. The fragment shows row 3 in progress with red stitches being created and blue stitches being discarded. The two blue stitches on the right needle are Slip Stitches, as is the red stitch on the left needle, which is about to be Knit and discarded. Also notice the preparatory row. As I mentioned above, Mosaic patterns generally instruct you to cast on and work one row. In

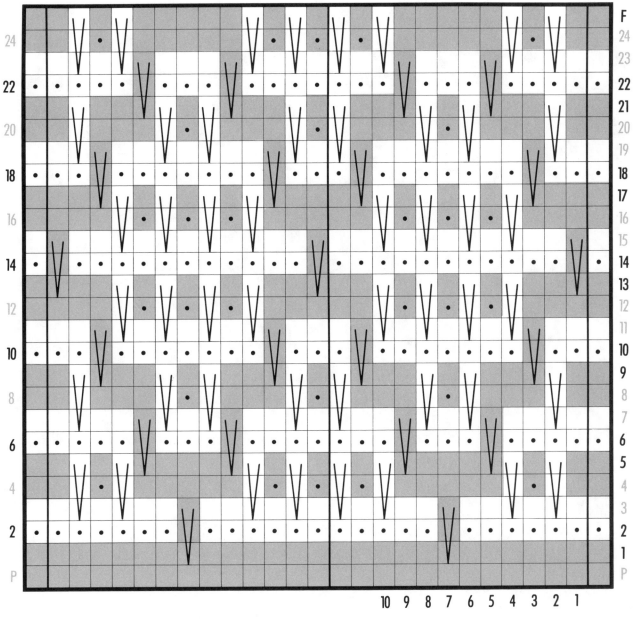

LATTICE MOSAIC/STANDARD CHARTING METHOD

this example, the red yarn was used to cast on. On the preparatory row, these red cast-on stitches are discarded and replaced with another row of red stitches. On row 1, red stitches were discarded and blue ones placed on the needle, except for the stitch in column 8, which was slipped. On row 2, blue stitches were discarded as Purl on the outside, and another row of blue stitches was placed on the needle, while the red stitch in column 8 was slipped again.

Actually, these color charts for Mosaics are most useful for seeing exactly what a particular color effect will be; however, you may find, as I do, that a chart of this sort is slightly disconcerting to work from; the col-

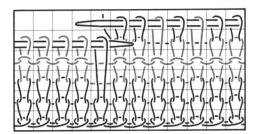

STRUCTURE OF LATTICE MOSAIC

LATTICE MOSAIC PATTERN

ors distract my eye, making the symbols hard to read. I find that Walker's charts are the easiest to use when all you're going to do is Stockinette or Garter Stitch. If you're going to mix things up a bit with some elements in Knit and some in Purl, it's best to work from a stitch pattern chart that has color designations on the row numbers but none on the stitches. For instance, if you look carefully at this chart, you will notice that in certain rows some of the stitches are in Knit and some are in Purl. This is not normal for a Mosaic pattern, but it is certainly possible to work this way. This sort of variation can be indicated on a color stitch chart or in written instructions, but there is no way to show it on the standard Mosaic chart.

Charting Special Techniques: There are several stitch techniques found in color patterns other than Mosaics that form important exceptions to the general rule of filling in each stitch with the color held on the row below.

• A Yarnover, Wrap, Stitch Pullover (not a Slip Stitch Pullover), Couching stitch or Bobble, and any yarn stranded on the outside of the fabric, will all be in the color used to knit the row with, because these all involve new stitches or strands made with the yarn in hand.

Because of their complexity, it is best to chart a color stitch pattern in pencil first and then trace over all of the numbers and symbols with colored pens to add the color portion of the pattern. Alternatively, the color pattern is more obvious if you use a black fine-point pen for all of the stitch symbols and then fill in the colors of the squares with a light overlay of crayon.

Let's look at a few examples of patterns making use of some of these techniques so you have a clear idea of what is required.

The first is a very charming pattern, Ringlet Diamond, employing a Wrap technique. The Wrap is done with the yarn currently in use, and lies at the base of the discarded, contrast-color stitches. The concept, of course, need not be restricted to a diamond shape as shown here—you can place the two-stitch Wrap units in any geometric configuration you like.

Next, Three Color Tweed contains Slip Stitches, some of which are stranded with the yarn on the outside to produce horizontal flecks of color across the elongated stitches. Barbara Walker has several lovely versions of this type of pattern in her books.

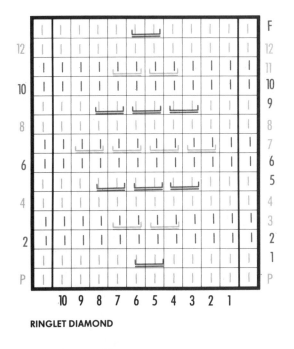

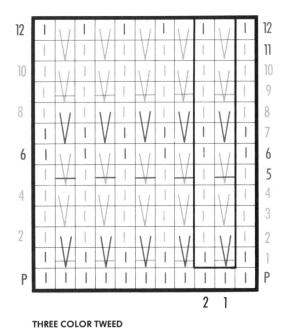

RINGLET DIAMOND

THREE COLOR TWEED

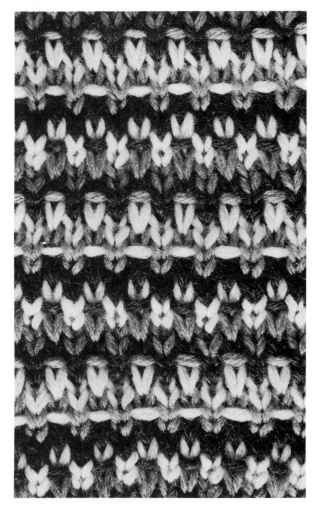

RINGLET DIAMOND

THREE COLOR TWEED

Displaying another aspect of Slip Stitches is Interlaced Stripe, a dramatic Lattice pattern in which the strand is pulled up over rows in the contrasting color.

Some of the most fascinating color interplays can be achieved with the wonderful Honeycomb patterns. Here is one example. Notice that the Slip Stitch portion of the symbol is in one color while the strand is in the other color. The pattern can be done with either Garter Stitch or the Reverse Stockinette shown between the columns of Slip Stitches, and it creates an interesting difference in the appearance of the fabric. The look is also changed if you use Garter Stitch, but place the Knit stitches on rows 1 and 3 and the Purl stitches on rows 2 and 4.

Finally, two versions of a Threaded technique, Fin-

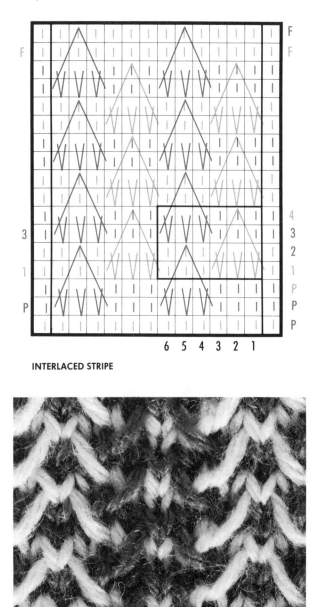

INTERLACED STRIPE

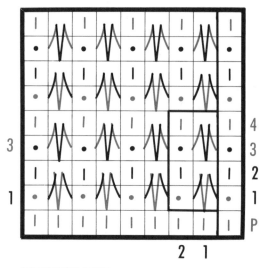

HONEYCOMB STRIPE

INTERLACED STRIPE

HONEYCOMB STRIPE

gertip Tweed, in which the facing stitch of the pair is slipped. Slipped once, it forms an irregular stripe; twice, a check. The pattern can further be varied by using either two or four colors instead of the three shown.

Charting Inlay Patterns

There is a small family of patterns that weave a con-trast-color yarn through the fabric by stranding it on the outside past certain stitches. This woven yarn is never used to form a stitch. The yarn can be handled either as for Double Stranding or as with Slip Stranding, and single or double strands may be used. That portion of the Slip Stitch symbol which indicates a yarn stranded on the outside of the fabric has been adapted to show

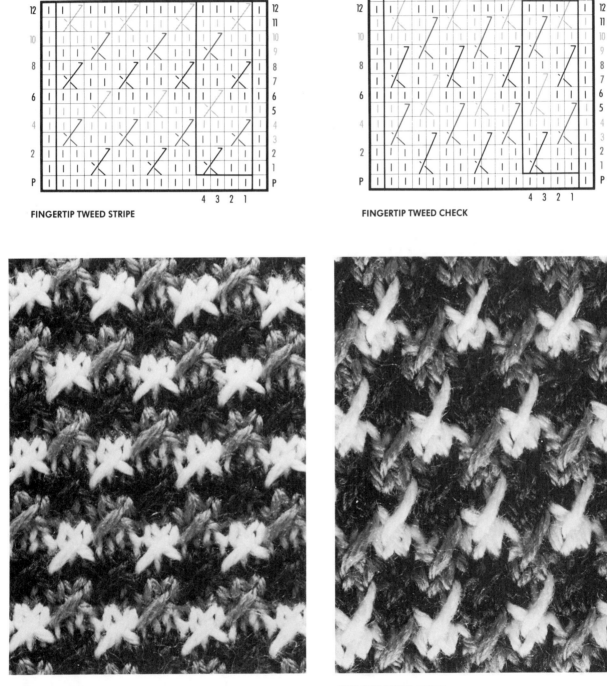

FINGERTIP TWEED STRIPE

FINGERTIP TWEED CHECK

FINGERTIP TWEED STRIPE

FINGERTIP TWEED CHECK

the weaving pattern. Here are some examples of charts for patterns of this sort.

In the first chart, the yarn is stranded across a background of Seed Stitch. The basic concept is easily varied; you could, for instance, strand the yarn past two Knit stitches instead of one and line them up in columns or on the diagonal.

Woven Polka Dot uses a double strand of yarn on every other row. These two yarns could be in contrasting colors and/or contrasting textures.

Charting Short Row Patterns

There are not very many color patterns that exploit the Short Row principles as a stitch technique, but there is no reason for them to be orphaned and out in the cold. They do present special problems, but the principle of using blank squares to indicate that stitches in certain columns are missing adapts itself quite well to indicating that portions of certain rows are missing. Here again, placing the empty squares within the chart serves very well when only a few rows are involved; with larger expanses, it is best to turn to the mini-chart concept instead.

In the first pattern shown, String of Purls, each little

Short Row section has just two turns, which are marked by a small arrow. When you come to the first arrow, you are to turn and work back four stitches. Turn at the second arrow and work those four stitches again, and then, when you come to the arrow that points down, you know that you can continue to work across the remaining stitches on the left needle. The two rows of squares on either side of the Short Row sections are left blank in order to make it clear exactly which columns of stitches have been worked with extra rows and which have not been. This solution to charting Short Rows is very precise about exactly what to do, but it doesn't give you a very good idea of what the fabric will look like.

In the next chart of the same pattern, the positions of the Short Row sections are marked on the pattern, with the manner of working those particular stitches indicated in the adjacent mini-chart. This gives you a much better idea of how things will look in the fabric, and since the Short Row pattern is so very simple to learn, having the instructions off to one side should present no problems.

Next is another example, Short Row Pattern, where the Short Row pattern is not only larger, but gradually

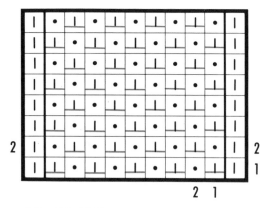

SEED STITCH INLAY

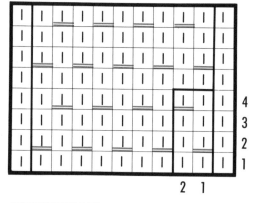

WOVEN POLKA DOT

SEED STITCH INLAY

WOVEN POLKA DOT

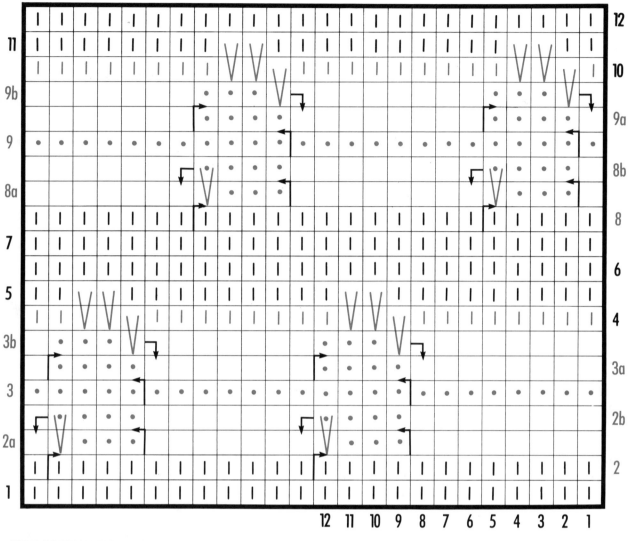

STRING OF PURLS WITH BLANK SQUARES

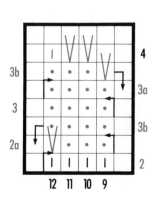

STRING OF PURLS WITH MINI-CHART

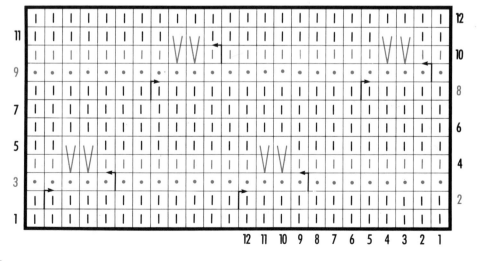

increases in size. When doing Short Rows as a stitch technique, you may or may not want to wrap the stitch at the turn. If you prefer to do that, you can clearly indicate this as shown in the mini-chart.

The same concept of charting Short Rows for a stitch technique is used when charting garment patterns that include the technique. (For more information, see page 532.)

Stranded Color Stitch Pattern Charts

As I mentioned, the method of charting color-stitch patterns described above works best for those patterns in which a single yarn is used on each row. Nevertheless, some very stunning effects can be had in knitting by combining stitch technique with Stranded color or Intarsia patterns. Purl, Crossed Stitch, Twist Stitch, and cluster stitches, all can be used to add texture to color.

In order to make up a chart for this method of working, fill in the color pattern first, then add the stitch techniques. In doing so, keep in mind what happens at a color change when Purl is on the outside of the fabric (see page 261). When you read the chart, you will have to read two rows at once—one row to find out what to do to the next stitch on the left needle and the row above to find out what color to make the new neutral stitch.

STRING OF PURLS

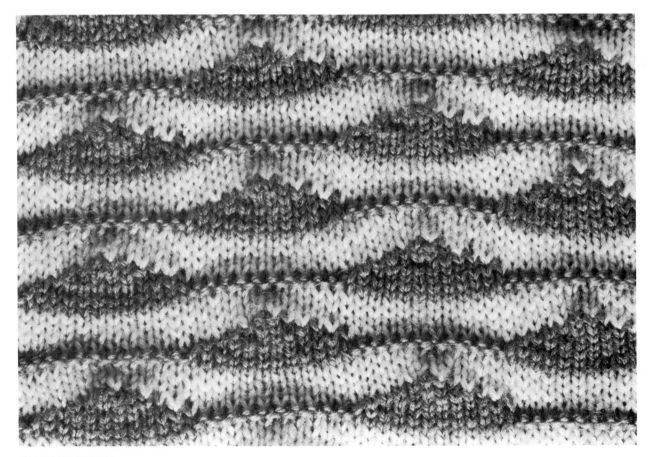

SHORT ROW PATTERN

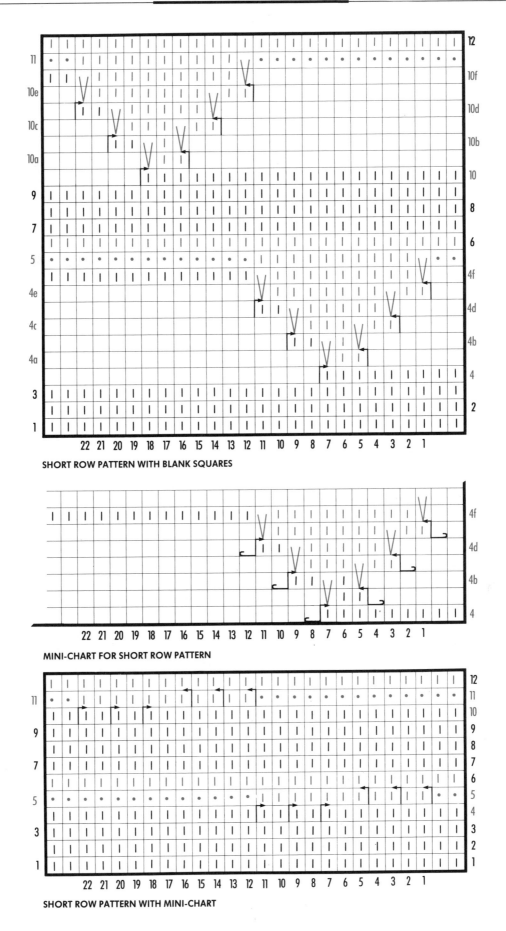

SHORT ROW PATTERN WITH BLANK SQUARES

MINI-CHART FOR SHORT ROW PATTERN

SHORT ROW PATTERN WITH MINI-CHART

Stranded Brocade Patterns

Stranded Brocade patterns can be done as solid-color texture patterns or as Stranded color patterns. They fall most easily within a discussion of color charts because they employ a stranding technique with two yarns. The chart for Brocade Diamond, shown first as it would be for use with a single color, illustrates how the symbol for this technique is used; the strand is always centered between two Purl stitches that are worked while holding the same yarn as the strand; the intervening stitch is worked with the other yarn.

Should you wish to work the pattern in color, filling in the chart is quite easy following the principles outlined above for any other color-stitch pattern chart, and the result is shown in the second chart of the same pat-

tern. Notice that the strand will be in the color currently in use, while the Purl stitches that flank each strand are discard stitches and will be in whatever color was used for that stitch in the row below. However, the stitch above every Purl stitch will be the same color as the strand. In this case, however, you need only read one row at a time, always using the contrast-color yarn for the Purl stitches.

With this particular pattern, the contrast-color yarn must occasionally strand past seven stitches; this is no problem in a fine yarn, but in a heavier yarn you might want to weave it in at the center of the span (see page 258).

Charting Color Patterns for Double Knit

The written instructions for one of these patterns can look formidable even to the experienced. Charting them takes a certain patience, but that, fortunately, need not be its own reward, for the process of doing so provides you with familiarity and understanding of the pattern before you ever start to knit, as well as the usual benefits of working from a clear graphic guide as you do. Actually, three charts are required—one to work from and two that show the structure and appearance of both faces of the finished fabric. The working chart looks unlike any other, but you will recognize the fabric charts for the standard color-stitch pattern charts that they are. I will give you examples of each major type of Double Knit color pattern so you can gain a clear understanding of how these charts are to be read and how you can convert written instructions to charted form.

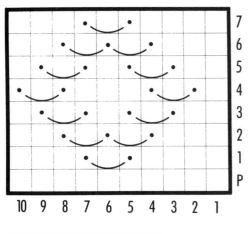

BASIC STRANDED BROCADE PATTERN

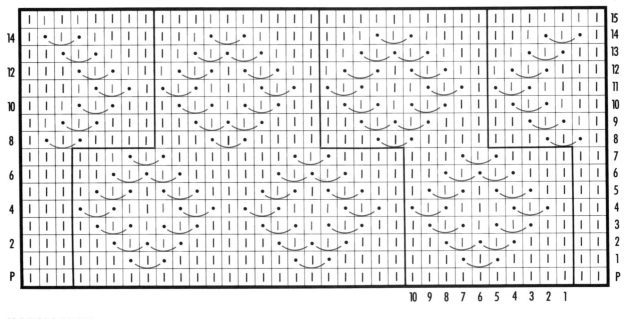

BROCADE DIAMOND

Reading Charts for Interwoven Patterns

In an Interwoven-type pattern, one yarn is used to knit all stitches of that color on the same rows in either face of the fabric; all stitches that must be in the other color are slipped. A second color is then used on another pass across the needle to fill in all the stitches that had been slipped. At the end of the two passes, every stitch in the two rows, one on each face, will have been worked.

The Working Chart

The working chart is basically a color pattern chart, and each square indicates what color the new stitches on the needle should be. Since it is designed to knit from, not to show the appearance of the finished fabric, it is only necessary to chart a single repeat.

Each pair of rows, one on each face of the fabric, is represented in this chart by a set of instructions containing two registers. The lower register of the set contains instructions regarding the stitches of one face of the fabric, called fabric A, while the upper register contains instructions for those of the other face, called fabric B.

The stitches represented by the two registers are, of course, actually interspersed on the needle, so as you work you must read first a square in one register, then a square in the other register, alternating back and forth, stitch by stitch across the row. Ignore the blank squares above or below each symbol as they do not represent stitches, just spaces that would be taken out if the symbols were interspersed side by side on a single row of the chart as the stitches they represent are while on the needle. The stitch column numbers at the bottom of the chart are also staggered to indicate that, say, even number of stitches on the needle belong to fabric A, odd number of stitches to fabric B.

Because virtually all of these patterns are in Stockinette, only two symbols are used, the Slip Stitch and the Knit. The Knit symbol is used in both registers because Knit is on the outside of both fabrics. The Slip Stitch symbol is used only for a true Slip Stitch, that is, one that remains in the fabric, and never for stitches that are slipped only as a means of handling two colors.

Two sets of numbers appear on the right side of these charts. The outer ones are used to number the register sets and are equivalent to one completed row on each fabric face. The inner set and those on the left side are used to indicate the color sequence and what direction to work in for each pass across the stitches when knitting flat; many of these patterns make use of Slides, and numbering may not alternate in the normal way. When working in the round, the numbers still indicate the color sequence, but you will, of course, work from right to left on every pass across the stitches. There may be up to four row numbers in each register, depending upon the number of different color yarns being used for the pattern.

The first example is a simple four-row pattern. The written instructions are provided to guide you.

Tiny Argyle

Cast on with Red. Slide.

Row 1: Blue: *K1, sl1yns, sl1yfs, p1, k1, sl1yns, sl1yfs, p1.*Turn

Row 2: Red: *Sl1yfs, p1, k1, sl1yns, sl1yfs, p1, k1, sl1yns.*Slide

Row 3: Blue: *Sl1yfs, p1, 3(k1, sl1yns).* Turn

Row 4: Red: *3(K1, sl1yns) sl1yfs, p1.* Slide

Row 5: Blue: Row 1. Turn

Row 6: Red: Row 2. Slide

Row 7: Blue: *2(K1, sl1yns) sl1yfs, p1, k1, sl1yns.* Turn

Row 8: Red: *K1, sl1yns, sl1yfs, p1, k1, sl1yns, k1, sl1yns.* Slide

Now let's look at these same instructions in a working chart. The outer numbers on the right indicate a four-row repeat. The inner numbers tell us there will be eight passes across the stitches, that Slides are employed every other row, and that the yarns alternate, first one color, then the other. The numbers across the bottom of the chart indicate an eight-stitch repeat, four to each fabric. To read the chart, work as follows:

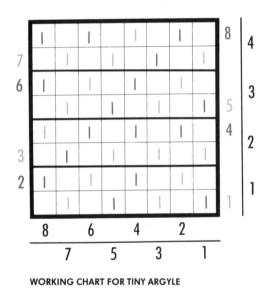

WORKING CHART FOR TINY ARGYLE

1. If the color number is on the right, read from right to left and work any stitch indicated in that color regardless of which register it is in. Knit the stitches that should be worked in the lower register, and Purl those to be worked in the upper register.

2. Slip any stitch indicated in the contrasting color. You must, of course, strand all yarns past these Slip Stitches between the two faces of the fabric, therefore bringing it nearside past any stitch in the upper register, and farside past any stitch of the lower register.

If you look at row 1 of this pattern, you will see that there are two blue and two red stitches in each register. The first pass across the stitches is with the blue yarn from right to left. When you read from right to left, fabric A will be facing you on the nearside, and all fabric A stitches must be Knit. Fabric B will be facing out on the farside, and in order for those stitches to be in Stockinette on the other side, they must be Purled on this side. You will therefore Knit stitches number one and five, Purl numbers four and eight, and slip all the others.

• If the color number is on the left, read from left to right in the same way, but knit all the stitches to be worked in the upper register, Purl those in the lower one. In this case, strand farside past any stitch of the upper register, nearside past any stitch of the lower register.

The second color number on this pattern is red, used left to right. That means fabric B will be facing you on the nearside. You must, therefore, Purl stitches seven and three, and Knit stitches six and two. This time, all the blue stitches will be slipped, stranding between the fabrics.

If you are knitting in the round, fabric A stitches will always be Knit, fabric B stitches will always be Purled.

The Fabric Charts

The next pair of charts show the two faces of the fabrics that result from this pattern. While not intended to Knit from, the charts are very useful. They give you a clear idea of what to expect, are invaluable for checking accuracy as you work, and provide a means of trying different color combinations during the planning process.

The fabric charts are transcribed from the working chart by taking all the symbols from register A rows for the fabric A chart, and all the symbols from register B rows for the fabric B chart. It may help for you to imagine that, as the stitches in each register of the working chart are discarded, they fall into place on one face or the other of the fabric charts. The column and row number for each stitch is the same in both the working chart and the fabric charts.

The two charts are set side by side, although they represent fabric faces that are actually back to back. It is as if the two faces were separated along the right edge and the one on the farside is flipped around next to the one on the nearside, with the two still joined along the left edge. Notice the stitch repeat numbers at the base of these charts. The odd numbers are on the right-hand chart, written from right to left. The even numbers are on the left-hand chart, written from left to right. This numbering is important in order to transcribe accurately the information from working chart to fabric chart. Keep in mind that in the fabric, stitch column 2 in fabric B lies directly behind stitch column 1 in Fabric A. Fabric charts should be done with at least two repeats in each dimension so you can see the way the pattern repeats fit together.

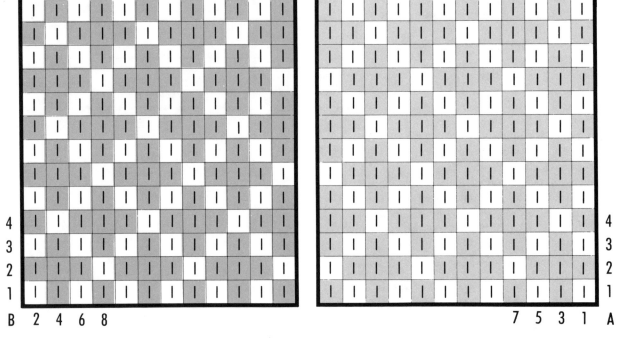

FABRIC CHART FOR TINY ARGYLE

There are some patterns for which it is really not worth the trouble to chart both faces. For those which are true reversibles, meaning they are the same on both sides, there is no reason to go to the trouble to make more than one of the fabric charts. The same thing is true for mirror reversals, where the pattern tilts up at opposite angles on each face. Actually, they look the same when either side faces you, but whichever one is facing away will be opposite. Since the fabric charts are done as if they were facing you, both charts would be the same. For patterns that are opposite reversible, meaning the pattern is the same but the colors are reversed, the second chart is optional but useful if you really want to see what the colors will do; sometimes the effects are surprising. For unlike reversibles, of course, two fabric charts are essential; however, many of these have one patterned side and one solid-color side, in which case you can eliminate the chart for the latter.

Writing an Interwoven Chart

Here is another, more complex Interwoven Double Knit pattern that we can use to go through the steps required to convert it to a chart. For space considerations, only a few lines of the written instructions are provided.

Enchained

> With color A, the dark yarn, cast on a multiple of twelve stitches. Slide.
> Row 1B: *2(k1, sl1yns), sl1yfs, p1, 3(k1, sl1yns).* Turn
> Row 2A: *3(k1, sl1yns), sl1yfs, p1, 2(k1, sl1yns).* Slide
> Row 3B: *2(sl1yfs, p1), 3(k1, sl1yns), sl1yfs, p1.* Turn
> Row 4A: *Sl1yfs, p1, 3(k1, sl1yns), 2(sl1yfs, p1).* Slide

Draw the vertical lines defining one stitch repeat, then draw the horizontal lines defining the registers, one set for each pair of rows in the instructions.

Now write the row numbers in whatever color should be used, starting on the lower right hand side. If it says "Turn" at the end of one row of instructions, mark the next row number on the other side; if it says "Slide," mark the next row number on the same side as the last one. (Actually, once the pattern is charted, you will see that there is generally some flexibility in how to work these patterns in this regard. Instead of the ABAB pattern shown, you may want to work ABBA.)

1. If you are writing a row from right to left, Fabric A will be facing on the nearside. Therefore, when the pattern calls for a Knit stitch, use the color indicated by the row number and mark a square in the bottom register, leaving the corresponding square above blank. When the pattern calls for a Purl stitch, mark a square in the top register, leaving the corresponding square below blank.

2. If you are working from left to right, fabric B will be facing on the nearside. Therefore, when the pattern calls for a Knit stitch, mark it in the upper register; if it calls for a Purl stitch, mark it in the lower register.

3. In all cases, skip a vertical pair of squares for every stitch that must be slipped.

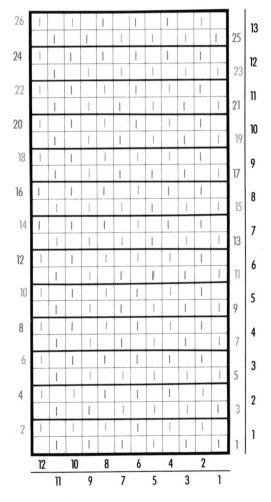

WORKING CHART FOR ENCHAINED

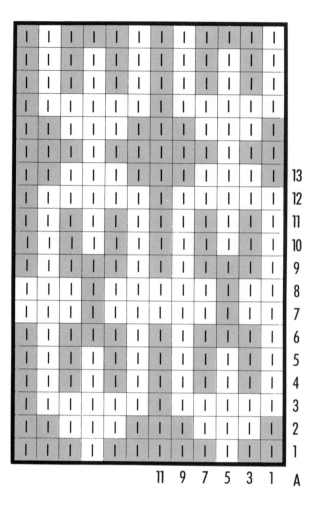

FABRIC CHART FOR ENCHAINED

When you have finished marking all the stitches, every vertical pair of squares should have one stitch mark.

Transcribing the information from working chart to fabric charts is quite straightforward. Transfer stitch information from all the lower registers from right to left in the right-hand chart, that from all the upper registers from left to right in the other. When the stitches are all in place on the fabric charts, color in the pattern.

Mosaic-Type Double Knit Charts

These patterns employ true Slip Stitches and therefore require a slight modification in the charting method. There are two clues that reveal the identity of one of these patterns. The same color is used on two consecutive rows of the pattern to work the same stitches, and some vertical pairs of squares will seem to be empty.

Here is a simple little pattern of this type with a Mosaic pattern on one side and plain horizontal stripes on the other.

Inscrutable Pagodas

With color A, light yarn, cast on a multiple of 8 stitches plus 3. Slide.
Row 1B: *K1, p1, sl1yfs, 2(p1,k1).* Turn
Row 2B: *2(p1, k1), sl1yns, k1, p1.* Slide
Row 3A: *Sl1yns, 3(k1, p1).* Turn
Row 4A: *3(k1, p1), sl1yns.* Slide

Notice that in this chart, the cast-on row occupies the first register. This is not only useful in terms of getting started, but as you will see, it is essential when it comes time to transcribe the information from working chart to fabric chart.

To Write the Working Chart

1. Write in one stitch in each column in the color used for casting on.
2. On the next register, write the first row number and fill in the squares from right to left according to the pattern.
3. The second row uses the same color as the first.

Should you try to write the stitches for row 2 into the same register as those for row 1, you would find the pertinent squares already occupied. Therefore, write the second row number in the next register and fill in the same pattern.

4. You will find that certain stitch columns contain no symbol. This indicates the presence of a slipped stitch and confirms that you are dealing with a Mosaic-type pattern. First, determine which face of the fabric the missing stitch belongs to. If you were working from right to left, the stitch in that position would belong to the near fabric if slipped yarn farside, to the far fabric if slipped yarn nearside. The opposite is true when working from left to right.

5. Since the Slip Stitches are carried up from the row below, they must continue in whatever color was last used to knit a stitch in that column. To determine the color of the Slip Stitch symbol, therefore, look at the color of the stitch is the same position in the register below. (Any Slip Stitch in the first register will be in the color used for casting on.) Write the symbol into the appropriate square using that color.

6. In the next register, when the Slip Stitch is finally worked, the square in that position will contain a Knit symbol.

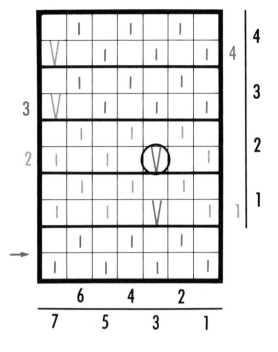

WORKING CHART FOR INSCRUTABLE PAGODAS

To Write the Fabric Charts: With the other kinds of Double Knit patterns, making the transition from a color-pattern chart in which each square shows the new stitch to a stitch-pattern chart in which each square shows the discard stitch is quite effortless, but a Mosaic chart is somewhat more challenging.

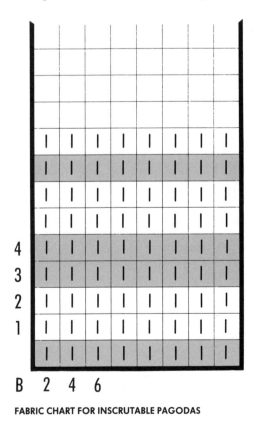

FABRIC CHART FOR INSCRUTABLE PAGODAS

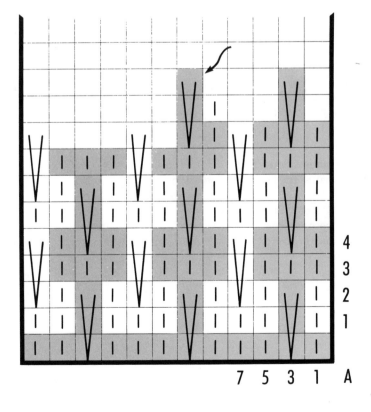

1. Work one fabric chart at a time; in other words, first transcribe the lower rows in each register to the right-hand chart, then transcribe those in the upper rows to the left-hand chart.

2. The row numbers of working chart and fabric chart should match. Leave the cast-on row unnumbered.

3. Check the first stitch in the register of the row you want to fill in. Look in the same column in the register above to see if that stitch was worked and discarded. If it was, write the stitch, in the same color, in the same column and row on the fabric chart.

4. If the square in the register above contains a Slip Stitch symbol, this means that stitch is still on the needle—it has not yet been worked and discarded. Leave the corresponding square in the fabric chart temporarily empty.

5. If you come to a Slip Stitch symbol in the working chart and the square in the register above contains another Slip Stitch symbol, this means that stitch is still on the needle and has not yet been worked and discarded. Skip another square on the fabric chart.

6. If you come to a Slip Stitch symbol in the working chart and the square in the register above contains the Knit symbol, that means the Slip Stitch is finally being worked and discarded. In the same column in the fabric chart, you will find several empty squares. Write in the Slip Stitch symbol, with the point in the lowest empty square and the top of the symbol in the square of the current row. In Mosaic patterns the Slip Stitches span three rows.

The fabric chart is shown partially filled in, and the next stitch to be written in is the Slip Stitch circled on the working chart in the third repeat of the pattern.

In a simple pattern such as this one, you could use one register for each pair of rows. I have written it up the long way to make perfectly clear what is at work.

Combination Patterns

The final chart is one of a pattern that has a little bit of everything. Two rows are done in one color as Single Rib, two rows are done with the Interwoven method, and two rows contain true Slip Stitches. The pattern is the same on both sides, so one fabric chart is sufficient.

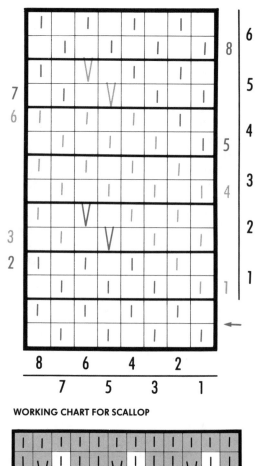

WORKING CHART FOR SCALLOP

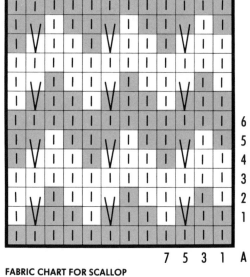

FABRIC CHART FOR SCALLOP

27
Schematic Drawings and Garment Pattern Charts

J ust as stitch-pattern charts make it far easier to follow a complex set of instructions, so it is with garment charts and schematic drawings. Most designing starts with a schematic, or outline drawing of the pattern, that establishes the basic proportions and stylistic details of the garment and shows how the different sections are assembled. The measurements of the design are then used in conjunction with the stitch gauge to either write the pattern out in words or put it into charted form.

A chart of each garment section, in effect a larger and more detailed schematic drawn on a grid, makes every step necessary to shape the fabric graphically clear. The relationship of stitch to garment pattern, the position and effect of every shaping unit, and the precise placement of elements such as buttonholes and pockets, color changes or Intarsia motifs are all made evident. Whether you are designing your own garment or working from a commercial pattern, you will find these charts and drawings an invaluable aid.

When this information is not given, I highly recommend that you use whatever written instructions are provided to "knit" the garment up on graph paper before you begin to work. In doing so, you will gain a vivid sense of how the pattern works before you start, and you will have the opportunity to make simple alterations and correct any problems should that be necessary. Once you are familiar with the conventions used, you will be able to translate any type of a pattern into the form you require, from written to schematic, from charted form to written, or from a schematic to a chart.

You will also be armed with everything you need to know in order to design your own garments. If you have always said you can't, here's where you discover you can. Usually the process of transformation from pattern knitter to designer comes about in a very practical way. Perhaps you have some very nice yarn in the closet, but

no longer like the pattern you purchased it for. Maybe you have found a beautiful yarn in a shop, but you did not like any of the patterns that were available for it. On the other hand, you might have found a pattern that you liked, but you are not happy with the yarn suggested, or you would prefer a different stitch pattern. Keep in mind that even a small change will create something that is uniquely yours, and that most professional designers are doing no more than changing the details and colors on a few very basic garment shapes.

With the help of the material here, plus some of the calculations found starting on page 433, you can design any shape and size garment that you want. However, even if you are not prepared to go to the trouble of designing or redesigning a pattern, you should be familiar with how to read schematics and charts because commercial patterns increasingly make use of them.

Schematic Drawings

Schematic drawings are small, abstract line drawings. The better commercial patterns will provide both a drawing of the assembled garment, which should include details (such as buttonholes, pockets, plackets, or collars) and the separate garment sections (such as a sweater front, back, and sleeve). Many patterns provide one or the other, but not both. Either on or next to these drawings, an assortment of basic measurements are given.

The drawing and the measurements are an excellent way to determine whether or not a given pattern is appropriate for what you have in mind, and whether or not it is likely to fit well. In addition, this information is useful for checking accuracy as you work, as a guide to assembly, and for checking dimensions when you clean the finished garment. And finally, you can use a schematic as a basis for developing a design of your own.

Using Existing Schematics for Design

Most of us are not trained in design and pattern drafting, and we don't have the knowledge or skills to establish the correct measurements and proportions required to translate our design ideas into a garment that will fit well. Fortunately, all that is necessary is to find a com-

mercial pattern in the desired style and size that provides a schematic you can work from. It does not matter what yarn or stitch gauge was used in the original design; what is important is that the design is what you have in mind.

Next you will want to select a yarn and a stitch pattern. While by no means essential, it is often a good idea to at least choose a yarn that is similar in size to that suggested by the pattern because it will then be suitable to the style, purpose, and drape of the garment, but it certainly need not be the same type or color. Once you have decided on a yarn and either a stitch or color pattern, knit a sample in order to obtain your gauge. Write down the details on needle sizes, the yarn to be used, the stitch gauge, and yardage requirements near the schematic so all of the basic data are in one place.

With the measurements provided on the schematic, and the stitch gauge that you develop for the yarn and stitch pattern you have chosen, you can quite easily work up either written or charted instructions from which to work (see "Drawing a Chart," below).

Alternatively, you can draw you own schematic based on measurements taken from the body, from an existing garment that fits well, or from a sewing pattern. For the latter, focus your attention particularly on those styles designed for knit fabrics, although you needn't

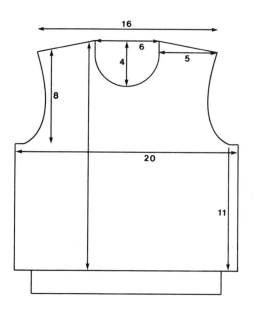

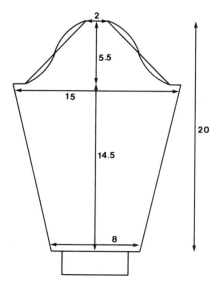

SCHEMATIC DRAWINGS OF BODICE AND SLEEVE

and curves; it is not necessary. On the sewing pattern, the vertical will be indicated by an arrow representing the "grain" line. On an existing garment, measure along the rows and columns of stitches. For some measurements it is easiest to use an L-rule; however, if you do not have one and you are measuring a sewing pattern, where necessary draw horizontal lines from which you can then measure straight up or down. If you are measuring a garment, use two rulers, one set horizontally along a row of stitches to form a line and one to measure vertically. If the garment has ribbed cuffs, waist, and neckline, do not include these in the measurements. Write down all of the measurements carefully, working according to the instructions, and save them for use in drawing up the schematic.

The example given is a typical pullover-type sweater. Once the basic principle is grasped you will be able to measure any type of garment.

Measuring the Bodice

1. Back Neck Width A–C: Measure straight across between points where the shoulders meet the neck.
2. Shoulder-to-Shoulder D–E: Measure straight across between the points where the shoulders meet the armholes.
3. Single Shoulder E–F: Subtract A–C from D–E and divide by 2.
4. Full Length A–P: Measure from where the shoulder meets the neck to the bottom edge.
5. Full Side Length D–N: Measure from where the shoulder meets the armhole to the bottom edge.
6. Shoulder Slope C–F: Subtract D–N from A–P or use an L-rule set out from the shoulder point at the armhole and up to the shoulder point at the neck.
7. Underarm Side Length J–M: Measure straight down from the underarm to the bottom edge. If the side slopes, use an L-rule set across from the armhole point and down to the bottom edge.
8. Armhole Length D–K: Subtract J–M from D–N, or use an L-rule set across from the underarm and up to the shoulder point at the armhole.
9. Center Front Length G–Q: Measure from the lowest point of the neckline to the bottom edge.
10. Neckline Depth B–G: Subtract G–Q from A–P or set an L-rule across from the center front opening and up to the shoulder point at the neck.
11. Upper Chest H–I: Measure horizontally at the narrowest width of the upper chest, usually halfway between the underarm and the lower shoulder point.
12. Chest J–L: Measure horizontally at the underarm across the widest portion of the chest.
13. Lower Body M–R: If the garment is tapered, measure the width at the bottom edge (on the garment, stretch the ribbing out as necessary).
14. Measure the length and width of the ribbing.

restrict yourself to them, for any design that fits like a knit, and has relatively simple lines and detailing, will work for a handknit fabric just as well. Sewing patterns are especially useful if you are familiar with how to alter a particular manufacturer's patterns to fit.

Following are the measurements you will need to take from an existing garment or a sewing pattern in order to develop a schematic drawing.

Measuring Garments or Patterns for a Schematic

The most important rule to follow is that all measurements must be taken perpendicular or parallel to the true vertical line of the garment. Never measure slopes

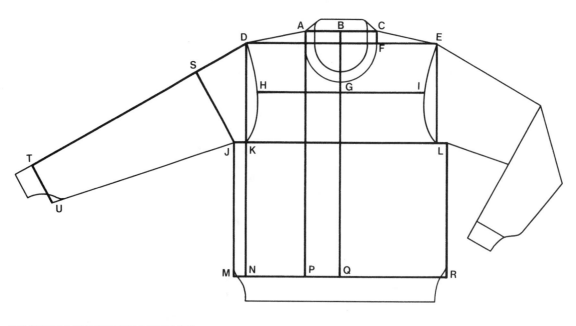

MEASURING A GARMENT FOR A SCHEMATIC

Measuring the Sleeve

1. Full Sleeve Length D–T: On a garment, measure down the vertical fold from where the sleeve meets the shoulder to the wrist. On a sewing pattern, measure down the center from the top of the sleeve cap to the base at the wrist.
2. Underarm Sleeve Length S–T: On a garment, set an L-rule out from the underarm and down the vertical foldline to the wrist. On a sewing pattern, draw a line between the armhole points and measure down from the line.
3. Cap Length D–S: On a garment, subtract S–T from D–T, or place an L-rule out from the underarm and up the vertical fold to the top of the cap. On a sewing pattern, measure up from the horizontal line between the armhole points.
4. Underarm Width S–J: On a garment, lay one side of an L-rule along the vertical fold in the sleeve, the other side along the row of stitches to the point at the underarm; multiply times 2. On a sewing pattern, measure across at the widest point.
5. Wrist width T–U: On a garment measure the width at the wrist, stretching out the ribbing if necessary; multiply times 2. On a sewing pattern, measure the narrowest width at the base of the sleeve.

Drawing a Schematic

While most commercial schematics are on a plain background, it is much easier to draw one yourself if you put it on graph paper. Use a grid about 5 squares to the inch, and let one square equal one inch of fabric. An 8.5 x 11-inch paper will have some 42 horizontal and 55 vertical lines, and this will obviously accommodate any pattern quite easily, especially since for most purposes you need only draw one vertical half of any particular garment section. After all, the left side of any garment is usually a mirror image of the right side. In much the same way, since the body, the armhole, and the shoulder line are frequently the same on both the back and the front of the garment, one drawing can often be used to show the details for both. If the garment is asymmetrical in design or detail, by all means draw the full width and, if necessary, both the back and front. The instructions are for a half-drawing; follow the same principles for a full version. Work as follows:

Schematic Drawing of a Bodice

1. Draw a vertical line down one side of the graph paper. This represents the center line of the garment front. Mark a point at the top of the line.
2. Count down the measurement of the shoulder slope and make a mark.
3. From the back neck point at the top, count down the depth of the neckline opening and make a mark.
4. From the shoulder slope point, count down the measurement of the armhole length and make a mark for the underarm.
5. From the underarm point, count down the measurement of the underarm side length and make a mark.
6. Check that the measurement from back neck point to bottom edge point equals the full garment length.
7. For the back neck, count from the point at the top

of the line straight across one-half the back neck width and make a mark; draw a horizontal line between the mark and the center front line.

8. For the shoulder width, count across from the shoulder slope point one-half the shoulder-to-shoulder measurement. From this point draw a sloped line connecting the armhole shoulder point with the shoulder point at the back neck.

9. For necklines, work as follows:
   • If the garment has a V neck, draw a line connecting the lower neck point on the center line with the point where the shoulder meets the back neck line.
   • If the neckline is a square opening, draw a line out from the lower neck point and up to the shoulder.
   • If the neckline is a round opening, draw a line across from the lower neck point one-third the width and another down from the shoulder neck point one-third the length; connect these two straight lines with a curved line.

10. For the chest width, count across one-half the full chest measurement from the underarm point on the center line and make a mark representing the underarm at the side.

11. For the simplest armhole shaping:
   • Draw a line straight down from the shoulder point at the armhole and straight across to the underarm point at the side.
   • Make marks one-third the way up the vertical line and one-third in from the outer underarm point on the horizontal line.
   • Connect these two marks with a deeply curved line.

12. To shape a curved armhole:
   • Make a mark on the center line halfway between the shoulder slope point and the underarm point.
   • From this mark, count across one-half the measurement of the upper chest width; make a mark.
   • Centered on this point, draw a vertical line one-third the measurement of the armhole length.
   • From the top of this line, draw a gentle curve out to the shoulder point at the armhole.
   • At the bottom of the line, make a mark, then continue the line straight down and then across to the underarm point at the side.
   • Divide this horizontal line in thirds and make a mark representing the amount to cast off for the underarm.
   • Draw a deeply curved line connecting this mark with the bottom mark on the vertical armhole line.

13. For the side line, work as follows:
   • If the side is straight, draw a line down from the underarm point the length of the side and then across from this point to the center line.
   • If the side is shaped, draw a line across from the bottom point on the center line the measurement of the bottom edge, then up to the underarm point.

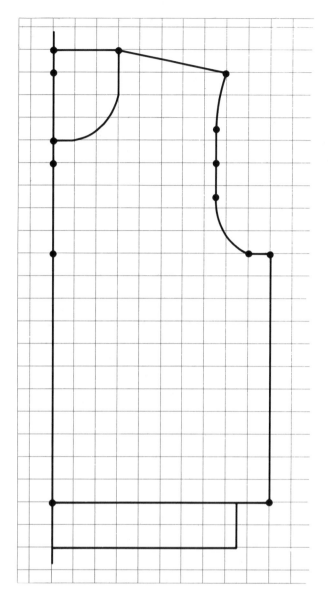

SCHEMATIC DRAWING OF A BODICE

Schematic Drawing of a Sleeve

1. Draw a center line. Make a mark representing the top of the cap.
2. Count down the line the measurement of the cap length and make a mark.
3. Count down the line the measurement of the underarm length and make a mark.
4. From the wrist point, count across for half the width, make a mark, and draw a horizontal line connecting the two points.
5. From the mark for the base of the cap, count across for half the width of the sleeve at the underarm. Draw a line connecting the underarm point to the wrist.
6. Count in from the underarm point the same length

Once you have the schematic drawn, it is a good idea to add the data on the measurements so you don't have to recount squares when you refer to the drawing.

Converting Written Instructions to Schematic Form

Should you come across a written knitting pattern that does not provide a schematic, it is relatively easy to draw one from the instructions. You may want to do this in order to check the size and shape of the pattern accurately before you begin work, or because you want to change the yarn or stitch pattern called for. In the latter case, developing the schematic would be an intermediate step in redesign. For converting a written pattern directly to a chart, see below.

- To find a width at any given point, divide the number of stitches that the instructions specify should be on the needle by the stitch gauge provided. If you want to draw one vertical half of the pattern, divide the results by 2.
- For a length, divide the number of rows called for by the row gauge.
- When the instructions call for shaping, always use the adjusted number of stitches on the needle for the calculations. For instance, if the instructions call for decreasing one stitch each side every other row five times, subtract ten stitches from the last known total on the needle (five on each side), then multiply by the stitch gauge to obtain the new width. Divide the answer by 2 if you are drawing one-half the pattern.

With a little care and attention to detail, the entire shape of the garment can be worked out and the schematic drawn as described above.

Measuring the Body

Design is a subject far too large to fit into this already big book, but for those of you who have the confidence to try, I can at least provide some basic instructions. However, there is no room for a discussion of how to create the multitude of variations on necklines and collars, sleeve and bodice styles. For these you must refer to existing garments, sewing patterns, and design books for ideas about how to work out the correct proportions. Nevertheless, if you understand how to take the appropriate measurements from the body and use them to develop a schematic drawing, you are well on your way to having a garment that has a custom fit and unique style. If you start with the simpler garment types, you will quickly gain confidence and move on to those that are more complex.

For any schematic, the measurements required are the same whether the source is an existing garment or pattern or the human body, but for the latter a different approach and a few additional steps are required. First it is necessary to take the actual measurements from the

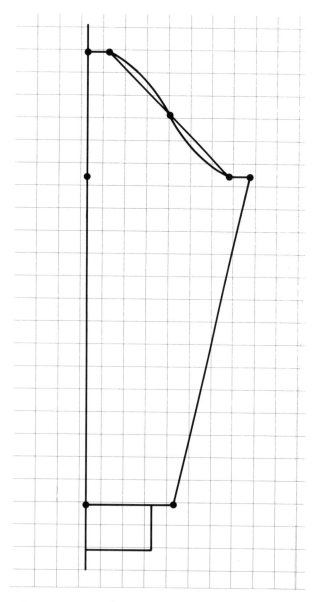

SCHEMATIC DRAWING OF A SLEEVE

as the amount removed for the underarm on the bodice.

7. For the flat portion at the top of the cap, count over one-half to one inch from the center line and make a mark.

8. Draw the horizontal line for the top of the cap, then a sloped line to the inner underarm point and another horizontal line to the outer underarm point.

9. To shape the cap:
   • Divide the sloped line in quarters.
   • At the point one-quarter of the way down, make a mark one-quarter inch out. At the point three-quarters of the way down, make a mark one-quarter inch in.
   • Draw an S-curve passing between the points from top to bottom.

body. To these measurements, certain amounts must be added for ease and design considerations before drawing up the schematic.

Ease is added to the actual measurements to provide for comfortable movement or to allow space for other garments worn underneath, most often at the chest, sleeve, armhole, hip, and in body and sleeve length. General guidelines for amounts to add are found below after the instructions for the basic measurements. In addition to ease, certain amounts may be added to the basic measurements for stylistic reasons. Body length measurements are taken to the waist, for instance, but frequently the garment will be designed to rest somewhere on the hip, and in drawing the schematic for a particular garment the appropriate amount must be added to the basic measurement.

It takes two people to obtain accurate measurements. Have the person to be measured stand in an erect but relaxed position wearing customary undergarments. It helps to have a string or soft belt tied at the natural waistline. On all circumferences, draw the measuring tape up firmly but not tightly. Always measure on the true horizontal and vertical. Work as follows:

Measuring for the Bodice

1. Back Neck Width: Hang the tape measure around the neck in the most comfortable position and allow the two ends to fall vertically down the front. With a straight rule, measure horizontally between the outer edges of the two ends.
2. Bodice Length: Leave the tape around the neck and pull the end down to the waist; note the measurement at the top of the shoulder.
3. Full Side Length: Center the end of the tape on top of the shoulder where it meets the arm and measure over the shoulder and straight down to the waist.
4. Armhole Length: Set a ruler horizontally under the arm. Holding the tape as for Full Side Length, above, measure down to the top of the ruler.
5. Underarm Side Length: Subtract Armhole Length from Full Side Length.
6. Shoulder Slope: Subtract Full Side Length from Bodice Length.
7. Center Front Length: Measure from the top of the sternum to the waist (find the hollow in the neck right above the bony plate in the center of the rib cage).
8. Neckline Depth: Subtract Center Front Length from Bodice Length.
9. Shoulder-to-Shoulder: Measure straight across the back between the outer points of the shoulder (find the end of the shoulder bone where it meets the arm).
10. Upper Chest: On the front, measure horizontally across the chest where the round bones of the upper arms meet the rib cage.
11. Full Chest: Place the tape under the arms at the fullest part of the chest/bust and measure the circumference; divide by 2.
12. Waist/Hip: Measure the circumference of the body where you plan the bottom of the garment to fall; divide by 2. (For a skirt, measure waist and both high hip, at the hip bone, and low hip, at the widest part).

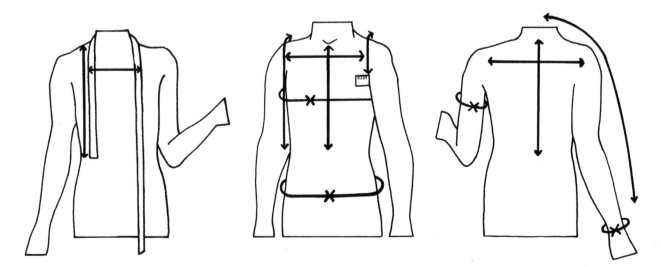

MEASURING FOR THE BODY

Measuring for the Sleeve

Sleeve width measurements are quite straightforward. Length measurements, however, depend not just on the length of your arm, but on where you plan to have the garment shoulder line fall and whether or not the sleeve will have a cap. The method of developing a sleeve cap requires a separate discussion, found below.

1. Upper Sleeve Width: Measure upper arm circumference with muscle flexed.
2. Wrist: Measure the circumference at the wrist bone; do not draw the tape tightly.
3. Neck-to-Wrist: The arm should hang naturally at the side; measure from the prominent bone in the neck across the shoulder and down to the wrist bone.

For a straight sleeve with no cap set on a drop shoulder, full sleeve length and underarm sleeve length are equal:

1. Hold up the arm and measure the narrowest width of the underarm; divide by 2. This is the amount to remove at the underarm of sleeve and bodice, A.
2. Subtract this figure from half the full chest width, B; this will be the shoulder width from center back to armhole, C.
3. Subtract the shoulder width from the neck-to-wrist measurement, D, to find the sleeve length, E.

For a set-in sleeve with a cap and a natural shoulder line:

1. Full Sleeve Length: Subtract half the shoulder-to-shoulder measurement, B, from the neck-to-wrist measurement, A.
2. Underarm Length: Once obtained, subtract cap length, D, from full sleeve length, C.

For a dropped shoulder with a cap sleeve:

1. Work as for a sleeve without cap to find full sleeve length.
2. For underarm sleeve length, subtract length of cap from Full Sleeve Length.

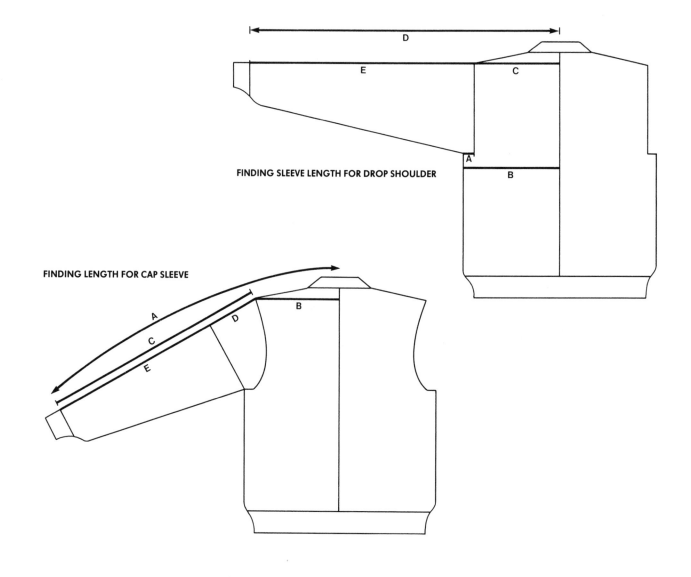

FINDING SLEEVE LENGTH FOR DROP SHOULDER

FINDING LENGTH FOR CAP SLEEVE

Adding Ease

Because a knitted fabric is elastic and resilient, ease is not actually essential and, in fact, some garments do not require any. Whether or not to add ease, and if so in what amount, is really a design decision based partly on style and partly on function. A mitten, for instance, needs no ease added to the actual measurement of the hand. A hat, on the contrary, should cling and might benefit from negative ease, meaning subtracting something from the actual head measurement (see "Average Gauge for Non-Ribs," page 437). Most sweaters, however, have at least a small amount of ease added for wearing comfort and drape. The following are general guidelines suitable for garments of any size, with the range running from moderate to very full.

- For average chest ease it is customary to add two to four inches to the full circumference, regardless of garment size. To give you some idea of what this means, for a man with a forty inch chest measurement, a garment measuring forty-four inches in circumference would allow you to "pinch an inch" at each side (one inch front and back at each side), allowing a comfortable, easy fit. In drafting, therefore, add one inch to full chest width (half the circumference) for a slim fit, two inches for average fit; three inches is full, more than three inches is considered oversize. The same amount works for children's or women's garments.

- On an upper sleeve width, average ease is two inches, allowing you to pinch an inch. On a slim short sleeve, one inch is adequate. On a long-sleeved garment, stylistic considerations play a large part, and many sleeves are wider.

- Armhole ease depends upon style and whether the sweater will be worn over another garment; average is two inches: In other words, if a woman's actual armhole length is six inches, a comfortable garment armhole length would be eight inches; less would be a slim, high armhole, more would be added only for design reasons. Subtract ease added to armhole length from underarm side length so overall side length does not change; what you want is just to lower the underarm point.

- In drafting the length of the bodice, add whatever design length is required to the shoulder-to-waist measurement. From this, subtract the depth of the ribbing, then add one to two inches for blousing if it is wanted. Work in the same way for sleeve length.

- If you are making a cardigan, remember that both the inner and outer button band should be centered on the center front line so they overlap; therefore, subtract half the width of the band from the half-front measurement.

Once you have these measurements, you can proceed to draw a schematic just as if the measurements had come from a paper pattern or an existing garment.

Designing a Sleeve Cap

A sleeve cap is designed to eliminate extra fabric at the underarm portion of the sleeve for wearing comfort. Sleeve caps are an aspect of design that frustrates and defeats many. The result is a lot of sweaters with drop shoulders and no sleeve caps whether that was what was wanted or not.

The difficulty is in determining the correct length of the cap. If it is too short, it will pull the sleeve up under the arm, and if it is too long, it will sag at the top of the arm below the shoulder. Most books that discuss this will provide some sort of simple guidelines suggesting a cap so many inches long for a child's garment, so many for a man's, etc. There are others that provide complex graphs, which contain various lengths depending upon the upper arm measurement. None of these are particularly accurate, as I'm sure many people have found to their dismay. The solution is really quite simple.

The length of the sleeve cap is related to shoulder width, depth of armhole and width of sleeve. As you know, these things change, not only in relation to the size of the person you are knitting for, but in relation to the design of the garment. If you are knitting for yourself, for instance, the measurement of your upper arm is likely to remain the same, but you may wish to make one garment with a high armhole and slim sleeve and another with a deep armhole and a loose sleeve. Further, some designs require a narrow shoulder, some a natural shoulder line, some a dropped shoulder. What you need is a formula for designing a sleeve cap regardless of what you are making, or what size the person you are making it for may be. Before proceeding, you must complete the schematic design of the garment bodice and then make a full-scale drawing of the armhole.

Calculating Length

For simplicity's sake, let us consider one-half the sleeve cap, all that is necessary for designing purposes. Most often, the cap will be decreased abruptly at the underarm in exactly the same way as at the underarm portion of the armhole. Then, decreases are worked according to a pattern to slope the side, and at the top a group of stitches is cast off flat. A measurement from the center across the top flat portion, down the slope, and across the bottom flat portion must equal the measurement of the armhole, including the flat portion cast off there for the underarm.

1. On the drawing of the armhole, mark off the flat portion at the bottom representing the stitches cast off at the underarm. Label this D.
2. Measure down from the top at the shoulder and make another mark that equals the width of the flat portion at the top of the sleeve, as shown. This is E.
3. Label the line between these two marks C. The measurement of this line equals the measurement of the

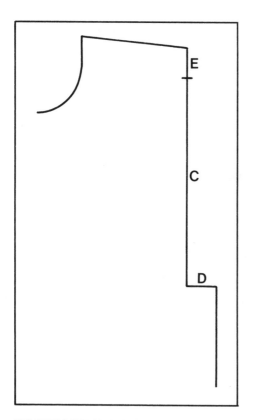

MEASURING ARMHOLE TO FIND SLEEVE CAP LENGTH

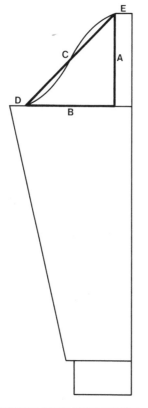

TRIANGLE DEFINING MEASUREMENTS FOR SLEEVE CAP

slope on the cap. If the armhole is curved, stand a tape measure on edge and "walk" it around the curve.

4. The slope on the cap is the hypotenuse of a triangle.
5. The base of this triangle is half the width of the sleeve less the width cast off at the underarm, less the width cast off at the top. (You can see the resulting triangle in the accompanying drawing.)

Now we know the measurement of the slope and the measurement of the base; the only thing missing is the height of this triangle—which is the length of the cap. There are two ways to work, one that requires the use of a calculator with a square root sign and some dim memories of high school geometry. The other is a purely mechanical approach, which you can use if you have neither of the former tools.

$$a^2 = c^2 - b^2$$

a^2 is the height, c^2 is the slope, and b^2 is the base of the triangle.

In other words, subtract the square of the base from the square of the slope and take the square root of the answer.

Measurement for Length

If you do not have a calculator, or have one without a square root sign, there is an alternative.

1. On the right side of the paper, draw a vertical line representing the center of the sleeve cap.
2. Draw a second line at a right angle to the base of the first that is equal in length to one-half the width of the sleeve at the underarm.
3. At the right end of this baseline, mark the width of the portion cast off at the underarm for D. At the left end, mark one-half the width of the portion cast off at the top of the cap for E.
4. Up from E, draw a line of any length parallel to the first vertical line.
5. On the drawing of the armhole, measure the length of C.
6. Place one end of the ruler at the inner underarm point on the baseline of the cap and hold it securely as you slide the other end down the inner parallel line until you reach the correct measurement. Draw the line representing the slope.
7. From the top of the slope, draw a horizontal line between the two parallel lines. This is the top of the cap.
8. Measure from the top of the cap to the baseline for the height of the cap. Use this figure times your row gauge to determine the number of rows in the pattern.

The cap described has a straight slope; if you would like to add a nice S-curve, by all means do so. The S-curve will add a slight amount of ease to the top of the sleeve, which helps it to fit more comfortably. Divide C

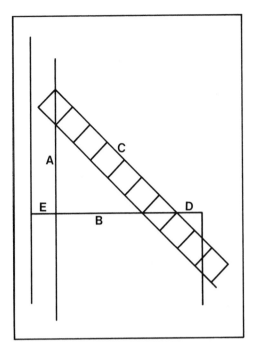

FINDING SLEEVE CAP LENGTH WITH RULER

in quarters, make a mark one-quarter inch out from the top quarter and another one-quarter inch in from the bottom quarter. Draw the S curve passing between these points and the center.

Should you want the sleeve to puff or gather slightly,

add a small amount of additional ease to the measurement of C before determining its slope. If you want pleats at the top, add the amount required to the measurement of E before you draw the parallel line.

I guarantee you, this will give the correct length cap for any sort of garment you can think of, for all those you haven't thought of yet, and for any size or shape person you might have occasion to knit for.

In designing a garment, however, keep in mind that there is a variable relationship between armhole length, sleeve width, and cap length; if one changes, one of the others must also change. As the sleeve circumference becomes smaller in relation to the armhole, the cap will lengthen. The same is true if the armhole lengthens in relation to the sleeve. The circumference of a sleeve with no cap must equal that of the armhole. There are, therefore, several ways to approach the design of this area of the garment. In addition to the approach described above, you could, for instance, determine the size of the cap and the depth of the armhole and then find what width sleeve will fit that configuration, or determine the size of the cap and the width of the sleeve and then determine armhole length.

Once you have a full-scale pattern draft for the shape of the cap, you can use it directly, or make a small scale schematic drawing, to create the garment chart from which to work, as described below. In doing so, the pattern of decreases required to form the slope or curve will be magically revealed.

Garment Charts

A garment chart is no more than an enlarged schematic of the pattern showing the exact contour of the edges of the fabric and any pertinent construction details. It is used as a substitute for written instructions, and you can knit directly from the information provided. Charts for garment sections worked flat are quite straightforward and serve well to introduce all the basic concepts; the discussion on charts for circular fabrics is found below.

Reading and Writing a Chart

Garment charts are like stitch charts in that one square on the paper represents one stitch in the fabric, but generally the grid is much smaller. (In fact, on commercial charts it can be very small indeed. You may find it help-

ful to take the chart to a place that has a copy machine that does enlargements.)

Just as with a schematic, it is generally not necessary to chart out the full width and length of a pattern, and so it is rarely done. For instance, there is no reason to chart a midriff section worked on a constant number of stitches. Similarly, if the right half is a mirror image of the left, the front just like the back, one chart will do for all, except perhaps for the back neck, which can be indicated on the chart above the front neck and be readily understood. The exceptions would be when a color pattern, a stitch pattern, or some eccentricity in the design must be carefully plotted on the entire width and length of the garment, such as might be the case with Intarsia designs or asymmetrical necklines.

In order to work from these partial charts, you must

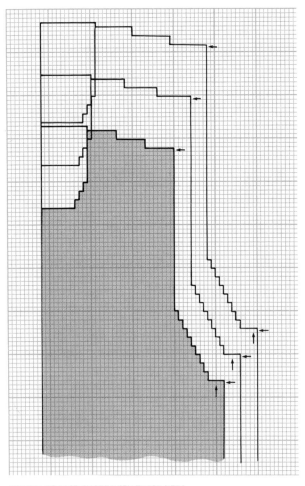

TYPICAL BODICE CHART WITH THREE SIZES

imagine the missing half of the pattern as it would be shown in a mirror. The chart, of course, shows only the outside of the garment section, and therefore each row must be read from the edge to the center and back out to the edge again, whether you are working on the inside or the outside of the fabric. While at first sight this seems as if it would be taxing, in fact it presents no problems at all because what is important are not the details of stitch technique, which should be available on a separate stitch chart, but the position of shaping techniques and stylistic details. It is a simple matter to glance at the chart to see if you are required to do anything on the next row, and if so, how many stitches are involved. Generally, what is done on one side, is done in precisely the same way on the other side.

As you can see in the example above, whenever a row contains a shaping unit, the edge of the chart jogs to show the number of stitches added or removed and the correct number remaining. Whenever the edge jogs in, you know that stitches have been removed and you must either cast off or decrease on that row. Whenever the edge jogs out, you will know that stitches must be added and you must either cast on or increase on that row. If it is not otherwise indicated with a symbol or

written instructions, you may select whatever techniques you prefer to use and place them as you like.

Keep in mind that any casting off must be done at the beginning of a row, so if this is required on the right side, it will be done on an outside row. However, in order to repeat the instruction on the left side, you will have to work to the end, turn, and then cast off the same number of stitches on the inside, one row up. This would be evident on a full garment chart, but must be understood on a partial one.

It is necessary for commercial patterns to indicate a range of sizes, and this is done by setting the charts for the smaller sizes inside those of the larger as shown. When knitting from one of these charts, you must work within whichever set of lines is appropriate for the size you have chosen, ignoring the lines for the smaller or larger sizes. Should you find that the stitches for the other sizes are visually distracting as you work, block them out with a marker or a tape, or use a highlight pen to mark the lines you must pay attention to. If you are charting your own pattern, of course, you will make it for just one size and have no lines to worry about.

Charting Symbols for Construction Details

While charts are concerned primarily with the contour at the edges, they can also be used to great advantage to provide graphically clear instruction regarding details worked within the fabric.

There are a variety of symbols that can be used to provide information about these different aspects of the construction of a fabric, although far fewer for this type of charting than is the case within stitch patterns. To a great extent these symbols are optional, but they are useful when it is necessary to indicate exactly which stitch is affected or which specific technique to use.

- Small arrows can be used to indicate the direction in which a row is worked.
- A curved arrow indicates where to reattach the yarn when the fabric has been divided, such as for a neck or pocket opening.
- Pickup symbols can be used at an edge to show precisely where to insert the needle and how many stitches to pick up.
- An opening for a buttonhole or pocket can be indicated by a line drawn across the appropriate squares or by the symbols for placing stitches on holders or for casting them off, or the squares can be colored in to indicate a Contrast-Color Yarn Opening.

Drawing a Chart

The material in the section on Calculations gives a very precise, mathematical way to work out a knitting pattern from the measurements on a schematic, and those results can then be either written or charted. Here is an alternate method of getting from schematic drawing to charted pattern that requires the minimum in calculations and is fast and accurate. This system makes it particularly easy to develop the instructions for any complex shaping such as an armhole curve or a sleeve cap.

Because you require one square per stitch for a garment chart, I suggest you use ten-square-per-inch graph paper. A one-inch overlay can be an aid to counting stitches and rows. On paper that is 8½ x 11 inches, you will be able to accommodate a pattern of up to 110 rows and 85 stitches. With an average stitch gauge of about 5 stitches and 7 rows per inch, this will allow room for a half garment section somewhat less then 17 inches wide and 15 inches long. Since for most purposes only partial charts are required, most of what you would want to chart will fit on paper of this size; however, the finer the gauge the more squares you will need. Should you require something larger, most business stationers or art supply stores carry 11 x 14 graph paper, or you can tape sheets together.

In order to transfer the shape of a schematic pattern to a chart, you must multiply all the basic pattern dimensions by the stitch and row gauges to find the number of stitches and rows required in the fabric. You must then count out an equal number of squares on the chart in order to draw the lines reproducing the schematic on a larger scale.

While one square on the chart represents a stitch, it does not accurately represent its shape, which is not a square but a rectangle. Therefore, while a schematic drawing of a pattern is an accurate rendition of the true proportions of the design, because of the shape of a stitch, when the schematic is converted to charted form, the proportions will be tall and narrow by comparison. For this reason, you cannot simply draw the contour of a neckline or an armhole directly on the chart as you wish it to be, count squares off and start to knit, because the fabric will not turn out to be the right size or shape. The steps from schematic measurements, to calculations, to chart are essential.

1. Draw a line on the chart representing the center front and establish all parallel and perpendicular lines in relation to it, counting out squares representing stitches and rows, just as you counted out the squares representing inches on the grid for the schematic.

2. Once the horizontal and vertical lines are in place, draw in any slopes or curves.

3. On top of these curved or sloped lines, draw a stepped line marking off the squares that follow the contour of the curve the most closely, as shown in the adjacent illustration. As much as possible, the stepped line should straddle the slope. It helps to establish whether you want to start or end the sequence with a shaping unit.

4. If you are dealing with an acute slope, which requires casting on or casting off, use arrows to establish the direction the rows will be worked in, as the latter

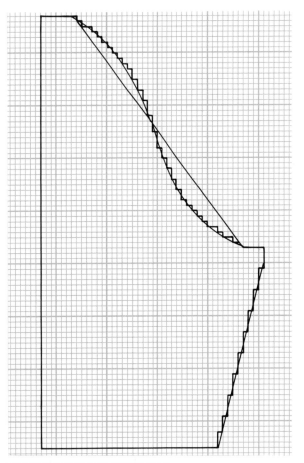

DRAWING SLOPED AND CURVED LINES

can only be done at the beginning of a row, the former only at the end. Keep in mind that stitches are worked before they are cast off, so the arrow should lie below the horizontal line indicating the number of stitches removed; it should lie above the line indicating stitches that are to be cast on. Also remember that there is one decrease on a row lying between two cast-off steps; there is no comparable intervening step when casting on.

The result is a finished garment chart that you can knit from; all you have to do is decide what kind of shaping units to use and where to place them.

From Written Instructions to Chart

Translating written knitting instructions to charted form is no more than "knitting" on paper, and you will find it very easy to do once you know how to read a chart.

• The instuctions will tell you how many stitches to place on the needle and how many rows to work. Count across for the stitches and up for the rows, then draw in the base and side lines to begin the chart. (If you are dealing with a partial chart, remember to divide the number of stitches given in half as necessary.)

- If the instructions call for you to knit up so many inches, use the row gauge to translate the measurement into a number of rows and count up this many squares on the chart.
- Whenever the instruction says to increase or decrease, cast on or cast off a certain number of stitches, jog the line over an equal number of squares, then up the number of rows. For instance, if it reads "Decrease one stitch every other row five times," you go over one, up two, over one, up two, etc.
- Whenever shaping units have been used, always check that the remaining number of stitches in the chart matches the number that should be on the needle. If they don't, you have misread the instructions, or jogged the line incorrectly.
- The final test comes when the lines for neck, shoulder line, and armhole must all connect.

The process of charting will give you a dry run through the pattern so when it comes time to actually knit, you will already be familiar with what is expected. In addition, it is much better to discover any problems with the instructions as you "knit" it onto a chart than with the yarn in your hands—erasing is much easier than ripping out stitches.

Alterations

Should you wish to alter a pattern, but don't want to go to the trouble of completely reworking it, there is still a great deal you can do to adjust the fit or to create something uniquely yours, and a chart makes this very easy to do. The limiting factor is that you must change nothing that would alter the stitch gauge.

There are, however, some very simple yet effective ways to alter a pattern that can be done right on an existing chart. Do keep in mind that you cannot mark off inches directly on the chart—*for any alteration you must always convert a measurement to a particular number of stitches and rows according to your gauge.* Draw your adjustment lines directly on the chart in a contrast-color pen so there is no confusion about which line to follow as you work. It is a good idea to make several copies of the original chart before you make any changes.

- At the very least, you could, for instance, introduce large color sections or stripes to an otherwise plain pattern (not color patterns, as these will have a different gauge). Just draw them in on the chart where you think they will be attractive.
- It is a relatively simple matter to alter the length of a midriff or sleeve. Use your stitch gauge to determine the number of rows or stitches that must be added or removed. The midriff section may not even be charted because it is worked plain from ribbing to armhole. In that case, just write a note on the chart indicating the correct number of rows to work.
- If you want to adjust the length of a shaped sleeve,

draw the baseline for the wrist in the new position, draw a new slope from wrist to armhole, and step off the slope to find the position of the shaping units.

- It is best to avoid altering the length of an armhole, because this requires a comparable adjustment in the shape of the sleeve cap. If you are dealing with a pattern for a simple drop shoulder with an unshaped sleeve top, however, there is little problem. Whatever measurement you add or subtract in rows to the length of the armhole must be added or subtracted in stitches from the width of the sleeve, or vice versa.
- Adjustments to the shape or size of a neckline are also quite simple. For instance, should you wish to raise or lower a V neckline by an inch, determine the number of rows required for the change, make a mark, and redraw the line from the lower point of the V to the shoulder, then step off the stitch/squares along this line. For a curved neckline, drop or raise the center front line as necessary, redraw the curve, and step off the new line. You can make the neckline wider or narrower at the shoulder line in the same way. Any change of this sort will, of course, require that you rewrite the pattern for any collar or ribbed border (see page 444 for information on working out pickup patterns).

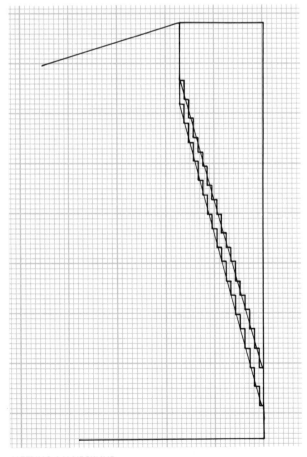

ALTERING A V-NECKLINE

• A pullover sweater can be transformed into a cardigan by centering a button band on the center front line. (Don't put the button band next to the center front line; you want one to overlap the other.) To change a cardigan into a pullover, draw a new center front line down the middle of the band. Take into consideration how a change of this kind alters the pattern for the collar or ribbed border on the neckline.

Coordinating Stitch and Garment Patterns

Whether you are designing your own or making alterations in a commercial pattern, you will want to take into consideration the relationship between the stitch pattern and the design lines and details of the garment pattern. This relationship was undoubtedly worked out carefully by the designer of a commercial pattern, and if you make any alterations, you can throw things off unless you make the proper adjustments. Equally with your own design, very likely you will be disappointed in the results if you just start working the stitch pattern in the bottom corner of the fabric and let things come out any way they will.

When a small, all-over stitch pattern is to be used, its relation to the garment pattern is so matter of fact little attention need be given to it. However, if the repeat is more than four stitches or rows, is distinctive in some way, or is to be used only on certain sections of the garment, care must be taken regarding how the stitch pattern relates to the garment. The aesthetic relationship between stitch pattern and garment is the most critical at eye level. For instance, it can make a great difference in the finished appearance of a garment if the stitch pattern is centered on the front below a key element such as the neckline or the yoke, on either side of a center front opening, or at the top of the sleeve cap.

Once the position of the pattern is established in a key area, repeats of the stitch pattern must be plotted down and across the garment chart to determine the precise stitch and row of the pattern with which to begin working. It would be difficult to write some of the more complex stitch patterns into the little spaces of ten-square-per-inch graph paper, and this is not necessary. All that is required are lines drawn on the garment chart to indicate where pattern repeats will fall horizontally and vertically. Then you can draw lines on the stitch chart indicating exactly where to start once you have worked it out. This is commonly done on commercial stitch charts that must indicate a range of sizes, with each starting on a different stitch and row of the pattern.

If the stitch pattern is complex, it is also a good idea to plot the repeats from the center out to any shaped area such as the armhole. This way you will know in advance if and when you must introduce plain stitches

should it become impossible to work certain stitch techniques as the armhole edge curves inward. You can do the same thing with vertical repeats at the shoulder line or along the neckline shaping. You may also want to determine the relationship of the stitch pattern to any decorative elements such as pocket openings to make sure they fall on a plain row rather than one containing complex stitch techniques.

As an added boon while you are knitting, having the lines of the stitch pattern repeats in a few key places like this can serve as a good indicator of whether your row count is accurate and that you are working as you should. This is particularly useful when the pattern offers you the opportunity of counting by repeats rather than rows. For instance, instead of having to count eighty-five rows to the armhole, you can knit to the fourth row of the sixth repeat; much easier.

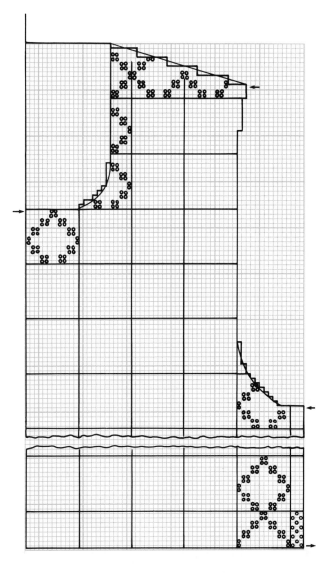

PLOTTING HORIZONTAL AND VERTICAL REPEATS

Plotting Vertical Repeats

Select a place on the garment section where you want to center the repeat and work down, as follows:

1. If you are working with a full-length garment chart, determine the number of rows in the stitch pattern repeat and mark off each repeat on the center front line, working down from the initial one.

2. If you are working with a partial garment chart, do this mathematically.
   • Use the schematic to find the length of the garment section from the top of the first repeat to the bottom and multiply times the row gauge to find the number of rows required.
   • Divide by the number of rows in the repeat to find the number of full repeats that will fit.

3. If there are rows left over, these must be filled by a partial repeat. On your stitch pattern count down the number of extra rows and draw a line indicating the row of the stitch pattern on which you must start knitting.

You may wish to add or subtract a few rows to your garment pattern in order to accommodate a full repeat at the bottom edge or to start the pattern on a plain row or in the exact middle, if not at the beginning.

Plotting Horizontal Repeats

In centering the pattern horizontally, you must decide whether to have the center stitch of a pattern repeat on the center stitch of the garment section, or a pair of repeats flanking the center stitch, or a center front opening. Once this is established, you can then plot the repeats out to the side edge to find which stitch of the pattern to begin working on. If you are dealing with a shaped side edge, determine the relationship of side edge and stitch pattern at the bottom right hand corner where you must start knitting. If you are dealing with a straight side edge, determine this on the partial chart wherever it is convenient, such as right below the armhole shaping.

• From the marks on the center front line that indicate the row repeats, draw a pair of parallel lines across to the side edge.

• Between these two lines, draw vertical lines marking off each stitch repeat.

• If there are squares left over, consider whether or not they must accommodate any required edge stitches. If not, they must be filled in with a partial stitch repeat to function as edge stitches, with some other sort of filler pattern, or eliminated or added to so the width accommodates only full repeats (see below).

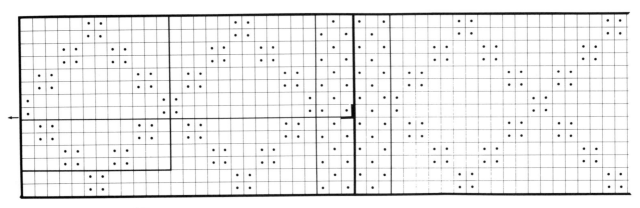

SEAM LINE CUTTING ACROSS STITCH PATTERN

FILL-IN PATTERN AT SEAM LINE

- If you must start working with a partial stitch repeat, draw a vertical line on the stitch pattern chart; the intersection of this line and the horizontal row line pinpoint the exact stitch you must start with.

Coordinating Stitch Pattern and Garment Width

Whenever you find you are dealing with a partial repeat at the side, you should take into consideration what the appearance will be once the garment is seamed. It is certainly tempting to add or subtract a few stitches to the garment in order to fit in a full stitch repeat, but this is generally not a good idea. If you think it through, you will see that the difference even a few stitches can make is by no means negligible when you take both sides and the front and back of the garment into consideration,

and frequently it is not just a matter of a few stitches. These situations are especially problematic when you are planning a circular garment. There are several possible solutions. In most cases, the situation can be handled in a creative and attractive way, and a problem turned to account.

- The easiest thing to do is to ignore the problem and work as many stitches in pattern as will fit at each side as edge stitches. If you are working flat, the seam will cut across the pattern, but that will be more or less hidden under the arm and no different from what would occur when seaming any fabric. On a circular fabric, a "seam stitch," a column of stitches worked in Purl or Slipped every other row and producing the illusion of a seam, serves the same purpose.
- You might find that the stitches join up along the seam

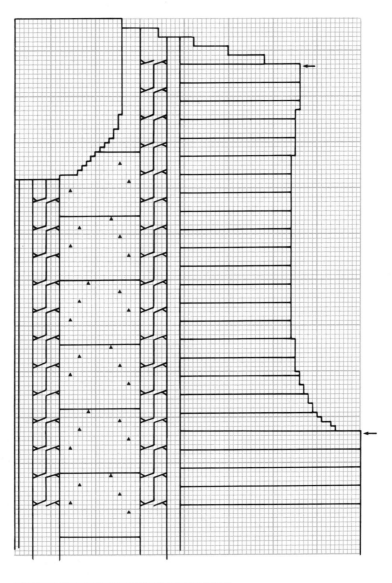

GARMENT CHART WITH MULTIPLE STITCH PATTERNS

more attractively if you change the way the pattern is centered on the garment; if you have a single repeat centered, see what will happen at the side if you flank two repeats on the center stitch instead. When you are working out a detail of this sort, it is helpful to do a pair of stitch pattern charts with a seam down the center, as shown, so you can see how things will look (or set a mirror down on the chart).

- Instead of working those edge stitches in pattern, you could do them in a plain or textured stitch instead. This is a particularly useful approach when working

color patterns in the round, especially when there will be shaping that can then be done within the plain portion rather than within the pattern.

- On the other hand, you can introduce another pattern instead, taking advantage of that odd bit of necessary space to add a contrasting decorative element.

Coordinating Multiple Stitch Patterns

When the stitch pattern changes on certain portions of a garment section, say just on the yoke and down the center front, the appropriate area should be delineated

A CHART FOR AN INTARSIA PATTERN

clearly so you know precisely when to switch from one to the other. If several different stitch patterns are to be used, as they are in the example shown here, they must be indicated in the correct positions, each of them centered correctly on the section they will occupy. In these cases, you will want to be alert to how the stitch patterns relate to one another as well as to the garment.

In some cases, it may be less important to center patterns on the garment than to create a satisfying relationship between the elements of two stitch patterns. Also consider how the stitch pattern falls within the fabric in relation to details such as buttonholes and pockets so you can plan for those elements to be worked on a plain row of the stitch pattern rather than one with techniques that might interfere. A color pattern should be handled in the same way as a stitch pattern.

Intarsia Patterns

Those glorious Intarsia patterns are really quite easy to work from a chart. It can, however, be time consuming to plot out every tiny detail. The Intarsia chart shown here is very economical in that the back, front, and sleeve are all superimposed on one another and on the color pattern, which, therefore, only needs to be plotted out once.

In order to read a complex chart of this sort, it is important to keep your place. Use contrast-color pens to mark off the lines for the different garment sections so you are clear about where to start and stop each row. Lay a ruler *above* the row that you are working on—if you place it below, you will obscure the visual clues from the stitches you will be working into.

If you have a chart for a garment worked in plain Stockinette, it is easy enough to add Intarsia designs— just fill in the squares. Remember, however, that if you are adapting a design from some other medium, or using something that you have drawn, you must first "distort" the drawing to fit your stitch gauge (see page 488).

Charts for Circular Fabrics

Many charts for flat fabrics serve equally well for working in the round. When knitting a sweater bodice, for instance, simply treat the right side seam as the beginning of the round. When the work must be divided at the armhole, you will be working flat in any case. However, when shaping occurs within a circular fabric, the chart must divide at that point to show the change, even though the fabric does not.

Multiple Shaping Lines

In order to shape the crown of a hat, a sock toe, a mitten tip, or a Medallion pattern, increases or decreases are placed along several vertical lines within the fabric. The adjacent chart for shaping a hat crown is an example of a pattern of this sort.

HAT CHART WITH SHAPED CROWN

The fabric is knit continuously in the round while the blank spaces on the chart between one section of fabric and another indicate where stitches have been removed by decreases. When the chart slopes or curves on one side of the gap but not on the other, this indicates the use of single decreases. When the chart slopes or curves on both sides of the gap, this indicates double decreases. The empty squares function in this case just as they do in a stitch chart (see page 475), and must not be misinterpreted to mean that the fabric itself is separated at that point.

Mittens

The second chart is for a mitten with a thumb Gusset (see page 229). There are other types of thumbs than the one shown here, but once you chart something of this sort, the others will also make sense.

The chart shows a mitten for the left hand and should be read from right to left; for the right hand mitten, read from left to right so it is mirror reversed.

The left half of the mitten represents the palm, the right half the back of the hand; the thumb is set to one side. Blank squares lie between the main Gusset and the mitten so the slope of the Gusset can be shown. The Gusset and the mitten are worked as one in the round; in referring to the chart, more or less ignore the blank squares and just pay attention to the pattern of increases forming the Gusset.

The thumb is, of course, worked separately. However, the bridge of stitches connecting thumb to mitten are those cast on for the Fourchette lying between thumb and hand, which are worked in the round with the mitten until the stitches are eliminated.

The other half of the Fourchette, worked on stitches

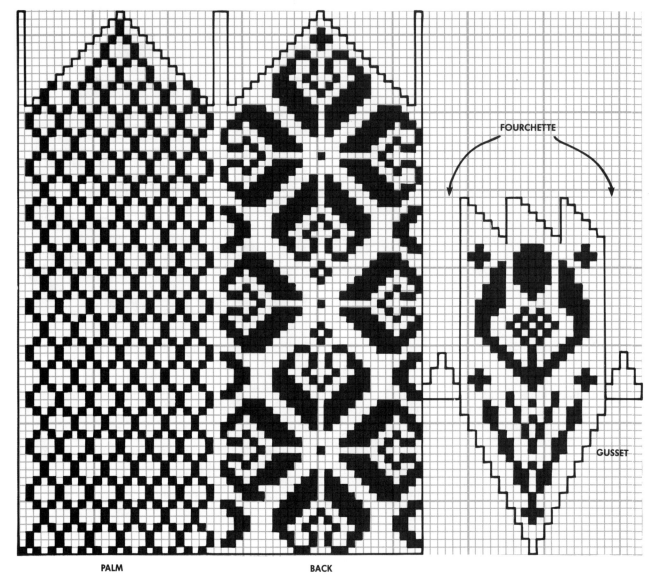

PALM   BACK

PATTERNED MITTEN WITH THUMB GUSSET AND FOURCHETTE

picked up along the first half's cast-on edge, appears to the right and is worked in the round with the thumb until those stitches are also eliminated.

Notice the shaping pattern at the top of the thumb and the top of the mitten.

For glove fingers, the chart would stop at the point where the mitten stitches are divided for the fingers, with the correct stitch division indicated. If you wanted to chart the fingers, they would each have to be done separately.

Socks

And finally, a chart for turning a sock heel. Few things are more confusing in written instructions than this, and a chart makes it nearly as easy to understand as having a good teacher sit and patiently show you how. The chart has three sections, one describing the calf portion worked in the round, the next showing the heel flap and cup worked flat; and then the portion for the foot and toe decreases.

The decreases shaping the leg portion of the sock are placed on either side of several plain stitches at the center back. Remember, the sock is worked in the round with only the chart divided to show the shaping pattern; therefore, read each round from right to left and simply skip over the blank squares.

On the heel cup, the sloped edges represent the pattern of decreases, the inner lines the pattern of the Short Rows, in this case for a wedge cup. However, although the side edge of the cup is stepped off to show the shaping, you must actually work the decreases right before the turning point; the stitches between the decrease and the side edge will begin to slope in.

Symbols are used here to show exactly where to pick up stitches along the selvedge of the heel flap in order to rejoin the sock into a round; however, once you are familiar with working a sock, these would be unnecessary, as it is always done in the same way.

Next, the chart is expanded to reflect the new number of stitches and then the pattern for the Gusset is shown. This portion is also worked in the round.

Once the Gusset is complete, the foot portion is worked on a constant number of stitches, and this can be indicated with a note regarding the number of rows required rather than charting the entire length. All that is really needed next is the toe shaping, which is shown worked in a natural shape.

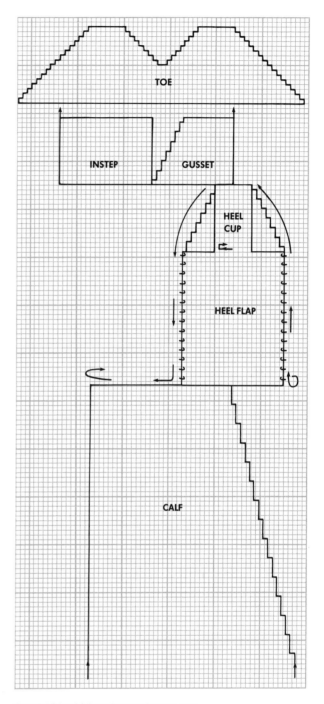

CHART FOR A SOCK WITH WEDGE HEEL CUP

Charting Short Rows

While the two Short Row patterns shown here are done on flat fabrics, the concepts used to represent them in a chart are very similar to those used for charting a circular fabric, and so I have put them at the end. In a sense they sum up the section in that they should prove to you that even the most complicated shape can be charted.

Curved Hemmed Corner

Here is a pattern for a lower corner of a cardigan. The corner is curved with Short Rows, and the bottom and center front edge are hemmed with fabric worked continuously with the garment section (see pages 182 and 207 for further explanation of how this is done).

The lower portion is the hem of the bottom edge and the curved corner. Next is the garment proper

showing the Short Row pattern that shapes the curved corner. The blank squares lying between the hem and the garment indicate that there are no rows of fabric in that position; however, the fabric itself is not divided, as the stitches along the top edge of the hem portion are still on the needle waiting to be reactivated. When the curved portion is complete, stitches are picked up along the bottom hem selvedge for the width of the vertical hem; notice the pickup symbols.

Curved Collar

Finally, another example of a Short Row pattern, here used to curve an entire fabric (see page 182), in this case a collar worked narrow and long. The wedges are the equivalent of the triangles seen above for the hat crown, but here laid on their side with blank squares represent missing rows, not missing stitches.

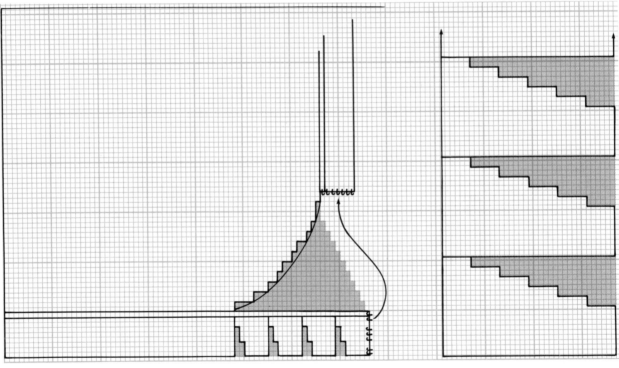

CURVED HEMMED CORNER WITH SHORT ROWS

SHORT ROW CHART FOR CURVED COLLAR

Glossary of Terms

Active Stitches
Those actually being worked; as opposed to those which are temporarily inactive. See Inactive Stitches.

Acute Slope
A sloped edge formed with casting on or casting off rather than with increases or decreases.

Average Gauge
A specialized form of stitch gauge used primarily for ribbed sections of fabric and for those that are intended to cling.

Back
In this text only used to refer to that section of the garment worn to the back. In some pattern instructions refers to the side of the fabric currently facing away from the knitter, or to that side of the stitch on the farside of the needle. See also Farside, Inside, and Outside.

Backing Stitch
The stitch or stitches of a Cable or decrease pulled past other stitches, and that are not visible on the outside of the fabric. See also Facing Stitch.

Band
A horizontal section of pattern.

Beading
A method of knitting beads into the fabric as it is formed; similar methods used for knitting in sequins.

Bias
Fabric knitted with the garment pattern set at a 45-degree angle to the columns of stitches. Also, a stitch technique that forces the columns of stitches to move at an angle.

Binding Off
See Casting Off.

Binding On
See Casting On.

Blocking
Method of stretching open a fabric with pins for air-drying or during steam finishing; used to display stitch pattern and establish proportions. See also Dressing.

Bobbin
A holder for a small supply of yarn; generally used in Intarsia work. See also Butterfly.

Bobble
A prominent knot of stitches on the surface of the fabric; also called a Popcorn. See also Knot.

Braid
A stitch technique forming a horizontal braid on the outside of the fabric; can also be done while casting on.

Brioche
See Honeycomb.

Brocade
Stitch patterns that form pattern through a combination of Knit and Purl stitches, exclusive of Rib patterns.

Butterfly
A small supply of yarn wrapped into a tiny skein and knotted against unraveling. See Bobbin.

Cable

A technique whereby one group of stitches changes places with another group to form a decorative, embossed pattern. See also Twist Stitch.

Cable Holder

A small hooked or bent needle used for making a Cable Stitch. Also called a Cable Needle.

Cable Needle.

See Cable Holder.

Casting Off

Various methods of simultaneously securing the stitches against unraveling and removing them from the needle. Also called Binding Off.

Casting On

Various methods by which the first stitches are placed on the needle. Also called Binding On.

Chart

A form of instructions for either a stitch or garment pattern done with a set of symbols or lines on graph paper.

Chevron

A stitch technique creating alternating columns of stitches moving on the bias.

Circular Knitting

Knitting a three-dimensional fabric without seams; the opposite of Flat Knitting. Also called Knitting in the Round.

Circular Needle

A type of double-point needle; a long, thin plastic cable with two metal or plastic knitting needle tips at each end. Used for both flat and circular knitting. Called "twin pins" in Great Britain.

Cluster

A group of stitches pulled tightly together.

Color Reversal Patterns

In stranded color work, where pattern and background colors are reversed in subsequent repeats.

Color Stitch Patterns

Patterns that combine color work with stitch techniques.

Continental Knitting

See Left-Finger Knitting.

Couching

A stitch technique that pulls a loop of yarn across the face of the fabric.

Crossed Stitch

A stitch crossed over on itself, or twisted on its axis; in some books called Twist Stitch. See also Twist Stitch.

Decrease

A stitch technique used structurally to reduce the number of stitches on the needle, and thereby the width of the fabric; also used decoratively when paired with Increases in many stitch patterns.

Discard Stitch

A stitch manipulated in a certain way as a new stitch is formed on it and then dropped from the needle into the fabric. See New Stitch.

Double Knit

A double-thick fabric with two outside faces; alternatively, a method of knitting two fabrics at the same time.

Double-Point Needles

Needles that are pointed at both ends; of different lengths, may be straight solid needles, or two needle points joined by a cable (see Circular Needle). Most often used for circular knitting.

Double Stranding

A method of working two-color Stranded patterns, with one yarn held in each hand.

Dressed Gauge

A stitch and row gauge taken from a tension sample that has been cleaned and smoothed out exactly the same way the finished fabric will be. Used for calculating stitches and rows required for fabric shape and size. See also Gauge, Stitch Gauge, Tension Sample, Undressed Gauge, and Weighted Gauge.

Dressing

Method of giving a knitted fabric a smooth, wearable finish and correct proportions after cleaning.

Drop

Lengthening of a garment caused by the hanging weight of the fabric in wear.

Dropped Stitch

A stitch that is either allowed to drop off the needle, or one that comes off accidentally.

Duplicate Stitch

An embroidery technique that is done on top of and

exactly duplicates the Knit stitches in the fabric; also used as a method of hiding ends during finishing.

Ease
In garment design, additional width or length added to body measurements to provide wearing ease.

Edge Stitch
A number of stitches at one or both sides of the fabric used to accommodate a stitch pattern multiple to fabric width, or to balance pattern elements.

Elongation
Process of making some stitches larger than others.

E-loop.
See Half-Hitch.

Embossing
Stitch patterns that create a raised surface on the fabric.

End
See Yarn End.

Eyelet
A small round opening in the fabric.

Face
A flat side of the fabric, as in the inside or outside face.

Facing Stitch
The stitch or stitches of a Cable or decrease that are pulled past other stitches and that are visible on the outside of the fabric. See also Backing Stitch.

Farside
A relative term referring to whichever side of the fabric is facing away from the knitter at any moment; also that half of a stitch on the needle which is the farthest from the knitter.

Felting
See Fulling.

Final Row
The last row of a stitch pattern that is only worked prior to casting off and is not a part of the row repeat.

Finishing
Methods of assembling individual sections into a completed garment.

Flat Gauge
Stitch gauge taken from a tension sample measured while lying flat. See also Weighted Gauge.

Flat Knitting
A method of working back and forth on rows of stitches to create a flat piece of fabric; opposite of Circular Knitting.

Foldline
A stitch technique used on a row or column of stitches that encourages the fabric to fold along that line.

Fourchette
A small diamond-shaped Gusset used between thumb and fingers of mittens or gloves to provide ease.

Front
In this text used only to refer to that section of a garment worn to the front.

Fulling
The process of felting a knitted wool fabric.

Gansey
See Guernsey.

Garter Stitch
An elementary stitch pattern that creates a highly elastic fabric with a horizontally corrugated appearance.

Gauge
The number of stitches and rows per inch or centimeter in a given fabric. See also Dressed Gauge, Flat Gauge, Stitch Gauge, Tension Sample, Undressed Gauge, and Weighted Gauge.

Gauge Swatch
See Tension Sample.

Gradual Slope
A sloped edge formed with increases and decreases. See Acute Slope.

Grafted Hemstitch
A method of sewing a hem that reproduces the form and resilience of Knit stitches; related to Grafting and to Duplicate Stitch.

Grafting
A sewing technique that re-creates the structure and appearance of knitting stitches; used as a means of invisibly joining the freed stitches of two fabrics as an alternative to a seam. Also called Kitchener Stitch.

Guernsey
A British word for a pullover sweater. The name apparently originated in the Channel Islands. Also called Gansey or Jersey.

Gusset
A triangle insert knitted into the fabric to provide ease, most commonly at the underarm or at the base of the thumb.

Half Drop
A stitch pattern that has elements that are staggered but partially overlapped.

Half-Hitch
A section of yarn looped back on itself around a needle or another stitch. Also called an e-loop from its appearance.

Honeycomb
A family of stitches that create a fabric with excellent thermal properties. Also called Brioche.

Inactive Stitches
Stitches on hold and not currently being worked; as opposed to Active Stitches (see above). Used in Short Rows or when fabric is temporarily divided.

Increase
A stitch technique used structurally to increase the number of stitches on the needle, and thereby the width of the fabric; also used decoratively when paired with decreases in many stitch patterns.

Inlay
A method of weaving in a second yarn that is not itself knitted; has decorative and technical applications.

Insertion
A column or band of openwork inserted into an otherwise solid fabric.

Inside
That face of the fabric not intended to be seen in wear or use; in many texts and patterns referred to as the "wrong side." See also Outside.

Intarsia
A method of creating a knitted fabric with different isolated sections of color, or with areas of figured color pattern; related to tapestry or brocade in appearance.

Interlock
A technique for preventing holes in the fabric where two sections of Intarsia color meet.

Interwoven
Type of color pattern in Double Knit.

Jersey
See Guernsey.

Joinery
Technique used for joining two sections of fabric with either decreases or casting off.

Kitchener Stitch
See Grafting.

Knit
Generically, the craft; specifically, one face of the basic stitch (see Purl). Also, a technique designed to place the Knit aspect of the stitch on the nearside of the fabric.

Knit Below
A stitch technique requiring that you work into a stitch a certain number of rows below the one on the needle.

Knit Farside
Method of working a normal stitch so it will cross, or a turned stitch so it will not; also done in Purl.

Knitting Belt
A belt with a padded section that supports a double-point needle.

Knitting in the Round
See Circular Knitting.

Knit Over
In Knitting a stitch, wrapping the yarn over the needle instead of under; results in a Turned Knit stitch. See Turned Stitch.

Knitwise
Describing insertion of the needle into the stitch as if to Knit.

Knot
Small version of a Bobble.

Lace
A patterned, openwork fabric.

Ladder
A vertical column of running threads within a fabric. May be formed accidentally by a dropped stitch, or deliberately as part of a stitch pattern.

Lattice
A stitch technique that pulls strands of yarn on the outside of the fabric into a lattice-like pattern with a resemblance to quilting.

Left-Finger Knitting

A method of knitting in which the yarn is carried on the left forefinger; often called Continental Knitting.

Left-Hand Knitting

For those who are left handed, knitting that is done from left to right.

Markers

Objects such as safety pins, small metal circles, or contrast-color thread or cord used to mark a fabric for measurement or counting.

Medallion

A flat knitted fabric worked in the round and having a circular or polygonal outer edge.

Mesh

An extremely open, netlike fabric.

Mini-Chart

A small stitch or garment chart adjacent to the main one that describes a particular technique or portion of the pattern.

Miter

A slope either within a fabric or at the edge of two fabrics that will be joined in order to form a corner.

Mosaic Pattern

A type of color stitch pattern based on two-row stripes and Slip Stitches.

Motif

A distinctive stitch or color pattern element within the fabric.

Multiple

The number of stitches and rows of a pattern that constitute a single unit and that may be repeated across the width or length of the fabric; in this sense, synonymous with Repeat. Also may refer to a decrease or increase that adds or removes several stitches at a time.

Narrow

An old term for reducing the width of a fabric.

Nearside

A relative term referring to whichever side of the fabric is facing the knitter at any moment; also that half of a stitch on the needle which is closest to the knitter. See also Farside.

Needles

The tools used to form the knitted fabric. Made in a variety of materials, sizes, and lengths, and pointed at one end or both. See Circular, Double-Point, and Single-Point Needles.

Needle Size

A number that refers to the circumference of the needle (see chart page 336).

Neutral Stitch

A stitch on the needle; not yet given a particular stitch form. See also New Stitch and Discard Stitch.

New Stitch

A loop of yarn pulled through an existing stitch to form a new, neutral stitch that sits on the needle until worked in its turn. See also Discard Stitch.

Opposite Direction Knitting

Picking up the running threads of released stitches and knitting down in the opposite direction from the original fabric.

Outside

That face of the fabric intended to be seen in wear or use; in many texts and patterns referred to as the "right side," a term here used only to refer to the opposite of "left side." See also Inside.

Over

An alternate term for a Yarnover; not used in this text.

Panel

A narrow, vertical stitch pattern, or narrow section of a garment worked in a particular pattern.

Pattern

May refer to written or charted instructions regarding either a particular configuration of stitches or a particular garment style.

Picking Up

The process of drawing new stitches through existing ones along the edge or within a completed fabric in order to knit another section of fabric in a different direction.

Picot

Usually refers to a tiny indentation at an edge created with combined increase and decrease techniques.

Ply

The number of separate, relatively fine strands that are brought together to make a single heavier strand of yarn.

Popcorn

See Bobble.

Preparatory Row
The first row of a stitch pattern that is subsequently not repeated.

Pullover
A stitch technique whereby one stitch is pulled over another and off the needle.

Purl
One face of the basic stitch; see Knit. Also, a technique designed to place the Purl aspect of the stitch on the nearside of the fabric. See also Stockinette.

Purl Farside
Method of working a normal stitch so it will cross, or a turned stitch so it will not; also done in Knit.

Purlwise
Describing the insertion of the needle into the stitch as if to Purl.

Regauging
A method of changing the width of the fabric without changing the number of stitches on the needle.

Repeat
A single complete stitch pattern unit, which may be repeated across the width and or length of the fabric; synonymous with Multiple.

Reverse Stockinette
The Purl side of a Stockinette fabric.

Ribbing
A variety of stitch patterns that create vertical welts and are more or less elastic; generally used for wrists, waistlines, and gathering. See also Welt.

Right-Finger Knitting
A method of knitting in which the yarn is carried and manipulated by the right forefinger.

Right-Hand Knitting
A method of knitting in which the yarn is held by the right thumb and forefinger.

Right Side
Used in some knitting instructions to refer to that face of the fabric which will be worn to the outside. Here used only in the common sense of a relative direction; opposite to left.

Rip
To pull out stitches or rows to correct an error or reduce the length of the fabric.

Round
A single row in circular knitting. See also Row.

Row
A single set of stitches lying horizontally, side by side from one edge of the fabric to the other; equivalent to a vertical stitch column. Knitting each and every stitch on the needle a single time forms one new row of fabric, and the number of rows determines the length of the fabric. See also Round.

Ruching
A method of creating horizontal bands of gathered fabric.

Run
A ladder of running threads left in the fabric where a stitch has unraveled.

Running Thread
That portion of the yarn that passes horizontally between one stitch and the next.

Running Thread Pattern
A technique that makes use of small horizontal strands of yarn on the outside of the fabric; found in Stranded Brocade and certain Slip Stitch patterns.

Schematic
A drawing of the pattern showing the configuration and assembly of sections of the garment and all pertinent measurements.

Seam Stitch
A column of stitches used to create the illusion of a seam; also a device permitting Intarsia patterns in circular knitting.

Selvedge
A stitch at a side edge that is either decorative or will eventually be encased in a seam.

Shaping Techniques
Increases and decreases used to contour or change the width of a fabric.

Short Rows
A technique for working partial rows in order to contour a fabric or slope an edge; sometimes called Turning Rows.

Single-Point Needles
Straight needles with a point at one end and capped at the other; used for flat knitting.

Skein
A long length of yarn wound into a large circle, then coiled and tied so it will not tangle.

Slide
A technique, used in flat knitting on double-point needles, in which the stitches are moved from one needle point to the other instead of the fabric being turned.

Slip Knot
A simple, sliding knot often used to begin casting on.

Slip Stitch
A stitch passed from one needle to the other without being worked.

Slip Stranding
In color-pattern knitting, a particular method of handling more than one yarn.

Slope
Using stitch techniques to create a sloping line either within or at the edge of a fabric.

Smocking
An embroidery technique that gathers fabric in a decorative manner.

Splice
Reducing the thickness of two ends of yarn, then plying them together so they resemble the appearance and diameter of a single strand.

Split Yarn
Yarn that has had one or more ply removed to make it finer.

Steek
An extra portion of fabric, worked in a manner similar to a Gusset, which is later secured against unraveling and then cut open. Used in circular knitting in some areas of the world for armholes and center front openings.

Steps and Points
A method of calculating the distribution of shaping techniques either at the edge or within a fabric, or to determine a pick-up pattern.

Stitch
A single loop of yarn within the fabric or on the needle; the number of stitches on the needle or in a row of fabric determines the width; the number of stitches in a single vertical column determines the length. See also Discard Stitch, Neutral Stitch, New Stitch, Turned Stitch.

Stitch Column
A single vertical column of stitches, one on top of the other; equivalent to a horizontal row. The number of stitch columns in a fabric determines the width.

Stitch Gauge
The number of stitches and rows per inch/cm produced by any unique combination of hands, yarn, needle, and stitch pattern; used to determine the number of stitches and rows required for a given width and length of fabrics. See also Tension Sample.

Stitch Gauge Ratio
A formula for translating instructions derived from one gauge to instructions based on another gauge.

Stitch Holder
A tool or cord used for holding stitches in waiting.

Stockinette
The most basic stitch pattern in knitting, with Knit used exclusively on the outside face of the fabric and Purl on the inside. Also called Stocking Stitch. The Purl face is referred to as Reverse Stockinette.

Stocking Stitch
See Stockinette.

Strand
Any short length of yarn which passes across a stitch or stitches on either the inside or the outside of the fabric.

Stranded Brocade
A type of Brocade pattern employing strands on the outside of the fabric; done with two yarns of same or different colors.

Stranded Color Patterns
A particular form of color knitting in which the yarn colors are interchanged, with the inactive yarn stranded past the stitches being formed with the active yarn; generally used to create geometric patterns in Stockinette.

Stranding
The technique of carrying a second yarn across the inside of the fabric in Stranded Color work.

Swatch
See Tension Sample.

Tail
A measured length of yarn used in certain methods of casting on.

Tapestry Needle
A blunt-tipped, wide-eyed needle used for sewing with yarns.

Tension

May be used to describe whether a knitted fabric was worked firmly or loosely, to refer to the tension placed on the yarn as one knits, or as a term equivalent to Gauge.

Tension Sample

A small sample of fabric worked with the same hands, yarn, needles, and stitch pattern to be used for the garment in order to determine the stitch gauge. May also be called Gauge Swatch.

Thermal

The properties of a fiber or a fabric that are conducive to capturing and preserving heat.

Threaded Stitch

A stitch technique in which one stitch is pulled through the center of another.

Tunisian

A form of knitting commonly employed in the Middle East, now generally a group of stitch techniques.

Turn

When working a flat fabric, to turn the work around at the end of the row in order to go back in the other direction.

Turned Stitch

A stitch which is not sitting on the needle in the normal position.

Turning Rows

See Short Rows.

Twice Knit

A stitch technique producing an extremely dense fabric.

Twist

The direction, either S-twist or Z-twist, and the degree of tightness given to several single yarns when wrapped together to form plied yarn.

Twist Stitch

Two stitches twisted around one another; closely related to a Cable Stitch. In some books used to refer to Crossed Stitch.

Tying On

Methods of attaching new supply of yarn as fabric is being worked.

Undressed Gauge

A stitch and row gauge taken from tension sample that has not been cleaned and smoothed; only used for comparison to work in progress.

Unravel

Literally, to disentangle. To pull yarn out of the fabric and thus reduce the number of completed stitches or rows. May occur accidentally or be done purposefully.

Weaving In

Catching a strand of yarn against the fabric when working Stranded Color patterns, or for warmth.

Weighted Gauge

A stitch gauge taken from a sample that is weighted to compensate for the drop exhibited by a garment in wear. See also Drop.

Welt

Here used to refer to any horizontal or vertical corded effect in a fabric. Also, British term for ribbing at waistline and wrist.

Work Even

To continue in an established pattern without change.

Wrap

Yarn wrapped around several stitches; also the method of wrapping the yarn around the needle to form a new stitch.

Wrong Side

Used in some knitting instructions to refer to that face of the fabric which is not intended to be seen. Not used in this text. See also Inside.

Yarn

Any of a wide variety of fibers, both natural and artificial, formed into a long continuous strand and used for knitting.

Yarn Butterfly

See Butterfly.

Yarn End

A relatively short length of yarn left hanging from the fabric generally as a result of casting on or off, or where one ball of yarn was exhausted and another begun. Hidden on the inside during finishing process.

Yarn Nearside/Farside

An instruction telling the knitter to pass the yarn between the needles to that side of the fabric which is currently facing the knitter, or that side which is facing away. In many texts and instructions this may be called "yarn front/back" or "yarn forward/back."

Yarnover

A decorative increase technique fundamental to knitted lace; leaves a hole in the fabric.

Bibliography

*These books are those that I particularly like and recommend. Of the others, some are difficult to find, some are quaint and therefore of limited use to the average knitter, and several contain information that is also found in other books. I have also passed over those that are primarily garment pattern books, favoring instead ones that contain stitch and color patterns for knitters to make use of in any way they choose. Many of my favorite choices also contain interesting and often inspiring information on the history of knitting in some particular region.

Abbey, Barbara. *The Complete Book of Knitting*. New York: Viking, 1971.

Aytes, Barbara. *Knitting Made Easy*. New York: Doubleday & Co., 1970.

—————. *Adventures in Knitting*, New York: Doubleday & Co., 1968.

Bennett, Helen. *Scottish Knitting*. Shire Album 164, Aylesbury, Bucks, U.K.: Shire Publications, 1986.

Susan Bates, Inc. *Learn To Knit: Knitting for Beginners*. Chester, Connecticut: Susan Bates, Inc., 1978.

Chatterton, Pauline. *Scandinavian Knitting Designs*. New York: Charles Scribner's Sons, 1977.

*Compton, Rae. *The Complete Book of Traditional Knitting*. New York: Charles Scribner's Sons, 1983.

Dandanell, Birgitta and Danielsson, Ulla. *Tvaandsstickat*. Stockholm: LTs Forlag, 1984.

Dexter, Janetta. *Traditional Nova Scotian Double-Knitting Patterns*. Halifax: Nova Scotia Museum, 1985.

*Don, Sarah. *The Art of Shetland Lace*. London: Bell & Hyman, Ltd., 1986.

—————. *Fair Isle Knitting*. New York: St. Martin's Press, 1979.

Duncan, Ida Riley. *The Complete Book of Progressive Knitting*. New York, London: Liveright, 1968 (1940).

Elalouf, Sian. *The Knitting Architect*. Knitting Fever, Inc., 1982.

*Fanderl, Lisl. *Bauerliches Stricken*. Rosenheimer, Germany.
*—————. *Bauerliches Stricken 2*. Rosenheimer, Germany.
*—————. *Bauerliches Stricken 3*. Rosenheimer, Germany.

Fee, Jacquelin. *The Sweater Workshop*. Loveland, Colorado: Interweave Press, Inc., 1983.

Gainford, Veronica. *Designs for Knitting Kilt Hose and Knickerbocker Stockings*. Edinburgh: Scottish Development Agency, 1978.

Gibson-Roberts, Priscilla A. *Knitting in the Old Way*. Loveland, Colorado: Interweave Press, 1985.

*Gottfridsson, Inger and Ingrid. *The Swedish Mitten Book*. Asheville, North Carolina: Lark Books, 1984.

Grayson, Martin, ed. *Encyclopedia of Textiles, Fibers and Nonwoven Fabrics*. New York: John Wiley & Sons, 1984.

Hansen, Robin. *Fox & Geese & Fences: A Collection of Maine Mittens*. Camden, Maine: Down East Books, 1983.

Hansen, Robin, with Janetta Dexter. *Flying Geese & Partridge Feet, More Mittens from Up North and Down East*. Camden, Maine: Down East Books, 1986.

Harrell, Betsy. *Anatolian Knitting Designs*. Istanbul: Redhouse Press, 1981.

Harvey, Michael and Compton, Rae. *Fisherman Knitting*. Shire Album #31, Aylesbury, Bucks, U.K.: Shire Publications, Inc., 1978.

Harvey, Michael. *Paton's: A Story of Handknitting*. Ascot, Berkshire: Springwood Books, 1985.

Hinchcliffe, Frances. *Knit One, Purl One*. London: Victoria & Albert Museum, Department of Textiles and Dress.

Hochberg, Bette. *Fiber Facts*. Santa Cruz, California: Privately printed, 1981.

——————. *Handspinner's Handbook*. Santa Cruz, California: Privately printed, 1980.

*Hollingworth, Shelagh. *The Complete Book of Traditional Aran Knitting*. New York: St. Martin's Press, 1985.

Huwitt, Furze and Daley, Billie. *Classic Knitted Cotton Edgings*. Kenthurst, Australia: Kangaroo Press. 1987.

Kinzel, Marianne. *First Book of Modern Lace Knitting*. New York: Dover Publications, Inc., 1972 (1953).

——————. *Second Book of Modern Lace Knitting*. New York: Dover Publications, Inc., 1972 (1961).

*Klift-Tellegen, Henriette van der. *Knitting from the Netherlands*. Asheville, North Carolina: Lark Books, 1985.

*Lind, Vibeke. *Knitting in the Nordic Tradition*. Asheville, North Carolina: Lark Books, 1984 (Denmark, 1981).

Lorant, Tessa. *The Batsford Book of Hand & Machine Knitted Laces*. London: B.T. Batsford, Ltd., 1982.

——————. *Knitted Lace Collars*. Somerset, U.K.: The Thorn Press, 1983.

——————. *Knitted Lace Doilies*. Somerset, U.K.: The Thorn Press, 1986.

——————. *Knitted Lace Edgings*. Somerset, U.K.: The Thorn Press, 1981.

——————. *Knitted Shawls and Wraps*. Somerset, U.K.: The Thorn Press, 1984.

——————. *Knitted Quilts and Flounces*. Somerset, U.K.: The Thorn Press, 1982.

Marshall Editions, Ltd. *The Knit Kit Book*. New York: Villard Books, 1985.

Matthews, Anne. *Vogue Dictionary of Knitting Stitches*. New York: Quill, 1984.

*McGregor, Sheila. *The Complete Book of Traditional Fair Isle Knitting*. New York: Charles Scribner's Sons, 1982.

*——————. *Traditional Knitting*. London: B.T. Batsford, Ltd., 1983.

*——————. *The Complete Book of Scandinavian Knitting*. New York: St. Martin's Press, 1984.

Meyers, Belle. *Knitting Know-How*. New York: Barnes & Noble Books, 1981.

Mon Tricot. *The Knitting Dictionary*, (translation by Margaret Hamilton-Hunt). New York: Crown Publishers, 1971.

——————. *The Knitter's Basic Book, Vol I and II*. Mon Tricot Monthly No. D17 and No. D18, Paris: Compagnie des Editions de l'Alma.

——————. *The Key to Success. Step by Step Knitting*. Paris: Ste. Ediclair et Cie, 1981.

*Neighbors, Jane F. *Reversible Two-Color Knitting*. New York: Charles Scribner's Sons, 1974.

Norbury, James. *Traditional Knitting Patterns*, New York: Dover Publications, Inc., 1973 (1962).

*Pearson, Michael. *Michael Pearson's Traditional Knitting*. New York: Van Nostrand Reinhold Co., Inc., 1984.

Phildar. *Hand Knitting Stitches*. France: Phildar Editeur, 1985.

Phillips, Mary Walker. *Creative Knitting: A New Art Form*. New York: Van Nostrand Reinhold Co., 1971.

Righetti, Maggie. *Knitting In Plain English*. New York: St. Martin's Press, 1986.

Robinson, Debby. *The Encyclopedia of Knitting Techniques*. Emmaus, Pennsylvania: Rodale Press, 1987.

*Rutt, Richard, Bishop of Leicester. *A History of Hand Knitting*. London: B.T. Batsford, Ltd., 1987.

Smith, Mary and Twatt, Maggie. *A Shetland Pattern Book*. Lerwick, Shetland: The Shetland Times, Ltd., 1986.

Stanley, Montse. *Creating and Knitting Your Own Designs for a Perfect Fit*. New York: Harper & Row, 1982.

Stewart, Evelyn Stiles. *The Right Way to Knit: A Manual for Basic Knitting*. Columbus, Ohio: Knit Services, 1967.

—————. *The Right Way to Knit. Basic Knits/How to Block and Finish*. Columbus, Ohio: Knit Services, 1969.

Taylor, Gertrude. *America's Knitting Book*. New York: Charles Scribner's Sons, 1968.

Thomas, Mary. *Mary Thomas's Knitting Book*. New York: Dover Publications, Inc., 1972 (1938).

—————. *Mary Thomas's Book of Knitting Patterns*. New York: Dover Publications, Inc., 1972 (1943).

Tortora, Phyllis G. *Understanding Textiles*. 2nd ed. New York: Macmillan Publishing Co., Inc., 1982.

*Thompson, Gladys. *Patterns for Guernseys, Jerseys & Arans*. New York: Dover Publications, 1979 (1969).

*Upitis, Lizbeth. *Latvian Mittens, Traditional Designs & Techniques*. St. Paul, Minnesota: Dos Tejedoras, 1981.

*Walker, Barbara. *A Treasury of Knitting Patterns*. New York: Charles Scribner's Sons, 1968.

*—————. *A Second Treasury of Knitting Patterns*. New York: Charles Scribner's Sons, 1970.

*—————. *Charted Knitting Designs*. New York: Charles Scribner's Sons, 1972.

*—————. *Knitting From the Top*. New York: Charles Scribner's Sons, 1972.

*Wright, Mary. *Cornish Guernseys and Knit-frocks*. Penzance, Cornwall: Alison Hodge in assoc. with Ethnographica Ltd., 1979.

Furuta, Yo, ed. *Yo's Needlecraft "How To": 101 Ways to Seam, Join, & Pick Up Stitches*. Vol. 3, no. 1, Tokyo: Nihon Vogue, Co., Ltd.

Zimmerman, Elizabeth. *Knitting Without Tears*. New York: Charles Scribner's Sons, 1971.

—————. *Knitting Workshop*. Pittsville, Wisconsin: Schoolhouse Press, 1981.

Index

Photograph Credits

Page 22. Dutch cotton petticoat by courtesy of the Trustees of the Victoria and Albert Museum, London, England.

Page 119. Silk lace medallion with beaded border. From the collection of Lacis, Berkeley, California.

Page 180. Cuffed wool socks © Dalarnas museum, Sweden.

Page 229. TOP. Wool mitten in the style of the District of Kurzeme. From the collection of Lizbeth Upitis, Minneapolis, Minnesota, knitted by Anna Mizens.
BOTTOM. Nineteenth century child's mittens in cotton lace, lined. From the collection of Lacis, Berkeley, California.

Page 255. Fair Isle sweater © Shetland Museum & Library. Knitted in 1925.

Page 262. Sixteenth century Italian silk tunic from the Metropolitan Museum of Art, Fletcher Fund, 1946. (46.156.117)

Page 266. Stranded brocade glove © Dalarnas museum, Sweden.

Page 269. Detail of Bohus pattern, sweater from the collection of Diane Baker, Albany, California.

Page 270. LEFT. Detail of Matisse dress—designed by Sandy Black, knitted in 100 percent cotton. Reproduced from Original Knitting by Sandy Black, published 1987 by Unwin Hyman and available in the USA from Westminster Trading Corp, 5 Northern Blvd., Amherst, New Hampshire 03031.
RIGHT. Detail of Gladiola coat—designed by Sandy Black, 1984, knitted in 100 percent Angora. Similar designs featured in Original Knitting (see above).

Page 271. Alsatian carpet by courtesy of the Trustees of the Victoria and Albert Museum, London, England.

Page 289. Embroidered gloves © Dalarna museum, Sweden.

Page 296. Beaded handbag from the collection of Joanna Lynch, Oakland, California.

Page 301. Beaded Victorian baby bonnet from the collection of Lacis, Berkeley, California.

Page 312. Shetland shawl from the collection of Lacis, Berkeley, California.
Detail, same as above.

Pages 313 to 320. Eight fiber photomicrograhs © Leo Barish and Albany International Research Company. All prints are about 750X.

Page 326. Detail of ribbon knit sweater knitted by Toshiko Sugiyama, Berkeley, California.

Page 338. Knitting sticks © The Welsh Folk Museum, The National Museum of Wales.

Page 344. Guernsey courtesy of The Manx Museum and National Trust, Douglas, Isle of Man.

Page 385. Fair Isle scarf from the collection of Maryann Zannini, San Francisco, California.

Page 392. Shetland shawl on stretcher © National Museums of Scotland.

Page 393. Fair Isle on stretcher © Shetland Museum & Library.

Page 403. Fulled, embroidered slippers © Dalarnas museum, Sweden, by K. G. Swensson.

Page 426. Aran sweater © National Museum of Ireland–Dublin.

Page 434. Swiss dolls from the collection of Christa Schreiber, Oakland, California.

About the Author

June Hiatt graduated Phi Beta Kappa with a degree in history from the University of California, Berkeley. She lives in Berkeley with her husband, Robert A. Hiatt, M.D., an epidemiologist, and their son, Jesse. This is her first book.